# EU Diplomatic Law

OXFORD EU LAW LIBRARY

The aim of the series is to publish important and original studies of the various branches of EU law. Each work provides a clear, concise, and critical exposition of the law in its social, economic, and political context, at a level which will interest the advanced student, the practitioner, the academic, and government officials.

OTHER TITLES IN THIS SERIES

**EU Constitutional Law**
Koen Lenaerts, Piet Van Nuffel, Tim Corthaut

**EU Customs Law**
*Third Edition*
Timothy Lyons

**Principles and Practice in EU Sports Law**
Stephen Weatherill

**EU Justice and Home Affairs Law**
*Fourth Edition*
Steve Peers

**EU Procedural Law**
Koen Lenaerts, Ignace Maselis, Kathleen Gutman, Janek Tomasz Nowak

**EU Anti-Discrimination Law**
*Second Edition*
Evelyn Ellis and Philippa Watson

**EU Securities and Financial Markets Regulation**
*Third Edition*
Niamh Moloney

**The EU Common Security and Defence Policy**
Panos Koutrakos

**EU External Relations Law**
*Second Edition*
Piet Eeckhout

**EU Employment Law**
*Fourth Edition*
Catherine Barnard

**The EU Common Fisheries Policy**
Robin Churchill and Daniel Owen

# EU Diplomatic Law

SANDERIJN DUQUET

*Belgian Diplomat and Associate Fellow of the Leuven Centre for Global Governance Studies, University of Leuven*

OXFORD
UNIVERSITY PRESS

OXFORD
UNIVERSITY PRESS

Great Clarendon Street, Oxford, OX2 6DP,
United Kingdom

Oxford University Press is a department of the University of Oxford.
It furthers the University's objective of excellence in research, scholarship,
and education by publishing worldwide. Oxford is a registered trade mark of
Oxford University Press in the UK and in certain other countries



First Edition published in 2022
Impression: 1



Published in the United States of America by Oxford University Press
198 Madison Avenue, New York, NY 10016, United States of America

British Library Cataloguing in Publication Data
Data available

Library of Congress Control Number: 2022940916

ISBN 978–0–19–284455–2

DOI: 10.1093/oso/9780192844552.001.0001

Printed and bound in the UK by
TJ Books Limited

# Contents

# Table of Cases

# List of Abbreviations

| | |
|---|---|
| ACCT | Agence de Coopération Culturelle et Technique |
| ACP | African, Caribbean, and Pacific countries |
| AFP | Agence France-Presse |
| AFSJ | Area of Freedom, Security and Justice |
| AG | Advocate-General |
| ai | *ad interim* |
| AL | Arab League (formally the League of Arab States) |
| APE | Commission des affaires politiques et des questions institutionnelles de l'Assemblée parlementaire européenne |
| ASEAN | Association of Southeast Asian Nations |
| AU | African Union |
| CAC | Common Application Centre |
| CARICOM | Caribbean Community and Common Market |
| CAT | Committee against Torture |
| CD | Conference on Disarmament |
| CD | Corps diplomatique |
| CEMAC | Communauté Économique et Monétaire des Etats de l'Afrique Centrale |
| CFSP | Common Foreign and Security Policy |
| CIA | Central Intelligence Agency |
| CIL | customary international law |
| CILSS | Comité inter-États de Lutte contre la Sécheresse au Sahel |
| CJEU | Court of Justice of the European Union |
| CoE | Council of Europe |
| COI | Commission de l'Océan Indien |
| COMESA | Common Market for Eastern and Southern Africa |
| Coreper | Comité des représentants permanents/Committee of Permanent Representatives |
| CPIUN | Convention on the Privileges and Immunities of the United Nations |
| CPIUN-SA | Convention on the Privileges and Immunities of the Specialized Agencies of the United Nations |
| CRSIO | Convention on the Representation of States in their Relations with International Organizations of a Universal Character |
| CSDP | Common Security and Defence Policy |
| CSM | Convention on Special Missions |
| CTBTO | Preparatory Commission for the Comprehensive Nuclear Test Ban Treaty Organisation |
| DG | Directorate General |
| DG RELEX | The European Commission's Directorate General for External Relations |
| DPRK | Democratic People's Republic of Korea |
| DRC | Democratic Republic of the Congo |
| EA | establishment agreement |
| EAC | East African Community |
| EC | European Community |

| | |
|---|---|
| ECCAS | Economic Community of Central African States |
| ECHR | European Convention for the Protection of Human Rights and Fundamental Freedoms |
| ECJ | European Court of Justice |
| EComHR | European Commission on Human Rights |
| ECOWAS | Economic Community of West African States |
| ECSC | European Coal and Steel Community |
| ECtHR | European Court of Human Rights |
| EDF | European Development Fund |
| EEAS | European External Action Service |
| EEC | European Economic Community |
| EETO | EU Economic and Trade Office |
| EFTA | European Free Trade Association |
| EIDHR | European Instrument for Democracy and Human Rights |
| ENP | European Neighbourhood Policy |
| EP | European Parliament |
| EPC | European Political Cooperation |
| EPO | European Patent Organization |
| EFTA | European Free Trade Association |
| ERTA/AETR | European Agreement concerning the Work of Crews of Vehicles Engaged in International Road Transport |
| ETD | emergency travel document |
| ETOO | European Economic and Trade Office |
| EU | European Union |
| EUD | European Union delegation |
| EUDEL | EU delegation |
| EULP | European Union Laissez-Passer |
| EURATOM | European Atomic Energy Community |
| EUSE | European Union Special Envoy |
| EUSR | European Union Special Representative |
| FAO | Food and Agriculture Organization |
| Frontex | European Agency for the Management of Operational Cooperation at the External Borders of the Member States of the European Union |
| G20 | Group of Twenty |
| GATT | General Agreement on Tariffs and Trade |
| GC | Gulf Cooperation Council |
| HCOC | Code of Conduct against Ballistic Missile Proliferation |
| HE | His/Her Excellency |
| HoD | Head of Delegation |
| HoM | Head of Mission |
| HoR | House of Representatives |
| HQ | Headquarters |
| HR | High Representative for Foreign Affairs and Security Policy |
| HRC | Human Rights Committee (ICCPR) |
| IAEA | International Atomic Energy Agency |
| IBRD | International Bank for Reconstruction and Development |
| ICAO | International Civil Aviation Organization |
| ICC | International Criminal Court |
| ICCPR | International Covenant on Civil and Political Rights |
| ICJ | International Court of Justice |

| | |
|---|---|
| ICMPD | International Centre for Migration Policy Development |
| ICRC | International Committee of the Red Cross |
| IDEA | International Institute for Democracy and Electoral Assistance (or International IDEA) |
| IFAD | International Fund for Agricultural Development |
| IGAD | Intergovernmental Authority on Development |
| IIASA | International Institute for Applied Systems Analysis |
| IIL | Institute of International Law |
| ILC | International Law Commission |
| ILO | International Labour Organization |
| IMF | International Monetary Fund |
| IMO | International Maritime Organization |
| IntAmComHR | Inter-American Commission of Human Rights |
| IntAmCtHR | Inter-American Court of Human Rights |
| INTERPOL | International Criminal Police Organization |
| IO | international organization |
| IOM | International Organization for Migration |
| IRENA | International Renewable Energy Agency |
| ISO | International Organization for Standardization |
| ITU | International Telecommunications Union |
| JPD | junior professional in delegation |
| LGBTQ+ | lesbian, gay, bisexual, transgender, queer or questioning, or another diverse gender identity |
| LoN | League of Nations |
| MEP | Member of the European Parliament |
| MFA | Ministry of Foreign Affairs |
| MFN | most-favoured nation |
| MoP | Meeting of Parties |
| MoU | memorandum of understanding |
| NATO | North Atlantic Treaty Organization |
| NGO | non-governmental organization |
| NSA | National Security Agency (US) |
| NSG | Nuclear Suppliers Group |
| OAS | Organization of American States |
| OCHA | United Nations Office for the Coordination of Humanitarian Affairs |
| OECD | Organisation for Economic Co-operation and Development |
| OECS | Organisation of Eastern Caribbean States |
| OEEC | Organisation for European Economic Co-operation |
| OHCHR | Office of the United Nations High Commissioner for Human Rights |
| OIC | Organisation of Islamic Cooperation (formerly Organization of the Islamic Conference) |
| OICP | International Organization for Criminal Police |
| OIF | Organisation Internationale de la Francophonie |
| OPEC | Organization of the Petroleum Exporting Countries |
| OSCE | Organization for Security and Co-operation in Europe |
| PCIJ | Permanent Court of International Justice |
| PermRep | permanent representation |
| PIL | public international law |
| PKD | Public Key Directory |
| PLO | Palestine Liberation Organization |

| | |
|---|---|
| PNA | Palestinian National Authority |
| PR | permanent representation |
| PRC | People's Republic of China |
| PSC | Political and Security Committee |
| RCC | Regional Cooperation Council |
| REIO | regional economic integration organization |
| RIO | Regional Integration Organization |
| ROC | Republic of China |
| SAARC | South Asian Association for Regional Cooperation |
| SACU | Southern African Customs Union |
| SADC | Southern African Development Community |
| SAR | Special Administrative Region |
| SE4All | Sustainable Energy for All Forum |
| SEA | Single European Act |
| SICA | Sistema de la Integración Centroamericana |
| SNE | seconded national expert |
| SOFA | status of forces agreement |
| SOMA | status of mission agreement |
| TEC | Treaty establishing the European Community |
| TEU | Treaty on European Union |
| TFEU | Treaty on the Functioning of the European Union |
| TTIP | Trade and Investment Partnership |
| UEMOA | Union Économique et Monétaire Quest-Africaine |
| UN | United Nations |
| UN Women | United Nations Entity for Gender Equality and the Empowerment of Women |
| UNAIDS | Joint United Nations Programme on HIV/Aids |
| UNCITRAL | United Nations Commission on International Trade Law |
| UNCLOS | United Nations Convention on the Law of the Sea |
| UNCOPUOS | United Nations Committee on the Peaceful Uses of Outer Space |
| UNCTAD | United Nations Conference on Trade and Development |
| UNDP | United Nations Development Programme |
| UNECE | United Nations Economic Commission for Europe |
| UNEP | United Nations Environment Programme |
| UNESCO | United Nations Educational, Scientific and Cultural Organization |
| UNFPA | United Nations Population Fund |
| UNGA | United Nations General Assembly |
| UN-Habitat | United Nations Human Settlements Programme |
| UNHCR | United Nations High Commissioner for Refugees |
| UNHRC | United Nations Human Right Council |
| UNICEF | United Nations Children's Fund |
| UNIDO | United Nations Industrial Development Organization |
| UNLP | United Nations Laissez-Passer |
| UNMIK | United Nation Interim Administration Mission in Kosovo |
| UNO | United Nations Organization |
| UNODC | United Nations Office on Drugs and Crime |
| UNOG | United Nations Office at Geneva |
| UNOPS | United Nations Office for Project Services |
| UNOV | United Nations Office at Vienna |
| UNRIC | United Nations Regional Information Centre |
| UNSA | United Nations Specialized Agency |

| | |
|---|---|
| UNSC | United Nations Security Council |
| UNSG | United Nations Secretary General |
| UNTS | United Nations Treaty Series |
| UPU | Universal Postal Union |
| VCCR | Vienna Convention on Consular Relations (1963) |
| VCDR | Vienna Convention on Diplomatic Relations (1961) |
| VCLT | Vienna Convention on the Law of Treaties (1969) |
| VCLT–IO | Vienna Convention on the Law of Treaties between States and International Organizations or between International Organizations (1986) |
| WA | Wassenaar Arrangement |
| WFP | World Food Programme |
| WHO | World Health Organization |
| WIPO | World Intellectual Property Organization |
| WMO | World Meteorological Organization |
| WTO | World Trade Organization |

# 1
# Introduction to EU Diplomacy and Diplomatic Law

## 1.1 The Essentials of Diplomacy

### 1.1.1 Why Do States Engage in Diplomatic Relations?

Diplomatic and consular intercourse is at the heart of international relations. It enables states to maintain mutual relations and to communicate with both nationals living or travelling abroad and foreign audiences. Virtually every state conducts permanent diplomatic relations with other states. To this end, it maintains an embassy in the capital city of a foreign country where an ambassador leads the state's representation in the receiving state. The ambassador interacts with official counterparts at the highest political level. A state may open one or more consulates per country, either in the capital or elsewhere. Consuls also function as the official representatives of one state in the territory of another, but compared to those of an ambassador or a diplomat, their tasks are of a more administrative and economic nature. A consulate maintains regular contacts with local authorities, businesses, and the nationals of the sending state; it also facilitates trade and friendship between two countries in a geographically limited area called the consular district.

The institution of diplomatic relations is praised for specific reasons. In a general understanding, diplomacy is a means of conducting foreign policy and an instrument of coexistence. Diplomacy tries to balance two ideas: on the one hand, diplomats represent their governments' priorities and their domestic constituencies' well-being; on the other hand, many issues are global in nature and cannot be solved by one country or one type of actor.[1] This relates to diplomacy's ultimate function to fortify relations between two (or more) nations, to define common interests, and to set up cooperation schemes.[2] Through diplomacy, political, economic, and cultural ties between countries are expanded.[3] Moreover, diplomacy is an excellent means for states to protect their interests, as well as those of their citizens and corporations, around the world.

Among the many functions of diplomacy, its commitment to the *preservation of peace* may be the most outspoken. Diplomacy has preventive (conflict prevention) and corrective (conflict resolution, peaceful settlement of disputes) dimensions. Accordingly, diplomacy is

[1] Brian Barder, 'Diplomacy, Ethics, and the National Interest: What Are Diplomats For?' (2010) 5 HJD 289; Joseph S Nye, 'Redefining the National Interest' (1999) Foreign Aff 22.

[2] Lloyd S Davis and Robert G Patman, *Science Diplomacy: New Day Or False Dawn* (World Scientific 2015); Maxime Verhagen and Henk Bleker, 'Economic Diplomacy in a Changing World' (2006) 1 HJD 171; Martina Topić and Siniša Rodin (eds), *Cultural Diplomacy and Cultural Imperialism: European Perspective(s)* (Peter Lang 2012).

[3] Andrew F Cooper, Jorge Heine, and Ramesh Thakur, 'The Challenges of 21st-Century Diplomacy' in Andrew F Cooper, Jorge Heine, and Ramesh Thakur (eds), *The Oxford Handbook of Modern Diplomacy* (OUP 2013) 3.

*EU Diplomatic Law*. Sanderijn Duquet, Oxford University Press. 
DOI: 10.1093/oso/9780192844552.003.0001

an alternative both to war and legal proceedings. In the words of the International Court of Justice (ICJ):

> [t]he institution of diplomacy [ ... ] proved to be an instrument essential for effective co-operation in the international community, and for enabling States, irrespective of their differing constitutional and social systems, to achieve mutual understanding and to resolve their differences by peaceful means. [4]

In its simplest sense, diplomacy is a primary and traditional means of communication between states[5]—it lies at the most formal end of the scale of international interactions.[6] Diplomacy is therefore not just an effective way to serenely solve quarrels but is also viewed as a *facilitator of inter-state communication*.[7] The International Law Commission (ILC) confirms this when it states that 'the maintenance of channels of communication between the two States concerned', and 'the resolution of the dispute between the parties' are essential functions of the diplomatic system.[8] Of subsidiary order (although gaining in importance), diplomacy also enables states to communicate with both nationals living or travelling abroad and foreign audiences.

## 1.1.2 A Brief History of Diplomacy

### 1.1.2.1 The Origins of Diplomacy

Diplomats sometimes claim their profession holds the prestigious title of 'world's second oldest profession'. The claim is wrong on a number of levels, but the quip serves as a reminder of diplomacy's long history.[9] Diplomatic envoys existed around the world for many years, although the literature is rife with varying time frames. The origins of diplomacy are connected to the emergence of political order, dating back at least to the kings of the Ancient Near East in the late fourth millennium BC.[10]

The history of diplomacy falls into two periods. In a first period largely covering antiquity and the Middle Ages, travelling ad hoc missions represented the interests of rulers. In a second period, which started around the thirteenth century and flourished from the fifteenth century onwards, missions were permanently installed in foreign nations.[11] Both types of diplomatic conduct have survived the test of time. Rules on the special protection, privileges, and status of envoys also remain an integral part of diplomatic and consular law

[4] *Case concerning United States Diplomatic and Consular Staff in Tehran (United States of America v Iran)* (Order) [1979] ICJ Rep 21, para 39.

[5] Chanaka Wickremasinghe, 'Immunities Enjoyed by Officials of States and International Organizations' in Malcolm D Evans (ed), *International Law* (4th edn, OUP 2014) 383.

[6] James Crawford, *Brownlie's Principles of Public International Law* (OUP 2012) 395.

[7] Christer Jönsson and Martin Hall, 'Communication: An Essential Aspect of Diplomacy' in Christer Jönsson and Richard Langhorne (eds), *Diplomacy* (2nd edn, Sage 2004); Alain Plantey, *Principes de Diplomatie* (2nd edn, Pedone 2000).

[8] ILC, 'Draft Articles on the Responsibility of States for Internationally Wrongful Acts with Commentaries' II(II) YBILC 131, 133.

[9] Robert Y Jennings and Arthur Watts (eds), *Oppenheim's International Law*, vol 1 (9th edn, Longman 1992) 1053; Biswanath Sen, *A Diplomat's Handbook of International Law and Practice* (3rd edn, Martinus Nijhoff 1988) 3.

[10] Ivor Roberts (ed), *Satow's Diplomatic Practice* (6th edn, OUP 2011) 5.

[11] Matthew S Anderson, *The Rise of Modern Diplomacy, 1450–1919* (Routledge 2005) 4.

today. Even in the earliest known civilizations, ambassadors were ceremoniously received and courteously treated, a custom originating from a belief that diplomats have a sacrosanct status in international relations.[12] In this sense, diplomatic customs predate modern international law.

### 1.1.2.2 Ad Hoc Missions

In ancient times, kings and emperors sent ad hoc representatives to their counterparts. The writings of Greek historians report that by the fifth century BC, a system had emerged regulating diplomatic contacts between city states and introducing definite principles of diplomatic practice and protocol. By way of illustration, Sir Harold Nicolson, a distinguished historian, has analysed the writings of Aristotle and Thucydides and described at length ceremonial practices as well as the legal system set up between the city states.[13] In Rome, too, foreign envoys on special mission were received with great respect, although Rome preferred to receive rather than to send ambassadors. In their active sending practices, Romans used *legati* for economic, trade, and political relations and *fetiales* for religious diplomacy as well as in negotiations on war and peace.[14] Cicero's *In Verrem* speeches contain ample references to the practice of sending and receiving ambassadors and the functions they fulfilled. In relation to the safe passage of diplomats, he stated: '[e]tenim nomen legati eius modi esse debet quod non modo inter sociorum iura, sed etiam inter hostium tela incolume versetur', which translates as 'the name of an envoy ought to be such as to pass in safety not only among the laws of allies, but even amid the arms of enemies'.[15] Because the Romans did not believe in 'sovereign equality' but in conquest and the extension of Pax Romana, diplomacy saw a relative decline during the Roman Empire. The Empire's disintegration, which had swallowed up practically the whole European continent, relaunched the development of the office of diplomacy.

The literature somewhat overlooks practices of non-European states. Yet, history records that princes of Asian states maintained diplomatic relations with their neighbours, as did China. There are accounts of Chinese countries exchanging diplomatic representatives among themselves, with ceremonial aspects carefully regulated.[16] The Laws of Manu for Ancient India provided a body of rules on foreign affairs that included diplomacy. Sen particularly notes that several Greek ambassadors were accredited to Pataliputra and that Indian kings also sent *dutas* to Greek courts.[17] In addition, both the Bible and the Quran contain references of instances of legation, which serve as proof of early diplomatic activity in the Middle East. King David sent and received ambassadors at his court (2 Samuel 8:10; 10:1–5), Moses sent messengers to the king of Edom and to Sihon (Numeri 28:14; 21:21), and the Prophet Muhammed sent emissaries on missions to Byzantium, Egypt, Persia, and Ethiopia either to declare Jihad or to negotiate treaties. In addition, the Prophet is said to have opposed the detention and the killing of a foreign envoy.[18]

[12] Charles Reichling, *Le Droit de Légation des Communautés Européennes* (UGA Éditions 1964) 7.
[13] Harold G Nicolson, *Diplomacy* (OUP 1988).
[14] Claude Eilers, *Diplomats and Diplomacy in the Roman World* (Brill 2009) 2.
[15] Marcus Tullius Cicero, *In Verrem*, 2.1, para 85.
[16] Graham Stuart, 'Le Droit et la Pratique Diplomatiques et Consulaires' in The Hague Academy of International Law (ed), *Collected Courses of The Hague Academy of International Law* (first published Librairie du Recueil Sirey 1935) 463.
[17] Sen (n 9) 4.
[18] Muhammad-Basheer Ismail, *Islamic Law and Transnational Diplomatic Law: A Quest for Complementarity in Divergent Legal Theories* (Palgrave Macmillan 2016) 79–112.

### 1.1.2.3 Permanent Missions

In the Middle Ages, the rulers of the eastern part of the Roman Empire, long before anywhere else in Europe, actively used their envoys for political reporting purposes and negotiations. Byzantine emperors exhibited a certain fondness for ceremonial aspects, as documented in a manual by Emperor Constantine VII, *De Ceremoniis*, dating from the tenth century. Today, Byzantine diplomacy has been recognized for its groundbreaking administrative organization and ceremonial practices. That diplomatic practice survived when the Ottoman Empire conquered the Byzantine Empire in the thirteenth century.[19]

In what is now known as Western and Central Europe, the first permanent representations made their appearance in the twelfth century, when trading nations and cities began appointing agents with representative tasks to one another's ports and commercial centres. Inspired by the Byzantine diplomatic organization practices, Venice became a nursing ground for the modern diplomatic system, 'l'école et la pierre de touche des ambassadeurs' [the school and touchstone for ambassadors].[20] From the beginning of the thirteenth century, the city state promulgated legislation to guide its resident ambassadors. Nys provides an interesting example of a 1236 decree that made the acceptance of favours or gifts for ambassadors at the court of Rome subject to prior approval.[21] Accredited in 1375 to the court of Visconti in Milan and to the court of Gongoza in Mantua, respectively, the first two resident ambassadors on record were Venetian, although even in 1322, the Pope claimed to have ambassadors in every quarter of the world. References to the life and work of those early ambassadors can still be found in the archives of the city of Mantua.[22] The use of permanent delegations was refined and diffused across Western Europe starting in the fifteenth century:[23] the Venetians stimulated principal Italian states and Papal Rome to also establish diplomatic relations with one another, a practice soon followed by other European powers.[24] The Papacy retained extensive reach throughout what was then the Christian world, which allowed it to introduce its negotiation and international communication model to the world.[25]

The birth of the modern nation-state gave new impetus to diplomacy.[26] The sixteenth century was marked by an increase in diplomatic activities across Europe.[27] The Treaty of 1520 between Henry VIII of England and Charles V of Spain, for instance, contained a clause on the mutual establishment of permanent missions and the exchange of ambassadors.[28] French diplomacy, first implemented under Louis XI, greatly developed under Henri IV (1553–1610) and Richelieu (1585–1642) and flourished under Louis XIV (1638–1715).[29]

[19] Charles Chatterjee, *International Law and Diplomacy* (Routledge 2007) 31; Marcellus Donald AR von Redlich, *The Law of Nations* (World League for Permanent Peace 1937) 221.

[20] Ernest Nys, *Les Origines de la Diplomatie et le Droit d'Ambassade Jusqu'a Grotius* (Librairie Européenne C Muquardt 1884 8–9.

[21] ibid 298.

[22] Garret Mattingly, *Renaissance Diplomacy* (Dover Publications 1988) 71–72.

[23] Harold G Nicolson, *The Evolution of Diplomatic Method: The Chichele Lectures Delivered at Oxford, November, 1953* (Greenwood Press 1954) 24.

[24] David Jayne Hill, *A History of Diplomacy in the International Development of Europe*, vol II (Longmans, Green & Co 1924) 309.

[25] Graham H Stuart, *American Diplomatic and Consular Practice* (Appleton-Century Co 1936) 8.

[26] Ludwik Dembinski, *The Modern Law of Diplomacy: External Missions of States and International Organizations* (Martinus Nijhoff 1988) 3.

[27] Mai'a K Davis Cross, *The European Diplomatic Corps: Diplomats and International Cooperation from Westphalia to Maastricht* (Palgrave Macmillan 2008) 37.

[28] Treaty between Henry VIII of England and Charles V of Spain, done at Calais on 14 July 1520 and described in Hill (n 24) 354.

[29] von Redlich (n 19) 223.

During the seventeenth and eighteenth centuries, French diplomatic methods and language dominated European diplomacy, when, increasingly, diplomacy was also recognized as a professional endeavour. Rules from that period, such as that on the confidentiality of diplomatic relations, are still observed in current diplomatic law.[30]

As the Holy Roman Empire underwent a reconfiguration of power relationships among its quasi-autonomous constituent states, the need for states to maintain permanent embassies became apparent. A turning point was the 1648 Peace of Westphalia. The negotiating meetings leading up to the Peace were the first of their kind formally involving diplomatic representatives ('plenipotentiary ambassadors'), while the Westphalian Treaties themselves brought about important changes in international political and commercial relations.[31] Westphalia embodied a new framework in Europe. It gave more than 300 entities the right to conduct their own foreign relations and restored the freedom of commerce, which boosted commercial ties and increased accreditation of consuls in other nations.[32] This makes the rules on diplomatic interactions 'one of the earliest expressions of international law'.[33]

The increasing exchange of permanent missions between states drove a need to further professionalize the diplomatic craft. In the eighteenth century, having a diplomatic service with career diplomats became a feature of the modern territorial state. Slowly, states started to recruit diplomats beyond aristocracy and to adopt internal rankings. It was Napoleon Bonaparte, in early nineteenth-century France, who amplified bureaucratic elements of the French diplomatic service's organization. By 1812, two out of three French diplomats undertook training organized by the state, an example followed by other European nations over the course of the century.[34] Although the act of diplomacy was not unknown to the rest of the world, European diplomatic methods spread across the globe, including through colonization.[35]

#### 1.1.2.4 Codification

Customary international law (CIL) was and continues to be the basis for the system of diplomatic and consular exchanges. The first attempts at codification were made in 1815, when the Congress of Vienna adopted a regulation on classifying heads of diplomatic missions and, in 1818, when the Congress of Aix-la-Chapelle adopted a protocol on diplomatic precedence and etiquette.[36] The 1815 Vienna Congress was a historically peculiar event in many ways. When it redrew the map of Europe, a deliberate effort was made to install a wartime coalition on the continent, including post-Napoleonic France.[37] The consequences for diplomacy, an expression of sovereignty, are noteworthy. It installed a new way of international communication in multilateral processes and adopted a diplomatic hierarchy in the form of a regulation on the classes of heads of diplomatic missions. Consequently, the Congress of Vienna was the first multilateral setting in which diplomatic norms were created.[38] The next

30 Chatterjee (n 19) 32.

31 Peace Treaty between the Holy Roman Emperor and the King of France and their respective Allies, done at Münster on 14–24 October 1648.

32 von Redlich (n 19) 263; Arthur Nussbaum, *A Concise History of the Law of Nations* (Macmillan 1954) 125.

33 Malcolm N Shaw, *International Law* (CUP 2014) 545.

34 Edward A Whitcomb, *Napoleon's Diplomatic Service* (Duke UP 1979) 152.

35 Chatterjee (n 19) 33.

36 Roberts (n 10) 11. On the origin if the rules of seniority, see Michael H Cardozo, *Diplomats in International Cooperation: Stepchildren of the Foreign Service* (Cornell UP 1962) 4.

37 Richard Langhorne, 'History and the Evolution of Diplomacy' in Jovan Kurbalija (ed), *Modern Diplomacy* (Diplofoundation 1998).

38 An initial codification can be read in Annex IV to the final act of the Vienna Regulation of 19 March 1815; Ignaz Seidl-Hohenveldern, *Völkerrecht* (9th edn, Carl Heymanns Verlag 1997) 187.

step in the course of codification was an academic exercise by the Institute of International Law (IIL). During its 1895 Cambridge session, the IIL adopted a regulation on diplomatic immunities.[39] The heightened scholarly interest in the topic did not translate into further results at the multilateral level. In the days of the League of Nations, diplomatic activities were still fairly limited. The League had concentrated mostly on issues of warfare, which in a way blocked attempts to develop rules on diplomacy. As a result, until the mid-twentieth century, diplomacy featured only in domestic law (eg the 1708 diplomatic privileges act by Queen Ann), bilateral treaties (establishing diplomatic relations and, since the end of the eighteenth century, defining consular exchanges), and the nineteenth-century Vienna and Aix-la-Chapelle Protocols. The rules of diplomatic and consular exchanges remained essentially customary until well after the Second World War.

In the early 1950s, the United Nations General Assembly (UNGA) selected the laws of diplomatic and consular intercourse as subjects ripe for further study by the ILC. Treaties on both subjects resulted: the 1961 Vienna Convention on Diplomatic Relations (VCDR)[40] and the 1963 Vienna Convention on Consular Relations (VCCR).[41] Concluded at the Hofburg in Vienna, the Conventions provide a complete framework for the establishment, maintenance, and termination of permanent relations on the basis of the principle of consent between independent sovereign states.[42] Measuring by the high degree of observance and their influence on the international and national legal orders, the VCDR and VCCR are among the most successful international instruments ever to be drawn up under the United Nations' (UN) auspices. To a large extent, the VCDR codified customary rules on bilateral diplomatic relations between states.[43] Meanwhile, 192 states became parties to the Convention and its provisions have largely become part of general international law.[44] The VCCR is not considered a simple codification of CIL, although its main provisions have acquired customary status over time and 180 states have ratified the Convention.[45]

Other attempts at codifying diplomatic law attempts were not nearly as successful. First, the United Nations (UN) sought to clarify the status, rights, and duties of missions performing specific tasks. In 1968, members of the UNGA's Sixth Legal Committee negotiated a

[39] Institute of International Law, 'Regulation on Diplomatic Immunities' in *IIL Yearbook* (IIL 1895, rev 1929) 242.

[40] Vienna Convention on Diplomatic Relations (opened for signature on 18 April 1961, entered into force on 24 April 1964) 500 UNTS 95 (hereafter VCDR). Two protocols were added to the Convention: the Optional Protocol to the Vienna Convention on Diplomatic Relations concerning Acquisition of Nationality, signed on 18 April 1961, entered into force 2 May 1964, 500 UNTS 223 and the Optional Protocol to the Vienna Convention on Diplomatic Relations concerning Compulsory Settlement of Disputes, signed on 18 April 1961, entered into force 2 May 1964, 500 UNTS 241.

[41] Vienna Convention on Consular Relations, opened for signature 24 April 1963, entered into force 19 March 1967, 596 UNTS 261 (hereafter VCCR). Two protocols were added to the Convention: the Optional Protocol to the Vienna Convention on Consular Relations concerning Acquisition of Nationality, signed on 24 April 1963, entered into force 19 March 1967, 596 UNTS 469 and the Optional Protocol to the Vienna Convention on Consular Relations concerning the Compulsory Settlement of Disputes, signed on 24 April 1963, entered into force 19 March 1967, 596 UNTS 487.

[42] Eileen Young (Denza), 'The Development of the Law of Diplomatic Relations' (1964) 40 BYIL 141; Leo J Harris, 'Diplomatic Privileges and Immunities: A New Regime Is Soon to Be Adopted by the United States' (1968) 62 AJIL 98. For a historical appraisal, see Kai Bruns, *A Cornerstone of Modern Diplomacy: Britain and the Negotiation of the 1961 Vienna Convention on Diplomatic Relations* (Bloomsbury Academic 2014).

[43] Geoff R Berridge, *Diplomacy: Theory and Practice* (5th edn, Palgrave Macmillan 2015) 121–22; Eileen Denza, *Diplomatic Law: Commentary on the Vienna Convention on Diplomatic Relations* (4th edn, OUP 2016) 2–5; Joe Verhoeven, *Droit International Public* (Larcier 2000) 106.

[44] *Case concerning United States Diplomatic and Consular Staff in Tehran (United States of America v Iran)* (Judgment) [1980] ICJ Rep 3, paras 45 and 62 *in fine*; *Case concerning the Arrest Warrant of 11 April 2000 (Democratic Republic of the Congo v Belgium)* (Judgment) [2002] ICJ Rep 3, para 52.

[45] Luke T Lee and John B Quigley, *Consular Law and Practice* (3rd edn, OUP 2008) 21–23.

Convention on Special Missions (New York Convention or CSM).[46] The scope of privileges and immunities largely followed those provided for in the VCDR. However, precisely this wide range of unassigned facilities by host states seems to have caused reluctance on the part of governments to ratify the CSM. Second, the UN also aimed to catch up with the diplomatic realities of a multilateral world. In 1958, the ILC identified a need to harmonize the field of permanent representation at international organizations (IOs). Accreditation practices, as well as rules on facilities, privileges, and immunities tended to differ from one IO to another. In 1975, a new Vienna Conference was convened to fill this legal gap.[47] At the time, there was a lack of genuine reciprocity and the smaller states were more interested in what they regarded as 'parity' than in negotiating a text that would be acceptable to the major host states. While the conference ultimately resulted in the Convention on the Representation of States in their Relations with International Organizations of a Universal Character (CRSIO), this treaty has not yet entered into force.[48]

The relative failures of the CSM and the CRSIO are connected to the legal and historical context in which codification took place.[49] UN efforts in the diplomatic and consular domain between 1961 and 1975 cannot be disconnected from the changes that were ongoing in the world at the time. Among those global events are the rise of newly independent states, the Cold War confrontation between East and West, and the steady rise of international organizations and global governance. The shift towards a politically and culturally more diverse world order influenced the codification processes as well as the content of the actual rules adopted. The success of the codification exercises in 1961 and 1963 lies in the fact that negotiators were able to focus on legal-technical issues—avoiding debates on the political issues that otherwise preoccupied the world.[50] That same technique was less successful in later episodes of multilateral law-making, when agreement had to be found on a larger number of issues. At the root of the failure both of the CSM and of the CRSIO is the different approach of small and new states, on the one hand, and long-established states, on the other.

Multilateral efforts to codify the rules on immunities of IOs, their staff, and representatives of member and other states remain rather disappointing. However, a plethora of agreements treating these subjects does exist, for instance in the form of headquarters agreements and the like. Over time, all sorts of IOs started demanding parity with the UN and sometimes even states, even though their functions and consequent need for protection from political harassment were substantially different and much less sensitive. Host states generally developed a functional approach towards such IOs and, at times, showed resistance to their demands for diplomatic status and threats to relocate if these were not met.[51]

[46] New York Convention on Special Missions (signed on 8 December 1969, entered into force 21 June 1985) 1400 UNTS 231 (thirty-eight state parties).

[47] Abdullah EL Erian, 'La Conférence et la Convention sur la Epresentation des Etats dans leurs Relations avec les Organisations Internationales: Analyse Générale' (1975) 21 AFDI 445; Wahe H Balekijan, 'Rechtsstatus Permanenter Missionen von Nichtmitgliedstaaten bei Internationalen Organisationen' (1976) 27 ZöR 67.

[48] Vienna Convention on the Representation of States in their Relations with International Organizations of a Universal Character (signed on 14 March 1975, not yet in force).

[49] Sanderijn Duquet and Jan Wouters 'Diplomatic and Consular Relations' in Simon Chesterman, David Malone, and Santiago Villalpando (eds), *The Oxford Handbook of United Nations Treaties* (OUP 2019).

[50] Bruns (n 42) 201.

[51] Resolution adopted by the Committee of Ministers of the Council of Europe on 26 September 1969 and explanatory report (Council of Europe 1970).

#### 1.1.2.5 Key Developments

Notwithstanding diplomacy's selling points, a debate emerges as to whether the conduct of formal diplomatic relations may (have) become obsolete.[52] Communication between states is no longer restricted to one-on-one meetings between diplomats: globalization, air travel, and technological advances connect diplomatic actors more than ever.[53] Faced with economic and financial realities, some countries may consider scaling back their diplomatic representations. Traditional diplomacy also increasingly faces competition from alternative fora and international cooperation schemes.[54] Based on formal hierarchies of governments, diplomatic institutions sometimes struggle to respond to ad hoc networks focused on expertise, legitimacy, and capacities. Changes relevant to diplomacy are quantitative, including an increase of the number of states and missions; they are also qualitative, as international society has witnessed increasing heterogeneity, a move from bilateralism to multilateralism, and changing citizens' expectations. Diplomacy has also transformed from within. Advancing foreign policy objectives is now the work of experts of many kinds, who often work in or with embassies. Driving this agenda is the sense that although diplomacy has changed over time, it is not evolving fast enough.

A final key development is the emergence of less traditional actors that have expanded their influence at the global level. This handbook studies the emergence of one particular non-traditional diplomatic and (to a certain extent) consular actor, the European Union (EU, or Union). The EU is not alone in this quest for diplomatic recognition. While in the past, actors that do not (strictly) classify as a state, such as city states and provinces, have attempted to set up legation practices, the frequency of such attempts has increased in recent years. With varying degrees of success and enthusiasm, sub-state entities (eg German *Länder*, Belgian federated entities, Spanish *comunidades autónomas* , and French regions), aspiring states (eg Kosovo and Palestine), international organizations, religious entities (eg the Holy See and the Sovereign Military Order of Saint John of Jerusalem), and non-governmental actors (eg the International Committee of the Red Cross) have made claims to the right to send and receive diplomatic and consular envoys.

However, diplomacy, despite (and even thanks to) its old and robust foundations and seemingly limited membership, is as relevant as ever. For one thing, media coverage on diplomats expediting foreign affairs events does not seem to decrease. Moreover, governments unequivocally choose to invest in a system where resident diplomats obtain insights on the host country that cannot be collected from a distance. Diplomacy is not a business: European states' missions are still expanding, despite budgetary constraints. In response to societal developments, traditional diplomacy changed and adapted working methods and priorities: globalization processes and technological advancements have brought about a major shift in how diplomacy is conducted.[55]

[52] Paul Sharp, 'Who Needs Diplomats? The Problem of Diplomatic Representation' in Jönsson and Langhorne (n 7).

[53] Wilfried Bolewski, *Diplomacy and International Law in Globalized Relations* (Springer 2007).

[54] Michelle M Betsill and Elisabeth Corell, *NGO Diplomacy: The Influence of Nongovernmental Organizations in International Environmental Negotiations* (MIT Press 2008).

[55] Scholarship therefore tends to study diplomacy in an evolutionary sense. See Alan K Henrikson, 'Diplomacy's Possible Futures' (2006) 1 HJD 3, 5; Jorge Heine, 'On the Manner of Practicing the New Diplomacy' [2006] CIGI 3; Ronald P Barston, *Modern Diplomacy* (4th edn, Pearson 2013) 96; Brian Hocking, 'Catalytic Diplomacy: Beyond "Newness" and "Decline"' in Jan Melissen (ed), *Innovation in Diplomatic Practice* (Palgrave Macmillan 1999); Jan Melissen (ed), *The New Public Diplomacy: Soft Power in International Relations* (Palgrave Macmillan 2005); Geoffrey R Wiseman, 'Polylateralism and New Modes of Global Dialogue' in Jönsson and Langhorne (n 7); Andrew F Cooper, 'The Changing Nature of Diplomacy' in Cooper, Heine, and Thakur (n 3).

On the legal side of things, an important observation is that the Vienna framework continues to show its durability, as evidenced by its universal application in diplomatic and consular practice around the world. For want of other multilateral legal instruments, the VCDR and VCCR also serve as reference instruments to deal with international relations that surpass those between states and the rights and duties of those participating. At the same time, society has evolved since the UN's latest codification efforts and questions arise as to just how bendable the international rules on diplomacy are to include, for instance, the diplomatic and consular activities of the Union.

## 1.2 The EU as a Diplomatic Actor

### 1.2.1 Why Does the EU Engage in Diplomatic Relations?

The EU has established a firm claim to diplomatic (and, to a lesser extent, consular) affairs, both in relation to the general international legal framework and in relation to its member states. What started over sixty years ago as a modest external representation of the High Authority of the European Coal and Steel Community (ECSC), and later of the European Commission , has become a fully grown diplomatic network. Unlike other IOs, which by and large only exercise a passive right of legation,[56] the broad array of competences of the EU's member states allocated to the Union has fuelled an active pursuit of common interests via diplomatic tools.[57] The EU maintains an anchored permanent diplomatic presence in 133 third countries—with 21 more accreditations to countries where it is represented through a neighbouring permanent delegation—and 4 regions not universally recognized as states. It has also installed nine permanent missions dedicated to representing the Union at IOs.

The EU is an integral part of the trends described in the previous sections. Not only did it emerge as a diplomatic actor even when the usefulness of diplomacy was challenged; in itself, the EU is also referred to as one of the challenges threatening the institution of diplomacy. Nevertheless, seeking diplomatic recognition is a logical consequence of the Union's positioning in the international scene. The Union's own history is driven by a desire of finding *peaceful solutions to international problems*. The Schuman Declaration, delivered by Robert Schuman on 9 May 1950, already contained ample references to world peace and peace among European states. The process of European integration exalts a modern society and resulted in the longest period without armed conflict among EU member states in written history. The EU's desire for peace was reiterated more recently, when, at the occasion of the receipt of the Nobel Peace Prize in 2012, Commission President José Barroso stated that '[a]s a community of nations that has overcome war and fought totalitarianism, we will always stand by those who are in pursuit of peace and human dignity'.

This pledge to peaceful international negotiations is equally reflected in external action: in the foundational Treaties, the Union commits to supporting peace and reconciliation. Article 3(5) of the Treaty on European Union (TEU) reads:[58]

[56] Henry G Schermers and Niels M Blokker, *International Institutional Law: Unity within Diversity* (5th edn, Martinus Nijhoff 2011) 1159.

[57] Brian Hocking and Michael Smith, 'An Emerging Diplomatic System for the EU? Frameworks and Issues' (2011) 44 Cuad Eurde Deusto 19; David Spence, 'Taking Stock: 50 Years of European Diplomacy' (2009) 4 HJD 235.

[58] See also Art 8(1) TEU and Art 21(2)(*c*) TEU.

> [i]n its relations with the wider world, the Union shall [ … ] contribute to peace, security, the sustainable development of the Earth, solidarity and mutual respect among peoples, free and fair trade, eradication of poverty and the protection of human rights, in particular the rights of the child, as well as to the strict observance and the development of international law, including respect for the principles of the United Nations Charter.

From this angle, the choice to invest in a diplomatic network is not at all surprising—it merely evidences the current and continued relevance of diplomacy as an institution of foreign relations.

But there are more tangible, functional, and practical reasons, too. The Union uses diplomacy to manage both its everyday interactions with foreign governments and more dramatic episodes, including international crises, wars, and disasters. It aims to build capacity and long-term relationships with host governments while looking for engagement-based solutions. Diplomacy provides it with an opportunity not only for convening knowledge, skills, and economic interests but also to assert values through packages of culturally resonant messages and more strategic narratives. Indeed, from a realist perspective, the Union engages diplomats in third countries and at IOs to exert power, defend its (citizens') interests, and to position itself as a truly global actor in international relations. Article 3(5) TEU says as much when it spells out that, in its international relations, the Union is to also 'uphold and promote its values and interests and contribute to the protection of its citizens'.

The EU's reasons for conducting diplomatic relations therefore do not fundamentally differ from those of nation states. As a new(er) international actor, it seeks changes in the practices of international relations that will permit it to acquire similar sorts of recognition and representation. In fact, securing representation rights is both a goal and a function of EU diplomacy.[59] Two additional elements push the Union towards its diplomatic actorness. First, the EU is required to conduct diplomatic relations in order to effectively exercise the many competences and powers attributed to it. Formal diplomatic relations are important tools for effectuating foreign policy and representational objectives. Building strong diplomatic ties is often a precursor to establishing bilateral and multilateral relations. Second, while it might have been possible for European states to individually protect their interests in the nineteenth century, the increasingly interconnected, post-Second World War world order has significantly reduced the benefits of this approach. Not only has Europe found itself in the midst of an increasing number of power blocs in a multipolar world, but also the ability of European states to individually protect their internal security and promote external stability has dramatically declined. A common representation—of states, citizens, the internal market—is detrimental to being perceived as a strong political actor and as a trade and development cooperation giant on the world stage.

### 1.2.2 A Brief History of EU Diplomacy

The following section gives a historical account of EU diplomacy.[60] Four phases will be distinguished: *(a)* the Union's first steps in diplomacy (1955–73); *(b)* the professionalization

[59] Paul Sharp, *Diplomatic Theory of International Relations* (CUP 2009) 1.

[60] European Commission DG External Relations, 'Taking Europe to the World. 50 Years of the European Commission's External Service' (European Commission 2004).

of diplomacy (1974–84); *(c)* the manifest expansion of diplomacy (1985–2009); and *(d)* the current stage, initiated by the entry into force of the Lisbon Treaty (2010 to date).

#### 1.2.2.1 Start Up and Informality

When the six founding nations of the ECSC created a closely unified economic union, it was agreed that political integration would be sought only in the longer term. The establishment of a legation practice, however, did not remain a theoretical possibility for a long time. Well before the Treaties of Rome were signed (1957), the ECSC had set up active and passive legation activities through the sending and receiving of diplomats. Missions of third states were received by the High Authority, which had concluded an agreement with the Grand Duchy of Luxembourg so that diplomatic privileges and immunities could be guaranteed to those countries' representatives. Following the creation of the European Economic Community (EEC) and the European Atomic Energy Community (EURATOM), a special committee treated accreditation requests from third countries, in agreement with the Council. The intervention of the Council was considered justified by the powers it had in the Treaties of Rome.[61] To facilitate interactions between missions of the Communities' member states, a Committee of Permanent Representatives (Coreper) was established consisting of their diplomatic representatives.[62]

In 1955, the ECSC opened its first foreign mission in London. An informal agreement on diplomatic relations was agreed between the High Authority (on the basis of the extensive powers under Articles 6 and 8 of the ECSC Treaty) and the United Kingdom but de facto extended to the whole ECSC.[63] From the very start, this mission considered it within its remit to diplomatically represent the ECSC and soon thereafter also the other Communities.[64] The United Kingdom accorded the mission certain privileges, including a CD license plate and immunities; the head of mission had ambassadorial status, in contrast to the staff, who enjoyed limited diplomatic privileges and immunities. However, it was mentioned at the end of London's diplomatic list, together with the personnel of international secretariats established in London.[65] Moreover, because the representative was accredited to the UK Government and not—as was common for foreign ambassadors—to the Court of St James, there were considerable inequalities. For instance, the head of mission was not allowed to participate in the meetings of the diplomatic corps. This caused some authors to raise doubts as to whether the mission in London was truly diplomatic in nature, and if so, whether it would be followed by the establishment of other missions.[66] However, as Smith argues in retrospect, '[s]ince the opening of the first European Commission delegation in London in 1955, the EU has been engaged in diplomatic activity even if it has not been considered or recognised as such'.[67]

[61] Commission des affaires politiques et des questions institutionnelles de l'Assemblée parlementaire européenne (APE), Rapport sur les problèmes que posent les relations des Communautés européennes avec l'extérieur, en particulier le droit de légation et de pavillon (Rapporteur: Marinus van der Goes van Naters) 9 November 1959, doc 87/1959 and Rapport complémentaire, 17 November 1960, doc 88/1960–61 (hereafter APE, Report on the Right of Legation).

[62] Cross (n 27) 143.

[63] Laurens J Brinkhorst, 'Permanent Missions of the EC in Third Countries: European Diplomacy in the Making' (1984) 10 LIEI 23, 26. See also the ECSC Act of 27 July 1955, discussed in Reichling (n 12) 38, 61.

[64] Assemblée parlementaire européenne, 'Droit de légation et de pavillon', 19 November 1960, 9.

[65] Schermers and Blokker (n 56) 1179.

[66] Rolando Quadri, 'La Personnalité International de la Communauté' in Michel Melchior (ed), *Les Relations Extérieurs de la Communauté Européenne Unifiée* (Institut d'Études Juridiques Européennes de la Faculté de Droit de l'Université de Liège 1969) 67.

[67] Michael H Smith, 'The EU as a Diplomatic Actor in the Post-Lisbon Era: Robust or Rootless Hybrid?' in Joachim Alexander Koops and Gjovalin Macaj (eds), *The European Union as a Diplomatic Actor* (Palgrave Macmillan 2014).

In the meantime, the High Authority had also signed an agreement with the United States to open a mission in Washington DC. For its first decades, the mission to the United States was officially operated as an 'information centre' registered under the US Foreign Agents Registration Act of 1938 and not as a diplomatic mission. The Act requires agents representing the interests of a foreign principal to disclose their relationship with that principal and information about their activities and finances.[68]

With the sprouting legation activities came a discussion concerning their legal qualification as well as the internal institutional aspects of the Communities' diplomacy.[69] The first was resolved rather easily[70] when the Parliamentary Assembly confirmed the diplomatic capacity of the Communities in 1960 in the following terms:[71]

> les Communautés européennes jouissent de par leur personnalité juridique internationale du droit de légation actif et passif.

However, the adoption of the Resolution did not settle the discussion as to who would then execute the diplomatic relations on behalf of the Communities. The Council's proposal to create a joint diplomatic representation was not withheld and the Commission became the dominant institution to deal with the active right of legation.[72] As a reaction, the Council opened its own liaison office in Geneva to deal with negotiations in the framework of the General Agreement on Tariffs and Trade (GATT).[73]

The passive right of legation was executed by both institutions: after an extraordinary meeting of the Council held in Luxembourg in January 1966, a statement was issued that credentials of the heads of missions of non-member states would from then on be submitted jointly to the President of the Council and the President of the Commission, meeting together for this purpose.[74] Paragraph 5 of the 1966 Luxemburg compromise read:

> [i]n 1959 the Council laid down the rules which, provisionally, were to govern the recognition of diplomatic missions accredited to the Community (letter of 25 July 1959 from MG Pella, President of the Council, to the President of the Commission). These rules amount to a sharing of prerogatives between the Council and the Commission. In particular, letters of credence are presented to the President of the Commission, who has instituted for these occasions a ceremony modelled on that used between states, whereas the Treaty of Rome

[68] Foreign Agents Registration Act (US) 22 USC § 611 et seq.

[69] APE, Report on the Right of Legation, para 10.

[70] The statement may not have accurately reflected PIL at the time; see Chapter 2 for a discussion.

[71] 'The European Communities enjoy the right of active and passive legation by virtue of its international legal personality' [own translation]; Résolution adoptée par l'Assemblée Parlementaire Européenne relative aux problèmes que posent les relations des Communautés européennes avec l'extérieur, en particulier le droit de légation et de pavillon, 29 November 1960, 761f/60 (Luxembourg) 707f/60 (Brussels) [1960] OJ 1496/60. For a discussion, see Carl A Ehrhardt, 'Das Diplomatische Korps bei Der EWG in Brüssel' (1962) 13 Aussenpolitik 659, 661.

[72] Michael Hardy, 'The Diplomatic Activities of International Organisations: The United Nations and the European Communities Contrasted' (1969) 5 RBDI 44, 56.

[73] David Spence, 'From the Convention to Lisbon: External Competence and the Uneasy Transition for Geneva Delegations' in David Spence and Jozef Bátora (eds), *The European External Action Service: European Diplomacy Post-Westphalia* (Palgrave Macmillan 2015) 227.

[74] Luxembourg compromise of 28 and 29 January 1966, Part a(3) [1966] 3 BullEC 10, referred to in Koen Lenaerts and Piet Van Nuffel, *European Union Law* (Robert Bray and Nathan Cambien eds, Sweet & Maxwell 2011) 955; Petrus Mathijsen and Peter Dyrberg, *Guide to European Union Law* (11th edn, Sweet & Maxwell 2013) 572.

lays down that the Council alone may commit the Community vis-à-vis non-member countries.

A sixth paragraph added: '[c]onsequently, any approaches by foreign representatives to the Commission must be reported to the Council'.

Following the installation period, diplomatic activity grew exponentially. Third states sought to intensify their relations with the Communities, primarily in the economic era, as a result of the Communities' growing competences. This triggered a need for both the establishment of autonomous representations in third states and the establishment of missions of third states in Brussels.[75] Within a period of ten years after the creation of the EEC in 1958, sixty-nine states had a mission accredited at the Communities.[76] In the meantime, Belgium had assumed the responsibility to accord foreign missions customary privileges and immunities.[77]

The Communities were slower in setting up a diplomatic service of their own.[78] During the 1960s and the early 1970s, Commission representations were more or less randomly established, with a preference for strategic partner countries and development cooperation partner countries. Multilateral missions were first established in Geneva (1961) and New York (1964). After being labelled Commission information and communication offices (*bureaux de presse et d'information*), the missions (in 1964 and 1974, respectively) officially became Commission delegations.[79] The United States only formally accorded the Commission delegation in Washington DC full diplomatic status in 1972—an offshoot of renewed transatlantic contacts during Henry Kissinger's 'Year of Europe'.

Another preference was to open delegationsin Africa, reflecting both individual member states' post-colonial interests and the desire to implement a common development policy. These 'aid' delegations were managed through the European Development Fund (EDF), which employed contract teams in associated states led by a *contrôleur technique* or a *controleur délégué*—hence the name 'delegations'. Hanses and Spence note that the presence of the Commission in Kinshasa (then Leopoldville) dates back from 1959 but was not upgraded to a diplomatic mission until 1988.[80] The offices primarily worked on low politics and developmental issues, but soon after were also assigned broader representational tasks that surpassed their development cooperation remit.[81] Host governments perceived the delegations as the Communities' political representatives and started bestowing them with certain privileges.[82] Much like the strategic missions in partner countries, the development

[75] Ramses A Wessel, *The European Union's Foreign and Security Policy: A Legal Institutional Perspective* (Kluwer 1999) 272.

[76] Keith Hamilton and Richard Langhorne, *The Practice of Diplomacy: Its Evolution, Theory and Administration* (Routledge 1995) 206. By 1969, eighty-one third states were accredited to the EEC; Jean Salmon, 'Les Représentations et Missions Permanentes auprès de le CEE et de l'Euratom' in Michel Virally, Pierre Gerbet, and Jean Salmon (eds) *Les Missions Permanentes auprès des Organisations Internationales*, vol I (Dotation Carnegie pour la Paix Internationale 1971) 720–21.

[77] Article 17 of the Merger Treaty (signed on 8 April 1965, entered into force 1 July 1967) [1967] OJ 152/2. The Merger Treaty installed a single Commission and a single Council for the Communities.

[78] Wessel (n 75) 272.

[79] Edith Drieskens, 'What's in a Name? Challenges to the Creation of EU Delegations' (2012) 7 HJD 51, 53.

[80] Bruno Hanses and David Spence, 'Structural Diplomacy and Foreign Policy: The Case of the EU Delegation in the Democratic Republic of the Congo' in Spence and Bátora (n 73).

[81] Jean Raux, *Les Relations Extérieures de La Communauté Économique Européenne* (Editions Cujas 1968).

[82] Hans Merket, 'From Commission to Union Delegations: A Legal-Institutionalist Analysis' [2014] European Union in International Affairs IV, Proceedings 2–3; Pia Kerres and Ramses A Wessel, 'Apples and Oranges? Comparing the European Union Delegations to National Embassies' (2015) Cleer Working Paper No 2. <https://www.asser.nl/media/2847/cleer15-2_web.pdf> accessed 1 June 2022..

cooperation missions were not immediately also recognized as diplomatic in nature but in general derived advantages and protection from the diplomatic regime that applied to other missions in the receiving state.

Experimentalism was demonstrated in two ways. First, in the absence of a strategy or template for negotiating the Commission delegations' privileges and immunities in a receiving state, the Commission and third states' governments agreed on the status of delegations informally. Much documentary evidence of these arrangements is not on hand, since the method that proved most effective involved simply requesting a third state to adopt a national law that predicated the application of diplomatic law. Second, the Community's foreign policy and external relations provisions in the Rome Treaties remained rather scarce. In securing a legal status for its missions in third countries, the Commission acted on its own authority.

### 1.2.2.2 Professionalization

In 1974, a second phase of EU diplomacy was entered into. During this period, the Commission put forward three different ways of achieving its aim of enjoying diplomatic status abroad: *(a)* through bilateral establishment agreements, *(b)* through unilateral concessions in domestic law, and *(c)* through a multilateral agreement. The Commission signed the first so-called Establishment Agreement (EA) with Japan and subsequently started using the Japan agreement as a template for negotiating the terms of its relations with other countries. This approach did not immediately result in the abandonment of the former technique of requesting third states to adapt their domestic laws to include a reference to the status of the Commission delegation. Several states hosting delegations—Canada (1976), Venezuela (1978), and Thailand (1979)—unilaterally accepted to accord diplomatic treatment without signing an agreement with the Commission.[83] Yet another approach was to deal with privileges and immunities collectively. In relation to African, Caribbean, and Pacific (ACP) countries, the diplomatic status of delegation was discussed in the multilateral Lomé framework.[84] The 1975 Lomé Convention, intended to boost trade and development aid, contained a Protocol on privileges and immunities that required partner states to accord diplomatic privileges and immunities to the Commission representations in signatory states.[85] Commission delegations enjoyed VCDR rights in Lomé countries,[86] where they executed what has been referred to as 'associative diplomacy'.[87]

At this point, things moved slower within the Communities. It was not until the 1970s that regular coordination between EEC member states in the field of international law took off; this informal cooperation between the embassies and consulates of the member states happened in the structures of the European Political Cooperation (EPC, established on 27 October 1970 following the Luxembourg compromise) and intensified with it.[88] Further, the 1973 Davignon Report sought progress by recommending that member states should

[83] For an overview of national laws treating the EU as a recipient of privileges and immunities, see Appendix 4; for an overview of all EAs concluded, see Appendix 3. Both are discussed in detail in Chapter 3.

[84] On the period preceding Lomé, see Ferdinand Leikam, 'A Matter of Preference: Commonwealth Africa, Britain and the EEC Association System, 1957–75' in Pascaline Winand, Andrea Benvenuti, and Max Guderzo (eds), *The External Relations of the European Union: Historical and Contemporary Perspectives* (PIE Peter Lang 2015).

[85] Protocol 5 of the ACP–EEC Convention of Lomé, signed on 28 February 1975 [1976] OJ L25/2.

[86] Brinkhorst (n 63) 25.

[87] Wessel (n 75) 274.

[88] Eileen Denza, *The Intergovernmental Pillars of the European Union* (OUP 2002) 165.

harmonize their views in foreign policy matters.[89] Thereto, it confirmed and made official an already existing practice of national diplomats aligning with the work of the EPC.[90] In the next phase, the 1981 London report pushed locally represented member states to jointly draft and send reports to the EPC, to 'regularly consider matters together', and to seek common positions.[91]

### 1.2.2.3 Manifest Expansion

In a third phase of EU diplomacy, experimentalism and differentiation in the active legation practices were replaced by a more calculated approach. The entry into force of the Maastricht Treaty of 1993 transformed the EPC into the Common Foreign and Security Policy (CFSP). Still, the CFSP was not intended to replace member states' sovereign conduct in diplomatic and consular relations nor their capacity to deal with foreign policy matters outside of the ambit of Community competences.[92] The informal cooperation between member state missions, developed under the EPC, was made a matter of legal obligation while practice also showed member states increasingly working together in the diplomatic domain. Maastricht introduced a requirement to cooperate in the implementation of Council common positions and joint actions, an obligation to exchange information and carry out joint assessments, and the entitlement to consular protection of unrepresented EU citizens as an element of that citizenship. The rotating presidency acted on behalf of the Union in third states where it was necessary to implement agreed policies.

The key focus of the Commission delegations continued to be the execution of its trade (mostly with strategic partners) and aid policies (mostly with ACP countries). The third Lomé Convention (1984) contained a reference leaving matters to bilateral arrangements, after which country-specific agreements on diplomatic relations were systematically sought with ACP countries.[93] In 1988, the Commission counted seventy delegations—six in strategic partner states and sixty-four in ACP countries. In 1989, a joint declaration was annexed to the Lomé Convention, reading: '[w]ithin the context of their respective regulations, the ACP Sates shall grant Commission delegations privileges and immunities similar to those granted to diplomatic missions so that they are able to carry out the functions incumbent on them under the Convention in a satisfactory and effective manner'. This caused an upgrade of representational offices to the level of Commission delegations, which came around the same time the Commission was seeking to establish diplomatic delegations in the capitals of its main trading partners.

For Lomé and non-Lomé countries alike, to enter into diplomatic relations, the Commission now exclusively relied on a template agreement it had first used to manage its diplomatic relations with Japan. This first model of EA was instrumental in standardizing the Commission's diplomatic practice. On its turn, the standardization fostered three developments. First, there was a manifest quantitative expansion of delegations, resulting in what can be best described as an EA boom: delegations were opened in the capitals of all of

[89] Christopher Hill and William Wallace, 'Diplomatic Trends in the European Community' (1979) 55 International Aff 47, 49, 53.

[90] Report on the Problems of Political Unification, prepared by the Davignon Committee [1970] 11 Bull EC 9–14.

[91] Report on European Political Cooperation, adopted in London [1981] Bull EC, Supp No 3, 14–17, para 8. See, for a discussion, Bernard R Bot, 'Co-operation between the Diplomatic Missions of the Ten in Third Countries and International Organisations' (1984) 10 LIEI 149.

[92] Denza, *Intergovernmental Pillars of the EU* (n 88) 86–90.

[93] Fourth ACP–EC Convention of Lomé, as revised by the agreement signed in Mauritius on 4 November 1995, Annex LXXIII, 295.

the EU's main trading partners and the relations with ACP delegations were upgraded.[94] Second, delegations' staff became more professional as their tasks extended to traditionally diplomatic tasks. Third, foreign countries increasingly accepted the Commission's role in representing the Community at the diplomatic level.[95]

Even at its height, the practice of concluding establishment agreements still lacked a constitutional mandate. Although the 1992 Maastricht Treaty counted quite a number of provisions on external relations and, for the first time, referred to the EU's diplomatic relations, it remained silent on *how* these relations had to be established; Article J.6 merely mentioned the existence of Commission delegations and that cooperation ought to take place: '[t]he diplomatic and consular missions of the Member States and the commission Delegations in third countries and international conferences, and their representations to international organizations, shall cooperate in ensuring that the common positions and common measures adopted by the Council are complied with and implemented'. Similarly, Article 20 (para 1) of the consolidated Amsterdam and Nice versions of the TEU refer to the gradual fostering of international cooperation between the member states and the Commission delegations without providing a clear legal basis for the conclusion of EAs that allow for the delegations to be established.

The Commission's organizational structure was adapted to accommodate diplomatic needs. The administrative reorganization dwelt on the idea that diplomatic representation was a manifestation of the Commission's general mandate and that it was to be executed by the relevant Commission Directorates General (DGs). Three DG were involved: DG I/DG External Relations), DG III/DG Development, and DG X/DG Press/Communication.[96] Maastricht divided the Commission's DG I, which formerly covered all external relations, into a DG I and a DG IA.[97] The latter took the responsibility for foreign policy issues but was soon overburdened with its new role in the CFSP. The institutional reform exposed that the Commission lacked knowledge, expertise, and manpower to keep up with the member states' diplomatic services. To deal with shortcomings, the possibility of establishing a common diplomatic training programme was first raised at this occasion. However, rather than training, efforts were put into a general reorganization of delegations and tasks to counter the critique that third states drew diplomatic advantage from the ambiguities in the Community's internal competences and organization. Nuttall argues that '[t]he confusion was compounded by the fact that the Commission's role varied not only over time, but also according to the area of policy concerned'.[98] Until then, Commission delegations had mainly dealt with issues over which the Commission held competence or shared competence, with a focus on trade, aid, and development. In 1999, the Relex Group of Commissioners—those responsible for external relations, economic and monetary affairs, development and humanitarian aid, enlargement and trade policy—launched an ambitious reform programme

[94] Michael Bruter, 'Diplomacy without a State: The External Delegations of the European Commission' (1999) 6 J Eur Public Policy 183.

[95] José Manuel Sobrino Heredia, 'La Actividad Diplomática de las Delegaciones de la Comisión en el Exterior de la Comunidad Europea' (1993) 20 Rev Inst Eur 485.

[96] Roberts (n 10) 407; Eduardo Vilariño Pintos, 'Representación Exterior y Cooperación Diplomática y Consular en el Tratado de la Unión Europea' (1995) 22 Rev Inst Eur 417.

[97] Reinhardt Rummel, 'The Intergovernmental Conference, 1966—How to Reform CFSP?' in Elfriede Regelsberger, Philippe De Schoutheete, and Wolfgang Wessels (eds), *Foreign Policy of the European Union: From EPC to CFSP and Beyond* (L Rienner 1997) 373.

[98] Simon J Nuttall, 'The Commission: Struggle for Legitimacy' in Christopher Hill (ed), *The Actors in Europe's Foreign Policy* (Routledge 1996) 130.

aimed at decentralizing administration and decision-making from Brussels to the delegations abroad.[99] The roles and functions of Commission delegations expanded accordingly: they became responsible for programme identification, programme preparation, and some procurement, as well as for technical, contractual, and financial implementation.[100]

Notwithstanding the Council's general mandate in common foreign policies, its role was reduced to that of a bystander in diplomatic relations when the Treaty of Maastricht formally separated CFSP methods from the first-pillar external relations procedures. Before 1989, the Commission informed the Council (in practice, Coreper) of its decision to open a Commission delegation and to appoint its head.[101] Together with the Parliament, the Council approved the budget to manage delegations. In 1989, the Commission placed its procedures on a more formal footing: it gave the Council the possibility to comment on choices made and declared itself willing to discuss those issues with member states if they so requested. As MacLeod, Hendry, and Hyett argued, '[t]he appointment of its overseas delegations is an administrative matter for the Commission but in practice the Council has a role in the decision to establish a delegation and in the appointment of the Head of Commission Delegations'.[102] The Council also moderately stepped up its own active legation activities. In 1994, following the coming into force of the Maastricht Treaty, a small Council liaison office was established in New York to serve as a support structure for the CFSP.[103] Much like the Council's Geneva office, the New York office was devoted to coordinating between member states and providing support to the rotating presidency.[104] To enjoy privileges and immunities, it was communicated to the host government that the delegation formed part of the Commission delegation.[105] Some ten years later, the offices of both institutions would move into the same premises, fitted with larger meeting rooms and a common entrance. In the late 1990s, the Council Secretariat's efforts to establish a liaison office in Vienna, parallel to the Council Secretariat office in Geneva and New York, ran aground.[106]

In this third phase of EU diplomacy, cooperation between member states also intensified. At the instigation of the United Kingdom, member states identified areas in which their posts abroad were to seek cooperation. These focus areas were subsequently attached to the Single European Act (SEA). The list mentioned administrative and practical problems, security and consular questions, health, education, information, and cultural affairs. In fact, the SEA did little more than to consolidate previous EPC practices. However, its Article 11 specified that officials employed in the newly created EPC Secretariat 'shall be treated in the same way as members of [member states'] diplomatic missions', thus foreshadowing immunity and privileges to which the European External Action Service (EEAS) would later also lay claim.[107]

[99] Damien Helly, Anna Knoll, and Greta Galeazzi, 'A Closer Look into EU's External Action Frontline: Framing the Challenges Ahead for EU Delegations' (2014) 62 ECDPM Briefing Note 3.

[100] Jonas Frederiksen and Heather Baser, 'Better Aid Delivery or Deconcentration of Bureaucracy? A Snapshot of the EC's Devolution Process' (European Centre for Development Policy Management 2004).

[101] Iain MacLeod, Ian D Hendry, and Stephen Hyett, *The External Relations of the European Communities: A Manual of Law and Practice* (OUP 1996) 216.

[102] ibid 209 and 216.

[103] Katie Verlin Laatikainen, 'The EU Delegation in New York: A Debut in High Political Drama' in Spence and Bátora (n 73) 195.

[104] Simon Duke, 'The Practices of Post-Lisbon Diplomacy' in Michael Smith, Stephan Keukeleire, and Sophie Vanhoonacker (eds), *The Diplomatic System of the European Union: Evolution, Change and Challenges* (Routledge 2016) 67; Allan Rosas and Lorna Armati, *EU Constitutional Law: An Introduction* (Bloomsbury 2012) 201.

[105] MacLeod, Hendry and Hyett (n 101) 225.

[106] Lars-Erik Lundin, 'Effective Multilateralism after Lisbon: The Added Value of the EEAS and the EU Delegation in Vienna' in Spence and Bátora (n 73) 246.

[107] Simon J Nuttall, *European Political Co-operation* (Clarendon Press 1992) 26–27; Federica Bicchi and Heidi Maurer, 'European Cooperation Abroad' (2017) 12 HJD 1.

National diplomats organized thematic meetings at more regular intervals,[108] engaged in joint reporting to capitals on local issues, and regularly issued joint démarches to host states.[109] National diplomats' rapprochement did not escape the Commission's notice, and it sought to collaborate with the member states, even in the EPC. Yet, the EPC had largely remained an intergovernmental activity designed to coordinate national foreign policies. The Commission's involvement was not self-evident; it was only in 1981 with the London report that this was accepted as a principle. The Commission collected information from various sources, including from its delegations, while setting up an autonomous input capacity.[110] From 1992 onwards, delegations were involved in the drafting of political reports together with locally represented member state embassies. Consequently, before 2009, the EU's diplomacy relied on multiple actors: the relevant Commission DGs, with a central position of DG Relex; the rotating presidency and the General Secretariat of the Council in CFSP matters; and the member states, all of which were represented in parallel.[111]

#### 1.2.2.4 Post-Lisbon

The entry into force of the Lisbon Treaty introduced a fourth phase, one that brought about the most radical change to EU diplomacy since its inception, aimed at upgrading the CFSP and the role of the EU at the global level.[112] The enhanced European external relations machinery resulted in more actors speaking and acting on the Union's behalf. This gave rise to a general criticism that the multitude of actors involved in the EU's public diplomacy results in a lack of consistency with regard to the messages brought by the Union, often referred to as the 'need to speak with one voice'.[113]

The Commission continues to represent the EU externally, with the exception of the CFSP and other cases provided for in the Treaties (Art 17(1) TEU). The Council remains responsible for the general external policymaking responsibilities conferred on it under the Treaties (Arts 16(1) and 26(2) TEU). New actors—the President of the European Council and the High Representative for Foreign Affairs and Security Policy (HR)—were called into existence. The President represents the EU on issues of CFSP, at his level and in that capacity (Art 15(6) TEU).[114] This is without prejudice to the powers of the HR, who tackles the more general mission of leading the EU's CFSP. Article 27(2) TEU provides that:

> the High Representative shall represent the Union for matters relating to the common foreign and security. He shall conduct political dialogue with third parties on the Union's behalf and shall express the Union's position in international organisations and at international conferences.

[108] Yannick Gérard, 'La Coopération Politique Européenne. Méthodes et Résultats' (1989) Rev du Marché Commun 466.

[109] MacLeod, Hendry, and Hyett (n 101) 219.

[110] Nuttall, *European Political Co-operation* (n 107) 141.

[111] Piet Eeckhout, *EU External Relations Law* (OUP 2011) 292.

[112] Simon Duke, 'Providing for European-Level Diplomacy after Lisbon: The Case of the European External Action Service' (2009) 4 HJD 211; Michael Emerson and others, *Upgrading the EU's Role as Global Actor* (Centre for European Policy Studies 2011); Jan Wouters, Dominic Coppens, and Bart De Meester, 'The European Union's External Relations after the Lisbon Treaty' in Stefan Griller and Jacques Ziller (eds), *The Lisbon Treaty: EU Constitutionalism without a Constitutional Treaty?* (Springer 2008).

[113] Steffen Bay Rasmussen, 'The Messages and Practices of the European Union's Public Diplomacy' (2010) 5 HJD 263, 282.

[114] *Council v Commission* [2016] ECLI:EU:C:2016:616, 33.

The HR also heads the newly established EEAS (Art 18 TEU). The EEAS is set up as a functionally autonomous body separate from the Commission and Council. The Service was launched on 1 December 2010 and became operational one month later, on the first day of 2011. Whereas the EEAS can be considered a 'Brussels-based machinery', its external bodies—the Union delegations or EUDELs—operate as the EU's diplomatic missions.[115] Article 221 of the Treaty on the Functioning of the European Union (TFEU) refers to the new Union delegations in the following terms:[116]

1. Union delegations in third countries and at international organisations shall represent the Union.
2. Union delegations shall be placed under the authority of the High Representative of the Union for Foreign Affairs and Security Policy. They shall act in close cooperation with Member States' diplomatic and consular missions.

The Treaties now, albeit in indirect terms, confirm the Union's general competence to establish and maintain its own diplomatic relations. In addition to the general obligation, there are specific obligations to share information and carry out joint assessments (Art 35, para 2 TEU); to contribute to the formulation and implementation of a common approach (Art 32 TEU), for example, by ensuring that decisions defining Union positions and actions are adopted in a manner pursuant to the CFSP (Art 35, para 1 TEU); and to cooperate in delivering consular protection to Union citizens in the territory of third countries (Art 35, para 3 TEU). Union diplomacy, however, must respect the distinctive character that the member states traditionally possess in diplomacy.[117]

All in all, the EEAS and EUDELs remain minimally described in primary law. They are, however, featured in the 2010 Council Decision on the organization and functioning of the EEAS.[118] This Decision is the outcome of intense discussions featuring institutional wrangling over the EEAS's composition and tasks, the balance between national diplomats and EU civil servants (with national diplomats tallying one-third and EU civil servants tallying two-thirds of the total workforce) and other traditional supranational versus intergovernmental debates.[119]

When, following Lisbon, Commission delegations converted into Union delegations, the EU sent notification letters to all diplomatic partners informing them of the transformation that would take place.[120] In New York and Geneva, the Council's liaison offices were

[115] Sophie Vanhoonacker and Natasja Reslow, 'The European External Action Service: Living Forwards by Understanding Backwards' (2010) 15 EFAR 1; Jozef Bátora, 'The "Mitrailleuse Effect": The EEAS as an Interstitial Organization and the Dynamics of Innovation in Diplomacy' (2013) 51 JCMS 598.

[116] See also Arts 20(2)(*c*) and 23 Consolidated Version of the Treaty on the Functioning of the European Union [2012] OJ C326/47 (hereafter TFEU)).

[117] Declarations Nos 13 and 14 concerning the Common Foreign and Security Policy attached to the Final Act of the Intergovernmental Conference which adopted the Treaty of Lisbon [2010] OJ C83/335.

[118] Steven Blockmans and Christophe Hillion (eds), *EEAS 2.0: A Legal Commentary on Council Decision 2010/427/EU Establishing the Organisation and Functioning of the European External Action Service* (Swedish Institute for European Policy Studies 2013).

[119] Robert Weiss, 'Remarks on the Draft Council Decision Establishing the Organisation and Functioning of the European External Action Service' in Sebastiano Faro, Mario P Chiti, and Erich Schweighofer (eds), *European Citizenship and Consular Protection: New Trends in European Law and National Law* (Editoriale Scientifica Napoli 2012).

[120] Council, Draft notification to third parties before the entry into force of the Treaty of Lisbon, Doc No 16654/1/09, 27 November 2009; Anne-Laure Vaurs-Chaumette, 'La Question de la Reconnaissance' in Myriam Benlolo-Carabot, Ulas Candas, and Eglantine Cujo (eds), *Union Européenne et Droit International* (Pedone 2012) 246.

absorbed into the new Union mission.[121] The reception of foreign missions is a matter still largely managed by the Commission. Yet, these missions are now also referred to, within and outside the EU, as 'accredited to the Union' rather than 'accredited to the Commission'.

With regard to the EU delegations, some have questioned whether the world is 'any different from that of the Commission delegations which preceded them'.[122] It is true that, through the years, the delegations' area of competence had already expanded from being strictly related to the Commission's commercial policy to a broad range of EU projects and programmes[123] and that high-level political tasks and diplomatic representation had been added pre-Lisbon.[124] However, there is more to the title 'Union delegation' and the label 'diplomatic service' than many might have foreseen. EUDELs are now fully authorized to represent and act on behalf of the EU, its institutions, and bodies.[125] Today, all EUDELs assume the responsibilities previously held by the rotating presidency, including the local co-ordination of EU positions, statements, and démarches.[126] The stronger internal mandate reflects the political importance of EUDELs: it supports the EU representatives' responsibility to carry the diplomatic weight of the Union and backs the EEAS's demands for its external arms to be treated as diplomatic missions. As a result, a transformation is noticeable, including in member states' attitudes.

Favourable conditions for further integrating European consular services have surfaced in recent years. The EU's consular aspirations find their origins in the concept of EU citizenship, which originates from the 1992 Treaty of Maastricht and includes the right to consular protection abroad (Art 20(2)(*c*) TFEU). Ever since, EUDELs have coordinated cooperation between the consular authorities of the member states and supported efforts in providing consular assistance to EU citizens. The delegations are also involved in information exchanges on topics such as the drawing of crisis contingency plans, the management of evacuations, the representation of unrepresented citizens, and the delivery of emergency travel documents.[127]

In terms of establishing the EU's global presence, the EEAS continued Commission practices and entered into establishment agreements that allowed it to open missions in Libya, South Sudan and Uzbekistan (2011), Myanmar and the United Arab Emirates (2013), Somalia (re-opening in 2014), and Mongolia (2017). The regionalised delegations in Ecuador, Laos, New Zealand, and Trinidad and Tobago became fully fledged delegations in 2016. In 2018, the EUDEL in Panama was opened and, in 2019, the EEAS strengthened its presence in the Middle East and in Central Asia with the opening of EUDELs in Kuwait and Turkmenistan. Due to shifting priorities, delegations were closed in 2013 in Croatia (one day before accession), New Caledonia, Surinam, and Vanuata, and in 2018 in the Solomon Islands.

121 Answer given by the Council to parliamentary question H-0407/03, 19 June 2003.

122 Paul Craig and Gráinne de Búrca, *EU Law: Text, Cases, and Materials* (6th edn, OUP 2015) 321.

123 Rohit Ambast and Vinay Tyagi, 'Ambassadors of Europe: An Insight into the Evolution of the European Union and International Diplomatic Law' (2008) 61 Studia Diplomatica 173, 16.

124 Cesare Onestini, 'A Hybrid Service: Organising Efficient EU Foreign Policy' in Spence and Bátora (n 73) 72–73.

125 David Spence, 'The EEAS and Its Epistemic Communities: The Challenges of Diplomatic Hybridism' in Spence and Bátora (n 73) 55.

126 EEAS, Report by the High Representative to the European Parliament, the Council and the Commission, 22 December 2011, para 16.

127 Council Directive 2015/637 on the coordination and cooperation measures to facilitate consular protection for unrepresented citizens of the Union in third countries [2015] OJ L106/1; Decision 96/409/CSFP on the establishment of an emergency travel document [1996] OJ L168/4.

Probably the most upsetting event for EU diplomacy since Lisbon has been the withdrawal of the United Kingdom from the Union ('Brexit'). The United Kingdom's exit was followed by the (re-)opening of the EU delegation in London in 2020 and discussions on the future cooperation on foreign and security policy. In addition to the much debated possible economic fallout (the United Kingdom is the EU's biggest trade partner), Brexit also caused a diplomatic fallout. The United Kingdom has a strong diplomatic tradition, culture, and global presence: it was the member state with the third most missions in third states (following France and Germany) and the sole member state with a resident diplomatic mission in remote places such as Guyana. Due to Brexit, the EU also lost one of the two member states holding a permanent seat on the UN Security Council and the United Kingdom's experience, assets, and security and defence capabilities. It is now up to the EUDEL in London to establish a new routine among EU ambassadors locally present and to establish a working relationship with the UK authorities. The United Kingdom, for its part, has lost its integration in a broader diplomatic network and practical cooperation modes, including on the protection of its unrepresented citizens.

## 1.2.3 The EU's Diplomatic Network

### 1.2.3.1 The EU's External Relations Machinery

Over the course of its integration, the EU has created a dense network of diplomatic relations with the outside world. These relations neither replace nor compete with national diplomacy; they should complement the diplomatic ties and historical resonance of member states with third states and at international organizations.

The EU maintains both an active and a passive legation practice. The Union's *active legation practice* is pursued through the management of its own diplomatic service, the EEAS. The EU is diplomatically present in most third countries and at international organizations through a worldwide network of 145 bilateral and multilateral missions and offices, called Union delegations since the Treaty of Lisbon. EUDELs coordinate EU external policies and perform diplomatic functions, the most prominent of which is the representation of the Union in third states and at IOs (cf Art 221 TFEU). Consequently, it is no longer possible to imagine a local *corps diplomatique* in which the Union is not represented. In the performance of diplomatic tasks, EUDELs protect the Union's interests as well as those of its citizens; they interact and promote friendly relations with local governments, IOs, and member states; and they report on the conditions in the receiving state or receiving IO. The EU engages in a particular type of ad hoc diplomacy through the appointment of Special Representatives (EUSRs) and Envoys (EUSEs), who each hold regional or thematic mandates.[128]

In its *passive legation practice*, the Union receives foreign diplomats, with whom it negotiates treaties, coordinates policies, and matches interests. Through the years, the scope and number of diplomatic missions with an accreditation to the EU in Brussels has significantly expanded. Three types of missions are present in Brussels: the permanent representations of EU member states, diplomatic missions of third states, and diplomatic missions of IOs and other non-state entities. Their representatives are accredited to the Union, enjoy diplomatic status, and exercise all normal diplomatic functions.[129]

[128] Dominik Tolksdorf, 'EU Special Representatives: An Intergovernmental Tool in the Post Lisbon Foreign Policy System?' (2013) 18 EFAR 471.

[129] Roberts (n 10) 408.

#### 1.2.3.2 Facts and Figures

The EU's network of *bilateral delegations* consists of 133 resident missions to third states.[130] At the time of writing, the delegations in Afghanistan, Syria, and Yemen were temporarily closed with the Head of Delegation (HoD) residing either in Brussels or in a neighbouring country. The EUDEL in Doha is the latest addition. Four more representations have the status of 'special representation offices' because they are accredited to non-globally recognized governments in Taipei (Taiwan), Hong Kong, Jerusalem and Gaza (Occupied Palestinian Territory), and Pristina (Kosovo) and not formally counted as diplomatic missions. The EU is present in twenty-one more countries through the multiple accreditation of a neighbouring delegation. The EUDEL to the Pacific is based in Fiji, for example, but it has accreditations to the Cook Islands, Kiribati, the Marshall Islands, Micronesia, Nauru, Niue, the Republic of Palau, Eastern Samoa, the Solomon Islands, Tonga, and Tuvalu. The EUDEL in Barbados is accredited to Antigua and Barbuda, Dominica, Grenada, Saint Kitts and Nevis, and Saint Vincent and the Grenadines. The delegation in India is responsible for Bhutan; the delegation to Switzerland for Liechtenstein; the delegation in Jamaica for the Bahamas and Belize; and the delegation in Sri Lanka for the Maldives. In fourteen third states, a resident member state mission executes the Union's diplomatic representation on a rotating basis. This is the case for Andorra, Bahrain, Brunei, the Comoros Islands, the Democratic People's Republic of Korea, Equatorial Guinee, Iran, Monaco, Oman, San Marino, Saint Lucia, the Seychelles, Suriname, and Vanuatu. Arrangements for the establishment of an EUDEL in Tehran are ongoing, following the green light from the Commission and the Council in 2015. Efforts towards ensuring the opening of an EU office in Saõ Tomé and Príncipe also continue. Such office is often the prelude to the opening of a fully-fledged delegation, although EU offices recently have also been opened in Gaziantep, Turkey (in 2014; together with the member states) and Erbil, Iraq (2015) to deal with a particular situation or with local authorities. EUDELs are located in the city where a third state's government has its seat, usually the capital. Only in two countries, Israel (Tel Aviv) and Myanmar (Yangon), is the EUDEL not located in the capital.

There are nine *multilateral delegations* accredited principally or exclusively to IOs. Four are based in EU member states (the EUDELs in Strasbourg, Paris, Rome, and Vienna) and five are based in third states (the EUDELs in New York, Addis Ababa, Geneva (two), and Jakarta).[131] Many of the bilateral EUDELs are also accredited to an IO headquartered in the host country. Since 2019, a liaison officer represents the Union at the IOs in The Hague.

The Union currently employs sixteen *ad hoc diplomats* that do not reside in a third country. There are six EUSRs with a regional mandate: EUSRs for the Horn of Africa, the South Caucasus and the crisis in Georgia, the Sahel, the Middle East Peace Process, Central Asia, and the Belgrade–Pristina Dialogue and other Western Balkan regional issues. Of the nine EUSRs, two are 'double-hatted' in the sense that they also head an EUDEL (the EUSRs in Bosnia-Herzegovina and Kosovo). One thematic EUSR is tasked with following up on human rights worldwide. The Council appoints EUSRs; while the HR (the EUSE for

[130] EEAS, 'Diplomatic Representation in Third Countries—1st Semester 2022', EEAS (2021)1319, 21 December 2021. For a schematic overview, see Appendix 1. This includes the EUDEL to the Holy See, that is also counted as one of the nine multilateral delegations.

[131] New York (UN), Geneva (UN), Geneva (WTO), Paris (UN, OECD), Vienna (UN, OSCE, IAEA), Rome (UN), Strasbourg (Council of Europe), Addis Ababa (African Union), and Jakarta (ASEAN). The EUDEL in Paris is also accredited to the Principalities of Andorra and Monaco. The EUDEL in Rome is also accredited to the Holy See, the Republic of San Marino, and the Order of Malta.

non-proliferation and disarmament, the EUSE to Somalia, the EUSE for Afghanistan, and the EUSE for the peace process in Colombia) and the Commission (the EUSE on freedom of religion or belief outside the EU, the EUSE on Space, and the EUSE on Afghanistan) can appoint EUSEs.

The *passive side of the network* counts 164 permanent missions of third states accredited to the Union. Further, thirty-three IOs, four non-state entities, and three private actors hold permanent missions in Brussels.[132]

According to 2020 numbers, 4,643 people were working for the EEAS, 2,286 of them at the Brussels Headquarters and 2,357 in the EUDELs.[133] EEAS staff is comprised of five main categories. At the end of 2020, 1,277 officials, 1,091 local agents, 539 contract agents, 472 seconded national experts (SNE's) and 370 temporary agents were working in the EEAS. In addition, 3,757 Commission staff members were posted in delegations. In 2019, the EEAS employed 33.7 per cent member state diplomats—this indicates that the EEAS has managed to maintain the statutory target of staffing at least one-third of the administrator level positions with officials from member state diplomatic services, an objective first reached in 2013. Local agents are hired for all sorts of activities of delegations, from logistical activities (driving, cooking, or secretariat jobs) to jobs demanding liaison activities and economic or political reporting. They are employed as technical and support staff, with conditions defined under local labour law; at the same time, local agents benefit from the EU's Framework Rules, which set minimum employment standards. The EEAS and the Commission jointly manage a junior experts programme, employing eighty junior professionals in delegations (JPDs) in 2020. There were also 385 trainees in 2020.

With regard to the HoDs, it is a general EEAS policy to try to have at least one diplomat from each member state in an HoD position. In 2019, only two member states did not have an HoD: Croatia and the United Kingdom (as a result of its decision to leave the EU). Likewise, successive HRs strived for gender parity and equality. Although the overall numerical gender balance of the EEAS is close to equal, with women representing almost half of the EEAS workforce, being 48,65 per cent in 2020, there still is a long way to go before gender is balanced in EEAS management positions. HR Mogherini had set the goal of having 40 per cent women in management positions, replicating Commissioner Kristalina Georgieva's pursuit to have 40 per cent women in the Commission's management by 2019. At present, female managers make up roughly one-third of all management positions and one-quarter of HoDs are female.[134]

Finally, the EU owns and rents 326 buildings in third countries (chancelleries, representation offices, residences, and other accommodation) as well as 750 service cars and 30 armoured vehicles.

#### 1.2.3.3 The Member States' Diplomatic Network in Third Countries

In 2021, member states tallied 1,548 resident diplomatic missions accredited to third countries. As one may expect, France (134) and Germany (127) have the most missions outside common borders, followed by Italy (101) and Spain (101) and the Netherlands (83). Malta (16) and Luxembourg (17) hold the fewest permanent external missions, followed closely

[132] See Appendix 5.

[133] The numbers printed in this section are drawn from the EEAS, Human Resources Annual Report 2019, Doc EEAS.DGBA.HR, <https://www.eeas.europa.eu/eeas/eeas-human-resources-reports-0_en> accessed 1 June 2022.

[134] Tereza Novotna, 'Women in the EEAS and EU Delegations: Another Post-Westphalia Change?' in Spence and Bátora (n 73).

by the Baltic trio (Estonia (18), Latvia (20), and Lithuania (22)) and Slovenia (23). There are five third countries in which all member states have a diplomatic representation: the People's Republic of China, the Republic of India, the Russian Federation, the United Kingdom, and the United States of America. Diplomatic presence is also high in Egypt and Israel (all but Luxembourg), in Japan (all but Malta), Turkey (all but Cyprus), in the United Arab Emirates (all but Croatia), in Australia (all but Latvia and Luxembourg), and in Canada and Ukraine (all but Luxembourg and Malta).

Conversely, in seventeen island states (the Bahamas, the Cook Islands, Dominica, Grenada, Kiribati, the Maldives, the Marshall Islands, Micronesia, Nauru, Niue, Palau, Saint Kitts and Nevis, Saint Vincent and Grenadines, Samoa, the Solomon Islands, Tonga, and Tuvalu), as well as in Belize, Bhutan, and Liechtenstein, neither the member states nor the EU maintain a resident mission. France is the only member state represented in the Comoros Islands, Saint Lucia, the Seychelles, and in Vanuatu. In San Marino (Italy) and São Tomé and Príncipe (Portugal) there also is just one European diplomatic mission. The EU has a delegation in two non-EU states where no member state keeps a permanent presence: Eswatini and Lesotho. A single member state joins the EUDEL in the Central African Republic (France) and in Timor Leste (Portugal). The EU also maintains its delegation in Somalia, while Germany, Sweden, and Italy are represented by an Ambassador resident in Nairobi.

## 1.3 The Structure of This Handbook

### 1.3.1 Uncovering the EU's Contribution to Diplomatic and Consular Law

In countless respects, EU diplomacy constitutes a remarkable legal experiment. The prevailing hypothesis in the literature is that, in terms of scope as well as exposure, EU diplomacy is a success story.[135] Yet, it remains unclear how innovations introduced by the EU stand in the bigger picture of diplomacy, both in a historical and contemporary sense. Scholarship's focus on the Union's diplomatic reach, achievements, and failures fits into fashionable research aims to measure efficiency and (good) organization. However, it tends to ignore the more fundamental legal determinants. The diplomatic and consular regimes are specific systems, even when judged against other legal regimes. The respect for diplomacy has its origins in its most basic characteristic, mutual dependency between equal and sovereign actors, which results in those actors' clear interest to keep the diplomatic system tight. The emergence of the EU as a diplomatic actor builds on a fundamental tension: the Union, in itself the result of a modern, multilateral, and integrative conception of the world order, introduces itself to a centuries-old legal regime that is thought to flourish because of its homogeneity.

This problem can be further translated into three substantive areas of tension between EU diplomacy and public international law (PIL); national laws and prerogatives of other states, including those of its member states; and global governance theory.[136]

[135] Bruter (n 94); Frauke Austermann, 'Towards Embassies for Europe? EU Delegations in the Union's Diplomatic System' Policy Paper 8 (Jean Monnet Multilateral Research Network 2012).

[136] Ben Rosamond, 'Conceptualizing the EU Model of Governance in World Politics' (2005) 10 EFAR 463; Michael Smith, 'The European Union and International Order: European and Global Dimensions' (2007) 12 EFAR 437.

First, the formal and permanent conduct of diplomatic and consular relations is associated with the birth of the modern nation state in the sixteenth and seventeenth centuries. Ever since, states appear to have been particularly protective of their rights to send and receive diplomatic and consular agents, an idea reflected in the 1961 VCDR and the 1963 VCCR. It is here that a fundamental legal problem arises: as a regional organization with far-reaching powers, the Union desires to employ diplomatic and consular means to pursue its competences. Indeed, by developing an extensive diplomatic practice, it challenges the basic premises of the Vienna framework. Barred from becoming a signatory party to the VCDR and VCCR, the Union must find legal solutions to enter into relations with foreign states.[137] A pragmatic solution was found in the EU's application of the 1961 Vienna Convention through numerous bilateral arrangements entered into with third states. Another challenge in this domain is the identifying of norms of CIL—a source of law originating from *state* practice and opinio juris. As regards the content of the rules on diplomacy, the EU's creative arrangements shake the foundations of diplomatic and consular law as these branches of international law are based on the principles of state sovereignty, equality, and non-interference.[138] Moreover, in practice, the EU is hindered by its inability to reciprocate: it cannot accord privileges and immunities to a third country's permanent mission to the EU that equal those offered to EU officials and premises in the country's territory.

Second, the Union's diplomatic aspirations are essentially an outgrowth of the Union's broader multinational process, in which competences are divided and levels of integration differ. Since the ECSC's foundation in 1952, a growing number of member states have mandated the Union to venture into thematic domains, which they believe are more efficiently addressed as a collective. To the benefit of the common European project, member states relinquish part of their sovereign powers. Yet, joining the Union does not entail that member states cease to be states as understood in PIL, nor must they surrender the whole of their sovereignty.[139] The EU's pursuit to develop its own diplomacy exists without the member states yielding the power to establish, conduct, and terminate their own diplomatic and consular relations. As a result, in a third country, a European citizen's interests are represented both by the bilateral mission of the member state of nationality and by an EUDEL. This means that at the international level, the emergence of EU diplomacy has not extinguished the diplomatic and consular rights and duties of its member states. EU nations continue to be represented individually, though their scope of action appears to be affected by EU law and EU diplomatic activities. This internal situation creates external effects. With the emergence of EU diplomacy arose an unusual situation in the international legal order: instead of states being fully fledged diplomatic actors, holding a monopoly over diplomatic and consular relations, there is now a plurality of actors sharing diplomatic competences and powers.

Third, European diplomacy can be considered a prime example of changes in global governance. Yet, collective diplomacy also affects the ideas of a pursuit of individual interests through diplomatic conduct, potentially threatening existing power balances. Moreover, European diplomacy contributes to the fragmentation of the unitary state and calls into question the continued relevance of the notion of sovereignty. Sovereignty, while itself subject to discussion and scepticism, remains a fundamental paradigm of international law and,

[137] Arts 48 and 50 VCDR; Art 74 VCCR.

[138] Julius Goebel, *The Equality of States: A Study in the History of Law* (WS Hein 2003); Paul Behrens, *Diplomatic Interference and the Law* (Hart 2016); Jens Bartelson, *A Genealogy of Sovereignty* (CUP 1995).

[139] *Van Gend & Loos* [1963] ECLI:EU:C:19 = 63:1; Robert Schütze, 'On "Federal" Ground: The European Union as an (Inter)national Phenomenon' (2009) 46 CML Rev 1069.

more specifically, of diplomatic and consular relations. The development of EU diplomacy is a well-established, though often contested, trend. It will be compared to broader trends in diplomacy in order to understand the extent to which legal novelties are part of a broader picture rather than merely a novelty therein. This includes problems related to the EU's adaptation to the 'Westphalian' world order and vice versa—an adaptation which entails augmenting the legal framework to fit in new actors such as the EU.

### 1.3.2 Focus

This handbook pursues general themes of EU diplomatic law by examining the EU's right of legation and qualifying its exercise on legal and historical lines. While this subject may seem broad, in many ways it is also confined. It is therefore apposite to briefly comment on the limits of this book and to list the omitted subjects or those not considered extensively.

First, this book examines the *formal* diplomatic and consular relations of the EU. Diplomacy is intentionally defined in legal terms and, consequently, limited in various ways. This work does not substantially investigate the validity of diplomatic and consular relations and the underlying assumptions on which these are based. It will neither venture into discussions on the political choices made with regard to Union delegations nor into substantive matters relating to the foreign policy they carry out. Those questions have been amply dealt with in the existing literature and are beyond the confines of this work.[140] In that sense, the focus is on the messenger rather than the message. 'Diplomacy' in this book therefore encompasses much less than in political science or the study of international relations, where the same concept is used as a synonym of foreign affairs.[141] In a legal sense, diplomatic relations never encompassed all types of contact that may occur between states or between states and other international actors. Rather, diplomacy is a particular medium for official agents to negotiate and to collect information—activities that are subject to a well-defined legal regime. This limitation has consequences for the demarcation of this book's subject matter. Notwithstanding, *tools* and *theories* of political science and public administration will be used to incorporate observations regarding an increased diversification of diplomatic actors.

Second, the handbook takes an *external* look at EU diplomacy. This adds a global dimension to the subject while also incorporating the interests and viewpoint of third states and IOs. The outsider perspective largely excludes the decisions and legal processes underlying EU diplomacy (ie the 'making of' questions). The internal decision-making of the EU and its external representation are different subjects, each worthy of study. Yet, the former is only examined if and when it is a necessary component for understanding or framing the latter. Consequentially, the book is also limited in the sense that EU law, including the law of the external relations of the Union, is only considered where it has consequences for the international legal order.

Finally, this work undoubtedly pays greater attention to *diplomatic law* than to consular law since the integration of EU consular services is still in its early stages. Within diplomatic law, the focus predominantly lies on *permanent representation* rather than ad hoc diplomacy.

[140] Smith, Keukeleire, and Vanhoonacker (n 104); Mai'a K Davis Cross and Jan Melissen, *European Public Diplomacy: Soft Power at Work* (Palgrave Macmillan 2013); Koops and Macaj (n 67); Stephen Woolcock, *European Union Economic Diplomacy: The Role of the EU in External Economic Relations* (Ashgate 2012).

[141] Stanisław Edward Nahlik, *Development of Diplomatic Law: Selected Problems* (Martinus Nijhoff 1990) 201 et seq.

### 1.3.3 Outline

The book is structured in six chapters, each divided into a number of sections. This first chapter functions as a prelude to the study and provides a short examination of the state of the art of EU diplomacy. Furthermore, it puts forward a glimpse into the historical, legal, and international context that defines it.

In order to carry out an analysis of EU diplomatic law, an enquiry into the broader, international legal context is required. Chapter 2 takes up this challenge. It studies the legitimacy of the EU's quest for diplomatic and consular recognition on the international plane. To build the necessary background, it looks at theories of PIL with regard to the right of legation, sovereignty, and functionalism. This allows a deeper delve into questions related to the structure and conditions of access to diplomatic and consular relations.

Chapter 3 focuses on the legal architecture of the EU's diplomatic framework. It addresses the patchwork of legal and political arrangements that the EU constructed to execute its diplomatic and consular roles. The chapter scrutinizes the EU's active and passive legation practice and maps its official relations with states, IOs, and other non-state entities.

Chapter 4 deals with substantive diplomatic law and examines in detail the EU's relation with international diplomatic norms. It tests the general suitability of the 1961 Vienna Convention to the EU's situation and, where necessary, expresses doubts about specific provisions in the Treaty. The study does not limit itself to a study of the application of the VCDR; it also explains the Union's urge to apply norms not covered by the Convention, including norms of protocol, CIL, and topics once considered unfit for codification.

Chapter 5 concerns the triangular relationship of the Union, its member states, and diplomatic and consular law. It starts with a study on coexisting norms that examines how the Court of Justice of the EU (CJEU) has addressed diplomatic and consular law in the EU legal order. This chapter ends by testing how rights of legation can coexist in the international legal order.

Finally, Chapter 6 offers conclusions. It makes the case for the Union functioning as a diplomatic actor in its own right, as an entity separate from the states that constitute the foundations of the Union. Concretely, it looks at the EU in the general international diplomatic legal system and the contributions made by the EU to diplomatic and consular law.

# 2
# Theoretical and Historical Perspectives

## 2.1 Defining the Right of Legation

### 2.1.1 Historical Account

Public international law (PIL) treats states as the most perfect of all international actors, bestowing upon them broad competences and enhanced responsibilities. States enjoy various rights by virtue of their status as sovereign entities.[1] Examples of such rights include but are not limited to the right to independence, the right to exercise jurisdiction over its territory and all persons therein, the right to sovereignty, the right to legal equality with other states, and the right of self-defence against armed attacks perpetrated upon it.[2] As a body of law created by nations to govern the conduct of and relations between one another, PIL holds in high regard the aforementioned rights in facilitating peaceful interactions and coexistence between sovereign states. Whether this means that a right of legation (ie the right to conduct formal diplomatic and consular relations) arises in light of this underlying rationale is debated.

Legal theories surrounding the right of legation predate modern international law and its doctrinal origins. Since the seventeenth century when the modern nation state is said to have emerged, many of the great classical international jurists addressed the topic. All treat the right of legation as a subject of prime importance: the concept not only informs the reading of international law from an academic perspective[3] but its study is also crucial in practical terms for states and governments (von Martens argues that 'Le droit d'ambassade [est] un droit essentiel du gouvernement').[4] Some authors even went as far as to accord legation an almost sacred character: according to Gentili's interpretation (1585), it is a right by virtue of a certain divine providence: immutable, of universal application, and admitted even by 'barbarous' peoples.[5] He speaks of the 'sanctum ius legationis' and 'gentibus barbaris', while finding support in the writings of Cicero, Caesar, and Tacitus, all of whom argued that the right of embassy is not just sacred but is also defended by a rampart of human and divine authority. Their manuscripts refer to the right of legation as the ius legationis; right of embassy,

[1] Matthew Craven, 'Statehood, Self-Determination, and Recognition' in Malcolm D Evans (ed), *International Law* (4th edn, OUP 2014) 201.

[2] UNGA Resolution 375 (IV) of 6 December 1949, UN Doc A/RES/375 (IV) (hereafter Draft Declaration on Rights and Duties of States); Convention on Rights and Duties of States, signed on 26 December 1933, entered into force 26 December 1934) 165 LNTS 20 (hereafter: Montevideo Convention). See Hans Kelsen, 'The Draft Declaration on Rights and Duties of States' (1950) 44 AJIL 259, 259; Philip Marshall Brown, 'The Rights of States under International Law' [1916] 26 Yale LJ 85, 85.

[3] Hugo Grotius, *De Iure Belli Ac Pacis, Libri Tres*, vol 2 (Paris 1625) Ch XVIII, 366, I.

[4] George Fréderic von Martens, *Précis du Droit des Gens Moderne de l'Europe Fondé sur les Traités et l'Usage* (2nd edn, Librairie de Dieterich 1801) 286.

[5] Alberico Gentili, *De Legationibus, Libri Tres* (Excudebat Thomas Vautrollerius 1585) 40.

*EU Diplomatic Law.* Sanderijn Duquet, Oxford University Press. © Sanderijn Duquet 2022.
DOI: 10.1093/oso/9780192844552.003.0002

*droit d'ambassade*, or *Gesandtschaftsrecht*.[6] The differences in terminology are symptomatic of the contradicting scholarly views developed about the content, scope, and identifiable holders of the right of legation. Importantly, however, the very existence of the ius legationis was not debated.

The right of legation was commonly believed to be directly linked to sovereignty by being its practical expression. De Wicquefort called the right to send ambassadors the most famous sign of sovereignty.[7] This resulted in its conceptualization as an open-ended, yet functional right. Emer de Vattel (1758) argued that every sovereign state has a *droit d'ambassade* which can be exercised to its likening.[8] Grotius draws a basic distinction in law between rights and obligations derived from nature (law of nature) and those derived from an authoritative will (volitional law). He categorized the right of legation under the volitional law of nations, being no more than the product of a pragmatic agreement between states.[9]

Another disagreement relates to the right of legation's content. Grotius distinguished between the right of ambassadors to be admitted into the territories to which they are sent and the rights of ambassadors to be granted certain privileges, including the freedom of violence. According to Vattel, it encompasses the right to send and receive public ministers but also to manage foreign affairs, enter into international transactions, and carry diplomatic correspondence.[10] Similarly to Grotius and Vattel, Henry Wheathon (1836), an American jurist and diplomat, referred to ius legationis in plural terms to mark its many different components.[11] Stockston (1914), finally, considered the special duties, special protection, and peculiar privileges enjoyed by diplomatic agents as part of the right of legation.[12]

A third point of contention concerns the right of legation's status. The very fact that the term 'ius legationis' includes a reference to the concept of law may by itself be perceived as problematic. Similarly to most branches of law, international law acknowledges that rights and duties are correlative and inseparable notions whereby a right possessed by a sovereign acquires a corresponding obligation to respect that right. The historically upheld doctrinal position, however, dictates that the right of legation exists without a direct corresponding obligation, provided that there is no treaty or other legal source to the contrary. Quite often, so-called Treaties of Friendship contained clauses on the exchange of diplomatic representatives.[13] Grotius was a strong supporter of this view, though he supplemented it by asserting that a state should have a just cause to refuse another state's proposal to establish diplomatic relations. The cause may be on the part of the sending as well as on the part of the receiving state.[14] Similarly, Vattel considers the refusal of a state to hear an envoy of a friendly power a serious offence under international law.[15] He was quite clear that the 'correlative duty' was

[6] Grotius (n 3) Ch XVIII; Emerich de Vattel, *Le Droit des Gens, du Principes de la Loi Naturelle, Appliqués à la Conduite et aux Affaires des Nations et des Souverains, Livre IV* (1758) Ch V.

[7] Abraham de Wicquefort, *L'Ambassadeur et ses Fonctions*, vol 1 (T Johnson 1724). In the same sense: Johann Caspar Bluntschli, *Das Moderne Völkerrecht der Civilisirten Staten* (Beck 1868) 126.

[8] de Vattel (n 6) para 57.

[9] Grotius (n 3) Ch XVIII, 366, I.

[10] de Vattel (n 6) para 57.

[11] Henry Wheaton, *Elements of International Law: With a Sketch of the History of the Science*, vol 1 (B Fellowes 1836) 257.

[12] Charles H Stockston, *Outlines of International Law* (Charles Scribner's Sons 1914) 197.

[13] The first edition of the Satow's handbook mentions such treaty concluded between Sweden and Holland in 1614; Ernest Satow, *A Guide to Diplomatic Practice*, vol 1 (1st edn, Longmans, Green & Co 1917) 175. Biswanath Sen, *A Diplomat's Handbook of International Law and Practice* (3rd edn, Nijhoff 1988) 22.

[14] Grotius (n 3) Ch XVIII, 368–69, III.

[15] ibid; de Vattel (n 6) para 64.

to listen—though listening to envoys could take place at the frontier. The contrary view defended by de Wicquefort (1677) provides that the law of nations rejects that a state should have or share its reasons for denying the establishment of a permanent mission on its territory.[16]

The idea that a denial of diplomatic relations has to be motivated by good reasons resurfaced in the early works of the nineteenth century. The Swiss jurist Bluntschli (1868) believed that states can only refuse to receive the envoys of recognized states when supported by exceptionally serious reasons for doing so. His reasoning is highly infused with moral arguments: states were thought to be bound by the rule out of a greater sense of international solidarity.[17] In opposition to Bluntschli's reasoning grounded upon the utopian ideas of the international community's functioning, Wheaton's views were central to realism. He perceived the obligation to entertain diplomatic relations as dependent on 'the nature and importance of the relations to be maintained between different states'.[18]

Twentieth-century writers did not redeem from calling the right of legation a 'right' and remained divided as to the obligations it created. Sir Ernest Satow (1917) categorically denied the presence of any corresponding duty on the part of other sovereigns;[19] and according to Fauchille, the ius legationis matches 'affaires de bons rapports, et non de droit strict'.[20] The contrary view was, however, prevalent among debates in 1905, where Lassa Oppenheim presented the following take on the matter:

> [o]bviously a State is not bound to send diplomatic envoys or to receive permanent envoys. But, on the other hand, the very existence of the Family of Nations makes it necessary for the members, or some of the members to negotiate occasionally on certain points. Such negotiation would be impossible in case one member could always, and under all circumstances, refuse to receive an envoy from the other members. The duty of every member to listen, under ordinary circumstances, to a message from another brought by a diplomatic envoy is therefore, an outcome of its very membership of the Family of Nations, and this duty corresponds to the right of every member to send envoys.[21]

Inspired by older literature on the existence of a de minimis duty to hear foreign envoys, Oppenheim identified an obligation under the right of legation both on the basis of courtesy and of the international order's very functioning.

## 2.1.2 The 1961 Vienna Convention on Diplomatic Relations

### 2.1.2.1 Negotiation History

In light of the historical significance of this topic, it is unsurprising that the discussion regarding the right of legation's existence in PIL, or the lack thereof, resurfaced when plans to

[16] Abraham de Wicquefort, *Mémoires Touchant les Ambassadeurs et les Ministres Publics* (chez Pierre Du Marteau 1677) 98.

[17] Bluntschli (n 7) 163.

[18] Wheaton (n 11) 258, 261.

[19] Dionisio Anzilotti, *Cours de Droit International* (French trans of 3rd Italian edn, Recueil Sirey 1929) 265.

[20] '[A] matter of good relations, not of strict law' [own translation]; Paul Fauchille, *Traité de Droit International Public*, vol 1, Pt 3 (Rousseau & C(ie) 1926) 37.

[21] Lassa Oppenheim, *International Law. A Treatise*, vol 1 (1st edn, Longmans, Green & Co 1905) 419. All first eight editions (up until 1992) of Oppenheim's magnum opus featured the quote.

codify diplomatic law emerged in the international community. In 1954, the International Law Commission (ILC) appointed Swedish Commissioner Emil Sandström as the Special Rapporteur on the codification of diplomatic privileges and immunities. Sandström, a traditionalist, devoted considerable attention to the topic. In the draft articles of what would later become the 1961 Vienna Convention on Diplomatic Relations (VCDR),[22] he proposed to directly refer to the ius legationis in the first of the twenty-eight provisions:[23]

> [si] deux Etats, ayant le droit de légation, sont d'accord pour établir entre eux des relations diplomatiques permanentes, chacun d'eux peut établir auprès de l'autre une mission diplomatique.

Draft Article 1 stated that those who possess the right of legation can seek the agreement to realize it. In principle, all sovereign states possess such right, although this is not entirely clear in Sandström's contention. Further, a distinction is made between the seeking of consent for the establishment of diplomatic relations and the seeking of consent for the establishment of a diplomatic mission.

When the ILC sent the draft articles to governments prior to the Vienna Conference asking for their feedback, it decided not to include the language as proposed by Sandström. The ILC Commissioners collectively raised two sets of objections. First, it was argued that a right of legation could only be included if it was adequately defined. Despite frequent references in doctrinal materials, it was not considered that this standard was met. Moreover, the ILC considered itself unable to pursue such challenge. The ius legationis was deemed too closely connected to the definition of statehood, a topic upon which the ILC traditionally had been reluctant to embark.[24] Second, ILC members questioned the status of the ius legationis as a right: no 'right' of legation 'can be exercised without agreement between the parties'.[25] The right of legation was therefore de facto unenforceable due to the lack of corresponding obligations enshrined therein on the part of the receiving state.[26]

After having received comments of states on the draft text, issues relating to the right of legation re-emerged. The Czechoslovak Government was among the fiercest supporters of including the right of legation in the treaty text as a true legal right.[27] Other governments argued that the concept's meaning was different in the Western literature when compared with the Czechoslovak contention, resulting in legal frictions between states as well as in a political divide between the East and the West.[28] Yet again, the final draft that was discussed in Vienna and prepared by the ILC does not reference to the right of legation. Rather, the ILC's Draft Article 2 merely stated that the establishment of diplomatic relations between two states, and in particular of permanent diplomatic missions, takes place by mutual agreement.[29]

[22] Vienna Convention on Diplomatic Relations, opened for signature 18 April 1961, entered into force on 24 April 1964, 500 UNTS 95 (hereafter VCDR).

[23] 'In case two states having the right of legation agree to establish permanent diplomatic relations between them, each of them may establish a diplomatic mission to the other' [own translation]; Emil Sandström, 'Report on Diplomatic Intercourse and Immunities' (1955) II YBILC, A/CN.4/91, 10.

[24] Eileen Denza, *Diplomatic Law: Commentary on the Vienna Convention on Diplomatic Relations* (4th edn, OUP 2016) 22.

[25] ILC, 'Text of the Draft Articles and Commentary'(1958) II YBILC, A/CN.4/117, 90.

[26] Remark of Mr Garcia Amador, 'General Debate on Diplomatic Intercourse and Immunities' (1957) I YBILC, A/CN.4/91, 9.

[27] Letter dated 10 March 1958 transmitted from the Permanent Representative of Czechoslovakia to the United Nations and published in ILC, 'Text of the Draft Articles and Commentary' (n 25) 117.

[28] Kai Bruns, *A Cornerstone of Modern Diplomacy: Britain and the Negotiation of the 1961 Vienna Convention on Diplomatic Relations* (Bloomsbury Academic 2014) 34, 107.

[29] ILC, 'Text of the Draft Articles and Commentary' (n 25) 90.

### 2.1.2.2 Silence in the Treaty Text

Having inherited an unsettled discussion, the Vienna Conference re-examined what had in the meantime become the ILC's Draft Article 2.[30] The driver for debate was, once again, the Czechoslovak delegation. The reason for Prague's persistence on this front related to its broader striving to protect equal rights among states and to ban any interstate discrimination in the spirit of the Charter of the United Nations (UN). The Czechoslovak delegation argued that a right of legation could help to prevent a state or a group of states from diplomatically isolating another state. It could, so it argued, avert states detrimentally excluding those that sought diplomatic cooperation.[31] The Czechoslovak proposal was openly supported by the Cuban and, to some extent, the Soviet delegates in Vienna. In contrast, the Turkish, Iraqi, Ghanaian, and Vietnamese delegations echoed the arguments put forward by the ILC, namely, that the focus of Article 2 should be on the principle of the establishment of diplomatic relations by mutual consent. The US delegation argued that the Czechoslovak fears of politically orientated discrimination in diplomacy were obsolete. States have always conducted diplomatic relations with equals whose constitutional, legal, and social systems differed from their own.[32] The delegate of Tunisia went as far as to argue that if the concept of a right of legation were to be included, the text would appear as 'unduly aggressive'.[33]

It became clear that the inclusion of the right of legation in Article 2 was unlikely to receive the necessary two-thirds majority in the Vienna Conference's plenary meeting. A compromise was reached in the agreement to embody a reference to the UN Charter principles on sovereign equality in the VCDR's preamble. Recitals 2 and 3 of the VCDR's preamble reflect this compromise: '[h]aving in mind the purposes and principles of the Charter of the United Nations concerning the sovereign equality of States, the maintenance of international peace and security, and the promotion of friendly relations among nations'; and '[b]elieving that an international convention on diplomatic intercourse, privileges and immunities would contribute to the development of friendly relations among nations, irrespective of their differing constitutional and social systems'.[34] The ILC's draft article was adopted unanimously without a reference to a 'right' to conduct diplomatic relations:

> [t]he establishment of diplomatic relations between States, and of permanent diplomatic missions, takes place by mutual consent.

The Czechoslovak delegate nevertheless added that '[h]is delegation firmly believed that the right of legation was a well-established principle of international law and hence it would be right to embody the principle in the text. However, in view of the differences of opinion it would withdraw its proposal.'

Article 2 stresses that the establishment of diplomatic relations exists by virtue of an agreement between states, denoting that there is neither a concrete right nor an entitlement to conduct diplomatic relations with another state under international law.[35] This means that a state cannot be forced to enter into diplomatic relations with another state and, further, that

[30] Official records of the United Nations Conference on Diplomatic Intercourse and Immunities (1961) II, A/Conf.20/C.1/L.6 and L.7, 8.
[31] ibid, paras 12 and 52.
[32] ibid, paras 11 and 58–59.
[33] ibid, para 49.
[34] ibid, para 50.
[35] See the mutual consent requirement as laid down in Art 2 of the New York Convention on Special Missions, signed on 8 December 1969, entered into force 21 June 1985, 1400 UNTS 231.

states are at liberty to end diplomatic relations as they wish under the relevant provisions (Art 45 VCDR). This was confirmed in 2005 by the Eritrea–Ethiopia Claims Commission when it underlined that 'Ethiopia was at all times free to terminate diplomatic relations with Eritrea and hence to close its mission.'[36] There are no other requirements than for the agreement to take place between states. The Vienna Convention does not lay down the form by which consent should be given or refused. Both the conduct of relations and the establishment of a mission in foreign territory are acts of political processes resting in the respective states' executive's hands.[37] However, the establishment of a permanent mission in another state's territory is probably the most concrete manner in which to enjoy newly established diplomatic relations.

#### 2.1.2.3 Shortcomings of the VCDR as a Standard to Define the Right of Legation

The VCDR takes a neutral position on the right of legation, therefore not addressing much of the discussion surrounding the actors in diplomacy. This is only logical. The Vienna Convention is merely a legal framework for the exercise of diplomatic relations. It does not define the right of legation nor accord it to certain actors; rather, it defines the actors bound by the substantive rules of diplomacy it establishes. In that sense, the VCDR encompasses no more than the rules of the game when played between certain players as defined specifically for the Convention's purposes. As an indirect consequence, this also means that the Convention does not preclude that other rules apply to other types of international relations nor that VCDR rules are copied and used in other (diplomatic or non-diplomatic) relations between entities.

Be that as it may, the concept of the right of legation is still central to the present-day diplomatic law and surrounding theories. The scholarly interest in theorizing the right of legation has become increasingly relevant in light of the emergence of new actors in the diplomatic arena.

### 2.1.3 Content

The prevailing scholarly view categorizes the right of legation as comprising two correlative elements: the passive right to receive foreign missions on a territory (*ius legationis passivum*) and the active right to establish missions in the territory of a foreign state (*ius legationis activum*) or '[c]eux qui ont le droit d'envoyer des ministres ont aussi celui d'en recevoir'.[38] Modern literature differentiates those active and passive elements from the prior act of establishing of diplomatic relations. The distinction is backed by Article 2 VCDR, which considers the establishment of diplomatic relations and the establishment of permanent missions as distinct legal acts.[39]

Although the notion of the right of legation is primarily used in the diplomatic context, the establishment of consular relations and missions is an integral part of it: states that decide to establish diplomatic relations concurrently imply the establishment of consular relations

[36] Eritrea–Ethiopia Claims Commission, Partial Award: Diplomatic Claim—Eritrea's Claim 20 (Eritrea/Ethiopia), decision of 19 December 2005, Report of International Arbitral Awards, vol XXVI 381, paras 46–47.

[37] Michael JL Hardy, *Modern Diplomatic Law* (Manchester UP 1968) 13.

[38] 'Those who have the right to send diplomats also have the right to receive them' [own translation]; von Martens (n 4) 286.

[39] Ivor Roberts (ed), *Satow's Diplomatic Practice* (6th edn, OUP 2011) 71.

unless stated the contrary (Art 2(2) VCCR).[40] Nevertheless, similarly to diplomatic relations, the establishment of consular relations and of consular posts is carried out by virtue of mutual consent (Art 2(1) VCCR). Consular relations can also be established regardless of existing diplomatic relations; an automatic agreement to establish diplomatic ties is not implied by the act of establishing consular relations.[41] The termination of diplomatic relations does not therefore *ipso facto* involve the severance or termination of consular relations; the reverse scenario is unlikely to unfold.[42]

### 2.1.4 Qualification

As is clear from the historical introduction to this chapter, one of the oldest jurisprudential debates is on the qualification of the right of legation and its enforcement.[43] Without having the intention of re-entering the entire debate, this section aims to clarify whether in current PIL the right of legation is a genuine right, an entitlement, a capacity that discretionally can be exercised, or simply an inaccurate label covering a tradition.

#### 2.1.4.1 The Right of Legation as a Right

There is no question that, by being subjects of international law, states enjoy international legal rights in addition to international legal obligations. Certain right and duties are considered more fundamental than others for being closely connected to sovereignty.[44] This is primarily so with the right of self-defence and various territorial rights, all of which originate from custom. The concept of fundamental sovereign rights revived in the twentieth century due to efforts made in the interest of codification. Both general and specific legal instruments began to list 'fundamental' sovereign rights. Such general attempts include the 1933 Montevideo Convention on the Rights and Duties of States and the 1949 Draft Declaration on the Rights and Duties of States.[45] In the latter instrument, the ILC listed four rights of a state, all of which relate to a state's independent character: the right of choice of the form of government, jurisdiction over state territory, equality in law, and equality of self-defence. The closest reference to diplomatic relations is found in Article 14 on the duty of a state 'to conduct its relations with other States in accordance with international law and with the principle that the sovereignty of each State is subject to the supremacy of international law'.[46] In other words, the provision repeats that when a state interacts with other states, including through diplomatic means, international law has to be respected. In the latter half of the twentieth century, these general conventions were supplemented by thematic legal sources on specific rights of states.[47]

[40] Vienna Convention on Consular Relations, opened for signature 24 April 1963, entered into force 19 March 1967, 596 UNTS 261 (hereafter VCCR).

[41] Roberts (n 39) 227.

[42] Luke T Lee and John B Quigley, *Consular Law and Practice* (3rd edn, OUP 2008) 66; Malcolm D Evans, 'The Restoration of Diplomatic Relations between Argentina and the United Kingdom' (1991) 40 ICLQ 473.

[43] On the enforcement paradigm in international law, see Jens David Ohlin, *The Assault on International Law* (OUP 2015).

[44] Daniel H Joyner and Marco Roscini, 'Is There Any Room for the Doctrine of Fundamental Rights of States in Today's International Law?' (2015) 4 CJICL 467, 468.

[45] Montevideo Convention; Draft Declaration on Rights and Duties of States.

[46] Kelsen, 'The Draft Declaration on Rights and Duties of States' (n 2) 276.

[47] See, e.g. the Declaration on the Granting of Independence to Colonial Countries and Peoples (UNGA Res 1514 (XV) 14 December 1960), the Declaration on Permanent Sovereignty over Natural Resources (UNGA Res 1803 (XVII) 14 December 1962), and more controversially, the Declaration for the Establishment of a New International Economic Order (UNGA Res 3201 (S-VI) 1 May 1974).

The right of legation shares a certain kinship with rights duly recognized as fundamental to sovereigns. Similarly to states' inalienable rights, the ius legationis has strong historical underpinnings. At the same time, the ius legationis also differs from those rights in not having benefitted from the twentieth-century codification wave that targeted fundamental state rights. The ius legationis was expressly featured only once in a multilateral instrument: Article 1 of the 1928 Havana Convention on Diplomatic Officers grants states the right to be represented before one another through the means of diplomatic officers.

A connection between sovereignty and the ius legationis, however, exists on a more conceptual level. As understood by the Permanent Court of International Justice in the *SS Wimbledon* case, sovereignty is used to describe legal capacities, powers, and liberties of states, including 'the right of entering into international engagements'.[48] Significantly, during the classical period of international legal scholarship between 1648 and 1815, the right of legation was seen as the logical deduction from the fundamental rights to independence and sovereignty. Many authors mentioned that the right of legation is an attribute of sovereignty, 'no matter whether the same is vested in a king, a president or in a senate or council acting in conjunction with such king or president'.[49] Its execution required equality between nations. As Brown argues, '[a]t a time when States were struggling to emerge and to assert their separate existence; when their claims and their diplomatic representatives were treated with contempt; it was expedient to insist on the equality of nations'.[50] The preamble to the 1961 VCDR too exemplifies this relationship between diplomacy and the right of sovereign equality. However, this does not necessarily bestow the right of legation with a special character in international law.

Much like in ancient times, the absence of a correlative duty is a point of discussion in modern literature.[51] Marcel Sibert is one of the few twentieth-century scholars who argues that the right of legation is a true right and who considers it an abuse of right when a state refuses to receive another state's envoy in times of peace.[52] Most others correctly argue that there is neither an obligation nor a duty to send or receive envoys, sometimes referred to as an 'accordable liberty', which overlaps with what Wesley Hohfeld called a 'legal privilege' or 'legal freedom' in his categorization of rights.[53] The Vienna Conventions also do not compel a receiving state to motivate a decision not to grant the necessary authorization to a foreign diplomat or consul (Art 4(2) VCDR and Art 12(2) VCCR). The right of legation nonetheless carries incidental obligations. First, the most obvious example of such corresponding duty is the international legal obligation not to act in serious prejudice to the right of legation; states that prevent another nation from sending or receiving ambassadors could trigger international responsibility.[54] Furthermore, these acts would be contrary to both the spirit and wording of the Vienna Convention: its preamble stresses the promotion of friendly relations among nations, a duty that is also codified in Article 40 VCDR. Second, states use legation to seek interaction and communication with others, making the ius legationis an enabler of the

[48] *SS Wimbledon (United Kingdom, France, Italy, and Japan v Germany)* (Judgment) [1923] PCIJ Ser A, No 1, 25. See for further reading, Craven (n 1) 212–13. James Crawford, *Brownlie's Principles of Public International Law* (OUP 2012) 448–49.

[49] Hannis Taylor, *A Treatise on International Public Law* (Callaghan & Co 1901) 324. See already Grotius (n 3) Ch XVIII, 326, II and De Wicquefort (n 16) 68. Elie RC Van Bogaert, *Volkenrecht* (Elsevier Sequoia 1973) 329.

[50] Brown (n 2) 91.

[51] Hans Kelsen, *General Theory of Law and State* (Harvard University Press 1945) 58–64; Jeremy Bentham, *Of Laws in General* (Athlone Press 1970).

[52] Marcel Sibert, *Traité de Droit International Public*, vol 2 (Dalloz 1951) 711.

[53] Hardy (n 37) 14.

[54] de Vattel (n 6) para 63.

ius communicandi.[55] The international legal order presupposes the existence of minimum relations between states; a complete diplomatic isolation of one state is therefore contrary to the very essence of international law and the principle of peaceful coexistence. This relates to Vattel's idea of a duty to hear envoys, even if it is just a quick conversation at the frontier, an idea that has become somewhat unreal in the context of modern communication. At the same time, one cannot but conclude that this obligation is in fact a limited one.[56]

#### 2.1.4.2 The Right of Legation as an Imperfect or Subjective Right

Having established that the right of legation's direct juridical implications are not sufficiently significant to deem the ius legationis a right under international law, alternative qualifications should be considered. Some academics accept that there are varying degrees of rights under international law. This account of law consists of norms backed by sanctions and some which are not, according to HLA Hart.[57] In similar vein, Schumaker places international rights on a spectrum whereby rights with corresponding duties enforced by law are considered as 'perfect' or 'strict' rights.[58] Obligations enforced by various social pressures are less perfect but still more perfect than norms that are unenforceable.[59]

The concept of imperfect rights can be applied to the right of legation. Apart from Carlos Calvo, there are few authors who have defended the view that the right of legation is 'un droit parfait en principe, mais imparfait dans la pratique'.[60] Nevertheless, as expressed earlier, older scholarship accords a considerable weight to the right of legation's moral aspects, the exercise of which is associated with a commitment to the peaceful functioning of the international order. In modern state practice, lengthily severed diplomatic relations and diplomatic relations being broken off completely are considered to be severe forms of international disagreement. A recent example of a shorter episode is Venezuela's 2014 breaking off, on the grounds of interference in internal affairs, and restoring of diplomatic ties with Panama. The countries did not have diplomatic relations between 5 March and 2 July 2014. A more sustained severance has been witnessed since Canada, in 2012, decided to close its Tehran Embassy and expel Iranian diplomats. To date, Switzerland serves its interests, while Oman represents Iranian interests in Canada. At the least, this represents the idea that states value the right of legation even when paired only with non-legally binding obligations. Alternatively, Reichling referred to the right of legation as a subjective right, without defining the consequences of such a label.[61] The theory of subjective rights originates in the thinking of opposability; the right of legation's exercise is indeed only opposable to other actors who have previously accepted it.[62] The ILC withheld neither qualification in 1958.[63]

[55] Charles Reichling, *Le Droit de Légation des Communautés Européennes* (UGA Éditions 1964) 12; Oppenheim (n 21) 419.

[56] Jean Salmon, *Manuel de Droit Diplomatique* (Bruylant 1994) 28.

[57] HLA Hart, *The Concept of Law* (3rd edn, eds Leslie Green and Joseph Raz, OUP 2012).

[58] Millard Schumaker, *Sharing without Reckoning: Imperfect Right and the Norms of Reciprocity* (Wilfrid Laurier UP 2006) 61.

[59] J Craig Barker, *International Law and International Relations* (Continuum 2000) 32–33.

[60] Carlos Calvo, *Le Droit International Théorique et Pratique*, vol 2 (Durand 1870) 556. See also Geraldo Eulálio do Nascimento e Silva, *Diplomacy in International Law* (AW Sijthoff 1972) 35.

[61] Reichling (n 55) 12.

[62] Ludwik Dembiński, *The Modern Law of Diplomacy: External Missions of States and International Organizations* (Martinus Nijhoff 1988) 29.

[63] ILC, 'Summary Records of the Tenth Session' (1958) I YBILC, A/CN.4/SER.A/1958, 91.

### 2.1.4.3 The Right of Legation as a Capacity

Most contemporary scholars do not define the right of legation as a right in the legal sense but as a matter of capacity or competence.[64] The term 'capacity' denotes an ability to do something; any reference to a legal commitment is absent.[65] The right of legation corresponds with this idea whereby states have a discretion to respectively exercise and accept it. Treating the ius legationis as a non-obligatory right has the advantage that corresponding legal and moral obligations do not follow. The active and passive acts of sending and receiving ambassadors become merely an activity that states can engage with to their likening, provided that an agreement to do so is reached with the state concerned. The argument's attractiveness lies in the fact that its conceptualization corresponds to the current practice, while also adhering to the strict views expressed in the earlier legal literature as well as in the VCDR's travaux préparatoires.

A remaining significant question, however, is whether the meaning of the term 'capacity' is sufficiently clear in the scope of public international law. The term has been used to mean international legal standing as well as a synonym of international rights.[66] Commonly, the notion of a 'capacity' is often preferred to a 'right' in the context of the foreign relations of states. The first example reverts to the 1933 Montevideo Convention, whereby Article 1 includes the requirement of '*capacity* to enter into relations with other States' [own emphasis], among other minimum qualifications which states ought to possess. A second use is seen in the foreign relations context, where it features in the Vienna Convention on the Law of Treaties (VCLT).[67] Article 6 of the Convention provides that '[e]very State possesses capacity to conclude treaties'. The ILC Commentary provides an interesting insight which provides that:

> [s]ome members of the Commission considered that there was no need for an article on capacity in international law to conclude treaties. They pointed out that capacity to enter into diplomatic relations had not been dealt with in the Vienna Convention on Diplomatic Relations and suggested that, if it were to be dealt with in the law of treaties, the Commission might find itself codifying the whole law concerning the 'subjects' of international law. Other members felt that the question of capacity was more prominent in the law of treaties than in the law of diplomatic intercourse and immunities and that the draft articles should contain at least some general provisions concerning capacity to conclude treaties.[68]

The Commissioners did not differentiate the nature of the ius tractatuum and the ius legationis. Instead, both were referred to as capacities assumed capable of resulting in similar consequences manifested as international right and duties.

The term 'capacity' also seems to be preferred to 'right' in the context of the competences of international organizations. When an organization exercises a right typically reserved for states in the traditional international legal order sense, that right may be referred to as

[64] Denza, *Diplomatic Law* (n 24) 23; Salmon (n 56) 28; Robert Y Jennings and Arthur Watts (eds), *Oppenheim's International Law*, vol 1 (9th edn, Longman 1992) 1056; Sen (n 13) 9; Georg Dahm, *Völkerrecht*, vol 1 (W Kohlhammer Verlag 1958) 309. See, a contrario, Sibert (n 52) 711 and Oppenheim (n 21) 419.

[65] See the Merriam-Webster Dictionary (2016) and the Oxford Dictionary of English (2015).

[66] Crawford, *Brownlie* (n 48) 57. Both meanings feature in the *Reparation for Injuries Suffered in the Service of the United Nations* (Advisory Opinion) [1949] ICJ Rep 174, 179.

[67] Vienna Convention on the Law of Treaties, opened for signature 23 May 1969, entered into force 27 January 1980, 1155 UNTS 331 (hereafter VCLT).

[68] ILC, 'Draft Articles on the Law of Treaties with Commentaries' (1966) II YBILC 192.

merely a capacity to strike the conceptual difference. In the *Reparation for Injuries* opinion, for example, the Court assessed the 'capacity' to bring a claim by an international organization on behalf of one of its officials. Generally, claims made under diplomatic protection are considered to be within the state competence, concerned with nationality as opposed to the organization per se.[69] A further example is found in the generally accepted notion that the UN has the capacity to accord limited recognition to a state 'at all events if it is necessary for it to do so for the performance of the functions for which the Organization was created'.[70]

### 2.1.5 Conceptualizing the Right of Legation

The nature and possession of the right of legation is subject to an ongoing discussion. Since the concept does not fit easily with some of the rights unquestionably possessed by sovereign states. Therefore, the ILC and the Vienna Conferences' negotiators shied away from referring to it in their codification efforts in the early 1960s. For this book's purposes, it nonetheless proved necessary to formulate a definition of the right of legation. In doing so, it was manifest that, despite its shaky foundations, the right of legation cannot be eliminated from scholarship nor general legal terminology. Moreover, establishing the underlying theories with regards to the right of legation's substance and significance assists in determining the challenges faced in the particular case of the European Union (EU, or Union) when conducting diplomatic and consular relations.

The first purpose of this chapter was to assess the right of legation's content. It determined that the ius legationis consists of three elements: *(a)* the establishment of diplomatic and possibly consular relations, *(b)* the sending of missions, and *(c)* the receiving of missions. In addition, PIL acknowledges numerous rights and duties which, when taken together, provide a framework for the right of legation's exercise without being strictly a part of it. Norms derived from the right of legation have become part of the general law between states and are codified in treaties, the Vienna Conventions being the most prominent example. Such subsidiary rules and duties are enforceable under international law as between the VCDR's signatory parties. The same is not true when the interactions involve at least one non-state actor, although other enforceable rules may be entered into in such case..

The second purpose of this chapter was to define the right of legation's nature. Theoretically, it can be either conceptualized as an imperfect right that is unenforceable by the holder or as a capacity which requires the agreement of counterparts to become exercised. There may be less difference between the two options than would appear at first glance. In both cases, the term 'right' is deceptive in the diplomatic context as its exercise requires an action by a counterparty. States do not have the obligation to either enter into relations with another state or to accept the opening of a mission on its territory. Equally, states do not have the right to open a mission in a foreign country without prior consent. Against the claim of being imperfect at best, but probably no more than a liberty, the right of legation is defined in this book as a capacity accorded to a certain entity which is to be used in agreement with other entities accorded the same ability.

[69] *Reparation for Injuries* (n 66) 182; see also the dissenting opinion by Judge Krylov, 217–19.

[70] Hans Aufricht, 'Principles and Practices of Recognition by International Organizations' (1949) 43 AJIL 679; Shabtai Rosenne, 'Recognition of States by the United Nations' (1949) 26 BYIL 437, 439.

## 2.2 The Holders of the Right of Legation

### 2.2.1 Historical Cracks in the State-Dominated System

#### 2.2.1.1 Practices

The previous section leaves no doubt that states possess a right of legation. An important question for the purpose of this handbook is whether and in accordance with what criteria non-state entities can also engage in legation activities that are fully recognized as such. The classic writers tend to be rather conservative: virtually all authors, including Grotius, Wheaton, and Satow, accord the right of legation to sovereign states only.[71] Some scholars even supported the hypothesis that the right is intrinsically connected to the sovereign in a personal capacity as opposed to the state they represent.[72]

This being said, historical practices tended to be more flexible than the doctrinal approaches from those days reflect. In the long history of diplomacy, states have always maintained official relations with non-state actors (even those whose international legal personality was not firmly established).[73] Equally, there have been cases where states were dependent on others for their diplomatic representation, where states jointly exercised a right of legation, where states temporary transferred their right of legation etc. Moreover, throughout history, city states, regions, and sometimes provinces have been diplomatically active.[74] The German Empire, for instance, consisted of states that enjoyed certain sovereign rights.[75] As a result, the Princes of the German Empire and later the German *Länder* exercised their rights of legation alongside the Emperor. This was changed in the 1871 Constitution: the *Länder* retained their right of legation, but the Emperor was named responsible for accrediting and nominating ambassadors and consuls. With the 1919 Weimar Constitution, *Länder* definitively lost their ius legationis. A single exercise of the ius legationis was observed, for example, by the United Kingdoms of Sweden and Norway (1815–1905) and the Austro-Hungarian Empire (1867–1918). In contrast, the Danish–Icelandic Union remained dualistic.[76]

In the decades leading up to the 1961 Vienna Conference and for a considerable period thereafter, the criteria of statehood and full sovereignty were increasingly questioned as being absolute requirements for and/or enablers of the exercise right of legation. This was mainly due to the colonial twentieth century, which showcased even more variations on the way to exercise the right. Statehood was no longer sufficient proof of sovereignty or independence, and this in turn affected the exercise of the right of legation.[77] At that time, a change in scholarly views is also observed: academics integrated the colonial logic to legitimize a temporary incapacity of certain states to exercise their right of legation. For example, Anzilotti argued in 1929 that the right of legation:

[71] Grotius (n 3) Ch XVIII, 326, I–II; Wheaton (n 11) 258.

[72] Charles de Martens, *Manuel Diplomatique ou Précis des Droits et des Fonctions des Agents Diplomatiques* (Treuttel et Würtz 1822) 18; de Wicquefort, *L'Ambassadeur* (n 7) 40.

[73] Jean-Paul Pancracio, *Droit et Institutions Diplomatiques* (Pedone 2007) 18.

[74] Bluntschli (n 7) 126.

[75] Jennings and Watts (n 64) 1057.

[76] Salmon (n 56) 35.

[77] James Crawford, *The Creation of States in International Law* (2nd edn, OUP 2006) 62–88; *Lotus (France v Turkey)* (Judgment) [1949] PCIJ Ser A, No 10, 18.

> appartient à tous les membres de la communauté internationale qui ne sont pas obligés à confirmer leur représentation diplomatique à un autre membre [ ... ] ou qui ne dépendent pas d'un autre Etat.[78]

As a result, the right of legation could be exercised by a mother state on behalf of another state. With regard to protectorates, the right of legation's exercise in concreto differed from one case to another. The former British Protectorate in current day Malaysia, for example, did not receive diplomatic representations until its independence in 1957, although foreign consular or commercial presence in the area was tolerated. In contrast, the member states of the Commonwealth of Nations exercised their own right of legation.[79]

The idea that the right of legation could be exercised collectively subsequently gained recognition in literature.[80] Anzilotti, on this point, pleaded for flexibility:

> parfois, à côté de l'exercice collectif pour les affaires d'intérêt commun, subsiste le droit individuel de chaque membre: le premier cas se produit, en règle, dans l'Union réelle [ ... ], le second dans la Confédération.[81]

One of the novelties was the fact that the right of legation could be recognized or regulated in a treaty or agreement between states or even in domestic laws.[82] For example, Article 80 of the 1977 USSR Constitution accepted that the Federal Republics had the right to establish diplomatic and consular relations.[83]

#### 2.2.1.2 Theories

Traditional academic literature clearly prefers to limit the right of legation's holders to sovereign states and fails to define what other entities than sovereigns can exercise the right of legation. Rather, it confines itself to listing the various *entities excluded from enjoying the right*. Among those mentioned are private persons, brigands, and pirates.[84] Grotius and Gentili legitimized this exclusion on the basis of the absence of any connection to sovereignty. An ambassador assumes equality with the sovereign, making it unthinkable for private groups (especially those with a vicious reputation) to equate with the noble protagonists of the international legal order.

Yet, when it comes to *positively defining* actors capable of exercising the right of legation, views varied.[85] Two attempts were made to theorize the debate. A first theory is attributable to Vattel and builds upon the idea of divisibility of sovereignty.[86] Vattel's contention is that rights derived from sovereignty are divisible and can be transferred to subordinate entities.

78 '[B]elongs to all members of the international community who are not obliged to seek confirmation for their diplomatic representation from another member [ ... ] or who are not dependent on another state' [own translation]; Anzilotti (n 19) 264.

79 Lorna Lloyd, *Diplomacy with a Difference: The Commonwealth Office of High Commissioner, 1880–2006* (Martinus Nijhoff 2007).

80 Stockston (n 12) 198.

81 '[S]ometimes, besides the collective exercise in relation to matters of common interest, an individual right of legation remains with each member: the first case occurs, as a rule, in a real union [ ... ], the second in a confederation of states' [own translation]; Anzilotti (n 19) 264–65.

82 do Nascimento e Silva (n 60) 36–37.

83 Danilo Turk, 'Recognition of States: A Comment' (1993) 4 EJIL 66, 71.

84 Gentili (n 5) 55, 59; Grotius (n 3) Ch XVIII, 368–69, III.

85 Silviya Lechner, 'What Difference Does Ius Inter Gentes Make? Changing Diplomatic Rights and Duties and the Modern European States-System' (2006) 1 HJD 235, 241–45.

86 de Vattel (n 6) para 62.

This partly overlaps with the 'model of divided sovereignty' that is put forward sometimes in discussions on the EU and regards the Union and its member states as partial sovereign entities within the sphere of their competences.[87]

The transfer of the right of legation by a sovereign actor should not be confused with a de facto transfer of sovereignty. Sovereignty is a unitary notion that can be acquired, transferred, or extinguished in its entirety only. The rights and capacities stemming from sovereignty can be divided, as can acts that do not affect the transferring state's sovereign status. Princes, communities, and states within a bigger constituency (eg an empire) can be granted (part of) a sovereign right but remain dependent on the transferring sovereign and/or constituency when executing it. Vattel considered the right of legation an example of such a sovereign right that could be attributed to a subordinate entity:

> le droit de traiter avec les Puissances Étrangères et de contracter avec elles des Alliances; ils ont incontestablement celui d'envoyer et de recevoir des Ministres Publics.[88]

The allocation could be either through an ad hoc concession or foreseen in a national constitution. Consequently, Vattels's model allows the right of embassy to be simultaneously exercised by the sovereign and subordinate subjects by way of agreement or law. The theory ties in well with some of the global developments at the time. The Holy Roman Empire of the German Nation had already demonstrated that the right of legation may be partly and for a specific purpose be transferred from the central power to its constituents. The model of pluralistic diplomacy was retained in the Final Act of the 1820 Viennese Ministerial Conferences and the establishment of the North German confederation.[89] The right of legation was vested in the Emperor, who received foreign diplomats and nominated German envoys on the basis of Article 11 of the 1867 Constitution. Yet, certain states of the Empire, such as Bavaria and Württemberg, retained the right of legation in matters not falling within the competence of the central power. At the same time, in practice, the non-linearity of the relationship between sovereignty, independence, and statehood is evidenced by the fact that certain states, when stripped of their right of legation, could continue to exercise other international rights and duties, for instance, in relation to their membership of international organizations.[90]

A second theory is functional in nature. Von Martens explained that:

> [l]e but propre et primitif des ambassades indique assez, I) que tous ceux qui sont autorisés à traiter en leur propre nom avec les puissances étrangères doivent aussi avoir le droit d'envoyer des ministres; que par conséquent non seulement les États entièrement souverains indépendamment des alliances égales *a*) ou inégales qui les unissent à d'autres États, mais aussi ceux qui comme les États de l'empire d'Allemagne *b*) et quelques autres

[87] Wildhaber L, 'Sovereignty and International Law' in Ronald SJ MacDonald and Douglas M Johnston (eds), *The Structure and Process of International Law: Essays in Legal Philosophy, Doctrine and Theory* (Martinus Nijhoff 1986) 425. Enzo Cannizzaro, 'Fragmented Sovereignty? The European Union and its Member States in the International Arena' (2003) 13 ItYBIL 35, 42.

[88] '[T]he right to negotiate with foreign powers, and to enter into alliances with them; they incontestably have the right to send and receive public ministers' [own translation]; de Vattel (n 6) para 59.

[89] Final Act of the Viennese Ministerial Conferences, done on 15 May 1820 and approved by the Frankfurt Confederal Assembly on 8 June 1820.

[90] Salmon (n 56) 34.

> États mi-souverains c), sans jouir d'une souveraineté entière sont en possession du droit de la guerre de la paix, et des alliances, doivent en jouir.[91]

Von Martens attributed an active right of legation to all entities authorized to conclude agreements in their own name with foreign powers. A fairly broad principle is tempered by Von Martens's list of entities capable of possessing the right of legation, all of which have a link with a sovereign power.[92] The line of reasoning, however, shares theoretical underpinnings with modern functionalist approaches that would later become prevalent in public international and institutional law.

## 2.2.2 Modern Cracks in the State-Dominated System

### 2.2.2.1 Parties to the 1961 Vienna Convention

Although the 1961 and 1963 Vienna Conferences took place in the midst of a shift towards an increasingly politically and culturally diverse global order, this did not result in the broadening of the diplomatic community as defined by the UN. The UN only invited sovereign states to participate in the Vienna Conferences. The text of the 1961 Vienna Convention is less restrictive. When defining the rules on who could sign the Convention, its drafters subtly moved away from the traditional criteria of independence and sovereignty. While the VCDR reserves its appurtenance and scope of application to states, the phrasing is quite specific. Article 48 VCDR reads:

> [t]he present Convention shall be open for signature by all States Members of the United Nations or of any of the specialized agencies or Parties to the Statute of the International Court of Justice, and by any other State invited by the General Assembly of the United Nations to become a Party to the Convention [ ... ].

Article 50 continues:

> [t]he present Convention shall remain open for accession by any State belonging to any of the four categories mentioned in Article 48. The instruments of accession shall be deposited with the Secretary-General of the United Nations.

The above articles limit the exercise of diplomatic relations to states belonging to one of four specific categories.[93] As a result, the Vienna Conventions left the ultimate determination of what qualifies as a 'state' in the UN's hands: its Specialized Agencies, the International Court of Justice (ICJ), and the UN General Assembly (UNGA) are entrusted with the responsibility

[91] [T]he original and primitive purpose of embassies indicates that all those who are authorized to act in their own name with foreign powers must also have the right to send envoys; "that" consequently, not only fully sovereign and independent states should enjoy equal or unequal which unite them with other states, but also states like those of the German Empire, and some other semi-sovereign states that—without enjoying full sovereignty—possess the right of the of war and peace, and of alliances, must enjoy this right [own translation].
von Martens (n 4) 284.

[92] See Fauchille (n 20) 33.

[93] See, similarly, Art 74 VCCR.

to define statehood, giving the community of states represented in the UN the power to decide who can join their diplomatic club.

Within the Vienna Conventions' membership, two actors stand out: the Holy See and the Palestinian Authority. The Holy See occupies a unique position in the international legal order. Some authors argue that the central organ of the Catholic Church is a sui generis subject of international law; others regard it as a state, albeit one with a very small territory and population.[94] Until 1870, the Pope headed the Papal States, in whose capacity diplomatic envoys were sent and received, entries into treaties were made, and representations at the international stage followed.[95] In the process of Italy's national unification, the Papal States were annexed, resulting in their population and territory, but not in their legation capacity. Most states sustained their legation practices with the Pontiff, whom they considered a sovereign. The 1871 Italian *Legge delle Guarentigie* (Law of Guarantees) attempted to settle the issue by giving the Pope a special sovereign status, the right to receive ambassadors, and the right to communicate freely with Roman Catholic bishops throughout the world. The Pontiff at the time, Pius IX, rejected the law, but his successors continued to enjoy the right of legation and the privileges that came with it. The Holy See's territorial basis in the Vatican City was recognized in the 1927 Lateran Treaty (which abrogated the Law of Guarantees);[96] as well as its power to conduct international relations: 'Italy recognizes the sovereignty of the Holy See in international matters as an inherent attribute in conformity with its traditions and the requirements of its mission to the world.'[97] The Holy See's apostolic pro-nuncios and nuncios continue to enjoy international rights and privileges in foreign states and it reciprocates to missions accredited to it.[98] The Holy See also has a permanent observer mission to the UN in New York, enjoys sovereign immunity form jurisdiction and execution, and has capacity to sign and ratify treaties.

Based on the Holy See's inherent diplomatic tradition and particular status in international affairs, it is unsurprising that states extended an invitation to the Holy See to take part in the 1961 and, subsequently, the 1963 negotiations on the codification of the law on diplomatic and consular relations. The Holy See was an active participant in Vienna and left substantial footprints on the final agreements.[99] One of the results is that Article 14(1) VCDR equates the legal position of the nuncios with ambassadors, reflecting the agreement reached in the 1815 Règlement de Vienne. Moreover, Article 16(3) on the precedence of diplomatic representatives provides that customary arrangements in force prior to the VCDR would be maintained between receiving states and the Holy See on the rank of the nuncio in the corps diplomatique. For many Roman Catholic countries, it is still common practice for the diplomatic representative of the Holy See to take precedence over heads of mission, regardless of their seniority in the diplomatic hierarchy. The nuncio functions as its dean.

Currently, the Holy See exercises full diplomatic relations with 176 states, the EU, and the Sovereign Military Order of Malta and enjoys 'special' relations with the Russian Federation and the Palestinian Authority. All EU member states recognize the Holy See's sui generis

[94] Crawford, *The Creation of States* (n 77) 223; Denza, *Diplomatic Law* (n 24) 23.

[95] Hyginus Eugene Cardinale, *The Holy See and the International Order* (Smythe 1976) 63.

[96] Article 2 of the Lateran Conciliation Treaty, signed in Rome on 11 February 1929, *Gazzetta Ufficiale*, 5 June 1929, No 130, as amended by the Agreement between the Italian Republic and the Holy See on 18 February 1984, 24 ILM 1589 (1985).

[97] Cedric Ryngaert, 'The Legal Status of the Holy See' (2011) 3 GoJIL 829.

[98] ibid 836.

[99] Roberts (n 39) 91.

position in international affairs and exchange diplomatic missions with the sovereign entity. The Holy See has missions in all member states but Denmark, Estonia, Finland, Latvia, and Luxembourg, for which neighbouring nunciatures are responsible. Full diplomatic relations with the United Kingdom were only restored in January 1982, two years before the United States accredited an envoy at ambassadorial level after a lapse of 117 years.[100]

The statehood of the Palestinian territories has been one of the more politically controversial issues of global affairs. Recent years have shown a wave of individual recognitions of the Palestinian National Authority (PNA) as well as its upgrade status in the multilateral settings.[101] The debate is ongoing in the EU context. The Union does not have the competence to recognize states, but the European Parliament supports 'in principle recognition of Palestinian statehood and the two state solution, and believes these should go hand in hand with the development of peace talks, which should be advanced'. In 2011, Palestine became a member of the United Nations Educational, Scientific and Cultural Organization (UNESCO), and in 2012 an impressive number of states (138) voted in favour of upgrading its status in the UN from permanent observer to a non-member observer state.[102] Whether Palestine is a state is a matter distinguished from the questions relating to Palestine's diplomatic capacity. Long before the UNGA vote, states started to receive permanent representatives of the Palestine Liberation Organization (PLO).[103] Most often, this was without a formal and explicit recognition of statehood.[104] By the early 1980s, the PLO claimed that it had more diplomatic missions than Israel.[105] The precise status and title of the representatives varied greatly in practice from one country to another. Some accorded it full diplomatic status, such as Austria in 1978, whereas others granted such status informally without recognizing the mission's diplomatic status, an example being Italy in 1974. Some yielded immunities informally along with diplomatic status to the head of mission but not to the personnel. Yet other states classified the mission as an 'other representation' rather than an 'embassy', for instance Spain in 1986.[106] By contrast in 2004, France refused to entitle diplomatic immunity to a Palestinian diplomat when his wife filed for divorce.[107]

The past ten years have seen an enhancement of the international community's interactions with the PNA, both in UN organs and bodies, as well as in bilateral diplomatic relations. EU member states upgraded the status of Palestine's representatives almost collectively, from 'Délégation générale' (France, 2010), or 'general representation' (Belgium, 2013) to an ambassadorial level. In a traditional conception, the upgrade amounts to a recognition of the right of legation, as well as to de facto recognition of statehood. Following the 2011 admission to UNESCO, a UN Specialized Agency, the State of Palestine joined the Vienna Conventions. In April 2014, it officially became the one-hundred-and-ninetieth signatory

[100] Sen (n 13) 20.

[101] European Parliament Resolution on Recognition of Palestine Statehood, 2014/2964(RSP), Strasbourg, 17 December 2014.

[102] The Status of Palestine in the United Nations (UNGA Resolution A/Res/67/19) adopted on 29 November 2012.

[103] James Crawford, 'Israel (1948–9) and Palestine (1998–9): Two Studies in the Creation of States' in Ian Brownlie, Guy S Goodwin-Gill, and Stefan Talmon (eds), *The Reality of International Law: Essays in Honour of Ian Brownlie* (OUP 1999) 121.

[104] Tamar Megiddo and Zohar Nevo, 'Palestinian Independence in a Post-Kosovo World' in Duncan French (ed), *Statehood and Self-Determination: Reconciling Tradition and Modernity in International Law* (CUP 2013) 200.

[105] John B Quigley, *The Statehood of Palestine: International Law in the Middle East Conflict* (CUP 2010) 151.

[106] ibid 152.

[107] Cour d'appel de Paris (FR) *Al Hassan v Nahila El Yafi* No 2001/18887 [2004] 108 RGDIP 1066, as referred to in Denza, *Diplomatic Law* (n 24) 20.

party to the VCDR and the one-hundred-and-seventy-seventh party to the VCCR. Palestine currently maintains diplomatic relations with 139 states.[108]

While the Vienna Conventions do not automatically apply to relations between states and non-states, they do not prevent non-states from becoming the holders of privileges and immunities either. For instance, headquarters agreements signed between international organizations and states that host them commonly grant permanent representation missions privileges and immunities similar to those enjoyed by bilateral diplomats. The interpretation of the rules also often follows the interpretation developed in the bilateral context. The same is observed in ad hoc diplomacy: when organizing a conference, the UN typically enters into a specific agreement with the host country that makes customary privileges and immunities applicable.[109] In such agreements, the host government commits to accord diplomatic representatives attending the conference privileges and immunities for the duration of the conference, often referring to the Convention on the Privileges and Immunities of the United Nations (CPIUN), which in turn refers to customary privileges and immunities as codified in the Vienna Conventions.[110] The Vienna Conventions therefore have a far broader scope and impact than what may be readily apparant at first glance.

### 2.2.2.2 Other Entities that Exercise Diplomacy

The broadening of the diplomatic community is observed beyond the Vienna Conventions. New forms of public and private cross-border interactions have emerged, gaining prominence in response to increasingly diverse and network-connected societies. Dwelling on the successes of the traditional bilateral diplomatic relations, a wide range of non-traditional actors put forth ambassadorial titles and functions, including governmental and non-governmental organizations, quasi-states, and regional actors, as well as business representatives.[111] Since the 2000s, there has been an increased use of terms and concepts traditionally associated with state-to-state diplomacy. The sheer abundance of UN goodwill ambassadors and Oxfam global ambassadors, as well as student, science, culture, and brand ambassadors who participate in people-to-people and soft diplomacy,[112] science and cultural diplomacy,[113] and independent diplomacy[114] testify to this trend. However, the phenomenon cannot be said to have impacted directly upon PIL principles. These actors do not exercise a legal right of legation for lack of a subjection to the international legal order's rules and responsibilities.

[108] See the list provided by the PA on its website: <http://palestineun.org/about-palestine/diplomatic-relations> accessed 29 April 2022.

[109] See, e.g. Art VI of the Agreement between the United Nations and the Government of Austria regarding the arrangements for the Vienna Conference on Consular Relations, signed at Vienna on 29 January 1963; Agreement between the United Nations and the Government of Kazakhstan regarding the arrangements for the International Ministerial Conference of Landlocked and Transit Developing Countries and Donor Countries and International Financial and Development Institutions on Transit Transport Cooperation, signed at New York on 27 June 2003.

[110] Convention on the Privileges and Immunities of the United Nations, opened for signature 13 February 1946, entered into force 17 September 1946, 1 UNTS 15 (hereafter CPIUN).

[111] Ronald P Barston, *Modern Diplomacy* (4th edn, Pearson 2013) 6; Kishore Mahbubani, 'Multilateral Diplomacy' in Andrew F Cooper, Jorge Heine, and Ramesh Thakur (eds), *The Oxford Handbook of Modern Diplomacy* (OUP 2013); Geoffrey R Wiseman, 'Polylateralism and New Modes of Global Dialogue' in Christer Jönsson and Richard Langhorne (eds), *Diplomacy*, vol 3 (2nd edn, Sage 2004).

[112] Matthieu Burnay, Joëlle Hivonnet, and Kolja Raube, 'Soft Diplomacy and People-to-People Dialogue between the EU and the PRC' (2014) 19 EFAR 35.

[113] Lloyd S Davis and Robert G Patman, *Science Diplomacy: New Day or False Dawn* (World Scientific 2015); Martina Topić and Siniša Rodin (eds), *Cultural Diplomacy and Cultural Imperialism: European Perspective(s)* (Peter Lang 2012).

[114] Michelle M Betsill and Elisabeth Corell, *NGO Diplomacy: The Influence of Nongovernmental Organizations in International Environmental Negotiations* (MIT Press 2008).

The distinction is more complex when it comes to actors involved in the exercise of public authority, which seek to represent that authority through diplomatic means. This section discusses four categories of international entities that are in some ways recognized as making a fair attempt at exercising the right of legation as understood in PIL.

*2.2.2.2.1 Those that aspire statehood*

The international legal order counts a number of non-states of which Hong Kong, Macau, Taiwan, and Kosovo may be the most known. These four entities enjoy a large degree of autonomy but still strive for broader recognition and representation.

**Hong Kong and Macau** Since 1997 and 1999, respectively, Hong Kong and Macau constitute Special Administrative Regions (SARs) of the People's Republic of China (PRC).[115] The SARs do not possess the right of legation but seek to be represented, nonetheless. With Beijing's authorization, the SARs can participate in 'external affairs', a term preferred over 'diplomatic affairs'.[116] Hong Kong has even acceded to international organizations, including the World Trade Organization. Many EU member states maintain consulates in Hong Kong and some in Macau. Those consulates often exercise a particular kind of lowered diplomatic and political relations.

**The Republic of China** The Republic of China (ROC) attended the 1961 Vienna Conference and contributed to the formulation of the VCDR as well as its Optional Protocol concerning the Compulsory Settlement of Disputes, subsequently signing and ratifying both. Yet the instrument of accession deposited on behalf of the Government of PRC on 25 November 1975 states that both the signature and ratification of the VCDR by the Chiang Kai-shek clique usurping the name of China were illegal, null, and void. Up to today, Taiwan insists that it is the Government of China. Yet most other states accept 'the position of the PRC that Taiwan is a province of China'—a carefully chosen form of words falling short of saying that they recognise Taiwan as a province of China. Since 1971, states' recognition of Taiwan as a state—and with it, its diplomatic recognition—has declined significantly.[117] States that no longer recognize Taiwan as a state also do not exercise diplomatic relations with it, or at least not officially.[118] During the first half of the twentieth century, over a hundred countries had formal diplomatic relations with Taiwan; today there are fourteen UN member states and the Holy See. The right of legation seems to be confirmed vis-à-vis those states that recognize Taiwan. To manage the bulk of its international exchanges with non-recognizing states, Taiwan has set up a parallel and informal system of representational offices.[119] Sixteen EU member states have established such non-diplomatic offices in Taipei.

[115] Article 151 of the Basic Law of the Hong Kong Special Administrative Region of the People's Republic of China, adopted at the Third Session of the Seventh National People's Congress on 4 April 1990, promulgated by Order No 26 of the President of the People's Republic of China on 4 April 1990, entered into force 1 July 1997.

[116] The line between the two terms is unclear; Simon Shen, 'Hong Kong's Sub-Sovereign Status and Its External Relations' in Per Sevastik (ed), *Aspects of Sovereignty: Sino-Swedish Reflections* (Martinus Nijhoff 2013) 102–03.

[117] Lung-chu Chen, *The US–Taiwan–China Relationship in International Law and Policy* (OUP 2016) 41.

[118] See generally Augusto Hernandez-Campos, 'The Criteria of Statehood in International Law and the Hallstein Doctrine: The Case of the Republic of China on Taiwan' (2006) 24 Chinese (Taiwan) YB Intl L&A ff 75.

[119] Linjun Wu, 'Limitations and Prospects of Taiwan's Informal Diplomacy' in Jean-Marie Henckaerts (ed), *The International Status of Taiwan in the New World Order* (Kluwer 1996) 37.

**Kosovo** As a recently self-declared state, Kosovo claims to be a diplomatic actor. Although Kosovo's assertions of statehood are not prohibited by international law, the validity and legal effects of such declaration are heavily debated.[120] The recognition record of Kosovo's statehood and its right of legation is mixed, even among EU member states.[121] In total, however, over a hundred countries recognize Kosovo as an independent and sovereign state, in which case the right of legation is no longer disputed. At present, sixty-nine countries have established diplomatic relations with Kosovo,[122] resulting in twenty-five Kosovar missions at ambassadorial level around the world, thirteen of which are located in EU member states. There are forty-four missions accredited at diplomatic level to the Kosovar Government (either resident or non-resident), thirteen of which fly the flag of an EU member state. Five more member states and the EU have opened a liaison office.

In the past, Kosovo was an interesting case for having exemplified an exercise of a legation practice by an international organization on a state's behalf. During the years of the UN's Interim Administration Mission in Kosovo (UNMIK), a complex system of civil reconstruction was set up under the UN's auspices.[123] UNMIK was mandated to adopt domestic legislation with immediate binding effect on private persons.[124] As a result, the UN had authority over the territory and people of Kosovo that would normally constitute the components of sovereignty, including its legislature, administration, judiciary, and diplomatic relations. Foreign diplomatic missions sought accreditation at the UNMIK; the credentials were presented to the Special Representative of the UN Secretary-General. This practice has since been replaced by a political procedure organized by the Government of Kosovo.

##### *2.2.2.2.2 A religious entity*

One of the most fascinating subjects of international law to have developed a legation practice is the Sovereign Military Order of Saint John of Jerusalem. Commonly known as the Order of Malta, this international confraternity is best described as a charitable organization that provides humanitarian assistance. Originally one of the two great military orders of chivalry of Jerusalem, it later moved to the islands of Rhodes and Malta. In early times, activities were carried out in accordance with the eight Priories spread out across Europe. It was recognized by the Pontiff as an autonomous organization in 1113. The Order is now referred to as a sui generis subject of international law.[125]

The nature of the Order of Malta's diplomatic relations has been disputed. Most academics argue that the Order of Malta has a right of legation, which is, however, subject to the limitations that result from the Order's specific nature and competences.[126] For sure, the legation practice is confined to activities in relation to the organization and humanitarian tasks. Others argue that privileges and immunities are accorded on the basis of courtesy rather than law. The Order's ius legationis resembles that of the Holy See as it is grounded in the

[120] Accordance with International Law of the Unilateral Declaration of Independence of Kosovo (Advisory Opinion) [2010] 403 ICJ Rep 49. See Marko Milanovic and Michael Wood (eds), *The Law and Politics of the Kosovo Advisory Opinion* (OUP 2015).

[121] EP Resolution of 5 February 2009 on Kosovo and the role of the EU [2010] OJ C-67 E/126; Eileen Denza, 'European Practice on the Recognition of States' (2011) 36 ELR 324.

[122] Richard A Brand, 'Kosovo after the ICJ Opinion' (2013) 74 U Pitt L Rev 591, 625.

[123] UNSC Resolution 1244 (1999) S/RES/1244, 10 June 1999.

[124] Regulation No 1 of 25 July 1999, on the Authority of the Interim Administration in Kosovo, UNMIK/REG/1999/1.

[125] Crawford, *The Creation of States* (n 77) 231.

[126] Noel Cox, 'The Acquisition of Sovereignty by Quasi-States: The Case of the Order of Malta' (2002) 6 MJLS 38; Arthur C Breycha-Vauthier and Michael Potulicki, 'The Order of St. John in International Law: A Forerunner of the Red Cross' (1954) 48 AJIL 554, 557.

combination of a unique history and some functional arguments flowing from the Order's humanitarian engagement. It differs from the Holy See's right of legation because it is disconnected from sovereignty, which is neither attributed nor transferred to the Order. Although its name denotes that the Order is a sovereign actor, such qualification is not universally accepted. However, sovereignty is still claimed by the Order, on its website among other places.[127] Certainly, the Order is a non-state, although material characteristics of statehood such as population, government, and territory were once satisfied. Whilst at present landless, the Order still has an administration that consists of regional offices and governmental elements. Since 1834, its headquarters have been in the Palazzo Malta in Rome.

Arguably the most visible manifestation of the unique position held by the Order in the international arena is its legation practice. These international relations were not abandoned when territorial sovereignty was lost by the Grand Master to Napoleon in 1798.[128] At present, the Order's envoys receive diplomatic immunities and privileges in countries that recognize it. Since the Order is unable to reciprocate a privileged status due to the lack of territory, countries tend to accredit an ambassador with another accreditation (eg their ambassador to Italy or the Holy See). Diplomatic recognition is broad, particularly in traditionally Christian states, but not global. The Order maintains diplomatic relations with 110 states, 18 of which are EU member states.[129] It also engages in non-diplomatic relations with Belgium, France, Germany, and Luxembourg. The treatment received by the Order in host states is broadly based on customary diplomatic privileges and immunities, although modifications exist.

*2.2.2.2.3 International organizations*

International governmental organizations (IOs) increasingly engage in diplomatic activities. Since the ICJ's *Reparation for Injuries* opinion, it is no longer disputed that states have the power to create organizations that possess an international legal personality.[130] The Court thereto introduced an objective benchmark[131] whereby an IO possesses international legal personality if it enjoys rights and responsibilities subject to international law.[132] Schermers and Blokker, however, argue that legal personality is not an absolute concept from which rights and obligations can be derived; rather, rights and obligations must be studied to decide whether an entity enjoys a legal personality.[133] Frequently cited examples of such rights include the right to enter into international agreements and the right to enter into relations with other international legal personae.[134] These international rights are either described in an IO's constituent document or derived from the functions assigned to it.[135] Subjective elements are also of key relevance. An international legal personality is ascertained expressly

127 See <www.orderofmalta.int> accessed 29 April 2022.

128 See, e.g. national cases in Italy and Hungary confirming the diplomatic recognition: Corte Suprema di Cassazione (IT) 13 March 1935, *Nanni and others v Pace and the Sovereign Order of Malta*, Ann Dig 2, 4–6 [No 2]; Case No 798, 12 May 12 1943 (HU) reported in [1949] 43 AJIL 537.

129 See, for an overview, <www.orderofmalta.int/diplomatic-activities/bilateral-relations> accessed 29 April 2022.

130 In *Reparation for Injuries* (n 66) 179; Jurisdiction of the European Commission of the Danube (Advisory Opinion) [1927] PCIJ Ser B, No 14.

131 Chittharanjan F Amerasinghe, *Principles of the Institutional Law of International Organizations* (2nd edn, CUP 2005) 86.

132 Peter HF Bekker, *The Legal Position of Intergovernmental Organizations* (Nijhoff 1994) 60.

133 Henry G Schermers and Niels M Blokker, *International Institutional Law: Unity within Diversity* (5th edn, Nijhoff 2011) 986–94.

134 ibid 1081.

135 For a functional approach, see *Reparation for Injuries* (n 66) 179.

or otherwise by virtue of international interactions with other legal persons.[136] An example of such express recognition would be a clause featuring in a treaty concluded with a non-member state. One observes that requests by organizations or their member states to recognize international legal personality have become more frequent over time. The determination of international legal personality is nevertheless undermined by circularity as there is no way of determining whether a particular right or obligation is, in fact, a cause or consequence of the observance of said personality.

The conduct of diplomatic relations by international organizations is a specific form of an institutional competence to act on the international arena.[137] As the introductory comments to the ILC 1958 Draft Articles on Diplomatic Relations state:

> [a]part from diplomatic relations between States, there are also relations between States and international organizations. Likewise, there is the question of the privileges and immunities of the organizations themselves. However, these matters are, as regards most of the organizations, governed by special conventions.

What stands out here is that the ILC does not refer to relations between states and international organizations as having a 'diplomatic' purpose.

When exercised by IOs, the type of diplomatic relations vary. Although not qualifying as diplomatic relations as such, formal interactions with the representatives of member states having established a permanent office at an IO are often viewed as a first step. The practice can be traced to the Brazilian Government's notification to the League of Nations (LoN) in March 1924 that it wanted to establish a permanent representation office in Geneva.[138] The Polish Government sent a similar note to the Secretary General only a month later.[139] Until then, states had instructed either their diplomatic representatives in Paris or Berne or their consuls in Geneva to act as liaison officers to maintain contact with the LoN. Yet, it was not long before other member states started copying the Brazilian and Polish example. Chile and Argentina were among the first to do so.[140] In spite of these changes, the LoN retained a dubious relationship with the permanent representatives accredited to it as it considered the practice's legal basis to be uncertain.[141] Nevertheless, Article 7 of the Covenant of the League of Nations, provided that:

> [r]epresentatives of the Members of the League and officials of the League when engaged on the business of the League shall enjoy diplomatic privileges and immunities. The buildings and other property occupied by the League or its officials or by Representatives attending its meetings shall be inviolable.

These provisions—the first of their kind to be featured in an IO's constitution—are rather general. Doctrine at the time furthermore agreed that this general expression referred only

[136] Philippe J Sands and Pierre Klein, *Bowett's Law of International Institutions* (6th edn, Sweet & Maxwell 2009) 475.

[137] ILC, Draft Articles on Diplomatic Intercourse and Immunities with Commentaries' (1958) II YBILC, introductory comments.

[138] do Nascimento e Silva (n 60) 40.

[139] Fauchille (n 20) 35.

[140] Pitman B Potter, 'Permanent Delegations to the League of Nations' [1931] 25 APSR 21, 26.

[141] Covenant of the League of Nations, drafted in Paris, 28 June 1919; Vittorio Mainetti, 'The League of Nations and the Emergence of Privileges and Immunities of International Organizations' in Roberto Virzo and Ivan Ingravallo (eds), *Evolutions in the Law of International Organizations* (Brill Nijhoff 2015) 326–28.

to persons appointed to the LoN by its members; the question of whether it applied to the IO's delegates too only came up at a later stage.

Sending states gave their permanent representatives an official character by providing them with diplomatic titles and ranks. Official letters addressed to the LoN gave notice of their appointment. This practice resembled that of various states represented in Washington or Rome which instructed their representatives there to keep in touch with the Pan-American Union or the Institute of Agriculture, although at those organizations too, establishing a more general right to receive diplomatic envoys was still rejected as being 'practically difficult'.[142] Be it as it may, the LoN's Secretariat would eventually acknowledge the practice and provide the missions with diplomatic treatment.

Formal diplomatic interactions with the LoN were limited to those with its own member. But even absent a sustained practice backing up this claim, certain authors argued that the League, being an international person sui generis, possessed the right to legation. The lingering doubts of passive legation practices in a multilateral setting raised in the LoN vanished with the birth of the UN. Article 105(2) of the UN Charter institutionalized the accreditation practice by providing that:

> [r]epresentatives of the Members of the United Nations and officials of the Organization shall similarly enjoy such privileges and immunities as are necessary for the independent exercise of their functions in connection with the Organization.

This language, insofar as it entails representations enjoying functional privileges and immunities, does not correspond to the practices of host states. Headquarters and host state agreements grant representatives of international organizations full diplomatic privileges and immunities, subject to certain minimal variations.

With the rise of the number of IOs came a plethora of (headquarter) agreements giving immunities to such organizations and all sorts of representatives. In 1975, an attempt was made to codify the status, privileges, and immunities of permanent representations to IOs. From the start, the UN Conference on the Representation of States in their Relations with International Organizations exemplified a strong divide between states hosting IOs and states sending permanent representatives to those IOs.[143] Host states were opposed to the uniform and broad regime of privileges and immunities as proposed in the ILC Draft. The Convention, although adopted, has not yet entered in force.[144] Even at the time of the final vote, the divide clearly showed: Belgium (host state of many UN bureaus and liaison offices) voted against; abstentions were recorded by the United States (UN headquarters); Switzerland (UN organs, ILO, World Health Organization (WHO), Universal Postal Union (UPU) ...), Austria (International Atomic Energy Agency (IAEA) and the United Nations Industrial Development Organization (UNIDO)), Canada (the International Civil Aviation Organization (ICAO)), France (UNESCO), and the United Kingdom (the International Maritime Organization (IMO)).

The Convention's Article 5 provides that member states may send permanent missions to international organizations if the IO's internal rules permit for it. The provisions do not grant

[142] Jan Klabbers, 'The Emergence of Functionalism in International Institutional Law: Colonial Inspirations' (2014) 25 EJIL 645, 663.

[143] Bekker (n 132) 20–23. See also Chapter 1.

[144] Vienna Convention on the Representation of States in their Relations with International Organizations of a Universal Character, signed on 14 March 1975.

a right of passive legation to an IO but rather accord an active legation right to the member states of the concerned organization to accredited a diplomatic mission. When unilaterally exercised, this right implies a corresponding duty for the IO to accept it, making it one of the few examples where (part of) a legation right corresponds with a legal obligation.[145] In that sense, despite the absence of a clear provision saying so, the member states' right to send representatives implies a passive capacity of legation, at least in relation with its member states.

While being perhaps the most evident form of diplomacy exercised by IOs, the accreditation of its own member states is not a true application of the right of legation. The relationship between IOs and member states are never entirely external, which makes comparison with bilateral relations difficult. The delegations' primary task is to represent own governments in the IO. However, another important task exercised by permanent representatives is to manage the IO's policymaking and administration, often in a committee that regularly meets. As such, they are an institutionalized part of the IO's machinery, making the right of legation prism the wrong way to study the relationship between an international organization and representatives to it.

A fully grown passive legation practice by an IO is only observed in those organizations that accredit representatives of non-member states and/or other international organizations. Quite a few IOs have sought accreditation from one another, creating some kind of institutional para-diplomacy.[146] Besides the EU, examples include the UN before the realization of universal membership and a number of regional IOs, including the Council of Europe, the African Union, and the League of Arab States.

Determining whether IOs are entitled to an active right of legation is even more difficult. Few IOs have ventured into an active legation practice. To this day, the EU's global diplomatic network constitutes the main exception, although others have also practiced active diplomacy on a more modest scale. The African Union operates a permanent bilateral mission accredited to the US Government in Washington DC and a number of missions accredited to IOs (the EU in Brussels, the UN in New York and Geneva, and the League of Arab States in Cairo).

#### *2.2.2.2.4 Federated and regional entities*

Regions, federated entities, provinces, and cities—just as they have done throughout history—forge links with states and with one another. Although there are some historical examples of successful exercises of legation practices by cities, in modern times they do not have a legal claim to a right of legation.[147] However, an increasing number of those subnational entities looks for ways to also be formally represented in the international arena.[148] Some have moved from words to deeds and established permanent missions in foreign countries. In the VCDR's original draft articles, proposed by Special Rapporteur Sandström, the right of legation had been foreseen for federated entities 'authorized by the sending State to engage in diplomatic activities proper'; this proposal was not followed by the other Committee members.[149] In contrast to IOs, which most frequently embrace passive legation practices, substate entities generally focus on building their own active legation

[145] Schermers and Blokker (n 133) 1159.

[146] On the accreditation of IOs and other entities to the EU, see Chapter 3.

[147] Yves Viltard, 'Conceptualiser la "diplomatie des villes": Ou l'obligation faite aux relations internationales de penser l'action extérieure des gouvernements locaux' (2008) 58 RFSP 511; Rogier van der Pluijm and Jan Melissen, *City Diplomacy: The Expanding Role of Cities in International Politics* (Clingendael 2007).

[148] Noé Cornago, 'On the Normalization of Sub-State Diplomacy' (2010) 5 HJD 11.

[149] ILC, 'Summary Records of the Tenth Session' (n 63) 90.

network. The international legal order does not expressly rule out the exercise of diplomatic or consular relations with such entities. However, such relations must be recognized by both the federal 'mother' state and the third state to be categorized as such.[150] First, the legal basis for the practice should be sought at first instance in domestic law: a constitution can provide for an internal mandate.[151] US states or Swiss cantons do not have the right of legation due to the lack of constitutional basis envisaging this. Federated entities may, however, entertain commercial or trade relations with foreign states and even set up permanent missions. The case of Chechnya also comes to mind. In an attempt to stress its independence from Russia, the region sought to appoint envoys in the mid-1990s. Russia argued that these did not have any ground in domestic law and the request was not met by other states. Second, there must be recognition of a right of legation at the international level.[152] Even when an internal mandate is present, third states have no obligation to recognize it and even when such international recognition is present, this does not necessarily create new rights. Rather, federated entities execute part of the right of legation allocated by the mother state.[153]

The fulfilment of these two conditions is rarely satisfied, making the exercise of autonomous rights of legation a rare occurrence in practice. Most federal constitutions list the ius legationis in the *domain réservé* of the central government, as is shown in Article 86 of the Constitution of Argentina, Article 10(2) of the Austrian Constitution, Article 167(1) of the Belgian Constitution, Article II(2), paragraph 2 of the US Constitution, Article 87 of the Italian Constitution, and Article 102(8) of the Swiss Constitution. The German Constitution does not recognize a right of legation of the *Länder* (see Arts 73(1) and 59(1)), and the Canadian Constitution does not address the right of legation at all, notwithstanding the fact that some of its provinces have established missions abroad. It is understood that its provinces require the approval of the federal government to engage in diplomatic/consular affairs.[154]

Even when external competences are granted to federal entities, the right of legation is rarely mentioned. Belgium serves as an example. At first glance, the conditions for recognizing a ius legationis on the part of the federated entities are favourable: Belgium's federal state structure exemplifies an advanced division of competences and constitutional provisions grant regions and communities full and exclusive competences over foreign policy on the basis of the adagio *in foro interno, in foro externo*.[155] The state's constituent parts are authorized to conduct external policies and are granted the right to conclude treaties and to establish own representations. The Flemish diplomatic network currently consists of twelve representatives and the Federation Wallonia-Brussels has fifteen *délégations générales*, with both entities having a representative to the EU. However, the federated entities do not exercise a right of legation different to that of the federal state. On the contrary, Belgian law determines that the overall responsibility to exercise Belgium's right of legation remains with the federal government. This view has been confirmed by the Belgian Constitutional Court's

[150] André Beirlaen, 'Répresentation diplomatique et consulaire' in Société Belge De Droit (SBDI) (ed), *Les Etats fédéraux dans les relations internationales* (Bruylant 1984) 183; Gleider Hernández, 'Federated Entities in International Law: Disaggregating the Federal State?' in Duncan French (ed), *Statehood and Self-Determination: Reconciling Tradition and Modernity in International Law* (CUP 2013) 491–512.

[151] Denza, *Diplomatic Law* (n 24) 20.

[152] Michael Richtsteig, *Wiener Übereinkommen über Diplomatische und Konsularische Beziehungen: Entstehungsgeschichte, Kommentierung, Praxis* (2nd edn, Nomos 2010) 17.

[153] Megiddo and Nevo (n 104) 509.

[154] Salmon (n 56) 36; Jacques-Yvan Morin, 'La Représentation des États Fédérés: L'Exemple du Québec' in Claude Blumann (ed), *Aspects Récents du Droit des Relations Diplomatiques* (Pedone 1989) 65 et seq.

[155] The principle is reinstated in Art 167(1) of the Belgian Constitution.

ruling that federal consular officers are authorized to exercise consular functions defined by PIL, even those in the economic fields, a domain normally reserved for the regions. The Court found support in the constitutional provisions granting the exclusive power to appoint diplomatic/consular officials (Art 107(2)) and to take the lead in the management of foreign relations (Art 167(1)) to the federal level.[156] Moreover, it was recalled that it is the federally appointed head of mission who preserves the diplomatic authority over *all* representatives and attachés. Consequently, all regional officials' personal and professional behaviour must be in accordance with the federal codes of conduct and diplomatic practices.[157]

To a great extent, PIL turns a blind eye to the federated state entities' diplomatic activities. As Malaczuk formulated it, '[i]nternational law is concerned only with states capable of carrying on international relations; consequently the federal state is regarded as a state for the purposes of international law, but the member states of the federation are not'.[158] The above is observed when studying privileges and immunities enjoyed by representatives of subnational entities. In order to receive privileges, a regional envoy will have to appear on the diplomatic list of the embassy of the 'mother state' and be notified through a note verbale, which indicates the regional affiliation of the person concerned (Art 10(1) VCDR). For instance, the Head of the General Representation of the Government of Flanders in New York receives consular privileges and immunities as he or she is mentioned on the list of Belgian officials provided by the Belgian Consulate to the US Government. At present, the building and archives of the office are not granted a specific protection. In practice, one also observes that regional executives' permanent missions often share diplomatic premises with national embassies.

EU member states are familiar with substate diplomacy: Austria, Belgium, Germany, Italy, Finland, and Spain house regional representatives or liaison officers in their Permanent Representation to the Union in Brussels. Other forms of representation are also possible: the Irish, Greek, and Hungarian permanent representations to the EU, for example, host representative(s) of the national parliaments. In turn, the EU recognizes permanent representations of member states' regional governments without attributing them a formal diplomatic status. Consequently, European regions do not receive an independent accreditation or an entry to the diplomatic list. Some authors even argue that the 'importance of these offices is exaggerated' and that the majority 'are lobbying organisations, although they do allow regions to remain informed'.[159] Staff working in such representations can be integrated into the staff of the mission of the member state concerned. Host state Belgium, however, does not consider the premises of their representational offices (when not integrated in the member state's permanent mission) to be part of the premises of a diplomatic mission.[160] The EU's seemingly unconcerned attitude towards the diplomatic endeavours of regions, while at first glance at odds with its own quest to seek diplomatic recognition, is not divergent from how PIL generally treats this question.

[156] Constitutional Court [BE] Judgment of 28 May 2015, No 80/2015, section B.7.2.

[157] See section B.5 of the judgment (ibid), which refers to Art 10(1–2) of the cooperation agreements dated 17 June 1994 and 18 May 1995 on the division of competences. Section B.7.1. refers to Arts 4 and 5 of the Law on the Consular Code of 21 December 2013 [BE] (Belgian State Gazette 30 April 2014).

[158] Peter Malanczuk, *Akehurst's Modern Introduction to International Law* (8th edn, Routledge 2002) 81.

[159] John Hopkins, *Devolution in Context: Regional, Federal and Devolved Government in the Member States of the European Union* (Cavendish Publishing 2002) 208.

[160] Response of the Minister of Foreign Affairs to the Parliamentary Question of MP Van Weert [BE] Bull QR, HR 2003–04.

### 2.2.3 Criteria to Exercise the Right of Legation

While a state-centred approach to diplomacy has the advantage of clarity, it provides for a one-dimensional, almost old-fashioned view on international law and its interactions. Diplomatic functions are part of a spectrum and many of them may be exercised informally by all sorts of actors acting internationally. The study of diplomacy solely in terms of an elitist system comprising only of states draws an incomplete picture. However, there is a legal distinction between those acknowledged to perform formal diplomatic functions and others. This section introduces other elements to determine actors capable of conducting diplomatic relations.

#### 2.2.3.1 Objective Criteria

##### *2.2.3.1.1 Condition ratione personae: having rights and duties under PIL*

A finding most obviously to emerge from the above analysis is that the right of legation's exercise requires entities to be capable of bearing international rights and/or duties. In this sense, Jean Salmon argued for the use of international legal personality rather than statehood as a conclusive element to determine the capability of being a diplomatic actor. Yet others, such as Alain Plantey, argue that sovereignty is a necessary condition of diplomacy.[161] Using the term 'subject of international law' may indeed provide a more pragmatic approach to determine a diplomatic actor[162] for it aims to distinguish entities relevant to the international legal system from those that are not.[163] To claim a diplomatic aptitude, the actor has to be capable of applying for, and be subject to, the international rules on diplomatic/consular relations. Clearly, if these competences are absent, the right of legation cannot exist.

The proposition is, however, not entirely free from delimitation issues and theoretical brainteasers. First, the concept of international legal personality has proven controversial, with the criteria to acquire it tending to be circular.[164] Since states occupy the central position in the international legal system, other entities can only acquire a derivative or secondary legal personality under the conditions recognized by states.[165] Consequently, states decide on both the recognition of an entity as a subject of international law and the entitlements it brings. Second, not all those having international personality are created equal. It may well be that an actor possessing international personality through recognition or for a functional reason in a specific context is fundamentally unfit to engage in diplomatic relations. As early as 1949, the ICJ pointed to the many shades an international actor can have when it stated that the 'subjects of law in any legal system are not necessarily identical in their nature or in the extent of their rights'.[166] The realization that the realm of diplomatic communication has not opened up to all subjects of the law of nations, even those that interact regularly on the international stage, necessitates an inquiry into possible additional criteria.

[161] Alain Plantey, *Principes de Diplomatie* (2nd edn, Pedone 2000) 20.

[162] Hersch Lauterpacht, 'The Subjects of the Law of Nations' (1947) 63 LQR 438, 444.

[163] Catherine Brölmann and Janne Nijmann, 'Legal Personality as a Fundamental Concept of International Law' in Jean d'Aspremont and Sahib Singh (eds), *Fundamental Concepts of International Law* (Edward Elgar 2017).

[164] *Reparation for Injuries* (n 66) 178.

[165] Roland Portmann, *Legal Personality in International Law* (CUP 2010) 13.

[166] *Reparation for Injuries* (n 66) 178.

#### *2.2.3.1.2 Conditions ratione materiae: internal and external autonomy*

**Independence** When looking for parallels between subjects of international law other than states that exercise formal diplomatic relations, common features are not overtly present. The one exception is their enjoyment of substantial independence from other international actors. The idea of independence as a condition for diplomacy reverts to the traditional school of thought that considered the right of legation to belong to *independent* and *sovereign* states only, and that the independence also had to be effective.[167] Independence is not a criterion used in the VCDR. Moreover, the autonomy of non-state entities in part seems to compensate for the absence of sovereignty. Though the notion of sovereignty has varied across history and remains controversial to the present day, here, it is given the meaning of a supreme authority in a political community.[168] The definition denotes two aspects of authority. This is first, to have a supreme power within the borders of a community, and second, to be independent from supreme authorities outside those borders.[169] It is only logical that non-sovereign diplomatic actors also have to possesses a sufficient ability of free and effective decision-making (*internal autonomy*), and the capability to define and monitor own international relations (*external autonomy*) to claim a right of legation. For sovereign states dependent on other states for the execution of part of their foreign policy (eg micro-states), the criterion does not apply: they are diplomatic actors by way of their status as state. Consequently, these features will function as objective subcriteria for actors to engage in diplomacy.

**The capacity to independently develop internal policies and general objectives** The right of legation presupposes a fairly general internal policymaking capacity. This notion encompasses two ideas. First, any aspiring diplomatic actor ought to exercise self-governance on a permanent basis, be it at the subnational, national, or international level. The conduct of diplomacy is reserved for public authorities able to autonomously determine the individual position of individuals, private associations, enterprises, or other public institutions through laws and regulations. Private interests of firms, non-governmental organizations (NGOs), or other associations that do not have public authority, cannot be represented through formal diplomacy.[170] Second, the internal policymaking capacity does not have to be perfect: the capacity to act independently in crucial policy domains suffices. The cases of diplomatically active IOs and federated entities showed that a decision-making mandate does not have to be general and all-encompassing, though it must be significant. One consequence, however, is that the representations' workload will be tied to such powers or domains. Therefore, even if possessing restricted powers does not necessarily hinder the ability to engage in diplomacy, it may have impact on its exercise.[171]

[167] Salmon (n 56) 33.

[168] Francs H Hinsley, *Sovereignty* (2nd edn, CUP 1986) 26. See, for a critique, Michael R Fowler and Julie M Bunck, *Law, Power, and the Sovereign State: The Evolution and Application of the Concept of Sovereignty* (Penn State Press 2010) 38 et seq; Neil Walker, 'Late Sovereignty in the European Union' in Neil Walker (ed), *Sovereignty in Transition* (Hart 2003).

[169] Helen Thompson, 'The Case for External Sovereignty' (2006) 12 Eur J Int Relat 251; Raia Prokhovnik, 'Internal/External: The State of Sovereignty' (1996) 2 Contemp Politics 7.

[170] See Grotius (n 3) and Gentili (n 5) on the exclusion of private groups.

[171] Kenneth W Abbott and Duncan Snidal, 'Why States Act through Formal International Organizations' (1998) 42 J Conflict Resolut 3, 5.

**The capacity to independently represent internal policies externally** The ius legationis also presupposes that those claiming the right of legation must be able and willing to represent their internal policies and interests externally. Hereafter, this principle will be referred to as the 'Guggenheim criterion'; a criterion named after the author who argued that a subject of international law can only acquire the power to exercise the right to active and passive legation when it has the capacity to conduct an independent foreign policy.[172] This idea consists of two notions: an entity must have the necessary *competences* as well as the necessary *tools* to engage in relations with other actors. The overwhelming majority of IOs, only knowing a passive legation practice, does not actively pursue a fully grown common foreign policy for which representation is required.

First, to be represented diplomatically in its own name, an entity has to prove that its competences necessitate interactions with others. The external competences can be, but are not necessarily, the logical external counterpart of the internal ones. Sufficiently evolved actors also have a fully grown foreign policy with purely external goals, not always strictly matching their internal competences. Similar to what was concluded in relation to internal policies and objectives, external competences ought to be pursued independently from the will of other subjects of international law. Therefore, no external power should be able to curtail the entity's foreign policy.

Second, if it wants to represent competences and objectives in a diplomatic manner, a subject of international law must possess a specific toolbox. To manage the passive right of legation, the entity must be able to accredit and recognize missions from other subjects of law. As seen in the cases of the Holy See, Palestine, and international organizations, the notion that such actions require the assistance of a third actor, most commonly a state, does not bar an entity from enjoying the right of legation. For example, a third state's involvement may be needed to guarantee that safe passage is granted to diplomats or to make the enjoyment of privileges possible. The role of the host state in the case of IOs, in the relationships between the Holy See and Vatican City as well as Italy and Israel and the State of Palestine, has been established.

The management of an active legation practice requires an even more extensive toolkit. The entity must have the appropriate instruments in place to allow it to acquire property abroad, enter into agreements with public and private entities in third states, request diplomatic visa for its representatives, and issue instruments typical to diplomacy.

### 2.2.3.2 Subjective Criteria

#### *2.2.3.2.1 Introduction*

Arguably more so than the objective criteria spelled out above, the subjective principle of recognition is of fundamental importance to the right of legation. A diplomatic actor exists only through the acknowledgement of others. The yardstick of the subjective criteria therefore is one of recognition. Over time, the subjective recognition can evolve into an objective fact if generally sustained for a sufficiently long period.

Recognition can be divided into five components, each constituting a separate legal act, as seen in Table 2.1.

[172] Paul Guggenheim, *Lehrbuch des Völkerrechts*, vol 1 (Verlag für Recht und Gesellschaft 1948) 452; do Nascimento e Silva (n 60) 36.

Table 2.1 The acts of recognition

| | State | Non-state actor |
|---|---|---|
| *Recognition 1*<br>Recognition of the entity | *Legal Act 1: Statehood*<br>Recognition of the entity on the basis of the rules of statehood | *Legal Act 1: Recognition as a subject of international law*<br>Recognition of the entity on the basis of its rights and duties under international law |
| *Recognition 2*<br>Recognition of the right of legation | Statehood by default brings about diplomatic capacity | *Legal Act 2: Recognition of a diplomatic capacity*<br>Through legal acts 2.1; 2.2 and/or 2.3—legal steps that often occur simultaneously |
| *Recognition 3*<br>Establishment of diplomatic relations | *Legal Act 2: Establishment of diplomatic relations*<br>Article 2 VCDR: consent | *Legal Act 2.1*<br>Separate agreement, often consisting of an agreement to establish diplomatic relations, the opening of a mission, and the applicable framework |
| *Recognition 4*<br>Establishment of a diplomatic mission | *Legal Act 3: Establishment of a diplomatic mission*<br>Article 2 VCDR: consent | *Legal Act 2.2*<br>Separate agreement, often consisting of an agreement to establish diplomatic relations and the opening of a mission |
| *Recognition 5*<br>Application of diplomatic law | *Legal Act 1: Statehood*<br>Statehood by default brings about the application of (customary) diplomatic law | *Legal Act 2.3*<br>Separate agreement, often consisting both of an agreement to establish diplomatic relations and the applicable framework |

#### 2.2.3.2.2 *The five acts of external recognition*

**The initial act of recognizing the subjects of international law** Diplomacy requires a recognition of a subject of international law in that capacity. Technically not part of the act of diplomatic recognition, it has its importance as the subjective counterpart to the objective ratione personae criterion discussed in section 2.2.3.1. The recognition of a state and a non-state is different. With regard to the former category, the rules on the recognition of statehood apply. Statehood is not automatically conferred; an act of recognition is required either in the form of an acceptance reflecting the reality on the ground, meaning that an entity satisfying the criteria for statehood has de facto come into being (*declaratory theory*) or in the form of collective action to endow an entity with its status of statehood (*constitutive theory*).[173] At the very least, this recognition implies the commitment to respect the sovereignty and territorial integrity of the state; however, it does not imply a desire to enter into diplomatic relations.[174] Non-states aspiring diplomatic relations go through a different type of recognition: one that

[173] Malcolm N Shaw, *International Law* (CUP 2014) 144–148.
[174] Article 7 Montevideo Convention.

focuses on international rights and duties already performed. In both cases, states are the central actors to either grant recognition or refuse it.

**The recognition of diplomatic capacity** The exercise of diplomatic relations necessitates the recognition of a diplomatic capacity. With states, such recognition automatically follows from the recognition of their statehood. All sovereign states possess an inherent right of legation; a separate recognition is unnecessary. An unrecognized government will not be able to exercise the right of legation on behalf of the state.[175] The obvious example of the Taliban in Afghanistan comes to mind. Following the Arab revolts that took place in 2011, Western countries recognized insurgents as 'legitimate representatives of the people', while leaving intact diplomatic relations with the incumbent regime. Such informal representatives were granted certain privileges in the receiving state that did not amount to the rights or privileges under the VCDR. However, a separate act of recognition is needed for non-states since the recognition as subject of international law does not imply the recognition of the right of legation.

Considerable misperceptions still exist about these two first acts of recognition. For states and non-states alike, the second recognition often serves as the best proof of the first. The establishment of a diplomatic mission in a newly established state can constitute an act of tacit recognition amounting to a de facto recognition of that state. The recognition of a state by itself does not necessarily entail the recognition of a government; contacts between a foreign mission and a new government, however, can be qualified as a recognition of such government.[176] This remains a delicate matter. The case of the Holy See and the Palestinian State, for instance, exemplifies that the recognition of statehood and diplomatic capacity have not been always perfectly synchronized. The Federal Republic of Yugoslavia in the 1990s provides another example: between the 'declaration' of the Republic by the remaining states of Serbia and Montenegro (27 April 1992) and the 'recognition' (April 1996) by EU member states, the entity was treated as a subject of international law nevertheless capable of conducting interactions in the international arena. Diplomatic relations were continued, albeit on a lower level. According to the EU member states, this only amounted to Yugoslavia's 'diplomatic recognition'.[177]

This provokes the question of whether the right of legation includes lowered diplomatic relations.[178] Due to a lack of a clear definition of the right of legation, alternative ways of conducting international relations (eg through liaison missions or consular relations) should not be unequivocally refused. It may be easier to accept that these relations can constitute a particular exercise of the legation capacity. Such a dynamic view on the right of legation could permit for different intensities of diplomatic relations. It is only when the international community as a whole does not accept an entity's diplomatic capacity that the right of legation must be unequivocally denied. The Order of Malta, Taiwan, and the State of Palestine (pre-VCDR accession) prove that universal recognition is not compulsory to the exercise right of legation. A historical example is provided by the Manchurian incident that gave rise to the Stimson Doctrine. During 1931, Japan unilaterally seized Manchuria, a region in north-eastern China. While only Germany and Italy joined Japan in recognizing the 'new

175 Richtsteig (n 152) 17 and Denza, *Diplomatic Law* (n 24) 20–21.
176 Salmon (n 56) 42.
177 Christian Hillgruber, 'The Admission of New States to the International Community' (1998) 9 EJIL 491, 499.
178 Salmon (n 56) 46.

state', other countries accepted the Manchurian consuls' mandate to inform their governments about current affairs and even to protect 'nationals'.[179]

**Mutual consent to enter into diplomatic relations** The mutual consent to establish diplomatic relations is the third component of recognition. For VCDR signatories, the acknowledgement corresponds with the Convention's Article 2 that contains a direct reference to mutual consent. Yet, especially in older literature, the recognition of statehood (*recognition 1*) is sometimes confused with the notion of consent.[180] Denza invokes the infrequency with which states formally recognize other states without establishing diplomatic relations as the reason for confusion between these two concepts.[181] States sometimes refuse to establish diplomatic relations with other states: France and Monaco decided to enter into diplomatic relations only in 2002, although Monaco's sovereign status was already been confirmed in the Franco-Monégasque Treaty of 1861.[182] In October 2005, Monaco became a signatory party to the VCDR. For the United States, there are three cases left where it has recognized a country without having established diplomatic relations with it: Bhutan, North-Korea, and Iran. In the first two instances, diplomatic relations have never been established; in the latter case, they have been broken off, but the interests of both countries are observed by the embassies of third countries. Nevertheless, it is obvious that diplomatic relations can be interrupted without the withdrawal of the recognition of an entity as a state.

For non-states, *recognition 2* (having a right of legation as an attribute of sovereignty) and *recognition 3* (the mutual consent to establish diplomatic relations) are tied together. While, theoretically, states can recognize the right of legation of an entity without entering into diplomatic relations with it, a recognition (eg of an international organization or a substate region) is generally only expressed at the time when a state establishes diplomatic relations with the entity.

**The consent to establish a permanent mission** The mutual consent to enter into diplomatic relations (*recognition 3*) is frequently accompanied or followed by the opening of a mission on both territories (*recognition 4*). Salmon even calls the consent to open a mission a modality of the consent to engage in diplomatic relations.[183] Especially for non-states, the establishment of a mission is usually the desired outcome of a decision to enter into diplomatic relations.

As between states, the decision to open a mission will often depend on policy and financial interests a country has in a particular region, or the number of its citizens residing there. The establishment of a permanent mission may be the most tangible way to maintain diplomatic relations, but it is not the only way.[184] Intermediate situations are common and include alternative methods such as a state trusting a third state mission with own interests being the host state, housing a one-person representation in another state's mission, or sending sporadic ad hoc or even virtual missions to the receiving state. In the first case, explicit consent is not required, although the receiving state has to be appropriately notified and has the right to object the exercise of diplomacy (Art 6 VCDR) or consular (Art 8 VCCR) functions by a

179 Daniel P O'Connell, *International Law*, vol 2 (2nd edn, Stevens 1970) 147.
180 Richtsteig (n 152) 17–18.
181 Denza, *Diplomatic Law* (n 24) 25.
182 Article 5 Traité destiné à adapter et à confirmer les rapports d'amitié et de coopération entre la République française et la Principauté de Monaco, signed on 24 October 2002 (published in [2003] RGDIP 19).
183 Salmon (n 56) 29.
184 Richtsteig (n 152) 17.

mission on behalf of third states. Article 2 of the New York Convention on Special Missions, however, confirms that consent is required for the sending of ad hoc missions. The practice of having 'laptop posts' and 'laptop diplomats' has been relatively well established, with the Netherlands having pioneered in it.[185]

When a state reopens a mission after a non-represented period in a particular receiving state, new consent is required. A receiving state will not lightly refuse a sending state to open a mission; such behaviour is, however, quite prevalent in the establishment of consular missions.[186]

Both states and non-states must gain permission to establish a permanent mission in a host state. For states, Article 2 VCDR serves again as the legal basis. The consent to establish a mission (Art 2 VCDR; Art 2 VCCR) should be distinguished from the act of *agrément* (Art 4 VCDR), *exequatur* (Art 12 VCCR), or the acceptance of the letters of credence of a specific diplomat (Art 13 VCDR). All of these can be refused without withdrawing the consent to establish a mission. In the VCDR context, a permission granted implies an authorization for the sending state to execute diplomatic functions on the receiving state's territory and the application of diplomatic law (see *recognition* 5). Most prominently, there is an obligation for the receiving state to accord privileges and immunities and the sending state to respect the duties provided (Arts 41–42 VCDR). When non-states are involved, these legal consequences cannot be assumed and a separate legal arrangement will be required.

**The recognition of the application of the law on diplomatic or consular relations** In inter-state relations, substantive rights and duties derived from the right of legation govern diplomatic and consular missions by default. The Vienna Conventions apply to signatory states and even other states (if still existing) as a matter of their status as rules of customary international law. The VCDR also continues to apply in the event of an armed conflict between the receiving state, the sending state, and/or a third state.[187]

Non-states have to make the rules on diplomacy expressly applicable to their mutual relations. For them, the fifth and final form of consent relates to the determination of the substantive legal framework to administer the newly established diplomatic relationship. The form of such arrangement is not prescribed by international law. States dealing with non-states have the discretion to grant envoys full diplomatic rights and duties (eg those common to IOs) or a selection of VCDR rights to a selection of people. This was the case for the representatives of the State of Palestine before its VCDR/VCCR accession and for the representatives of the Baltic states in the United Kingdom following the annexation by the Soviet Union in 1940. The United Kingdom recognized the annexation de facto, giving Baltic diplomats only 'courtesy' treatment when the United Kingdom passed the 1964 Diplomatic Privileges Act. Alternatively, states may opt to accord a more restricted consular scheme of privileges and immunities (eg Hong Kong). In an inter-state context, such à la carte application of diplomatic and consular law would be irreconcilable with the provisions not to discriminate between states spelled out in Articles 47 VCDR and 72 VCCR.

[185] Dutch Ministry of Foreign Affairs, 'Nota modernisering Nederlandse diplomatie', 8 April 2011, 9, 23.

[186] Denza, *Diplomatic Law* (n 24) 26.

[187] *Case concerning United States Diplomatic and Consular Staff in Tehran* (*United States of America v Iran*) (Judgment) [1980] ICJ Rep 3, para 40; *Case concerning Armed Activities on the Territory of the Congo* (*Democratic Republic of the Congo v Uganda*) (Judgment) [2005] ICJ Rep 168, para 324.

*2.2.3.2.3 Recognition: the role of the UN Security Council*

Recognition is a discretionary legal act perpetrated by states. However, this recognition is not entirely unbridled. The principle of consent can be trumped by other rules of international law and by binding decisions of the UN Security Council (UNSC).[188] States' discretion in diplomacy can be subjected to a decision by the UNSC. Article 41 UN Charter provides that the UNSC may call upon the UN Members to severe diplomatic relations.[189] A 1992 Resolution provides a practical example, where the UNSC demands UN member states to:[190]

> [s]ignificantly reduce the number and the level of the staff at Libyan diplomatic missions and consular posts and restrict or control the movement within their territory of all such staff who remain.

Apart from decisions regarding the size of missions and application of freedom of movement of diplomats as provided in Article 26 VCDR, the decision to establish, suspend, or terminate diplomatic relations is also not entirely free. The UNSC has the power to adopt measures including the prohibition to recognize illegal situations, the establishment of diplomatic relations, diplomatic missions, and the severance of diplomatic relations. The Security Council executed this power on a few occasions, including in Resolution 217 of 20 November 1965 on the declaration of independence of Southern Rhodesia. In the Resolution, the UNSC called:

> upon all States not to recognize this illegal authority and not to entertain any diplomatic or other relations with it.

*2.2.3.2.4 Common features of recognition*

Recognition lies at the hearth of the diplomatic system and ties with an idea that the right of legation depends on the will of the parties involved. Some general observations can be made. First, the right of legation can be acquired in different ways and variations; by custom or by treaty. All five components of recognition can be expressed tacitly in the form of a written agreement or any alternative way the actors agree fit. In the absence of formal requirements, the act of seeking consent constitutes a diplomatic act in itself. The form of consent given in an interstate context does not differ all that much from that used in other encounters. Frequently, the relations that exist between the subjects of international law determine whether recognition will be uncomplicated or hampered with complexities. Second, as often happens, the different steps of recognition can take place at once. Drawing a line between the components requires a certain decoding of political and legal acts. Third, when recognition is achieved, the right of legation is observed either in the general sense (ie when the recognition is broad or stems from the plurinational customary tradition) or, on a lesser strength, in a bilateral relationship.

[188] Shaw (n 173) 547.

[189] Charter of the United Nations, opened for signature on 26 June 1945, entry into force 24 October 1945, 1 UNTS XVI (hereafter UN Charter).

[190] UNSC Resolution 748, S/RES/748 (1992), adopted on 31 March 1992.

### 2.2.4 The Monopoly of States Revisited

The concept of sovereignty existed long before 1648 and has undergone significant alterations since. Changes in the international society after 1945 specifically contribute to the perception that Westphalian sovereignty has decreased. Amidst these changes, the tradition of diplomacy has always stood out by its endurance.[191] But diplomacy is no stranger to change either. The increased prominence of actors in diplomatic relations that includes international organizations, aspiring states, and regions may create the idea that states' monopoly in diplomacy is equally crumbling. An increasingly diverse set of actors participate in international negotiations and informally exercise diplomatic functions. The key question is whether the phenomenon has fundamentally changed the primary role of states in diplomatic relations. The following paragraphs examine, first, whether the state monopoly still exists and, second, whether sovereignty is still of relevance to diplomacy.

The state monopoly remains intact in two ways. First, the mandate to conduct diplomacy is still granted by states: by fellow states in the case of a state that has nearly obtained statehood, member states in the case of an international organization, by the federal state in the case of a federated entity, and by state-created customs in the case of a sui generis subject of international law. While both objective and subjective criteria are reliable in predicting the existence of a right of legation, the latter benchmark trumps the former. This is of relevance since it is precisely this subjective 'recognition' criterion that guarantees the continuation of the primacy of states in diplomatic relations. A state remains at liberty to establish relations with an entity without attaching much importance to its legal personality, its degree of independence, or the existence of a foreign policy. Second, states are the drivers behind creating conditionality to the exercise of diplomatic relations by states. States can facilitate or hinder this exercise by either granting or withholding privileges and immunities. Even in cases where non-states have established diplomatic interactions among each other (eg the relations between the EU and a federated region), a state's intervention will be necessary for diplomatic rights to be put into practice.

The decision by states to allow new participants in diplomatic affairs results in a more stable and inclusive international system and ultimately preserves their monopolist position. When interacting with emerging actors, states force such actors to accept their traditionally established system and the norms thereof, thereby ultimately asserting and strengthening the sovereign and central status of states in the international order. States are driven by the search for predictability, calculability, and the protection of their sovereign interests.[192] The diplomatic system satisfies these desires: it enables independent states to pursue self-interests without destroying one another and/or the international system. However, to think that this order comes from the benevolent workings of an invisible hand would be a misconception. The system's success lies in deliberate acts of states to respect it as well as in its systematic and coherent practice and organization. The inclusion of non-states in diplomatic relations is not a given nor a right; it is a choice. This casts diplomacy as the prime example of the potential of the Westphalian system to reassert itself.

[191] Christopher Harding and CL Lim, 'The Significance of Westphalia: An Archaeology of the International Legal Order' in Christopher Harding and CL Lim (eds), *Renegotiating Westphalia: Essays and Commentary on the European and Conceptual Foundations of Modern International Law* (Martinus Nijhoff 1999) 2.

[192] Jens Bartelson, *A Genealogy of Sovereignty* (CUP 1995) 181.

## 2.3 The EU's Right of Legation

### 2.3.1 Introduction

As early as the late 1950s, the European Communities sought to assert diplomatic claims. Over the years, the Union has gradually built its own permanent bilateral and multilateral diplomatic network. The legitimation of EU diplomacy is often sought through the unique status attributed to it at the international level. This book recognizes and embraces the Union's uniqueness. However, the discussion is taken beyond the mere notion that the EU is unrivalled by other international organizations in its diplomatic practices. Rather, it aims to pin down a tangible legitimation for the EU's diplomatic endeavours. An evaluation of the Union's competences and tools is made against the objective and subjective criteria introduced in section 2, to define whether the EU possesses the right and capacity of legation.

### 2.3.2 The Origins of the EU's Right of Legation

#### 2.3.2.1 First Traces

The High Authority of the European Coal and Steel Community (ECSC) broke new ground in the mid-1950s by engaging in diplomatic relations with third countries. At the time, the High Authority acted at its own discretion without being backed by a legal mandate. It was only after the entry into force of the Rome Treaties that the sprouting legation activities attracted the attention of the other European institutions. In 1959, the European Parliamentary Assembly subjected the newly established diplomatic relations to a legal review.

When the members of the Parliamentary Assembly decided to examine—for the first time in history—the Communities' right of legation, their aim was to support the emerging practice with the necessary legal legitimacy. The Assembly engaged the *Commission des affaires politiques et des questions institutionnelles* to study the European Communities' relations with third countries in general, and the '*droit de légation et de pavillon*' in particular.[193] Dutch lawyer and member of the Assembly Marinus van der Goes van Naters was appointed rapporteur. His work focused on whether and to what extent the Communities possessed an active and passive right of legation vis-à-vis third countries. This resulted in a 1959 report, on the basis of which the Parliamentary Assembly later adopted Resolution 761f/60. In the Resolution, dated 19 November 1960, the Assembly declared that:

> les Communautés européennes jouissent de par leur personnalité juridique internationale du droit de légation actif et passif.[194]

[193] Commission des affaires politiques et des questions institutionnelles de l'Assemblée parlementaire européenne (APE), Rapport sur les problèmes que posent les relations des Communautés européennes avec l'extérieur, en particulier le droit de légation et de pavillon (Rapporteur: Marinus van der Goes van Naters) 9 November 1959, Doc 87/1959, and Rapport complémentaire, 17 November 1960, Doc. 88/1960–61 (hereafter APE, Report on the Right of Legation).

[194] Résolution adoptée par l'Assemblée Parlementaire Européenne relative aux problèmes que posent les relations des Communautés européennes avec l'extérieur, en particulier le droit de légation et de pavillon, 29 November 1960, 761f/60 (Luxembourg) 707f/60 (Brussels) [1960] OJ 1496/60: '[t]he European Communities enjoy the right of active and passive legation by virtue of its international legal personality' [own translation].

This is a particularly strong statement, promulgated at a time when the Communities' active component of the right of legation had been exercised only to a very limited extent.

To come to its conclusion, the Assembly had sought support in PIL.[195] At the time, it was already clear that the Communities were subject to international law, as confirmed by several provisions of the founding treaties. In the debate that took place in the Assemblée parlementaire européenne, Rapporteur van der Goes van Naters explicitly mentioned that the political and legal status of the Communities in the world is not disputed. Despite this position, saying that the Communities were bound by international diplomatic law was not without complication. In the late 1950s, diplomatic law had not yet been codified and international institutional law was immature. The report also mentions this, where it states that the general development of international institutional law is still too underdeveloped to come to firm conclusions about the IOs' competences. While, at the time, it was clear that international legal personality was no longer limited to states, the theory on what other subjects could possess it stood in its infancy.[196] Moreover, the majority of international organizations had only just started to cautiously experiment with passive legation practices.

This probably explains why the report struggles with legal ambiguities. However, the experimental character of the work carried out by the Parliamentary Assembly also had its advantages. In the lack of a codified body of diplomatic and institutional law, the Assembly could adopt an avant-garde position on the topic—one that may not have been the same if it had been adopted after diplomatic law's codification in 1961.

### 2.3.2.2 The European Assembly

#### *2.3.2.2.1 The European Communities and legal personality*

The direct reference to the Communities' legal personality in Resolution 761f/60 exemplifies that the Assembly attached particular importance to this criterion to define the holders of the right of legation. The Resolution reflects the 1959 report on this point, which had studied the subject at length.[197] The report recalls the 1954 decision by the High Authority to open its London delegation and the fact that this decision was taken on the basis of Article 6*j*.8 of the ECSC Treaty. Article 6 lays down the legal personality of the ECSC and a general capacity to exercise functions accorded to it by the member states. Article 8 provides a mandate for the High Authority to ensure the fulfilment of the objectives set out in the Treaty.[198] Support for the theory that the ECSC possessed legal personality (and therefore, diplomatic capacity) was thus sought in its founding treaty, which confirmed the ECSC's *internal legal personality*.

The 1959 report nevertheless made an important remark, stating that a diplomatic actor also necessitates an *international personality*. Without much discussion, it was accepted that the Communities possessed both features. The report asserted that an international legal personality was not 'a given' nor dependent on the will or objective behaviour of an international organization. This approach contrasts with the ICJ's efforts in *Reparation for Injuries* to introduce objective and functional benchmarks to determine international legal personality. Rather, the Assembly relied on subjective criteria: the Communities' international personality was the result of a series of acts of recognition by third states. A self-proclaimed legal

[195] APE, 'Droit de légation et de pavillon', 19 November 1960, 86 (hereafter APE, Right of Legation Parliamentary Debate).

[196] APE, Report on the Right of Legation, para 2.

[197] ibid, para 6.

[198] See the remarks of Albert Wehrer, Member of the High Authority of the ECSC, during the 1960 APE, Right of Legation Parliamentary Debate, 9. For a discussion on Art 6, Ricardo Monaco, 'Les Relations Extérieures de la CECA' in *Annuaire Européen/European Yearbook* (Springer 1958) 78–79.

personality emanating from the will of the member states as also expressed in the founding treaties was deemed irrelevant. For non-member states, these treaties are a *res inter alios acta* that cannot impose obligations on them without their consent (Art 34 VCLT). Consequently, the Communities' international legal personality was relegated to being a purely political fact without reference to the rights and duties held by the Communities at the time.[199]

All in all, the most problematic aspect of the report remains the false causal conjunction it makes between legal personality and the right of legation, captured in the single phrase 'le droit de légation [ ... ] découle de la personnalité juridique'.[200] It would be incorrect to contend that when third countries recognized the Communities' international legal personality, they automatically also accepted its right of legation. Legal personality is not an absolute concept that creates concrete international rights and duties. Rather, these rights and duties are acts that evidence an international legal personality.[201] The idea that the Communities enjoy the right of legation *by virtue of* their legal personality was nevertheless incorporated to Resolution 761f/60.

In the course of the 1959 discussions, another questionable argument arose. The Assembly members suggested that since the European Communities were mandated by the member states to carry out tasks on their behalf, they behaved more similarly to states than to international organizations. Some therefore argued that the fact that the Communities had state-like features sufficed to deduce a right of legation. Rapporteur van der Goes van Naters was in favour of this argument and contended that the right of legation 'parvient à la Communauté d'une facon naturelle' because it increasingly resembled a nation state.[202] This legal reasoning was rightfully rejected and the argument was not further explored or used.[203] Van der Goes van Naters drew other, more useful parallels between the diplomatic relations of the Communities and those of states, such as the fact that the Communities required a recognition 'n'éloigne pas du statut étatique. Aussi, un Etat a-t-il besoin de cette reconnaissance.'[204]

#### *2.3.2.2.2 The European Communities and recognition*

The 1959 report did not limit itself to third states' recognition of the Communities as an international actor but also looked into the acts of recognition of a diplomatic capacity. The Communities' passive right of legation was observed: the Treaties of Rome ensured member states' missions accredited to the Communities customary privileges and immunities, whereas the ECSC Treaty had been silent on this matter: Article 16, Chapter 6 of the Protocol on the privileges and immunities attached to the EEC and Euratom Treaties read: '[t]he Member State in whose territory the Community has its seat shall accord the customary diplomatic immunities to missions of third countries accredited to the Community'. The member states did not unequivocally create a legal competence to actively pursue legation. However, the report mentions active legation to be consequential to the Communities'

[199] APE, Report on the Right of Legation, para 6.

[200] ibid, para 2: '[t]he right of legation [ ... ] derives from legal personality' [own translation]. See, in the same sense, para 6: '[d]ans la mesure où les États tiers reconnaissent les Communautés, il n'y a pas de sérieuses difficultés à reconnaître à celles-ci la personnalité juridique et—*par voie de conséquence*—le droit de légation' [own emphasis]. See, for a critical remark, the intervention of Fernand Dehousse during the APE's Right of Legation Parliamentary Debate, 88–89.

[201] Schermers and Blokker (n 133) 1166; Pierre Pescatore, 'Les Relations Extérieurs de la Communauté Européenne' (1961) 1 Hague Recueil 103, 190; Hardy (n 37) 48.

[202] 'Comes to the Community naturally' [own translation].

[203] APE, Right of Legation Parliamentary Debate, 86.

[204] ibid 86: 'does not take away from statehood. A state needs this recognition too' [own translation].

external competences. In turn, these external relations were found to be sufficiently broad to comprise the right of legation:

> [o]n peut en conclure que conformément à la volonté des États membres telle qu'elle s'est exprimée par la pratique au sein de la CECA par les textes des traités de Rome et par la pratique dans les nouvelles Communautés, le droit de légation existe. La doctrine est d'ailleurs unanime dans ce sens.[205]

*2.3.2.2.3 The necessity of the right of legation for the Communities*

Perhaps surprisingly, the already existent internal competences of the Communities were not used as a legitimation in the 1959 report.[206] The report was produced well before the CJEU's landmark decision in *Van Gend & Loos* on the existence of a new legal order and in limited fields the transfer of sovereignty by the member states. It does not contain much of the theory later developed by the Court. Rather, the report relied on the existence of an independent foreign policy.[207] Assembly members already envisaged a greater role for European external cooperation:

> [c]ette tendance sera encore renforcée si la politique extérieure des six pays sera, tout au moins en partie, mise en commun, ce qui se produira de plus en plus, car la politique commerciale amène nécessairement à une politique extérieure commune.[208]

Emphasis on the functional necessity of a diplomatic practice was a bit (more prominent) in the parliamentary debate that followed the report's release. Rapporteur van der Goes van Naters submitted evidence in the Assembly of a developing common foreign policy perhaps requiring a diplomatic outreach. Other members took a less prudent approach and pointed to foreign policies already being developed and requiring diplomatic action such as the common commercial policy or association relations with third states.[209] The then Vice-President of the Commission, Giuseppe Caron, qualified the right of legation as an essential and effective instrument to realizing economic integration objectives. He argued that the delegations in London and Washington DC were established that so qualified representatives could help to solve the problems which arose in the collaboration with major countries such as the United States and the United Kingdom. Clearly, such problems concerned the Communities as a whole and therefore had to be be faced by the Communities as a whole in a direct dialogue with the interested interlocutors.[210] The Assembly's members, however, did not explicitly refer to the possible existence of implied powers to engage with diplomacy.[211]

[205] APE, Report on the Right of Legation, para 5: 'it can be concluded, in accordance with the will of the member states as reflected in the ECSC's practices, in the texts of the Treaties of Rome, and in the new Communities' practices, that the right of legation exists. The doctrine is moreover unanimous in this sense' [own translation].

[206] *Van Gend & Loos v Administratie der Belastingen* [1963] ECLI:EU:C:1963:1, para 3.

[207] Introduced earlier as the Guggenheim criterion; Report on the Right of Legation, para 8.

[208] ibid: 'this trend will be further strengthened if the foreign policy of the six countries is, at least in part, pooled, which will happen more and more, because trade policy necessarily leads to a common foreign policy' [own translation].

[209] APE, Right of Legation Parliamentary Debate, 86.

[210] See the remarks of Giuseppe Caron, Vice-President of the EEC Commission (ibid at 91). The functional point of view was echoed by Member Stassen (p 92).

[211] The notion of implied powers already features in *Fédération Charbonnière de Belgique v High Authority* [1956] ECLI:EU:C:1956:11 and was further refined in subsequent case law, most notably in *Commission v Council* (AETR/ERTA) [1971] ECLI:EU:C:1971:32 and *Cornelius Kramer and others* [1976] ECLI:EU:C:1976:114.

Overall, the functional arguments were developed sporadically in comparison to arguments based on legal personality. Moreover, arguments were largely reduced to mere political considerations:

> [e]n conclusion, le problème du droit de légation paraît se présenter sous une forme beaucoup plus politique que juridique. Les bases juridiques dans la doctrine et dans la pratique paraissent solides, mais elles ne peuvent avoir de prise sur les considérations politiques.[212]

On other occasions, the right of legation was considered as factually given:

> la Commission n'invente rien; elle ne prétend rien; elle suit, avec modération, une pratique qui se réalise chaque jour.[213]

One explanation may be that the decision to establish a representation in a particular country still differed according to the Communities' needs; the urgency was determined on a scale between opportunity and possibility reliant upon a political rather than legal appreciation.[214]

#### 2.3.2.3 Early Literature

When the European Parliamentary Assembly confirmed the right of legation's existence in a legal instrument, a broad and general legation practice was still illusory. Rightfully, the reasoning and conclusion reached in the 1960 Resolution were not shared by all observers of the European project. In the early days of European integration, a substantial amount of literature expressed doubts as to whether the ECSC, and later the Communities, possessed the right of legation.[215]

The right of legation was challenged in its entirety by Italian Professor Ricardo Monaco. In his 1958 seminal article, he argued that:

> la légation est instituée entre deux Etats sur une base de parité absolue; elle comporte la négociation de toutes les questions qui peuvent se rapporter aux relations entre les deux Etats; elle a un caractère réciproque, puisque, à l'envoi de représentants diplomatiques, de la part d'un Etat, auprès de l'autre, correspond un envoi parallèle de la part de ce dernier [ … ] Le rapport particulier de représentation diplomatique entre la C.E.C.A. et les Etats tiers n'est donc pas directement comparable au rapport qui tire son origine de l'exercice du droit de légation active et passive de la part des Etats. Et cela aussi parce que la C.E.C.A. n'est pas dotée d'une sphère de souveraineté territoriale, et ne peut donc pas garantir certaines immunités et certaines exemptions à des organes d'un Etat étranger qui se trouvent résider et agir sur le territoire d'un de ses Etats membres. Pas plus qu'elle n'a, aux termes du Traite, le pouvoir d'imposer à l'Etat membre l'obligation de réserver à des représentants donnés le traitement diplomatique.[216]

212 APE, Report on the Right of Legation, para 12: '[i]n conclusion, the problem of the right of legation appears to be of a much more political than legal nature. The legal bases in doctrine and in practice appear solid, but they cannot do without political considerations' [own translation].

213 APE, Report of Legaton Parliamentary Debate, 86. The Commission is not inventing anything; it is not claiming anything; it is following, with moderation, a practice that is carried out every day.

214 APE, Report on the Right of Legation, para 9.

215 Werner Feld, 'The Competences of the European Communities for the Conduct of External Relations' (1965) 43 Tex Law Rev 891, 922–23.

216 Monaco (n 198) 80:

> [l]egation is instituted between two states on an absolute equal basis. It involves the negotiation of all questions which may relate to the relations between two states. It is of a reciprocal nature, since

Professor Monaco raises two types of objections. First, he notes that the new legation practices give rise to a sense of unease with regard to international law and states' position in the international legal order. The criticism was that the European Assembly approached the revolution in diplomacy caused by European practices unjustifiably lightly. Second, Professor Monaco expressed concerns about the practical hurdles for a non-state actor in diplomacy. In retrospect, such issues did not turn out to be an impassable barrier. Monaco particularly underestimated the Communities'' powers to legally oblige member states to perform tasks on its behalf in the international sphere.

Accepting the passive component of the Communities' right of legation, Pierre Pescatore challenged the Communities' claim to an active legation capacity. His main objections boiled down to more practical reluctance when he considered especially the absence of a right in the ECSC's internal law to reciprocate the accreditation of missions to be problematic. He argued that the establishment of a mission in a third state would therefore lack the relevant legal basis.[217] Moreover, Pescatore assumed that the ECSC delegation in London was an isolated example that did not evidence an existence of emerging practice.[218] Yet, he fully realized that a further European integration could increase the needs of the Communities to become diplomatically active.[219]

Scholarly suspicion decreased in the mid-1960s. Charles Reichling was one of the first to support both the active and passive components of the right of legation.[220] Agreeing with Pescatore that the limited active legation was problematic to fully prove a decisive exercise of the right of active legation, Reichling also submitted that legal and political arguments were in place that compensated for the absence of an established practice. He pointed to the recognition by third states and their reciprocal behaviour.[221] Furthermore, Reichling justified the right of legation on functional grounds:

> [l]a nécessité fonctionnelle constitue [ ... ] une partie importante de la base juridique de droit de légation sur laquelle se fonde son existence, tant pour l'élément actif que passif. La nécessité politique de droit de légation actif, par contre, en ce qu'elle suppose l'initiative des Communautés, justifie son exercice effectif.[222]

diplomatic representations from one state to the other correspond to a parallel dispatch [ ... ] The diplomatic exchanges between the ECSC and third states is therefore not directly comparable to those that have their origin in the exercise of the right of active and passive legation on the part of states. One of the reasons is that the ECSC does not possess territorial sovereignty and therefore cannot guarantee the granting of immunities and exemptions to organs of a foreign state residing and acting in the territory of one of its member states. Nor has it, under the terms of the Treaty, the power to impose on the member state the obligation to accord diplomatic treatment to such representatives' [own translation].

217 Pierre Pescatore, 'La Personnalité Internationale de la Communauté' in Michel Melchior (ed), *Les Relations Extérieurs de la Communauté Européenne Unifiée* (Institut d'Études Juridiques Européennes de la Faculté de Droit de l'Université de Liège 1969) 98.

218 *Fédération Charbonnière* (n 211); Pescatore, 'Les Relations Extérieurs de La Communauté Européenne' (n 201) 195.

219 Pescatore, 'Les Relations Extérieurs de la Communauté Européenne' (n 201) 196.

220 Reichling (n 55) 64.

221 ibid 63–64.

222 ibid 64: '[t]he functional necessity constitutes an important part of the legal basis of the right of legation on which its existence is founded, both for active and passive elements. The political necessity of the right of active legation, in contrast, inasmuch as it presupposes an initiative of the Communities, justifies its effective exercise' [own translation].

This point of view was echoed by Werner Feld in 1965, who argued that the Communities increasingly trod in international fields 'such as the raising of funds in the financial markets of third countries, the acquisition and exchange of technical information, or the conclusion of international freight rate agreements'; all requiring continuous contacts in the world's capitals to achieve the ECSC Treaty objectives.[223] Likewise, four years earlier, Pescatore had taken the view that the need for European diplomacy would only truly arise when a common commercial policy was fully developed.[224] In this sense, scholarship provided a more dynamic justification for the right of legation based on functional necessity, a contrast to the static approach adopted by the Assembly based on the Communities' legal personality.

### 2.3.3 Validity and Legitimacy of the EU's Right of Legation

The European landscape looks different when compared to the 1960s. The EU now plays a substantially more active role in international affairs, with implications for the European, national, and international legal orders. The Union's claim to the right of legation has consequently gained strength. This section re-evaluates the Union's current-day features, institutional set-up, functional needs, and global recognition in order to further legitimize its diplomatic capacity.

#### 2.3.3.1 Objective Criteria

##### *2.3.3.1.1 The EU as a subject of international law*

For a considerable time, European scholarship pointed to the ambiguity surrounding the EU's international legal personality. There is no doubt, however, that the EU enjoys international legal personality.[225] Since the Lisbon Treaty's entry into force, Article 47 TEU even explicitly recognizes that '[t]he Union shall have legal personality'.[226] Although this provision primarily deals with the Union's internal personality, it also serves as a legal basis for the Union to perform its functions in the international sphere. Indeed, the main function of the personality mentioned in primary law is to confirm the Union's status as an independent entity in its own right in the EU legal order as well as in the domestic legal orders of its member states. But Article 47 TEU also indirectly enhances the Union's capacity to enter into relations with third states and international organizations by emphasizing the Union's unique position in the international legal order as well as its identity as an entity capable of acting independently from its member states.[227] Some authors, however, argue that Article 47 TEU did little to raise the EU's profile on the international arena.[228]

The EU's international legal personality is exemplified most visibly by the Union's exercise of international rights and duties such as its entering into legal agreements with other

[223] Feld (n 215) 923.

[224] Pescatore, 'Les Relations Extérieurs de la Communauté Européenne' (n 201) 196.

[225] Ramses A Wessel, 'Revisiting the International Legal Status of the EU' (2000) 5 EFAR 507, 507; Henri de Waele and Jan-Jaap Kuipers, 'The Emerging International Identity of the European Union—Some Preliminary Observations' in Henri de Waele and Jan-Jaap Kuipers (eds), *The European Union's Emerging International Identity: Views from the Global Arena* (Martinus Nijhoff 2013) 2. For a historical overview, see Niels Blokker, 'International Legal Personality of the European Communities and the European Union: Inspirations from Public International Law' (2016) 35 Yearb Eur Law 471.

[226] Article 47 of the Consolidated Version of the Treaty on European Union [2012] OJ C326/01 (hereafter TEU); see previously Art 6(1) ECSC Treaty, Art 205(1) EC Treaty, and Art 184 Euratom Treaty.

[227] Philippe De Schoutheete and Sami Andoura, 'The Legal Personality of the European Union' (2007) LX Studia Diplomatica 5.

[228] De Waele and Kuipers (n 225) 2.

international actors (*ius tractatuum*) and its participating in international organizations. The recognition of these capacities by third countries indubitably supports the Union's international position. The Union fulfils the criteria for an IO to enjoy international legal personality set out by the 1949 *Reparation for Injuries* opinion.[229] Following the CJEU's finding in the 1971 *ERTA* case that (former) Article 281 of the Treaty establishing the European Community (TEC) entailed the Community's capacity to establish contractual links with third countries, the matter was also considered settled academically.[230]

While not strictly necessary from the point of view of international law, over the years, the Union also explicitly proclaimed the existence of its international legal personality. Remarkably, it did so through its diplomatic practice. At the Lisbon Treaty's entry into force in 2009, the Union reiterated its international legal personality by informing the world of the changes the Union was going through. In a notification sent to all third states, the Council and the Commission jointly announced that the European Union would replace and succeed the European Community, and that therefore would:

> exercise all rights and duties and assume all obligations of the European Community whilst continuing to exercise existing rights and assume obligations of the European Union.[231]

The agreements concluded with third countries establishing diplomatic relations also contain a formal confirmation of the Union's legal personality on the territory of the contracting state. In Article 2(2) of the model agreement used by the EU to establish such diplomatic relations, the more concrete consequences of its international legal personality are spelled out:

> [t]he European Union and the EAEC shall have the capacity to conclude contracts, to acquire and dispose of immovable and movable property as necessary for the effective fulfilment of their duties, in accordance with the procedural and administrative requirements imposed by the law of [country X], and to conduct legal proceedings, and shall be represented for that purpose by the European Commission.[232]

When entering into diplomatic agreements with the EU, third states recognize the Union's personality within their territories by way of this provision as well as the consequences that derive from such recognition in their national contexts.

#### *2.3.3.1.2 The EU as an independent actor exercising public authority*

The intensity of the European integration process and the results that followed therefrom require only a light introduction. The Union has no equal in the world of international organizations in the way it develops policies, pursues its own objectives, and even enforces them. One of the most remarkable aspects of the Union has been the creation of its own European legal order.[233] Ever since its inception, EU law has been an integral part of the member states'

[229] Philippe Gautier, 'Reparation for Injuries Case Revisited: The Personality of the European Union' (2000) 4 Max Planck UNYB 331.

[230] *AETR/ERTA* (n 211). See also Henri de Waele, *Layered Global Player: Legal Dynamics of EU External Relations* (Springer 2011) 4.

[231] Council, Notification to third parties before the entry into force of the Treaty of Lisbon, Document of the Council No 16654/1/09, 27 November 2009.

[232] Model agreement (reprinted in Appendix 2), also reproduced in Jan Wouters and others, *The Law of EU External Relations* (3rd edn, OUP 2021) 44–45. See Chapter 3 of this book for a discussion.

[233] *Van Gend & Loos* (n 206) para 3.

legal systems:[234] domestic courts are bound to apply EU law, including its 'essential characteristics' such as the principles of primacy and direct effect.[235] Independence also shows in the European legislative processes, which include multiple independent elements such as the Commission's exclusive right of initiative and the co-legislative role of the directly elected European Parliament.[236] The European system is furthermore unique for EU citizenship ensures that European citizens can directly enjoy rights when working, travelling, studying, or participating in elections.

The supranational elements of EU policymaking and law-making have been backed by institutional evolutions. At first, the High Authority of the ECSC, and later the Commission, Council, Parliament, and the Court of Justice of the European Union (CJEU) were established to exercise executive, legislative, and judicial powers.[237] Every Union institution has an autonomous will. The Lisbon Treaty reinforced the Union's international status by enhancing its international actorness and by upgrading its competences.[238] First, Lisbon altered the institutional landscape with the creation of the High Representative for Foreign Affairs and Security Policy (hereafter High Representative or HR) and the European External Action Service (EEAS).[239] The way the EEAS is set up—as a functionally autonomous body, separate from the Commission and Council—can be seen as an institutionalization of a long-existing active legation practice. With the transformation of Commission delegations into EU delegations (EUDELs) came the constitutional confirmation of the existence of EU missions abroad with a representational finality.[240] Article 221(1) of the TFEU reads: 'Union delegations in third countries and at international organisations shall represent the Union.' In 2014, the diplomatic finality was confirmed by the CJEU in two civil servant cases: '[i]t is clear from Article 221 TFEU and from Article 5 [EEAS Decision] that the delegations provide the Union's diplomatic representation in accordance with the Vienna Convention on Diplomatic Relations of 18 April 1961'.[241] Second, Lisbon also clarified the roles of actors acting on the Union's behalf.[242] The Commission continues to represent the Union externally; that the President of the European Council represents the EU on issues of the Common Foreign and Security Policy (CFSP) at his level and in that capacity (Art 15(6) TEU); and that the HR has the more general mission of taking the lead in the EU's CFSP (Arts 18 and 27(2) TEU).

Furthermore, the Union has its own administration, which is to be distinguished from its member states' administrations. The EU therefore manages its own governance activities

234 *Variola v Amministrazione Italiana delle Finanze* [1973] ECLI:EU:C:1973:101, para 10; *Politi SAS v Italian Ministry of Finance* [1971] ECLI:EU:C:1971:122, para 9.

235 *Flaminio Costa v ENEL* [1964] ECLI:EU:C:1964:66, 593; Opinion 1/91 *EEA Agreement* [1991] ECLI:EU:C:1991:490, para 21.

236 See Arts 17(2), 16(3), and 14(1) and (3) TEU.

237 Magdalena Ličková, 'European Exceptionalism in International Law' (2008) 19 EJIL 463, 464.

238 Simon Duke, 'Providing for European-Level Diplomacy after Lisbon: The Case of the European External Action Service' (2009) 4 HJD 211; Jan Wouters, Dominic Coppens, and Bart De Meester, 'The European Union's External Relations after the Lisbon Treaty' in Stefan Griller and Jacques Ziller (eds), *The Lisbon Treaty: EU Constitutionalism without a Constitutional Treaty?* (Springer 2008); Michael Emerson and others, *Upgrading the EU's Role as Global Actor* (Centre for European Policy Studies 2011).

239 Article 1(2) of the Council Decision 2010/427/EU establishing the organization and functioning of the European External Action Service [2010] OJ L201/30 (hereafter 'EEAS Decision').

240 Article 221 Consolidated Version of the Treaty on the Functioning of the European Union [2012] OJ C326/47 (hereafter TFEU).

241 *De Loecker v EEAS* [2014] ECLI:EU:F:2014:246, para 4 and *Delcroix v EEAS* [2014] ECLI:EU:F:2014:9, para 1.

242 Steffen Bay Rasmussen, 'The Messages and Practices of the European Union's Public Diplomacy' (2010) 5 HJD 263, 282.

on an ongoing basis. When taken together, such activities constitute the exercise of public authority.

*2.3.3.1.3 The EU as a sovereign actor*

The completion of the European integration process rests on a unique premise, being the division of sovereignty between the EU and the member states.[243] The Union enjoys 'real powers stemming from a limitation of sovereignty or a transfer of powers from the States to the [Union]'.[244] In turn, the member states have 'limited their sovereign rights, albeit within limited fields'.[245]

Despite the fact that the Union is not a state, its competences and set-up are also much more advanced than those of any other IO. Quite a number of the Union's key policies, including the single currency and the common commercial policy, have become examples of supranationalism par excellence. The Union has also acted in external domains traditionally reserved for states, ranging from defence, police cooperation, and border control to foreign policy at large. Scholars have also noted that the Union's growing engagement with the international order resulted in a state-like behaviour.[246] Mike Smith noticed this pattern in the global political economy as well as in the global security order,[247] whilst Sen refers to the more traditional Union competences when he states that:

> the basis on which the claim of the EEC appear to have been sustained is that under the instrument constituting that body, some of the governmental functions of the Community states have been conceded in favour of the Community, such as in the field of fisheries, and accordingly the representation of the Community is analogous to the representation of governments.[248]

The ius legationis, being a capacity rather than a competence, did not have to be 'transferred' to the Union as was the case for other domains. Rather, the question becomes whether the member states accepted or admitted to the enjoyment of a diplomatic capacity by the Union to be sovereignly executed. Both law and practice strongly suggest that they did. The EU constitutional treaties recognize, albeit indirectly, the right of legation through references to privileges and immunities (passive legation) and the Union delegations (active legation). In other words, they facilitate the exercise of a right of legation. Arguably more importantly, throughout the years, the member states have never protested against the diplomatic representation of the competences they allocated to the Union.

*2.3.3.1.4 The EU as a functional actor*

Functionalism is often relied upon in international institutional law to explain why rights and duties are attributed to IOs. The EU's right of legation can also be explained relying on

[243] Pierre Pescatore, *The Law of Integration: Emergence of a New Phenomenon in International Relations, Based on the Experience of the European Communities* (Sijthoff 1974) 30; Robert Schütze, *From Dual to Cooperative Federalism: The Changing Structure of European Law* (OUP 2009) 72–73.

[244] *Costa v ENEL* (n 235) 593.

[245] *Van Gend & Loos* (n 206) para 3.

[246] Teija Tiilikainen, 'To Be or Not to Be?: An Analysis of the Legal and Political Elements of Statehood in the EU's External Identity' (2001) 6 EFAR 223, 228.

[247] Michael Smith, 'The European Union and International Order: European and Global Dimensions' (2007) 12 EFAR 437, 452.

[248] Sen (n 13) 17.

these more dynamic functional arguments.[249] As a subject of international law with a highly integrated political and legal system, the EU has a concrete and well-established functional need to interact with other subjects of international law, including via diplomatic relations.[250] In 1969, Jean Rey pointed to this need, while being still relatively humble:

> [i]l est devenue nécessaire que la Communauté fusionnée ait la possibilité d'entretenir des représentants diplomatiques à l'étranger. Il ne s'agit pas de disperser cent ou cent-dix ambassadeurs un peu partout dans le monde, mais de posséder un représentant diplomatique dans les quelques grands centres où se fait la politique mondiale et où, par conséquent, nous avons-nous, comme Communauté, des intérêts essentiels à défendre.

Over time, a growing range of thematic areas has been governed by the Union, internally as well as externally.[251] In those different domains, it is in the interest both of the Union and the member states that the Union can meaningfully exercise the functions granted.

The power to conduct diplomatic relations can therefore be derived, in accordance with the principle of '*effet utile*', directly from the competences and objectives of the Union.[252] To effectively perform its powers, to attain its goals, and to exercise the functions as enshrined in the treaties the Union can rely on different instrumental powers, even if these are only implied.[253] This is the case for all IOs: implied powers give effect to explicit powers and help an IO to exercise those powers effectively. The Treaties' wording is clear about the importance of the EU's general engagement with the outside world, whereby the conduct of international relations is not just a possible venue for action but also a legal obligation. Suffice it to point to the EU's legal obligation to contribute to peace, security, and the strict observance and the development of international law as spelled out in Article 3(5) TEU. Additionally, the EU is entrusted with the general responsibility to represent the community of states, their common policies, and interests in international relations.[254] In social science literature, moreover, the EU is increasingly seen as a 'normative power', a vigorous promoter of a strong international legal order that benefits all of its constituents. It uses this responsibility to influence international law and policymaking and to export its own normative preferences to external actors.

What constitutes as 'effective' in this context may be debated. The Treaties are not conclusive as to whether diplomatic relations categorize as 'effective' or even 'appropriate'

[249] A strong case for functionalism is made by Schermers and Blokker (n 225); and Sands and Klein (n 136). A more critical approach is taken by Finn Seyersted, *Common Law of International Organizations* (Nijhoff 2008).

[250] Jean Rey, 'La Politique Commerciale de la Communauté Européenne' in Michel Melchior (ed), *Les Relations Extérieurs de la Communauté Européenne Unifiée* (Institut d'Études Juridiques Européennes de la Faculté de Droit de l'Université de Liège 1969) 255:

> it has become necessary for the merged Community to have the possibility of maintaining diplomatic representatives abroad. This is not a question of scattering one hundred or one hundred and ten ambassadors all over the world, but of having a diplomatic representative in the few major centres where world politics are made and where, therefore, we have, as a Community, essential interests to defend [own translation].

[251] Roberts (n 39) 399; Antonio Tizzano, 'The Foreign Relations Law of the EU between Supranationality and Intergovernmental Model' in Enzo Cannizzaro (ed), *The European Union as an Actor in International Relations* (Kluwer 2002) 136.

[252] Rachel Frid, *The Relations between the EC and International Organizations: Legal Theory and Practice* (Martinus Nijhoff 1995) 35–36.

[253] See the ICJ's broad interpretation in *Reparation for Injuries* (n 66); Amerasinghe (n 131) 24 et seq; AIL Campbell, 'The Limits of the Powers of International Organisations' (1983) 32 ICLQ 523.

[254] Ian Manners, 'Normative Power Europe: A Contradiction in Terms?' (2002) 40 J Com Mar St 235; Richard Whitman (ed), *Normative Power Europe: Empirical and Theoretical Perspectives* (Palgrave Macmillan 2011).

instruments to realize powers. In Article 3(6) TEU, for instance, it is said that '[t]he Union shall pursue its objectives *by appropriate means* commensurate with the competences which are conferred upon it in the Treaties' [own emphasis]. The member states seem to have envisaged a degree of discretion in the choice of the means the Union can use to accomplish its objectives. In the absence of constitutional provisions obliging the Union to engage in formal diplomacy, the theoretical possibility exists that objectives can be met through other channels than those of diplomatic relations—potential alternatives include the conduct of informal relations or the diplomatic representation of the EU via its member states, to name a couple. In the *Reparation for Injuries* opinion, it entailed the bringing of an international claim. There is no reason why this should be the only option available. In fact, legal proceedings should be a matter of last resort and always be preceded by diplomatic efforts.[255]

The idea that there would be a complete freedom as to the choice of means to realize internal and external objectives on the international arena is deceptive. In addition to its own ambitions, external forces also require the Union to be a fully equipped international actor. Even with a wide range of tools and instruments available in external relations, the most effective way to attain some international goals will be through the conduct of formal diplomacy. International circumstances often impose the framework on how international relations take place. By not engaging in the most basic systems familiar to other public actors to intermingle internationally, the Union would exemplify a lack of cognisance of the world's established norms, functions, and demands. As noted by Leo Tindemans in his 1976 report:

> [r]ecent developments of international life show that economic, industrial, financial and commercial questions will all in the future be the subject of negotiations, the significance of which will be highly political. If the European Union did not have the means to cover all aspects of our external relations, it would not be equal to its task. The Union must have a comprehensive and coherent outlook and act accordingly.[256]

#### 2.3.3.2 Subjective Criteria

There are several objective reasons to conclude that the EU is particularly and objectively fit to be considered a diplomatic actor. However, this does not automatically provide it with such abilities. The relationship between an internal competence and an external capacity is not one of correspondence: the sharing of powers between the Union and its member states remains a primarily internal matter.[257]

The possession of the right of legation requires a subjective element in the form of recognition by diplomatic counterparts. In the Union's case, recognition was triggered in response to acts initiated by it. The Union entered into negotiations with third states, leading to the acceptance of the Union's diplomatic capacity by those states. Third states' recognition has been formalized in arrangements made at the time of establishment of the EU's missions abroad, often taking the form of an Establishment Agreement (EA) signed and ratified by third states. The EAs are discussed in more detail in Chapter 3. However, it is important to note here that the agreements contain four key provisions. They confirm the Union's international legal personality, provide the conditions for when an EU mission will be established

[255] *Reparation for Injuries* (n 66) 179.
[256] Report by Leo Tindemans to the European Council [1976] Bull EC, Supp 1/76, 14.
[257] Cannizzaro, 'Fragmented Sovereignty?' (n 87) 42.

in the third states, make the VCDR applicable to diplomatic relations, and grant reciprocal rights to third states missions accredited to the Union in Brussels. As a result, this single instrument confirms all five dimensions of diplomatic recognition.

The global recognition of the EU's right of legation also stems from decades of overwhelming state practice. Union delegations are diplomatically present in over 130 third countries and accredited to some 160 government actors. As a result, all those third countries acknowledge the EU as a legitimate and direct diplomatic counterpart.

### 2.3.4 Legal Controversies Surrounding the EU's Right of Legation

When, in 1960, the European Parliamentary Assembly concluded that the right of legation existed on behalf of the Communities, it also pointed out a number of legal controversies and practical difficulties the newly established right would likely give rise to. The first type of complications were of a political nature. These hurdles were largely time-bound and had to do with recognition in the context of IOs in which the USSR was represented. More relevantly, a second set of legal complications was identified resulting from the Communities' inherent inability to be fully assimilated with a state despite the exercise of certain sovereign functions. Many of these legal struggles remain relevant today.

#### 2.3.4.1 Reciprocity

The principle of reciprocity is central to diplomatic law. Diplomatic and consular exchanges are historically grounded in reciprocity and the Vienna Conventions adhere to a balance between rights and duties of receiving and sending states. The principle of reciprocity is based on states' desire to see the protection offered to foreign diplomats on their territory accorded equally to the diplomats they send to other countries.[258] Because of such mutual dependency, immunities, inviolabilities, and privileges are generally well respected in international relations.[259]

In 1960, the Assembly noted that the Communities were hindered by their inability to reciprocate in diplomatic relations. Until this day, the EU does not possess territorial jurisdiction as is required to grant privileges and immunities. Its 'territory' is derived from and does not go beyond the member states' territories.[260] The Assembly's report therefore rightly concluded that an exchange of diplomats between the Communities and third states could never take place in a climate of perfect reciprocity. Domestic laws of third states exclusively refer the representatives of states as recipients of privileges and immunities. Consequently, the enjoyment by European officials would be by the grace of third countries. The fact that the EU does not have the full competence to control the access to a territory of a member state in general nor the access to a territory by diplomats in particular still causes friction.[261]

The inability has been dealt with in a pragmatic way from the beginning. With regards to the first missions only accredited to the ECSC, the matter was settled without complication. In 1955, an agreement was reached between the High Authority and the Grand Duchy of Luxembourg tasking the host state to fulfil the diplomatic obligations on behalf of the

[258] Plantey (n 161) 207–08.

[259] Marjoleine Zieck, 'Diplomatiek en Consulair Recht' in Nathalie Horbach, René Lefeber, and Olivier Ribbelink (eds), *Handboek Internationaal Recht* (TMC Asser Press 2007) 291.

[260] Allan Rosas and Lorna Armati, *EU Constitutional Law: An Introduction* (Bloomsbury Publishing 2012) 14.

[261] See *Hungary v Slovak Republic* [2012] ECLI:EU:C:2012:630 and the Opinion of AG Bot in the same case, ECLI:EU:C:2012:124, point 34.

ECSC, after which the duty was integrated into Luxembourg's domestic law. When the other Communities were established, the idea of a member state executing this task for the Union was copied into the Rome Treaties. Article 16 of the then Protocol 13 on Privileges and Immunities read:

> The Member State in whose territory the Community has its seat shall accord the customary diplomatic immunities to missions of third countries accredited to the Community.

The Article guarantees that the growing number of third states' missions in Brussels would enjoy privileges and immunities and encourages that third states would reciprocate protection offered to the Communities' staff abroad. This perhaps unorthodox system survived to the modern day. Article 16 of what is now Protocol 7 on the privileges and immunities of the Union requires Belgium 'to accord the customary diplomatic immunities and privileges to missions of third countries accredited to the Union'.[262] In the establishment agreements signed with third states to allow for diplomatic exchanges, the EU explicitly refers to this provision of EU law as well as to the principle of reciprocity.

#### 2.3.4.2 The Exercise of Diplomatic Functions

A second issue identified by the Assembly concerned the scope of the functions exercised by European diplomats. Article 3(1) VCDR stipulates that the functions of diplomatic missions consist of inter alia the representation, protection of interests, negotiation, observation, and promotion of friendly relations.[263] While states possesses the totality of international rights and capabilities recognized by international law, the EU's rights and capabilities depend on the purposes and functions specified or implied in its Treaties and as developed in practice.[264]

The drafters of the 1959 report already noted that, as a result of the allocated powers theory, the European competences in diplomacy would be restricted to issues affecting the Communities. Originally, Commission delegations indeed mainly dealt with issues where the Commission possessed broad competences. A few minority expressions in the early literature even denied the exercise of politically diplomatic tasks all together and stated that European missions were confined to economic or development aid responsibilities, depending on the place of operation.[265] Such restricted view did not reflect the reality on the ground. Although functions relating to trade and aid made up the centre of gravity until the 1980s, the Commission missions' focus expanded well before the Treaty of Lisbon transformation and were competent in fields of agriculture, fisheries, environment, transport, health and safety, and so on.[266] Commission delegations coordinated common European positions and negotiated on behalf of member states in cooperation with the Council presidency in areas of shared competences.[267] Without underestimating the variance due to differing circumstances in third countries, the delegations have generally benefitted from the consecutive transfers of competences to perform an increasing number of diplomatic

[262] Protocol No 7 on the Privileges and Immunities of the European Union, attached to the EU Treaties [2012] OJ C326/266.
[263] Denza, *Diplomatic Law* (n 24) 30.
[264] *Reparation for Injuries* (n 66) 180.
[265] Reichling (n 55) 33.
[266] Rohit Ambast and Vinay Tyagi, 'Ambassadors of Europe: An Insight into the Evolution of the European Union and International Diplomatic Law' (2008) 61 Studia Diplomatica 173, 16.
[267] Michael Smith, 'Still Rooted in Maastricht: EU External Relations as a "Third-Generation Hybrid"' (2012) 34 J Eur Integr 699.

and representational tasks. The most tangible adjustment happened at the time of the transformation of Commission delegations into Union delegations. Union delegations have since taken over the coordinating role and functions previously undertaken by member states' embassies holding the rotating presidency. Notwithstanding that the delegations' tasks were never confined to the common commercial policy, the formal broadening of tasks of the EUDELs was considered an important challenge. High Representative Ashton acknowledged in her foreword to the 2013 EEAS review that 'delegations in the field had to transform themselves overnight taking on new roles with no extra resources and without consolidated instructions or advice'.[268]

### 2.3.4.3 Who Holds the EU's Right of Legation?

A third uncertainty in the early days of European diplomacy was the question of ownership of the right of legation. As regards the first delegation in London, on the basis of its broad competences and high level of independence, the High Authority executed the right of legation on the ECSC's behalf.[269] Following the changes introduced by the Rome Treaties, the Assembly's Resolution 761f/60 accorded the right of legation to the Communities, although it was executed by the Commission.[270] Indeed, for many decades, the Commission was the primary actor in conducting active legation practice. Yet, for a considerable time, the Council also operated two delegations of its own in New York and Geneva. Moreover, the passive counterpart, the Commission, shared competences with the Council. The issue was ultimately resolved by the entry into force of the Lisbon Treaty. The right of legation is now claimed and enjoyed by the EU as a whole.

### 2.3.4.4 The Recognition of States

The penultimate legal question identified concerned the inability of international organizations to recognize states, a preliminary condition to enter into diplomatic relations.[271] The Union has been involved in acts of recognition and has voiced opinions on questions of statehood for various political reasons through its institutions.[272] An illustration can be found in the 1991 Declaration on the 'Guidelines on the Recognition of New States in Eastern Europe and in the Soviet Union' promising the 'recognition by the Community and its Member States and to the establishment of diplomatic relations'. However, the member states have retained the exclusive competence to recognize states and/or governments. Given that recognition is a condition to exercise diplomatic relations, the possibility emerges that views between member states on the statehood of a particular entity may vary, rendering the EU inapt to exercise the capacity of legation.

This issue was not featured in the original analysis of the right of legation, which is interesting since the Assembly's Resolution was passed during a time when quite a few newly independent states were emerging. Compared to the late 1950s and early 1960s, attempts at secession and declarations of independence have become rare. However, the legal issues did not vanish. As evidenced by the Palestinian Territories, Kosovo and, to some extent, Taiwan, Hong Kong, and Macau, the various approaches taken by the member states in recognition

268 High Representative, 'EEAS Review', July 2013.
269 Reichling (n 55) 67.
270 See the remarks of Albert Wehrer, Member of the High Authority of the ECSC, during the Right of Legation Parliamentary Debate (n 195) 9.
271 Denza, *Diplomatic Law* (n 24) 24; Plantey (n 161) 204.
272 Reprinted in Turk, 'Recognition of States' (n 90) 72. See also the non-binding European Parliament Resolution on Recognition of Palestine Statehood (n 101).

debates impact the EU's conduct of external relations. At present, the Union cannot open a diplomatic mission in third countries not recognized by all twenty-seven member states. The pragmatic solution has been to establish representative offices in Taipei, Hong Kong, Jerusalem, and Pristina rather than diplomatic missions. Formally lacking diplomatic status, these missions are given facilities that mimic those granted to embassies. Similarly, the representatives of the said regions are accredited to the Union not in a diplomatic capacity but rather as 'other representatives'.

A related issue touched upon in 1959 concerns the question whether the Communities could accredit representatives opposed by one or more member states.[273] One of the more interesting solutions proposed at the time was the establishment of a European district in which the Communities could receive and accredit foreigners to their liking. A second proposal to intensify cooperation and communication between the Communities and the member states was rightly given more support. The cooperative approach still forms the basis for the current-day success of EU diplomacy.

### 2.3.5 Does the EU Possess the Right of Legation?

The European continent has been fertile soil for the growth and development of diplomatic interactions. Greek city states were the first to send and receive envoys, European writers such as Grotius and Vattel were the first to write systematically on issues of diplomatic law, and it was in Vienna that the rules on diplomacy were finally codified. Even today, European states still traditionally maintain large and influential networks of permanent missions. It is no surprise that in Europe too a new type of diplomatic actor has set afoot that even in 1960 claimed the right of legation under PIL.

The diplomatic system is created for and by states. States are particularly protective of rights resulting from their monopoly position, which explains why international law on diplomatic relations preserved a strong state-orientated attitude. However, sovereignty is not in itself a necessary condition to conduct formal diplomatic relations as the two determining factors are *(a)* whether a mandate is granted by a sovereign actor, and *(b)* whether the new diplomatic actor is recognized by other sovereigns. This presupposes the idea that the right of legation can be split between individual entities and assigned to be executed in fields in which they exercise authority. On the basis of these conditions, this chapter researched the arguments for the EU to possess the capability to establish, conduct, and maintain diplomatic relations. It was found that in 1960 the Parliamentary Assembly concluded prematurely that the Communities had a right of legation, whereby many underlying legal controversies were ignored and fundamental questions left unanswered. Yet, the discussion's records already show a strong ideological appeal to the notion of a common European diplomacy.

The legal justification of the constantly developing diplomatic practice was reinforced over the years. Today, the Union can comfortably claim a right of legation on the basis of *(a)* its functional needs; *(b)* a transfer of powers by its member states; and *(c)* the quasi-universal acceptance by third states of the EU's diplomatic status, rights, and duties. The EU's right of legation is no longer self-imposed or political. Rather, it is the result of multiple and continuous legal acts of various internal and external actors. The Union's endeavours are

[273] APE, Report on the Right of Legation, para 12.

supported by its organizational set-up and instruments, which facilitate and contribute to the fulfilment of the right of legation.

Still today, oddly, there is no reference *expressis verbis* to the Union's right of legation in EU primary law. The closest indication of a ius legationis is perhaps Article 221(1) TEU, whereby it is noted that the:

> Union delegations in third countries and at international organisations shall represent the Union.

This notion is inadequate in two ways. First, Article 221(1) TEU does not directly refer to the *diplomatic* character of the activities undertaken by the EUDELs. Representative tasks can be executed in numerous ways; engaging with diplomatic relations is just a singular example of representation. Second, 'representation' connotes an *active* form of being; Article 221(1) TEU thus does not capture the passive counterpart of the Union's right of legation.

EU diplomacy is not the first to challenge PIL's understanding that diplomacy is a *domaine réservé* of states. Yet, its diplomatic claims and successes clearly surpass that of other (regional) IOs that have set foot in diplomacy. One of the major consequences is that the exercise of the right of legation is not without complication. Legal issues identified in 1959 are remarkably similar to those regularly invoked well over six decades later. They will therefore be subject to a more intense review in the chapters to follow, although it may already be concluded now that some of these will remain inherent challenges by reason of the EU's lack of statehood. It will also be shown that the Union embraced its imperfections in diplomacy, rather than resolving them, and found and perfected resolutions along the way. One could therefore even argue that those struggles have become characteristic of EU diplomacy. Due to its coping mechanisms, the Union may well be the only IO equipped to fully live up to the requirements associated with formal diplomacy.

# 3

# The EU's Diplomatic Framework

## 3.1 The Active Right of Legation: Bilateral Arrangements

### 3.1.1 Legal Framework

Article 221 of the Treaty on the Functioning of the European Union (EU, or Union) states that Union delegations (EUDELs) in third countries and at international organizations (IOs) shall represent the Union.[1] As of 1 January 2010, the responsibility of the diplomatic representation of the EU has been performed by the EUDELs, replacing the Commission delegations who had performed this task until then. The delegations are placed under the authority of the High Representative of the Union for Foreign Affairs and Security Policy (HR). Still, there are a number of countries where the EU has (not yet) opened a delegation of its own. As regards the representation of the EU in those remaining third countries, a 2006 Council decision on the practical arrangements relating to the rotating presidency in third countries continues to apply.[2] These arrangements are based on the order in which member states exercise the presidency of the Council: in case the presidency (nor the succeeding presidency) has a resident accredited representative, the Union will be represented in rotation, for a period of six months, by another member state represented in the country. As a result, the EU's diplomatic representation in third countries may be performed by *(a)* an accredited and resident EU delegation, *(b)* an accredited but not resident EU delegation, or *(c)* a member state.

To establish diplomatic relations with third countries, the European Commission and, since the Lisbon Treaty, the HR sought to conclude bilateral establishment agreements (EAs) with receiving states. As was explained in this book's historical introduction in Chapter 1, the Commission thereto relied upon a model agreement—reprinted in Appendix 2—that was used all over the world and only slightly adapted following the Lisbon Treaty's entry into force. Lisbon's major innovation is having given this practice for the first time a legal basis. The 2010 Council Decision on the organization and functioning of the European External Action Service (EEAS) presents EU law's first and (up to now) only reference to the EAs.[3] Pursuant to its Article 5(6):

> [t]he High Representative shall enter into the *necessary arrangements* with the host country, the international organisation, or the third country concerned. In particular, the High Representative shall take the necessary measures to ensure that host States grant the Union delegations, their staff and their property, privileges and immunities equivalent to

[1] Article 221(2) of the Consolidated Version of the Treaty on the Functioning of the European Union [2012] OJ C326/47 (hereafter TFEU).

[2] Council Decision of 20 December 2006 on the arrangements establishing a system according to which Member States are to take on the functions of the Presidency in third countries, Council Doc 16568/06.

[3] Council Decision 2010/427/EU of 26 July 2010 establishing the Organization and Functioning of the European External Action Service [2010] OJ L201/30 (hereafter EEAS Decision).

*EU Diplomatic Law.* Sanderijn Duquet, Oxford University Press. © Sanderijn Duquet 2022.
DOI: 10.1093/oso/9780192844552.003.0003

those referred to in the Vienna Convention on Diplomatic Relations of 18 April 1961 [own emphasis].

The article refers to 'arrangements' and 'measures', but in practice the Commission-drafted model EA is still in use.[4] The 2010 EEAS Decision, in that sense, confirms Commission practices that had been in existence for decades. The High Representative has relied on the Council Decision's mandate ten times: to conclude formal EAs with Libya (2010), South Sudan and Uzbekistan (2011), Myanmar (2012), United Arab Emirates and Turkmenistan (2013), Somalia (2015), Mongolia (2017), Kuwait (2019), and Qatar (2022). Informal arrangements with the United Kingdom also kicked off in 2021. It is worthwhile to also point out that the diplomatic agreements concluded by the Commission are still operative and bring about the same legal effects as those entered into by the HR. With this in mind, after the entry into force of the Lisbon Treaty, the EU sent a note to third countries explaining the change in name and reassuring diplomatic partners that, since this would not cause a substantial alteration in the existing diplomatic relations, no change of the title of the EA or its provisions was required.

To date, there are records of well over a hundred different arrangements entered into. Not all diplomatic partners signed an EA with the EU. Before the first EA was signed with Japan, and for a considerable period thereafter, the Commission requested third states to unilaterally grant the Union privileges and immunities. Several states hosting Union delegations—among others the United States (1972), Canada (1976), Venezuela (1978), Thailand (1979), Australia (1980), and Switzerland (2005)—adapted their national laws in that sense.[5] Those states often never entered into an EA later on, and, as a result, the only reference to the diplomatic status of EU missions and its officials in aforementioned countries exists in domestic law. The unilateral concessions granted largely bring about consequences similar to those of EAs. Still, one must be mindful of small particularities in those laws: Canadian law for instance indicates that diplomatic privileges and immunities will only be granted if necessary for the EU representatives' performance of their functions.

Following the withdrawal of the United Kingdom from the Union and the end of the transition period in December 2020, a diplomatic row emerged between the EU and the former member state. The United Kingdom had made clear that it would not grant the newly established EUDEL in Smith Square, London, full diplomatic status. London insisted that the

[4] Steven Blockmans and Christophe Hillion (eds), *EEAS 2.0: A Legal Commentary on Council Decision 2010/427/EU Establishing the Organisation and Functioning of the European External Action Service* (Swedish Institute for European Policy Studies 2013) 61.

[5] Act to extend diplomatic privileges and immunities to the Mission to the United States of America of the Commission of the European Communities and to members thereof, Pub L No 92-499, 86 Stat 815 [1972] and Exec Order No 11689, 37 CFR 25987 [1972] (United States); European Communities Privileges and Immunities Order of 23 December 1976, Foreign Missions and International Organizations Act, Consolidated Regulations of Canada 1308, Canada Gazette Part II, Vol 111, No 1, 12 January 1977; Resolución por la cual gozarán individualmente en el territorio nacional de personalidad jurídica y en consecuencia podrán celebrar los actos jurídicos que se requieran para el normal desarrollo de sus actividades, la Comunidad Europea del Carbón, del Acero y de la Energía Atómica, denominadas globalmente las Comunidades Europeas (No 104), 15 December 1977, *Gaceta official de la Republica de Venezuela*, December 1977, No 31385, 236337–38 (Venezuela); and the Act protecting the operations of the European Economic Community and the European Economic Community Commission in Thailand (BE 2522), *Government Gazette*, Part 42, vol 96, 25 March 1979 (Thailand); Section 5A in the Diplomatic Privileges and Immunities Act No 16 of 1967, 10 April 1980 (Australia); Décision du 26 Octobre 2005 du Conseil federal autorisant la Commission à ouvrir une Délégation permanente à Berne, the Decree of the Swiss Federal Council of 31 March 1948, as amended on 20 May 1958 and on 3 November 1967, and the Declaration of the Swiss Federal Council of 20 May 1958 (Switzerland).

EU's ambassador should be seen as representing an IO rather than being treated as a national envoy. The United Kingdom's view on the matter was remarkable since records show that the country in the late 1980s had been quite insistent on extending the EA technique when it came to third countries. In the first months following Brexit, the UK Government argued that immunity is a derogation from the principle of the rule of law that should be restrictively applied provoking a certain irritation on the part of the Union. The incident was finally settled in May 2021 with the United Kingdom's granting of diplomatic immunities and privileges to the EU delegation and its staff in London. At the time of writing, no legal text had been entered into to formalize this arrangement.

The following sections study in more depth the remaining 128 written arrangements that take the form of separate agreements. Most of the EAs (122) are written contracts and are referred to as an 'agreement' by the parties; in six cases, the diplomatic relations between the Commission exist on the basis of an exchange of letters. This is the case for EAs concluded with Sudan (1985), the Holy See (1970), the Republic of North Macedonia (2000), North Korea (2002), Singapore (2002), and Panama (2003). In the EA concluded with the Republic of North Macedonia (then the Former Yugoslav Republic of Macedonia (FYROM)), the parties acknowledge that the letters 'constitute an agreement between the Government of the Republic of Macedonia and the European Commission'. Similarly, the Singapore's EA reads that the Commission's letter and its confirmation by the Government 'will together constitute an agreement between the Republic of Singapore and the Commission of the European Communities'. Taken together, however, the 128 EAs provide a good sample of the law on EU diplomacy.

## 3.1.2 Common Features of EAs

### 3.1.2.1 Main Characteristics

The main goal of an establishment agreement is to enable an EUDEL to assume diplomatic functions and enjoy full diplomatic privileges and immunities in a third state. Over time, the EAs were only moderately altered: the few implemented improvements concern the EAs' format and language rather than their content or envisioned effects, both of which have remained remarkably constant throughout the years. The post-Lisbon EA template is a relatively short written document comprising three constituent elements: a heading, a number of substantive clauses, and a number of final phrases. The exact number of articles and phrasing varies between EAs, but the features discussed in this section form part of all EAs unless explicitly specified to the contrary.

All agreements are produced in an official language shared between one of the member states and the contracting third state; additionally, they may as well be drawn up in another local language. If there is more than one language version, the EAs spell out that all texts have equal validity. In the recent cases of Kyrgyzstan (2004; in English, Russian, and Kyrgyz), Tajikistan (2004; in English, Russian, and Tajik), Mongolia (2013, in English and Mongolian), Turkmenistan (2013, in English and Turkmen), and Kuwait (2019, in English and Arabic), the agreement spells out that the English version will prevail when the wording does not seem clear or it is not immediately apparent. There is no such provision in the EA concluded with China (1987, drafted in English, French, and Mandarin) and Serbia (1980; drafted in the English, French, and Serbo-Croat languages and officially entered into with the Socialist Federal Republic of Yugoslavia).

#### 3.1.2.2 Heading

All EAs feature a heading comprising the agreement's title, a preamble, and the names of the parties.[6] The title—'Agreement between the Government of [the Kingdom/Republic of] XXX and the European Union on the Establishment and the Privileges and Immunities of the Delegation of the European Union in [idem] XXX'—insists on the use of the term 'agreement', giving it a certain formality. It does so in a larger and bold font, in some cases accompanied by the EU flag and, although less commonly, the third state's flag or emblem.

In the preamble, parties further introduce the topic of the agreement, state the reasons for concluding it, and stress the identity of parties in the following terms:

> The Government of [third state] and the European Union,
>
> Desirous of further strengthening and developing the friendly relations and co-operation between [idem] and the European Union,
>
> Wishing to lay down terms concerning the establishment on the territory of [idem] of a Delegation of the European Union and concerning the privileges and immunities of that Delegation, have agreed as follows

Depending on the bilateral relationship between the Union and the third country, the preamble may also refer to other legal instruments concluded between the parties. See, by way of example, the reference in the preamble of the EA concluded with Serbia (1979): '[h]aving regard to the cooperation agreements signed in Belgrade'; and that in the EA with Syria (1979): '[d]ésireux [ ... ] de faciliter la rélaisation des objectifs de l'Accord de cooperation [desiring to facilitate the achievement of the objectives of the Cooperation Agreement]'. Other EAs mention a national law on diplomatic relations; see, for instance, the reference in the preamble of the Vietnamese EA (1995) to the national 'Ordinance on the Privileges and Immunities of Diplomatic Missions'. It is common for EAs concluded with African, Caribbean, and Pacific (ACP) countries that a reference is made to the Lomé Convention. An example is provided by the 1991 EA concluded with Zambia, of which the preamble reads: '[d]esirous of stipulating existing relations between the Government of the Republic of Zambia and the European Communities and facilitating attainment of the objectives of the ACP–EEC Cooperation Agreements, especially the Lomé Convention'. The more recent EAs with Somalia and South Sudan no longer feature such reference to their ACP status. This was already the case for some pre-Lisbon agreements with countries from the region (eg the 1993 South Africa EA).

#### 3.1.2.3 Substantive Clauses

The EAs contain a limited numbered of substantive clauses. In Article 1, a third state agrees to the establishment on its territory of an EUDEL. A few EAs contain a slightly different phrasing because they were concluded at a time when diplomatic relations were (not yet) observed through a permanent delegation but rather through the accreditation of a non-resident EU Head of Delegation (HoD). The EA with Turkmenistan, concluded in 2013, for instance, reads that the Government 'agrees to the posting on its territory of Officials and other Servants of the Institutions of the European Union'. In 2019, the HR signed a second

[6] Lars Ole Petersen, *Europäisierung der Diplomatie: Völker- und Duroparechtliche Rahmenbedingungen* (Duncker & Humblot 2011) 93.

agreement with Turkmenistan to establish a 'full EU' delegation in Ashgabat; a formal review of the original EA was not deemed necessary.

Article 2 of the model EA comprises a formal confirmation of the Union's legal personality. The EA concluded with Zaire (still in force for the Democratic Republic of the Congo (DRC)), mistakenly reads that the Commission (instead of the Communities) has legal personality. The other agreements mention the legal personality of the Communities (sixty-four), the E(E)C and Euratom (sixty-two), and the EU (nine). Article 2 permits EU diplomats to conclude contracts, to acquire and dispose of immovable and movable property, and to conduct legal proceedings on the EU's behalf in the receiving state. The provision is somewhat redundant: Article 3 model EA makes the entire 1961 Vienna Convention on Diplomatic Relations (VCDR)[7] applicable, including the exercise of all diplomatic functions by EU diplomats.

To do this, the EA employs a simple and effective *renvoi* provision to the VCDR. Article 3(1) of the post-Lisbon template provides:

> [t]he Delegation of the European Union, its Head and its members, as well as the members of their families forming part of their respective households, shall, on the territory of XXX, enjoy such rights, privileges and immunities and be subject to such obligations as correspond to those laid down in the Vienna Convention on Diplomatic Relations of 18 April 1961 and respectively accorded to and assumed by Diplomatic Missions accredited to XXX, the heads and members of those Missions, as well as the members of their families forming part of their respective households.

There is a direct reference to the VCDR, albeit the wording may differ depending on the EA, with the exception of the agreements with Sudan (1985) and Singapore (2002). Notwithstanding, provisions in those two EAs still accord full diplomatic status to the Delegation and its staff. When a country unilaterally grants the EU diplomatic immunities in its national law (see the six cases referred to), a direct reference to the VCDR is also lacking. Generally speaking, the VCDR's description of diplomatic functions is sufficiently broad to comprise all kinds of legal representational functions (listed in Art 3 VCDR). The EA concluded with Uzbekistan (2011) goes even further. In its Article 4, the EA reiterates that the VCDR clauses on staff having the citizenship of the receiving State will apply; in its Article 6, it recalls that the VCDR provides that the receiving state is informed about the arrival of new members of the delegation; in its Article 7, it evokes that purpose of such privileges and immunities is not to benefit individuals and that the diplomats cannot engage in commercial activities.

To be absolutely clear, Article 3(2) of the template agreement spells out that the application of the VCDR is not limited to the enjoyment of privileges and immunities by EUDELs and their diplomats but extends to the full text of the Convention: '[t]he other provisions of the Vienna Convention on Diplomatic Relations of 18 April 1961 shall be applicable *mutatis mutandis*'.

The EU's establishment agreements go well beyond merely stipulating the advantages and protection for EU delegations and officials abroad. The phrase *mutatis mutandis* makes the entire Vienna Convention govern the EU diplomatic practice. Not all EAs have a *mutatis mutandis* clause because this was introduced to the model template at a later stage. Yet,

[7] Vienna Convention on Diplomatic Relations, opened for signature 18 April 1961, entered into force 24 April 1964, 500 UNTS 95 (hereafter VCDR).

in practice, all third states accept that the VCDR applies in full unless specified otherwise. Canadian law provides an interesting example by referring in its European Communities Privileges and Immunities Order to the privileges and immunities of EU diplomats in the following manner:

> senior officials shall have in Canada, to such extent as may be necessary for the performance of their functions, the privileges and immunities referred to and specified in section 19 of [the 1946 Convention on Privileges and Immunities of the United Nations [CPIUN].[8]

As such, it is the only instance known where EU diplomats and their families are granted privileges and immunities similar as those accorded to the UN Secretary General (via a clause in the CPIUN referring to 'diplomatic envoys' and thus customary international law as codified in the VCDR) but only to the extent that these are necessary 'for the performance of their functions'.

In essence, the large majority of EAs referring to the VCDR directly is the confirmation of the Union's choice to be subjected to the international legal regime without formally being a signatory party to the Vienna Convention. Moreover, its application is reciprocal. Through another *renvoi* clause in Article 3(3) of the EA, the Union guarantees that diplomatic privileges and immunities of third state missions accredited to it will be respected. Reference is made to Article 16 of the Protocol 7 on the Privileges and Immunities of the European Union annexed to the EU Treaties. This provision mandates the member state in whose territory the EU has its seat (ie Belgium) 'to accord the customary diplomatic immunities and privileges to missions of third countries accredited to the Union'. Some EAs, such as the one concluded with Yemen (2003), refer to the granting of privileges and immunities by *all* Member States, an interpretation of Protocol No 7 on the Privileges and Immunities of the European Union, attached to the EU Treaties [2012] OJ C326/266 (hereafter Protocol No 7), that is not complied with in practice.[9] In the case of the EA concluded with Kuwait in 2019, a reference to reciprocity and Protocol No 7 is missing.

Article 4 of the model EA contains a clause on third states' recognition of travel documents issued by the EU to its officials stationed abroad, the so-called laissez-passer.[10] Since the issuing of (diplomatic) passports is a competence that does not belong to the EU but to the member states, the EU laissez-passer (EULP) has been used as an alternative. Over the past fifty years, the EULP has proven to be an invaluable working tool for EU civil servants when travelling to third countries. The Treaties task the Commission to have the EULP accepted by third countries: the second subparagraph of Article 6 of the Protocol No 7 on the Privileges and Immunities of the European Communities of 8 April 1965, states in this regard that 'the EC may conclude agreements for these laissez-passer to be recognized as valid travel documents within the territory of third countries'.[11] The EULP does not grant diplomatic status to its holders; rather, it determines the agent's quality as an EU official posted to a delegation, and eases the delivery of visas in third countries that recognize it.[12] Such recognition can be but is not necessarily expressed in an EA. Article 4 model EA reads:

[8] Convention on Privileges and Immunities of the United Nations, done at New York, 13 February 1946, entered into force 17 September 1946, 1 UNTS 15 (hereafter CPIUN).

[9] Protocol No 7 on the Privileges and Immunities of the European Union, attached to the EU Treaties [2012] OJ C326/266 (hereafter Protocol No 7).

[10] See, for a discussion on the EULP, Chapter 4.

[11] See Art 6 Protocol No 7.

[12] See generally <www.laissez-passer.eu> accessed 1 May 2022.

> [t]he Government of [XXX] hereby recognises the laissez-passer issued by the European Union to officials and other servants of its institutions as valid travel documents.

Currently, 91 out of the 128 EAs feature an EULP clause. However, the actual number of recognizing states may be different. A small number of states that signed into a Article 4 clause (eg New Zealand and Somalia) do not or no longer recognize the EULP. There are states (eg Brazil) that do not formally recognize the laissez-passer but nevertheless accept it in practice. Yet other countries recognize the EULP not on the basis of the EA but through another agreement entered into with the Commission. This is the case for twenty-five third states. This leaves us with a total of only thirteen countries that do not recognize the EULP either in the EA in practice or in any other agreement. Their reasons for non-acceptance typically relate to security concerns. To remedy this, the EU recently upgraded its LP to match international minimum aviation security standards. The upgrade was deemed necessary both to comply with security standards in civil aviation and to facilitate the use, in extraordinary situations, of this travel document by family members of Union officials working in delegations.[13] Council Regulation No 1417/2013 provides the EULP with a form and features having long-lasting value, including International Civil Aviation Organization (ICAO)-compliant machine readability and inclusion of biometrics data. It remains to be seen whether these upgrades will facilitate EULP acceptance.

#### 3.1.2.4 Final Clauses

A third and final part of the model EA encompasses a formulation concerning the practicalities of the newly established contractual relationship, its implementation, and entry into force. More than half (ninety-one) of the EAs contain some sort of provision that deals with the settlement of disputes arising from the interpretation of the EA. While no agreements refer to a specific form of compulsory judicial or arbitral adjudication, they stipulate that disputes will be settled via consultations between their parties with the aim of arriving at a conciliation (Art 5).

All but seven EAs have a clause on the entry into force of the agreement. This is not the case for the EAs concluded with the Republic of North Macedonia (2000), the Holy See (1970), Israel (1980), North Korea (2002), São Tomé e Príncipe (1988), Singapore (2002), and Sri Lanka (1995). Article 6 model EA provides that each contracting party has to notify the other of the completion of the procedures necessary for the approval of the EA, which will enter into force on the date of reception of the second notification. This formulation is most commonly used in practice, although fifty-two EAs—to a large extent those concluded with ACP countries—provide that the agreement will enter into force on the date of signing. Thirteen EAs also provide for a provisional application of the agreement upon the date of signature. New Zealand notes that its agreement 'entered into force' a month after the date of signing.

The EAs do not generally include a termination or amendment clause. A provision of the first type appears only in two agreements concluded in 2004 with New Zealand and Tajikistan and in the 2011 EA concluded with Uzbekistan. Article 7 of the New Zealand EA reads that this '[a]greement may be terminated by either Contracting Party on giving 12 months' notice in writing to the other Contracting Party'. In the Tajik EA, a clause is added to Article 6 that reads that the 'terms of validity of the present Agreement shall expire one year after a

[13] Council Regulation No 1417/2013 of 17 December 2013 laying down the form of the laissez-passer issued by the EU [2013] OJ L353/26; see also Chapter 4.

written notification of either Party expressing its willingness to terminate it'. Article 10(2) of the Uzbek EA spells out that the Agreement 'is concluded for an indefinite period and shall be terminated after six months following the notification by either of the Parties through diplomatic channels about the intention to terminate the Agreement'.

One possible explanation is that the signatory parties wanted to commit to establish norms of conduct relating to a wider sphere of relations for a long or indefinite periods of time. The lack of a termination clause does not mean that diplomatic relations between the EU and a third state cannot be terminated or suspended. This is possible, for example, in times of war or as a side effect of a general souring of relations. Under public international law (PIL), the termination of diplomatic relations, the closing of a permanent mission, and the termination of a constituent agreement are different legal acts. The act of ending diplomatic relations also does not entail a withdrawal from the VCDR. Quite to the contrary, Article 45 VCDR spells out receiving states' obligations in case a mission is permanently or temporarily recalled. Similarly, the EU (or a third state) can suspend or terminate diplomatic relations or (temporarily) close a delegation without cancelling the EA or the application of the VCDR. For instance, in reaction to the civil war in Syria, the EUDEL scaled down its activities in the host country and temporarily closed its premises. The HoD temporarily resides in Beirut. A termination of the EA in such circumstances would be uncalled for and would go against the general principles of diplomacy.

An amendment provision features only in the EAs concluded with Burundi (1988), Kyrgyzstan (2004), New Zealand (2004), Tajikistan (2004), and Uzbekistan (2011). By way of example, Article XI of the 1988 Burundi EA reads: '[à] la demande de l'une des deux parties, le présent Accord peut être amendé par voie de négociation, et tout amendement ne devient applicable qu'après une échange de notes'. Article 9 of the 2011 Uzbek EA states that '[b]y mutual agreement of the Parties, this Agreement may be amended and modified by separate protocols which shall form an internal part of this Agreement'. The revision of an EA is not excluded in the other agreements. In 2004, the 1987 Turkish EA was amended in mutual agreement through an official exchange of letters. The letters allowed for the upgrade of the representation office of a full delegation. The first letter reads '[t]his letter and your confirmation shall together constitute an Agreement modifying our Establishment Agreement signed in Brussels, on 4 February 1987'. This reflects the general rule of international treaty law that an agreement may be adjusted when its signatory parties so decide.

At the end of the model EA, the following phrase is added: 'in witness whereof, the undersigned, duly authorized to this effect, have signed this Agreement'. A blank space ensures that the date and place of signing as well as the signature of the representative of the third state can be added; in practice, this is usually at the level of ambassador or minister. In most EAs, initials are placed in the corner of each page and a full signature is provided at the bottom of the document. On the EU side, the pre-Lisbon EAs were signed either by the Commissioner responsible for external relations or, in the case of the ACP countries, the Commissioner responsible for development cooperation. As a general rule, the High Representative signs the EAs post-Lisbon, although the task has also been delegated. The 2011 EA entered into with Uzbekistan, for instance, is signed by Mr Pierre Vimont, in his function as Executive Secretary General of the EEAS. HR Ashton in that case expressly authorized Mr Vimont to sign the agreement on her behalf in a separate letter, done at Istanbul on 21 January 2011. Remarkably, in the cases of Sierra Leone (1989), Costa Rica (1991), and Laos (2003), it was the (future) head of the Commission delegation to the country that signed the EA. Likewise, the 2017 EA with Mongolia and the 2019 EA with Kuwait were signed by the non-resident EU ambassadors to the countries. This entails that the ambassador was granted the capacity to enter into a binding agreement even before the EUDEL was formally established and the ambassador's role fully recognized accordingly.

### 3.1.2.5 Special Cases

The Union maintains sub-diplomatic relations with a number of non-state entities. These relations are governed by specific legal frameworks and executed by a third (or 'mother') state. The Union concluded EAs with the People's Republic of China on the operating of a single EU Office to *Hong Kong* and *Macao*, based in the former, and an EU Economic and Trade Office (EETO) in *Taiwan*.[14] The Hong Kong office is the only EU mission governed by the 1963 Vienna Convention on Consular Relations (VCCR) rather than the VCDR.[15] Conversely, although there is no diplomatic status accorded, the mission in Taiwan enjoys a limited set of inviolabilities relating to the protection of its archives and communication. For instance, the mission is allowed to use sealed bags as a replacement for the traditional diplomatic bag. Further, the office staff are exempt from customs duties, taxes, and duties imposed by central and local authorities; they also receive special identity cards and CD licence plates.

In Pristina, *Kosovo*, the Union operates a technical office that is not a full diplomatic delegation. The staff are granted immunities through an accreditation in the Republic of North Macedonia. This accreditation is required for practical reasons such as to be able to request a diplomatic licence plate that enables the Office's cars to drive to Belgrade.

The EU mission in *Jerusalem*—officially the EU Technical Assistance Office—is neither a fully fledged delegation nor a diplomatic representation.[16] Before it opened, the EU maintained a 'special advisor' to the Palestinian National Authority (PNA); interactions were best defined as a donor–recipient relationship. Over time, the office gradually assumed broader representational tasks and became known as the 'Office of the EU Representative'. Currently, diplomatic privileges and immunities are accorded to the head of office as a matter of courtesy by the Israeli Government; some staff enjoy functional immunity on this basis.[17] The agreement between the EU and Israel, however, makes the enjoyment of privileges and immunities conditional on the functions of the office being limited to the delivery of humanitarian aid. In a note verbale dated 14 November 1994, the Commission and Israel agreed on the following principle '[t]he ECTAO [ … ] will deal strictly with the channeling of assistance. It will not enjoy diplomatic or consular status. In addition, the ECTAO will not have or carry out any diplomatic or consular functions.' It is doubtful that, following Palestine's accession to the VCDR, such functional limitation posed by a third state legally holds.

Finally, the EU has two accreditations at religious entities. The *EUDEL to the Holy See*, which has only had a full official accreditation since 2006, receives privileges and immunities on the basis of reciprocity.[18] The Holy See has appointed a diplomatic nuncio to the EU's corps diplomatique in Brussels since 1970; those privileges and immunities are reciprocated

[14] Exchange of letters, dated 25 and 29 June 1997, between the European Commission and the Government of the People's Republic of China on the office in Hong Kong. For a short while, until the end of his appointment, the first head of the office enjoyed diplomatic privileges and immunities. The status of office in Taiwan is governed by an Exchange of letters dated 27 November 2002 between the European Commission and the Government of the Republic of China.

[15] Vienna Convention on Consular Relations, opened for signature on 24 April 1963, entered into force 19 March 1967, 596 UNTS 261 (hereafter VCCR).

[16] Sanford R Silverburg, 'Diplomatic Recognition of States in Statu Nascendi: The Case of Palestine' in Sanford R Silverburg (ed), *Palestine and International Law: Essays on Politics and Economics* (McFarland & Co 2002) 20.

[17] Exchange of notes between the European Commission and the Government of Israel dated 7 February 1992 and 14 November 1994.

[18] Note verbale dated 30 July 1970 and the exchange of letters that followed between the Commission and the Nonciature Apostolique in Belgium.

to the EUDEL located in Rome. As is provided for in the Lateran Pacts of 1929, Italy recognizes the missions accredited by foreign governments to the Holy See and ensures that these enjoy all the prerogatives of immunity enjoyed within its territory by diplomatic agents under international law. Importantly for the EU, the diplomatic status of an entity is recognized even if Italy itself does not entertain diplomatic relations with it. In 2007, the head of the EU delegation in Rome—officially known as the delegation to the Holy See, the Republic of San Marino, and to the United Nations—was also accredited to the Order of Malta. Ever since, credentials have been presented to the Grand Master of the Order of Malta.[19]

### 3.1.3 The Status of EAs under PIL

#### 3.1.3.1 IOs and Treaty-Making

The understanding in older case law that only states possess treaty-making capacities by virtue of their sovereignty has lost validity and prominence for almost a century. The International Court of Justice (ICJ) formally accepted a more functional understanding of general competences of IOs in the *Reparation for Injuries* opinion.[20] States have since created numerous IOs that more or less function as independent legal entities in the international arena and as such possess treaty-making powers. The legal basis for an IO's *ius tractatuum* is derived from the competencies allocated to it in its constituent instrument.[21] When this is required to facilitate the fulfilment of their purposes, it is accepted that IOs also enjoy a more general capacity to enter into treaties beyond their constitutional basis. As the preamble of the Vienna Convention on the Law of Treaties between States and International Organizations or between International Organizations states, '[n]oting that international organizations possess the capacity to conclude treaties, which is necessary for the exercise of their functions and the fulfilment of their purposes'. The absence of a competent organ to conclude these agreements does not prevent the organization from enjoying this inherent right.[22]

In the case of the EU, treaty-making authority emanates explicitly from primary law—Article 216(1) Treaty on the Functioning of the European Union (TFEU) provides that the Union 'may conclude an agreement with one or more third countries or international organisations [ ... ]'[23]—and is implied on topics that relate to the broad spectrum of its objectives.

[19] See the memorandum of understanding between the Commission and the Sovereign Military Hospitaller Order of Saint John of Jerusalem of Rhodes and of Malta, signed in Brussels, 17 February 2009.

[20] *Reparation for Injuries Suffered in the Service of the United Nations* (Advisory Opinion) [1949] ICJ Rep 174, 179. See, for older case law, *SS Wimbledon* (*United Kingdom, France, Italy, and Japan v Germany*) (Judgment) [1923] PCIJ Ser A, No 1, 25.

[21] See Kirsten Schmalenbach, 'Article 6: The Capacity of States to Conclude Treaties' in Oliver Dörr and Kirsten Schmalenbach (eds), *Vienna Convention on the Law of Treaties: A Commentary* (Springer 2012) 113; Vera Gowlland Debbas, 'The Role of the International Court of Justice in the Development of the Contemporary Law of Treaties' in Christian J Tams and James Sloan (eds), *The Development of International Law by the International Court of Justice* (OUP 2013) 31; Finn Seyersted, 'Treaty-Making Capacity of International Organizations: Article 6 of the International Law Commission's Draft Articles on the Law of Treaties between States and International Organizations or between International Organizations' (1983) 34 ZöR 261.

[22] *Reparation for Injuries* (n 20);Vienna Convention on the Law of Treaties between States and International Organizations or between International Organizations, done in Vienna on 21 March 1986, not entered into force yet (hereafter VCLT–IO)). See Henry G Schermers and Niels M Blokker, *International Institutional Law: Unity Within Diversity* (5th edn, Nijhoff 2011) 1127, 1139.

[23] See also Arts 3(2) and 218 TFEU and Art 37 of the Consolidated Version of the Treaty on European Union [2012] OJ C326/01 (hereafter TEU).

The CJEU introduced an implied powers doctrine in the 1971 *ERTA* case. In Opinion 1/94, the Court's vision bears resemblance to the 'functional necessity' adopted by the ICJ in its *Reparation for Injuries* opinion. This case law was later codified in Article 216(1) TFEU, providing the implied powers theory with a Treaty basis.[24]

While it is undoubted that the EU has a general capacity to negotiate and conclude treaties with third countries, it is another thing to say that all arrangements entered into by the Union are treaties under PIL. This is by no means an issue original to the Union; many international agreements have had their treaty status questioned before national and international courts and panels.[25] The objective of the following sections is to analyse whether the EAs qualify as international treaties.

### 3.1.3.2 PIL's Definition of a Treaty

In the past, the question of what constitutes a treaty provoked intense debates within the International Law Commission (ILC), the broader academic community, and courts around the world. Prior to the codification of the law of treaties, the ILC studied the meaning of the term for over sixteen years.[26] Agreement, so it seems, could only be found on what are a treaty's basic characteristics. Irrespective of its name, by virtue of the customary international law (CIL) definition, a treaty takes the form of a consensual arrangement between two or more international legal subjects that creates rights and duties enforceable under PIL. As a result, CIL is not concerned with formalities. As the ICJ concluded in an oft-quoted phrase, a treaty may 'take a number of forms and be given a diversity of names'. The Permanent Court of International Justice (PCIJ) observed similar flexibility when it ruled that 'engagements may be taken in the form of treaties, conventions, declarations, agreements, protocols, or exchanges of notes'.[27] Paradoxically, the simplest way for parties to express a meeting of the minds is by writing it down. The Vienna Convention on the Law of Treaties (VCLT) incorporates this idea in Article 2(1)(*a*), defining a treaty as:

> an international agreement concluded between States in written form and governed by international law, whether embodied in a single instrument or in two or more related instruments and whatever its particular designation.[28]

It should be clear that the above definition only exists for the purposes of the VCLT. While the written from is not an intrinsic requirement of a treaty, for instance, oral agreements are excluded from the scope of the law of treaties as codified in the Vienna Convention.[29] At the same time, the definition's resonance in the international legal order clearly surpasses

[24] *Commission v Council (AETR/ERTA)* [1971] ECLI:EU:C:1971:32; Opinion 1/94 *Competence of the Community to conclude international agreements concerning services and the protection of intellectual property* [1994] ECLI:EU:C:1994:384. See, for a critical review of the codification, Robert Schütze, *European Constitutional Law* (2nd edn, CUP 2015) 272.

[25] See the illustrations provided by Jan Klabbers, *The Concept of Treaty in International Law* (Kluwer Law International 1996) 2–3.

[26] Mark E Villiger, *Commentary on the 1969 Vienna Convention on the Law of Treaties* (Martinus Nijhoff 2009) 13.

[27] *Maritime Delimination and Territorial Questions Case (Qatar v Bahrain)* (Judgment) [1994] ICJ Rep 112, paras 23–29; *Customs Regime between Germany and Austria* (Advisory Opinion) [1931] PCIJ Ser A/B, No 41, 14. See also ILC, 'Draft Articles on the Law of Treaties with Commentaries' (1966) II YBILC 188.

[28] Vienna Convention on the Law of Treaties, done in Vienna on 23 May 1969, entered into force 27 January 1980, 1155 UNTS 331.

[29] *Legal Status of Eastern Greenland (Denmark v Norway)* (Judgment) [1933] PCIJ Ser A/B, No 53; *Case Concerning the Temple of Preah Vihear (Cambodia v Thailand)* (Judgment) [1961] ICJ Rep 31.

the VCLT as it is widely used in the international practice, which includes not only states but also IOs. Article 2(1)(*a*) VCLT is grounded in CIL and over time has obtained the status of general law.[30] The VCLT's reference to states as the only possible parties to international agreements does not mean that an agreement concluded by an IO cannot constitute a treaty, nor that other components of the above definition are of no relevance to the EU or EAs. This is acknowledged in the Convention. For example, Article 3 VCLT confirms the validity and legal force of international agreements not covered by it. Therefore, the VCLT does not exclude the application of rules to EAs.[31]

Further, as is commonly known, the more recent 1986 Vienna Convention on the Law of Treaties between States and International Organizations or between International Organizations only (VCLT–IO), introduces an almost identical definition of treaties to the VCLT, confirming that a treaty is not substantially different when entered into by IOs. The observations made with regard to Article 2 of the 1969 Vienna Convention are *mutatis mutandis* applicable. The same goes for the other articles of the VCLT–IO, which make only minor concessions to match the special features of IOs.[32] The European Economic Community (EEC) participated in the 1986 conference but neither signed nor ratified the Convention. Hoffmeister argues that the reason why the Union has not yet ratified that 1986 Convention relates to the assessment that its specific rules did not fit the Community structure, as opposed to those of the 1969 Convention.[33] Likewise, the Court of Justice of the European Union (CJEU) is inclined to refer to the VCLT rather than the VCLT–IO when asked to rule on the law of treaties, including cases concerning agreements to which the EU is a signatory.[34] A similar observation was made with regard to the practice of other EU institutions.[35]

#### 3.1.3.3 Are EAs Treaties?

It transpires from the above introduced definition that three features must be present to refer to EAs as treaties under international law: they must create legal rights and obligations, they must be governed by PIL, and they must express consent. With regard to the last requirement, it can be observed that the ICJ in some case law replaced the notion of consent by that of a good faith acceptance.[36] The following section demonstrates that EAs fulfil all three conditions.

[30] Jan Klabbers, 'Qatar v Bahrain: The Concept of "Treaty" in International Law' (1995) 33 AVR 361, 366; Anthony Aust, *Modern Treaty Law and Practice* (3rd edn, CUP 2013) 14.

[31] Villiger (n 26) 59.

[32] Philippe Gautier, 'Article 2—Convention de 1986' in Olivier Corten and Pierre Klein (eds), *Les Conventions de Vienne sur le Droit des Traités* (Bruylant 2006) 83; Philippa Webb, 'Treaties and International Organizations: Uneasy Analogies' in Christian J Tams, Antonios Tzanakopoulos, and Andreas Zimmermann (eds), *Research Handbook on the Law of Treaties* (Edward Elgar 2014569.

[33] Philippe Manin, 'The European Communities and the Vienna Convention on the Law of Treaties between States and International Organizations or between International Organizations' (1987) 24 CML Rev 457; Catherine Brölmann, 'The 1986 Vienna Convention on the Law of Treaties: The History of Draft Article 36bis' in Jan Klabbers and René Lefeber (eds), *Essays on the Law of Treaties: A Collection of Essays in Honour of Bert Vierdag* (Martinus Nijhoff 1998); Frank Hoffmeister, 'The Contribution of EU Practice to International Law' in Marise Cremona (ed), *Developments in EU External Relations Law* (OUP 2008) 57.

[34] See the references to the VCLT in *Racke GmbH & Co v Hauptzollamt Mainz* [1998] ECLI:EU:C:1998:293, paras 49, 53, 58–59; *France v Commission* [1994] ECLI:EU:C:1994:305, paras 25, 27; and Opinion 1/13 *Convention on the civil aspects of child abduction* [2014] ECLI:EU:C:2014:2303, para 37.

[35] Pieter Jan Kuijper, 'The European Courts and the Law of Treaties: The Continuing Story' in Enzo Cannizzaro (ed), *The Law of Treaties beyond the Vienna Convention* (OUP 2011) 256.

[36] *Qatar v Bahrain* (n 27) para 27 and the *Nuclear Test Case (New Zealand v France)* (Judgment) [1974] ICJ Rep 457, 253.

*3.1.3.3.1 The design of establishment agreements*

PIL does not prescribe the procedure to conclude a treaty, nor does it matter how the treaty is formulated, what name it is given, and whether it is signed or not.[37] Over the years, a number of exotic forms of agreement have been accepted by international courts as treaties. In all of those cases, the context in which the treaties came about was crucial to establish that there was a joint will to enter into binding obligations.[38] Yet, and notwithstanding the more unconventional examples occasionally provided in international case law, most treaties actually look like treaties. The reason should be clear: a standardized format complete with a preamble, provisions, and signatures allows parties, government agents, and lawyers to recognize a treaty when they see one. International treaty law embodies the idea that formalities express the will to be bound. Article 11 VCLT lists a number of indicative means: an expression of consent by signature, an exchange of instruments constituting a treaty, ratification, acceptance, or approval, are all the accepted benchmarks.

The EU and third states negotiated a text on the establishment of diplomatic relations and wrote down the results of this process; an effort that shows they considered written evidence important to denote intentions. The EAs reflect a mutual will of the parties, notwithstanding one party's (the EU's) dominant position as exemplified by the general template imposed on third states.[39] Studying the EAs, one actually sees that the negotiation process allowed derivations from the template in terms of country-specific alterations and clauses. This includes small alterations to, or clarifications of, the general regime on immunities and privileges. Article 5 of the 1989 EA concluded with Guinee, for instance, repeats a general principle of international law when it explicitly states that persons enjoying privileges and immunities shall not be entitled to invoke immunity from the jurisdiction of the court in respect of any counterclaim arising out of the same legal relationship or facts as the principal claim.

The consistency with which formalistic elements are included is a strong indicator of the parties' intention to assume binding obligations. This goes both for EAs drafted in one document and those taking the form of an exchange of letters. The EAs adhere to Article 11 VLT for they include final phrases, signatures of the parties, and furthermore specify when the agreement enters into force.

A provision on the entry into force signposts not just the legally binding character of an agreement but also its consensual nature: the parties jointly decide on a date to start assuming rights and obligations. With the exception of seven EAs, the agreements concluded with the Holy See (exchange of letters, 1970), Israel (1980), Sudan (1985), São Tomé e Príncipe (1988), the Republic of North Macedonia (2000), North Korea (exchange of letters, 2002), and Panama (2013), all EAs contain said provision and refer to the fact that the relevant national or European procedures will be followed for the agreement to legitimately enter into force. Even with regard to the seven agreements mentioned, it must be highlighted that these are fully executed despite the lack of detail on the implementation.

[37] See the ILC (n 27) 188–89; Malcolm N Shaw, *International Law* (CUP 2014) 908.

[38] Signed minutes of a meeting among ministers of foreign affairs (*Qatar v Bahrain* (n 27) para 30), an exchange of letters (ibid paras 22 and 30), an oral promise (*Denmark v Norway* (n 29) 22–23), a joint press communiqué (*Pulp Mills on the River Uruguay (Argentina v Uruguay)* (Judgment) [2010] ICJ Rep 14, paras 138–40; *Aegean Sea Continental Shelf Case (Greece v Turkey)* (Judgment) [1978] ICJ Rep 3, para 96; *Ambatielos Case (Greece v United Kingdom)* (Preliminary objections) [1952] ICJ Rep 28, 44), a declaration which was later regretted by a party (*Delimitation of the Czechoslovak-Polish Frontier* (Advisory Opinion) [1923] PCIJ Ser B, No 8, paras 29–30), and a resolution adopted by the Council of the League of Nations (*Railway traffic between Lithuania and Poland* (Advisory Opinion) [1923] PCIJ Ser A/B, No 42, para 28).

[39] Anne-Laure Vaurs-Chaumette, 'La Question de la Reconnaissance' in Myriam Benlolo-Carabot, Ulas Candas, and Eglantine Cujo (eds), *Union Européenne et Droit International* (Pedone 2012) 248.

Furthermore, the careful listing of numbered provisions called 'rights and privileges' (Art 3 model EA) indicates the parties' intentions to adopt a legally binding framework. The most obvious sign of consent can be found in Article 1 model EA, for it literally spells out that the agreement that exists between parties to establish a diplomatic mission: '[t]he Government of [X] hereby agrees to the establishment on its territory of a Delegation of the European Union'.

While linguistic formalities are not a defining criterion per se, the language used in the EAs is particular. Typical treaty jargon is employed throughout the model EA. The agreements consciously use words specific to legal documents such as the verbs 'shall', 'agree', 'undertake', and 'enter into force'. All articles and subsections of the EA template employ the word 'shall', with the exception of Article 4, which uses '[t]he Government of [X] *hereby recognizes* [ . . . ]'. Article 2(1) states that the EU and the European Atomic Energy Community (EAEC) '*shall* each have legal personality on the territory of [X]'; and Article 2(2) mentions that they '*shall* have the capacity to conclude contracts, to acquire and dispose of immovable and movable property'. Moreover, the parties identify themselves as 'the contracting parties' (Arts 5–6), indicating that the obligations are not entered into loosely. In other words, formal features serve as the lingua franca of treaty-making, and the EAs speak it. If parties intended to conclude a memorandum of understanding (MoU), they probably would have been more inclined to use 'will' rather than 'shall' and to omit references to an entry into force.[40] The mandatory language supports the claim that EAs should be distinguished from normative gentlemen's agreements and other varieties of soft law and that parties willingly contracted in a specific and legally binding transaction. There does not seem to be many alternative ways to qualify international legal obligations. As Jan Klabbers puts it, 'a commitment is either legal, or it is no commitment at all'.[41]

*3.1.3.3.2 The content of establishment agreements*

The consensual nature of EAs stems not just from their outlook and wording; it equally transpires from the substance of clauses. A contextualized reading reveals that for both parties the primary purpose of an EA is to enter into diplomatic relations with one another and to identify general diplomatic law as the framework governing those. The embodiment of an exchange—a quid pro quo—in a treaty is not requisite under PIL, as confirmed by the CJEU.[42] It is nonetheless important to note that in an EA parties mutually pledge to a certain behaviour that would not be legally required in its absence. New rights and obligations are thus created. An assumption put forward by the ICJ is that the will to be bound in law contains a strong indicator of the legal bindingness in itself. While consent can be derived from an intentional act of the parties to enter into a transaction, it does not stand alone. The consensual nature of a treaty requires an obligatory element, an expression of the will to be bound in law rather than morally or politically.[43]

All but two of the EAs based on the model agreement explicitly refer to the 1961 Vienna Convention—a well-respected multilateral instrument that undoubtedly constitutes a treaty—as the go-to body of law. Through the technique of *renvoi*, EAs make the entire

[40] Aust (n 30) 30.

[41] Klabbers, *The Concept of Treaty* (n 25) 13.

[42] *Parliament v Council and Commission v Council* [2014] ECLI:EU:C:2014:2400 (hereafter *Venezuelan Fishing Rights*); Klabbers, *The Concept of Treaty* (n 25) 86.

[43] *Qatar v Bahrain* (n 27) para 30. In its opinion on the *Interpretation of the Agreement of 25 March 1951 between the WHO and Egypt* (Advisory Opinion) [1980] ICJ Rep 73, para 37, the ICJ confirmed that the requirement that parties are bound by the provisions of treaties to which they have adhered applies to IOs.

international legal regime applicable to relations that would normally not be covered by it. One may argue that the reference to the instrument also implies an agreement on the application of the interpretation of the Convention. The two exceptions are the arrangements entered into with Sudan (1985) and Singapore (2002). In both cases, the EU is given privileges and immunities that correspond to those accorded to other diplomats accredited to the host state. Since both are party to the VCDR and legally obliged to treat diplomats according to the Convention's standards, the EU will be granted VCDR privileges and immunities indirectly.

The VCDR's rights and obligations have not lost their binding character when applied in the relationship between the EU and third states. In fact, the EAs mention what happens in case of non-compliance by parties. First, more than half of the EAs contain a clause installing a quasi-judicial dispute settlement procedure that aims to arrive at conciliation in case of dispute. Such conciliation is a common mechanism to deal with disagreement in the diplomatic context. Second (and this goes for all EAs), a sanction mechanism is provided through the reciprocal character of rights and obligations embodied. Reciprocity is the oldest and most fundamentally known compliance mechanism in international diplomatic law. Denza notes that it 'forms a constant and effective sanction for the observance of nearly all the rules of the Convention'.[44] Reciprocity indeed serves as a powerful tool to ensure that the other party applies the standards of protection to foreign diplomats. In the event of a breach of EA by one party, retaliatory measures can be taken by the other party to the agreement. One could think of the restrictive reading of certain privileges accorded to the mission, a countermeasure often used to express a certain discontent in diplomatic relations.[45]

*3.1.3.3.3 Reception of establishment agreements by contracting parties*

A third way to discern consent and international legal commitments is to look at how parties treat EAs after their conclusion. Observations reveal that the EU exercises an active and passive right of legation.[46] Since missions in Brussels and abroad are granted diplomatic status and the accompanying privileges and immunities, the EAs produce the expected results. Their meticulous execution throughout the years furthermore exemplifies parties' commitment to abide by the respective obligations.

When international agreements are ratified, registered, or published in the official national journals, it leaves little doubt regarding the parties' intention to endow them with a binding character. States independently define how PIL impacts their national legal order; hence, diverse implementation practices are evident. For example, as the United States, Australia, Canada, and New Zealand show, there is a preference of common law tradition countries to transpose EA clauses in general codes on diplomatic privileges and immunities. Other countries publish the agreement in full, either in an official journal or national treaty series. In Norway, the EA is published in full in the Norwegian Treaty Series, for instance.[47] New Zealand combines a number of these techniques: the EA was presented to the House of Representatives, published in the Treaty Series, and inserted in the general privileges and

[44] Eileen Denza, *Diplomatic Law: Commentary on the Vienna Convention on Diplomatic Relations* (4th edn, OUP 2016) 2; Andrew L Odell, 'Enforcing Reciprocity in U.S. Diplomatic Relations: The Foreign Missions Act of 1982' (1984) 17 NYUJILP 817.

[45] Sanderijn Duquet and Jan Wouters, 'Legal Duties of Diplomats Today' in Paul Behrens (ed), *Diplomatic Law in a New Millennium* (OUP 2017).

[46] For a list of missions accredited to the Union, see the EEAS' Protocol Service's website, <https://www.europa.eu/eeas/diplomatic-list-missions-accredited-european-union_en> accessed 2 June 2022.

[47] For an overview, see Appendix 4.

immunities act, after which it entered into force officially. In certain cases, an entry into force requires an implementing act to be approved by the national parliament (eg Egypt) or approved by the executive (eg Nicaragua). In some countries, the entry into force of the EA requires both parliamentary and presidential approval (eg the Kyrgyz Republic). The differences in acceptance and ratification procedures relate to national constitutional systems and in principle are not of concern to PIL. What matters is that the fulfilment of procedural arrangements articulates the will of third states to be legally bound by them.

The EU's practices as regards the ratification and publication of EAs are perhaps surprising in light of the stakes involved. The EU's general practice on the reception and publication of international agreements is not applied to EAs. The Council does not adopt a final decision to conclude EAs; a procedure that would otherwise formally mark ratification. Moreover, the agreements are neither published in the EU Treaty Database nor the Official Journal. In fact, the Union merely informs third states of the 'completion' of its internal approval procedures after having entered into an EA, which internationally is an adequate way to express that a treaty exists in its internal sphere. One example is the Commission's note verbale addressed to the Mission of Albania to the European Communities, dated 17 September 1993. In this note, the Commission had 'the honour to inform the Mission of the completion by the Commission of the procedures necessary to the *approval* of the [EA]'. The same phrase was used in the note verbales addressed to the missions of Bangladesh (6 November 1989) and Eritrea (14 December 1994). In a note verbale addressed to the Mission of Ecuador, dated 20 April 2004, the Commission stated that 'all necessary steps have been completed so as to allow the Agreement to enter into force'. Similarly, a note verbale (dated 25 February 1998) addressed to the Ministry of Foreign Affairs (MFA) of Guatemala read that the agreement would enter into force on 23 January 1998. While it generally suffices that parties to an agreement sent a notification of approval to be bound by it, it remains disappointing that the EAs have not gone through more formal steps that would also allow for transparency and democratic control.

Somewhat surprisingly, none of the EAs is officially registered with the UN. This possibility, foreseen in Article 102 of the UN Charter, generally serves as a sound indicator of legally binding force.[48] In the absence of such registration, notwithstanding that the numerous clauses in the EAs, combined with their signing and execution, indicate a will to be bound in law, the discussion on legal bindingness may never be completely settled.

### 3.1.3.4 The EAs' Effects and Validity

The acceptance of EAs as treaties creates international legal consequences. It can be inferred that the EAs have become sources of PIL and that customary rules on the interpretation and execution of treaties apply to them. This is the case for the most basic principle regarding observance of treaties, that is, the principle of *pacta sunt servanda*. The rule that EAs must be respected and implemented in good faith is no more than a logical consequence of their consensual features.[49] A number of other rules that acquired CIL status equally bind EA parties. Without striving for completeness, this is the case for rules on the application of the treaties *ratione temporis* and *ratione loci*: Article 25 VCLT, for instance, allows the provisional application of treaties with the consent of the parties and Article 28 VCLT states that

[48] Charter of the United Nations, opened for signature on 26 June 1945, entered into force 24 October 1945, 1 UNTS XVI (hereafter UN Charter).

[49] Article 26 VCLT; *Certain German Interests in Polish Upper Silesia* (*Germany v Poland*) (Judgment) [1925] PCIJ Ser A, No 6, 30, 39; *Gabčíkovo-Nagymaros Project (Hungary v Slovakia)* (Judgment) [1997] ICJ Rep 7, para 114.

treaties cannot be retroactively applied unless a different intention appears from the treaty or is otherwise established. A treaty is binding in respect of the entire territory unless a different intention appears from the treaty or is otherwise established (Art 29 VCLT). The EAs establish such different intention with regard to the privileges and immunities to missions accredited to the Union in Brussels. It follows from the EA that the enjoyment is granted by Belgium and limited to the Belgian territory.

Other rules apply as well, such as those on the interpretation of treaties on the rules on the use of different language versions.[50] When a treaty has multiple language versions, the text is equally authoritative in each language unless the treaty provides otherwise (Art 33(1) VCLT). The EAs comply with this rule, as was explained earlier. However, one may question how Article 63 VCLT, which deals with the effects of a treaty termination, would play out in a situation in which an EA is terminated. With regard to changes in treaties after they have entered into force, it is interesting to note that CIL recognizes the possibility to amend treaties by tacit consent following a pattern of consistent behaviour.[51] The post-Lisbon transformation of Commission delegations into Union delegations in the absence of a formal amendment can be viewed as an example of such tacit change: third countries did not object to the EU's post-Lisbon notification that this change would take place. The continuity of the conduct of diplomatic relations was preserved accordingly. Although the change was significant for the EU's internal structure, it did not amount to a *rebus sic stantibus* situation under PIL. Ultimately, the circumstances only changed with regard to the institution that was represented (the Union instead of just the Commission), which for third countries arguably did not make that much of a difference. Yet another VCLT rule states that it is prohibited to create obligations for third states without their consent. Here, the EAs run up against the bounds of the parallel and bilateral application of a multilateral treaty. The VCDR spells out obligations that third states have to observe. While Article 40(1) can be enforced in a multilateral treaty system, it brings about complications in bilateral relationships. A third state is not bound by the EA concluded between the EU and another state, not even when it has concluded an EA of its own with the EU.

Occasionally, treaties are deemed invalid. This is a rare event since invalidity must be invoked by one of the parties on the ground of error, fraud, corruption, coercion, or because a consent to be bound was effected in a manner that violated domestic law in a manifest way.[52] Taking into account the purpose and effect of EAs, such claims are unlikely to be made. The subjects of international law are entitled to conclude an agreement on any subject matter with only two exceptions. First, when concluding a treaty, the parties cannot contravene a peremptory norm of international law (Art 53 VCLT), and second, the parties cannot set rights and obligations that conflict with those which the member states have undertaken under the UN Charter (Art 103 UN Charter). No EA violates either restriction. The UN Charter contains few references to diplomatic relations, yet Article 41 spells out the right of the UN Security Council (UNSC) 'to decide what measures not involving the use of armed force are to be employed to give effect to its decisions', which may include 'the severance of diplomatic relations'. Consequently, the EAs cannot (and do not) limit this right.

[50] Olivier Corten and Pierre Klein, *The Vienna Conventions on the Law of Treaties: A Commentary* (OUP 2011) 681.

[51] Richard D Kearney and Robert E Dalton, 'The Treaty on Treaties' (1970) 64 AJIL 495, 525.

[52] Article 46 VCLT.

### 3.1.3.5 UN and EU Practices Compared

Over the years, many IOs have entered into agreements on rights and privileges of their staff and representatives. Every IO enjoys the so-called inherent right to manage its own status, implying the power to enter into such treaties.[53] An example would be the administrative agreements on diplomatic privileges and immunities concluded by the UN. The exact point of reference is a particular category of agreements concluded by the UN in the late 1940s and early 1950s. At the time, similarly to EUDELs today, UN missions in non-member states executed a general representational task whereby the staff received diplomatic status from the host government. In the absence of a clear delegation of powers, the UN Secretary General (UNSG) used their general competences as the UN's chief administrative officer to enter into agreements, the purpose of which was to define the status of UN offices and of its personnel on the territories of third states. Such agreements with UN member states are governed, first, by Articles 104 and 105 of the UN Charter, which apply as between the UN and its members, and second, by the provisions of the 1946 CPIUN. The UN Charter does not accord the UNSG the power to conduct an independent foreign policy. However, successive holders of the office have held that they were entitled to send diplomatic representatives. The UNSG concluded agreements with Switzerland and Japan[54] and exchanged letters with the Republic of Korea[55] and the Italian representatives of Somaliland,[56] all concerning the immunities, privileges, and right of entry into the host state of officials posted in UN permanent missions.[57] While in principle a formal agreement on the cooperation of the UN with other entities requires the express authorization of the UN General Assembly (UNGA) or another competent deliberative organ, this is not necessarily the case with regard to agreements on the privileges and immunities of staff abroad. In the absence of such appropriate authority, the UN office of legal affairs recommends that 'these relationships be based on an informal memorandum of understanding and not on a formal agreement'.[58]

The resemblance in design and content of the older UN's agreements to the EAs is striking. It leads one to believe that the Commission's legal service strongly relied upon them when drafting their own EAs. First, the UNSG arrangements define the UN's capacity *(a)* to contract, *(b)* to acquire and dispose of immovable and movable property, and *(c)* to institute legal proceedings. This enumeration sounds familiar. The EAs grant the same three competences to EU Heads of Delegation. One notes that the origins of the phrase lie in Article I (section 1) of the Convention on Privileges and Immunities of the United Nations (CPIUN). Second, the agreements explicitly state that the UN 'shall possess juridical personality'. Third, the agreements implement Article VII of the CPIUN on the facilities to be accorded to the holders of the UN laissez-passer (UNLP). The wording of Article VII CPIUN is contained

[53] Schermers and Blokker (n 22) 1127, 1139.

[54] See the interim arrangements on privileges and immunities of the UN, concluded between the UNSG and the Swiss Federal Council, signed on 11 June 1946, 1 UNTS 165 and the UNSG and Japan, signed on 25 July 1952, 135 UNTS 373.

[55] Exchange of Letters constituting an Agreement between the UN Secretary-General and the Republic of Korea regarding Privileges and Immunities to be enjoyed by the United Nations in Korea, signed on 21 September 1951, 104 UNTS 323.

[56] Exchange of Letters constituting an Agreement between UN Secretary-General and the Italian Observer to the UN on Privileges and Immunities of the Advisory Council for Somaliland, as reprinted in the *Handbook on the Legal Status, Privileges and Immunities of the United Nations*, 77–91.

[57] Jean Aimé Stoll, 'Le Statut Juridique du Représentant-Résident du Bureau de l'Assistance Technique des Nations Unies dans l'État où il est Accrédité' (1964) 10 AFDI 14.

[58] Michael Hardy, 'The Diplomatic Activities of International Organisations: The United Nations and the European Communities Contrasted' (1969) 5 RBDI 44, 51–55; and UNYearb 1981 at 149, as referred to in Schermers and Blokker (n 22) 1137–38.

in the Swiss Interim Arrangement. Japan, Korea, and Italy (for Somaliland) similarly recognized and accepted the laissez-passer as a valid travel document in accordance with the provisions of Article VII CPIUN. All of the above elements appear more or less word for word in the EAs. Fourth, and more practically, a comparison can be drawn in that the agreements are dominated by one party (the UNSG, respectively the Commission/HR) and based upon a model agreement, subject to some minor deviations depending on the case.

Further comparison between EAs and the UNSG's agreements also reveals dissimilarities. In contrast to the EAs, the UN agreements are not diplomatic but administrative in nature. They merely indicate the existence of an early practice of permanent technical missions of IOs, the main objective of which was the proper functioning of the (almost universal) organization in non-member states. The agreements' purpose was to allow for missions of personnel to those states while also ensuring their protection—only incidentally did this result in the enjoyment of diplomatic privileges and immunities. The UN agreements do not feature the possibility of a formal diplomatic accreditation of the UN mission to the host state. The only section in the EAs that is truly unilateral and, in a way, administrative, is the one on the recognition of the EU laissez-passer. The EA's scope is much broader: the agreements properly establish full diplomatic relations with third states and therefore cannot be reduced to a mere application of the inherent right of IOs to deal with the organization's or their staff's status. Moreover, the EAs establish reciprocal rights and obligations. For these reasons, the UNSG's agreements should be distinguished from the EAs, even though under the former agreements of individual staff members may equally have enjoyed diplomatic privileges and immunities. Other VCDR principles only applied when it was specifically agreed, while the EAs' *renvoi* provision makes the entire Vienna Convention applicable.

## 3.1.4 The Status of EAs under EU Law

### 3.1.4.1 Introduction

The previous section revealed that there are few objections to recognizing the EAs as treaties for the purposes of PIL. Dealing with the same issue under EU law provokes more glitches. To successfully interact with other international subjects, the Union uses a predefined set of instruments. In Article 288 TFEU, such instruments at the disposal of the Union institutions (thus excluding the HR) are listed without preventing those institutions from producing legal effects by means of other instruments.[59] In simplified terms: if legally binding effects are not desired, the EU adopts MoUs or joint declarations; where legally binding effects are intended, it enacts international agreements or autonomous acts. When concluding both binding and non-binding instruments, the Union has to respect the principle of conferral of powers and the division of competences between institutions.[60]

The EU's diplomatic arrangements with third countries do not fit easily with the aforementioned typology of instruments. Some diplomatic arrangements simply lie outside the remit of EU law. This is true for cases where the Commission requested third states to adopt or adapt national laws. As far as EU law is concerned, these qualify as unilateral concessions of host states.[61] This is different for the EAs, which conceptually come close to 'international

[59] Bart Van Vooren and Ramses A Wessel, *EU External Relations Law: Text, Cases and Materials* (CUP 2014) 34.
[60] *Council v Commission* [2016] ECLI:EU:C:2016:616, paras 25, 40.
[61] But see *Venezuelan Fishing Rights* (n 42).

agreements': there are strong indications of the legal force of EAs in the international legal order, thereby precluding their soft law nature; moreover, they are of a bilateral nature and thereby not merely unilateral positions.

yet, none of the EAs was concluded as an 'international agreement' on the basis of the treaty-making procedure laid down in EU law. The reason why is somewhat unclear but most likely relates to the practical considerations of avoiding the procedural burden associated with treaty-making procedures that slow down the process or require additional efforts. The following sections examine whether legal rules exist(ed) that impede EAs' adoption as treaties and/or whether alternative qualifications are opportune and legally acceptable.

### 3.1.4.2 The Road Not Taken: EAs as International Agreements

#### *3.1.4.2.1 What is a treaty in the EU legal order?*

The CJEU has on various occasions defined the concept of an international agreement for the purposes of EU law. Doing so, the Court relies on PIL's holistic definition of a treaty and interprets the term in a general and functional sense.[62] The influence of international law is clear via the Court's echoing that an international agreement is 'any undertaking entered into by entities subject to international law which has binding force, whatever its formal designation'.[63] According to the Court, a treaty's legally binding character stems from the parties' intention as expressed in the text or by context. Much like in international case law, the use of specific terms such as 'should' or 'will' rather than 'shall' are deemed less conclusive factors. However, it is clear that when the will of the parties not to enter in a legally binding instrument is reiterated throughout the negotiations, this may lead to the conclusion that the instrument is not an international agreement.[64] Later case law establishes the criterion of consent more explicitly. The Court now requires international agreements to reflect a 'meeting of the minds' or to express 'the convergence of intent on the part of two or more subjects of international law'. Such 'convergence of intent' can be established on the basis of an offer and acceptance in an agreement without it being necessary that performances of the parties are equal.[65]

Based on the CJEU's jurisprudence, nothing outwardly excludes EAs from bearing the label of an international agreement. An EA reflects the Union's and a third state's joint will to exchange diplomatic representatives on a permanent basis and incorporates commitments that facilitate such interactions. Moreover, the topic of diplomatic privileges and immunities is far from new to EU treaty-making rules. Under the Common Security and Defence Policy (CSDP), the Union regularly concludes international agreements that lay down the rights and duties of forces and personnel in third states.[66] So-called status of forces agreements and status of mission agreements (SOFAs/SOMAs), often taking the form of an exchange of letters, grant military or civilian missions a similar status to diplomatic missions in countries of posting for a specific period of time whereby the top-ranking staff also often enjoys

[62] Piet Eeckhout, *EU External Relations Law* (OUP 2011) 195; Panos Koutrakos, *EU International Relations Law* (2nd edn, Hart 2015) 137.

[63] Opinion 1/75 *Draft Understanding on a Local Cost Standard drawn up under the auspices of the OECD* [1975] ECLI:EU:C:1975:145, 1360; Opinion 2/92 *Competence of the Community or one of its institutions to participate in the Third Revised Decision of the OECD on national treatment* [1995] ECLI:EU:C:1995:83, para 8; *France v Commission* [1994] ECLI:ECLI:EU:C:1994:305, para 27; *Venezuelan Fishing Rights* (n 42) para 83.

[64] Case C-233/02 *France v Commission* [2004] ECLI:EU:C:2004:173, paras 42–44.

[65] Opinion 1/13 (n 34) para 37; and especially *Venezuelan Fishing Rights* (n 42) paras 71–73, 96.

[66] Panos Koutrakos, 'International Agreements in the Area of the EU's Common Security and Defence Policy' in Enzo Cannizzaro, Paolo Palchetti, and Ramses A Wessel (eds), *International Law as Law of the European Union* (Martinus Nijhoff 2012) 175 et seq.

diplomatic privileges and immunities. The granting of privileges and immunities equivalent to that of a diplomatic mission and diplomatic personnel is commonly only reserved for the top officials of a mission.[67] Older SOFAs/SOMAs contained a *renvoi* to the 1961 Vienna Convention, a feature no longer present in later agreements, and had a much broader application, which was also criticized.[68] In recent SOFAs/SOMAs, privileges and immunities often are stripped from the reference to the VCDR.[69] A second example of agreements applying diplomatic privileges and immunities concerns international agreements facilitating the sending of EU Special Representatives to third countries. Through agreements with host states, these ad hoc representatives acquire VCDR privileges and immunities in the course of the missions so that their status is comparable to states' ad hoc diplomats.[70]

Two observations lead to the conclusion that EAs fulfil the conditions of international agreements in the EU legal order. First, EAs purposely create consensual international rights and obligations, and second, the topic of diplomatic privileges and immunities is suitable for codification. However, for the EU to conclude such international agreements, a legal basis must be established and appropriate procedures must be observed.

#### *3.1.4.2.2 First-generation EAs*

EU primary law defines the Union's treaty-making competences. In the complex system of legal provisions scattered across EU treaties, there is no obvious legal basis for the EU to conclude international agreements establishing diplomatic relations. When the Commission kicked off its legation practice, EU external relations law was still rather undeveloped. The original version of the European Economic Community (EEC) Treaty comprised of only two legal basis expressly authorizing the Community to enter into international agreements. One was what later became Article 207 TFEU on the Common Commercial Policy; the other one was (the current) Article 217 TFEU on association agreements.[71] However, even when the number of explicit external relations legal bases increased, the EU legal regime remained silent on the possible forms of action available to the Commission in pursuing its diplomatic aspirations.[72]

In the absence of an explicit Treaty provision, it is worthwhile to research whether the EAs could have been concluded on another legal basis. A first possibility is the conclusion on the basis of implied treaty-making powers. Especially in its early days, the Commission structured and ran its delegations as extension of the Brussels-based administration. This was quite logical since Commission delegations initially only represented the EEC; only after 1993 did they follow the hybrid EU foreign policy system.[73] Delegations were largely

[67] Frederik Naert, *International Law Aspects of the EU's Security and Defence Policy* (Intersentia 2010) 250; Aurel Sari, 'Status of Forces and Status of Mission Agreements under the ESDP: The EU's Evolving Practice' (2008) 19 EJIL 67, 78–79.

[68] Council, 'Generic Status of Force Agreement for police missions—Immunities and privileges for EU Mission personnel', 17 December 2002.

[69] See Art 6 of the Agreement between the EU and the Republic of Niger on the status of the EU mission in Niger CSDP (EUCAP Sahel Niger) [2013] OJ L242/2; Art 5 of the Agreement between the EU and Ukraine on the status of the EU Advisory Mission for Civilian Security Sector Reform Ukraine (EUAM Ukraine) [2004] OJ L334/3.

[70] See, by way of example, Art 2 of the Agreement between the EU and the Government of Georgia on the status of the EU Special Representative for the South Caucasus [2004] OJ L135/14.

[71] Ex-Arts 113–14 and 238 Treaty Establishing the European Economic Community, 25 March 1957 (hereafter EEC Treaty). See, for further reading, Alan Dashwood, 'The Attribution of External Relations Competence' in Alan Dashwood and Christophe Hillion (eds), *The General Law of EC External Relations* (Sweet & Maxwell 2000) 119.

[72] Anthony Arnull and Derrick Wyatt (eds), *Wyatt and Dashwood's European Union Law* (6th edn, Hart 2011) 910.

[73] Michael H Smith, 'Does the Flag Still Follow Trade? Implications for European Union Diplomatic Practices in Third Countries' (2018) 13 HJD 41.

occupied with administering Commission programmes, budgets, and instruments abroad. In other words, the Commission's delegations were a vehicle through which internal competences were realized.

The question arises how well this argument is supported in case law on implied powers. The Court recognized the existence of implied external competences on the basis of two principles. First, in its 1979 European Free Trade Association (ERTA) judgment, the Court decided that the inability of member states to act internationally in cases where the EU exercises internal competence to adopt common rules is compensated by the existence of implied external competences to be used by the Union. The decision gave the Commission a certain leeway to conclude treaties in domains where it was the competent internal actor to prevent member states' external action affecting common policies: 'such authority arises not only from an express conferment by the Treaty [ ... ] but may equally flow from other provisions of the treaty and from measures adopted, within the framework of those provisions, by the Community institutions'.[74] Second, the Court introduced the complementarity principle in its Opinion 1/76. Complementarity means that whenever EU law confers internal competences on the institutions to attain a specific objective, the Union can enter into the necessary international commitments to attain those objective even in the absence of any express provision to that effect.[75] Complementarity applies even in the absence of prior EU internal legislation.[76] Yet, the threshold for corresponding external competences is rather high. Complementarity only surfaces when internal Union competences are truly indispensable. Both the ERTA and the complementarity theory introduced a more flexible reading of primary law, allowing the Community to enter into treaties in its own authority. Nevertheless, the strict conditions for such an undertaking reflect that implied external competences have a special status and are, in fact, the exception to the rule. Over the years, the Commission made several attempts at extending the principles on implied external competences beyond the bounds set by the Court. To enlarge its playing field, the Commission constructed an argument whereby a general parallelism exists between the Union's internal and external fields. This '*in foro interno, in foro externo*' reasoning has been repeatedly rejected by the Court and therefore the Union cannot be said to enjoy implied external competence beyond the two pre-defined circumstances as per the relevant case law.[77]

On the basis of the Luxembourg case law, it is difficult to argue that the ERTA ruling and the complementarity principle provided the Commission with a definite legal basis for the conclusion of EAs. The ERTA effect is only at play when common internal rules are established. Diplomatic relations do not fit easily in the definition of 'common rules'. They are not related to a particular policy but should be conceived as a means of taking action in respect of a panoply of competences conferred to the Union. Moreover, member states remain diplomatic actors in their own right while also acting alongside the Union to diplomatically

[74] *AETR/ERTA* (n 24) para 16. See also Opinion 1/03 *Lugano Convention* [2006] ECLI:EU:C:2006:81. Generally, Theodore Konstadinidies, 'EU Foreign Policy under the Doctrine of Implied Powers: Codification Drawbacks and Constitutional Limitations' (2014) 39 ELR 511.

[75] Opinion 1/76 *Inland Waterway Vessels* [1977] ECLI:EU:C:1977:63, para 3; Opinion 2/94 *Accession by the Community to the European Convention for the Protection of Human Rights and Fundamental Freedoms* [1996] ECLI:EU:C:1996:140, para 26. See also: Pieter Jan Kuijper, 'The Evolution of the Third Pillar from Maastricht to the European Constitution: Institutional Aspects' [2004] 41 CML Rev 609.

[76] Geert De Baere, *Constitutional Principles of EU External Relations* (OUP 2008) 52–58; Christophe Hillion and Ramses A Wessel, 'Competence Distribution in EU External Relations after Ecowas: Clarification or Continued Fuzziness?' (2009) 46 CML Rev 551.

[77] Javier Roldán Barbero, 'The Relationship of the Member States' International Agreements with the EU', in Piet Eeckhout and Manuel Lopez-Escudero (eds), *The European Union's External Action in Times of Crisis* (Bloomsbury 2016) 264.

defend individual interests. Given that the conduct of diplomatic relations *an sich* is not construed as necessarily exclusive, the risk that member state action affects the general conduct of EU diplomacy is therefore limited. Finally, the ERTA ruling is on the subject of the agreement itself, on the finding of a legal basis, but it does not say much about the potential effect the EAs may have on the external exercise of common rules. In its 2017 Opinion 2/15 on the Singapore Agreement, the Court explained that its quest to look for a legal basis is 'entirely without prejudice to the question whether the content of the agreement's provisions is compatible with EU law'.[78]

At least in its pre-2009 understanding, complementarity required the existence of a shared or exclusive objective that could not be reasonably exercised without external action. Generally, diplomacy satisfies the external Community objectives: the exercise of Commission competences via diplomatic relations responds well to the general needs of multilateral and bilateral relations. However, for complementarity to apply it needs to be accepted that the Union's internal competences could not have been exercised without the establishment of diplomatic relations and consequently the conclusion of EAs. When member states entrusted competences to the Union, an attendant discretion on their exercise was included. The Treaties are not conclusive on the means to execute international relations and how these measure up. Article 3(6) TEU merely states that '[t]he Union shall pursue its objectives by appropriate means commensurate with the competences which are conferred upon it in the Treaties'. However, in Chapter 2, it was concluded that failing to engage in diplomacy would show a lack of cognizance to the world's functioning and demands. It therefore could have been argued that the necessity for the Commission to conduct diplomatic relations satisfied the complementarity criteria.

As an alternative, older literature sometimes presented a third potential implied legal basis for Commission EAs. It introduced the idea that diplomatic relations could have been established on the basis of the former Article 235 of EEC Treaty ('the flexibility clause') and its successors, which reads:

> [i]f any action by the Community appears necessary to achieve, in the functioning of the Common Market, one of the aims of the Community in cases where this Treaty has not provided for the requisite powers of action, the Council, acting by means of a unanimous vote on a proposal of the Commission and after the Assembly has been consulted, shall enact the appropriate provisions.[79]

The provision enabled the Community to achieve its internal objectives at the international level where the Treaties were silent on the matter. Opinion 1/94 explains that the provision: 'enables the Community to cope with any insufficiency in the powers conferred on it, expressly or by implication, for the achievement of its objectives, that article cannot in itself vest exclusive competence in the Community at international level'.[80] Pescatore argued in 1961 that the only way to create common external bodies without formally revising the Treaties was through Article 235 EEC.[81] The contrasting view was upheld by Verwey, who

[78] Opinion 1/03 *Lugano Convention* (n 74) para 120; Opinion 2/15 *Singapore Agreement* [2017] ECLI:ECLI:EU:C:2017:376, para 30.

[79] Subsequently Art 235 TEC (1992 Maastricht Treaty); Art 308 TEC (1997 Amsterdam Treaty), now Art 352(1) TFEU.

[80] Opinion 1/94 (n 24) para 89.

[81] Pierre Pescatore, 'Les Relations Extérieurs de la Communauté Européenne' (1961) 103 Hague Recueil 1, 195.

argued that treaty-making procedures are too precisely formulated to include the EA practice in the article.[82]

Using the flexibility provision as a legal basis to conclude EAs would have required the satisfaction of three conditions. First, one has to accept that the Commission delegations facilitated the functioning of the internal market.[83] Second, even though over the years it was accorded wide interpretations, Article 235 EEC Treaty in principle could not be used to enlarge the scope of Community competences.[84] The final and strongest reason against the use of Article 235 EEC Treaty is its subsidiary character: the use of the provision assumes a true lacuna in the Treaties.[85] In other words, it required a confirmation that diplomatic relations were *not* an implied power but in fact a completely new competence not yet transferred by the member states.[86]

#### *3.1.4.2.3 Second-generation EAs*

The HR concludes EAs in a new legal context. Delegations shifted from housing civil servants of the Commission that administered budgets and instruments via diplomatic means to fully fledged diplomatic missions that represent the entire Union even if the EUDELs were never completely freed from operational task.[87] The rebranding of delegations moreover emphasizes their CFSP label: the Treaties promote the interaction of and cooperation between the diplomatic missions of the member states and the EUDELs in third countries (Art 32 TEU). Moreover, the task of representing the EU externally for CFSP matters, transferred from the rotating presidency to the HR (Arts 18 and 27(2) TEU). In the meantime, the EU Treaties also clarified the Union's competence to conclude international agreements and the applicable procedures. According to Article 216(1) TFEU, codifying the case law in the field, the Union can close an agreement with one or more third countries not just *(a)* 'where the Treaties so provide' but also *(b)* when the Treaties imply such competence.

With regard to *(a)*, it should be reiterated that similarly to its predecessors, the Lisbon Treaty does not introduce a specific legal basis for the conclusion of EAs. However, the Treaties now contain a general competence to conclude international agreements in the CFSP domain (Art 37 TEU) providing that the 'Union may conclude agreements with one or more States or international organisations in areas covered by this Chapter'. The competence is not derived from an internal power and rests on the autonomous role given to the Union in Article 24 TEU. Barents argues that Article 24(1)'s phrasing 'all areas of foreign policy' means that the Union's policy has the same scope but not necessarily the same substance as the foreign policy of a state.[88] Certainly, the role is sufficiently broad to encompass the diplomatic relations of the EU in its present form. The provision has also already been relied upon by the Union to conclude treaties dealing with ad hoc diplomacy. Agreements concluded with third countries on the status of EU Special Representatives, for instance, find their legal basis in

[82] Delano R Verwey, *The European Community, the European Union, and the International Law of Treaties* (TMC Asser Press 2004) 43.

[83] Opinion 2/94 (n 75) para 29.

[84] ibid, paras 34–35; *Kadi and Al Barakaat International Foundation v Council* [2008] ECLI:EU:C:2008:461, para 224; Opinion 2/15 (n 78).

[85] Rachel Frid, *The Relations between the EC and International Organizations: Legal Theory and Practice* (Martinus Nijhoff 1995) 90–91.

[86] Opinion 2/94 (n 75) para 28.

[87] Simon Duke, 'The Practices of Post-Lisbon Diplomacy' in Michael Smith, Stephan Keukeleire, and Sophie Vanhoonacker (eds), *The Diplomatic System of the European Union: Evolution, Change and Challenges* (Routledge 2016) 64.

[88] René Barents, *Het Verdrag van Lissabon: Achtergronden en Commentaar* (Kluwer 2008) 647–48; Schütze, *European Constitutional Law* (n 24) 108.

Article 37 TEU.[89] It is only agreements in the diplomatic field dealing with practicalities such as visas for third-country diplomats that have been concluded on the basis of Article 77(2)(*a*) TEU on the common policies on border checks, asylum, and immigration.[90] This leads to the conclusion that, if it had wanted to, the Union could have also concluded the agreements regarding its permanent diplomatic relations on the basis of Article 37 TEU.

Possibility *(b)* reverts to the discussion on implied external powers. Article 216(1) TFEU is the Treaty basis for implied competences in the post-Lisbon era. It provides three scenarios whereby an international agreement (i) is likely to affect common rules or alter their scope (*ERTA*), (ii) is necessary to achieve one of the objectives referred to in the Treaties (*complementarity*), or (iii) is provided in a legally binding Union Act.

Scenario (i) codifies the *ERTA* doctrine discussed earlier.[91] Article 216(1) TFEU promulgates that:

> [t]he Union may conclude an agreement with one or more third countries or international organisations [ . . . ] where the conclusion of an agreement [ . . . ] is likely to affect common rules or alter their scope.

The text is ambiguous on whether the requirement that an international agreement 'may affect' common EU rules carries a different meaning than the one given to it by the Court. Scholarship pointed out that the wording was not particularly favourable to the existence of shared implied powers. If, as Article 216(1)'s text suggests, it only applies to exclusive competences, the conclusion of international agreements on the Union's diplomatic relations may not, or no longer, find their legal basis in the ERTA doctrine.[92]

The rule on complementarity found its way to Article 216(1) TFEU in scenario (ii), providing that:

> [t]he Union may conclude an agreement with one or more third countries or international organisations [ . . . ] where the conclusion of an agreement is necessary in order to achieve, within the framework of the Union's policies, one of the objectives referred to in the Treaties [ . . . ].

Article 216(1) TFEU clarifies that the complementarity theory ensures the optimal exercise of EU objectives. More so than ever, the Treaties now indeed inextricably link action in diplomatic relations to the Union's objectives. The Union is legally obliged to 'develop relations and build partnerships with third countries, and international, regional or global organisations which share the principles referred to in the first subparagraph [of Article 21(1) TEU]'. The conduct of diplomacy is not just an objective in itself but a vehicle through which the broad spectrum of foreign policy objectives of Article 21(2) TEU is expressed. Similarly to diplomatic missions of states, EUDELs protect the Union's interests abroad and realize the objectives to safeguard the Union's 'values, fundamental interests,

[89] See the EU–Georgia Agreement (n 70).

[90] See, eg the Agreement between the EU and the Federative Republic of Brazil on short-stay visa waiver for holders of diplomatic, service or official passports [2011] OJ L66/2; Agreement between the EU and the People's Republic of China on the short-stay visa waiver for holders of diplomatic passports [2016] OJ L76/19.

[91] Thomas Verellen, 'The ERTA Doctrine in the Post-Lisbon Era: Note under Judgment in Commission v Council (C-114/12) and Opinion 1/13' (2013) 21 Colum J EurL 383.

[92] Marise Cremona, 'A Constitutional Basis for Effective External Action?' (2006) EUI Working Paper 1, 10–11; Robert Schütze, 'Lisbon and the Federal Order of Competences: A Prospective Analysis' (2008) 33 ELR 709, 713.

security, independence and integrity'. Moreover, European actors are legally obliged to work towards the realization of specific objectives such as the promotion of peace, values, interests, and the protection of citizens (Art 3(5) TEU). Often, the most effective way to attain these goals in highly political or sensitive circumstances (eg the negotiation of a peace agreement or a nuclear deal) is through the conduct of diplomatic relations. With the EU's increasingly engaged role on the global arena, the means of diplomatic relations have become indispensable in obtaining goals on the international scene. The EAs permitting for long-lasting relationships with external actors can therefore find their legal basis in the complementarity principle.

In scenario (iii), Article 216(1) TFEU enables the Union to conclude international agreements when this 'is provided for in a legally binding Union act'. Doing so encompasses the possibility for secondary EU law to provide a mandate for international action. As discussed in section 3.1.1, the 2010 EEAS Decision adopted in the wake of the Lisbon reform gives the HR permission to enter into the 'necessary arrangements' related to the Union's diplomatic relations. The power to initiate diplomatic arrangement therefore flows from the Council's delegation of power to the HR. It is undisputed that the EEAS Decision qualifies as a legally binding Union Act as understood in Article 216(1) TFEU. Rather, the issue here seems to be whether the language of Article 5(6) EEAS Decision—'arrangements'—is sufficiently clear to serve as the legal basis to conclude EAs amounting to international agreements.

The wording of the EEAS Decision in different languages deserves close scrutiny. In the Italian version 'accordi' is used, whilst the Spanish version uses 'acuerdos'; exactly the same terms in those languages as feature in Article 218 TFEU. Linguistic resemblances with the term 'agreements' are much more significant when compared to the English version's reference to 'arrangements' and even more so when compared to the weaker French notions of 'mesures' and the Dutch 'maatregelen'. The German version uses 'Vereinbarungen', while Article 218 TFEU refers to 'Übereinkünfte'. The only certainty resulting from this babelesque discussion is that the Council Decision did not unequivocally opt to conclude EAs as international agreements but did not rule out the possibility either. This provides the necessary policy space on the part of the EU institutions and bodies but nevertheless raises the question of how Article 5(6) EEAS Decision can be reconciled with Article 216(1) TFEU. Moreover, the chances of successfully invoking the flexibility clause of Article 352(1) TFEU (the successor to Art 235 EEC Treaty and Art 308 EC Treaty) as a legal basis are even fewer than before 2009: Article 352(4) TFEU (*cf* Art 40, second paragraph, TEU) provides that the flexibility clause cannot be invoked to attain objectives pertaining to the CFSP nor can the implementation of CFSP policies affect the application of established treaty-making procedures.

Finally, it has to be pointed out that the use of an external instrument not explicitly foreseen in the EU Treaties is not exceptional. In the past, much less obvious instruments have been regarded as international agreement by the CJEU. For example, the Court considered a unilaterally binding declaration in the *Venezuelan Fishing Rights* judgment to constitute an international agreement for the purposes of Article 218 TFEU.[93] The judgment also invalidated the hypothesis that rules on international agreements can be applied to external action instruments not foreseen in the Treaties by analogy, without requalifying such instruments as treaties.[94]

[93] *Venezuelan Fishing Rights* (n 42) paras 83–85.
[94] Opinion of AG Sharpston in *Venezuelan Fishing Rights* [2014] ECLI:EU:C:2014:334.

*3.1.4.2.4 Procedural questions*

Based on the above, there do not appear to be convincing reasons for denying that EAs could have been concluded as international agreements on the basis of the implied competences of the Community/Union or, later on, potentially even on the basis of the mandate provided for in the EEAS Decision. Accepting that EAs are international agreements, in any of the above legal scenarios, has an automatic consequence that EU treaty-making procedures should have been followed. The exact procedure applicable would have depended on the preliminary choice of the substantive legal basis for the adoption of the EA. Both aspects are inherently linked to each other since the legal basis of an action determines the procedures to be followed within the options presented by Article 218 TFEU.[95] By itself, the absence of a separate procedure for the conclusion of EAs should not cause a problem, as in the past the Court has found ways to adapt the application of the Treaties to the needs of the EU's external relations.[96]

Finding the precise procedural basis for the EAs is challenging. When competences are implied, the procedural rules relied upon are the same as those governing explicit action. EAs give effect to both CFSP and non-CFSP competences since they facilitate the establishment of delegations representing the whole Union. On the one hand, EUDELs are the prime CFSP actors placed under the authority and control of the HR in its role as EEAS chief. On the other hand, partly due to the historical kinship, EUDELs also represent the Commission's non-CFSP competences. Furthermore, practice shows that in many delegations over half the staff engage in trade policy and/or development cooperation, the Commission's playground.

As various objectives are inseparably linked without being incidental to the others, the question arises whether EAs should have been based on two, or more, legal bases. Longstanding CJEU case law accepts the use of a dual legal basis, combining CFSP and non-CFSP competences of EU external actions, when objective factors (eg the aims and content of Union instruments) so require. However, a dual legal basis is not possible where these legal bases require procedures that are irreconcilable.[97] For instruments simultaneously triggering procedurally incompatible procedures, the Court gives priority to the main or overarching legal basis.[98] When the Commission's overall involvement in diplomacy was much more prominent in the past, a non-CFSP legal basis probably could have been selected (former Art 228 EEC Treaty). The Commission would have been the logical choice to conduct negotiations on the agreements, with the Council concluding them in name of the Community.[99] However, in their current form EAs increasingly relate to CFSP.[100] The hypothesis contains an element of paradox: while it is unsure how the Court would have interpreted the legal basis question and if/how it would have applied the so-called 'centre of gravity test', Article

[95] Opinion of AG Bot in *Parliament v Council ('Somali Pirates I')* [2014] ECLI:EU:C:2014:41, para 19.

[96] Opinion in *Venezuelan Fishing Rights* (n 94) paras 104–13.

[97] *Parliament v Council* [2012] ECLI:EU:C:2012:472, paras 42–45 and case law cited therein (hereafter *Restrictive Measures against Bin Laden and others*); *Commission v Council* [2014] ECLI:EU:C:2014:1903, para 34 (hereafter *Philippines Agreement*).

[98] For a critical appraisal, see Geert De Baere and Tina Van den Sanden, 'Interinstitutional Gravity and Pirates of the Parliament on Stranger Tides: The Continued Constitutional Significance of the Choice of Legal Basis in Post-Lisbon External Action' (2016) 12 EU Const 85.

[99] Simon Denys, 'Les Relations Extérieures de la Communauté Economique Européenne à la Lumière de l'Arrêt de la Cour de Justice des Communautés "Commission Contre Conseil" (AETR)' in Enrico Grillo Pasquerelli, Nicole Kleman, and Simon Denys (eds), *La Communauté Economique Européenne dans les Relations Internationales* (Centre Européen Universitaire 1972) 49.

[100] See, for an assessment by the Court on whether an agreement relates exclusively, principally, or incidentally to the CFSP, *Commission v Council ('Small Arms/ECOWAS')* [2008] ECLI:EU:C:2008:288, paras 76–77; *Restrictive Measures against Bin Laden and others* (n 97) paras 42–49.

5(6) EEAS Decision nevertheless seems to suggest that, in the conclusion of EAs, CFSP procedures prevail.[101] Under those CFSP procedures, it would have been for the HR to submit recommendations to the Council to open negotiations and appoint a Union negotiator (Art 218(3) TFEU). Presumably, the HR would then also be appointed the head the negotiating team. Therefore this procedure perhaps unintentionally corresponds to the EEAS Decision's suggestion that the HR should take up the negotiating role.[102]

### 3.1.4.3 The More Unusual Solution: EAs as Administrative Agreements

#### *3.1.4.3.1 Introduction to an alternative theory*

The EAs were not concluded as international agreements. Rather, although it was never formally stated, the Commission, and subsequently the HR, seem to have concluded EAs as administrative agreements. An administrative agreement is an international instrument without formal basis in EU law.[103] As a reminder, PIL also does not have a special category of administrative agreements.[104] Regardless of the EU's definition for internal reasons, the international effects would be alike. The only real lead on the existence of this presumably separate category of international instruments is provided in CJEU case law and the EU's institutional practice. Despite their incidental status in law, EU actors can conclude administrative agreements when certain conditions are respected. However, various well-founded objections exist against employing the instrument to establish diplomatic ties with third states.

#### *3.1.4.3.2 First-generation EAs*

In the early 1990s, France was the first member state to take issue with a particular administrative agreement and accordingly to question the legality of the instrument under EU law. At stake was an administrative agreement between the Commission and the United States signed on 23 September 1991 concerning the application of competition rules. The CJEU sided with France and annulled the Commission's decision nominating Commissioner Brittan as the head of its negotiating team. The arguments presented by the Commission and Advocate General, as well as the final judgment, provide important insights on a possible legal basis for the EA practice. Up to then, the Commission had regularly entered into administrative agreements with foreign governments and IOs. The Commission found recourse to such agreements particularly when setting up collaboration schemes and in developing practical exchanges.[105] In fact, administrative agreements were commonly used by the Commission to deal with known bugs in the EU legal system as the general EU treaty-making procedures for the Commission to execute its broad mandate were rigorous and explicit legal bases few.

**The AG's Opinion in *France v Commission* (1994): the three-criteria theory** In *France v Commission* (1994), the Commission contended that it was competent to conclude administrative agreements. It was argued that these instruments have the three following essential

[101] In *Parliament v Council* [2016] ECLI:EU:C:2016:435 (hereafter *Somali Pirates II*), the CJEU ruled in favour of a CFSP-only legal basis after having applied a traditional centre of gravity test.

[102] Eeckhout (n 62) 42, 196; Koutrakos, *International Relations Law* (n 62) 139–40.

[103] Opinion of AG Tesauro in *France v Commission* [1993] ECLI:EU:C:1993:941, para 22.

[104] Opinion of AG Alber in *France v Commission* [2003] ECLI:EU:C:2003:503, para 64.

[105] Elisa Baroncini, 'The Treaty Making Power of the European Commission' in Marianne Dony and Lucia Serena Rossi (eds), *Démocratie, Cohérence et Transparence: Principes Constitutionnels de l'Union Européenne* (Éditions ULB 2008) 199.

characteristics: the agreements *(a)* give rise to limited international legal obligations that can be discharged in full by the Commission alone; *(b)* are implemented within the limits set by the Commission's budget so that they do not impose further financial obligations, and *(c)* do not make the Community liable for non-performance since any failure to discharge obligations will exclusively lead to the termination of the agreement.[106] The definition placed a strong emphasis on the fact that the administrative agreements were simply by-products of the Commission's internal organization, which the Commission sought to legitimize on the basis of functional necessity.[107] In its arguments, the Commission referred to no less than twenty-five different types of administrative bilateral cooperation agreements with non-member countries that it had already concluded, of which the EAs were but one kind.[108] The Commission therefore assumed *(a)* that it had a general competence to conclude administrative agreements and *(b)* that EAs qualified as such. Advocate General (AG) Tesauro accepted both claims. As regards the second claim, he was of the opinion that:

> on the one hand, the establishment of delegations in non-member countries may be deemed to fall within the Commission's power to organize its own departments and, on the other, there is in any event tacit approval by the budgetary authorities (Council and Parliament) which can be inferred from the adoption of the appropriations necessary for them to function.[109]

In addition to the Council's and Parliament's tacit acceptance, the member states never formally objected to the Commission's diplomatic practices.[110] Yet, the question arises whether inferred approvals via budgetary oversight can circumvent well-established procedures. It is even more fundamental to ask whether the nature of the pre-Lisbon EAs actually conformed to the three general characteristics attributed to administrative agreements by the Commission, as resonated by AG Tesauro.[111]

The first criterion on the Commission's sole execution is problematic. Unlike administrative agreements, the EAs created legal obligations the Commission could not discharge under its own power. Most prominently, Article 16, Protocol No 7 obliges Belgium to accord diplomatic rights to missions accredited to the Union and accordingly to assume corresponding obligations. On this basis, Belgium accords 'customary privileges, immunities and facilities' (or the 'privilèges, immunités ou facilités d'usage' in French, 'gebruikelijke diplomatieke immuniteiten en voorrechten' in Dutch, 'inmunidades y privilegios diplomáticos habituales' in Spanish, and 'die üblichen diplomatischen Vorrechte und Befreiungen' in German). In practice, these are the very same privileges, immunities, and inviolabilities as those granted to bilateral diplomatic missions on its territory. The VCDR spells out such obligations for receiving states such as the facilitation of the acquisition of premises for the mission and the finding of suitable accommodation for its members on its territory (Art 21), the offering of full facilities for the performance of the functions of the mission (Art 25), and the principle of non-discrimination between missions (Art 47). The second criterion equally did not stand the test of time. The cost of maintaining a diplomatic network accelerated with

[106] Opinion in Case C-327/91 *France v Commission* (n 103) para 30.
[107] ibid, para 17; Case C-327/91 *France v Commission* (n 63) para 29.
[108] Opinion in Case C-327/91 *France v Commission* (n 103) para 28.
[109] ibid, n 28.
[110] See Baroncini (n 105) 207; Iain MacLeod, Ian D Hendry, and Stephen Hyett, *The External Relations of the European Communities: A Manual of Law and Practice* (OUP 1996) 209.
[111] Petersen (n 6) 94.

its steady growth, giving rise to new financial obligations on the part of the Community as a whole. The third criterion bans the idea that rights and obligations are created under PIL by virtue of administrative agreements. This does not correspond with the text of the EAs, which resulted in reciprocal obligations under international law, the breach whereof can trigger international legal responsibility.

**Judgment in *France v Commission* (1994): the express legal basis theory** When the matter appeared before the Court, the idea that the Commission possessed a general competence to conclude administrative agreements was not conclusively ruled out. However, the Court gave a rather restrictive reading to the three-criteria-theory. In *France v Commission*, the CJEU re-qualified the administrative agreement at hand as a binding international agreement that produced legal effects under international law.[112] Although the Commission was referred to as a party to the agreement, the Court held that it was the Community that had committed itself at the international level: 'it is the Community alone, having legal personality pursuant to Article 210 of the Treaty, which has the capacity to bind itself by concluding agreements with a non-member country or an international organization'.[113] Only the Community has legal personality; it is the sole possessor of capacity to bind itself by concluding agreements with non-member states. Consequently, whenever legally binding commitments are entered into on behalf of the Community, the Commission must avail itself with the common constitutional procedures on treaty-making.

In the 1994 *France v Commission* case, the Commission tested two arguments. First, the Commission argued that it possessed an implied competence to conclude administrative agreements on the basis of the European Atomic Energy Community Treaty (Euratom). Second, it was submitted that in any event the power could be grounded in its own past practice—a practice in itself developed on the basis of an interpretation of the French wording of a competence provided for in Article 101 of the Euratom Treaty and the treaty-making procedure of Article 228 EC Treaty (Maastricht consolidated version). At the hearing, the Commission argued 'that the new wording of Article 228, in so far as it confers on the Commission the power to modify the technical aspects of pre-existing agreements concluded by the Council, does not concern or encroach on the power, already vested in it, to conclude administrative arrangements'.[114]

The Court disagreed with both views. The horizontal application of the conferral of powers means that each institution must act within the limits of its conferred Treaty powers.[115] The theory of implied powers therefore cannot be relied upon to legitimize the use of an instrument unforeseen by the Treaties. Moreover, although the Commission's EA practice was well established and tacitly approved by the Council and European Parliament (EP), the Court confirmed its own case law stating that 'in any event, a mere practice cannot override the provisions of the Treaty'.[116] Rather, the selection of a legal basis should be based on objective factors amenable to judicial review: this is not a matter of pure institutional choice or

[112] Case C-327/91 *France v Commission* (n 63) paras 22–27.

[113] ibid, paras 24–25. See also the Opinion in Case C-327/91 *France v Commission* (n 103) para 22.

[114] Opinion in Case C-327/91 *France v Commission* (n 103) paras 23–24.

[115] Case C-327/91 *France v Commission* (n 63) para 34 refers to former Art 4(1), para 2 EEC Treaty (current Art 13(2) TEU).

[116] Case C-327/91 *France v Commission* (n 63) para 36. See also Opinion 1/94 (n 24) paras 52, 61; *France v Commission* [2007] ECLI:EU:T:2007:290, para 45. The Court has confirmed the principle also with regard to Council practices; see the judgments in *United Kingdom v Council* [1988] ECLI:EU:C:1988:85, para 24; *Germany v Council* [1995] ECLI:EU:C:1995:367, para 21.

behaviour, it is a matter of law.[117] As a result, the Commission was barred from using administrative agreements to circumvent the principles of conferral and the institutional balance. The *France v Commission* judgment also rejected the PIL doctrine on treaty revision through mere uncontested subsequent practice.[118] This being said, one cannot but observe that an EU practice can still survive as long as it is simply not challenged in Court, especially when it does not directly affect the interest of the member states or a body with the relevant locus standi to challenge it.

The French Government did not contest the very fact that the instrument of administrative agreements exist in EU law. The member state conceded that powers were vested in the Commission to conclude administrative or working agreements in at least two situations:[119] agreements that enabled recognition of the Community laissez-passer (in Art 6, Protocol 7 on the Privileges and Immunities) and agreements establishing relations with the UN and other international organizations pursuant to Article 302 EC Treaty, currently Article 220(1) TFEU. The question becomes whether these examples—and their explicit legal bases—could be extended to the EAs.

The first example of an administrative agreement that has a firm legal basis relates to diplomat's travel documents. Pursuant to Article 6, Protocol No 7:

> [t]he Commission may conclude agreements for these laissez-passer to be recognised as valid travel documents within the territory of third countries.

As discussed above, nearly half of the diplomatic partners of the EU signed an EA that contains provisions on the laissez-passer. In such cases, EAs serve as the replacement of the administrative agreement that the Commission is expressly permitted to sign. The EAs should, however, be distinguished from those laissez-passer agreements: by encompassing a *ius repraesentationis omnimodae*, the object and purpose of EAs is much wider.[120] The *ius repraesentationis omnimodae* is the right to represent another person or entity with respect to all matters and allows for legation in the broadest sense thinkable. The single clause on the EULP is incidental to the overall goal of EAs. For that reason, EAs do not qualify as Article 6, Protocol 7 administrative agreements.

The second legal basis concerns the Commission's relations with IOs. Article 229 TEC as consolidated in 1992 Maastricht version and its successors, permitted the Commission to enter into administrative arrangements with other IOs:

> [i]t shall be for the Commission to ensure the maintenance of all appropriate relations with the organs of the United Nations, of its specialized agencies and of the General Agreement on Tariffs and Trade.
>
> The Commission shall also maintain such relations as are appropriate with all international organizations.[121]

[117] *Parliament v Council* [1996] ECLI:EU:C:1996:133, para 24; *Commission v Council* [2009] ECLI:EU:C:2009:590, para 54.

[118] Georg Nolte, *Treaties and Subsequent Practice* (OUP 2013).

[119] Case C-327/91 *France v Commission* (n 63) para 29.

[120] José Manuel Sobrino Heredia, 'La Actividad Diplomatica de las Delegationes de la Comision en el Exterior de la Comunitad Europea' (1993) 20 Rev Inst Eur 485, 489.

[121] See also Arts 230–31 TEC Treaty (1992 Maastricht Treaty), Arts 302–04 TEC Treaty (1997 Amsterdam Treaty), and Arts 302–04 EC (2001 Nice Treaty).

The provision enables the Commission to manage international relations and to set up international cooperation. The duty was first codified in the Maastricht Treaty but arguably already existed in practice before 1992 as part of the Commission's general competences. The current version of Article 220(1) TFEU allocates this competence to the Union rather than the Commission. Although the scope is limited to international institutional partners, the provision may be the closest form of authorization the Commission had to conclude administrative agreements relating to management of both general and permanent international relations. It has indeed been suggested in the academic literature that the EA system was modelled after the practice of Article 229 TEC/Article 220(1) TFEU.[122] Yet this legal basis does not include the power to conclude international agreements.[123]

The Commission, and since the Lisbon Treaty also the HR, used this article on numerous occasions to conclude administrative arrangements.[124] Besides the obvious issue that the provision does not refer to either to states or the establishment of permanent missions, using the provision as a legal basis for diplomatic relations raises other concerns.[125] One such concern is that the provision was introduced in the Maastricht Treaty when numerous EAs were already concluded. When Maastricht entered into force on 1 November 1993, the Commission had concluded 101 diplomatic arrangements with third states. It cannot serve as an express legal basis for the pre-1993 EAs. If it were to be argued that Article 229 TEC was relevant before November 1993 insofar as the provision was implied (eg on the basis that all IOs enjoy rights to conclude functional cooperation agreements with one another), this seems to exclude diplomatic relations with third countries in any event since such relations are not commonly exercised by IOs.

**Judgment in *France v Commission* (2004): confirmation of the express legal basis theory** In the aftermath of the 1994 judgment, a new classification for the EAs had to be found. A remarkable proposal can be found in the handbook by MacLeod, Hendry, and Hyett. The authors argued in 1996 that it 'may be best to regard agreements or arrangements of that kind as, in essence, unilateral concessions by the host State'.[126] They reasoned that if an EA imposed obligations or conferred rights to the Community, the Council's involvement would be required in accordance with the normal treaty-making procedures. However, this is a false deduction as EAs *are* reciprocal in nature as they facilitate an exchange of diplomatic missions and staff.

The Commission found an alternative solution to maintain its administrative practices; it rebranded them. Instead of abandoning practices, the Commission simply stated that its administrative agreements were non-binding and of a political nature only.[127] This change was purely rhetorical as the EAs were not subjected to a lexical revision; the Commission continued to rely on the model EA until it was replaced, after the conclusion of the Commission's last EA on 16 November 2009 with Iceland and the entry into force of the Lisbon Treaty, with a similar model to be used by the HR.

[122] Baroncini (n 105) 199.

[123] Verwey (n 82) 97.

[124] See, eg the Framework Administrative Agreement for Capacity Development Cooperation between the Commission and the International Monetary Fund, signed 21 May 2015; Administration Agreement between the Commission and the International Bank for Reconstruction and Development concerning the EC IPA Sarajevo Waste Water Treatment Plant (Butila) Single-Donor Trust Fund, signed on 24 July 2015.

[125] Laurens J Brinkhorst, 'Permanent Missions of the EC in Third Countries: European Diplomacy in the Making' (1984) 10 LIEI 23, 26.

[126] MacLeod, Hendry, and Hyett (n 110) 95.

[127] Baroncini (n 105) 200.

In 2004, a different post-1994 administrative agreement that had been marked legally non-binding by the Commission became the object of a judgment concerning (once again) France and the Commission. The case concerned a Commission–US agreement referred to as the 'Guidelines on Regulatory Cooperation and Transparency', on which the Commission insisted that no rights or obligations at the international level were created.[128] In the judgment, the difference between the binding or non-binding label did not in itself appear to be decisive. The Court recalled that principles of EU law apply *whenever* the Commission acts on the international scene. As the Court stated, '[t]his judgment cannot be construed as upholding the Commission's argument that the fact that a measure such as the Guidelines is not binding is sufficient to confer on that institution the competence to adopt it [ … ]'.[129] The Court further held that the Commission's competences permitted the conclusion of both legally binding and non-legally binding international instruments, provided such actions respect 'the division of powers and the institutional balance established by the Treaty'.

*3.1.4.3.3 Second-generation establishment agreements*

The HR concluded ten EAs, using the same model EA, between 2010 and 2022. The idea that this is a simple continuation of an old practice is partly illusory. Rather, the post-Lisbon practice awakened old discrepancies and raises new questions.

The legal position and capacities of the EEAS and the HR differ from the Commission's. Unlike the Commission, the EEAS is not an EU institution (Art 13 TEU). The extent to which the HR has a general power to conclude administrative agreements is equally ambiguous, whether personally in its role of heading the EEAS or as the Vice-President of the Commission. The most recent Treaty version provides at least one instance of the HR's ability to enter into administrative agreements, confirming that the capacity can be allocated to the HR: originally conceived for the Commission to establish cooperation with other IOs as discussed prior, Article 220(1) TFEU now allocates the competence to enter into arrangements to the Commission and the HR.

Lisbon did not appoint the HR as the responsible actor for the conclusion of administrative agreements pursuant to Article 6 Protocol No 7 concerning the EULP. To the present day, the Commission and not the HR holds the responsibility for negotiating and concluding EULP arrangements with third states. However, the Treaty text does not correspond to post-Lisbon practices as all of the EAs concluded under the authority of the HR contain a provision on the EULP. The failure to adjust Protocol No 7 to the HR's new role in the general foreign affairs management could be either a drafting negligence or, alternatively, a conscious choice to limit the administrative practices of the newly established diplomatic service of the Union. Both hypotheses result in a *contra legem* practice to be remedied at a future constitutional revision.

The following question is whether Article 5(6) EEAS Decision can be used as legal basis to conclude EAs in the form of administrative agreements. On the face of it, the Council authorized the HR to carry on the Commission's established practice. The wording of 'necessary arrangements'/'necessary measures' indicates that the Council had in mind an instrument other than an international agreement for the EU to enter into diplomatic relations. However, as indicated earlier, using a certain name does not mean that a new category of

[128] Case C-233/02 *France v Commission* (n 64) para 11.
[129] ibid, para 40.

international instruments is created.[130] Yet, in itself, Article 5(6) EEAS Decision does not indisputably state that EAs are to be concluded as administrative agreements either.

When interpreting Article 5(6) EEAS Decision in light of the discussed case law, the argument that post-Lisbon EAs qualify as administrative agreements fails. The 1994 and 2004 *France v Commission* judgments revealed that the Commission can conclude administrative agreements as the external manifestation of its own activities in certain circumstances only. These circumstances, dubiously present pre-Lisbon, now definitely no longer existing. As a reminder, it can be recalled that Advocate General Tesauro argued that because the agreement under review in 1994 designated the Community as a contracting party it was *not* an administrative agreement: 'the terms of the Agreement are clear: the Community has bound itself at international level, and the Community must be regarded as the true contracting party'.[131] The HR's role is fundamentally different from the Commission's since, in steering the EUDELs, the HR now definitely acts on behalf of the whole Union. The activities of Union delegations are no longer linked to a singular institution. The HR's mandate to conclude 'arrangements' on its sole authority can therefore not be read as an authorization to conclude administrative agreements. If this was so, Article 5(6) EEAS Decision would have fundamentally modified the concept of administrative agreements as developed in case law. The decision to enter into an EA is also fundamentally different from the decision to open or close an EUDEL, which has to be adopted in agreement with the Council and the Commission (Art 5(1) EEAS Decision) and is of a more administrative nature.

#### 3.1.4.4 International or Administrative Agreements: What Difference Does It Make?

The grey zone position of EAs in EU law results in a grey zone with regard to supervision and control as well: there are virtually no legal obligations to disclose information on the EAs and public scrutiny is denied as EAs are not published in the Official Journal or in the EU Treaty Database and are entered into with little parliamentary or judicial oversight. This is striking since the EU generally has a good track record in responding to public demands for openness, transparency, and review.[132]

The choice to conclude EAs either following the established treaty-making procedures or as an administrative agreement on the basis of Article 5(6) EEAS Decision affects the jurisdiction of the CJEU. As a reminder, the Court is generally excluded from reviewing CFSP instruments including international agreements (Art 24(1) TEU). The CJEU decided that the scope of the exception in Article 24(1) TEU 'must be interpreted narrowly'.[133] This is arguably part of a broader trend instigated by the Court to further embed the CFSP into the EU legal order.[134] Its jurisdiction is further limited by Article 275, paragraph 1, TFEU on CFSP matters laid down in the Treaties and Acts adopted pursuant to it (such as acts adopted on the basis of Art 5(6) EEAS Decision).[135] However, as confirmed by recent case law, just because a measure is concluded on the legal basis of CFSP does not automatically preclude the Court from conducting a review. The Court can still deliver an opinion on an international agreement's compatibility with the Treaties, including on matters of competence. One of

130 Declaration No 8 on Art 109 of the Treaty Establishing the European Community, annexed to the Treaty on European Union [1992] OJ C191/99; De Baere (n 76) 78.

131 Opinion in Case C-327/91 *France v Commission* (n 103) para 19.

132 Brölmann (n 33) 121.

133 *Parliament v Council* [2014] ECLI:EU:C:2014:2025, para 70 (hereafter *Somali Pirates I*). This is arguably part of a broader trend instigated by the Court to further embed the CFSP into the EU legal order, as exemplified in

134 *Philippines Agreement* (n 97); *Somali Pirates II* (n 101); and *H v Council* [2016] ECLI:EU:C:2016:569.

135 De Baere and Van den Sanden (n 98); Andrea Ott, 'The Legal Bases for International Agreements Post-Lisbon: Of Pirates and the Philippines' (2014) 21 MJECL 739.

the purposes of such an opinion is to clarify competence issues as soon as negotiations start.[136] However, this is only so when a member state, the EP, the Commission, or the Council asks for it *and* if it is decided that the legal basis of such an agreement is in the CFSP and when it is accepted that Article 218(11) TFEU applies to CFSP agreements.[137] When so requested, the Court could deliver its opinion on the EAs with regard to questions that 'give rise to doubt either as to the substantive or formal validity of the agreement with regard to the treaty'. In 1975, for instance, the Court deemed a draft 'Understanding on a local Cost Standard' drawn up under the auspices of the Organisation for Economic Co-operation and Development (OECD) to fulfil the conditions of an international agreement. It contained a 'standard' in the sense of 'a rule of conduct, covering a specific field, determined by precise provisions, which is binding upon the participants'.[138] Furthermore, the Court has full jurisdiction to give a preliminary ruling on an interpretation where agreements encompass CFSP matters partly or entirely. Judicial oversight is also possible in cases where the arguments relate to procedural points outside of the CFSP Articles in Title V TEU.[139] Moreover, Article 24 TEU introduces an exception to the general limits whereby the Court has jurisdiction to monitor compliance with Article 40 TEU on the division between CFSP and other domains. Finally, in *H v Council* (2016), the Court interpreted Article 275 TFEU narrowly, at the same time expressing that the rule of law principles require the possibility of effective judicial review in the EU.[140] The EAs therefore can be judicially reviewed even if the decision to enter into an EA is adopted on the basis of a single substantive legal basis that falls within CFSP.

A second discrepancy arises with regard to the legally binding character of EAs, knowing that as a general rule, where international agreements are concluded by the EU they are binding for member states and EU institutions.[141] This problem is not merely theoretical. One could, for instance, question whether, when a third-country diplomat travels to Brussels to take up its functions as a representative to the EU passing through territories of other member states, those member states are bound by the EA to grant VCDR treatment to such a diplomat. Since the Union is not a VCDR party, the rules on diplomatic protection in transit only apply through the EA and its *renvoi* clause to the VCDR. Member states are not parties to the EAs, which are in fact instruments adopted outside of the applicable treaty-making procedures. If EAs qualify as international agreements, they are an integral part of EU law (Art 216(2) TFEU).[142] In the EU hierarchy of norms, if the EAs were to be accepted as international agreements, these would have primacy over acts of secondary law.[143] However, if EAs do not qualify as such, it is unclear to what extent member states other than host state Belgium (Protocol No 7) must duly ensure compliance with EAs in the municipal legal order.[144] The general

[136] Opinion 1/78 *International Agreement on Natural Rubber* [1979] ECLI:EU:C:1979:224, para 35; Opinion 2/94 (n 75) paras 16–18; Koutrakos, *International Relations Law* (n 62) 209–10.

[137] Koen Lenaerts, Ignace Maselis, and Kathleen Gutman, *EU Procedural Law* (OUP 2014) 552–53.

[138] Opinion 1/75 (n 63) 1360–61.

[139] *Somali Pirates I* (n 133) paras 69–73; Maria-Gisella Garbagnati Ketvel, 'The Jurisdiction of the European Court of Justice in Respect of the Common Foreign and Security Policy' [2006] 55 ICLQ 77.

[140] *H v Council* (n 134) paras 40–41.

[141] *Air Transport Association of America (ATAA) and others v Secretary of State for Energy and Climate Change* [2011] ECLI:EU:C:2011:864, para 50 and case law cited therein.

[142] *Haegeman v Belgium* [1974] ECLI:EU:C:1974:41, para 5; Koutrakos, *International Relations Law* (n 62) 209–10.

[143] *Commission v Germany* [1996] ECLI:EU:C:1996:313, para 52; *Soysal and Savatli v Germany* [2009] ECLI:EU:C:2009:101, para 59.

[144] *Hauptzollamt Mainz v CA Kupferberg* [1982] ECLI:EU:C:1982:362; *Simuntenkov v Ministerio de Educación y Cultura and Real Federación Española de Fútbol* [2005] ECLI:EU:C:2005:213.

principle of sincere cooperation in EU law surely applies and will probably be more helpful to solve this type of question than a reasoning based on the hierarchy of EU law sources.

The constitutional importance of the choice of legal basis for EU external action should be stressed, once again, for it also determines how far the right of Parliament to provide democratic scrutiny reaches. The Parliament does not need to be consulted in cases where international agreements relate exclusively to the CFSP (Art 218(6) TFEU), although an obligation to inform stands (Art 218(10) TFEU).[145] Parliamentary control is a vital part of executive democratic accountability, although oversight on matters of diplomacy is generally less than with other areas. For the moment, the conclusion of an EA is a matter not discussed in the EP. A certain parliamentary role is guaranteed on the basis of a number of rules and working arrangements. The HR is obliged regularly to inform the Parliament of its activities (Art 36 TEU). Moreover, due to the post-Lisbon Declaration on Political Accountability, the EP has an increased scrutiny role over foreign affairs, including negotiations of international agreements at all stages. Furthermore, the Members of Parliament informally exchange views in the Foreign Affairs Committee with EU diplomats appointed as HoDs before taking their posts. Finally, the EP is empowered to question the HR on the (continuation of) diplomatic relations with countries having questionable human rights records.

Finally, it should be noted that in its relations with third states, the EU's choice between an international or administrative agreement may not be a determining factor. Internal quarrels cannot be invoked by the Union as justification for an international non-performance. For example, an act or omission on the part of Belgium causing harm to a third state representative to the Union are attributable to the Union and not Belgium. However, the Commission would be able take up a case of non-performance (Art 17 TEU and Art 258 TFEU), possibly leading to a procedure before the CJEU on Belgium's compliance with Protocol No 7 on Privileges and Immunities. If the Court were to invalidate an EA for being wrongly concluded in disregard of the treaty-making procedures, the international legal consequences would be limited. The Court recognizes under its settled jurisprudence that international agreements which do not satisfy EU legal requirements on competence and procedure nevertheless bind the Union under international law.[146] If this were to happen, the CJEU annuls the contested internal decision that adopted the agreement but maintains its effects on the grounds of legal certainty and avoidance of any negative consequences for the Union's relationship with third countries, whether practical or political. The Court has held in this regard that the effects of such an act may be maintained in particular where the immediate effects of its annulment would give rise to serious negative consequences for the persons concerned and where the lawfulness of the act in question is contested not because of its aim or content but on grounds of lack of competence or infringement of an essential procedural requirement.[147] The second paragraph of Article 264 TFEU provides the Court with the opportunity to specify which effects of the void act are definitive. This allows the Court

145 De Baere and Van den Sanden (n 98).

146 Case C-327/91 *France v Commission* (n 63) para 25; Koen Lenaerts and Eddy De Smijter, 'The European Union as an Actor under International Law' (1999) 19 Yearb Eur Law 95, 102.

147 *Parliament and Commission v Council* [2014] ECLI:EU:C:2014:2400, para 90.

to manage the potentially negative consequences of an annulment.[148] The Union will then be required to act again using the correct legal basis and the applicable procedures.[149]

Looking at the EAs, the above scenario is destined to remain a purely theoretical discussion for two reasons. First, in light of the established practices, the chances of the EU's international commitment being called into question by third parties, member states, or the institutions are limited. Part of the reason why the choice of instrument discussion attracts little attention relates to the fact that the agreements have created the desired results for the parties and only occasionally directly impact individuals in the EU or abroad. Second, it is undesirable for the Union or third states to renegotiate the existing EAs. Opening up such debate could stir up discussions between parties on the exact rights and privileges the EU is entitled to since states are not obliged under international law to grant the EU VCDR treatment. Considering the quasi-universal application of the VCDR in its diplomatic relations today, the EU has more to lose than to gain.

## 3.2 The Active Right of Legation: Multilateral Arrangements

### 3.2.1 The EU's Diplomatic Representation at Other IOs

Of the 145 Union delegations, 9 are accredited principally or exclusively to other international organizations, including regional organizations, UN bodies, programmes, and funds. In addition, twenty-one EU HoDs combine a bilateral engagement in the country of posting with an accreditation at one or more IOs headquartered in the same country. In addition, the Union is regularly represented in ad hoc settings such as multilateral summits and gatherings.

A permanent mission of one IO to another IO can only be compared to a state's mission when the institutional representation meets the following three conditions:[150] the IO's mission is permanent; represents executive powers; and is granted a general competence, even though the sending organization's competence may be thematically restricted by its own member states.[151] The nine multilateral missions of the Union satisfy these standards. By opening multilateral missions, the Union seeks to establish permanent structures that interact with the secretariat of the relevant IO, its principal organs, and the diplomatic representatives of states to the IO (including with representatives sent by its own member states). Similarly to activities in bilateral settings, a multilateral Union delegation represents the EU, protects its interests, and engages in negotiations at the host IO.

Functional needs resulted in the Union requesting diplomatic recognition at the various multilateral settings where it is formally represented. Much like states, the nature of the EU's representational activities at IOs requires a specific type of protection that enables the mission and its staff to execute tasks independently and free from interference. This functional equivalence legitimates the EU requesting equivalent treatment for its delegations. Yet, the

[148] *Parliament v Council and Commission* [2006] ECLI:EU:C:2006:346; Case C-327/91 *France v Commission* (n 63).

[149] *Council v Commission* [2016] ECLI:ECLI:EU:C:2016:616, para 54.

[150] Vincent Pouliot, 'Diplomats as Permanent Representatives: The Practical Logics of the Multilateral Pecking Order' (2011) 66 Int J 543.

[151] Charles Reichling, *Le Droit de Légation des Communautés Européennes* (UGA Éditions 1964) 42.

proposition of granting missions of IOs to other IOs privileges and immunities raises legal and practical issues, which have not been fully tackled in international institutional law.[152]

Quite a number of questions arise. A first issue concerns the legal entitlement to accreditation. Practice unequivocally confirms that states have a right to establish permanent representations to IOs where they are full members.[153] Little doubt exists regarding the fact that the same goes for IOs in a similar situation: in case of membership, the status of a delegation rests on an institutional obligation of the accrediting IOs rather than the right of legation.[154] For instance, this is the case with the EUDEL to the World Trade Organization (WTO) in Geneva. More often than not, however, IOs do not enjoy membership at other IOs and are instead granted some form of (enhanced) observer status or even choose to maintain relations without becoming part of the IO. It is for each IO to determine the rules on membership, observer status, and outsiders. As a result, and much like non-member states to an organization, a non-member IO has to seek the consent of the accrediting IO to establish a permanent representation. Privileges and immunities in such case do not result from an institutional obligation.

A second point concerns the diplomatic status of IOs' permanent missions. Following accreditation, the exact modalities of immunities and privileges accorded will have to be determined. Multiple legal sources can determine their exact content: IOs commonly established their own internal rules on the treatment of permanent missions. Often, the IO's constituent instrument (eg the organization's constitution or charter) features a clause on permanent representations of the members and, less commonly, of observers. Specialized treaties also target the legal status of representatives to IOs. The most prominent example is the UN's 1946 CPIUN, which has served as a model for the privileges and immunities of the UN Specialized Agencies (CPIUN–SA)[155] and numerous other IOs, including the North Atlantic Treaty Organization (NATO) and the Council of Europe (CoE).[156] Host states play a prominent role in granting diplomatic status to permanent representations. Therefore, headquarters or seat agreements are one (if not the most important) source for rules on the status of permanent representations to IOs. The host state operates as an executing third party in the relation between an IO and sending states/IOs, meaning that it has a say in allocating diplomatic advantages and the manner in which they are enjoyed on its territory, for example, through domestic legislation and practices. Although most headquarters agreements require a host state to provide diplomatic status to missions the IO accredits, this has not completely ruled out frictions. A host state's margin of appreciation is even more significant in cases of accreditation of non-member states or in the absence of a legal obligation requiring the state to grant diplomatic status in the headquarters agreement.

A third complication concerns the number of parties involved in this diplomatic relationship. Unlike in bilateral diplomacy, where two parties consisting of the sending and receiving state take part in a diplomatic relationship, multilateral diplomacy results in tripartite or arguably quadruple relationships. This fourth relationship is the one between the sending IO and its own member states. These states allow the IO to exercise an active right of legation

[152] See the attempt made in the Vienna Convention on the Representation of States in their Relations with International Organizations of a Universal Character, signed on 14 March 1975, not yet entered into force, UN Doc A/CONF.67/16 (hereafter CRSIO).

[153] ibid, Art 5(2); Schermers and Blokker (n 22) 1159.

[154] Reichling (n 151) 41.

[155] Convention on the Privileges and Immunities of the Specialized Agencies, signed on 21 November 1947, entered into force 2 December 1948, 33 UNTS 261 (hereafter CPIUN–SA).

[156] Ivor Roberts (ed), *Satow's Diplomatic Practice* (6th edn, OUP 2011) 299.

and can significantly curtail such a right, for example, on the basis of a competence (not) transferred. In the case of the EU, three legal relationships prove to be relevant to determining the status of a multilateral EUDEL: the relationship between the Union and the IO, the relationship between the EU and the host state, and the relationship between the IO and host state. It was presented earlier that since the rules on bilateral diplomatic relations do not apply by default (neither through the VCDR directly nor through a system of EAs referring to the VCDR), there is no general legal framework on the status, rights, and privileges of Union delegations to IOs. Moreover, the many actors involved complicate the implementation of diplomatic law's basic concepts. For example, it is unclear whether and how the principle of reciprocity limits the diplomatic relations between the EU and other IOs.

The following sections explore in more detail the Union's permanent active legation practice in an international institutional setting. The status of the EU in an IO (its membership) and the diplomatic status of the EU's delegation in the country hosting that IO are two separate legal issues. This book focuses on the second issue by studying legal techniques pioneered by the EU that permit its permanent representatives to be accredited to other IOs and to enjoy diplomatic status, immunities, inviolabilities, and privileges.[157]

### 3.2.2 Multilateral EUDELs in Third Countries

The EU maintains five delegations in four third countries, accredited exclusively to one or more international organization. The EUDEL in New York represents the Union in UN Headquarters, while the multilateral EUDEL in Addis Ababa observes diplomatic functions in the African Union (AU); and the multilateral EUDEL in Jakarta coordinates the EU's expanding cooperation activities with the Association of Southeast Asian Nations (ASEAN). A first EUDEL in Geneva is accredited to the WTO; a second EUDEL based in the same city is accredited to the International Committee of the Red Cross (ICRC), the Geneva-based UN bodies, funds, and agencies, as well as to a number of other organizations working on disarmament and non-proliferation related matters: the Conference on Disarmament (CD), the Human Rights Council (UNHRC), the Office of the High Commissioner for Human Rights (OHCHR), the Office for the Coordination of Humanitarian Affairs (OCHA), the UN High Commissioner for Refugees (UNHCR), UN Conference on Trade and Development (UNCTAD), the World Health Organization (WHO), the International Labour Organization (ILO), the World Intellectual Property Organization (WIPO), the UN Economic Commission for Europe (UNECE), the International Organization for Migration (IOM), the Joint UN Programme on HIV/AIDS (UNAIDS) and, as far as possible, the International Telecommunications Union (ITU) and the World Meteorological Organization (WMO). In addition, the EUDEL may take up a role as a formal observer at meetings of state parties to various international conventions to interact with their secretariats. In other countries, the Union has also opened offices that maintain relations with IOs

[157] For a the first type of question, see Jan Wouters, Jed Odermatt, and Thomas Ramopoulos, 'The EU in the World of International Organizations: Diplomatic Aspirations, Legal Hurdles and Political Realities' in Smith, Keukeleire, and Vanhoonacker (n 87); Eric Hayes, 'EU Delegations: Europe's Link to the World' in Knud Erik Jørgensen and Kartie Verlin Laatikainen (eds), *Routledge Handbook on the European Union and International Institutions: Performance, Policy, Power* (Routledge 2013); Alan Hervé, 'The Participation of the European Union in Global Economic Governance Fora' (2012) 18 ELJ 143; Frank Hoffmeister and Pieter Jan Kuijper, 'The Status of the European Union at the United Nations' in Jan Wouters, Frank Hoffmeister, and Tom Ruys (eds), *The United Nations and the European Union: An Ever Stronger Partnership* (TMC Asser Press 2006).

(eg the EU Office in Montréal that deals with the ICAO). This section gives an account of the legal framework the EUDELs operate under in the United States, Switzerland, Ethiopia, and Indonesia. It shows that the delegations are largely accorded customary diplomatic immunities and privileges in third countries, subject to some notable exceptions.

### 3.2.2.1 The EUDEL in New York City

#### *3.2.2.1.1 The history and status of the mission*

While being formally represented at the UN Headquarters in New York City, the Union has no official status with nor is it accredited to the UN. Instead, the EU and, in some cases, the Commission sought recognition with different UN organs and bodies on a case-by-case basis. Rules on membership are defined under Articles 3–4 of the UN Charter. According to these rules, membership is open to states only and requires the approval of the UNGA. However, the UN has a long history of allowing non-member states to observe its activities: the Swiss Government maintained a permanent observer mission from as early as 1946 until it became a UN member state and the Holy See has appointed permanent observers both at New York and at Geneva since the 1960s. At the UNGA, the EU enjoys an enhanced observer status. The EC became the first entity other than a state to enjoy permanent observer status at the UNGA by Resolution 3208 of 11 October 1974. The EU's status was upgraded with UNGA Resolution A/65/276, adopted on 3 May 2011.[158] At the UNSC, EU positions are represented by the elected or permanent EU member states or, upon invitation, by the EUDEL. EU member states sitting on the Council have to 'concert and keep the other Member States and the High Representative fully informed' (Art 34(2) TEU).

Both the HoD and deputy HoD are accredited at the level of the ambassador, a ceremonial title in the UN context. In addition to the two ambassadors, thirty members of the EUDEL to the UN are recognized as members of the diplomatic staff and accorded the common diplomatic titles such as Minister Counsellor, (First) Counsellor, (First) Secretary, and Attaché. The EUDEL communicates changes in its personnel to the UN's Protocol and Liaison Service (UNGA Res 257 (III)). Whenever the HoD departs its duty station in New York, either permanently or on a temporary basis, the EUDEL is required by UNGA Resolution 257 A (III) to notify the UNSG of the name of the Chargé d'affaires.[159] The actual number of diplomats representing the Union is even higher, given that the delegation is reinforced by seconded national experts (SNEs) from EU member states' foreign ministries remaining on their country's diplomatic list. The delegation also employs non-diplomatic staff, including locally hired staff. They enjoy a functional immunity only and no personal inviolability.[160] In case of an issue arising, the EU can express its views in meetings of the Committee on Relations with the Host Country. This is a subsidiary Committee of the Sixth (Legal) Committee of the UNGA which was established in 1971 by UNGA Resolution 2819 (XXVI).

European diplomatic activities in New York are long-standing. The first Commission Information Office established in 1964 already enjoyed diplomatic status. Around the same time, the Council opened its own liaison office. A decade later, in 1974, when the EEC was

[158] Heidi Panke, 'The European Union in the United Nations: An Effective External Actor?' (2014) 21 J Eur Public Policy 1050; and Jan Wouters, Anna-Luise Chané, Jed Odermatt, and Thomas Ramopoulos, 'Improving the EU's Status in the UN and the UN System: An Objective without a Strategy?' in Christine Kaddous (ed), *The European Union in International Organisations and Global Governance* (Hart 2015).

[159] Chief of Protocol, Executive Office of the UNSG, note verbale, 10 November 2014.

[160] Annex C of the US Department of State Office of Foreign Missions, *Diplomatic and Consular Immunity: Guidance for Law Enforcement and Judicial Authorities*, revised May 2015, <www.state.gov/documents/organization/150546.pdf> accessed 2 May 2022 (hereafter US Department of State Office of Foreign Missions Guide).

granted a standing invitation to participate as an observer in the UNGA,[161] the Commission's mission got its a first upgrade:[162] the information office officially became a Commission delegation and was accredited to the UN Secretariat as a permanent observer mission. The UNSG has no authority to deny such status to non-member states (Art 5(2) CRSIO) but retained this right with regard to non-member IOs. From that point onwards, the representation has been listed in the official UN Blue Book on Permanent Missions. The EU is mentioned in the category 'Intergovernmental organizations having received a standing invitation to participate as observers in the sessions and the work of the General Assembly and maintaining permanent offices at Headquarters'.[163] The Blue Book is circulated for information purposes and to facilitate communication. Nevertheless, inclusion does serve as prima facie evidence of diplomatic status.[164]

*3.2.2.1.2 Host state policies*

Although not expressly stated in the UN–US Headquarters Agreement, it is assumed that the United States is obligated to allow UN members to establish a permanent mission in New York. In 1988, a US District Court refused to enforce a government decision to close, on the basis of the Terrorism Act, the offices of the Palestine Liberation Organization (PLO) as these were also used to house the PLO mission at the UN, at the time recognized by the UN as an observing non-governmental organization (NGO) rather than an observing state. The Court found that the United States had an international legal obligation under section 11 of the Headquarters Agreement to permit UN invitees to maintain permanent offices.[165] In contrast, the status of observer missions depends on the host state's decision. Until 1975, the United States applied a so-called a discretionary 'New York formula' to accord privileges and immunities; since 1976, the so-called 'Vienna formula' has gained ground, on the basis of which extensive privileges and immunities are accorded to observer missions. As a result, their status is largely equated with that of permanent representations of states on the basis of the functional necessity theory.[166] Section 15 of the Headquarters Agreement gives the US Government a discretionary right to recognize 'other permanent representatives' as diplomatic representatives and accordingly grant them diplomatic privileges and immunities.[167] The consequences are twofold: the status of non-member states remains a matter of courtesy rather than legal obligation and the host state can define the status's modalities. As a result, if a diplomat represents a state not recognized by the United States, the Headquarters Agreement allows for a territorial delimitation: they will be immune from legal process only within the Headquarters District, mission offices, and residences, and when in transit (section 15). The United States does not consider the EU as a non-recognized state, considering that it maintains full bilateral diplomatic relations with the Union.

[161] Victor-Yves Ghebali, 'Le Role des Missions Permanentes auprès des Organisations Internationales Universelles' in Société Française pour le Droit International (ed), *Aspects Récents du Droit des Relations Diplomatiques* (Pédone 1989).

[162] Melissa Thomas, 'When the Guests Move In: Permanent Observers to the United Nations Gain the Right to Establish Permanent Missions in the United States' (1990) 78 Cal L Rev 197, 223.

[163] UN Blue Book of the Permanent Missions to the United Nations (New York), No 306, April 2021, ST/PLS/SER.A/306.

[164] Leo Gross, 'Immunities and Privileges of Delegations to the United Nations' (1962) 16 Int Organ 483, 491.

[165] *District Court (NY) [US] United States v Palestine Liberation Organization*, 695 F Supp 1456 [1988].

[166] Seung Hwan Choi, 'The Status, Rights, and Duties of Observers for Non-Member States of the United Nations' (1991) 19 Korean J Comp L 135, 159.

[167] UN–US Agreement regarding the Headquarters of the United Nations, signed on 26 June 1947, entered into force 31 October 1947, 11 UNTS 11 (hereafter UN–US Headquarters Agreement).

In the past, the UN's legal office has pleaded with the United States to grant permanent missions of non-members a functional protection.[168] According to the legal office, such protection could be derived directly from the immunity of the UN (Art 105 UN Charter) with which the observer mission has established a relationship. Moreover, the office took the view that while permanent observers were not entitled to diplomatic privileges in the host state, it was possible for them to enjoy immunities in the United States through an appointment in the bilateral mission to the country. This cautious view quickly became outdated. Since 1988, the United States has accepted that the Commission delegation (and later the EUDEL) enjoys full diplomatic rights and privileges, as do UN member state missions.

The legal basis for these arrangements is rather complex. Neither Article 105 UN Charter, nor the CPIUN, nor UNGA Resolution 257 (III) of 3 December 1948 on permanent missions even mention the establishment of permanent representations by non-UN members.[169] In its Draft Articles on representatives of States to international organizations, the ILC concluded that, by lack of a general legal basis for permanent observers, '[t]heir status, therefore, has been determined by practice'.[170]

The EUDEL's status finds its legal basis in statutory provisions of the host state.[171] In a 1988 Executive Order, President Ronald Reagan granted:

> to the Permanent Observer Mission of the Delegation of the Commission of the European Communities to the United Nations the same privileges and immunities as are accorded to permanent observer missions of states to the United Nations.

President Reagan also extended:

> to the members of the diplomatic staff of that mission assigned to New York to observe the work of the United Nations and duly notified to the United States Government and the United Nations in that capacity, and to their families, the same privileges and immunities, subject to corresponding conditions and obligations, as are accorded to members of the diplomatic staff of missions accredited to the United Nations.

The Order further stated that it is not intended to abridge in any respect privileges, exemptions, or immunities that the delegation had already acquired or may acquire by international agreement or by Congressional action. Prior to the issuing of this Executive Order, the 1972 Act granting the bilateral Commission delegation in Washington DC diplomatic status was amended.[172] This was to allow the US President to also 'extend diplomatic privileges and immunities to *other offices* of the Commission of the European Communities which are established in the United States and the members thereof'.[173] Neither the Act nor the Executive

[168] Memorandum (22 August 1962) of the UN Legal Counsel, 'Accreditation of Permanent Observers by non-members at United Nations Headquarter' (1962) UN Jur Yearb, 237.

[169] UNGA, 'Permanent Missions to the United Nations', 3 December 1949, A/RES/371.

[170] International Law Commission (ILC), 'Draft Articles on Representatives of States to International Organizations, with Commentaries (1970) II YBILC 6.

[171] See the discussion in Petersen (n 6) 99–102.

[172] Act to extend diplomatic privileges and immunities to the Mission to the United States of America of the Commission of the European Communities and to members thereof, PL 92-499, 18 October 1972, 86 STAT 815; Executive Order No 11689, 5 December 1972, 37 FR 25987, issued by President Richard Nixon.

[173] Section 741 of the Foreign Relations Authorization Act, PL 100-204, 101 STAT 1331, 22 December 1987, 101 STAT 1331. The amendment was identical to the legislative proposal in the form of a bill introduced in the House of Representatives on 31 March 1987 by Representative Lantos (Dem).

Order were amended following the entering into force of the Treaty of Lisbon and the accompanying transformation of the Commission delegation(s) in EU delegation(s).

The 1988 Executive Order makes a distinction between the mission's status whereby reference is made to the status of observer missions of states, and the status of diplomatic staff and their families, which takes the permanent missions of UN member states as a benchmark. In practice, however, the distinction does not have any direct consequences. Since 1948, seventeen states have maintained permanent observer missions to the UN, all receiving privileges and immunities similar to UN member states' permanent missions. Most states eventually became full members. Switzerland, the first non-member state to have established a permanent observer mission, did not become a UN member state until 2002, but its permanent observer mission received diplomatic privileges and immunities long before that time. A similar diplomatic status is granted to the two remaining missions of non-member states maintaining permanent observer missions at the UN Headquarters, the Holy See, and the State of Palestine.[174]

The EUDEL's diplomatic staff enjoy privileges and immunities and are subject to the corresponding obligations. Under section 15 of the Headquarters Agreement, the United States entitles principal resident representatives of such missions:

> in the territory of the United States to the same privileges and immunities, subject to corresponding conditions and obligations, as it accords to diplomatic envoys accredited to it.

The provision speaks of 'the principal resident representative with the rank of Ambassador or minister plenipotentiary', but in fact all members of the diplomatic staff are granted full diplomatic privileges and immunities.[175] It is a consistent practice of the UN Secretariat to request, and for the US Government to grant, representations of UN members a treatment equivalent to that of bilateral missions. This privilege is extended to the EUDEL. Executive Order 12851 confirms this interpretation by referring to 'diplomatic' staff of the EUDEL. The EUDEL's treatment therefore largely coincides with that of states' missions, as codified in the CPIUN and VCDR.

The differences in treatment between the EUDEL and permanent missions of member states are few and strictly administrative. One example is the State Department's distinction in the type of visas accorded to the Union delegation staff. The type of visa granted to observers is at the discretion of the host state to the extent that it does not bar the recipient from performing official functions.[176] To enter US territory to take up their duties, European officials receive a G-3 status; a visa granted to 'representatives of non-recognized or non-member foreign governments to international organizations'. A national diplomat seconded to the delegation is either considered a member of its national diplomatic mission to the United States and granted an A-1 visa or a member of its national permanent representation to the UN and granted a G-1 visa. The difference does not amount to significant consequences or differences in treatment at the US airports. Following registration at the State Department, much like national representatives, US authorities provide the EUDEL's diplomatic staff with a diplomatic identity card and designated driver's licence.[177]

[174] Executive Order 13427, Extending Privileges and Immunities to the Permanent Observer Mission of the Holy See to the United Nations, 7 March 2007.

[175] See the practices of the *State Department and District Court (NY) [US] United States v Fitzpatrick*, 214 F Supp 425, 441–42 [1963]; *District Court (NY) [US] United States v Melekh*, 190 F Supp 67, 84 [1960]; *District Court (NY) [US] United States v Egorov*, 222 F Supp 106 [1963].

[176] Choi (n 166) 148.

[177] Section 13(*a*) of the UN–US Headquarters Agreement.

In its capacity as host state, the United States nevertheless reserves a right to control the entrance of aliens into its territory. The state asserts the right to deny visas to temporary and permanent delegates and the right to require a representative of member governments to leave its territory in cases of abuse of privileges in conducting non-official duties.[178] Section 8(*b*) of the International Organizations Immunities Act also foresees a possible withdrawal of immunity by the Secretary of State upon a finding that the continued presence in the United States of a representative is undesirable. All the above claimed rights are subject to heavy discussion. This is especially so since the United States retains the right to declare a permanent representative persona non grata following an abuse of diplomatic status—a right arguably belonging solely to the UN. The United States justifies this 'Reservation Clause' on the basis of national security and has invoked it, famously, in the case of a temporary visit of Yasser Arafat, and more recently, in the case of Hamid Aboutalebi, Iran's chosen permanent delegate to the UN, because of his alleged involvement in the Tehran Hostages Crisis.[179] In case a problem arises with members of the EUDEL and before taking drastic measures, the US State Department will, however, first notify the UN and ask the EU to waive the immunity of such member or to withdraw them.[180]

In the matter of tax exemptions, the host state policies of the United States are less generous for the EUDEL. The host state applies a 'strict reciprocity' policy meaning that concessions that go further than the VCDR (eg certain tax privileges, privileges regarding the import or purchase of certain goods free of customs duties, and related charges) are granted on the same basis as what foreign governments accord to US diplomatic missions and staff. The tax privilege regime for the diplomats of a particular country accredited to the UN adopts the regime for bilateral diplomats of that same country to the United States. Owing to considerations based on reciprocity, some missions do not enjoy an exemption from sales tax in the United States, while a significant number of others enjoy it to a certain extent. The Department of State issues 'tax exemption cards' both to missions and to their diplomatic staff. Different animals shown on the front correspond with the level of privileges. EUDEL diplomatic staff are accorded a card with a deer, which provides the bearer a nationwide exemption with regard to taxes imposed on purchases over 100 USD, including hotel stays and restaurant meals.[181] The application of reciprocal treatment by the United States in its role as host state is legitimized by referral to section 15 of the Headquarters Agreement, whereby it grants privileges 'as it accords to diplomatic envoys accredited to it'. Section 15, however, seems to be the source of more than one inconsistency. It has been criticized for that reason. In a 1967 study, the UN Secretariat found 'that the privileges and immunities granted should generally be those afforded to the whole diplomatic corps, and should not be subject to particular conditions imposed, on a basis of reciprocity, upon the diplomatic missions of particular States'. However, the Headquarters Agreement unquestionably serves as the *lex specialis* regarding the status of permanent representatives in New York.[182] In practice, the US Government takes the treatment of its own diplomats in Brussels (ie by the Belgian

[178] ibid, section 13(*b*); 'United States Jurisdiction over Representatives to the United Nations' (1963) 63 Colum L Rev 1066, 1074.

[179] Section 6, Joint Resolution of the US Congress, Public Law 357, 4 August 1947; Department of State Statement on the Determination by the Secretary of State on Visa Application of Yasser Arafat, 26 November 1988.

[180] Report of the Sixth Committee to the General Assembly, Official Records of the General Assembly, Second Session, Doc A/427.

[181] Annex A of the US Department of State Office of Foreign Missions Guide (n 160).

[182] UN Secretariat, 'The Practice of the UN, the Specialized Agencies and the International Atomic Energy concerning their Status, Privileges and Immunities', UN Doc A/CN 4/L 118 (1967) II YBILC, para 96 (hereafter 1967 UN Secretariat Study on Specialized Agencies).

Government) as a point of reference for the tax exemptions granted to the EUDEL. Quite obviously, the EU has little control over the exact quota and privileges granted by the Belgian Government on its territory beyond the minimum threshold set by the VCDR. Arguably, it would be more correct to calculate the EUDELs' exemptions on the basis of traditional international courtesy.

#### 3.2.2.2 The EUDELs in Geneva

##### *3.2.2.2.1 The history and status of the missions*

Since 1961, and three years before the establishment of the New York information office, a Geneva-based European information and communication office had been operational.[183] In February 1964, the Commission of the EEC notified the Swiss Confederation that it wished to open a fully fledged permanent delegation to the UN offices in Geneva, simultaneously requiring the office to receive diplomatic privileges and immunities.[184] Compared to the situation in New York City at the time, the status of permanent representatives in Geneva was established more firmly. The Swiss Government's host state policy is built on the practices which had been in force when the League of Nations (LoN) maintained its headquarters in Geneva. From as early as 1922, the country granted diplomatic status to the permanent representatives of both member and non-member states. These representations were established to keep the sending state informed on the League's business. In 1920, Poland was the first country to set up a specific permanent delegation in Geneva.[185]

When the UN set up a regional office in Geneva, permanent delegations were awarded the rights and facilities similar to those of bilateral diplomatic missions accredited to Switzerland in Bern.[186] The Swiss law on privileges and immunities was revised soon after the VCDR had come into force in Switzerland and introduced an even more homologous application of privileges and immunities. The fact that Switzerland in those days maintained an active *ius legationis* as a neutral observer to IOs missions makes it plausible that it was sympathetic to considering similar claims of other actors. Switzerland sent an ad hoc observation delegation to the first session of the UNGA in London and to its second session in New York. In 1946, a liaison office was set up within the Consulate General in New York, which was converted into an observer mission in 1948.[187]

The Commission's request presented a challenging question from a legal-technical point of view, in the absence of any reference to permanent representations in the arrangements entered into by the UN and the Swiss Federal Council. Negotiators had not included this topic as it had been expected that member states would establish delegations at the New York headquarters only.[188] It just so happens that while still considering the Commission's February 1964 request, the Swiss Federal Council entered into a headquarters agreement with the United Nations Organization on 19 April 1964. This agreement introduced an Article IV

[183] Edith Drieskens, 'What's in a Name? Challenges to the Creation of EU Delegations' [2012] 7 HJD 51, 53.

[184] Exchange of Notes Verbales between the Swiss Mission to the European Communities and the European Commission, dated 11 February and 28 July 1964 and the Exchange of Notes Verbales between the Swiss Embassy in Brussels and DG Relex, dated 19 August and 26 October 2005.

[185] Harold Tobin, 'The Problem of Permanent Representation at the League of Nations' (1964) 48 Polit Sci Q 481.

[186] Decree of the Swiss Federal Council of 31 March 1948, as amended on 20 May 1958 and on 3 November 1967.

[187] Choi (n 166) 135.

[188] Amadeo Perez, 'The System of Privileges and Immunities Applicable to the International Organisations in Switzerland and to the Permanent Foreign Delegations in Geneva' (Eidgenössisches Departement für auswärtige Angelegenheiten 1997) 23.

on 'Representatives of Members of the United Nations' that accorded the representatives *(customary)*:

> privileges, immunities and facilities [ ... ] as diplomatic envoys enjoy, except that they shall have no right to claim exemption from customs duties on articles imported (otherwise than as part of their personal baggage) or from indirect taxes or sales taxes.

When the Swiss Federal Council then also conceded to the Commission's request on 28 July 1964 in an exchange of notes verbales, it announced that the Commission's delegation would enjoy the same status as missions of states accredited to international organizations on the Swiss territory.[189] The Swiss Government in return demanded to be informed of the name, rank, function, and end and start dates of posting of diplomatic staff in the Commission delegation.

Unlike in the United States, where the privileges and immunities are granted to observer missions following a case-by-case decision of the host state, in Switzerland all missions (of member and non-member states) are de facto accorded diplomatic immunities.[190] In the past, the exact privileges tended to vary slightly from one mission to another because of the mirroring of the status of the Bern diplomatic missions whose status was based on reciprocity. However, this appears to be less the case now.[191] Over time, the Federal Council also removed remaining differences between the bilateral missions in Bern and the multilateral delegations in Geneva.[192] All representatives in Geneva are granted tax exemptions in respect of direct taxes such as driving licences, car registration fees, and sales tax on duty-free goods (including liquors and tobacco). An exemption is not granted, as is common in receiving states, from taxes incorporated in the price of goods.

#### *3.2.2.2.2 The tale of two delegations*

The European Commission originally operated just one mission in Geneva, having as a main task the representation of the Commission in the UN. However, the delegation slowly but consistently began to execute liaison activities at other IOs located in the city. The delegation also participated in the work of the General Agreement on Tariffs and Trade ('GATT') from the very beginning. After having acquired full WTO membership in 1995, the Commission informed the Director General of the WTO of its intention to establish a permanent delegation to be integrated into the existing Commission delegation in Geneva. The number of personnel assigned to both missions increased: the mission to GATT grew from nine (diplomatic) members in 1982 to eighteen in 1992; the mission to the WTO had twenty-one members in 2002 (then the largest mission to the WTO), fifteen in 2012, and sixteen in 2017 (including the HoD).[193] This resulted in the focus of the entire Commission's delegation becoming trade-orientated; the UN section of the delegation was said to have become secondary and even understaffed.[194] Yet, it took until the establishment of the EEAS in January 2011 to split the delegation into one EUDEL to the WTO and another EUDEL to the UN

[189] Decision of the Swiss Federal Council, 14 July 1964.
[190] UN Doc A/CN 4/SER A/1967/Add 1, para 170.
[191] See the 1967 UN Secretariat Study on Specialized Agencies (n 182) para 63.
[192] ibid, para 148.
[193] Craig Van Grasstek, *The History and Future of the World Trade Organization* (World Trade Organization 2013) 83, 90–91.
[194] Paul Taylor, 'The EU in Geneva: Coordinating Policy in the Economic and Social Arrangements of the United Nations System' in Katie Verlin Laatikainen and Karen E Smith (eds), *The European Union at the United Nations: Intersecting Multilateralisms* (Palgrave Macmillan 2006).

and other IOs, dealing with multilateralism and all non-trade issues.[195] As also happened in New York, the new missions absorbed the Geneva Council liaison office established in the late 1960s.

In the past, the Swiss Federal Department of Foreign Affairs was a strong advocate of the 'one-mission' rule, but this principle was abandoned when the WTO was established. In a note verbale, dated 20 May 1994, Switzerland informed sending states that they could accredit multiple missions to the UN organizations and United Nations Specialized Agencies (UNSAs), the Conference of Disarmament (which has its own ambassadorial arrangements), and the WTO if they so wished.[196] On this basis, Switzerland does not oppose that the EU is represented by two missions in one city (three in the country if one counts the bilateral EUDEL in Bern). Both the multilateral missions and their members receive full diplomatic status.[197] The EUDELs operate in parallel and are both headed by an HoD at ambassadorial level. However, they share a joint administrative section, formally attached to the EUDEL to the WTO.[198] The fact that the EU is 'only' an observer to the UN activities and has membership in the WTO does not result in a difference in treatment: the WTO Headquarters Agreement refers to the CPIUN with regard to the privileges and immunities enjoyed by the representatives of the members.[199] The delegation to the UN and other IOs in Geneva counts twenty-nine staff members with diplomatic status, whereby the delegation to the WTO operates with sixteen diplomatic staff members. In both missions, the VCDR classification system and titles are used.[200] In comparison, the EU's mission to Switzerland counts six diplomats.

The EUDEL to the UN represents the EU at a great number of fora and each comes with their own accreditation practices, rules of procedure, and seating and speaking arrangements.[201] Internally, this is reflected in the EUDEL's structure consisting of five sections, all staffed with diplomats working on particular themes. The HoD and staff coordinate the actions of the human rights, economic affairs, health and social affairs, humanitarian and migration, and the disarmament sections. Each of those is tasked to follow-up on the particular relations with the UN Office and other IOs in Geneva on particular themes, for example, the EUDEL social affairs counsellor in Geneva, who will liaise with the ILO. Similarly, the EUDEL is represented at conferences of the parties to treaties taking place in Geneva. By way of example, the Union delegation to the fourth Conference of the Convention on Conventional Weapons (2011), was led by the Deputy HoD, accompanied by disarmament

[195] Commission, 'Communication from the Commission to the Council and the European Parliament: Establishment of an EU Delegation to the UN in Geneva', 2010, COM(2010)287 final; David Spence, 'From the Convention to Lisbon: External Competence and the Uneasy Transition for Geneva Delegations' in David Spence and Jozef Bátora (eds), *The European External Action Service: European Diplomacy Post-Westphalia* (Palgrave Macmillan 2015) 225.

[196] Perez (n 188) 14.

[197] Caterina Carta, 'The EU in Geneva: The Diplomatic Representation of a System of Governance' (2013) 9 J Contemp Eur Res 406, 416.

[198] Spence (n 195) 228, 233.

[199] Art VIII(4) Agreement establishing the World Trade Organization, signed on 15 April 1994, 1867 UNTS 4 (hereafter WTO Headquarters Agreement).

[200] UN Blue Book, Missions Permanentes auprès des Nations Unies (Geneva), No 119, 2021.

[201] Rudi Delarue, 'The EU–ILO Partnership and the Global Identity of the Union's Social Model' in Henri de Waele and Jan-Jaap Kuipers (eds), *The European Union's Emerging International Identity: Views from the Global Arena Studies in EU External Relations* (Martinus Nijhoff 2013). See, for a discussion at the UN Human Rights Council, Karen E Smith, 'Speaking with One Voice? European Union Co-ordination on Human Rights Issues at the United Nations' (2006) 44 JCMS 113; Jan Wouters and Katrien Meuwissen, 'The European Union at the UN Human Rights Council. Multilateral Human Rights Protection Coming of Age?' (2014) 2 Eur Hum Rights Law Rev 135.

desk officer from the delegation and an EEAS expert on disarmament.[202] The Union delegation is referred to in the Geneva edition of the UN Blue Book as one of the fifteen intergovernmental organizations to have received a standing invitation to participate as an observer in the sessions.

The EUDEL to the WTO has a more specific mission and operation modus. The WTO stands as an example of an effective Treaty-created international organization with, at its core, an effective adjudication process that is complied with.[203] This requires a permanent presence of highly specialized trade diplomats in the EUDEL. The delegation represents the Commission's exclusive trade competences but it also serves the broader external representation on the part of the Commission in particular and of other institutions in matters of shared or parallel competences. These realities have also resulted in diplomatic arrangements on the ground in terms of pooling together of diplomatic resources and the framing of negotiating positions between the EU institutions as well as between the EU and its member states.[204]

Specific WTO instruments further define the diplomatic status of the EUDEL. The 1994 Agreement establishing the World Trade Organization institutes a functional immunity based on the CPIUN–SA: '[t]he officials of the WTO and the representatives of the Members shall similarly be accorded by each of its Members such privileges and immunities as are necessary for the independent exercise of their functions in connection with the WTO'. These 'shall be similar to the privileges and immunities stipulated in the Convention on the Privileges and Immunities of the Specialized Agencies'.[205] The most tangible benefit of the agreement is that representatives travelling to other member states enjoy functional privileges and immunities in all WTO member states. The EU is able to abide by this rule because its member states are WTO members too; when visiting the EU institutions, third country representatives to the WTO will find themselves on Belgian, French, or Luxembourgian territory and be granted immunities by the respective governments. As regards representatives residing in Geneva, the 1961 VCDR applies by analogy on the basis of the 1995 Agreement as between the World Trade Organization and the Swiss Confederation Headquarters Agreement.[206] Article 17 of the Agreement provides that:

> [p]ermanent missions shall enjoy privileges and immunities in accordance with customary law, the Vienna Convention on Diplomatic Relations of 18 April 1961, which applies by analogy, and relevant provisions of this Agreement.

To a large extent, the application of reciprocity with regards to tax and custom privileges is excluded by the Agreement. Tax privileges are granted in accordance with the VCDR and a fixed lower limit is introduced which applies to all missions for the exemption from value-added tax (VAT): '[t]his exemption shall be granted by means of deduction at source for amounts of not less than 100 francs per invoice, without upper limit [ ... ] VAT shall be

[202] Answer given by the High Representative to parliamentary question P-009808/2011, 6 December 2011.

[203] Marina Foltea, *International Organizations in WTO Dispute Settlement: How Much Institutional Sensitivity?* (CUP 2012) 9 et seq.

[204] Michael H Smith, 'The EU as a Diplomatic Actor in the Post-Lisbon Era: Robust or Rootless Hybrid?' in Joachim Alexander Koops and Gjovalin Macaj (eds), *The European Union as a Diplomatic Actor* (Palgrave Macmillan 2014); Xavier Pierre and Rytis Paulauskas, 'Enhancing Teamwork within the European Union Diplomacy and Including Key External Partners in the EU Coordination Process in Geneva' (2014) 12 Lith Foreign Policy Rev 106.

[205] Art VIII (3–4) WTO Headquarters Agreement.

[206] Agreement between the World Trade Organization and the Swiss Confederation, signed on 17 May 1995.

deducted without lower limit from the bills of the PTT and *services industriels* (utilities).'[207] Furthermore, the Swiss Federal Council grants permanent missions privileges 'at least as favourable' as those provided by the national Ordinance of 13 November 1985 concerning preferential customs treatment of states in their relations with IOs.[208] In addition, members of permanent missions who have diplomatic status have the right to import and use a second duty-free car subject to an unlimited undertaking for as long as they remain the owner thereof.

#### 3.2.2.3 The EUDEL in Addis Ababa

##### *3.2.2.3.1 The history and status of the mission*

The Commission opened a new delegation in Addis Ababa in 2007 where the African Union's headquarters are located.[209] Since then, the EU operates two delegations in the Ethiopian capital, a bilateral and a multilateral EUDEL, each headed by an HoD at the level of ambassador. The division of labour between the two is clear. The EUDEL accredited to the Ethiopian Government deals with bilateral issues (eg the monitoring of fair and transparent trials and humane conditions of detention), while the multilateral delegation monitors the relations with the AU.[210] The first delegation was established in 1991 and accredited to the Ethiopian Government, while the second represents the EU at the AU. While the EU collaborates intensively with different organs of the AU, it has no formal observer status in the organization.[211] It is formally marked a 'regional integration and international organization'. The intensity of the AU–EU relationship should not be underestimated, however: EU financial commitments to the AU for activities contracted in 2014 and 2015 amounted to EUR 717.9 million. Cooperation is mainly pursued in the framework of the EU–Africa partnership, which contains a number of thematic policy dialogues such as the Africa–EU Migration and Mobility Dialogue. The AU equally maintains a diplomatic mission to the EU.

##### *3.2.2.3.2 Host state policies*

Prior to the EUDEL's opening, the Union sent an ad hoc diplomat to Addis Ababa in the form of the EU Special Representative for the Great Lakes region, whose tasks then included the maintenance of links between the EU and the AU. The first HoD to the AU—then appointed by the Commission—was also 'double hatted' in the sense that he also observed the function of EU Special Representative to the AU—a mandate issued by the Council. The latter function has been fully integrated in the former since the Lisbon Treaty.[212] The formal enhancement of a permanent European diplomatic presence to deepen relations with the AU was nevertheless welcomed by Ethiopia as the host state; one needs only to look at the local government's decision to grant the new mission and its members full diplomatic immunities and privileges. It has helped, of course, that the AU had opened a mission of its own in Brussels a year earlier, which was granted diplomatic privileges and immunities.[213]

[207] ibid, Arts 18 and 24.

[208] ibid, Arts 19 and 25.

[209] Julia Lieb, *Diplomatie Jenseits des Staates: Die EU-Außenvertretung Gegenüber Drittstaaten und der Europäische Auswärtige Dienst*, vol 80 (1st edn, Nomos 2013) 126–34.

[210] Answer given by the Commission to parliamentary question P-0790/2007, 16 April 2007.

[211] Answer given by the Commission to parliamentary question P-015699/2015, 27 January 2016.

[212] Natividad Fernández Sola, 'The Stakes of the European External Action Service. What is Needed in Order to Become a European Diplomatic Corps?' in José María Beneyto (ed), *La Unión Europea como Actor Global: Las Nuevas Dimensiones de la Política Exterior Europea* (Instituto Universitario de Estudios Europeos de la Universidad CEU 2011) 51.

[213] Headquarters Agreement between the Kingdom of Belgium and the Organization of African Unity, signed in Brussels on 9 October 1985 and the Exchanges of Letters of 9 October 1985 and 29 June 1998 between the

The Ethiopian Government instantaneously decided to place the new mission on an equal footing with the Commission's bilateral mission in Addis Ababa. The host state informed the Commission that it would make existing bilateral arrangements applicable to the multilateral Commission delegation to the AU, specifically the 1991 EA between the Commission and Ethiopia.[214] Ethiopia did this in a written reply taking the form of a letter to a diplomatic note sent by the Commission, which requested agreement for the establishment of a permanent delegation to the AU. As to the legal qualification of these instruments, one could argue that taken together, the two letters constitute an exchange of letters that represents an understanding between the Ethiopian Government and the European Commission.[215] The instrument meets the criteria of Article 13 VCLT of a treaty in the form of an exchange of notes since it encapsulates a consent of the parties to be bound. The consent lies in the express extension by the host state upon request of the Commission of the conditions provided in the 1991 EA on the bilateral delegation to the multilateral delegation. In that regard, the host state's reply reproducing part of the text of the Commission's letter, is interesting:

> [t]he Ministry is pleased to inform the Commission of the European Communities that the Government of Ethiopia agrees to the establishment of a new EUDEL to the African Union in Addis Ababa. The Ministry also agrees that the Agreement signed between the Government of Ethiopia and the Commission of the European Communities on the Establishment and on the Privileges and Immunities on 22nd February 1991, would be applicable to the premises of the EUDEL to the AU, its HoD, its members as well as their families forming part of their respective households.

The text of the exchange of letters is rather concise as it only refers to the 1991 EA as valid law. To the present date, the exchange of letters is the only formal evidence in writing of the recognition by the host state of the delegation and its diplomatic status.

### 3.2.2.4 The EUDEL in Jakarta

#### *3.2.2.4.1 The history and status of the mission*

The multilateral EUDEL in Jakarta is the latest acquisition in the EU's multilateral diplomatic network. The mission was opened on 8 August 2015, a symbolic date for ASEAN, which celebrated its forty-eighth anniversary that day. Since 2014, a dedicated Ambassador to ASEAN had been preparing the EUDEL's establishment, in close cooperation with the bilateral EUDEL in Jakarta, accredited to the Indonesian Government. ASEAN does not have a similar mission accredited to the EU: its interests are represented by its member states and ad hoc missions. According to Article 45(2) of the ASEAN Charter, it is up to the ASEAN Coordinating Council to decide on the form the external relations with other regional IOs will take.

The establishment of the EUDEL reflects the EU's growing engagement with ASEAN and underlines its ambition to upgrade the partnership to a strategic one. The diplomatic efforts, including the formal upgrade of the mission, certainly contributed to the fact that, as of 1

Kingdom of Belgium and the Organization of African Unity (adopted by Belgian law 21 February 2006: Belgian State Gazette, 21 February 2006).

[214] Agreement between the Government of the People's Democratic Republic of Ethiopia and the European Commission on the establishment of the Commission delegation, 22 February 1991.

[215] Commission, External Relations DG, note verbale, K6/D(07)511257, 1 August 2007 and Federal Democratic Republic of Ethiopia, Ministry of Foreign Affairs, Letter, No IG-Rt/23/11/05, 26 October 2007.

December 2020, the Union became a strategic partner of ASEAN. Prior to that, it was a 'dialogue partner' of the IO (cf Art 44 of the ASEAN Charter).

Indonesia and the EU share important and promising ties in trade and investment. The EU is one of the largest trading partners of Indonesia and the second largest investor. There is vast untapped potential, as exemplified by ongoing trade agreements negotiations with several ASEAN countries, and, eventually, the prospect of concluding a region-to-region free trade agreement.[216] In addition, the EU and ASEAN discuss matters as diverse as climate change, sustainability and biodiversity, counter-terrorism, maritime issues, education, science and technology, and disaster management.

While the topic of the establishment of permanent missions of non-member states is not discussed in the ASEAN Charter, the founding document leaves the necessary policy space to the IO to decide on its external relations.[217] ASEAN considers the EUDEL as a diplomatic mission; the EU Ambassador presents their letter of credence to the Secretary General of ASEAN.

*3.2.2.4.2 Host state policies*

In 2014, the HR informed Indonesia about its intention to establish a dedicated mission to ASEAN in Jakarta on the basis of the Host Country Agreement between the ASEAN Secretariat and Indonesia. In order to make the VCDR applicable, the HR requested the extension of rights, privileges, and immunities, mentioned in the EA signed between the Government of Indonesia and the EU on 6 September 1988, to the premises and staff of the EUDEL to ASEAN, which host state Indonesia accepted. With regard to the missions of member states, Article 19 of the ASEAN Charter spells out that permanent representatives of the member states 'enjoy such immunities and privileges as are necessary for the exercise of their functions' and are governed by the 1961 VCDR. The mission and its ambassador enjoy full diplomatic privileges and immunities and are treated in a similar way as the EUDEL accredited to the Indonesian Government. This puts the EUDEL in a better position than what is foreseen in Article 19 of the ASEAN Charter with regard to the missions of the member states, which spells out that those permanent representatives 'enjoy such immunities and privileges as are necessary for the exercise of their functions', although their status is governed by the 1961 VCDR too.

### 3.2.3 Multilateral EUDELs in EU Member States

The EU maintains four permanent delegations to IOs headquartered 'at home' in EU member states. The diplomatic duty stations are located in Paris, Strasbourg, Vienna, and Rome.

In Paris, the Commission is granted an observer status in the OECD and at the UN Educational, Scientific and Cultural Organization (UNESCO) The status of the EU in UNESCO can be upgraded for specific purposes. For example, in the negotiations of the Convention on the Protection and Promotion of the Diversity of Cultural Expressions, the Commission was granted the right to 'participate actively and as fully as appropriate'.[218]

[216] See EU–ASEAN Strategic Partnership 2022,: *EU–ASEAN Natural Partners*, <https://www.eeas.europa.eu/sites/default/files/documents/EU-ASEAN%20Blue%20Book%202022.pdf> accessed 2 May 2022.

[217] Articles 41(6), 44(2), and 45 of the ASEAN Charter.

[218] UNESCO, Executive Board, 171 EX/Decisions, 25 May 2005, 72.

The EU regularly participates in CoE meetings and working groups without formally being granted an observer status. Accession to the European Convention on Human Rights is foreseen in Article 6(2) TEU but received a negative opinion by the Court in 2014.[219] On 7 October 2019, after it received a written contribution from the Commission which addresses all the objections raised by the Court, the Council reaffirmed its commitment to the accession and agreed to supplementary negotiating directives in order to allow for a swift resumption of negotiations with the CoE.

The EUDEL in Vienna represents the Union at a vast number of Vienna-based UN bodies, funds, and agencies. It concerns the International Atomic Energy Agency (IAEA), UN Office on Drugs and Crime (UNODC), the UN Industrial Development Organization (UNIDO), the UN Commission on International Trade Law (UNCITRAL), and the UN Committee on the Peaceful Uses of Outer Space (UNCOPUOS). The EU is a fully fledged party to a number of Conventions (and participates as such in the sessions of the Conferences of Parties) which are within the remit of the UNODC (ie the UN Convention against Illicit Traffic of Narcotic Drugs and Psychotropic Substances, the UN Convention against Transnational Organized Crime, and the UN Convention against Corruption, as well as a number of Protocols to these Conventions). The modalities adopted regarding the EU's enhanced observer status at the UNGA in Resolution GA/65/276 apply to UNCITRAL but not to other UN organizations. The EU has been invited to observe the meetings of the IAEA Governing Bodies (General Conference and Board of Governors), UNCOPUOS, and UNCITRAL Working Groups. In the IAEA, EURATOM (but not the EU) has an observer status. Also in Vienna, the EUDEL is active in the Organization for Security and Co-operation in Europe (OSCE). The role of the EU in the OSCE has never been formally defined and is based on a number of practices. The EUDEL is regarded as being part of the delegation of the member state holding the rotating presidency of the Council, which allows it to participate in all proceedings, to speak (even on behalf of the member states), and to intervene unless the issue under discussion clearly is not an EU competence. The Union is represented in other Vienna-based international organizations too: it is an observer in the Zangger Committee and the Nuclear Suppliers Group (NSG). The EU works closely together with the Preparatory Commission for the Comprehensive Nuclear Test Ban Treaty Organisation (CTBTO), the Wassenaar Arrangement (WA); the Code of Conduct against Ballistic Missile Proliferation (HCOC); the Organization of the Petroleum Exporting Countries (OPEC), the Sustainable Energy for All Forum (SE4All), the Energy Community, the International Centre for Migration Policy Development (ICMPD), and the International Institute for Applied Systems Analysis (IIASA).

In Rome, the EUDEL represents the Union in the Food and Agriculture Organization (FAO).[220] The FAO was the first and, up to today, is the only UNSA that recognizes the EU as a full member. Through a 'Regional Economic Integration Organization' (REIO) clause in the FAO Constitution, the EU enjoys similar rights and obligations as state parties. The Commission is a special observer of the World Food Programme's (WFP) Executive Board. Its permanent seat in the Board comes with the right to speak, which can be exercised only after the member states of the Board have spoken. Also in Rome, the EU is an observer in the Governing Council of the International Fund for Agricultural Development (IFAD). The

[219] Opinion 2/13 *Accession by the European Union to the European Convention for the Protection of Human Rights and Fundamental Freedoms* [2014] ECLI:EU:C:2014:2454.

[220] Commission Communication, 'The Role of the European Union in the Food and Agriculture Organization (FAO) after the Treaty of Lisbon', COM(2013)333, 13.

Delegation also represents the Union at the Holy See, the Order of Malta, and the Republic of San Marino.

The dynamics between the Union and the host states are cooperative. Acquainted with the Union's institutional set-up and diplomatic aspirations, Austria, France, and Italy act responsively to the requests for diplomatic treatment by the Union. However, the conduct of diplomacy within the territory of member states raises specific legal questions compared to that in third states. Confusion tends to emerge most prominently over the nature of the legal framework applicable to EUDELs. If it is accepted that the EU is an independent diplomatic actor, it follows that the international (customary) law, not EU law, governs the status of EUDELs in Austria, Italy, and France as regards the privileges and immunities. A further consequence is that the decision-making power of the host state can be curtailed by the (headquarters) agreements entered into by the EU and the accrediting IO.

The above has been accepted by the member states in principle but occasionally contested in practice. It is not always possible to make an abstraction of the diplomatic relations of the Union and to view it as an actor external to the member states in need of a protection as if it was a third party. One could argue that EU officials, archives, communication, and premises are sufficiently protected by EU law and that therefore it is not necessary for member states to grant the Union diplomatic privileges and immunities. Personal immunity would in that case be limited to the execution of official functions and not be extended to the official's family but would exist in the territory of each member state, irrelevant of the nationality of the official. In diplomatic law, host states commonly restrict or do not grant privileges and immunities to nationals and permanent residents. It is recommended not to appoint nationals to the diplomatic staff (see also Art 8(1) VCDR). If a national would still be appointed, consent of the host state must be sought (Art 8(2–3) VCDR); the diplomat will granted functional immunity (Art 38 VCDR). In EU law, all EU officials receive personal immunity on the basis of Article 11(*a*) Protocol No 7 on Privileges and Immunities, which provides that Union officials are 'immune from legal proceedings in respect of acts performed by them in their official capacity, including their words spoken or written'. Officials continue to enjoy this immunity after they have ceased to hold office.

Moreover, member states may be reluctant to grant EU diplomats personal privileges in the form of tax and customs exemptions exceeding those which are granted pursuant to Protocol No 7. Although Protocol No 7 on Privileges and Immunities foresees the right to import and export furniture free of duty (Art 12 (*d*)); the right to import free of duty a motor car for their personal use (Art 12 (*e*)); and an exemption from national taxes on salaries, wages, and emoluments paid by the Union (Art 13), its privileges are less extensive than those of the Vienna Convention. The VCDR's fiscal exemptions include all dues and taxes, personal or real, national, regional, or municipal, and custom duties (Arts 23, 34, 36). The EU itself is exempt from all direct taxes (Art 3); and all customs duties, prohibitions, and restrictions on imports and exports in respect of articles intended for its official use (Art 4) in the territory of the member states on the basis of Protocol No 7.

Against this background, the following sections study how Austria, Italy, and France have dealt with their role as host state to an EUDEL. It will be shown that the field of tension between international diplomatic law and EU law has resulted in different legal arrangements.

### 3.2.3.1 The EUDEL in Vienna

In its vibrant capital, Austria hosts a Union delegation that plays a key role in the development of multilateral relations. Since 1979, the EUDEL has ensured the common European representation at an impressive number of IOs, of which the most important are the Vienna

UN Office (UNOV) and the OSCE. The HoD and the deputy HoD are granted the personal rank of ambassador whereby the first is accredited to the UNOV and the latter functions as the EU permanent representative to the OSCE. In addition, delegation staff take part in all sorts of (institutionalized and ad hoc) meetings of parties to international conventions having a secretariat in Vienna, as well as meetings of more informal groups of friends and international alliances.[221] During an eighteen-month transition period after the entry into force of the Lisbon Treaty, the EUDEL pushed hard for a staffing level in line with that typical for large member states' presidencies and additional resources, as well as a second dedicated ambassador, to deal with its important multilateral agenda. The EUDEL had grown to twice the size of the pre-Lisbon Commission delegation by 2014, which clearly enhanced visibility.[222]

The host state accepts that the EUDEL is a diplomatic mission, the status of which is governed by international law. Austria is the only member state with which the EU has concluded an establishment agreement to that effect. The legal instrument, dated 15 October 1987, is a perfect copy of the diplomatic arrangements entered into with third states.[223] It contains standard clauses on the recognition by the host state of the Union's legal personality and its capacity to conclude contracts and acquire and dispose of immovable and movable property in Austria (Art 2). On the basis of the EA, the delegation, its head and members, as well as the members of their families forming part of their respective households, enjoy such rights, privileges, and immunities and are subject to such obligations that correspond to those laid down in the VCDR. The Vienna Convention's other provisions are applicable *mutatis mutandis* (Art 3). Consequently, the EUDEL to Vienna-based IOs is granted diplomatic privileges and immunities as if it were a bilateral mission to Austria, although it is not being a multilateral mission accredited to a number of international organizations.

One provision in the Commission–Austria EA warrants closer scrutiny because it introduces a reciprocity clause. Article 4 of the 1987 EA reads:

> [c]es privilèges et immunités sont reconnus à la condition que, conformément aux dispositions de [article 16 of Protocol No 7], les Etats membres des Communautés européennes accordant les mêmes privilèges et immunités à la Mission de la République d'Autriche auprès des Communautés européennes, à son chef et aux membres de son personnel ainsi qu'aux membres de leurs familles qui font partie de leurs ménages respectifs.

While useful in an EU–third state bilateral context, the reciprocity provision provokes friction when applied to the relationship between the Union and Austria. At first glance, it would appear that the accordance of diplomatic privileges and immunities by Austria to the EU is subject to the enjoyment of similar rights of mission to the EU in other member states. There are two issues with such a reading. First, the reference in the EA to *the duty of (all) member states* should be nuanced. The obligation to grant member states' representatives diplomatic status primarily targets host state Belgium, where such mission would be based. Further,

221 Answer given by the High Representative to parliamentary question E-002524-13, 5 March 2013.

222 Lars-Erik Lundin, 'Effective Multilateralism after Lisbon: The Added Value of the EEAS and the EU Delegation in Vienna' in Spence and Bátora (n 195) 250.

223 Accord entre la Commission de Communautés européennes et le Gouvernement de la République d'Autriche sur l'établissement ainsi que les privileges et immunités de la Délegation de la Commission de Communautés européennes en République d'Autriche, signed on 15 October 1978, entered into force 1 January 1988. See also the Exchange of Letters between the Commission and the Republic of Austria with regard to the recognition of the laissez-passer of EU officials (dated 11 July 1980).

the representatives receive privileges and immunities of 'diplomats in transit' when visiting EU institutions in Luxembourg and France and travelling to and from EU meetings (Art 10, Protocol No 7). Second, a member state's permanent representation in Brussels is legally entitled to diplomatic status. The EU Treaties recognize the right of member states to open a permanent representation to the EU. Those missions enjoy the customary diplomatic privileges and immunities on the basis of Article 10, Protocol No 7. The entitlement stems from the bilateral and institutional relationship between the Union and its member states; it is not a diplomatic reciprocal entitlement. In other words, a member state's mission enjoys diplomatic status regardless of whether an EUDEL is located on its territory, whether accredited to one or more IOs, what rights it enjoys, and how well these are respected. Permanent representations of the member states are fully covered under Article 11 of Protocol No 7 on Privileges and Immunities, where it is stated that '[r]epresentatives of Member States taking part in the work of the institutions of the Union, their advisers and technical experts shall, in the performance of their duties and during their travel to and from the place of meeting, enjoy the customary privileges, immunities and facilities'. Member states receive this protection because of their status as EU members, not because they may or may not have parallel relations with the Union in their role of host states. A hypothetical Austrian failure to comply with the terms of the EA should never result in the taking of countermeasures by either the Union or host state Belgium. Some may suggest that the reciprocity clause of the EA has some practical value as it grants Austria a more pronounced enforcement mechanism when compared to other member states to mitigate a hypothetical Belgian failure to comply with its obligations under the EU Treaties vis-à-vis permanent representations. However, in such a case, Austria should find recourse in well-established EU procedures to denounce violations of EU law rather than in a separate international agreement entered into with the Union. The Commission, and even Austria, can bring an infringement action against Belgium on the basis of Article 258 TFEU. If Austria would choose not to follow this road and to take reciprocal measures on the basis of the EA, the country can only target the EUDEL; Belgian diplomatic representatives in Vienna (either those accredited to the government or to IOs) should not be made the object of reciprocal sanctioning. The only reasoned conclusion is that any invocation of Article 4 of the 1987 EA risks creating undesired political and diplomatic consequences and is therefore appropriately avoided.

#### 3.2.3.2 The EUDEL in Rome

Officially the delegation to the Holy See, the Order of Malta, the Republic of San Marino, and the UN, the EU's Rome mission serves both bilateral and multilateral purposes. When created in 1993, the delegation's focus was the development of general relations with Rome-based IOs; over time, relations with the FAO, the WFP, and IFAD were deepened. In 2006, the Head of the EUDEL was accredited to the Holy See and, in 2007, to the Order of Malta.[224] The legal framework under which the EUDEL operates differs substantially from Austria's. The EU did not enter into an EA nor an accord de siège with the Italian Republic. In effect, the delegation and its staff enjoy full diplomatic privileges and immunities via the Union's accreditation to the FAO, of which it has been a full member since 1991. When the European Economic Community was accepted as a full member of the FAO (Rome), it was the first time it had been recognized as a full voting member by a UN agency. The Union now serves as the FAO's biggest contributing partner. In secondary order, the Union also enjoys

[224] See the 1970 exchange of letters with the Holy See (n 18) and the 2009 MoU with the Order of Malta (n 19).

reciprocal privileges and immunities in reciprocity as a consequence of the diplomatic status it grants Holy See envoys in Brussels.

Being a member of a UNSA in Rome, the EU is subjected to the terms of the CPIUN–SA on the privileges and immunities of permanent representations. More specific rules are contained in the FAO Headquarters Agreement concluded between Italy and the organization.[225] The Agreement grants every person designated by a member as its principal resident representative to the FAO and the members of its mission, whether residing inside or outside Rome, the same privileges and immunities within the Italian territory, subject to corresponding the conditions and obligations 'as the Government accords to diplomatic envoys and members of their missions of comparable rank accredited to the Government' (Art XI, section 24(*a*)). The Agreement's reference to member 'nations' has been interpreted to include member organizations such as the EU. This leads to the full application of the rights of the VCDR to the EUDEL in Rome and its members, including the corresponding obligations that transpire from it. A specific clause of section 24(*b*) targets governments which are not recognized by the Italian Republic. It grants them such privileges and immunities 'only within the headquarters seat, at their residences and offices outside the headquarters seat, in transit between the headquarters seat and such residences and offices, and in transit on official business to or from foreign countries'. The provision, including its geographical limits, does not apply to the EU.

Section 24(*c*) grants Italy the right to accord a more limited functional immunity to diplomats when these are Italian citizens (without mentioning its applicability to permanent residents) or when engaged in commercial activities in Italy. Article XI, section 24(*c*) reads in full: '[w]henever the resident representatives of the Member Nations or members of their missions are Italian citizens, or are engaged in any trade or industry within the Italian Republic, the privileges and immunities recognized by international law shall apply to the extent authorized by international law as accepted by the Government'. The reference to commercial activities has become somewhat redundant now that the Vienna Convention, and with it CIL, deal with the matter in greater detail. Article 42 VCDR forbids diplomatic agents to perform commercial activity in the receiving state. Spouses (after an authorization by the receiving state) and non-diplomatic personnel may engage in such activities, but their immunity from civil and administrative jurisdiction does not apply to acts arising from the performance of the activity and their immunity from execution does not apply to judicial decisions related to such acts (Arts 31(1)(*c*), 31(3), 37(1) VCDR).

Section 25 deals with ad hoc representatives of the members. In a similar fashion to the provisions of the CPIUN–SA, the clause grants them the privileges and immunities allowing them to take part in meetings in Rome. For this category, similar to the CPIUN–SA, a duty rather than a right to waive exists when the immunity of the Delegation or one of its members would impede the course of justice (section 26). For the permanent representatives, the VCDR rules on the waiving of immunity apply.

The EU's accreditation at the Holy See provides a second legal source for the enjoyment of diplomatic rights and immunities of the Rome delegation and its staff. As signatory party to the VCDR, the Holy See has sent a Diplomatic Nuncio to the EU's corps diplomatique since 1970. The privileges and immunities accorded to the Nuncio since are reciprocated with regard to the EUDEL to the Holy See in Rome.[226] On the basis of the Lateran Pacts of

[225] Agreement between the Government of the Italian Republic and the FAO regarding the headquarters of the Food and Agriculture Organization of the United Nations, signed on 31 October 1950, 1409 UNTS 521.

[226] Exchange of letters between the Commission and the Holy See (n 18).

1929, Italy recognizes the missions accredited by foreign governments to the Holy See and ensures that within its territory they also enjoy the prerogatives of immunity held by diplomatic agents under international law.[227] Similarly, the missions' headquarters may be located within the Italian territory.[228] The rule that Italy must recognize the diplomatic status of an entity even when it does not conduct diplomatic relations with that entity itself certainly facilitates the recognition of this status on the part of the Union.

### 3.2.3.3 The EUDELs in France

#### *3.2.3.3.1 Host state policies*

The EU is diplomatically represented in Paris and Strasbourg by two multilateral delegations. Host state France does not oppose the EUDEL's activities in its territory and accords them the core diplomatic privileges and immunities. However, the French Government adopts a more restrictive reading of diplomatic law in its relations with the Union than do Austria and Italy. In comparison to those host (member) states, France is less expeditious in its recognition of the applicability of the VCDR or CIL. This is exemplified by the fact that France has not yet responded to the Union's call for the conclusion of an EA or an alternative legal instrument governing the status of the EUDELs. The French position probably originates from the pre-2009 situation, when the Union was represented by a Paris-based Commission Representation. This mission was in charge of coordinating all issues falling under Community competences and therefore functioned as a satellite office of the Commission, which could have been confused with the (non-diplomatic) information office that the Commission also operated in the same city (as it does in all member states' capitals). To this day, the French Government does not entirely distinguish between the status of the EU delegations and that of the Commission's Information Office.

By not entering into an establishment agreement with the EU, France effectively retains its prerogative to decide who is accorded diplomatic treatment and its ability to define the scope of privileges and immunities. Additionally, France retains the capacity to revoke them. Further, since the host state never formally accepted that PIL creates obligations on its part, privileges and immunities are negotiated on a case-by-case basis, permitting dissimilar treatment even between the Paris and Strasbourg missions.

#### *3.2.3.3.2 The EUDEL in Paris*

The Paris-based delegation represents the Union at the OECD[229] and UNESCO, and is also accredited to the Principalities of Andorra and Monaco.[230] The Union's diplomatic link with the OECD is particularly strong: a mission was established by the ECSC High Authority as early as 1952 on the basis of an exchange of letters.[231] In supplementary Protocol No 1 to the 1960 OECD Convention, signatory parties expressly allowed for the three Communities to establish an official representation at the OECD (Art 1) and to participate in its work (Art

[227] Article 12 of the Lateran Conciliation Treaty, signed on 11 February 1929 (published 5 June 1929 in the Gazzetta Ufficiale No 130) as amended by the Agreement between the Italian Republic and the Holy See, signed on 18 February 1984, 24 ILM 1589 [1985].

[228] Cedric Ryngaert, 'The Legal Status of the Holy See' (2011) 3 GoJIL 829.

[229] Convention on the Organisation for Economic Co-operation and Development and Supplementary Protocols, signed on 14 December 1960, entered into force 30 September 1961, 888 UNTS 179 (hereafter OECD Convention).

[230] Article 18 of the Agreement regarding the headquarters of the United Nations Educational, Scientific and Cultural Organization and the privileges and immunities of the Organization on French Territory, signed on 2 July 1954, entered into force 23 November 1955 (hereafter UNESCO Headquarters Agreement).

[231] Reichling (n 151) 42.

2).[232] Although it is not a member, the EU's legal status in the OECD goes well beyond that of a mere observer and is often referred to as a 'quasi-membership'.[233] The Union, for instance, has voting rights except in the case when decisions and recommendations are presented before the Council. In the OECD's Development and Assistance Committee, moreover, the EU enjoys a full membership.

However, when it comes to the entitlement to diplomatic privileges and immunities, only the representatives of full OECD members are mentioned. Protocol No 2 (1960) refers to the privileges, exemptions, and immunities described in the 1948 OEEC Convention. Article 9 of said Convention grants representatives 'the privileges, immunities and facilities normally enjoyed by diplomatic envoys of comparable rank', while Article 11 excludes the application between a representative and the state of their nationality or of which 'he is or has been the representative'.[234] Similarly, Articles 18–21 on diplomatic privileges, immunities, and facilities of the UNESCO Headquarters Agreement limit their scope to the representatives of the member states.[235] In the IOs' internal sphere, EU representatives and member state representatives nevertheless receive equal treatment. The EUDEL uses note verbales and démarches, participates in diplomatic activities, and its HoD is addressed by the courtesy title of ambassador. The consequences are more significant in the EU's relations with the French Government. France, not having assumed an obligation to grant the EUDEL diplomatic status, has been willing to recognize the vast majority of privileges and immunities that would result from it as matter of courtesy. Consequently, the delegation receives similar treatment to other diplomatic missions in Paris, for example, with regard to the issuance of diplomatic license plates, the use of the diplomatic bag, and the inviolability of the mission's premises, documents, and archives. Both the HoD and the Deputy HoD are granted diplomatic status and a diplomatic identity card, which reads on the back that the VCDR applies to their personal situation. The diplomatic identity cards of other diplomatic agents of the delegation reflect the VCDR nomenclature in terms of the functions exercised by the members of the mission, yet do not declare that the status of the holder is regulated by international diplomatic law. The latter signposts retained policy space on the part of the host state. It can therefore be deduced that France accepts that certain privileges and immunities operate in the Union's favour but that these facilities are granted on the basis of a functional necessity and do not arise ipso jure from PIL.[236]

The voluntary nature of the arrangements does not impede the members of the EUDEL in Paris from enjoying the normal diplomatic tax privileges, that is, on their income but also on purchased products such as fuel or alcoholic beverages. Nevertheless, not all taxes are lifted by the French Government in the same manner as for other diplomatic missions. Examples include local residential and audio-visual taxes (*taxe d'habitation* and the *contribution à l'audiovisuel public*), which the French authorities continue to collect from EUDEL staff; members of other Parisian diplomatic and consular missions of foreign nationality who do not have permanent residence in France are exempt from such direct personal taxes on the basis of Article 34 VCDR. In the past, the Commission was strongly opposed to this discrimination. Because the Commission could not find an amicable solution through negotiations,

[232] Supplementary Protocol No 1 to the OECD Convention.

[233] see: Joren Verschaeve and Tamara Takács, 'The EU's International Identity: The Curious Case of the OECD' in de Waele and Kuipers (n 201) 194–95.

[234] Convention on the Organisation for European Economic Co-operation (OEEC) and its Supplementary Protocol No 1 on the Legal Capacity, Privileges and Immunities of the Organisation, signed 16 April 1948).

[235] UNESCO Headquarters Agreement.

[236] Reichling (n 151) 43.

it even took the matter to court. In 2006, in an appeal procedure, the French *Conseil d'Etat* upheld the earlier judgment of the Administrative Court of Paris denying that a discrimination existed. The position of the then deputy HoD ruled not to be within the scope of Article 1408, II, 3 of the French *Code Général des Impôts*, which frees diplomatic agents from local residential taxes.[237] The Tribunal further rejected the Commission's claim to assimilate its status in the OECD with that of a member state in the sense of the aforementioned Protocol No 2 to the 1960 OECD Convention and Protocol No 1 to the 1960 Convention on the Organization of the OECD. It further observed that although diplomatic identity cards were issued to the then Commission delegation by the *Ministère des Affaires étrangères*, the mission's diplomatic staff were not accredited to the French Government. According to the local court, the granting of customary diplomatic privileges and immunities in such situation is an act upon the discretion of the member state.

The proceedings before French national courts were unsatisfactory from the point of view of the EUDEL and leave ample questions of EU and international law unanswered, especially on the relationship between France in its capacity of host state and the Union. With regards to the specific problem of the residence tax, a pragmatic solution was found in a yearly reimbursement to officials by the Commission of taxes paid in Paris.

#### *3.2.3.3.3 The EUDEL in Strasbourg*

A permanent delegation represents the interests of the EU at the Council of Europe. Although the Commission has been represented in Strasbourg since 1987, the Union only opened a delegation there in January 2011. Discussions on the strengthening of the diplomatic ties between Europe's two most prominent IOs are even older.[238] The CoE's Liaison Office in Brussels was established as early as 1974 and later upgraded with the appointment of a permanent Special Representative of its Secretary General, carrying the title of ambassador.[239] On the part of the EU, the opening of a Strasbourg permanent mission was coupled with the envisioned accession to the CoE, as foreseen in the Lisbon Treaty.[240] As soon as the HR took office in 2009, she launched a formal request to that effect. The French Government replied positively to the call to open a new delegation but hesitated to agree with the request to conclude an agreement that would make the VCDR's regime applicable. Initial resistance was followed by a notification that the decision would be postponed. The issue has not been adequately addressed since.[241]

Under the CoE's Protocol to the General Agreement on Privileges and Immunities, France is legally obliged to grant members' permanent representatives diplomatic privileges and immunities; the obligatory character with regard to a privileged status of non-members is, however, less clear.[242] When the EUDEL first assumed operations in 2011, the French

[237] Conseil d'Etat [FR] 25 January 2006, No 271 365, Spatolisano (appeal against Tribunal administratif de Paris, 28 June 2004) [2006] 1058 Revue de Jurisprudence Fiscale 8-9. See also *Ministre délégué, chargé du budget v Pazdziej* [2015] ECLI:EU:C:2015:338.

[238] See the MoU between the Council of Europe and the European Union, done at Strasbourg on 11 May 2007.

[239] CoE, CoM Resolution (74) 13, adopted on 6 May 1974 and the Supplementary Agreement, signed in Strasbourg on 3 December 1974 to the General Agreement on Privileges and Immunities of the Council of Europe on 2 September 1949. See also Thomas Streinz, 'Fraternal Twins: The European Union and the Council of Europe' in de Waele and Kuipers (n 201) 111.

[240] Jed Odermatt, 'The EU's Accession to the European Convention on Human Rights: An International Law Perspective' (2014) 47 NYUJILP 59.

[241] Exchange of letters between the French Ministry of Foreign Affairs and the High Representative, dated 16 November 2008, 5 February 2010, and 23 April 2010.

[242] Article 4 of the first Protocol to the General Agreement on Privileges and Immunities of the Council of Europe, signed on 6 November 1952.

Government did not automatically make the Paris arrangements effective in Strasbourg. Yet, over time, informal agreements were reached on the accordance of the most important privileges and immunities. For certain issues, the sense of urgency proved less urgent than others. For example, the archives, documents, and communication of the EUDEL are adequately protected under EU law as under the VCDR.

The CoE's Protocol Office now communicates the names of diplomatic members of the EUDEL to the French Government, which uses the information to grant privileges and immunities. Following requests made by the EUDEL through the CoE's Protocol Office, since 2013, the French Government accords the mission's premises inviolability in the sense of Article 22(1) VCDR, issues diplomatic licence plates, and provides a designated parking spot to the mission. Since 2014, the HoD also receives a diplomatic identity card. The other staff's identity cards mention that their status is governed under the EU Treaties.[243] Most tax privileges are granted to the mission and its members, including the *taxe d'habitation* that had been the object of discussion in Paris. Issues still subject to negotiations concern certain taxes on income, purchases, and services. The pragmatic solution is for EUDEL members to send receipts to the EEAS headquarters, which in turn make an annual request for refunds to the French Government. Similarly to the situation in Paris, the Commission covers taxes that could not be reclaimed.

### 3.2.4 Double-Hatted EUDELs

Multilateral diplomacy is not only practiced in the multilateral Union delegations. A number of bilateral EUDELs in third countries also represent the Union at an IO located in the country of posting. Diplomatic law does not oppose such practice: the multiple accreditation of a single ambassador in a receiving state is foreseen by Article 5 VCDR. With regards to an extra accreditation to an IO, Article 5(3) confirms that:

> [a] head of mission or any member of the diplomatic staff of the mission may act as representative of the sending State to any international organization.

Many bilateral EUDELs also have an accreditation at IOs headquartered in the same capital: Barbados (Organisation of Eastern Caribbean States, OECS and the Caribbean Community and Common Market, CARICOM); Botswana (Southern African Development Community, SADC); Burkina Faso (Union Économique et Monétaire Ouest-Africaine, UEMOA; Comité Inter-États de Lutte contre la Sécheresse au Sahel, CILSS); Central African Republic (Communauté Économique et Monétaire des Etats de l'Afrique Centrale, CEMAC); Djibouti (Intergovernmental Authority on Development, IGAD); Egypt (AL); Gabon (Economic Community of Central African States, ECCAS); Guyana (Caribbean Community and Common Market, CARICOM); Kenya (United Nations Environment Programme (UNEP) and United Nations Human Settlements Programme (UN-HABITAT)); Mauritius (Commission de l'Océan Indien, COI); Namibia (Southern African Customs Union, SACU); Nepal (South Asian Association for Regional Cooperation, SAARC); Nicaragua (Sistema de la Integración Centroamericana, SICA); Nigeria (Economic Community of West African States, ECOWAS); Saudi Arabia (GCC); Tanzania (East African Community, EAC); United

[243] Protocol No 7 on Privileges and Immunities.

Arab Emirates (International Renewable Energy Agency, IRENA); United States of America (Organization of American States, OAS); Zambia (Common Market for Eastern and Southern Africa, COMESA). One notes an EU preference for accreditation at IOs that have an economic integration objective. Diplomatic representation is often also urged when the EU is granted a special status in an IO. For example, the EU accredited its HoD in Nairobi to UNEP when it received observer status.[244]

EU diplomatic presence depends on a decision of the IO or its executive body agreeing to an accreditation, often followed by a formal ceremony in which a high-ranking IO representative accepts an EU ambassador's credentials. An *agréation* (acceptance of diplomatic mission) is only possible when the IO's rules of procedure allow for it. If this is not the case, the Union will be duly represented by its member states (with a preference for the one holding the rotating presidency) to either put an EU official (often a member of the bilateral EUDEL) on their own national diplomatic list or to represent the Union's interests directly.[245] A double-hatted HoD enjoys privileges and immunities through its accreditation to the host state. There is no need to renegotiate rights differently than those foreseen in the VCDR.

Receiving states may require that they be informed in advance of an accreditation to an IO. Article 5(1) VCDR foresees a system of prior notification and a possibility for the receiving state to refuse multiple accreditations. It provides that:

> [t]he sending State may, after it has given due notification to the receiving States concerned, accredit a head of mission or assign any member of the diplomatic staff, as the case may be, to more than one State, unless there is express objection by any of the receiving States.

Being developed in a bilateral context, the text of Article 5(1) VCDR is not entirely clear as to whether a receiving state has the competence to oppose an extra accreditation to an IO located in its capital. Practice, however, seems to confirm this right of a host state since there are states which object to double accreditation, for example, the United States.

### 3.3 The Passive Right of Legation

Academic scholarship is divided on the question as to whether IOs enjoy a passive right of legation by way of CIL. The discussions leading up to the VCDR only refer to the customary nature of the right on the part of sovereign states notwithstanding the fact that IOs like the LoN and the European Coal and Steel Community (ECSC) had already established a passive practice.[246] Be it as it may, such practices have only increased. The EU in the meantime developed an impressive passive legation practice through receiving and accrediting foreign diplomats in Brussels.[247] Throughout the years, the scope and number of those diplomatic missions to the EU strongly expanded. Three types of permanent diplomatic actors with an accreditation to the EU in Brussels can be discerned: *(a)* the permanent representations of

[244] Chad Damro, 'EU–UN Environmental Relations: Shared Competence and Effective Multilateralism' in Laatikainen and Smith (n 194) 181.

[245] Carta (n 197) 418.

[246] ILC, Memorandum prepared by the Secretariat relating to Diplomatic Intercourse and Immunities, A/CN.4/98, 21 February 1956, paras 168–75. For a positive answer with regard to IOs, see Reichling (n 151) 26–30. For a negative answer to the same question, see Chittharanjan F Amerasinghe, *Principles of the Institutional Law of International Organizations* (2nd edn, CUP 2005) 315.

[247] Arnaud Tournier, 'Le Droit de Légation Passive de l'Union Européenne' in Benlolo-Carabot, Candas, and Cujo (n 39) 236.

EU member states, *(b)* permanent missions of third states, and *(c)* permanent missions of IOs and other non-state entities. While the first type of missions are not considered part of the right of legation of the Union, they are studied here for the sake of completeness.

## 3.3.1 Member States

### 3.3.1.1 Between Diplomacy and Policy

Each EU member state operates a permanent representation (PR, or PermRep) at the EU in Brussels. These national missions manage interactions between the national and European levels, represent national preferences and opinions, develop friendly relations with fellow member states and third states, and take part in negotiations. When performing the above tasks, the PermReps largely act similarly to permanent diplomatic missions accredited to other IOs. However, their job description also entails responsibilities generally unknown to multilateral diplomacy: in the Permanent Representatives Committee (Comité des représentants permanents or Coreper; Art 240 TFEU), member state representatives with the rank of ambassador prepare the (legislative) work of the Council.[248] By taking an active part in the Union, they surpass the representation of national interests to seek common solutions and attain common goals in an institutionalized manner.[249] As a result, member states' missions are an integral part of the Union's machinery more than they are external to it. Jean Salmon even speaks of the '*double qualité*' of a permanent representative.[250]

The PRs' double role within the Union leads to the scholarly conclusion regarding their status. The accreditation of member states missions is not a part of the Union's exercise of a passive right of legation. This is confirmed by the fact that, unlike third states' diplomatic missions to the EU, the establishment of a member state's mission and the appointment of its members including the ambassador(s), is a national act not subject to approval by the EU institutions or the Belgian authorities.[251] Consequently, the EU also does not hold a right to issue an agrément or to declare a member of the PR persona non grata. Finally, an element of reciprocity is also lacking in the relationship between the EU and the member states (and their missions): the Union does not exercise an active right of legation in its own member states, at least not with the view of accrediting an EU diplomat to their national governments. The EU exercises an active right of legation only in Austria, France, and Italy, where it has accredited missions to IOs headquartered in those countries. The reason why the PermReps are discussed in this handbook is solely due to their status, privileges, and immunities largely corresponding with those granted to diplomatic missions proper. However, some authors do distinguish between a right of passive legation *sensu lato* (including permanent delegations of member states) and a right of passive legation *sensu stricto* (which only includes third states' missions).[252]

[248] Mai'a K Davis Cross, *The European Diplomatic Corps: Diplomats and International Cooperation from Westphalia to Maastricht* (Palgrave Macmillan 2008) 143 et seq.

[249] Les Metcalfe, 'International Policy Co-ordination and Public Management Reform' (1994) 60 IRAS 271.

[250] Jean Salmon, 'Les Représentations et Missions Permanentes auprès de le CEE et de l'Euratom', *Les Missions Permanentes auprès des Organisations Internationales*, vol I (Dotation Carnegie pour la Paix Internationale 1971) 569.

[251] ibid, 571–77.

[252] Tournier (n 247) 238.

#### 3.3.1.2 Duties

Coreper provides a forum for missions acting on behalf of instructing member states to discuss the very core of EU policies. It consists of representatives from the EU countries with the rank of ambassador and is chaired by the EU country holding the Council presidency. In Coreper, diplomatic and political tasks are blurred: it serves as a forum for dialogue (among the PermReps and between them and their respective national capitals), as well as a means of policymaking (when preparing the Council's agenda and work) and political control (providing guidance and supervising the work of the expert groups; carrying out scrutiny of acts tabled by the Commission).[253]

Member state missions are headed by an 'ambassador extraordinary and plenipotentiary' who has overall responsibility for the mission and takes charge of Coreper II business. Member states can appoint a second or a third representative in an ambassadorial rank. In such a case, the ambassador's title will be carried by the deputy permanent representative representing the country in Coreper I and/or by the country's diplomatic representative to the Political and Security Committee (PSC). Representatives in Coreper I or the PSC that do not carry the ambassadorial title are commonly appointed as Minister Plenipotentiary or First Counsellor. Within national foreign affairs ministries, these positions are seen as prestigious postings in their own right; governments usually appoint as their ambassadors to the EU persons with excellent credentials hailing from the diplomatic service with wide-ranging experience in Union affairs.[254]

PermReps to the EU operate under the umbrella of their national ministry of foreign affairs (MFA), but represent the entire member state.[255] Because of the kaleidoscopic range of expert topics dealt with in EU settings, the missions tend to be large in size and employ civil servants from many different ministries and agencies.[256] However, within the PRs, grades, titles, and functions largely correspond with those of bilateral missions.

#### 3.3.1.3 Permanent Representations and Diplomatic Law

Permanent representations and their staff enjoy customary diplomatic privileges and immunities. For the members of the mission, this is confirmed in Article 10 of Protocol No 7, which provides that:

> [r]epresentatives of Member States taking part in the work of the institutions of the Union, their advisers and technical experts shall, in the performance of their duties and during their travel to and from the place of meeting, enjoy the customary privileges, immunities and facilities.

It is common for IOs to have this type of provision in their constitutional treaties, referring to Article 105 UN Charter.[257] Yet the EU's version warrants some further discussion with regard to the interpretation of the phrases *(a)* 'customary privileges, immunities and facilities' and *(b)* 'the performance of their duties and during their travel to and from the place of

[253] Jaap W de Zwaan, *The Permanent Representatives Committee: Its Role in European Union Decision-Making* (Elsevier 1995).
[254] ibid 15.
[255] See the contributions in Brian Hocking and David Spence, *Foreign Ministries in the European Union: Integrating Diplomats* (Palgrave Macmillan 2016).
[256] Hussein Kassim and others (eds), *The National Co-ordination of EU Policy* (OUP 2001).
[257] Petersen (n 6) 85.

meeting'; and the applicability of this provision *(c)* to the mission itself, as well as *(d)* to the Belgian PR and its staff.

First, when interpreting the expression 'customary' privileges, immunities, and facilities, one should keep in mind that when this clause entered into force in 1958, the VCDR had not yet been negotiated. In other words, *all* diplomatic privileges, immunities, and facilities at the time were of a customary nature. In 1958, the Belgian Government confirmed that it considers this provision—directly applicable in the Belgian legal order—to cover the permanent representatives to the EU.[258] Furthermore, it stated that a fellow member state's mission would enjoy the same privileges and immunities as are enjoyed by the member state's diplomatic representation accredited to the kingdom.[259] This resulted in a perfect equalization of the two legal regimes.[260] Consequently, on the basis of reciprocity, Belgium grants the PRs on its territory those privileges and facilities that the Belgian Embassy receives in a particular co-member state.

Second, the phrase 'in the performance of their duties' should not be interpreted restrictively. The mission's staff is accorded full diplomatic privileges and immunities and not merely functional ones, as one may expect reading this phrase. The primordial role and responsibility to accord these rests with Belgium, but other member states have certain legal obligations too: the diplomatic status and the accompanying facilities are to be granted in the performance of the representatives' duties *wherever* they take place. While most meetings occur in Brussels, where envoys are based and registered, they may also be organized in EU institutions in Luxembourg and Strasbourg or in decentralized EU agencies; and a PR represents its member state at the Union in its entirety. Moreover, all member states have obligations under EU law towards a PermRep's staff passing through their territory on their way to and from such meeting. This is confirmed by the phrase 'to and from the place of meeting'. Duties for member states other than Belgium are, however, less stringent. The PR officials' status, when present in a member state on official business or travelling to and from the place of meeting, is assimilated to that of 'diplomats in transit'. The latter is a term borrowed from the VCDR's Article 40(1)–(2), which tasks third states to accord inviolability and such other immunities as may be required to facilitate and ensure a transit or return of a diplomatic agent passing through or being in their territory. Likewise, EU member states must ensure the safe passage of members of PermReps to the EU and accord them the necessary inviolability and immunities. There also is a general obligation to accord official correspondence, diplomatic bags, and communications in transit (including messages in code or cipher) the freedom and protection as is accorded to their diplomatic partners (Art 40(3) VCDR). One important limitation is that members of the PRs, their communications, and bags will not receive privileges and immunities in their own member state. This corresponds with the regime for diplomats in transit under the VCDR, which also does not foresee a specials status for diplomats in their own sending state.

Third, although the Treaties remain silent on the status of the PermRep itself (including its communication, vehicles, archives, etc), Belgium has shown its readiness to accord those missions privileges, immunities, and facilities laid down in the VCDR and CIL. The legal regime applicable to missions accredited by a member state to the Union is therefore analogous to that of bilateral missions of that member state accredited to the Kingdom of Belgium.

[258] Salmon (n 250) 572–74.
[259] Tournier (n 247) 239.
[260] See, eg the Circular Note [BE] 'Instruction sur les immunités diplomatiques et les régimes assimilés', 1962, para 207.

An example of a non-VCDR facility granted is the accordance of diplomatic licence plates (CD) to the mission.

Fourth, in terms of privileges and immunities, the Belgian Government does not treat its own PR as a diplomatic mission. This is somewhat paradoxical because, with its 160 staff members, it is the largest Belgian diplomatic post in the world.[261] Instead, the status of members of the representation in Brussels is assimilated with that of national civil servants.[262] It is not unusual for a host/receiving state to limit the privileges and immunities of nationals working in diplomatic missions on its territory; Article 38 VCDR provides that these will be granted functional immunity only. However, Belgium denies the Belgian mission and its staff any form of diplomatic protection or tax privileges, neither does there exist an immunity from legal process in respect of words spoken or written or acts done in an official capacity or the inviolability for archives, papers, and documents. As such, the Belgian diplomats at the PR to the EU receive less protection than civil servants of Belgian nationality working for the EU (functional immunity), their MFA colleagues taking up tasks abroad (full diplomatic immunity and important personal tax privileges), or Belgians working for foreign missions in Belgium (functional immunity). As a favour by the Belgian MFA, a CD licence plate is assigned to the PR's ambassadors—the same goes for Belgium's mission to NATO. The rationale for this strict approach is the absence of a ground for immunity: the PR officials obviously do not have to fear interference from the host state, equally their employer. Moreover, the PR and its staff, as organs of the Belgian state, are covered by Belgium's sovereign immunity when their acts would be challenged in court.

## 3.3.2 Third States

### 3.3.2.1 Diplomatic Missions to the EU and Euratom

There are 164 permanent missions of third states accredited to the EU.[263] Of these, 153 are also accredited to the EAEC or Euratom, an international organization which is legally distinct from the EU but comprises the same membership. Quite frequently, the third country will be represented in Brussels by a single mission accredited to the Kingdom of Belgium and the EU and be located in the same premises and headed by an ambassador with a double (or triple) accreditation.

Third state missions accredited to the Union present a genuine exercise of the Union's passive right of legation.[264] The EU does not grant observer status to third states, which would allow observers to attend meetings of the IO's organs and to speak without the right to vote. The missions of third states are truly external to the Union. This is in line with Article 5(2) CRSIO, which stipulates that the reception of non-member state missions is not by right.

[261] Benjamin Robinet, *La Représentation Permanente Belge auprès de l'Union Européenne: Une Cheffe d'Orchestre à Bruxelles* (Presses Universitaires de Louvain 2021).

[262] Salmon (n 250) 573–75; Tournier (n 247) 239.

[263] See the list of all missions accredited to the EU as updated in June 2022, <https://www.eeas.europa.eu/eeas/diplomatic-list-missions-accredited-european-union_en> accessed 2 June 2022.

[264] Commission des affaires politiques et des questions institutionnelles de l'Assemblée parlementaire européenne (APE), Rapport sur les problèmes que posent les relations des Communautés européennes avec l'extérieur, en particulier le droit de légation et de pavillon (Rapporteur: Marinus van der Goes van Naters) 9 November 1959, Doc 87/1959, para 4.

#### 3.3.2.2 Duties

Third state missions to the EU ensure the representation of the sending state, safeguard its interest, and promote cooperation between their country and the Union. Such a job description fits in with the general functions of non-member states to IOs as described in Article 7 CRSIO. Third state missions are generally banned from attending the EU's internal deliberations. Important exceptions exist that allow third states to actively negotiate or attend meetings.[265] Specific organs and advisory committees have been established to discuss EU policy vis-à-vis certain regions.[266] Examples are legion, and third states' participation with the Union may differ depending on whether they are *candidates for accession* (Art 212 TFEU—may be invited to member state-only meetings);[267] whether they have entered into an *association agreement* (Art 217 TFEU); or whether they are considered part of the *African, Caribbean and Pacific Group of States* (ACP, in the sense of the Cotonou Agreement of 23 June 2000), the *European Neighbourhood Policy* (ENP), or a *Strategic Partnership* (SP). Diplomats from European Free Trade Association (EFTA) states Iceland, Liechtenstein, and Norway are invited to attend certain truly internal EU committees and even Council meetings;[268] the same goes for diplomatic representatives of Schengen associated states participating in discussions on the Schengen acquis. Obviously, there are also third countries that do not fall into any of the above categories.

#### 3.3.2.3 Permanent Missions and Diplomatic Law

The privileges and immunities of non-member states missions to the EU are governed by EU primary law. Article 16 of Protocol No 7 attached to the Treaties thereto provides that:

> [t]he Member State in whose territory the Union has its seat shall accord the customary diplomatic immunities and privileges to missions of third countries accredited to the Union.

As a reminder, Article 16 Protocol No 7 is also the clause referred to (through a *renvoi*) in the EAs (Art 3(3) model EA). By sending a diplomatic mission to Brussels, third states assent to the idea of the VCDR and CIL governing their relations with the Union under the agreed conditions of the EA.

Article 16 differs from Article 10 of the same Protocol No 7 on the status of permanent representations of the member states. First, Article 16 does not link the receiving of privileges and immunities to the exercise of certain functions at the EU. However, due to Belgium's rather generous reading of Article 10, the difference in treatment between member states and non-member states is minimal, if not non-existent. Belgium in both cases interprets the phrase 'customary diplomatic immunities and privileges' to mean all diplomatic privileges and immunities enshrined in the VCDR and general diplomatic law. Belgium therefore grants the permanent mission of a third state the same treatment as that state's embassy accredited to the Kingdom of Belgium, including those going beyond the privileges spelled out in the VCDR such as the quota for duty-free import of alcohol and tobacco, the CD-licence plates accorded to the mission, and restrictions regarding the size of the mission. The host

265 Schermers and Blokker (n 22) 1161.

266 Koen Lenaerts and Piet Van Nuffel, *European Union Law* (Robert Bray and Nathan Cambien eds, Sweet & Maxwell 2011) 955.

267 José M Magone, 'The Portuguese Permanent Representation in Brussels: The Institutionalization of a Simple System' in Kassim and others (n 256) 171.

268 Sven Norberg and Martin Johansson, 'The History of the EEA Agreement and the First Twenty Years of Its Existence' in Carl Baudenbacher (ed), The Handbook of EEA Law (Springer 2016).

state has accepted that the word 'customary' entails that there will be no discrimination between two missions of the same country on its territory.[269] This is not all that clear from the Treaties: different language versions (in French, '*d'usage*'; in German '*üblichen*'; in Spanish '*habituales*'; in Dutch '*gebruikelijke*') do not translate the English 'customary' as necessarily referring to CIL status.

Similarly to the relationship between the EU and its member states' missions, there is no perfect reciprocity in the relations between the EU and third states. In a normal exchange of diplomatic missions, the sending and receiving entities are in a mutual relationship. As regards the EU, reciprocity is only observed in the sense that it exchanges missions with a particular third country.[270] If Belgium does not have a mission in a third state establishing a mission to the EU, the treatment of fellow member states by the third state is looked at rather than the EUDEL's treatment in order to define 'reciprocal treatment'.[271]

Second, the obligation in Article 16 is geographically limited as Article 16 targets host state Belgium only, remaining silent on the obligations of other member states. Some EAs, such as the one concluded with Yemen (2003), refer to the granting of privileges and immunities by *all* member states, an interpretation of Protocol No 7 on Privileges and Immunities that goes beyond what EU law provides. As such, in this case as well as for the other relations with third countries, the question arises as to the legal duty for member states to treat third state missions to the Union as 'diplomats in transit' as defined in the VCDR. There is no direct obligation stemming from EU law, in contrast to Article 10 Protocol No 7 on member state representatives; neither is there an obligation on the basis of diplomatic law, given that the Union is not a VCDR signatory party. The only legal obligation therefore stems from the duty of sincere cooperation as formulated in EU law. As a minimum, member states should allow for the safe passage and grant appropriate treatment of third state diplomats going to or returning from their post in Brussels. Bilateral accreditations of third states' ambassadors to Belgium (or even Luxembourg or other neighbouring countries as they commonly do) certainly facilitate the enjoyment of transit rights in other member states and even allow for the direct application of the VCDR.

### 3.3.3 IOs and Other Representations

#### 3.3.3.1 The Passive Right of Legation *Sensu Lato*

Forty IOs and other non-state entities maintain some kind of permanent representation at the EU in Belgium.[272] Of those IOs, the UN family (consisting of the UN, its bodies, funds, programmes and specialized agencies) is by far the most visibly present as it currently operates twenty-two offices in Brussels. This includes liaison offices of UN programmes, funds, and agencies. Other IOs with a formal diplomatic representation in Brussels are the Arab League (AL), the African Union (AU), the Organisation of Islamic Cooperation (OIC), Organisation Internationale de la Francophonie (OIF), the CoE, EFTA, the European Patent Organization

269 Salmon (n 250) 573.
270 Frid (n 85) 31.
271 Salmon (n 250) 722.
272 See Appendix 5 for an overview.

(EPO), and the Gulf Cooperation Council (GCC).[273] The group of 'other' non-states presents a colourful mix of entities and regional organizations, including the International Committee of the Red Cross (ICRC) (a private association formed under the Swiss Civil Code with a hybrid international status), the International Institute for Democracy and Electoral Assistance (International IDEA, a think tank), the Regional Cooperation Council (RCC, an informal regional cooperative framework), and the Sovereign Military Hospitaller Order of Saint John of Jerusalem of Rhodes and of Malta (which claims possession of a sovereign status in the international legal order). The precise name of IO and non-state missions to the Union varies. The majority is referred to as a 'liaison office' (thirty-three) but the EU also accredits several 'permanent missions', an 'economic and trade office' (Hong Kong) and an 'information office' (the UN's Regional Information Centre, UNRIC).

There is no common regulatory framework dealing with missions and liaison offices of international organizations and other non-state entities. The Union should not seek the Belgian Government's consent to accredit a non-state actor. At the same time, there are no direct obligations for Belgium stemming from EU law to treat a non-state mission in a prescribed manner. The legal regime on missions of IOs accredited to the Union has therefore essentially developed via practice and ad hoc arrangements. Host state Belgium has entered into multiple agreements—applying its general host state policy—with the entities the EU accredits. The individual agreements consequently share similar structures and linguistic features, though noteworthy differences exist, which require a careful study. It is noteworthy that the agreements concluded by Belgium generally do not contain a clause on reciprocity (on behalf of the Union). A practical consequence of this is that the EUDEL to the AU in Addis Ababa is accorded more elaborate privileges and immunities on the basis of the VCDR than the AU's mission to the EU in Brussels.

#### 3.3.3.2 Duties

Most non-state entities operate small representation offices ranging from one to three officials in Brussels. With the exception of Palestine and the Order of Malta, representations for which it was concluded earlier that they come close to being diplomatic missions in the proper sense, none of these entities missions is truly diplomatic in nature.[274] Arguably, some missions of IOs (the AU, AL, OIC, and OIF), all of which are established as a 'permanent mission' headed by an ambassador, share important characteristics with diplomatic missions. The Belgium Government reserves the title of ambassador for heads of bilateral missions (embassies) who have presented their credentials to the King; it will not address representatives of other missions as ambassadors. For other IOs, a more diffuse terminology is employed: the Gulf Cooperation Council and the Council of Europe have established 'liaison offices', of which the representatives bear the title of ambassador. In effect, the mission's name or the use of the title of 'ambassador' do not grant the mission or its representative diplomatic status, although it may be a sign of the more intense relation the entity has established with the Union. In certain cases, the use of a diplomatic titles may be the result of a reciprocal gesture when the EU HoD is also referred to as 'ambassador'.

[273] See, for a complete list, 'International Organisations and Other Representations to the European Union', <https://www.eeas.europa.eu/eeas/international-organisations-and-other-representations-european-union_en>, accessed 2 May 2022.

[274] Frid (n 85) 29; Reichling (n 151) 42.

### 3.3.3.3 International Organizations

Protocol No 7 does not cover the status of missions of IOs and other non-state entities to the EU. As a result, there is no general obligation for Belgium to treat non-state representations in a prescribed manner. Indeed, the legal status of the different moulds of non-state missions to the EU depends upon special agreements entered into by the host state and the organization or entity at hand or, alternatively, on unilateral concessions made by the Belgian Government. In the past, a Luxembourg law on the granting of certain privileges to the ECSC also did not solve the problem of the privileges and immunities to be granted to representatives of international organizations.[275] Although the missions' status is far from consistent across individual measures, Belgium generally grants protection to missions of IOs' premises, assets, archives, and communication. Personal inviolabilities and immunities are generally accorded to the highest-ranking representative of the mission. The next sections highlight some of the specificities governing missions and liaison offices of IOs and other non-state entities in Brussels.

#### *3.3.3.3.1 Belgium is a member state of the IO*

When the EU accredits a mission of an IO of which Belgium is a member, the host state is bound by the rules of that organization regarding the IO's privileges and immunities. In such a case, Belgium grants a special status to the IO's mission on the basis of international institutional law and not necessarily because a diplomatic relation has been established between the Union and the IO. The topic of privileges and immunities commonly features in the IO's constitution or in a separate agreement on privileges and immunities.

**The UN family** Both the UN Charter and the CPIUN prescribe the obligations of member states in relation to offices of UN organs and bodies located in the member states' territories, while the CPIUN–SA does the same with regard to the offices of UN Specialized Agencies. Article 105 of the UN Charter states in this regard that '[t]he Organization shall enjoy in the territory of each of its Members such privileges and immunities as are necessary for the fulfilment of its purposes'. In addition, constitutional documents and special agreements have been concluded that impact the status of UN missions.[276]

The General Conventions install an immunity from jurisdiction and execution, without a geographical restriction while all the UN's premises, documents, and archives are inviolable.[277] On the immunity from of the UN, the CPIUN, for instance, reads: '[t]he property assets of the United Nations, wherever located and by whomsoever held, shall be immune from search, requisition, confiscation, expropriation and any other form of interference, whether by executive, administrative, judicial or legislative action'.[278] Furthermore, member

[275] Reichling (n 151) 42

[276] See, for those UNSAs accredited to the Union, Art VIII(4) Constitution of the Food and Agricultural Organization of the United Nations, signed on 16 October 1945, UNYearb 693; Art 40 Constitution of the International Labour Organization, opened for signature on 9 October 1946, entered into force 28 May 1947, 38 UNTS 583; Art IX of the Articles of Agreement of the International Monetary Fund, opened for signature on 22 July 1944, entered into force 27 December 1945; Art XII of the Constitution of the United Nations Educational, Scientific and Cultural Organization, opened for signature on 16 November 1945, entered into force 4 November 1946, 4 UNTS 52; Art 21 Constitution of the United Nations Industrial Development Organization, opened for signature on 8 April 1979, entered into force 21 June 1985; Art VII of the Articles of Agreement of the International Bank for Reconstruction and Development, opened for signature on 22 July 1944, entered into force 27 December 1945, 2 UNTS 134; Chapter XV of the Constitution of the World Health Organization, opened for signature on 22 July 1946, entered into force 7 April 1948, 4 UNTS 221.

[277] Article II, section 3–4 CPIUN; Art III CPIUN–SA.

[278] Article II, section 3 CPIUN.

states are obliged to provide inviolability and facilities in respect of communications and correspondence: the Conventions are formulated in such way that the VCDR regime (Art 27) applies de facto to the UN/UNSAs' permanent missions.[279] The missions are even explicitly allowed to use codes and to dispatch and receive its correspondence by diplomatic couriers and bags (Art III CPIUN; Art IV CPIUN-SA). Finally, the CPIUN and CPIUN-SA also provide a number of substantive protections to be guaranteed by each member state. These mostly take the form of tax exemptions for the offices and their staff (Art II, section 5, 7–8 CPIUN; Art III, section 7 CPIUN-SA). Salaries paid by the UN are exempt from taxation. When staff takes up their post, they have the right to bring their furniture and effects duty free into Belgium but further have little to no customs exemptions.[280] At the bare minimum, UN officials are accorded a range of privileges and immunities in Belgium which enable them to perform their job independently of any control or interference (Art V CPIUN; Art VI CPIUN-SA). The only UN officials who are granted diplomatic immunity in the meaning of the 1961 VCDR are the UNSG and the Under-UNSGs (Art V, section 19 CPIUN). When certain conditions are fulfilled, the UNSG has the right to waive the immunity of officials (Art V CPIUN) and UN property (Art II CPIUN). UN liaison staff generally enjoys travel facilities, including a UNLP, that enable them to travel to and from the place of posting (Art VII CPIUN; Art VIII CPIUN-SA). Both General UN Conventions also protect the property and assets of the UN and the UNSAs *wherever located and by whomsoever held* (Art II CPIUN; Art III CPIUN-SA).

In addition to the aforementioned general instruments to which Belgium is bound in its capacity as a member state, the host state has also entered into specific agreements with the UN/UNSAs. These supplement the General Privileges and Immunities Conventions and for that reason do not repeat the principles already covered in the general instruments, for example, with regard to the inviolability of premises or the right to use the diplomatic bag. In 1977, Belgium concluded such agreement with the United Nations Organization (UNO),[281] the raison d'être of which was to determine the exact privileges and immunities necessary for the functioning of the newly established 1975 UN Liaison Office in Brussels. The decision to establish such an office was a direct response to the obtained observer status of the EEC in the UNGA but also reflected the UNSG's recognition of the EEC's increased role in international (economic) relations as well as a desire on the part of the EEC to expand its diplomatic network.[282] In the *travaux préparatoires*, the Belgian legislator clarified the host state's preference for a uniform policy with regards to all missions of IOs within its jurisdiction. It is furthermore explained that the agreement's content mirrors that of agreements concluded with the ILO and the CoE. According to Article 1, the Agreement applies not just to the UNO Office but also to any office on the Belgian territory which depends either on the UN or another organism that is an integral part of this organization. The number of UN bodies, programmes, and funds with liaison offices in Brussels has grown exponentially over the years, all of which are covered by the Agreement. The Belgian Government preferred this over the conclusion of separate agreements with all these UN entities. Originally, the 1977 agreement was interpreted to also cover UNSAs' offices. However, in the meantime all Specialized Agencies but UNESCO—Article XII of the UNESCO Constitution is also

279 Article III, section 9 CPIUN. See, for a similar protection, Art IV CPIUN-SA.

280 Article V CPIUN; Art VI CPIUN-SA.

281 Agreement between the Kingdom of Belgium and the United Nations Organization, on the Privileges to the General Agreement and immunities of the United Nations, signed on 22 January 1976, adopted by Belgian law 22 May 1978, and supplementary exchange of letters (hereafter Belgium-UN Agreement).

282 House of Representatives [BE], Explanatory Memorandum, 117 No 1 (1977–78), 20 October 1977, 1.

relatively brief on the subject, referring only to Articles 104 and 105 of the UN Charter—concluded similar supplementary headquarters agreements of their own. This is the case for the ILO,[283] the World Bank Group,[284] the International Monetary Fund (IMF),[285] WHO,[286] FAO,[287] and UNIDO.[288]

While the supplementary agreements are more generous than the general conventions, the privileges and immunities they encompass are still rather limited when compared to those of diplomatic missions. Certain agreements instal a more elaborate system on customs exemptions than others. The Protocol to the Belgium–International Bank for Reconstruction and Development (IBRD) Agreement, for instance, allows officials appointed by the Liaison Office, within the twelve months following the date on which they start observing their duties in Belgium, to import furniture and motor vehicles for personal use free of import duties, or to purchase those locally free from tax on added value. Note that the Protocol refers to Belgium's duty to respect EU law: '[s]ans préjudice des obligations qui découlent pour la Belgique des dispositions des traités concernant l'Union européenne et de l'application des dispositions légales et réglementaires'.[289]

The supplementary agreements generally limit the enjoyment of diplomatic privileges and immunities to the head of the mission.[290] They are accorded a VAT exemption when they *(a)* are not a Belgian national/permanent resident and *(b)* do not engage in commercial activities. Belgian citizens/permanent residents that would take up such functions are covered by Article V, section 18 CPIUN and Article VI, section 19 CPIUN–SA. With the exception of the FAO Representative's case,[291] family members forming part of a head of office's household enjoy the same status. Since the inclusion of family members is standard when diplomatic immunities are accorded (see Art 37 VCDR), chances are that the silence in the FAO Agreement is due to forgetfulness on the part of contracting parties. Two conditions are nevertheless added, which do not feature in Article 37(1) VCDR: the children of the head of mission of the UN, World Bank, WHO, UNIDO, and IMF liaison offices have to *(a)* be living with the head of office and *(b)* be minors to enjoy protection.[292] With regard to the VCDR, the Belgian Court of Cassation has held that Article 37(1) VCDR's expression 'forming part

[283] Agreement between the Kingdom of Belgium and the International Labour Organization on the establishment in Belgium of the Office of the Organization and the exchange of letters, signed on 4 November 197, adopted by Belgian law 31 July 1978.

[284] Agreement between the Kingdom of Belgium and the International Bank for Reconstruction and Development on the establishment in Belgium of a liaison office of this organization, signed on 26 April 1999, adopted by Belgian law 4 March 2002, and the Additional Protocol of 28 February 2005, adopted by Belgian law 3 April 2013 (hereafter Belgium–IBRD Agreement).

[285] Agreement between the Kingdom of Belgium and the International Monetary Fund on the establishment in Belgium of a Liaison Office of the Organization, signed on 16 March 2004, adopted by Belgian law 29 July 2014 (hereafter Belgium–IMF Agreement).

[286] Agreement between the Kingdom of Belgium and the World Health Organization concerning the establishment in Belgium of a liaison office of this organization, signed on 6 January 1999, adopted by Belgian law 24 January 2002 (hereafter Belgium–WHO Agreement).

[287] Agreement between the Kingdom of Belgium and the Food and Agriculture Organization of the United Nations on the establishment in Belgium of a Liaison Office of the Organization, signed on 5 February 1997, adopted by Belgian law 3 July 2000 (hereafter Belgium–FAO Agreement).

[288] Agreement between the Kingdom of Belgium and the United Nations Industrial Development concerning the establishment in Belgium of a Liaison Office of the Organization, signed on 20 February 2006, adopted by Belgian law 29 June 2014 (hereafter Belgium–UNIDO Agreement).

[289] See also ibid, Art 3(1): 'without prejudice to the obligations of Belgium under the provisions of the EU Treaties and the application of legal and regulatory provisions' [own translation].

[290] Article 3 Belgium–UN Agreement. See also Art 1 Belgium–IMF Agreement; Art 1 Belgium–IBRD Agreement; Art 1 Belgium–WHO Agreement; Art 1 Belgium–UNIDO Agreement.

[291] Article 1 Belgium–FAO Agreement.

[292] Cour de Cassation [BE] 28 March 1990, Pas, 1990, I, 885.

of his household' cannot be interpreted as referring only to cohabitation and should rather be understood as entailing the existence among the persons concerned of a 'domestic community'. The term 'household' is interpreted in the Belgian MFA as only including the spouse, the unmarried legal partner, and the children that are dependent of the diplomatic agent. This approach seems to be in contradiction with the flexibility intended by the Convention's authors, who did not wish to exclude certain special circumstances. This discussion seems settled in the supplementary agreements discussed here, in which the narrow approach clearly prevails.

The UNO Agreement provides that immunity granted to officials does not cover the legal disputes arising out of private agreements (eg a lease). It also contains an exception to immunity in case of violations of Belgian traffic laws or damage caused by motor vehicles.[293] Even more common is a provision that reminds staff of liaison offices to respect Belgian road traffic laws and regulations and obliges them to obtain a compulsory insurance against civil liability in respect of motor vehicles.[294] The same requirement exists for members of diplomatic missions and can be considered part of Belgium's general host state policy. Moreover, the insurance is required in order for diplomats to enjoy the customs exemption for fuel.[295] The Belgium–FAO Agreement, Belgium–WHO Agreement, and Belgium–IMF Agreement do not contain the same requirement.

One of the supplementary agreements' goals is to require missions to get the highest possible level of social protection for the office's staff. They thereto contain a so-called social clause, of which the name and terms differ. The World Bank, WHO, and IMF agreements, for instance, allow staff members to opt for a subjection to the UNSAs' social security systems and to be exempted from the obligatory subscription to the Belgian social security system.[296] The FAO Agreement is formulated slightly differently as it allows staff members to voluntarily subscribe to the public health insurance under the Belgian social security system. This system is more beneficial than the recent interpretations of the VCDR regarding social security. As of 1 January 2014, Belgium no longer allows staff members of diplomatic missions who are exempt from social security provisions in force in Belgium (Arts 33 and 37(2) VCDR) to voluntarily subscribe to health insurance through a health insurance fund (*mutualité*). This exclusion is consistent with Article 33(4) VCDR.[297] Interestingly, a few recent agreements also contain a provision on the protection of patients' privacy and on medical ethics.[298]

**The Council of Europe** As one of the founding members, Belgium signed the CoE's General Agreement on Privileges and Immunities on 2 September 1949.[299] The Convention contains standard clauses with regard to the immunity of the organization's property and assets, wherever located and by whomsoever held (Arts 3 and 7) and the inviolability of premises,

293 Exchange of letters Belgium–UN (n 281).

294 Article 2 Belgium–IBRD Agreement; Art 4 Belgium–UNIDO Agreement.

295 Law of 21 November 1989 [BE], Belgian State Gazette 8 December 1989; circular note of 1 September 2013 on the annual duty-free quotas for diplomatic purchases.

296 Article 6 Belgium–IMF Agreement; Art 4 Belgium–IBRD Agreement; Art 3 Belgium–WHO Agreement; Art 6 Belgium–UNIDO Agreement; Belgium–UN Agreement.

297 Article 3 Belgium–FAO Agreement. See also circular note of 1 August 2013 [BE] on Health insurance; Frédéric Dopagne, Sanderijn Duquet, and Bertold Theeuwes, *Diplomatiek Recht Toegepast in België* (Maklu 2014) 123.

298 Article 4 Belgium–IBRD Agreement; Art 3 Belgium–FAO Agreement; Art 3 Belgium–WHO Agreement. Such a clause does not feature in the Belgium–UNIDO Agreement.

299 General Agreement on Privileges and Immunities of the Council of Europe, opened for signature on 2 September 1952, entered into force 10 September 1952, ETS No 2.

communication, and archives (Arts 4–5 and 8). Under the General Agreement, CoE officials are granted functional immunity and certain tax privileges. Only the Secretary General and Deputy Secretary General enjoy privileges and immunities, exemptions, and facilities similar to those of diplomatic envoys (Art 16).

The CoE wished to extend and specify the personal protection of its representatives in Brussels.[300] It did so in a supplementary agreement concluded with host state Belgium, the content of which bears resemblance with arrangements that apply to other IOs' missions in Brussels.[301] The Belgian legislator indicates in its explanatory memorandum that it continues to (and in the future will) respect a policy line in which all IO representations and their staff on the Belgian territory are granted similar advantages. To this end, the status of the CoE mission mirrors that of the missions of the UNO and the ILO, which requested the opening of a representation around the same time. The CoE office's head enjoys diplomatic privileges and immunities except if they hold Belgian nationality, in which case functional immunities are accorded, as provided in Article 18 of the 1949 General Agreement.

**IOM** Belgium is member of IOM, a 'related organization' of the UN. Article 23 of the IOM's Constitution only briefly touches upon the privileges and immunities of the IO: Article 23(3) spells out that these are to be defined in 'agreements between the Organization and the States concerned or through other measures taken by these States'.[302] The IOM entered into such an agreement with Belgium as early as 1973 (the Geneva Accord), which was subsequently revised and updated in 1996 (the London Accord).[303] One of the London Accord's innovations concerns the exemption from any form of taxation on salaries for Belgian staff at the IOM office in Brussels, as had been the applicable rule for foreign employees since the Geneva Accord. This way, Belgian officials and permanent residents are no longer subject to a double taxation.[304] Belgium is not obliged to grant any other privileges and immunities to its own nationals or permanent residents, with the exception of an immunity from jurisdiction for action in the performance of their duties (Art 5 London Accord). Interestingly, the accords stipulate an obligation for IOM to provide the Belgian tax authorities with annual data on salaries and other allowances received by the beneficiaries of the tax exemption (Art 3 London Accord, introducing an Art 18*bis* in the Geneva Accord). The latter duty of information is a provision which increasingly features in Belgian headquarters (HQ) agreements.

**EPO** Although all EU member states are EPO member states, the organization is entirely independent from the Union. Belgium has not entered into an HQ agreement with the IO, but relies on a fairly general Protocol on Privileges and Immunities to the EPO Constitutional

[300] HoR, *Explanatory Memorandum* (n 282) 1. See the reference to Art 220 Treaty of Rome, which probably should be a reference to Art 230 of the same Treaty (current Art 220(1) TFEU), which then read: 'The Community shall establish all appropriate forms of cooperation with the Council of Europe.'

[301] See the CoE Supplementary Agreement (n 239) adopted by Belgian law 5 November 1990, Belgian State Gazette, 30 April 1991. The Supplementary Agreement is retroactively applied to the date of establishment of the CoE mission.

[302] Constitution of 19 October 1953 of the (then) Intergovernmental Committee for European Migration, entered into force on 30 November 1954 (as amended).

[303] Agreement between the Kingdom of Belgium and the International Organization for Migration on the privileges and immunities of the organization in Belgium, signed on 4 December 1996) amending the Agreement between the Kingdom of Belgium and the Intergovernmental Committee for European Migration, signed on 2 July 1973, adopted by Belgian law 2 July 1973.

[304] Article 2 London Accord, amending Arts 18–21 Geneva Accord; Senate [BE] Explanatory Memorandum, 2-760/1 (2000–01), 21 May 2001, 3.

Treaty of 1973 to determine the status of its mission in Brussels.[305] Traditional inviolabilities (Art 2 on the archives), privileges (Art 4 on tax exemptions within the scope of official activities; Art 5 on custom duties), and functional immunities (Art 3) are accorded. All EPO employees enjoy immunity from jurisdiction in respect of acts done in the exercise of their functions, but there is no specific provision relating to the diplomatic status of the offices' heads in the member states.[306] This immunity does not apply in the case of a motor traffic offence committed by an EPO employee, nor in the case of damage caused by a motor vehicle belonging to or driven by an employee. Remarkably, the Protocol provides that in time of international crises EPO employees and the members of their family enjoy the same repatriation facilities as diplomatic agents (Art 14(*f*)).

**International Criminal Police Organization** Interpol's Constitution does not feature a clause on the status, privileges, and immunities of the organization in its member states.[307] This legal void was only addressed recently by an agreement in the form of an exchange of letters.[308] The HQ agreement grants the traditional diplomatic rights and immunities to the Brussels liaison office's head and their deputy. Other officials enjoy an exemption from taxes on salaries, emoluments, and fees, as well as personal inviolability. There is but one notable difference with other agreements of this kind: the social security provision was omitted on Interpol's request.

**Organisation Internationale de la Francophonie** The OIF is a linguistic community, structured as an international organization with member states, including Belgium, that have French as an official language. The OIF was created in 1970 as the Agence de Coopération Culturelle et Technique (ACCT).[309] In 1998, the Agency was renamed the *Agence Intergouvernementale de la Francophonie* (Intergovernmental Agency of the Francophonie), before it got its current name in 2005. It currently maintains four permanent representations, among which is the one to the EU in Brussels. The OIF is also represented in Addis Ababa (at the AU and at the United Nations Economic Commission for Africa), in New York, and in Geneva (at the UN). The status of the Brussels office is governed by a 1995 HQ agreement entered into with Belgium.[310] The agreement echoes provisions of other HQ agreements, including the diplomatic status for the head of the office and their deputy (Art 15), the inviolability of the parts of the premises used for official activities (Art 2), and of the archives and communication (Art 4). It differs from most HQ agreements in that the OIF Agreement specifies that Belgium is not internationally responsible for the work, acts, or omissions of the OIF or its officials in its territory (Art 29).

[305] Protocol on Privileges and Immunities of the European Patent Organisation to the Convention on the Grant of European Patents, signed on 5 October 1973, adopted by Belgian law 15 December 1975.

[306] ibid, Art 14(*a*).

[307] Constitution of the International Criminal Police Organization, signed on 1 June 1956 and entered into force 13 June 1956.

[308] Headquarters Agreement (by exchange of letters) between the Kingdom of Belgium and the International Organization for Criminal Police, signed on 14 and 24 October 2014.

[309] Article 8 Convention portant création de l'Agence de Coopération Culturelle et Technique, signed on 20 March 1970.

[310] Headquarters Agreement between the Kingdom of Belgium and the Agency for Cultural and Technical Cooperation, signed on 16 November 1995, adopted by Belgian law 5 June 1998.

*3.3.3.3.2 Belgium is not a member state of the accredited international organization*

Upon request, Belgium also welcomes missions of organizations of which it is not a member 'given the presence of the institutions of the Community in Belgium'.[311] The missions' status is determined by the conditions set out in an HQ agreement concluded between the IO and Belgium. The Belgian Government has adopted a policy line that extends the regime applicable to missions of IOs of which it is a member to missions of other IOs. Consequently, although laid down in different instruments, the privileges and immunities do not differ greatly between those two types. However, it is notable that the second type of HQ agreement is significantly longer. The explanation is simple: the agreements also have to cover those privileges and immunities that traditionally feature in the constitutional treaties or general privileges and immunities conventions but which do not automatically apply to non-member state Belgium. The agreements with IOs of which Belgium is a member typically do not deal with the general immunity of the IO, its archives, or communication (which are overall well covered in other treaties) but focus on the individual status of the staff of the mission. This section summarizes the legal framework applicable to missions of the AU,[312] GCC,[313] Arab League,[314] the OIC,[315] and EFTA,[316] while also paying attention to the specificities of each regime. The last case is an interesting one: Belgium is not a member of the EFTA, and as such not bound by the terms on privileges and immunities of its Constitution; to remedy this, it entered into an HQ agreement. The EEA, of which Belgium is a member, does not have its own representation in Brussels, nor does it refer to privileges and immunities in the EEA Agreement.

The protection of archives, communications, and correspondence of the liaison offices matches customary diplomatic law standards as well as the language of the CPIUN(–SA).[317] There are two discrepancies. First, the EFTA and GCC Agreements stipulate that only communications for official use are unrestricted. Second, unlike the case for UN and UNSA Offices (and stipulated in Art 27 VCDR), the HQ agreements generally do not establish a right for the liaison offices to use a diplomatic bag or messages in cipher or code. The OIC constitutes an exception: under Article 16(1)(*d*) of its HQ agreement, the Brussels office has the right to use codes and to send and receive correspondence and official documents by courier or in sealed bags for their communications with the OIC. Note that the word 'diplomatic' is not used and that the sender/recipient of those communications is limited expressly to the mother IO.

[311] Senate [BE] Explanatory Memorandum, 1-1086/1 (1997–98) 3 August 1998, 2.

[312] Headquarters Agreement between the Kingdom of Belgium and the Organization of African Unity, signed on 9 October 1985; exchanges of letters of 9 October 1985 and 29 June 1998 between the Kingdom of Belgium and the Organization of African Unity, adopted by Belgian law 21 February 2006 (hereafter Belgium–AU Agreement).

[313] Headquarters Agreement between the Kingdom of Belgium and the Cooperation Council of the Arab States of the Gulf, signed on 11 May 1993, adopted by Belgian law 22 January 1999) (hereafter Belgium–GCC Agreement).

[314] Headquarters Agreement between the Kingdom of Belgium and the League of Arab States, signed on 16 November 1995, adopted by Belgian law 9 June 1999 (Belgian State Gazette, 4 November 1999) (hereafter Belgium–AL Agreement).

[315] Headquarters Agreement between the Kingdom of Belgium and the Organization of the Islamic Conference, signed on 4 February 201, adopted by Belgian law 16 January 2016 (hereafter Belgium–OIC Agreement).

[316] Convention establishing the European Free Trade Association, signed on 4 January 1960, revised by the Vaduz Convention of 21 June 2001; Headquarters Agreement with the European Free Trade Association, done at Brussels on 27 January 1993, adopted by Belgian law 9 February 1999 (hereafter Belgium–EFTA Agreement).

[317] Articles 6 and 14 Belgium–AU Agreement; Arts 4 and 13 Belgium–EFTA Agreement; Arts 4 and 13 Belgium–GCC Agreement; Arts 4 and 13 Belgium–AL Agreement; Arts 4 and 14 Belgium–OIC Agreement.

As is the case for other liaison offices to the Union, Belgium does not easily accord diplomatic status to all of the IOs' representatives: generally, only the office's representative or director (and their respective households) are granted privileges and immunities that equal the VCDR's. The Belgium–AU Agreement, Belgium–AL Agreement, and Belgium–GCC Agreement mention the head and deputy. The Belgium–OIC Agreement extends this to the head and *deputies* and the Belgium–EFTA Agreement to the head and deputy, as well as officials that had a diplomatic status in Geneva prior to moving to Belgium. The remarks made with regard to the interpretation of the term 'household' made earlier apply here too. Other staff are immune from civil and criminal jurisdiction in respect of words spoken or written and all acts performed by them in an official capacity,[318] a limitation that by definition applies to Belgians working in the office.[319] Similar to the UNO Agreement, the HQ agreements contain a general exception for accidents caused by motor vehicles belonging to the mission or operated on the mission's behalf or in the case of a traffic violation or accident caused by such a vehicle.[320] In the Belgium–OIC Agreement, it is made explicit that this restriction of immunity also applies to the head of mission, who enjoys diplomatic privileges and immunities.

Some agreements are more detailed than others on the question of whether there is an obligation for the IO to waive immunity in certain circumstances. For instance, Article 22 of the Arab League HQ Agreement stipulates that the AL Secretary General is under a duty to waive the immunity of its representative in any case where the immunity would impede the course of justice, and it can be waived without prejudice to the purpose for which the immunity is accorded; language that reminds us of section 14 CPIUN.[321] All officials, as well as the mission itself, enjoy extensive privileges in the form of an exemption from direct taxes, an exemption from indirect taxes for the good for official use, and in relation to the import of goods.[322] A social security provision features in each of the agreements.[323]

The HQ agreements have their own restrictive interpretation of the concept of 'premises of the mission' and the accompanying concept of 'inviolability'. First, only the parts of the building used for official business are protected.[324] Second, in diplomatic law, the term 'inviolability' entails, on the one hand, a special positive duty of protection for the receiving state and, on the other hand, a negative duty for the latter to abstain from exercising any sovereign right, in particular enforcement rights.[325] The HQ agreements give a different meaning to this term, when they provide that the:

> buildings may only be accessed with the consent of the IO. Such consent shall be deemed to have been obtained in case of fire or other disaster requiring immediate protection measures require.

[318] Arts 18-21 Belgium–AU Agreement; Arts 16–21 Belgium–EFTA Agreement; Arts 15–21 Belgium–GCC Agreement; Arts 16–21 Belgium–AL Agreement.

[319] See, eg Art 21 Belgium–AL Agreement.

[320] Article 25 Belgium–AU Agreement; Art 3 Belgium–EFTA Agreement; Art 3 Belgium–GCC Agreement; Art 3 Belgium–AL Agreement; Art 27 Belgium–OIC Agreement.

[321] See also Art 25 Belgium–OIC Agreement.

[322] Articles 7–13 Belgium–AU Agreement; Arts 6–12 Belgium–EFTA Agreement; Arts 6–12 Belgium–GCC Agreement; Arts 6–12 Belgium–AL Agreement; Arts 6–13 Belgium–OIC Agreement.

[323] Article 19 Belgium–AL Agreement: head and deputy; Art 24 Belgium–OIC Agreement.

[324] Article 3 Belgium–AU Agreement; Art 2 Belgium–EFTA Agreement; Art 2 Belgium–GCC Agreement; Art 2 Belgium–AL Agreement; Art 5 Belgium–OIC Agreement.

[325] Denza (n 44) 40; Marjoleine Zieck, 'Diplomatiek en Consulair Recht' in Nathalie Horbach, René Lefeber, and Olivier Ribbelink (eds), *Handboek Internationaal Recht* (TMC Asser Press 2007) 284.

This clause is less extensive than the protection granted to diplomatic missions in Belgium. According to the VCDR, the receiving state's agents may not enter the mission without the head of mission's express consent (Art 22(1) VCDR); that consent, unless agreed to the contrary, is not presumed, not even in emergency or exceptional situations such as a fire. In fact, the HQ agreements grants a protection that reminds of the consular protection of premises. Under Article 32(2) VCCR, the prohibition to enter consular premises only applies to sections used exclusively for the purpose of consular work. Consequently, other parts (eg a kitchen) can be entered in accordance with local rules. Moreover, in consular law too, the head of the consular post's consent may be assumed in case of a fire or another disaster requiring prompt action. Article 3 of the Belgium–AU Agreement also mentions the inviolability of the residence of the head of mission, as is standard in bilateral diplomacy; other agreements are silent on the matter. In some HQ agreements, Belgium explicitly commits to protecting the mission's premises from external threats, a formulation that neither features in the VCDR nor VCCR but can be seen as Belgium's pledge to reiterate the interpretation of inviolability under diplomatic/consular law comprising a negative and a positive duty.[326] One could argue that even in absence of such clause, the general meaning of inviolability entails an obligation on the part of Belgium to protect the IO's offices.

Property and assets of liaison offices in Belgium enjoy immunity from legal process when used in the course of official duties.[327] The HQ agreements derogate from the VCDR and CPIUN, which grants immunity to all assets and property of a sending state the UN used for whatever purpose in the territory of one of the member states. An IO can decline its entitlements under an HQ agreement, but each measure will require a separate waiver of immunity. With regard to the waiver, the HQ agreements' language corresponds to section 2 of the CPIUN and customary diplomatic law.

Finally, some agreements contain an obligation on the part of the liaison office to annually inform the Belgian tax administration about salaries, emoluments, remuneration, or pensions received by the staff of the mission by the IO.[328] In the AU's case, the inclusion of information duty came with a struggle. During the agreement's negotiations, the AU indicated that it considered the mandatory production of such a document a violation of its 'sovereignty'. A discussion on the issue postponed the entering into force of Articles 17 and 29 regarding the information duty. A later agreement in the form of an exchange of letters dated 29 June 1998 encompasses a compromise on the issue. All provisions of the HQ agreement are now executed.

#### 3.3.3.4 Non-State Entities

Four non-state entities feature in the Union's diplomatic 'b-list', a list containing representational missions of IO's and other entities. *Hong Kong* and *Macao* each manage an Economic and Trade Office in Brussels. Neither of those offices functions at ambassadorial level. However, arrangements with Belgium allow for the exercise of a somewhat lowered diplomatic capacity. The *Order of Malta*'s permanent representation in Brussels is accredited exclusively to the Union; its head is granted the courtesy title of ambassador.

[326] Article 2 Belgium–GCC Agreement; Art 2 Belgium–AL Agreement; Art 5(3) Belgium–OIC Agreement.

[327] Article 4 Belgium–AU Agreement; Arts 1 and 3 Belgium–EFTA Agreement; Arts 1 and 3 Belgium–GCC Agreement; Art 1 Belgium–AL Agreement; Art 2 Belgium–OIC Agreement.

[328] Articles 17*j*–29 Belgium–AU Agreement; Art 27 Belgium–AL Agreement; Art 27 Belgium–OIC Agreement. The GCC and EFTA Agreements do not contain such a clause.

The *general delegation of Palestine to the EU* is also included in the b-list as it awaits formal recognition as a diplomatic mission, which will be granted as soon as its statehood is firmly recognized by all member states.[329] Belgium, however, recognizes the general delegation as a diplomatic mission. Since Palestine's accession to the VCDR, it enjoys diplomatic status and the accompanying privileges and immunities.

As of yet, *Taiwan* and *Kosovo* have not opened liaison offices to the EU in Brussels.

#### 3.3.3.5 Non-Governmental and Private Actors

Belgium entered into an HQ agreement with the ICRC in 1999.[330] Similar to IOs, this happened in response to a request by the ICRC President to expand the relations of the Committee with the EU. It was the first time that Belgium had concluded an HQ agreement with a non-state entity that is not an IO. This resulted in a lively debate in the Belgian Parliament on the ICRC's status under PIL, which was settled by Belgium's treatment of the ICRC as having a functional international legal personality. The recognition of the ICRC's rights and duties allowed for the conclusion of the HQ agreement and the opening of a liaison office. In the travaux préparatoires, the Belgian legislator relied on the criteria for legal personality laid down in the ICJ's *Reparation for Injuries* opinion and applied these to the ICRC.[331] The agreement's structure largely follows that of agreements on liaison offices of IOs to which Belgium is not a member, as does the applicable legal regime. Consequently, the mission's head and deputy are granted a diplomatic status, provided that they do not possess Belgian nationality (Art 16).

Belgium used the example of the ICRC HQ Agreement as a model for agreements with two other entities. In 2008, an HQ agreement was entered into with the RCC, an informal regional cooperative framework for countries in Southeast Europe in which the EU participates,[332] and in 2014 an HQ agreement was entered into with the International IDEA—a think tank with an intergovernmental structure.[333] Both agreements are still awaiting ratification and entry into force.

329 See <http://diplomatie.belgium.be/nl/Diensten/Protocol/adresgegevens_diplomatiek_corps> accessed 2 May 2022.

330 Headquarters Agreement between the Kingdom of Belgium and the International Committee of the Red Cross, signed on 19 April 1999, adopted by Belgian law 4 March 2002).

331 Senate [BE], Explanatory Memorandum, 2-839/1 (2000/2001), 9 July 2001, 2–3.

332 Headquarters Agreement between the Kingdom of Belgium and the Secretariat of the Regional Cooperation Council, signed on 29 August 2008, not yet entered into force.

333 Headquarters Agreement between the Kingdom of Belgium and the International Institute for Democracy and Electoral Assistance, signed on 15 May 2014, not yet entered into force.

# 4

# The EU's Application of Diplomatic Law

## 4.1 General Principles

The European Union (EU, or Union) has constructed a dense legal framework within which to conduct diplomatic relations. However creative and pragmatic this arrangement may be, it is still undecided whether and to what extent an age-old and comprehensive set of international legal rules codified in a multilateral treaty—but also captured in customary international law (CIL), behavioural norms, practices, and rules of protocol—is transferable, and if so, whether a simple *renvoi* to the Vienna Convention on Diplomatic Relations (VCDR) in bilateral instruments can accomplish a perfectly equivalent application of the body of diplomatic law.[1]

Despite all the changes that have occurred in global affairs over the past centuries, diplomacy still trades in secrecy and seclusion while avoiding intrusions and other actions that could upset balances and the idea of equality in international relations. Contemporary diplomacy is built on ancient foundations, understandings, and practices. These have given rise to a number of key characteristics and principles underpinning the diplomatic regime, all of which are fundamentally connected to how diplomatic law has been conceptualized in the past few centuries: its self-contained character, as well as the principles of non-discrimination and reciprocity; the principle of non-interference; and the idea that diplomatic interactions must take place in secrecy.

### 4.1.1 A Self-Contained System?

Diplomatic law can be characterized as a fairly closed system within international law in which actors (states) and rules, including the so-called non-discrimination and reciprocity principles, are well-defined. Yet, the extent to which the diplomatic system is impenetrable has been the object of considerable debate. In scholarly writings, diplomatic law has been characterized as a 'closed system',[2] a 'strong form of lex specialis',[3] as well as 'a non-institutionalized special regime'.[4] The discussion centres on whether diplomatic law is to be treated as some sort of autonomous subsystem within international law and, if so, the legal effects this brings about. Much confusion has its origins in the *Tehran Hostages* judgment of the International Court of Justice (ICJ). In this well-known case, the ICJ affirmed that the interpretation and application of diplomatic law requires a specific approach.[5] In paragraph

[1] Vienna Convention on Diplomatic Relations, opened for signature on 18 April 1961, entered into force 24 April 1964, 500 UNTS 95 (hereafter VCDR).

[2] Karel Wellens, 'Diversity in Secondary Rules and the Unity of International Law: Some Reflections on Current Trends' (1994) 25 Neth Yearb Int Law 3, 4.

[3] International Law Commission (ILC), 'Draft Articles on the Responsibility of States for Internationally Wrongful Acts with Commentaries' (2001) II YBILC 104.

[4] Axel Marschik, 'Too Much Order? The Impact of Special Secondary Norms on the Unity and Efficacy of the International Legal System' (1998) 9 EJIL 212, 215.

[5] Bruno Simma, 'Self-Contained Regimes' (1985) 16 Neth Yearb Int Law 111; Jean Salmon, *Manuel de Droit Diplomatique* (Bruylant 1994) 480–81.

*EU Diplomatic Law*. Sanderijn Duquet, Oxford University Press. © Sanderijn Duquet 2022.
DOI: 10.1093/oso/9780192844552.003.0004

86, the ICJ referred to the diplomatic system as a *self-contained system*, the rules of which must be understood in line with the specific rationale of diplomatic law:

> [T]he rules of diplomatic law, in short, constitute a self-contained regime which, on the one hand, lays down the receiving State's obligations regarding the facilities, privileges and immunities to be accorded to the diplomatic missions and, on the other, foresees their possible abuse by members of the mission and specifies the means at the disposal of the receiving State to counter any such abuse. These means are by their nature, entirely efficacious. [6]

The ICJ judgment provoked considerable criticism.[7] Some argued that it adds to the fragmentation of public international law (PIL) and that there exists no such thing as a self-contained regime in international law.[8] Concerns also arose in part from the lack of consistent usage of the notion itself and the consequences this brings about for other (international) legal regimes.

To understand the self-contained regime reference, it is crucial to recall the particular issue addressed by the ICJ. The dictum in *Tehran Hostages* merely relates to the conditions for and limitations on the taking of countermeasures by an injured state in the diplomatic context.[9] It confirms that, when a wrongdoing occurs, a receiving state has to resort to the means of defence and sanctions provided for in diplomatic law itself.[10] Being representatives of their home state in a foreign country, envoys are placed in a vulnerable position for the greater good of the international office. International law does not allow them to be a standing target for countermeasures. Consequently, only diplomatic retorsions (ie 'unfriendly' conduct not inconsistent with any international obligation and by definition allowed under diplomatic law) are justifiable.[11] Based on functional grounds, the ICJ excluded the taking of countermeasures infringing diplomatic or consular law;[12] countermeasures are only allowed as long as these 'respect the inviolability of diplomatic or consular agents, premises, archives and documents'.[13] The ICJ makes the point that the diplomatic system lays down particular obligations for participating states and identifies wrongdoings as well as a limited number of specific means to address them.[14] In relation to the EU's diplomatic practice, it should be kept in mind that the Court has never referred to the 'self-contained' finding

[6] *United States Diplomatic and Consular Staff in Tehran (United States of America v Iran)* (Judgment) [1980] ICJ Rep 3, para 86 (hereafter *Tehran Hostage* case).

[7] Anja Lindroos and Michael Mehling, 'Dispelling the Chimera of "Self-Contained Regimes" in International Law and the WTO' (2005) 16 EJIL 857; Bruno Simma and Dirk Pulkowski, 'Of Planets and the Universe: Self-Contained Regimes in International Law' (2006) 17 EJIL 483.

[8] ILC Study Group, 'Fragmentation of International Law: Difficulties Arising from the Diversification and Expansion of International Law' (2006) UN Doc A/CN.4/L.682, paras 192–93; Martti Koskenniemi and Päivi Leino, 'Fragmentation of International Law. Postmodern Anxieties?' (2002) 15 LJIL 553; Ralf Michaels and Joost Pauwelyn, 'Conflict of Norms or Conflict of Laws?: Different Techniques in the Fragmentation of Public International Law' (2012) 22 Duke J Comp & Intl L 349.

[9] *Tehran Hostage* case (n 6) para 83.

[10] ibid, para 87.

[11] Salmon, *Droit Diplomatique* (n 5) 481.

[12] ILC, 'Draft Articles on State Responsibility' (n 3) 134. See also: James Crawford, *The International Law Commission's Articles on State Responsibility: Introduction, Text and Commentaries* (CUP 2002) 293.

[13] Art 50(2)(*b*) of the ILC, 'Draft Articles on State Responsibility' (n 3) 131.

[14] LANM (Bert) Barnhoorn, 'Diplomatic Law and Unilateral Remedies' (1994) 25 Neth Yearb Int Law 39; Robert D Sloane, 'On the Use and Abuse of Necessity in the Law of State Responsibility' (2012) 106 AJIL 447, 492; James Crawford, *State Responsibility: The General Part* (CUP 2013) 697.

beyond the topic of the taking of reprisals.[15] Jean Salmon also correctly recalls that the ICJ never excluded the taking of countermeasures in a non-diplomatic context, which would be perfectly legal.[16]

On a broader level, the diplomatic system's 'closed' nature should also not be overstated. Self-contained regimes are no more than a conventional way to disregard the more general and standard rules of international law to the benefit of rules developed in an area of functional specialization within general international law (eg diplomatic law or EU law, for that matter). In that sense, states use diplomatic law to partially opt out of (certain) rules of state responsibility in light of the diplomatic domain's specific characteristics: diplomatic law serves a specific, 'functional' purpose, limits the number of participating members, relies on an interlinked set of rules, and allows only specific sanctions. This is an important part of what makes diplomatic law 'special'; not in the sense of being in some way outside of PIL but of being an elaborate form of lex specialis. This also has the consequence that, in case the self-contained subsystem as a whole would fail (eg a state refuses to comply with the normal diplomatic sanctions enforcement), a fallback on the general regime of state responsibility is unavoidable.[17]

### 4.1.2 Non-Discrimination and Reciprocity

In the application of international diplomatic law, the principle of non-discrimination is closely observed.[18] The Vienna Convention was designed to avoid a system based solely on reciprocity, typical to traditional bilateral diplomatic relations before the VCDR came into force. Yet reciprocity continues to live in the sense that it makes it in a state's own best interest to apply the appropriate standard of protection to foreign diplomats within their territory so that its own diplomats abroad receive an equal protection. The VCDR itself adheres to a certain balance between rights and duties of receiving and sending states, which enables the diplomatic and consular systems to function. Yet, the system is not in every aspect based on mutual obligations. Strict adherence to the reciprocity principle might hinder equal treatment of diplomatic missions as it would enable states to discriminate according to privileges received by their own missions abroad.[19] Consequently, the general non-discrimination rule benefits the multilateral system as a whole while the reciprocity principle benefits the collective of bilateral relations.

In the current state of law, the principle of non-discrimination as it has emerged under CIL is accurately reflected in the text and logic of Article 47(1) VCDR; the article contains a straightforward prohibition for parties to discriminate between states. The VCDR refers to non-discrimination in two other instances. First, Article 11(2) allows a host state to refuse to accept officials of a particular category on a non-discriminatory basis. Second, Article 13(1) states that the practice of the presentation of the credentials of new heads of mission must be applied in a uniform manner in a host state. These provisions can be regarded as concrete applications of the general non-discrimination clause of Article 47 VCDR. That

[15] Salmon, *Droit Diplomatique* (n 5) 54; Eileen Denza, *Diplomatic Law: Commentary on the Vienna Convention on Diplomatic Relations* (4th edn, OUP 2016) 420.
[16] Salmon, *Droit Diplomatique* (n 5) 481.
[17] Simma and Pulkowski (n 7) 507.
[18] Salmon, *Droit Diplomatique* (n 5) 52–54.
[19] Andrew L Odell, 'Enforcing Reciprocity in U.S. Diplomatic Relations: The Foreign Missions Act of 1982' (1984) 17 NYUJILP 817.

provision should be understood as the duty of receiving states to treat all diplomats within their territory according to a general standard of treatment, both in law and in practice. It does not, however, prohibit a receiving state, under the specific circumstances spelled out in Article 47(2) VCDR, from granting treatment more favourable than the general standard to particular sending states, nor from applying diplomatic privileges restrictively because of a restrictive application of that provision to its own missions in the sending state.[20] The non-discrimination principle is not limited to the field of immunities and privileges: it applies to the Convention as a whole.[21]

The reciprocity principle continues to live on as an exception to the principle of non-discrimination. Article 47 VCDR, in its second part, elaborates on this by allowing, in certain circumstances and based on reciprocal rights, less favourable treatment and more favourable treatment. First, a receiving state may apply a Convention provision 'restrictively because of a restrictive application of that provision to its mission in the sending State' (Article 47(2)(*a*) VCDR). Consequently, it allows for retorsions as well as for a restrictive reading of provisions of the Vienna Convention, although the latter cannot be breached.[22] Second, no discrimination takes place when states 'extend to each other more favourable treatment' than is required by the VCDR (Art 47(2)(*b*) VCDR). The legal basis for a more generous treatment may either be a rule of custom or an agreement between states. Such arrangements may be construed as a 'most-favoured-nation' clause. In fact, in bilateral agreements between states establishing diplomatic, consular, or other missions or extending privileges and immunities and treatment in general, these so-called MFN clauses are commonplace. They are mostly granted on a reciprocal basis.[23] However, neither the existence of a treaty or custom nor an explicit reference to a reciprocal scheme are required as a condition for the application of more favourable treatment. Nonetheless, in practice, the main reason why states grant additional privileges will be because their missions abroad are receiving such rights.[24] Interestingly, conventions governing the status of diplomatic missions to IOs do not allow for the discriminatory treatment of different foreign missions on grounds of reciprocity. The UN Secretariat argues that the privileges and immunities granted should generally be those accorded to the diplomatic corps as a whole and should not be subject to particular conditions imposed, on a basis of reciprocity, upon the diplomatic missions of particular states.[25]

Article 47(1) explicitly refers to states as the beneficiaries of non-discriminatory treatment. This choice of wording—the treaty drafters could have referred to 'diplomatic missions' rather than 'states'—is not favourable to EU delegations (EUDELs). A choice for the more neutral term 'diplomatic agents' was preferred in the ILC's 2001 Draft Articles on responsibility of states with regard to Article 50 on obligations not to be affected by countermeasures. The ILC commentary elaborates on the wording of the draft article and explains that there did not need to be an explicit reference to multilateral diplomacy since the representatives of states to international organizations are covered by the reference to diplomatic agents. The more restrictive wording in the Vienna Convention is, however, but a logical consequence of the idea that the principle reflects the general rule inherent in the

[20] Joe Verhoeven, *Droit International Public* (Éditions Larcier 2000) 106.
[21] Salmon, *Droit Diplomatique* (n 5) 53.
[22] Holger P Hestermeyer, 'Vienna Convention on Diplomatic Relations (1961)' in Anne Peters (ed) *Max Planck Encyclopedia of Public International Law*, para 41, <https://opil.ouplaw.com/home/mpil> accessed 3 May 2022.
[23] International Law Commission (ILC), 'Draft Articles on Most-Favored-Nation Clauses with Commentaries' (1978) II YBILC 21, 37.
[24] Denza, *Diplomatic Law* (n 15) 409.
[25] Abdullah El-Erian, 'Fourth Report on Relations between States and International Organizations', UN Doc A/Cn.4/218, reprinted in 1969 II YBILC 11, 18.

sovereign equality of states.[26] For Union delegations to adhere to the VCDR in the same non-discriminatory way as state missions is a challenge. The Headquarters of the European External Action Service (EEAS) has to perform the vital task of requesting and ensuring that EUDELs are treated equally with state missions in receiving states.

The rights of diplomatic missions and their staff are conceptualized as immunities, inviolabilities, privileges, and entitlements. As a result, state parties accept restrictions on the exclusive jurisdiction over their own territory,[27] as certain laws and regulations either do not apply these, as is the case with privileges, or they cannot be enforced, as is the case with immunities and inviolabilities. The far-reaching restrictions on the sovereignty of states would not have withstood the test of time if there were not certain strings attached. The quasi-unchallengeable rights of diplomats and, to a lesser extent, of consuls bring about obligations that need to be observed when stationed abroad. Therefore, academic literature often notes that most if not all duties of diplomats serve as the corollary of the immunities. In other words, diplomatic and consular rights and duties are seen as corresponding notions.[28] However, the International Law Commission (ILC) ruled out the idea that a state only has to grant immunities if an envoy fulfils their duties in the receiving state. In the 1958 Commentary to the Draft Articles on Diplomatic Intercourse and Immunities, the ILC submitted that '[f]ailure by a diplomatic agent to fulfil his obligations does not absolve the receiving State from its duty to respect the agent's immunity'.[29]

The diplomatic legal framework, as a consequence of its self-contained characteristics, has the capacity to be self-enforcing. In this system, the principle of reciprocity can also be conceptualized as a *mechanism fostering compliance*. Typically, reciprocity is seen as the embodiment of the states' desire to see the protection they offer to foreign diplomats in their territory equally accorded to their own diplomats who are accredited in another country.[30] In other words, reciprocity serves as the incentive for state parties to the VCDR to apply the highest standards of protection.[31] In this sense, Bruno Simma and Dirk Pulkowski noted that 'at least at the time when the Vienna Convention was drafted, the ILC appears to have been of the view that the symmetry of its obligations would allow reciprocal reprisals'.[32] The reciprocity principle also has a *preventive nature*. Most states, in their practice as sending states, instruct their diplomats to respect obligations under the VCDR. As such, a state will want to avoid the failure of its diplomats to meet their obligations under the Vienna Convention since it may cause the receiving state to react. Similarly, protocol services of receiving states are keen to draw the diplomatic duties embodied in Articles 41 and 42 VCDR to the attention of the corps diplomatique present in a certain capital.

Reverting to EU practice, establishment agreements (EAs) refer to the VCDR without indicating how the concepts of non-discrimination (as the general rule) and reciprocity (as the exception) are to be applied in relation to the Union: the general *mutatis mutandis* clause provides the only guidance. Despite the references made in the EAs to the multilateral system, the principle of reciprocity seems to be of a more defining nature in the EU's

[26] ILC, 'Report Covering the Work of the ILC's Twelfth Session: 25 April to 1 July 1960 A/4425' (1960) II YBILC 178.

[27] James Crawford, *Brownlie's Principles of Public International Law* (OUP 2012) 204.

[28] Ivor Roberts (ed), *Satow's Diplomatic Practice* (6th edn, OUP 2011) 150.

[29] International Law Commission (ILC), 'Draft Articles on Diplomatic Intercourse and Immunities with Commentaries' (1958) II YBILC 104.

[30] Alain Plantey, *Principes de Diplomatie* (2nd edn, Pedone 2000) 207–08.

[31] Silviya Lechner, 'What Difference Does Ius Inter Gentes Make? Changing Diplomatic Rights and Duties and the Modern European States-System' (2006) 1 HJD 235, 245.

[32] Simma and Pulkowski (n 7) 513, referring to the ILC's 'Draft Articles on State Responsibility (n 3) 105.

diplomatic relations than the non-discrimination standard. This stems from the bilateral design of the EU's legal framework for the conduct of diplomatic relations. Reciprocity serves as a powerful tool for the Union to ensure that its delegations receive treatment equal to that granted to diplomatic missions in Brussels.[33] The non-discrimination principle, on the other hand, is closely associated with the multilateral system. The following sections discuss some practical consequences of these legal issues and present some interesting trends in the application of the VCDR in the daily diplomatic activities of the EEAS.

### 4.1.3 Non-Interference

A receiving state's status as a sovereign member of the international community calls for limitations to diplomatic conduct which threaten the status or rights derived from it.[34] Consequently, diplomats have to abstain from interfering in the domestic policies of the country they are accredited to. The rule featured in draft codes on diplomatic relations in the nineteenth and early twentieth century,[35] was first assessed by the ICJ in the 1950 *Asylum* case,[36] and eventually codified in Article 41(1) VCDR. The last sentence of that provision speaks of the duty for persons enjoying immunities to not 'interfere in the internal affairs' of the receiving state. Nevertheless, as is the case for states wanting to be outspoken on topics of human rights, democracy, and the rule of law, a certain tension emerges when the EU uses its formal diplomacy to speak out about such topics. Indeed, an EUDEL that presents itself as a strong supporter of democracy by weighing on political processes or supporting political actors may be at unease with PIL's duty not to interfere in a receiving state. An additional layer of complexity is caused by the fact that the Union is legally obliged to uphold and promote its values (Art 21 TEU).[37] Whether this implies that EUDELs can or even have to publicly condemn a receiving state (eg for a general lack of democracy or a gross rule of law violation) is not quite clear and has never been truly tested under Union law. However, Jozef Bátora and David Spence go as far as to argue that:

> [i]ntervention in domestic affairs of third countries has been the rule of the game for the EU and its institutional predecessors ever since it developed embryonic forms of diplomatic actorness in the 1960s.[38]

Different discussions in the sections to come (eg on the exercise of diplomatic functions, diplomatic visas, and diplomatic asylum) support the above quote and showcase the tension between the EU defending its own values in its external relations and the basic principles of diplomatic relations that require a certain restraint.

[33] Jan Wouters and Sanderijn Duquet, 'The EU and International Diplomatic Law: New Horizons?' (2012) 7 HJD 31, 34.

[34] See generally, Paul Behrens, *Diplomatic Interference and the Law* (Hart 2016) 31.

[35] ibid 33–34. See also the Draft Code by Johann Caspar Bluntschi (1868); Pasquale Fliori (1890); the Project of the American Institute of International Law (1925); and the Project of the International Commission of American Jurists (1927), all published in [1932] 26 AJIL 161–73.

[36] *Asylum Case (Colombia v Peru)* (Judgment) [1950] ICJ Rep 266.

[37] Consolidated Version of the Treaty on European Union [2012] OJ C326/01 (hereafter TEU).

[38] Jozef Bátora and David Spence, 'The EEAS as a Catalyst of Diplomatic Innovation' in David Spence and Jozef Bátora (eds), *The European External Action Service: European Diplomacy Post-Westphalia* (Palgrave Macmillan 2015) 9.

A first area of tension is the potential interference in the receiving state's internal politics. The 1958 ILC Commentary gives as an example that it is prohibited for diplomats to take part in political campaigns.[39] Instances of direct meddling in political campaigns are rare, although some states do continue to exert influence in other states' elections, including through their diplomatic presence on the ground.[40] But receiving states may consider diplomats who sit together with opposition leaders in violation of Article 41(1).[41] This is much more common in modern practice and in EU practices. In March 2021, for instance, the EU Delegation and EU Special Representative met with representatives of opposition parties following the arrest of an opposition leader in February of that same year. Since the opposition is also an important source of information and is also seen as an integral part of the system, these actions are increasingly tolerated. Whether an ambassador can make statements after elections will depend on the context at hand. Generally, in the wake of elections, it is advisable that missions only release neutral statements, for example, to congratulate the people of the sending state on holding a peaceful election or to have the sending state's government convey a message of congratulations through the embassy. Criticizing a third state, which is strictly speaking not an interference in the 'internal' affairs of the receiving state, is also not allowed if it would jeopardize the relations between the host state and that third state.[42]

A second tension exists between the principle of non-interference and the freedom of communication (Art 27 VCDR) as well as the diplomatic function to protect the interests of the sending state (Art 3(1) VCDR). In the 1958 ILC Commentary, it was explicitly accepted that:

> [t]he making of representations for the purpose of protecting the interests of the diplomatic agent's country or of its nationals in accordance with international law does not constitute an interference in the internal affairs of the receiving State within the meaning of this provision.[43]

For the Union, freedom of expression, free press, and media pluralism are crucial guarantees for an open and free democratic debate. These values guide the EU's action internally and externally and are considered a part of its own interests in its wider relations with third countries. In July 2020, a joint column by the EUDEL and national EU Ambassadors to China on the occasion of the forty-fifth anniversary of EU–China diplomatic relations was censored before being published by the *China Daily*. Still, the full and unedited piece was published on the EUDEL's social media channels and also distributed to Chinese media outlets 'to pass EU messages to the Chinese public' in spite of the obvious challenges.

A third tension between the duty of non-interference and general obligations of external relations exists in the area of human rights. Legal scholars express doubts as to whether formally criticizing internal (human rights) matters is permitted—let alone appropriate—in a

[39] ILC, 'Draft Articles on Diplomatic Intercourse' (n 29) 104.

[40] See, for a discussion, Sanderijn Duquet and Jan Wouters, 'Legal Duties of Diplomats Today' in Paul Behrens (ed), *Diplomatic Law in a New Millennium* (OUP 2017).

[41] Paul Behrens, 'None of Their Business?: Diplomatic Involvement in Human Rights' (2014) 15 Melb U L Rev 190; Roberts, *Satow* (n 28) 153.

[42] Michael Richtsteig, *Wiener Übereinkommen über Diplomatische und Konsularische Beziehungen: Entstehungsgeschichte, Kommentierung, Praxis* (2nd edn, Nomos 2010) 102.

[43] ILC, 'Draft Articles on Diplomatic Intercourse' (n 29) 104.

diplomatic context.[44] Yet the EU (as do member states) remains a frontrunner in engaging its delegations in the direct support of democracy initiatives and the protection of local human rights' defenders. Answers to parliamentary questions reveal that the High Representative (HR) frequently instructs the delegations to keep track of blasphemy cases; to inform individuals on possible legal defence avenues; to request local authorities to hold investigations when human rights defenders are attacked; to urge the local government to establish a political environment in which all opposition parties, civil society, and media can operate freely; to promote the abolition of the death penalty and the freedom of belief; and to visit human rights activists in prison or attend their trials (if allowed by the host state).[45] In other cases, the decision to intervene or showcase support for human rights is left to the discretion of the Head of Delegation (HoD), who is best placed to judge on whether the local situation allows for such display. A concrete example is the decision of EUDELs on whether or not to raise the rainbow flag and to take part in pride marches to commemorate the International Day against Homophobia. In 2017, around forty-five EU delegations around the world raised the rainbow flag. Actions can be set up with or without member states. Frauke Austermann provides the example of the HoD in Beijing, who drafted a common statement on a human rights situation with ambassadors of EU member states but who was the only one who signed it in the end.[46] Sometimes, EU actions even take the form of diplomatic activism. In September 2020, diplomats from EU member states and the EUDEL kept a round-the-clock guard at the home of a Belarusian writer and opposition activist, amid fears for her safety, forming a diplomatic cordon.

The inherent contradiction as described above presents issues of both diplomacy and diplomatic law to the Union that have not been fully addressed in diplomatic practice or in academic literature. What is clear, however, is that balancing non-interference in internal affairs of host states and actively upholding EU values simultaneously is tricky even for the most seasoned of diplomats. Although it can build on Commission practices, the EEAS is still a relatively new diplomatic actor and in many ways is learning the true limits of its duty not to interfere. Reconciling competing principles from its own internal legal order and the external characteristics of international law will remain a challenge for the EU's future diplomatic endeavours but will also define the kind of diplomatic actor the Union wishes to be.

### 4.1.4 Secrecy

Secrecy and confidentiality are an integral part of diplomatic relations.[47] Stereotypically, a diplomatic agent distrusts diplomatic counterparts and treads carefully in order to avoid the dissemination of classified information. In order not to do so, the stereotype continues,

[44] Salmon, *Droit Diplomatique* (n 5) 129; Richtsteig (n 42) 103.

[45] Answers given by High Representative to question E-001991/2019 (EUDEL Pakistan; 6 June 2019); E-001877/2019 (EUDEL Brazil; 2 July 2019); E-000156/2019 (EUDEL Cambodia; 2 April 2019); E-006129/2018 (EUDEL Sudan; 1 February 2019); E-007102/2020 (EUDEL China/EU Office in Hong Kong; 26 February 2021); E-005000-15 (23 September 2015); E-006706/2014 (EUDEL Indonesia; 7 January 2015); and E-002335/2017 (17 June 2017).

[46] Frauke Austermann, 'Representing the EU in China: European Bilateral Diplomacy in a Competitive Diplomatic Environment' in Spence and Bátora (n 38) 301.

[47] Geoff R Berridge, *Diplomacy: Theory and Practice* (5th edn, Palgrave Macmillan 2015) 150. See, for further reading, Sanderijn Duquet and Jan Wouters, 'Diplomacy, Secrecy, and the Law' in Corneliu Bjola and Steve Murray (eds), *Secret Diplomacy: Concepts, Contexts and Cases* (Routledge 2016) and 'What the Eye Cannot See: Justifying Limits to Freedom of Information in the Diplomatic Context', in Dorota Mokrosinska (ed), *Transparency and Secrecy in European Democracies: Contested Trade-Offs* (Routledge 2020).

the diplomat has a specific toolbox. Diplomatic bags and couriers, backroom diplomacy, and coded messages are just a number of ways to protect intelligence from acts of espionage or disclosure in the media. The picture painted is that of a Cold War understanding of diplomacy. It would appear that the way in which diplomats handle information has now changed. Technological developments that allow for the fast and uncomplicated distribution of data have been introduced to diplomatic correspondence and negotiations, increasing both efficiency and vulnerability. Moreover, diplomats are increasingly working together in a manner that requires trust and loyalty rather than distrust and the shielding of information. Similarly, a greater degree of openness can be seen in the relationship between diplomats, on the one hand, and the press and the public, on the other. Nowadays, diplomatic missions establish dialogues, actively using both old and new media, to inform and engage with domestic and foreign publics.[48] In addition to the aforementioned changes, internal and external pressures that pose a more fundamental threat to the culture of secrecy in diplomacy can be discerned.[49] Recent years have seen a rise in demands for openness and transparency in diplomacy, especially where human rights are at stake. Such demands have been echoed in judicial proceedings, in which the interests of diplomacy and the public have had to be balanced. The EU is an integral part of these changes. Intelligence is shared between member states and institutions *within* the Union constellation, but Union actors also share information through the participation in institutionalized diplomatic fora (eg the UN) and in less formalized coalitions (eg G20). Especially in recent years, the EU has become rather responsive to public demands to access documents, to individual information rights, to effective judicial review, to be governed by a transparent administration, and, more generally, to public scrutiny and democratic accountability.

Nevertheless, it would be wrong to state that secrecy is no longer a topic in diplomacy and international law. To the contrary, diplomatic agents are well aware that they are sitting on information that may damage their sending state/entity or its partners. The majority of bilateral and multilateral negotiations continue to happen behind closed doors, in settings with predefined rules on confidentiality. Moreover, rules protecting secrecy that have been translated in the Vienna Convention remain fundamental to the way in which diplomacy is conducted. Therefore, it is recognized that the EU's diplomatic service still operates in a culture of secretiveness. As will be shown in the sections to follow, the Union also uses traditional means of diplomatic communication (eg the diplomatic bag) to keep its content as protected as possible.

## 4.2 The 1961 VCDR

The 1961 VCDR is the cornerstone of modern diplomatic relations. Measuring by the high degree of observance and its influence on the international and national legal orders, it is among the most successful international instruments ever to be drawn up. The Convention serves as the general framework on diplomatic life: it covers all its aspects, from the establishment of a diplomatic mission, over questions of accreditation and rights and duties of sending and receiving state, to the suspension and even termination of diplomatic relations.

[48] Ronald P Barston, *Modern Diplomacy* (4th edn, Pearson 2013) 90.

[49] Andrew F Cooper, 'The Changing Nature of Diplomacy' in Andrew F Cooper, Jorge Heine, and Ramesh Thakur (eds), *The Oxford Handbook of Modern Diplomacy* (OUP 2013) 46–47.

This section is designed as an introductory guide to how the EU applies the 1961 Vienna Convention in its active and passive diplomatic relations. It is therefore not intended to be a full doctrinal study of the general aspects of the law of contemporary diplomatic relations. Rather, it will pinpoint to the remaining frictions the EU experiences in diplomacy.

## 4.2.1 The Establishment and Termination of Diplomatic Relations

### 4.2.1.1 Establishing Diplomatic Relations

As explained in Chapter 2, the establishment of diplomatic relations and the establishment of a permanent mission are separate international legal acts, both of which are carried out by mutual consent (Art 2 VCDR). To establish relations or a mission, most commonly a formal request is made by the sending state's ministry of foreign affairs (MFA) to the receiving state's authorities.[50] Such decisions are commonly taken in close cooperation with or under the approval of the head of state or government. Subsequently, the receiving state is obliged to either facilitate the acquisition—in accordance with local laws (Art 41 VCDR)—on its territory of premises or assist in obtaining accommodation in some other way (Art 21(1) VCDR); the sending state may not, without the receiving state's prior express consent, establish offices forming part of the mission in localities other than those in which the mission itself is established (Art 12 VCDR).

The EU uses similar methods to establish diplomatic relations. In the past, it was the European Commission that reached out to third states in that regard. Although the 2010 EEAS Decision does not explicitly say so, it can be assumed that this function has been taken over by the High Representative of the Union for Foreign Affairs and Security Policy (HR) since Lisbon—although there aren't too many states left with which no relations are entertained.[51] The EU has not yet signed an EA with Cuba, the Democratic People's Republic of Korea (DPRK), and Iran and does not have an EUDEL in Havana, Pyongyang, or Teheran. However, those countries' representatives are accredited to the Union in Brussels and the EU's local representation is exercised by a member state mission on a rotating basis, showcasing that diplomatic relations are in fact established.

With regard to the establishment of an EU, Article 5(1) EEAS Decision stipulates:

> [t]he decision to open or close a delegation shall be adopted by the High Representative, in agreement with the Council and the Commission.

The HR must thereto enter into 'the necessary practical arrangements' with the receiving state or the international organization (IO) concerned (Art 5(6) EEAS Decision). Agreement on the establishment of diplomatic relations is sought through the EAs. In turn, the Model EA includes an Article 1 on the establishment of a Union delegation:

> [t]he Government of [third state] hereby agrees to the establishment on its territory of a Delegation of the European Union.[52]

[50] Biswanath Sen, *A Diplomat's Handbook of International Law and Practice* (Martinus Nijhoff 1988) 22.

[51] Council Decision 2010/427/EU of 26 July 2010 establishing the Organization and Functioning of the European External Action Service [2010] OJ L201/30 (hereafter EEAS Decision).

[52] Elisa Baroncini, 'Le Delegazioni dell'Unione Europea Dopo Il Trattato Di Lisbona. Struttura, Status E Funzioni' (2014) 6 CDT 68, 99.

As a result, in the EAs, third states consent both to the establishment of diplomatic relations and of a mission.

This does not necessarily mean they consent to a second office being opened in the same country: in the aftermath of Brexit, the United Kingdom—which in any event has not signed an EA with the EU yet—twice refused the opening of a permanent EU Belfast office of a limited size to oversee its trade and customs relations with Northern Ireland. In fact, in diplomatic law, the opening of a consular mission also warrants the express consent of the host state. The most recent EA (signed with Kuwait in 2019) is interesting because there is an explicit clause about it in the agreement. In its Article 1(3), Kuwait grants the Union 'the possibility to open offices forming part of its Delegation in localities other than those in which that Delegation is established'. The Union, for its part, commits in clear terms to notify the host state of its intention to open such offices, 'which may not be established without the prior express consent of Kuwait'. This language does not fundamentally differ from what the Vienna Convention spells out on the topic but was nevertheless copied in the EA.

In other cases too, the establishment of diplomatic relations and the establishment of an EUDEL do not always take place at the same time. For instance, the Commission HoD was given full ambassadorial status in Sudan in 1985; when the Commission opened a delegation in Juba in 2006, the Sudanese Government had to consent to the establishment of the mission. The EU may also opt to accredit a diplomat in a neighbouring country to conduct relations with a third state. By way of example, the EUDEL for the Pacific, based in Fiji, maintains relations with the receiving state and no less than eleven other island states: the Cook Islands, Kiribati, the Marshall Islands, Micronesia, Nauru, Niue, the Republic of Palau, Eastern Samoa, the Solomon Islands, Tonga, and Tuvalu. In other instances, diplomatic relations are established but executed by a locally represented member state on a rotating basis. Suriname serves as an example: the country entered into an EA that allows for the establishment of an EUDEL, but this has not yet been put into practice:[53] the French (first half) and Dutch (second half) continued to represent the EU in 2022 in the country.[54] The diplomatic interests of the EU in Andorra and Monaco are represented on a rotating basis by the French, Spanish, and Italian consular missions. Yet, the EU HoD to the Organisation for Economic Co-operation and Development (OECD) and the United Nations Educational, Scientific and Cultural Organization (UNESCO) based in Paris is accredited to both countries. In extraordinary cases, the EUDEL has been closed temporarily due to security concerns and awaiting a political decision on the future relations with certain regimes: the delegation in Damascus (Syria) relocated its staff to Brussels and Beirut, the EU HoD accredited to Afghanistan currently resides in Brussels, while the EU HoD to Yemen resides in Amman.

Third states and other entities wanting to establish diplomatic relations with the EU or to accredit a mission in Brussels need to obtain the Union's agreement. This happens through a procedure involving the EEAS, the Commission, and even the member states represented in the Council. Pre-Lisbon, decisions were taken by the Commission's Directorate General for External Relations (DG RELEX) and the Council's Committee of Permanent Representatives (Coreper).[55] Establishing diplomatic relations with any or all member states is not a prerequisite for an entity to engage in diplomatic relations with the EU. For example,

[53] Article 1 of the EA between the European Commission and the Republic of Suriname (1989).

[54] EEAS, 'Diplomatic Representation in Third Countries—1st Semester 2022', EEAS(2021)1319, 21 December 2021.

[55] Rachel Frid, *The Relations between the EC and International Organizations: Legal Theory and Practice* (Martinus Nijhoff 1995) 34.

the mission of the Order of Malta to the EU in Brussels does not have an accreditation to the host state Belgium and many other member states.

### 4.2.1.2 Terminating Diplomatic Relations

The EAs do not, as a standard, include a termination or amendment clause. A provision of the first type appears only in the agreements concluded in 2004 with New Zealand and Tajikistan and in the 2011 EA concluded with Uzbekistan. Article 7 of the New Zealand EA reads that this 'agreement may be terminated by either Contracting Party on giving 12 months' notice in writing to the other Contracting Party'. In the Tajik EA, a clause is added to Article 6 that reads that the 'terms of validity of the present Agreement shall expire one year after a written notification of either Party expressing its willingness to terminate it'. Article 10(2) of the Uzbek EA spells out that the Agreement 'is concluded for an indefinite period and shall be terminated after six months following the notification by either of the Parties through diplomatic channels about the intention to terminate the Agreement'.

The absence of a termination clause in the vast majority of EAs can be explained by the intention of the signatory parties to commit to establishing norms of conduct relating to a wider sphere of relations for a long, even indefinite, period of time. The lack of a termination clause, moreover, does not entail that diplomatic relations between the EU and a third state cannot be terminated or suspended, for example, in times of war or as a side effect of a general souring of relations. Under international law, the termination of diplomatic relations, the closing of a permanent mission, and the termination of the agreement on which these are based are different legal acts. As a result, the breaking off of diplomatic relations between two states does not have as a consequence that the VCDR is terminated. Quite to the contrary, Article 45 VCDR spells out a receiving state's obligations in case a mission is permanently or temporarily recalled.[56] In a similar vein, the EU can suspend or terminate diplomatic relations or temporarily close a delegation without this affecting the status of the EA. A termination of the EA in cases where the EU temporarily closes its mission for safety reasons (cf practices in Syria or Afghanistan at the time of writing) would be uncalled for and would go against the general principles of diplomacy. The same goes for the closing of a Union Delegation for managerial reasons. When in 2018 the EEAS closed the EUDEL in the Solomon Islands and added it to the jurisdiction of the EUDEL in Fiji, it did so without recalling the EA with the former country.

Although there has not been a case yet involving the EU, in extraordinary cases, a breach of diplomatic relations can occur. For these extraordinary occasions, EUDELs have contingency plans for an evacuation, usually involving a member state's embassy. If the EA or other arrangements are not terminated, the receiving state has an obligation to continue to respect and protect the EUDELs' premises, property, and archives (Art 45(*a*) and staff enjoying privileges and immunities (Art 39(2) VCDR). Where diplomatic relations are broken off by the EU, it would also be expected that it would ask a member state, under Article 45 VCDR, to protect its interests. It is doubtful whether the VCDR obligations would continue to apply if a third state were to cancel the legal basis on which they were founded. Whether diplomatic law would apply as customary international law applies is a question addressed in section 4.5 of this chapter.

[56] See J Craig Barker, 'The Function of Diplomatic Missions in Times of Armed Conflict or Foreign Armed Intervention' (2012) 81 Nord J Int Law 387.

## 4.2.2 The Accreditation and the End of Functions

### 4.2.2.1 Diplomatic Law

International diplomatic law and practice govern the accreditation of diplomatic agents, which is a rather complex process.[57] When the sending state appoints a new ambassador, it will informally (through the MFA or the envoy who will be replaced) announce their name to the MFA. If there are no objects on the part of the host state, a formal application for *agrément*, or consent, is made by the MFA. The VCDR does not prescribe a form or method to be used for the agrément.[58] The newly appointed ambassador will be announced in a 'letter of credence' signed by its head of state and addressed to the head of the receiving state.[59] A copy of this letter is sent to the foreign minister and sometimes other ministers of the government too for information purposes. Other members of a mission are simply notified, which does not require prior agrément of the receiving state (Art 7 VCDR); a notification by note verbale suffices. However, the MFA of the receiving state does need to be notified of the details of the appointment of the other members' arrival (Art 10 VCDR). The VCDR does not compel a receiving state to give reasons for a decision not to grant the necessary authorization to a foreign diplomat (Art 4(2) VCDR).

It is the sending state who decides on the exact diplomatic rank an agent will take; the receiving state can only raise an eyebrow if it thinks there is abuse or, in more extreme circumstances, not accept a diplomat or declare the official persona non grata. The receiving state may, however, require the names of military, naval, or air attachés to be submitted in advance for approval (Art 7 VCDR); require that the size of the mission be kept within limits it considers reasonable (Art 11 VCDR); or refuse to accept officials of a particular category, within similar bounds and on a non-discriminatory basis (Art 11 VCDR).

The head of a diplomatic mission is considered as having taken up their functions in the receiving state either following the presentation of their credentials or following a notification of their arrival and the presentation of a true (certified) copy of the credentials to the MFA of the receiving state (Art 13(1) VCDR). The credentials ceremony is a formal act of inauguration in the hands of the receiving state's protocol service, the details of which vary from one country to another. The EEAS asks all its HoDs, following the presentation of their credentials to the head of state, to send an account of the presentation ceremony to the High Representative, with copies addressed to the offices of the Presidents of the European Council and the Commission and relevant EEAS departments. Until the presentation of the credentials, the head of mission (HoM) will be addressed formally as ambassador-designate. The order of presentation of credentials or of a true copy thereof will be determined by the date and time of the arrival of the new HoM. Article 16 establishes that heads of mission are to take precedence in their respective classes in the order of the date and time of taking up their functions in accordance with Article 13. When the functions of a person enjoying privileges and immunities come to an end, such privileges and immunities cease at the moment when they leave the country or on expiry of a reasonable period in which to do so—even in case of armed conflict (Art 39(2) VCDR).

[57] Malcolm N Shaw, *International Law* (CUP 2014) 547.
[58] Denza, *Diplomatic Law* (n 15) 40.
[59] Sen (n 50) 50; Crawford, *Brownlie's Principles* (n 27) 400.

#### 4.2.2.2 EUDELs in Third States

Following the appointment of a new HoD, the chargé d'affaires ad interim (ai) informs the receiving state's MFA of the imminent arrival by note verbale. The HoD starts enjoying privileges and immunities from the moment they enter the territory of the receiving state or, if already in, from the moment when the appointment has been notified to the local authorities (Art 39 VCDR). Between the time of arrival and the ceremony of presentation of the credentials the appointed HoD is in a delicate legal position (*in spe legationis*), which calls for a degree of discretion. During this period, diplomatic custom prescribes that the HoD is formally barred from participating in official events. A visit to the doyen of the corps diplomatique can be made but other authorities can only be visited when accompanied by the chargé d'affaires ai. In the relations with locally represented member states (so, internally) these rules of diplomatic custom are not adhered to: it is common for the HoD-designate to visit colleagues from member states, take part in EU working groups, reply to member states' formal invitations, and participate in working visits by officials from the EEAS Headquarters. During this period, the HoD is in charge of managing the EUDEL and has taken up duties as far as the EEAS is concerned.[60] The chargé d'affaires ai, however, continues to represent the EUDEL towards the outside world. The formal visits to external partners should start with the local minister for foreign affairs and/or the protocol service, followed by visits to fellow ambassadors, if possible starting with the Dean.

The EU developed a practice in which it duplicates state-to-state procedures for accrediting HoDs and other members of the staff. For internal purposes, the Union has laid down the EU administrative grades that it considers to correspond with diplomatic titles. The EEAS notifies the sending state of the rank of a new member of the staff.[61] Accreditation procedures and letters have been used by the Commission since the 1970s.[62] The post-Lisbon practice has been one where the letters of credence are co-signed by the President of the European Council and the President of the Commission—not by the High Representative.[63] This is remarkable, bearing in mind the general mission of the HR as stated in Article 18 TEU, but coincides with international practice. The fact that both EU presidents are considered the equivalent of a head of state when signing letters of credence is a legacy of the Commission delegations: before the Lisbon Treaty came into force, letters of credence for heads of Commission delegations were signed by the Commission only. The Union's protocol service seems to consider prestige important in this matter: the letters of credence are presented to a head of state in a blue leather folder with the new HoD's credentials displayed on the right hand side and the predecessor's letters of recall on the left. A third country is requested in the letter of credence to give credit to everything that the HoD may say in the name of the EU, as is common in state practice too.[64]

At any time, even before an arrival, the receiving state may declare the head or a member of the diplomatic staff of the mission persona non grata or notify it that any other member of the staff of the mission is not acceptable (Art 9 VCDR). Examples of EU diplomats being declared persona non grata in third countries are few but seemingly more common over

[60] EEAS, 'Business Process Policy: Diplomacy and Protocol' (2013, on file with author).

[61] See Appendix 8 for an equivalency table.

[62] Véronique Dimier, *The Invention of a European Development Aid Bureaucracy: Recycling Empire* (Palgrave Macmillan 2014) 496; Jan Wouters and others, *The Law of EU External Relations: Cases, Materials, and Commentary on the EU as an International Legal Actor* (3rd ed OUP 2021) 40.

[63] See Appendix 6 for the EU's model letter of credence, also reproduced in Wouters and others, *The Law of EU External Relations* (n 62) 44.

[64] Roberts, *Satow* (n 28) 62.

the past couple of years. In December 2018, the Democratic Republic of the Congo (DRC) ordered the EU ambassador to leave the country 'within 48 hours' after he had expressed doubts about the organization of the Congolese general elections. In December 2019, Benin expelled the EU HoD following accusations of unwarranted interference in domestic political affairs. In February 2021, the EU HoD was declared persona non grata by Venezuela in response to EU sanctions imposed against Venezuelan officials. The decision was announced to the EU ambassador in a meeting with the Venezuelan minister of foreign affairs, which also included diplomatic representatives from member states France, Spain, the Netherlands, and Germany. The HoD was given seventy-two hours to leave the country. The minister did not accede to the Venezuelan National Assembly's request to revise the EU's presence in Venezuela altogether, which allowed the EUDEL to continue its operations even with the HoD gone. In the last two cases, the Union followed suit by declaring the ambassadors of Benin and Venezuela persona non grata in a diplomatic tit-for-tat move.[65] While it was not legally obliged to do so, the Union decided to state its reasons in two statements claiming that the declaration was a response to the decision by the local government to declare the head of the EU delegation persona non grata: 'the EU considers this declaration as wholly unwarranted and contrary to the EU's objective of developing relations and building partnerships in third countries'. Because of her accreditation in Belgium and Luxembourg, the Venezuelan ambassador, however, continued to be posted in Brussels after having lost her accreditation to the EU. This in itself shows a difference between EU and state practices and is an example of how the absence territorial sovereignty can play out in a diplomatic context.

The EU also has the possibility of recalling its ambassadors or staff before the end of their function—a decision taken by the HR as an exercise of its general management functions—for either political or internal managerial reasons. An example of the first would be the decision in November 2018 to recall the EU HoD to Tanzania, citing 'the deterioration of the human rights and rule of law situation' in the East African country following state-led violence against lesbian, gay, bisexual, transgender, and queer (LGBTQ+) Tanzanians. An example of the second happened in December 2019, when the EU HoD unexpectedly left Malawi and the HR insisted that this was a purely internal management decision, although there the country also faced political unrests. Under EU law, the HoD can file an appeal against such recall decision. In the 2020 *EEAS v Hebberecht* case, the Court sided with a staff member contending that the EEAS's refusal of a request for an extension of her posting as HoD in Ethiopia was contrary to the interests and continuity of the service, transparency, equal treatment, and compliance with positive discrimination measures in favour of women.[66] The discretion of the HR to takes such management decisions is thus not unbridled and subject to judicial review.

#### 4.2.2.3 EUDELs at IOs

Many IOs have installed a ceremony in which the head of a permanent mission is received by the chief of protocol, a director, or the head of the international secretariat when taking up their functions. Typically, such a ceremony is modelled after the formalities used in bilateral diplomacy. Because IOs formally do not exercise the right to agrément, legally speaking the accreditation practices and accompanying customs are purely ceremonial in nature and do not bring about additional rights and obligations for the accrediting IO (such as the right to

[65] Statements by the Council, 'Benin: head of mission to the EU declared persona non grata', 19 December 2019 and 'Venezuela: head of mission to the EU declared persona non grata', 25 February 2021.

[66] *EEAS v Hebberecht* [2020] ECLI:EU:C:2020:946.

control and reject an HoM) unless sovereign nations have conceded such right to the IO.[67] Importantly, the host state also does not have the right of agrément, which implies prior approval and national control. Consequently, in theory it can neither object to the appointment of an HoM to an IO nor declare that person persona non grata. All a host state can do is to informally request a removal, without there being an obligation to remove (on the part of the IO) or to recall (on the part of the sending state/the Union). Sometimes, a provision in an agreement on privileges and immunities says otherwise. Section 25 of the Convention on the Privileges and Immunities of the Specialized Agencies (CPIUN–SA), states with regard to ad hoc representatives that they can:

> [ ... ] not be required by the territorial authorities to leave the country in which they are performing their functions on account of any activities by them in their official capacity. In the case, however, of abuse of privileges of residence committed by any such person in activities in that country outside his official functions, he may be required to leave by the Government of that country [ ... ]

provided that the diplomatic procedure applicable for the removal of diplomatic envoys accredited to that country is followed. Given that the Convention on the Privileges and Immunities of the UN (CPIUN) grants those ad hoc representatives immunity only with regard to functions performed, it can be argued that the same rule applies to the United Nations (UN) itself.[68]

This subsection discusses how the accreditation takes place for the EUDELs at IOs. To be permanently represented at IOs based in other cities around the world, as well as to take part in special conferences and meetings organized by IOs, the EUDEL will have to seek an accreditation. For example, the International Labour Organization (ILO) uses an online accreditation system for the ILO Conferences to which credentials issued by and bearing the signature of an authority with power to bind the state can be uploaded.[69]

At the UN Headquarters in *New York City*, the Union (for the HoD) and the HoD (for all other diplomatic members of the mission) have to formally request the UN Secretary General (UNSG) and the UN chief of protocol for an accreditation.[70] UNGA Resolution 257 (III) sets out a process that is not completely unlike an agrément procedure (although formally, it is not necessary to secure agrément) for permanent representatives of the member states.[71] Different than the ambassadors of permanent representations of UN member states, who present their credentials upon first arrival to the UNSG during a ceremony (or in its absence, the Chef de Cabinet), the Union merely announces the arrival of a new HoD in a signed letter of notification. The UNSG will not formally receive the HoD for the purpose of a presentation of credentials, as is the case for the permanent representatives of member

67 Leo Gross, 'Immunities and Privileges of Delegations to the United Nations' (1962) 16 Int Organ 483, 491.

68 Convention on the Privileges and Immunities of the Specialized Agencies, done at New York on 21 November 1947, entered into force 2 December 1948, 33 UNTS 261; Convention on the Privileges and Immunities of the UN, done at New York on 13 February 1946, entered into force 17 September 1946, 1 UNTS 15; Yu-Long Ling, 'A Comparative Study of the Privileges and Immunities of United Nations Member Representatives and Officials with the Traditional Privileges and Immunities of Diplomatic Agents' (1976) 33 Wash & Lee L Rev 127, 125.

69 International Labour Organization (ILO), 'Submission of Credentials', <www.ilo.org/ilc/Credentials/lang--en/index.htm> accessed 4 May 2022.

70 See, generally, Dan Ciobanu, 'Credentials of Delegations and Representation of Member States at the United Nations' (1976) 25 ICLQ 351.

71 UNGA Resolution 257 A (III) of 3 December 1948 regarding permanent missions of Member States to the United Nations, para 1; Memorandum to the Chef de Cabinet, Executive Office of the Secretary General, reprinted in [1986] UNJY 272.

states, but an informal meeting will take place.[72] The HoD is granted protocol assistance by analogy to other permanent missions: the UN's chief of protocol forwards the notification letter to the permanent mission of the United States to the UN's office of host country affairs.[73] After a reply is given by the US State Department, the EUDEL is informed by way of a standard letter, giving details of the privileges, immunities, and the various tax exemptions granted.[74] All diplomatic staff and their family members (in the sense of the Art 37(1) VCDR) receive a (blue) diplomatic identity card and a special driver's licence. The identity card has some interesting language on it to point out to local authorities that its holder enjoys 'immunity from criminal jurisdiction'. Furthermore, they 'shall not be liable to any form of arrest or detention, but may be given a notice of violation'. It also contains instructions for US police officers and a telephone number they can call at State Department when they have inquiries on how they should treat the holder. The EUDEL is listed in the UN Blue Book in New York (as well as in those in Geneva and Vienna). These blue books are used for internal reasons of protocol but are formally not a diplomatic list.

The UN's Legal Office holds the view that an accreditation to the UNSG in New York does not extend to the UN Offices in *Geneva* and *Vienna*.[75] In the UN office in Geneva, it is customary for the EU HoD to present credentials during an informal ceremony to the Director General of the UN Geneva Office (UNOG), to whom the UNSG has permanently delegated the competence to receive new heads of mission: '[w]henever the Secretary-General receives credentials accrediting a permanent representative at Geneva, Protocol takes note and transmits to Geneva'.[76] At the World Trade Organization (WTO), the EUDEL enjoys a fully fledged diplomatic status in terms of protocol and accreditation practices corresponding to its membership.[77] The credentials of the EU ambassador are addressed to the WTO's Director General, according to the standard internal procedure. It is customary for a new permanent representative to inform other permanent representatives to the WTO that credentials were presented to the WTO's DG. The Swiss Mission to the WTO has competence for issues regarding Switzerland's policies towards the WTO.

As far as the UN Viennese Office (UNOV) is concerned, corresponding to Genevan practices, the UNSG has delegated the competence to accept the accreditation of permanent representatives to the Director General for UNOV. The HoD's credentials are therefore addressed to the UNSG but accepted on their behalf by their direct representative in Vienna.[78] In accordance with their respective rules of procedure, the HoD is invited to an official visit by the executing Directors of the International Atomic Energy Agency (IAEA), the Preparatory Commission for the Comprehensive Nuclear Test Ban Treaty Organisation (CTBTO), Wassenaar Arrangement, Nuclear Suppliers Group (NSG), and the Organization

[72] Seung Hwan Choi, 'The Status, Rights, and Duties of Observers for Non-Member States of the United Nations' (1991) 19 Korean J Comp L 135, 143; Eric Suy, 'The Status of Observers in International Organizations' (1978) 160 Recueil des Cours de l'Academie de Droit International 75, 155–56.

[73] Chief of Protocol, Note verbale PRO/NV/Requests for Privileges and Immunities, 12 November 2012.

[74] Study by the UN Secretariat, 'The Practice of the UN, the Specialized Agencies and the International Atomic Energy concerning their Status, Privileges and Immunities' [1976] UN Doc A/CN4/L118, II YBILC, para 53.

[75] Memorandum to the Chief of Protocol, 23 October 1979, reprinted in UNJY [1979] 168–69.

[76] Marcel André Boisard, Evgeny M Chossudovsky, and Jacques Lemoine (eds), 'Guide de la Pratique Diplomatique à Genève' in Chef de protocole, UNOG (ed) *La Diplomatie Multilatérale* (Martinus Nijhoff 1998) 419.

[77] Swiss Confederation, 'Practical Manual of the Regime of Privileges and Immunities and Other Facilities', <www.eda.admin.ch/missions/mission-onu-geneve/en/home/manual-regime-privileges-and-immunities/introduction/manual-opening-mission/mission-wto.html> accessed 4 May 2022.

[78] UN Protocol and Liaison Office, 'Manual of Protocol', <www.un.int/protocol/pm/manual-protocol> accessed 4 May 2022.

for Petroleum Exporting Countries (OPEC) at the start of its mandate but will not be invited to submit formal credentials.

The practices applicable to the multilateral delegation in *Addis Ababa* have their own particularities. The HoD is accredited to the African Union (AU) but takes part in the ordinary order of precedence of ambassadors, alongside all (bilateral) diplomatic missions present in the city.[79] The consequence is that the EU appears on the same list twice: once for its bilateral delegation to Ethiopia and once for the delegation to the AU. This practice is not reciprocated to the mission the AU maintains in Brussels. In *Jakarta*, the HoD of the multilateral mission is included in the list of ambassadors representing non-Association of Southeast Asian Nations (ASEAN) member states and relevant intergovernmental organizations.

When appointing a new HoD in *Rome*, the EEAS transmits their name and diplomatic rank to the Food and Agriculture Organization (FAO) beforehand. Once arrived, the EU representative provides an official copy of its credentials to the FAO's Director General. For the other members of the mission, it suffices that their names and rank are notified in an official letter of the HoD addressed to the Director General.[80] The HoD in Rome also presents credentials to the Pope (Holy See) and to the Grand Master of the Order of Malta. From the early days onwards, the idea was for FAO members to select, wherever possible, their resident representatives to the organization from the diplomatic staff of their missions accredited to the Italian Government or, alternatively, to include them in the bilateral mission afterwards.[81] Since the Union does not maintain a bilateral diplomatic mission to Italy, an additional set of rules concerning non-bilateral diplomats applies. The FAO Director-General, after having received the information on the name and rank of the HR's nominee, formally has to seek advice from the Italian Government.[82] FAO Resolution 54/53 prescribes that the host government can voice an opinion or make a recommendation if it so wishes. However, in light of EU law, any Italian opposition to an EU nomination could be seen as a violation of the duty of sincere cooperation (Art 4(3) TEU).

In *Paris*, the HoD presents their credentials to the Chairpersons of the OECD and UNESCO. The practice of the OECD's protocol service, which functions as an interlocutor, has been to request the Ministère des Affaires étrangères to accord the EUDEL diplomatic status as well as the formalities that go with it. The HoD is mentioned on the diplomatic lists either right after the member states (OECD) or, in a position less favourable to the EU, with the other IOs (UNESCO). In *Strasbourg*, the HoD presents a letter of credence to the Secretary General of the Council of Europe (CoE). When other diplomatic staff are added to the EUDEL, a note verbale mentioning their function and rank is sent to the CoE's protocol office. The Union has a sui generis status on the CoE's diplomatic list—it is neither mentioned with CoE member states nor with the observers.

### 4.2.2.4 The Corps Diplomatique Accredited to the Union

#### *4.2.2.4.1 Missions of member states*

The missions of member states are not part of the EU's passive right of legation and are a mere application of international institutional law. The establishment of a mission by a member

[79] Federal Democratic Republic of Ethiopia, Ministry of Foreign Affairs, Diplomatic List prepared by the Protocol Directorate, February 2012, Addis Ababa.

[80] FAO, 'Procédure pour l'accréditation des représentants permanents auprès de la FAO ainsi que des membres de leur mission' [1992] paras 1–3.

[81] See recital 4 of FAO Resolution 54/53 on Resident Representatives, adopted at the seventh session of the Conference in Rome, 11 December 1953.

[82] ibid, Recital 5.

state to an IO and the appointment of an HoM are unilateral acts. An example would be the Belgian Royal Decree of 4 June 1959 creating the country's permanent representation to the Communities.[83] An agrément therefore does not have to be obtained: a permanent representative is included ex officio in Coreper, without a formal procedure needing to be followed.[84] In a note verbale, member states merely inform the Presidents of the Commission and the European Council of the appointment of new ambassadors. It is, however, customary for a member state's newly arrived ambassador to make a courtesy visit to both presidents as well as to the other permanent representatives when taking up functions.[85]

*4.2.2.4.2 Missions of third states, IOs, and other non-state entities*

The diplomatic corps accredited to the EU consists of missions of third states, IOs, and other non-state entities. These have to abide by the Union's accreditation rules and practices. After having obtained the Union's agreement to establish a mission, a sending entity needs to obtain the agreement on the person proposed to head the mission.[86] The EU has its own accreditation procedures for non-member states.[87] A request for agrément has to be submitted to the Union by the ministry of foreign affairs of the sending state. The request is sent by note verbale directed to the Union's protocol service and accompanied by the curriculum vitae of the head of the mission. The final decision implies the approval from the Commission, the Council, and the EEAS.[88] The member states weigh in via their representation in the Council. The approval can take up to eight weeks. Once agrément is given, the Union's protocol service notifies, by note verbale, the mission or the sending state's MFA. The Belgian protocol directorate will subsequently be asked by the Commission to provide them with a diplomatic identity card on the basis of documents submitted by the mission. Until recently, the Belgian Government has never on record objected to the accreditation of a foreign diplomat to the EU. The topic was subject to a parliamentary question as early as 1964, when Belgium confirmed the EEC's accreditation of the ambassador of Taiwan. The Belgian minister of foreign affairs at the time replied that he did see any reason to object to the accreditation since Belgium entertained diplomatic relations with the Republic of China itself.[89]

After the arrival of the HoM in Belgium but before the presentation of credentials, the appointed HoM visits the Commission's head of protocol. The appointee will offer a facsimile of their letter of credence and the letter of recall of their predecessor.[90] They may also pay a visit to the Doyen of the diplomatic corps; other contacts with diplomats in Brussels are considered of an informal nature until the ambassador has presented their credentials.

The letters of credence of the newly appointed HoM of a third country are signed by its head of state. Two identical originals of the letters must be drawn up, one addressed to the President of the European Council, the other to the President of the European Commission.

[83] Belgian State Gazette, 18 June 1959, 4563.

[84] Jaap W de Zwaan, *The Permanent Representatives Committee: Its Role in European Union Decision-Making* (Elsevier 1995) 16.

[85] Arnaud Tournier, 'Le Droit de Légation Passive de l'Union Européenne' in Myriam Benlolo-Carabot, Ulas Candas, and Eglantine Cujo (eds), *L'Union Européenne et Droit International* (Pedone 2013) 238, 242.

[86] Frid (n 55) 34.

[87] Salmon, *Droit Diplomatique* (n 5) 723; Carl A Ehrhardt, 'Das Diplomatische Korps bei Der EWG in Brüssel' (1962) 13 Aussenpolitik 659.

[88] Frédéric Dopagne, Sanderijn Duquet, and Bertold Theeuwes, *Diplomatiek Recht toegepast in België* (Maklu 2014) 39. For a description of the procedure, see Charles Reichling, *Le Droit de Légation des Communautés Européennes* (UGA Éditions 1964) 55.

[89] Answer to parliamentary question [BE] of MP Glinne, 17 March 1964 [1963–64] Bull QR, n 16.

[90] EEAS, 'Vade Mecum for the Use of the Diplomatic Corps', <https://www.eeas.europa.eu/eeas/diplomatic-corps_en>.

Between 1959 and 1960, the Official Journal published a short report on the ceremony. The first one was published in October 1959 and read:

> M Walter Hallstein, président de la Commission de la Communauté Économique Européenne, a reçu le lundi 19 octobre 1959 Son Excellence M l'ambassadeur Eiji Wajima qui lui a remis les lettres l'accréditant en qualité de chef de la mission du Japon auprès de la Communauté Économique Européenne.[91]

Nowadays, it is common for both the sending state and the Council's General Secretariat to publish a press statement on the event.[92]

Until 1966, credentials were presented solely to the Commission president. As a result of an internal discussion, the letters have since been presented to the Commission and Council president in a joint meeting. The 1966 Luxembourg Compromise states in this regard: '[t]he credentials of Heads of Missions of non-member states accredited to the Community will be submitted jointly to the President of the Council and to the President of the Commission, meeting together for this purpose'.[93] In a first period following Lisbon, the appointed HoM was still received in an official audience by the President of the European Council and the President of the Commission in order to present their credentials and the letters of recall of their predecessor. These visits were organized both 'simultaneously and separately'. In the official guidelines, it is clarified that no speeches are made during the official visit, that ambassadors are expected to wear either a dark suit or national costume, and that a photo report is made.[94] Commission President Jean-Claude Juncker at a certain point renounced his right to receive the ambassadors; the practice was reinstalled by Commission President von der Leyen.

In accordance with Article 13(1) VCDR, the new ambassador is considered as having taken up their functions at the date and time of the presentation of their credentials. Duties of the other diplomatic staff start on the date that the mission's note verbale is sent to the Union's protocol service announcing that the person concerned is commencing their duties or at a later date if indicated in the said note verbale. When two visits are organized on separate dates, the second date of submitting credentials is the decisive date for the official commencement of functions.

A declaration persona non grata (Art 9 VCDR) is taken at the initiative of the HR and approved by the Council. Much like what happens during the agrément procedure, the members states (and, importantly, host state Belgium) have an opportunity to voice their opinion, as was show in the example of the Venezuelan ambassador being declared persona non grata in February 2021 (discussed above). Following a declaration of persona non grata by the EU, the third state's ambassador will lose its accreditation to the Union. This decision in itself does not imply an automatic expulsion from the Belgian territory, which remains in the hands of the Belgian authorities. When the diplomat is also a member of a bilateral mission to Belgium, it may occur that an ambassador declared persona non grata is not expulsed and

[91] Commission, 'Informations' [1959] OJ 1127/59: 'Mr Walter Hallstein, President of the Commission of the European Economic Community, received on Monday 19 October 1959 His Excellency Ambassador Eiji Wajima who presented him with the letters accrediting him as Head of the Japanese Mission to the European Economic Community' [own translation].

[92] See, eg General Secretariat of the Council, 'Presentation of letters of credentials to the President of the European Council Herman Van Rompuy', press release EUCO 242/14, Brussels, 4 November 2014.

[93] Final Communiqué of the extraordinary session of the Council [1966] Bull EC 3.

[94] EAAS, 'Vade-Mecum for the Use of the Diplomatic Corps' (n 90) para III.

can continue to represent the sending state in bilateral affairs in Belgium and, in the event of accreditation, at the North Atlantic Treaty Organization (NATO) and/or other member states as a non-resident ambassador.

#### *4.2.2.4.3 Multiple accreditations*

All three types of missions (those of member states, third states, and IOs/other entities) may be simultaneously accredited to Belgium and/or other IOs with headquarters in Belgium (Art 5(3) VCDR). Based on research conducted in 2017 of the third states' missions to the EU, 151 had an additional accreditation to the Kingdom of Belgium, 94 had an accreditation to Luxembourg, and 57 had an accreditation to the Netherlands. Quite a few ambassadors are simultaneously accredited to NATO; the ambassadors of Bhutan and Benin were even accredited to the IOs in Geneva.[95] The EU accepts the representation of a state by an ambassador having their residence in the sending state, a member state, or a third state but making regular visits to Brussels. In 2017, the diplomatic representative of the DPRK was based in London; the former ambassador was based in Berlin. An ambassador simultaneously accredited to the Kingdom of Belgium and to the EU gives priority to the king of the Belgians in presenting their credentials.[96]

## 4.2.3 The Exercise of Diplomatic Functions

### 4.2.3.1 The Job Description of an EU Diplomat

At the time of the establishment of the EEAS, no substantial discussion took place on the functions that EUDELs ought to perform. David Spence even argues: '[s]ignificantly, there was no intensive discussion about what a diplomat was, though everyone was keen to point out that diplomacy was changing'.[97] Accordingly, to characterize EU diplomats' tasks abroad, one has to revert to general legal conceptions. The job description of diplomats in the Union's primary law is minimal. Article 221(1) TFEU merely states that 'Union delegations in third countries and at international organizations shall represent the Union'.[98] A closer look at the diplomatic practice, therefore, is not just enlightening, but required. At first sight, EUDELs' activities do not differ substantially from those of national diplomatic representations. In a host state, the Union's and EU citizens' interests are represented and protected. Union diplomats promote friendly relations between the EU and the local government, and they interact with representatives of third states as well as with those of EU member states.[99]

These observations only tell part of the story. While EUDELs are keen to take the diplomatic helm, they are also legally limited in their functions. It is necessary to examine where legal constraints lie in order to identify the activities that EUDELs are meant to do or should refrain from doing. However, a looming risk of diplomatic overreach is inherent in the EU's attempts to don the cloak of an international actor.

95 See the EEAS' Protocol Service's website, <https://www.eeas.europa.eu/eeas/diplomatic-list-missions-accredited-european-union_en> accessed 2 June 2022.

96 Dopagne, Duquet, and Theeuwes (n 88) 40–41.

97 David Spence, 'The EEAS and Its Epistemic Communities: The Challenges of Diplomatic Hybridism' in Spence and Bátora (n 38) 50.

98 Consolidated Version of the Treaty on the Functioning of the European Union [2012] OJ C326/47 (hereafter TFEU).

99 Paul Craig and Gráinne de Búrca, *EU Law: Text, Cases, and Materials* (6th edn, OUP 2015) 321; Koen Lenaerts and Piet Van Nuffel, *European Union Law* (Robert Bray and Nathan Cambien eds, Sweet & Maxwell 2011) 955.

#### 4.2.3.2 International and EU Legal Constraints

Both PIL and EU law impose limitations on the conduct of diplomacy by European actors. Exactly like states, the Union is subject to the Convention's definition of diplomatic functions in its Article 3 and to the provisions spelling out how these functions should be observed. The most articulate sections on the general obligations of diplomats and diplomatic missions are Articles 41 and 42 VCDR for these include, among other elements, the principle of non-interference, an obligation to respect local laws and to conduct official business with or through the receiving state's ministry of foreign affairs, and the prohibition of diplomats engaging in commercial activities.

As will be further explained in this handbook's Chapter 5, diplomatic representation does not affect the distribution of competences, to be derived from the EU Treaties with their limits governed by the principle of conferral, nor can it be invoked to claim new powers.[100] Consequently, the EUDELs' exercise of diplomatic functions hinges on the particularities of the division of competences between the Union and the member states. The selection of EU diplomacy's priority areas—backed by the necessary accompanying legal basis in EU law—clearly reflects this. When exercising diplomatic functions, there is a thematic predominance with regard to matters in which the EU enjoys broad competences.[101] Moreover, the EUDELs must respect the principles of subsidiarity and proportionality (Art 5 TEU) and abide by the obligation of consistency (Art 21(3) TEU). Beyond constitutional hurdles, the EU's Staff Regulations also specify how functions are to be performed: those working in delegations must carry out duties solely with the Union's interests in mind.[102] They cannot seek nor take instructions from governments of member or third states (Art 11), nor accept any favour or gift without the consent of the EEAS Headquarters while exercising a diplomatic assignment.[103]

Finally, and stemming from the interplay between EU and international law, the Union must embrace its member states as sovereign diplomatic actors with broad powers in their own right.[104] This entails, on the one hand, a mutual (positive) duty of cooperation,[105] and, on the other hand, a (negative) duty for the EU to respect the diplomatic prerogatives held by the member states and protected both by international and EU law.[106] The legal obligations showing deference to the national performance of diplomatic functions, to distinct national diplomatic methods, and to long-established partnerships are not entirely clear.

The sum of these factors dictates that constraints originating from the EU's relationship with its member states are more tangible than those imposed by international diplomatic law that apply equally to the Union and states. The following sections discuss how this legal framework is reflected *in concreto* in the day-to-day actions of EUDELs. The analysis is

[100] Marise Cremona, 'EU External Relations: Unity and Conferral of Powers' in Loïc Azouli (ed), *The Question of Competence in the European Union* (OUP 2014) 66.

[101] See, for a discussion, Chapter 5.

[102] Regulation No 31 (EEC), 11 (EAEC), laying down the Staff Regulations of Officials and the Conditions of Employment of Other Servants of the European Economic Community and the European Atomic Energy Community, as amended (hereafter 'EU Staff Regulations').

[103] Decision of the High Representative establishing the rules applicable to national experts seconded to the European External Action Service [2012] OJ C12/8.

[104] Ramses A Wessel, 'Can the European Union Replace Its Member States in International Affairs? An International Law Perspective' in Inge Govaere and others (eds), *The European Union in the World: Essays in Honour of Marc Maresceau* (Martinus Nijhoff 2013).

[105] Article 35 TEU; Art 221(2) TFEU.

[106] Article 4(2) TEU on the 'essential state functions' of the EU member states, as well as Declarations 13 and 14 attached to the Treaties.

undertaken in two steps: first, the performance of traditional diplomatic tasks is evaluated and, second, the execution of those functions that are specific to the EU is examined.

### 4.2.3.3 Diplomatic Tasks

The functions of diplomatic missions, as formalistically defined in legal instruments, must be distinguished from the broader purpose of diplomacy, which includes all 'conduct of business between states by peaceful means'.[107] According to Article 3(1) VCDR, the functions of a diplomatic mission consist, inter alia, of the representation, protection of interests, negotiation, observation, and promotion of friendly relations. The non-exhaustiveness of Article 3's list ('inter alia') and the absence of many details on how functions are to be performed allow for a certain degree of flexibility in its interpretation. While diplomats' basic functions may have changed (surprisingly) little since 1961, the room for manoeuvre left by the Convention has been effectively used by states and the Union alike to keep up with challenges posed by a changing global context.[108]

#### *4.2.3.3.1 Representation*

The representational function (Art 3(1)(*a*) VCDR) lies at the foundation of the institution of diplomacy, but it proves difficult to delineate the concept. According to the ILC, the representational task 'characterizes the whole activity of the mission'.[109] Three other diplomatic functions (protection, negotiation, and observation) are considered to be integral parts of it, although these functions also feature as independent functions in Article 3 VCDR.[110] Representation *per se* is of particular importance to EU diplomacy—it is both a goal and a function thereof.[111] Moreover, representation is the only diplomatic function explicitly mentioned in the EU Treaties: it is featured in Article 221(1) TFEU and elaborated upon in Article 5(8) EEAS Decision. According to Paul Sharp, representation in a traditional understanding involves at least three actors: 'the sovereign'; the 'ambassador as a person'; and the 'ambassador in his representative capacity as the sovereign'.[112]

In the case of the EU, discerning an identity equivalent to a 'sovereign' is complex. The Union is a much more fragmented diplomatic actor than the model described above. The EUDELs operate as a single interlocutor with multiple instructing principals.[113] Placed under the overall authority of the HR, delegations receive instructions from either the Commission (for non-Common Foreign and Security Policy (CFSP) matters) or the HR (for CFSP matters). In both domains, EUDELs perform representational tasks, but the concrete implementation depends on the directions received from the EEAS or the relevant Commission Directorate General (DG), which come with a specific modus operandi and a different chain of loyalty.[114] To complicate matters even further, EUDELs may also be given the mandate to speak on behalf of member states where there is such an agreement. The

[107] Denza, *Diplomatic Law* (n 15) 30.

[108] Sasson Sofer, 'Old and New Diplomacy: A Debate Revisited' in Christer Jönsson and Richard Langhorne (eds), *Diplomacy*, vol 3 (2nd edn, Sage 2004) 395; Roberts, *Satow* (n 28) 77.

[109] ILC, 'Draft Articles on Diplomatic Intercourse' (n 29) 90.

[110] Roberts, *Satow* (n 28) 77; Denza, *Diplomatic Law* (n 15) 30.

[111] Berridge (n 47) 114.

[112] Paul Sharp, 'Who Needs Diplomats? The Problem of Diplomatic Representation' in Jönsson and Langhorne (n 108).

[113] Rosa Balfour and Kristi Raik, 'Equipping the European Union for the 21st Century' in *National Diplomacies, the European External Action Service and the Making of EU Foreign Policy* (The Finnish Institute of International Affairs 2013) 36, 43.

[114] David Spence, 'From the Convention to Lisbon: External Competence and the Uneasy Transition for Geneva Delegations' in Spence and Bátora (n 38) 228.

inherent risk to inconsistency is tackled in a number of internal working arrangements between the Commission and the EEAS in relation to external relations issues.[115]

Representation presents a source of authority for diplomats. The mission serves as a sending state's proverbial figurehead in a receiving state and, as such, operates as its legal and political representative. In accordance with general diplomatic practice, in which the ambassador embodies the representational task, the HoD acts as the direct envoy representing the EU.[116] The EU ambassador has the capacity to conclude contracts, is authorized to sign off on financial transactions, and is empowered to bring or defend legal proceedings on behalf of the Union.[117] Equally so, EUDELs ensure the EU's political representation in local meetings and at conferences. These political functions have expanded since the entry into force of the Lisbon Treaty,[118] although even before 2009 the Commission had set itself a target of allocating at least one political attaché per duty station.[119]

Representation furthermore comprises an outreach and communication function. The ILC recognized in 1958 that:

> [ ... ] the mission, and in particular the head of the mission, is the spokesman for its Government in communications with the receiving Government, or in any discussions with that Government to which relations between the two States may give rise.[120]

This is no different for an EUDEL, which will communicate official positions through the HoD directly or through common diplomatic means such as démarches and notes verbales.[121] EUDELs also act similarly to states when it comes to communication through symbolism: delegations fly the European flag on the premises of their missions, play the European anthem, and enter HoDs on the diplomatic list. As was previously the case for the Commission's DG for External Relations (RELEX), the EEAS established a Protocol Unit to advise delegations on formal diplomatic behaviour. Ultimately, the idea is that communication through visible assimilation with the diplomatic tradition contributes to the establishment of a higher profile for the EU, both in the diplomatic circuit and beyond.[122] Over time, contemporary interactions with media and the general public have surpassed the provisions of Article 3 VCDR. Embracing this development, most EUDELs fulfil public diplomacy and spokesperson functions and, more recently, use social media platforms as a source to disseminate the latest information on EU affairs.[123]

The EU's division of competences leaves its mark on the exercise of the representational function on the ground. Distinction is made between the representation of the EU itself and

[115] Commission and EEAS, Internal working arrangements on external relations issues (SEC(2012)48) 13 January 2012.

[116] Jean-Paul Pancracio, *Droit et Institutions Diplomatiques* (Pedone 2007) 166.

[117] Steven Blockmans and Christophe Hillion (eds), *EEAS 2.0: A Legal Commentary on Council Decision 2010/427/EU Establishing the Organisation and Functioning of the European External Action Service* (Swedish Institute for European Policy Studies 2013) 35.

[118] Federica Bicchi and Heidi Maurer, 'European Cooperation Abroad' (2017) 12 HJD 1; Rohit Ambast and Vinay Tyagi, 'Ambassadors of Europe: An Insight into the Evolution of the European Union and International Diplomatic Law' (2008) 61 Studia Diplomatica 173, 173.

[119] Cesare Onestini, 'A Hybrid Service: Organising Efficient EU Foreign Policy' in Spence and Bátora (n 38) 73.

[120] ILC, 'Draft Articles on Diplomatic Intercourse' (n 29) 90.

[121] For templates, see Wouters and others, *The Law of EU External Relations* (n 62).

[122] Barston (n 48) 2.

[123] See, eg Commission Communication on a 'European Agenda for Culture in a Globalizing World', Brussels 10 May 2007, COM(2007)242; see, for a discussion on the EUDELs' 'Internetpräsentation', Stephanie Frimmer, *Delegationen Der Europaischen Union* (Grin Verlag 2013) 71.

the representation of EU policies. While the delegation has carte blanche to inform foreign governments (including in legal proceedings) and citizens about what the EU is and does, its representational functions are more limited when it comes to presenting, explaining, and implementing concrete policies. Only in cases where the Union does not enjoy broad competences does EU law indirectly turn the delegation's representational role into a less active, observatory role.

*4.2.3.3.2 Protection*

Within the limits permitted by international law, diplomats can protect the interests of the sending state and of its nationals (Art 3(1)(*b*) VCDR). The VCDR's language matches that of the Union's external objectives. The first sentence of Article 3(5) TEU obliges the European Union to 'uphold and promote its values and interests and contribute to the protection of its citizens' in its relations with the wider world.

The resemblance is partly illusory, however. First, while the VCDR predominantly refers to political or trade interests, the EU's definition is more value-laden.[124] Article 3(5) TEU continues by imposing the duty upon the Union to contribute to 'peace, security, the sustainable development, solidarity and mutual respect among peoples, free and fair trade, eradication of poverty and the protection of human rights'. The realization of a number of these European interests via formal diplomatic means is potentially problematic.[125] Many states do not appreciate ambassadors taking sides in, or openly discussing, matters that they consider to be domestic politics.[126] Union diplomats displaying interest in a human rights case must anticipate accusations of interference or the violation of local laws (Art 41(1) VCDR). Practice shows that the EU is not immune from the Vienna Convention's constraints on what diplomats can say or do when posted abroad. A 2007 incident with the Commission delegation in Sudan ended with the expulsion of the HoD for what the local government regarded as 'unacceptable contacts with opposition leaders'.[127] That same year, the Zimbabwean Government summoned several ambassadors, including the Union's, to utter disapproval of their apparent support of the opposition.[128] Moreover, media reports indicate that EU diplomats making comments (eg criticizing policies which favoured ethnic Malays in Malaysia) resulted in accusations of meddling.[129] Such accusations have become more common over the past couple of years, as is showcased by a number of persona non grata declarations by third states, discussed above. More generally, it is fair to say that receiving states have varying standards regarding EU meddling: the concept of non-intervention 'soit un concept relatif susceptible d'avoir un contenu variable dans le temps et dans l'espace'.[130] What some states consider inappropriate diplomatic behaviour will not necessarily lead to an invocation of the rights under the Vienna Convention in another state. However, when they choose to do so, host states have tools of diplomatic law

[124] Joris Larik, *Foreign Policy Objectives in European Constitutional Law* (OUP 2016).

[125] Behrens, 'None of Their Business?' (n 41) 192.

[126] In its 'Draft Articles on Diplomatic Intercourse' (n 29) 104, the ILC also considers this to be a form of interference.

[127] Agence France-Presse, 'EU Trying to "Resolve" Envoy Expulsion with Sudan', *Sudan Tribune*, 25 August 2007, <www.sudantribune.com/spip.php?article23432> accessed 4 May 2022.

[128] Behrens, *Diplomatic Interference* (n 34) 19.

[129] BBC News, 'Malaysia Fury at EU Envoy Remarks', 25 June 2007, <http://news.bbc.co.uk/1/hi/world/asia-pacific/6237328.stm> accessed 4 May 2022.

[130] '[I]s a relative concept likely to have a variable content in time and space' [own translation]; Salmon, *Droit Diplomatique* (n 5) 129.

at hand in the form of sanctions to halt overly active diplomatic missions, including those of the EU.[131]

In other cases, countries have requested the EU to get involved in law-making and policymaking. The EUDEL in Bangladesh, for example, contributed to the writing of a new version of a local law that was prone to restrict operational space for local non-governmental organizations (NGOs).[132] In enlargement policies, EUDELs have been monitoring changes in legislation and steering government reforms. This type of derogation of the VCDR—those that happen with the receiving state's approval—do not cause too many distortions in the diplomatic relations between the Union and receiving states that are eligible for the EU's neighbour(hood) treatment.[133]

Second, the EU's constitutional obligation to protect its own interests is stronger than its obligation to protect the interests of its citizens. Note, for example, that Article 3(5) TEU states that the Union will only 'contribute' to the protection of its citizens. The legal construct of European citizenship does not equal that of nationality under international law. As a result, it is not obvious in either EU law or PIL that the delegations can offer diplomatic and/or consular protection. Sometimes confused (the EU Treaties could also have been formulated more clearly in this regard),[134] these are two different concepts.[135] Under CIL, *diplomatic protection* is a right that a state can exercise following a wrongful act committed by another state against one of its nationals. The 2006 ILC Draft Articles on this topic spell out a number of conditions such as the exhaustion of local remedies by the individual.[136] Despite its name, a diplomatic mission's involvement is not required. Diplomatic protection can be enforced through diplomatic action that involves the invocation of another state's legal responsibility and through international judicial proceedings.[137] The EU's exercise of these actions is improbable for at least three reasons. First, the 2010 EEAS Decision's reference to legal proceedings instigated by the HoD only provides for legal action on behalf of the Union without mentioning citizens. Second, any action by the EU would imply that the member state of nationality was not willing or able to take up an action itself.[138] Finally, the right to diplomatic protection is largely governed by CIL, which establishes no clear right for IOs in this matter. Neither do the ILC's Draft Articles on Diplomatic Protection deal with the protection of an agent by an international organization.

*Consular assistance* relates to answering requests for medical or legal assistance abroad, for evacuation, for repatriation, and similar situations. Nothing in the Vienna Convention prevents the performance of consular functions by a diplomatic mission (Art 3(2) VCDR). However, the EU is neither a signatory party to the 1963 Vienna Convention on Consular Relations (VCCR) nor has entered into bilateral agreements on the topic. Relevant articles

[131] Behrens, 'None of Their Business?' (n 41) 200.

[132] Concord, 'EU Delegations Report 2015: Mutual Engagement between EU Delegations and Civil Society Organisations: Lessons from the Field', 2015, <http://news.bbc.co.uk/2/hi/asia-pacific/6237328.stm> accessed 4 May 2022.

[133] Bátora and Spence, 'The EEAS as a Catalyst of Diplomatic Innovation' (n 38) 10.

[134] Elisabeth Tichy-Fisslberger, 'Der Schutz Der EU-Bürger durch Die Diplomatischen und Konsularischen Vertretungsbehörden' (2012) 13 Europarecht 217, 217.

[135] *LaGrand (Germany* v *United States of America)* [2001] ICJ Rep 466 and *Avena and other Mexican Nationals (Mexico v United States of America)* [2004] ICJ Rep 12.

[136] International Law Commission (ILC), 'Draft Articles on Diplomatic Protection with Commentaries' (2006) II YBILC 26.

[137] John Dugard, 'Diplomatic Protection' in Anne Peters (ed) *Max Planck Encyclopaedia of Public International Law*, 2009, <http://www.mpepil.com> accessed 4 May 2022.

[138] Pia Kerres and Ramses A Wessel, 'Apples and Oranges? Comparing the European Union Delegations to National Embassies' (2015) Cleer Working Paper No 2, 21.

are Article 8 on the exercise of consular functions on behalf of a third state and Article 18 on the appointment of the consul by two or more states.[139] Inside the Union, the issue has been debated ever since the Treaties linked consular protection to Union citizenship in the 1992 Treaty of Maastricht.[140] Recent legislative initiatives confirm, however, that missions of EU member states remain the primary actors in consular affairs.[141] Article 5(10) of the EEAS Decision and the 2015 Council Directive on consular protection envisage only a supportive role for the EUDELs, which is nevertheless interpreted more broadly in times of crisis.[142] However, it has been suggested that the protective aspect of consular functions is where the EU can contribute most concretely and visibly.[143]

#### *4.2.3.3.3 Negotiation*

International diplomatic law allows the sending state to negotiate with the receiving state's government (Art 3(1)(*c*) VCDR). This function is covered by EU law as, during the course of the European integration process, the EU gathered unprecedented competences that enable it to negotiate and conclude treaties with one or more third countries or IOs (Art 218 TFEU).[144] The Commission, the HR, and even the EU member states can provide the EUDEL's staff with a mandate to negotiate on their behalf in a third state. Similar to their national colleagues, EU diplomats negotiate in accordance with that mandate.[145] The high level of specialization that characterizes modern treaty negotiations means that EUDELs are more likely to be involved in informal talks or discussions leading up to the opening of formal negotiations. The mission's staff, however, may be invited to join a temporary expert negotiation delegation from Brussels. Permanent diplomats are generally well informed of the conditions on the ground, the political climate, and the personalities and interests of the diplomatic counterparts at the negotiation table—for these reasons, permanent diplomats are an important tool for the EU. HoDs have a role in the final and ceremonial phase of negotiations when they are mandated by the Union to sign a treaty or a memorandum of understanding. By way of example, the HoD in Delhi in 2012 signed an EU–India memorandum of understanding (MoU).[146] Interestingly, when the Council designated the Portuguese Ambassador as the person empowered to sign a Protocol to the Fisheries Partnership Agreement with Gabon, the Commission brought an action against the Council.[147] By not appointing the HoD to conclude the agreement, the Commission argued that the Council violated the Commission's external representation powers under Article 17 TEU, principles of the inter-institutional balance, and the requirement of the unity of external representation.

[139] Vienna Convention on Consular Relations, opened for signature on 24 April 1963, entered into force 19 March 1967, 596 UNTS 261 (hereafter VCCR). See Jan Wouters, Sanderijn Duquet, and Katrien Meuwissen, 'Caring for Citizens Abroad: The European Union and Consular Tasks' (2014) 19 EFAR 563, 578.

[140] Annemarieke Vermeer-Künzli, 'Where the Law Becomes Irrelevant: Consular Assistance and the European Union' (2011) 60 ICLQ 965, 965.

[141] Articles 20(2)(*c*) and 23 TFEU.

[142] Council Directive 2015/637 on the coordination and cooperation measures to facilitate consular protection for unrepresented citizens of the Union in third countries and repealing Decision 95/553/EC [2015] OJ L106/1; Council, 'Consular démarches: toolkit on procedural issues', 26 April 2016.

[143] Eileen Denza, 'Art 46—Diplomatic and Consular Protection' in Steve Peers and others (eds), *The EU Charter of Fundamental Rights: A Commentary* (Hart 2014).

[144] Article 37 TEU and Arts 3(2), 216, and 218 TFEU.

[145] Charles Chatterjee, *International Law and Diplomacy* (Routledge 2007) 85.

[146] Press release 6409/12 on the 12th EU–India summit, New Delhi, 10 February 2012, <http://europa.eu/rapid/press-release_PRES-12-44_en.htm> accessed 4 May 2022.

[147] See the pending case, *Commission v Council* [2021] OJ L242/3.

*4.2.3.3.4 Observation and reporting*

An official function of a diplomatic mission is to ascertain conditions and developments in the receiving state and to report these details to the sending state's government (Art 3(1)(*d*) VCDR). The proviso that the mission may use only lawful means is a restatement of Article 41(1) VCDR. The observation function primarily includes tasks related to the monitoring of information including the political, cultural, social, and economic activities of the country, and (in general) all aspects of life that may be of interest.[148] The acquisition and assessment of information is further enabled by the freedom of communication (Art 27 VCDR) and the freedom of movement (Art 26 VCDR).[149]

The observation function forms a significant part of the responsibilities that EU policy-makers and member states are comfortable outsourcing to EUDELs—that is, providing commentary to the local press and briefing Brussels on developments in the host country.[150] All official reporting from delegations is produced under the authority of the HoD. EUDELs' reports and briefings are drawn up in English or French and sent via diplomatic cables to the EEAS Headquarters and the relevant Commission DGs. They can be shared with the member states via internal information-sharing tools:[151] sensitive, restricted, confidential, and secret reports are sent via the appropriate secure communication systems. In 2016, the EEAS and the European Parliament also agreed that political reporting regarding certain countries would be shared by the European Parliament (up to the classification level of 'restricted' information). Reporting should be frank and clear, analyse developments using insights and contacts rather than merely factually reporting about them, and convey a clear political assessment. Delegations are encouraged to be daring in their analyses. The EEAS wants reporting to be political and as forward-looking as possible. They may contains analyses, recommendations, or requests for action or input from headquarters.[152] These reports are true examples of diplomatic reporting, which exist in parallel with informal emails exchanges with headquarters.

An original European interpretation of the customary functions of diplomatic missions is witnessed here: when EUDELs exercise the diplomatic function relating to the collection and transfer of information captured in Article 3(1)(*d*) VCDR, they do so to increase the collective benefit. EUDELs are even encouraged to generously share, in a non-reciprocal manner, their political reporting with resident member state embassies. Unlike most diplomatic actors, the EU is even obliged to make observations available to other diplomatic actors, including the missions and foreign affairs ministries of EU member states (Art 35 TEU; see also Chapter 5 for a discussion of the concrete obligations). From an international point of view, the idea of intensive information exchanges with other diplomatic personae in an environment where secrecy and confidentiality reign is almost revolutionary.

The maintenance of lines of communication with opposition groups, NGOs, and citizens of the receiving state also tends to be ambiguous. Although receiving states generally allow foreign diplomatic agents to interact with members of parliament and representatives from business, academia, civil society organizations, the arts, and so on, this is not the case

[148] ILC, 'Draft Articles on Diplomatic Intercourse' (n 29) 90.

[149] Barston (n 48) 3; Pancracio (n 116) 177.

[150] Steffen Bay Rasmussen, 'The Messages and Practices of the European Union's Public Diplomacy' (2010) 5 HJD 263, 274.

[151] Doc EEAS.sg.1(2016)2601452); Damien Helly, Anna Knoll, and Greta Galeazzi, 'A Closer Look into EU's External Action Frontline: Framing the Challenges Ahead for EU Delegations' [2014] No 62 ECDPM Briefing Note (hereafter Helly and others, 'Challenges Ahead for EUDELs'). See also Chapter 5 of this handbook on the obligation to share information.

[152] EEAS, Guidelines on Political Reporting, ARES (2016) 2106827.

everywhere. Union delegations nevertheless have a tradition of treating civil society as a source of information. In 2017, the website of the EUDEL in Beijing explicitly stated that 'in order to get a full picture of the situation in China, the European Union Delegation in Beijing is not just dealing with government officials but also with international and local non-governmental organisations, European and Chinese business representatives and others'. In a Brazilian case, the HR instructed the EUDEL 'to stay in contact with civil society organisations'.[153] Both the Council and Commission encourage EUDELs to engage with local groups and to enter into consultation practices.[154] Such relations are generally accepted in modern diplomatic practice.[155] Yet, it is one thing to have such contacts, to observe and to report on local struggles, and quite another to encourage them.[156] The case of the EU ambassador in Cambodia, who invited local organizations to report government intimidations relating to land-grabbing issues provides an example of a type of activism that may not be tolerated by the host state.[157]

#### *4.2.3.3.5 Promotion of friendly relations*

Finally, diplomatic missions promote friendly relations and develop economic, cultural, and scientific partnerships between the sending and receiving state (Art 3(1)(*e*) VCDR). The EU embraces the idea that friendly relations must be promoted in both internal and external policies. Yet cultural and scientific relations—and even economic relations—are arguably rather underdeveloped at this stage. EUDELs have traditionally interacted with local governments and other stakeholders on issues concerning market access, regulatory issues, investment, and international trade, all of which are hallmarks of the EU's trade-orientated diplomacy. Nonetheless, EU member states' interests constrain the EUDELs' broader economic diplomacy. EUDELs are increasingly taking up the role of disseminating information on European culture and science, organizing activities that give locals a taste of Europe's cultural heritage. Even in that case, however, the promotion of 'common' European symbols may be subject to local arrangements that protect the member states' promotion of their own artists, cuisines, and cultural heritage. The joint organization of cultural activities, or on a rotating basis, with EU member states' embassies is a good example. Less controversial is the EUDELs' role in promoting EU awareness through initiatives such as the occasion of Europe Day, the accession of a new member state, or the launch of new policy plans. Using techniques of public diplomacy that are remarkably similar to those used by national diplomatic missions, EUDELs contribute to the visibility and promotion of the common identity. All in all, the Union delegations embrace their role as the public face of the European Union abroad—a diplomatic function *par excellence*—both in relations with foreign governments and publics.

### 4.2.3.4 Non-Diplomatic Tasks

Beyond these diplomatic tasks, Union delegations also execute administrative and managerial tasks. Over the years, EUDELs shifted from housing Commission civil servants, to administering budgets and instruments, to fully fledged diplomatic missions that were

[153] Answer given by High Representative to written question E-001877/2019, 2 July 2019.
[154] Commission Communication, 'The Roots of Democracy and Sustainable Development: Europe's Engagement with Civil Society in External Relations', Brussels [2012] COM(2012) 492.
[155] Roberts, *Satow* (n 28) 153.
[156] Brian Barder, 'Diplomacy, Ethics, and the National Interest: What Are Diplomats For?' (2010) 5 HJD 289, 291.
[157] Concord (n 132) 25.

never freed from operational tasks. Simon Duke notes that these administrative functions are something 'member states were loath to do'.[158] Functions funnel together under the umbrella of the EUDELs—functions that, at national level, are generally performed not only by a ministry of foreign affairs and embassies but also by operational offices of defence ministries and development agencies.[159] Absorbing these functions prompted the EUDELs' title of 'hybrid constructs'.[160] While not strictly prohibited under the VCDR regime, the Vienna Convention provides receiving states with tools to restrict the execution of public administration activities by diplomatic missions. This section studies two tasks of delegations that are not explicitly mentioned in the VCDR: the implementation of development cooperation policies and the coordination with and between EU member states.

*4.2.3.4.1 The implementation of development cooperation*

The EU runs a large number of programmes aimed at promoting democracy locally, the management of which is in the hands of delegation staff. Under the umbrella of these programmes, EU officials work closely together with and have become an important source of funding for civil society actors in host states. The delegations' permanent presence on the ground is considered an asset in the decentralized context of development aid.[161] Representing the world's largest aid donor, the EUDELs inherited tasks as well as expertise from the Commission delegations.[162] In those states receiving EU funding, the work of EUDELs continues to be largely influenced by the work, modes of thinking, and legal competences of the Commission stretching back to the 1970s. EUDELs perform both political (eg in-country aid programming) and operational tasks such as the selection of recipients of Commission project resources. In the Arab region, for example, EUDELs are involved in the monitoring of local projects under the European Instrument for Democracy and Human Rights (EIDHR) programme.[163] The first function—the policy dialogue and management cycle tasks—is largely administered by the EEAS in Brussels but executed by Commission staff on the ground. Negotiated at (the beginning of) the end of an era of colonialism, the VCDR does not address development cooperation. However, the political aspects of development cooperation can surely be considered an exercise of the normal diplomatic functions of negotiation and observation.[164] The operational component departs further from traditional diplomatic functions. The Commission tasks its staff in delegations with streamlining the application process for funding schemes, reviewing draft proposals, identifying and selecting local projects, and implementing aid programmes, tasks for which the legal basis in European law is clearer than in diplomatic law.[165]

The EU's broad interpretation of the dimensions of diplomatic functions in development aid has certain advantages. Not only are resources pooled but also political issues and implementation are dealt with by the same staff, allowing for a comprehensive foreign policy in a

[158] Simon Duke, 'The Practices of Post-Lisbon Diplomacy' in Michael Smith, Stephan Keukeleire, and Sophie Vanhoonacker (eds), *The Diplomatic System of the European Union: Evolution, Change and Challenges* (Routledge 2016) 64.

[159] For instance, the German *Gesellschaft für Internationale Zusammenarbeit* has 130 offices abroad.

[160] Helly and others, 'Challenges Ahead for EUDELs' (n 151) 4.

[161] ibid 3.

[162] Dimier (n 62).

[163] Jan Wouters and Sanderijn Duquet, 'The Arab Uprisings and the European Union: In Search of a Comprehensive Strategy' (2013) 32 Yearb Eur Law 230.

[164] Isabelle Tannous, 'The EEAS, EU External Assistance and Development Aid: Institutional Dissonance or Inter-Service Harmony?' in Spence and Bátora (n 38) 130.

[165] Articles 5(9) and 9 EEAS Decision.

third state. The combination of various organizational and policy elements under one roof makes the EEAS an innovative diplomatic agency.[166] This dynamism, however, does not always sit well in the diplomatic system, which was created by states for particular purposes. From the legal perspective, Article 41(1) VCDR situations may arise. Non-diplomatic tasks can only be performed through diplomatic missions because—and as long as—a host state tolerates them. In most cases, the receiving state benefits from EU funding (direct aid) and will not object to diplomats providing funds to local actors (indirect aid). When used to circumvent interaction with government bodies, more involved development cooperation techniques, especially those that cement strong ties with civil society, remain susceptible to accusations of intermeddling. The Serbian Government, for instance, uttered disapproval in 2015 after the EUDEL in Belgrade funded the Balkan Investigative Reporting Network, a network of NGOs promoting freedom of speech, human rights, and democratic values in Southern and Eastern Europe.[167]

*4.2.3.4.2 Coordination with member states*

European cooperation abroad kicked off well before the entry into force of the Lisbon Treaty. The Treaty of Maastricht (Art J.6 EC Treaty) already included a constitutional obligation to cooperate. Yet, since the Treaty of Lisbon came into force in 2009, duties for EUDELs to foster close cooperation with the EU member states' diplomatic/consular missions (Art 35 TEU; Art 221(2) TFEU; 3(1) EEAS Decision), to share information, and to carry out joint assessments (Art 5(9–10) EEAS Decision) are scattered throughout the Treaties as well as in secondary law. This is but a practical application of the principle of sincere cooperation (Art 4(3) TEU). It is important to note that, while seemingly parallel to the VCDR's negotiation function, EU coordination differs from negotiation in that it targets not the host state but other states represented in the country. Synchronization exercises between diplomatic missions also exist in other constituencies (think of the G7, G20, or Commonwealth missions). It is the intensity with which coordination is carried out—almost contradicting the fact that countries pursuing their own interests traditionally occupy the diplomatic domain—that makes EU diplomacy unique.

From an international relations perspective, coordination by EU diplomats boasts numerous advantages. It comes with an unprecedented strategic advantage, contributes to the EU's visibility and is a source of negotiation power. From a legal perspective, two issues nevertheless arise. First, in cases when the EUDEL protects the interests of an EU member state that is not locally represented, strictly speaking, prior consent must be obtained from the receiving state (Art 46 VCDR). Even when a state is locally present, diplomatic law, to the letter of the Convention, stipulates that a sending state can only represent itself and protect its own interests (Art 3(1)(*a–b*) VCDR). Second, and recalling principles of EU law, a certain tension exists between the obligation to coordinate (Art 35 TEU) and the obligation to respect the essential state functions of EU member states (Art 4(2) TEU). Member states that perceive an overly active EUDEL as depriving them of influence can call upon the latter principle at any time. In practice, such internal quarrels are mostly solved informally in the regular interactions between the EUDEL and the member states.

[166] Jozef Bátora, 'The "Mitrailleuse Effect": The EEAS as an Interstitial Organization and the Dynamics of Innovation in Diplomacy' (2013) 51 JCMS 598, 610.

[167] Answer given by the Commission to parliamentary question E-000611/2015, 23 March 2015.

#### 4.2.3.5 Conclusion

EUDELs execute most of the traditional functions of diplomatic missions, as well as a number of other tasks, in third countries. This section examined the extent to which Union practices in diplomacy are compatible with the existing legal frameworks. It was found that the EU fits the state-based system, although the range of tasks performed by EUDELs is both broader and more restricted than that of states. Over time, Union delegations have more actively pursued diplomatic and political functions, with the Lisbon Treaty as the definite tipping point, while at the same time the scope of non-diplomatic endeavours also broadened. Comparatively speaking, the EU spends more resources on coordination activities and on information-sharing, to the benefit of other diplomatic missions. The value added by European cooperation is both internal, as Union delegations contribute to the idea of a common European identity abroad, and external, as EUDELs introduce new cooperative techniques to deal with common problems to an international diplomatic system that has traditionally been defined by the pursuit of individual national interests.

EUDELs are also used as pawns to execute a large number of Commission policies on the international stage. Fitting all the activities that EUDELs have on their plate into the language of Article 3 VCDR requires a broad reading of international diplomatic law, of which concrete execution depends both on the nature and scale of the relationship with the host country as well as the intensity of the diplomacy carried out by member states. Yet, the execution and implementation of common policies and shared competences also contribute to the specific character of the EUDELs compared to national missions, resulting in foreign actors' recognition of expertise and even authority in distinct policy domains.

Two sets of rules can be invoked by states to oppose more innovative EU diplomatic practices: PIL (both by third states and member states) and the law of the EU (by member states). This section furthermore demonstrates the EU's modern interpretation of the principle of non-interference (which makes room for public diplomacy and human rights policies carried out by diplomats); its building of all-round missions that represent a broad range of policies (going beyond the representation of interests in, for instance, trade to also include the dissemination of values, science, and culture); and its institutionalization of a cooperative relationship with other diplomatic representations. Although their activities are markedly confined in multiple ways, Union delegations are able to meet the multifaceted demands of modern diplomatic relations and have even contributed to the altering of diplomatic practice altogether.

### 4.2.4 The Enjoyment of Immunities, Inviolability, and Privileges

#### 4.2.4.1 Definitions

The 1961 Vienna Convention covers a wide variety of topics that relate to the sending and receiving of diplomats. The majority of these provisions concern the rights of the missions and their staff, conceptualized as immunities, inviolabilities, and privileges. The VCDR does not define these terms. In general, a distinction between the different concepts has been made as follows: *immunity* encompasses the immunity from jurisdiction (Art 31(1) VCDR) and the immunity from execution (Art 31(3) VCDR). It should be reminded that the Union itself enjoys jurisdictional immunity on the basis of the customary rule which recognizes that like states, IOs are exempted from the local jurisdiction of municipal judicial or administrative authorities and therefore are not subject to suits, claims, or enforcement proceedings in such domestic forums. While in common speak the term 'immunities' is often used in an umbrella sense to mean any kind of protection or exemption from local authority, its meaning is more restricted in PIL, where it is distinguished from other types of privileges granted to diplomatic personnel. Such other legal advantages include *inviolabilities*, which bring about the protection of a particular good or a person. They entail, on the one hand, a special positive duty of protection for the receiving state and, on the other hand, a negative duty for the latter to abstain from exercising any sovereign right, in particular enforcement rights. Immunities do not encompass such positive duty of protection. Inviolability and immunity sometimes overlap, yet the former is concerned about questions of infringement or trespass whereas the latter is applied to jurisdictional matters.[168] The concepts have in common that they confer a procedural protection from the enforcement processes in the receiving state without affecting any underlying substantive liability. The ICJ confirmed that the law of immunity is essentially procedural in nature.[169] This is different for the *exemptions* listed in the VCDR, which are substantive rights that have for a consequence that laws and regulations do not apply. *Freedoms* and *facilities*, in turn, are positively formulated rights that are granted by the receiving state to smoothen the functioning of diplomats and consuls on their territory.

The rules laid down in the VCDR regarding diplomatic privileges, immunities, and inviolability are mainly based on CIL and have become international custom themselves.[170] The preamble to the VCDR states that the 'purpose of such privileges and immunities is not to benefit individuals but to ensure the efficient performance of the functions' of 'diplomatic missions as representing States'.[171] Indeed, there is no doubt that the privileges, immunities, and inviolability enjoyed by diplomats, members of the mission, and their family members, serve a functional need. The purpose of privileges and immunities is not to benefit individuals but to ensure the efficient performance of their respective functions. This is shown in the preambles of the VCDR and VCCR, which contain a formulation reflecting that in the 1960s a compromise needed to be found between two theoretical bases that historically have been used to justify diplomatic benefits: the functional necessity theory (diplomatic advantages serve a functional need) and the representative character principle (diplomats are the direct representatives of the sending state). The functional necessity theory has clearly prevailed. This explains why, although the rationale for diplomatic and consular immunities is similar; the scope of diplomatic and consular immunity varies according to the content of diplomatic and consular functions performed: the more sensitive work carried out by diplomats requires a more extensive protection and a guaranteed confidentiality.[172]

### 4.2.4.2 Privileges and Immunities of Union Diplomats

#### *4.2.4.2.1 General*

The VCDR accords quasi-absolute immunities to diplomatic agents and their family members. Diplomats enjoy personal immunity (Art 31 VCDR), which encompasses criminal as

[168] Sanderijn Duquet, 'Immunities of Diplomatic and Consular Personnel' in Tom Ruys, Nicolas Angelet, and Luca Ferro (eds), *The Cambridge Handbook of Immunities and International Law* (CUP 2019); Denza, *Diplomatic Law* (n 15) 105–06; Roberts, *Satow* (n 28) 121–22.

[169] *Case Concerning the Arrest Warrant of 11 April 2000 (Democratic Republic of the Congo v Belgium)* (Judgment) [2002] ICJ Rep 1, para 60 (hereafter *Arrest Warrant* case) and, in the context of state immunity, (*Jurisdictional Immunities of the State (Germany v. Italy: Greece intervening)* (Merits) [2012] ICJ Rep 99, para 93.

[170] *Arrest Warrant* case (ibid). para 52; *Tehran Hostage* case (n 6) para 62. See also Verhoeven (n 20) 106.

[171] See also Art 25 VCDR.

[172] Salmon, *Droit Diplomatique* (n 5) 521–22.

well as civil and administrative immunity from jurisdiction and the immunity from execution. Members of the diplomatic agent's family 'forming part of the respective household' who are not nationals of the receiving state also enjoy the privileges and immunities described in Articles 29–36 VCDR. Members of the administrative and technical staff of the mission (and their families) do not enjoy immunity from civil and administrative jurisdiction in regard to acts performed outside the course of their duties; the service staff of the mission enjoy immunity for official acts only; private servants are exempted from taxes and social security obligation but do not receive any form of immunity (Art 37 VCDR).

The *immunity from jurisdiction* is broad and applies to legal proceedings based upon official acts but also in the private sphere (eg an application for a divorce or a dispute stemming from the rental of personal accommodation). The diplomatic immunity from criminal jurisdiction is absolute, while the VCDR formulates three exceptions with regard to civil and administrative jurisdiction concerning *(a)* real actions relating to private immovable property, *(b)* actions relating to private succession matters, *(c)* actions relating to professional or commercial activities exercised by the diplomatic agent.[173] American case law accepts that the term 'commercial activity' as used in the VCDR does not have so broad a meaning as to include occasional service contracts but rather relates only to trade or business activity engaged in for personal profit.[174]

In addition to immunity from jurisdiction, diplomats enjoy *immunity from execution* (Art 31(3) VCDR) to which the three exceptions referred to in the field of civil and administrative immunity also apply. Diplomatic immunity continues to exist after the termination of the diplomatic function (Art 39(2) VCDR) with the caveat that for acts not performed by the diplomat in the exercise of official functions, the immunity only continues until the agent leaves the country or until a 'reasonable period' to do so has expired (Art 39(2) VCDR).[175] Diplomatic agents enjoy a personal inviolability and are not liable to any form of arrest or detention (Art 29 VCDR). The receiving state is under the positive obligation to treat the diplomat with due respect and has to take all appropriate steps to prevent any attack on their person, freedom, or dignity (Art 29 VCDR) by its authorities as well as by individuals. The 1973 Convention on the Prevention and Punishment of Crimes against Internationally Protected Persons, including Diplomatic Agents, may be mentioned in this regard. Committing a murder, a kidnapping, or another attack against the person or liberty of a diplomatic agent, as well as the threat, attempt, or participation in such an attack (Art 2(1)(*a*) and (*c*)–(*e*) of that Convention), are subject to punishment in states party to the Convention.[176] Diplomats also enjoy exemptions from social security (Art 33 VCDR), taxation (albeit with some exceptions; Art 34 VCDR), and custom duties (Art 36 VCDR).

The rules on immunities, privileges, and inviolabilities of diplomatic and consular agents are among the oldest in international law and indispensable for the functioning of international relations. It has frequently been observed that there is generally good compliance with the law of diplomatic and consular immunity by receiving states. The EU follows this trend: Belgium grants diplomats of third state missions accredited to the Union the same privileges and immunities as it accords their counterparts accredited to the kingdom. Likewise, there is a firm practice in receiving states of granting the EU and its diplomats

173 Article 31(1) VCDR; Pancracio (n 116) 217–18; Salmon, *Droit Diplomatique* (n 5) 309–16; Roberts, *Satow* (n 28) 130–32.

174 *US District Court of Columbia [US] Sabbithi v Al Saleh*, 605 F Supp 2d 122 [2009].

175 Richtsteig (n 42) 96–99.

176 Convention on the Prevention and Punishment of Crimes against Internationally Protected Persons, including Diplomatic Agents, adopted on 14 December 1973, entered into force 20 February 1977, 1035 UNTS 167.

privileges, immunities, and inviolabilities.[177] There are no publicly reported cases of EU diplomats not paying rent or committing traffic offences—abuses of immunity that occasionally occur but receive ample attention in the media when committed on a large scale or as part of a pattern.[178] Any statements on this subject remain unsubstantiated now that data are lacking. However, speculatively, the absence of known incidents could have something to do with the instructions from the EEAS encouraging diplomats to pay (traffic) fines and private debts and to respect local laws in the receiving state. This is important, considering the distress an abuse of immunities can cause to citizens and/or society—a situation a relatively new actor in diplomacy may want to avoid.[179] The obligation to respect local laws is, of course, a legal obligation and features in Article 41(1) VCDR.

#### *4.2.4.2.2 Nationality*

It has always been regarded desirable that a diplomat should be a national of the sending state. Article 8 VCDR reflects this and introduces a requirement of consent of the receiving state to appoint non-national diplomatic staff. Article 38(1) provides that diplomatic agents and family members that are nationals and/or permanent residents of the receiving state have immunity and inviolability only for official acts carried out in the exercise of their functions, even if they simultaneously hold the nationality of another state. Additional privileges and immunities can, but rarely are, granted to this category by the receiving state/state of nationality. Building on state practices, the EU almost exclusively recruits EU citizens for diplomatic functions although—like most states—staff performing non-diplomatic functions are frequently locally hired and are either national or permanent residents of the receiving state. Nationals among local staff do not have immunity, including relating to taxation, except to the extent allowed for by the receiving state. However, upon a closer look, small frictions arise with regard to the definition of 'nationality' in the VCDR and the equation with the concept of EU citizenship. The rules with regard to nationality have to be modified to fit the EU practice.

In its *active legation practice*, the EUDEL is subjected to the VCDR rules with regard to nationality. There are three issues at stake: first, with regard to the multilateral delegations in member states Austria, France, and Italy, EU citizenship can overlap with the nationality of the host state. In such cases, agreements will have to be entered into with host states on the privileges and immunities of the EUDEL staff. Second, technically speaking, the EU does not send its own nationals but nationals of its member states to represent the Union abroad, which can be considered third state nationals by the receiving state. Prior to the VCDR, there were no clear rules about the practice of appointing third state nationals; now they are subject to the same consent requirement as nationals of the sending state (Art 8(3) VCDR).[180] Interestingly, the Union upheld the nationality rule after the United Kingdom's withdrawal by explicitly referring to Article 8 VCDR: UK nationals working in EUDELs were either recalled or barred from exercising diplomatic functions. Staff with UK nationality were transferred back to the EEAS Headquarters in accordance with the Staff Regulations and Article 8

[177] Myriam Benlolo-Carabot, 'Les Immunités des Communautés Européennes' (2008) 54 AFDI 549; Ramses A Wessel, 'Immunities of the European Union' (2013) 10 IOLR 395.

[178] Cour de Cassation [BE] 28 October 2016, No C.16.0039.N.

[179] Francisco Orrego Vicuna, 'Diplomatic and Consular Immunities and Human Rights' (1991) 40 International and Comparative Law Q 34; Rosalyn Higgins, 'The Abuse of Diplomatic Privileges and Immunities: Recent United Kingdom Experience' (1985) 79 AJIL 641; William G Morris, 'Constitutional Solutions to the Problem of Diplomatic Crime and Immunity' (2007) 36 Hofstra Law Rev 601; Jonathan G Carter, *Diplomatic Immunity: Privileges and Abuses* (Nova Science 2011).

[180] Denza, *Diplomatic Law* (n 15) 59–60.

VCDR. HoDs, as well as other senior staff representing the EU, having UK nationality only, returned by 29 March 2019, the day the United Kingdom left the Union. All other British officials were transferred back in September 2019 in the context of the normal yearly rotation.[181] Third, oddly enough, 49 EAs contain an addendum that is stricter than what the VCDR provides with regard to nationals. The 1988 EA with Zimbabwe, for instance, reads in Article 3(2):

> [t]he privileges and immunities accorded to the head and members of the Commission Delegation and to the members of their families who form part of their respective households in accordance with the provisions of the foregoing paragraph shall not be granted to those who are not member state of the European Communities or who have the Zimbabwean nationality.

In a way, the agreement introduces the concept of EU citizenship to international diplomacy and compares it with the nationality of a sending state. Yet the phrasing contains multiple restrictions and is unnecessarily strict: it denies nationals *as well as* non-EU citizens *all* privileges and immunities. It reads as if non-EU citizens as well as Zimbabwean citizens can never be entitled to diplomatic immunities. This does not correspond with PIL: diplomatic staff who have the nationality of the receiving state and/or are permanently resident under the VCDR regime still enjoy immunity and inviolability for official acts. Moreover, in theory, a country can appoint a third state national to its mission. The provision gives the Zimbabwean government significant leverage to refuse privileges and immunities (Art 38(1) VCDR).

In the *passive legation practice*, the idea of EU citizenship is less prominently present. Host state Belgium abides by the VCDR rules as if it were the receiving state: the appointment of non-sending state nationals, in particular of Belgians in the diplomatic staff of missions of third states to the EU, requires consent (Art 8 VCDR). Those Belgian citizens will receive privileges and immunities only with regard to the execution of their functions (Art 38 VCDR).

#### *4.2.4.2.3 Diplomatic confidentiality*

Since a diplomatic agent cannot be judged in the civil or criminal courts of a receiving state nor be the object of any act of investigation or prosecution they cannot be forced to give up secret knowledge in a court of law. Equally, the agent cannot be required to give evidence as a witness (Art 31(2) VCDR). The sending state can waive the aforementioned immunities if it deems that the diplomatic confidentiality is not at risk. Such a waiver has to be explicit and the testimony must be requested through the ministry of foreign affairs of the receiving state transmitting the request to the relevant mission for the agent concerned.[182] Diplomats who testify as a witness after their sending state has waived its right to object the testimony of its diplomatic agent still have tools at hand to protect secrecy if needed. Due to their immunity from criminal jurisdiction, a diplomat cannot be prosecuted for perjury without a new and specific waiver by the sending state. As a practical result, the value of a diplomatic testimony may be uncertain. Accordingly, in criminal cases, this legal regime has been questioned in light of the right to a fair trial of others.

[181] Commission and EEAS, 'Note for the attention of EEAS and Commission staff of UK nationality', 27 July 2018, Ares (2018) 3987013.

[182] Salmon, *Droit Diplomatique* (n 5) 320.

The European Court of Human Rights (ECtHR) dealt with the issue in *Meier v Switzerland*. The case concerned the 1999 interrogation by a prosecutor of the district of Zürich of Korean diplomats. Partly on the basis of those pre-trial testimonies, the applicant was convicted for fraud offences and sentenced to twenty-seven months in prison. The applicant argued that the admittance of the testimonies violated Article 6(1) European Convention for the Protection of Human Rights and Fundamental Freedoms (ECHR). Moreover, so he argued, the statements should have been disregarded by the Swiss courts since, for the reasons outlined above, diplomats are under no threat of prosecution for false testimony. By a decision of 18 June 2013, the Chamber declared the case inadmissible for reasons unrelated to the issue of diplomatic testimonies (para 54). In an obiter dictum, however, the Chamber noted that the ECHR does not, as such, prohibit the taking into account of statements of diplomats who are under no threat of criminal penalties for perjury. It added that such diplomatic testimonies would require increased attentiveness on the part of the prosecuting authorities and courts of law.[183]

In addition to these rights, EU diplomats enjoy supplementary privileges and immunities to protect information in the EU member states, which originate not from diplomatic but from institutional law. The rationale for the special protection of EU civil servants (Art 11) is also functional: it ensures that official activities are shielded from examination by member states under their domestic laws so that the Union's diplomatic activities may be carried out in full freedom.[184] Where an EU diplomat is called to give evidence before a national court on a subject related to their official capacity, prior permission must be obtained from the EEAS or, depending on the case, the Commission. As confirmed in case law, no distinction is to be made in this respect between information covered or not covered by the duty which prohibits EU officials from disclosing confidential information obtained from third parties.[185] Finally, there is a duty of discretion for all EU official with regard to facts and information coming to their knowledge in the course of their duties. In order to comply, officials must be able to justify any information they may pass on to an interest group, for reasons of transparency, as serving the interests of the Union. Prior permission must be sought by the HoD and the EEAS for any publication related to the work of the EU.[186]

#### *4.2.4.2.4 Case study: the EU in the UK*

The most mediatized case of non-compliance with the VCDR is that of the EU Delegation in London, (re-)opened after the UK's withdrawal from the Union. Since 2019, the HR is trying to negotiate an establishment agreement with the United Kingdom's Foreign and Commonwealth Office and several proposals were exchanged between the two actors. When it was clear that the United Kingdom would not be easily convinced to sign an EA referring to the VCDR, the HR disputed the United Kingdom's choice in a November 2020 letter to the British Foreign Secretary. It was argued that EUDELs, due to the specificities of the Union, enjoy privileges and immunities equivalent to those of diplomatic missions under the VCDR. This status in external relations and its resulting diplomatic status are widely recognized.

[183] *Meier v Switzerland*, App No 11590/08, 18 June 2013; ECHR, signed on 4 November 1950, entered into force 3 September 1953, 213 UNTS 222.

[184] *Sayag and SA Zurich v Leduc, Thonnon, and SA La Concorde* [1968] ECLI:EU:C:1968:42, 402.

[185] *Weddel & Co BV v Commission* [1992] ECLI:EU:C:1992:75, para 20.

[186] Article 17 EU Staff Regulations.

For two years, the British argued that the EU is an IO with limited and functional competences, entitled only to functional immunities. In itself, such point of view is not unlawful as the Union (not a VCDR signatory party) and the host state have to agree on the immunities of the EU office. Under section 4B of the EU Future Relationship Act 2020 of 31 December 2020, the British Government 'may decide' that the Union, its organs and offices, and its staff, shall be granted such privileges and immunities as 'it is in the opinion of Her Majesty in Council appropriate to confer on them'. In practice, the EU ambassador was not constrained to exercise his function in any way. Politically, however, the matter strained relations between the two sides, which had an unwanted effect on the important talks still being conducted on the future relationship between the United Kingdom and the EU. The Union started actively considering taking certain retorsions. A first action was the 'postponement' of an inaugural meeting between the United Kingdom's new HoM to the Union and senior EU officials in Brussels in January 2021. In May 2021, the UK Government recognized the corrosive effects of its position and after two years accepted that it would grant the EUDEL in London and its staff full diplomatic status, including privileges and immunities commonly received by bilateral missions. The discussion, settled for now, exposes one of the weak points of EU diplomacy and is particularly sensitive to the Union.[187] It leaves no doubt that the Union will repeat its question to have an agreement in writing on the matter.

#### 4.2.4.3 Inviolability of Communication, Archives, Diplomatic Bags, and Correspondence

##### *4.2.4.3.1 Premises*

The provisions on the inviolability of diplomatic premises and their correspondence, archives, and documents are among those that are most relevant. The premises of the mission enjoy a special status under PIL. The diplomatic mission is inviolable and agents of the receiving state may not enter them except with the consent of the HoM (Art 22(1) VCDR). Similarly to the personal inviolability of the diplomatic agent, the receiving state is under a special duty to take all appropriate steps to protect the mission against any intrusion—including acts that would violate its secret intelligence (Art 22(2) VCDR). The protection offered ranges from preventive measures to the taking of criminal sanctions post factum. The inviolability is to be respected in emergencies and exceptional situations, even in cases of suspected criminal activity within the premises of the mission.[188] Crucial for the protection of physical documents as well as electronic apparatus, the prohibition on coercive measures by local authorities extends to the furnishings and other property found on the diplomatic premises, as well as the means of transport of the mission (Art 22(3) VCDR).[189] The inviolability of the EU's diplomatic premises is generally well respected. Premises have been violated during protests, however. In September 2019, the lobby of the EUDEL in Tel Aviv was vandalized with threatening slogans on the walls. The Israeli Foreign Minister condemned the action and stated that Israel is committed to maintaining the security of all diplomatic missions. Observing the VCDR rules, an official investigation was launched by the host state.

[187] Mauro Gatti, 'Diplomats or Fonctionnaires? The Contested Status of the EU's "Embassy" in the UK', 1 March 2021, blog post at EJIL, <www.ejiltalk.org/diplomats-or-fonctionnaires-the-contested-status-of-the-eus-embassy-in-the-uk> accessed 4 May 2022.

[188] Roberts, *Satow* (n 28) 102.

[189] Richtsteig (n 42) 47.

*4.2.4.3.2 Communication*

One of the principles of the Vienna Convention is to facilitate and protect interstate communication, including its secret character. Denza describes the free and secret communication (Art 27(1) VCDR) between a mission and its sending state as 'probably the most important of all privileges and immunities accorded under international diplomatic law' for it enables the mission to carry out its functions, notably the reporting and negotiation function.[190] This relates to the idea that if diplomatic communication is not kept secret its very purpose vanishes. Article 27(1) VCDR sets out a general obligation for the receiving state 'to permit and protect free communication on the part of the mission for all official purposes'. The provision continues by stipulating that, in communicating with its sending state, 'the mission may employ all appropriate means, including diplomatic couriers and messages in code or cipher'. This is the sole instance in which the Convention directly refers to secret operation modes of a mission by explicitly allowing methods to transform a message into an obscured form so that it cannot be understood by other actors. While the use of such codes is allowed, the consent of the receiving state is imperative for the installation and use of wireless transmitters (Art 27(1) VCDR). Due to the technological evolution since the introduction of the VCDR, communication has changed significantly. Yet, it is accepted that 'all appropriate means' includes modern means of communication such as (mobile) telecommunication and email.[191]

Article 27(2) VCDR stipulates that all official correspondence relating to the mission and its functions is inviolable. The protection of correspondence includes both official correspondence from the mission and correspondence addressed to it and is not limited by its physical location. For example, mail cannot be intercepted even if it is not located in the diplomatic premises. The inviolability of diplomatic archives and documents entails that they cannot be opened, searched, or requisitioned without consent 'at all times and wherever they may be' (Art 24 VCDR). Further, they cannot be used as evidence in legal proceedings. These principles were confirmed in a judgment of the Court of Appeal of Brussels in the context of a criminal investigation which involved seizure (outside the premises of the mission) of correspondence exchanged with a diplomatic mission in Brussels. Since a seizure of a mission's official correspondence is void regardless of its physical location, the mail had to be returned to the diplomatic mission.[192] The term 'archives' is neither further described in the VCDR nor in the commentaries to the ILC's 1958 Draft Articles on Diplomatic Intercourse and Immunities. However, the 1963 Convention on Consular Relations (VCCR) provides inspiration. In the latter Convention, the term 'consular archives' is defined as including 'all the papers, documents, correspondence, books, films, tapes and registers of the consular post, together with the ciphers and codes, the card-indexes and any article of furniture intended for their protection or safe keeping' (Art 1(1)(*k*) VCCR). Scholars have argued that the broad definition applies by analogy to diplomatic archives but does not exclude other forms of information and modern forms of storage such as computer files and USB keys.[193] The issue was discussed in the UN's Host State Committee, where the EUDEL presented the Union's

[190] Denza, *Diplomatic Law* (n 15) 178.

[191] Won-Mog Choi, 'Diplomatic and Consular Law in the Internet Age' (2006) 10 SYBIL 117.

[192] Jean Salmon, 'Les Représentations et Missions Permanentes Auprès de Le CEE et de l'Euratom' in Michel Virally, Pierre Gerbet, and Jean Salmon (eds) *Les Missions Permanentes auprès des Organisations Internationales*, vol 1 (Dotation Carnegie 1971) 210; Court of Appeal Brussels [BE] 22 December 2010, No 4970, unreported.

[193] Salmon, *Droit Diplomatique* (n 5) 209; Denza, *Diplomatic Law* (n 15) 160–61; Roberts, *Satow* (n 28) 113; Choi, 'Diplomatic and Consular Law' (n 191) 117.

views on the matter and confirmed by the UN General Assembly.[194] The Resolution featured the first express confirmation of a broad understanding of diplomatic documents and archives, where it notes:

> that diplomatic and consular missions may maintain archives and documents in various forms, that official correspondence may take a variety of forms and that diplomatic and consular missions may use a variety of means of communication.

The interception of, or any attempt to become acquainted with, the content of diplomatic or consular communication is prohibited. Yet, observers of international relations provide ample examples of receiving states that have installed listening devices or bugged telephones of diplomatic missions on their territory.[195] The Vienna Convention does not expressly deal with the reverse situation, namely, secret intelligence gathering by diplomats and consuls in the receiving state. Espionage as such is not prohibited under PIL and state-led surveillance operations seem to be ever-present.[196] However, the ICJ has considered acts of espionage by diplomatic agents to be an 'abuse of [diplomatic] functions', making their performance by diplomatic agents unlawful.[197] With more states possessing the technical capability for interception, it has been suggested that such practices are even on the rise.[198] The EUDELs are well equipped in that regard: premises have soundproof isolation rooms, regular inspections of the mission premises' interior are conducted by experienced technicians, and there are strict security instructions for classified correspondence and receiving visitors.

Interestingly, the US National Security Agency's (NSA) scandal was a catalyser for the coming into being of Resolution 69/121 of the UN General Assembly (UNGA). Edward Snowden's 2013 leak of classified NSA documents revealed the conduct of acts of espionage from the rooftop of the US Embassy in Berlin by a special unit of the Central Intelligence Agency (CIA) and NSA, which allegedly monitored telephone communication in Germany's government quarter. In 2013, it was reported that the Agency's efforts to intercept global communication had targeted a number of permanent representations to the UN in New York, including the EUDEL. The Union's reaction was that of a mature diplomatic actor. First, the HR raised concerns in notes verbales—the diplomatic communication channel par excellence—and in person on several occasions with the US authorities, including the Secretary of State and the US President's National Security Advisor, and requested clarifications and assurances in this regard.[199] Second, the EU supported legal initiatives in the UNGA Sixth (Legal) Committee, instigated by the Brazilian representation in New York and brokered by member state Finland, with cooperation of the EUDEL, which led to UNGA Resolution 69/121. In the UNGA Resolution, the international community reminds fellow receiving states of the obligations of diplomatic law with regard to the protection of secrecy. It is not a restatement of the Vienna Convention; the innovative character of the Resolution lies in the confirmation of the modern definition of diplomatic documents and archives to

[194] UNGA Resolution 69/121, adopted on 10 December 2014, on the consideration of effective measures to enhance the protection, security and safety of diplomatic and consular missions and representatives, A/RES/69/121.

[195] Richtsteig (n 42) 61.

[196] Aurélien Colson, 'The Ambassador between Light and Shade: The Emergence of Secrecy as the Norm for International Negotiation' (2008) 13 Int Negot 179, 179.

[197] *Tehran Hostage* case (n 6) para 84.

[198] Barston (n 48) 11.

[199] Answer given by the High Representative to parliamentary questions E-010707/2013 and E-010708/2013, 13 December 2013.

include electronic means. The Resolution is 'concerned at the failure to respect the inviolability of diplomatic and consular missions and representatives' without specifying that only states enjoy these privileges. A broad definition is introduced in paragraph 2, which speaks of 'diplomatic and consular missions and representatives, as well as against missions and representatives to international intergovernmental organizations and officials of such organizations'. The protection applies to all missions, including the EU observer mission in New York and EUDELs in third countries.

The example also points to a wider trend in the contribution of the EU to law-making in diplomatic and consular relations via the UN. In New York, the EUDEL actively engages in the discussions in the Sixth Committee's Committee on Relations with the Host State. The range of issues the Committee deals with, though often practical in nature and targeted to the United States, goes to the heart of preserving the general diplomatic regime that outlines the rights and obligations of diplomatic agents. The Committee's work often surpasses the relations with the host state and ventures out to a variety of issues the diplomatic community at large faces. In fact, the Committee has become the most important technical forum for discussing international diplomatic and consular law on a regular basis. Because activities of permanent *and* observer missions to the UN and their staff are discussed, the EUDEL has leverage to fully participate in debates and, as such, influence discussions on the application and interpretation of diplomatic CIL and the VCDR. It is helped by the fact that the Committee adopts draft resolutions with consensus (ie without voting) so that influence can be exerted by coordinating between member states and facilitating between third states. The UNGA Resolution is but one recent outcome of the Host State Committee's work. Another notable contribution to general diplomatic law was made by the EUDEL in a Resolution on bank accounts held by diplomatic missions.[200] The discussion was instigated by Bolivia after certain countries could no longer open bank accounts in the United States as a result of economic or personal sanctions.[201] Sending states by the US Government were informed that since banks are private actors, the State Department could not make them accept clients. The EUDEL was very present in finding a solution—the UN bank started offering services to representatives of the members and to observers—and negotiating the UNGA Resolution and has followed up on the issue in later statements.[202]

#### *4.2.4.3.3 The diplomatic bag*

The Vienna Conventions protect diplomatic and consular bags if they bear visible external marks (Art 27(4) VCDR; Art 35(4) VCCR). Specifically, the diplomatic bag cannot be opened or detained (Art 27(3) VCDR). To add to its protection, states can opt to have the bag carried by a diplomatic or consular courier (Art 27(5) VCDR). The competent authorities of a receiving state can, however, always request a sending state's authorized representative to open it in their presence (Art 35(3) VCCR).[203] In a 2006 Dutch case, the interception of a 'diplomatic' bag that contained cocaine was deemed lawful. Although sealed, the bag did not bear visible external marks and for that reason did not meet the VCDR's requirements.[204]

[200] UNGA Resolution 68/306, adopted on 9 September 2014, UN Doc A/RES/68/306.

[201] UNGA, Host State Committee discussions, 10 December 2014, UN Doc A/69/PV.68.

[202] EU Statement in the Committee on the Relations with the Host Country, 14 November 2014; EU Statement in the Committee on the Relations with the Host Country, 3 November 2016, New York.

[203] See: Jeffrey F Addicott, 'The Status of the Diplomatic Bag: A Proposed United States Position' (1991) 13 Houst J Int Law 221, 224–225; Wilfried Bolewski, 'Diplomatischer Kurier: Völkerrechtliches Instrument und Gefahren Seines Missbrauchs' (2005) 43 AVR 537.

[204] Court of First Instance (Haarlem) [NL] 23 June 2006, No 15/500349-06, <www.rechtspraak.nl> accessed 4 May 2022.

The EU equally looks to protect flows of diplomatic information between the Brussels Headquarters and missions in third states. The diplomatic bag has therefore become an established means of communication between the EEAS and EUDELs, which must always be handled by or in the presence of a delegation official. As is common nowadays, diplomatic bags are mostly transported by a private shipment company. The Union's diplomatic pouch has some particular features: it is blue bag carrying the EU's emblem and official seal. On average, the EUDELs, weekly or biweekly, send a bag to the EEAS HQs, where it is opened in a special office and delivered to the destined person.

The prohibition to open the diplomatic bag is subject to controversy as it leads to abuses such as drug or weapon trafficking.[205] Several states entered into reservations seeking to limit the diplomatic bag's inviolability while reserving the right to open or return it in specific circumstances.[206] Other states objected to these reservations,[207] arguing inter alia that these go against the object and purpose of the VCDR[208] and, for that reason, are invalid.[209] As a measure to protect airspace and air traffic, certain states started to scan diplomatic bags at airports, with the Vienna Convention not being entirely clear on the legality of the specific act of doing so.[210] Modern scholarship argues that the VCDR does not prohibit the scanning of a diplomatic pouch as Article 27(3) VCDR is silent on any external controls of pouches, while Article 27(4) VCDR spells out that the diplomatic bags may only contain articles intended for official use.[211] However, screening methods that exist today go beyond the mere search for explosives or weapons, allowing the contents of a bag to be detected without opening the bag. In its own practice, EU diplomats are instructed that under no circumstance must their briefcase be opened, although it must be offered for X-ray examination, if required by local regulations. With regard to practices at member states' airports (including Brussels airport, where third state representatives to the Union commonly arrive), EU legislation provides that member states are entitled to policy space to decide whether they want to subject diplomatic pouches to scanning. A national authority 'may allow a diplomatic bag to be exempted from screening or to be subjected to special security procedures provided that the requirements of the Vienna Convention on Diplomatic Relations are met'.[212]

### 4.2.4.4 Access to Diplomatic Information in the EU Context

#### *4.2.4.4.1 Side-lining the general public?*

The special status afforded to diplomatic documents and communication affects outsiders to the diplomatic system. The VCDR, which was set up to govern relations between states, does not directly tackle questions such as whether diplomatic intelligence may be consulted by the public, whether it may be reported on by media, or whether it may be used as evidence

[205] Salmon, *Droit Diplomatique* (n 5) 247–49; Amy Zeidman, 'The Abuse of the Diplomatic Bag: A Proposed Solution' (1989) 11 Cardozo L Rev 427.

[206] See the reservations of Bahrain, Qatar, Kuwait, Libya, and Saudi-Arabia; UN Treaty Collection, <https://treaties.un.org/Pages/ViewDetails.aspx?src=IND&mtdsg_no=III-3&chapter=3&clang=_en> accessed 4 May 2022.

[207] ibid. See, in particular, the objections of Australia, France, the Unite Kingdom, Ireland, and the United States.

[208] See, in this regard, the objections of Mongolia, Poland, and the Soviet Union.

[209] See Art 19(c) Vienna Convention on the Law of Treaties, done 23 May 1969, entered into force 27 January 1980, 1155 UNTS 331.

[210] Christine M Nelson, '"Opening" Pandora's Box: The Status of the Diplomatic Bag in International Relations' (1988) 12 Fordham Int Law J 494.

[211] Denza, *Diplomatic Law* (n 15) 202; Roberts, *Satow* (n 28) 117.

[212] Annex, 4.1.2.11 to Commission Regulation (EU) No 185/2010 of 4 March 2010 on common basic standards of aviation security [2010] OJ L55/1.

in court cases. Since diplomatic law is silent on the matter, this section scrutinizes how the EU has dealt with increased demands from its citizens seeking access to information held by its diplomats.

Diplomats operate largely outside the scrutiny of the public, with little oversight by parliaments.[213] The special status granted to diplomacy goes against the trend of 'open government', recognized in human rights law and constitutional provisions across the world. Indeed, most general human rights treaties contain a right to seek, receive, and impart information and ideas.[214] These provisions are increasingly interpreted by the relevant enforcement bodies as protecting a right of access to official documents.[215] Further pioneering work on the issue has been carried out in the context of the United Nations Economic Commission for Europe (UNECE) Convention on access to information, public participation in decision-making, and access to justice in environmental matters—the famous Aarhus Convention.[216] The Council of Europe's 2008 Convention on Access to Official Documents, however, is the first international treaty fully dedicated to the topic.[217] The 2008 Convention explicitly recognizes a general right of access to official documents held by public authorities (Art 2). Limitations on the right of access to official documents are only permitted in order to protect certain interests. In Article 3(1)(*a*–*b*), which reflects the relevant ECtHR case law, the 2008 Convention provides that state parties may limit the right of access to official documents only when three conditions are met. The limitations have to be: *set down precisely in law*; *necessary* in a democratic society; and *proportionate* to the aim of protecting international relations, national security, and public security. Diplomatic cables serve as a classic example of documents that are potentially harmful to international relations as well as to national security interests. The application of these three conditions may be observed in (case) law at the national and EU level.

#### *4.2.4.4.2 The diplomatic exception is set down in law*

Member states commonly recognize a right to access to information in their domestic laws and virtually all of them also incorporate a 'diplomatic exception' in one form or another. This exception has been referred to as the public interest immunity or the principle of *secret diplomatique* (France). Most member states formulated the diplomatic exception in fairly general and all-encompassing terms. The 1991 Dutch Government Information Act contains a wide-ranging exception for all documents on diplomatic relations of the Netherlands with other states and IOs;[218] the 1978 French administrative transparency law refers to *la politique extérieure de la France*[219] as an exception to access to information rights.[220] The

[213] Andraž Zidar, *Diplomatie Contemporaine: Entre Secret et Publicité, Secrets et Le Droit* (Universités de Berne, Fribourg, Genève, Lausanne, et Neuchâtel 2004) 419–43.

[214] See, eg Art 19 Universal Declaration of Human Rights, Art 19 International Covenant on Civil and Political Rights, Art 10 ECHR, and Art 13 American Convention on Human Rights.

[215] Maeve McDonagh, 'The Right to Information in International Human Rights Law' (2013) 13 Hum Rights Law Rev 25, 26. See, for ECtHR case law, *Österreichische Vereinigung zur Erhaltung v Austria*, App No 39534/07, 28 November 2013, paras 37–48; *Roşiianu v Romania*, App No 27329/06, 24 June 2014, paras 61–68.

[216] Convention on Access to Information, Public Participation in Decision-Making and Access to Justice in Environmental Matters, done at Aarhus on 25 June 1998, entered into force 30 October 2001, 2161 UNTS 447.

[217] Council of Europe Convention on Access to Official Documents, done on 18 June 2009, entered into force 1 December 2020, CETS No 205.

[218] Article 10(2.1) Wet houdende regelen betreffende de openbaarheid van bestuur [NL] Law of 31 October 1991 on freedom of information.

[219] Article 6(I)(2)(*c*) Law No 78-753 [FR] portant diverses mesures d'amélioration des relations entre l'administration et le public et diverses dispositions d'ordre administratif, social et fiscal, 17 July 1978.

[220] The US Freedom of Information Act speaks of information on 'foreign policy'; Freedom of Information Act [US] 5 USC Sect 552, as amended by public law No 104-231, 110 Stat 3048 §552, b(1)(A).

EU provides an atypical example of an organization which has made special efforts with regard to access to information. Unlike states, IOs do not commonly recognize a general right to information. However, a trend can be discerned towards more openness. The WTO, the World Bank Group, and the International Monetary Fund (IMF) have cautiously adopted a number of disclosure policies.[221] EU law on the topic resembles national regulations: it has as a starting point a general recognition of the right to access, with a diplomatic exception laid down in law.[222] In its Treaties, the EU commits to take decisions as openly as possible (Art 10(3) TEU) and to maintain an open, transparent, and regular dialogue with representative associations and civil society (Art 11(2) TEU). Moreover, the right of EU citizens to access to documents of the Union's institutions, bodies, offices, and agencies (Art 15 TEU) is included in the Charter of Fundamental Rights of the EU (Art 42). The right of access also applies to documents relating to the CFSP.[223] However, similarly to states, EU institutions and the EEAS will refuse access to a document where disclosure would undermine the protection of the public interest as regards public security, defence and military matters, and international relations.[224]

The Court of Justice of the European Union (CJEU) has ruled on these exceptions on a number of occasions. In *Sison v Council*, the CJEU confirmed that 'international cooperation concerning terrorism presupposes a confidence on the part of states in the confidential treatment accorded to information which they have passed on to the Council'.[225] In view of the nature of the document requested, in this case, the Council had rightly considered that disclosure could compromise the position of the EU in international cooperation concerning the fight against terrorism. In *Jurašinović v Council*, the Court decided that access can be denied to a Union citizen on the basis of Article 4(1)(*a*) Regulation 1049/2001, even if the documents in question have been made available to a third party, *in casu* the International Criminal Tribunal for the former Yugoslavia, established by the United Nations.[226]

#### *4.2.4.4.3 The diplomatic exception is necessary in a democratic society*

Limits to the access to public documents have to be *necessary in a democratic society*. Non-disclosure is commonly defended on realist grounds. The preservation of a culture of secrecy is considered necessary to enable diplomats to negotiate effectively at the international level.[227] Moreover, confidentiality is deemed required to earn the trust of diplomatic partners.[228] While this rationale is easily understandable, it impedes citizens from discovering how their governments fare in conducting diplomatic relations. A paradox can be identified: the disclosure of diplomatic knowledge is sacrificed for the goal of political effectiveness in foreign relations, but, as a result, it is virtually impossible for the general public and, one may add, members of parliament, to ascertain whether this goal is reached or even pursued. Parliamentary control and scrutiny are a vital part of the democratic accountability

[221] Alasdair Roberts, 'A Partial Revolution: The Diplomatic Ethos and Transparency in Intergovernmental Organizations' (2004) 64 Public Adm Rev 410.

[222] See the EU rules on access to documents, in particular, Regulation (EC) No 1049/2001 of the European Parliament and of the Council regarding public access to European Parliament, Council and Commission documents [2001] OJ L145/43 (hereafter Regulation 1049/2001). Pursuant to Art 11(1) EEAS Decision, this regulation also applies to the EEAS. See also Council Decision 2011/292/EU on the security rules for protecting EU classified information [2011] OJ L141/17.

[223] Recital 7 of Regulation 1049/2001.

[224] ibid Art 4(1)(*a*).

[225] *Jose Maria Sison v Council* [2007] ECLI:EU:C:2007:75, para 20.

[226] *Ivan Jurašinović v Council* [2013] ECLI:EU:C:2013:777, para 65.

[227] Barston (n 48) 90.

[228] Colson (n 196) 186.

of governments and executive agents. However, on matters of diplomacy, the obligations for executives to justify their decisions and implementation to parliaments seem less demanding than for other policies. While, in general, democratic accountability is seen as a necessary means to control diplomatic services, in literature it is also argued that democratic control does not automatically exert a consistently positive effect on diplomacy. Lieberfeld, for example, point outs out that '[s]ecrecy reduces incentives for negotiators to grandstand and speak mainly for the benefit of domestic audiences'.[229] Domestic systems deal with the issue in various ways. In the United States, oversight by Congress, comparatively speaking, is one of the strongest systems of parliamentary accountability in foreign policymaking.[230] The House and Senate Committees on Foreign Affairs review and consider diplomatic nominations, legislation relating to foreign policy and policy decisions of the US President and are responsible for overviewing foreign policy agencies of the US Government, including the Department of State. Yet, even here national courts have recognized the President's authority to classify information bearing on national security or foreign affairs.[231]

Parliamentary accountability is also an issue in the EU context.[232] An interesting case before the CJEU concerned a Member of the European Parliament (MEP) who was denied full access to a document containing an opinion of the Council's Legal Service (*Council v in't Veld*).[233] The requested opinion discussed the opening of negotiations between the EU and the United States to make financial messaging data available to the US Treasury Department in the framework of the so-called SWIFT Agreement. The Council's refusal decision was taken on the ground of the exceptions laid down in the third indent of Article 4(1)(*a*) relating to the protection of the public interest as regards international relations and the second indent of Article 4(2) of Regulation No 1049/2001, which provides protection for legal advice. The Council argued that a disclosure of the document would reveal to the public information relating to certain provisions in the Agreement and, consequently, would negatively impact on the EU's negotiating position and would also damage the climate of confidence in the ongoing negotiations.[234] In 2012, the General Court had ruled that the fact that negotiations were ongoing was not conclusive in ascertaining whether there exists any overriding public interest justifying non-disclosure,[235] which the CJEU confirmed in its appeal judgment.[236] Furthermore, the judgment backed the General Court in its assessment that legal advice on external relations is not automatically exempt from EU transparency requirements and that the Council must give specific reasons why the access would undermine the Council's interest to show that these are not purely hypothetical.[237] As a matter of principle, the fact that this judgment confirmed that it is possible to apply for access to legal opinions related to international negotiations constitutes a modest step forward for democratic accountability in the EU. In light of the relatively high number of international negotiations conducted by EU actors for which access to information for MEPs has not been self-evident,

229 Daniel Lieberfeld, 'Secrecy and "Two-Level Games" in the Oslo Accord: What the Primary Sources Tell Us' (2008) 13 Int Negot 133, 137.

230 Corneliu Bjola and Markus Kornprobst, *Understanding International Diplomacy: Theory, Practice and Ethics* (Routledge 2013) 31.

231 David E Pozen, 'Deep Secrecy' (2010) 62 Stan L Rev 257, 322.

232 Jan Wouters and Kolja Raube, 'Towards an Inter-Parliamentary Scrutiny of CSDP' (2012) 47 The International Spectator 149.

233 *Council v Sophie in 't Veld* [2014] ECLI:EU:C:2014:2039.

234 ibid, para 8.

235 ibid, paras 73–76.

236 ibid, para 110.

237 ibid, para 104.

the judgment may potentially have a considerable impact. One can think of the cases of the ongoing transatlantic talks on the topic of genetically modified organisms, data protection, and trade relations.

#### *4.2.4.4.4 The diplomatic exception is proportionate to the aim of protecting international relations*

A government's decision to restrict access to documents has to be *proportionate*. Generally, there are two main requirements for a state to deny access based on diplomatic grounds. First, in national laws such as the ones referred to above, it is clear that, in order to come to a decision regarding access, the authorities need to engage in a balancing exercise. Second, an authority denying access to a diplomatic document has to state its reasons for doing so. In general, this means that a public authority has to weigh the interests of the citizen requesting access, as well as those of the public at large, in being informed on government policies vis-à-vis the state protecting its interests in diplomacy. While there are no strict rules regarding how the proportionality test should be performed, studying state practices highlights a number of elements which are generally relied upon.

A first set of criteria concerns the *age of the document* and the *sensitivity of the information* contained. The sensitivity of a document decreases significantly with time. Moreover, many countries have rules governing the preservation and the disclosure of diplomatic papers, including archives of embassies and consular offices, after a fixed number of years, while others always require prior authorization. It goes without saying that truly sensitive data are rarely disclosed by diplomats. At the same time, not all diplomatic documents are protected by all-encompassing classifications such as 'national security' or 'secret'. Moreover, non-sensitive information is increasingly shared through a number of channels. One medium to inform the public is the publication of official announcements such as an announcement in the official gazette or a government information document. Numerous diplomatic missions have a website, an official Facebook page, and/or Twitter and Instagram accounts, all of which contribute to public diplomacy efforts.[238]

In certain cases, a citizen may have a legitimate interest in gaining access to a particular document. This is the case when the document is of relevance to the exercise of their *individual rights*. A recent example can be found in the EU practice. In September 2014, Rosneft—Russia's main state-owned oil company—was hit with economic sanctions by the EU.[239] The company requested that the Belgian Government provide Rosneft, under Belgian law, access to information that would disclose the facts relied upon in the EU's sanctions decision. In other words, the company was interested to learn the rationale for the measures taken and the evidence upon which sanctions were based. Moreover, Rosneft demanded access to sensitive information of a diplomatic nature. It requested access to *(a)* European communications with third countries, in particular the United States of America; *(b)* information on the voting of EU member states when adopting the restrictive measures; and *(c)* the EU member states' anticipated reaction 'of the Government of the Russian Federation to the implementation of the measures, and in particular with regard to its foreign policy objectives in relation to the Ukraine'. The Belgian Government denied access on the basis of (i) Belgium's

[238] Jan Melissen (ed), *The New Public Diplomacy: Soft Power in International Relations* (Palgrave Macmillan 2005) 13.

[239] Council Regulation (EU) No 960/2014 of 8 September 2014 amending Regulation (EU) No 833/2014 concerning restrictive measures in view of Russia's actions destabilizing the situation in Ukraine [2014] OJ L271/3, Annex 3.

general international relations exception in its access to information law (ie its version of the 'diplomatic exception') and (ii) reasons of national security. The applicant was not satisfied with the government's answer and filed an administrative appeal with the Belgian Commission for the access to and the re-use of administrative documents.[240] In its report, the Commission restated national and international case law to find that, in principle, administrative documents are public and that a rejection has to be based on a ground provided by law and necessary to protect the interests of the state.[241] The Commission did not consider that the third criterion of proportionality had been met. Although it recognized that diplomatic relations constitute a possible legal basis for a denial of access, the Commission found that the administrative decision-maker had failed to give sufficient reasons for its decision in the present case. The mere fact that the subject of the requested documents touched upon the diplomatic domain was not considered satisfactory by the Commission to justify a ruling that denial of access was proportionate. A balancing exercise has to be carried out and motivated at all times. In deciding on the access to diplomatic documents, a government has to assess, on the one hand, the interest served by making the document public for the applicant and society at large and, on the other hand, the protection of Belgium's international relations. The original decision was struck down and the government was required to retake the decision.

The *Rosneft* case highlights a final criterion, here referred to as the *rule of diplomatic counterpart control*. Disclosure by one country may affect diplomatic counterparts. In settings such as the EU, where member states cooperate in fairly integrated ways, even in external relations, there is also a risk of forum shopping. Individuals can 'shop' around in order to find the national laws that give the broadest access to information on common diplomatic actions of member states.[242] Similarly, under EU legislation, documents originating from third countries or IOs, classified as '(top)secret' or '*confidentiel*' are considered to be sensitive and can only be released with the consent of the originator.[243] Even in bilateral relations, the decision of one state to make diplomatic archives public may bring discomfort to other nations. In 2005, when South Korea released diplomatic documents detailing behind-the-scenes negotiations between Japan and South Korea concerning reparations for Korean victims during Japan's colonial rule, a diplomatic incident ensued. To this day, the Japanese Government has a policy of keeping its pertinent documents on the 1965 Treaty on Basic Relations between Japan and the Republic of Korea secret. In general, national governments have a duty of vigilance in their treatment of information received in confidence from diplomatic counterparts. Access to official documents is often denied when it is potentially harmful to other governments. In Canada, this limitation is expressly confirmed by law: its Access to Information Act foresees exemptions for information supplied by a government in confidence or which could reasonably be expected to result in financial loss, loss of a competitive position, or interference with contractual or other negotiations

#### 4.2.4.5 Enforcement

In cases where jurisdictional immunity will need to be invoked in foreign local courts or administrative tribunals, the EEAS or the Commission, depending on the case, will task the

[240] Commission d'accès aux et de réutilisation des documents administratifs [BE] Avis No 2014-93, 24 November 2014.
[241] ibid 4.
[242] Article 20(1) of the Access to Information Act [CA] RSC, 1985, c A-1.
[243] Article 9 Regulation 1049/2001.

EUDEL to inform the local Ministry of Foreign Affairs. Usually, a note verbale will be sent asking the MFA to take the appropriate steps to confirm with local courts that immunity is invoked. Where considered necessary or useful, local counsel will be appointed to follow the proceedings and to invoke the immunity or inviolability on behalf of the EU and/or its staff.

## 4.3 Diplomatic Protocol, Practices, and Procedures

### 4.3.1 The Rules on International Politeness

Diplomatic actors attach great value to international courtesy.[244] A set of global formalities has therefore emerged based on considerations of mutual respect, hospitality, and decency. Fundamentally, institutionalized behaviour in diplomacy serves to connect equals with one another. Receiving and sending states will prevent any diplomatic incidents from arising in connection with questions of protocol or equality between missions. They spare no expense to devise protocol arrangements: a seating or title error is a diplomatic error, the seriousness of which varies according to the rank and susceptibility of the victim. A seating error can even be a legal error, as was showcased during the so-called 'sofagate'. When Turkish President Erdogan invited the Presidents of the European Council and the Commission in April 2021, the former assumed that he was entitled to the only seat available, side-lining his (female) colleague. EU law does not spell out a hierarchy between the presidents of different institutions, placing them at the same level to represent the Union in their different capacities. EU protocol is a little more dubious on the question, suggesting that the European Council indeed takes precedence. In light of the media attention that went to the seating discussion rather than the actual visit and the strong feelings it provoked, the incident exposed a need for better inter-institutional coordination on protocol, which does not require a formal change of the Treaties.

When adhering to international comity, states do so on silent agreement, empirical expediency, and general practices, but also on law. The Vienna Convention only briefly addresses the topic of international politeness: it sets out basic rules for overcoming discrepancies between national traditions with the aim of protecting the principle of equality between states. The VCDR leaves concrete questions of international etiquette to general practice, the legal value of which is unclear at times. The use of official titles, the priority and ranking of diplomats, and the use of symbols are but some of the examples of aspects of the diplomatic life which feature in the Convention but are by and large regulated by diplomatic protocol. These topics are considered part of the playing field of protocol services of foreign ministries around the world. The Union is no stranger to diplomatic protocol, customs, and practices. Both in its active and its passive practices, general understandings and informal rules are adhered to. This understanding is important for two reasons. First, symbols and protocol in diplomatic relations are intended to create a shared sense of belonging between sending and receiving states and diplomats themselves. They motivate a common esprit de corps across borders and influence the position of individuals participating in diplomatic practice.[245] In

[244] Jean Serres, *Manuel Pratique de Protocole* (De La Bievre 2016); Mary Jane McCaffree, Pauline Innis, and Richard M Sand, *Protocol: The Complete Handbook of Diplomatic, Official & Social Usage* (Durban House 2002); Emmanuel Coppieters, *Protocole: National et International/Protocol Nationaal en Internationaal* (Institut Royal des Relations Internationales 1989).

[245] Alisher Faizullaev, 'Diplomacy and Symbolism' (2013) 8 HJD 91.

other words, it has an interactionist and group function. Second, the use of symbols and titles visualize the presence of a diplomatic actor abroad. It can be argued that this contributes to one of the most important diplomatic functions, namely, representation: government agents in receiving states as well as local residents will become increasingly familiar with a diplomatic actor's symbols. Protocol and symbolism also serve a branding function.

### 4.3.2 Diplomatic Nomenclature

Diplomacy has its own nomenclature. A sending state uses diplomatic titles to inform the authorities of the receiving state of the title and rank it wishes to see granted to its staff. The EU, like sending states, respects the categories of mission personnel mentioned in Article 1 VCDR in order to avoid confusion between the statuses. Diplomatic grades are the following: minister plenipotentiary, minister (-counsellor), (first or second) counsellor, (first, second or third) secretary, attaché, assistant attaché. The host state is also allowed to limit the size of the mission and to refuse to accept officials of a particular category (Art 11 VCDR).

HoMs are divided into three classes: ambassadors (or nuncios, accredited to the head of state); envoys (or ministers and internuncios, also accredited to the head of state); and chargés d'affaires (accredited to the minister of foreign affairs) (Art 14(1) VCDR). The fact that EU heads of delegation belong to the first category is clear-cut. HoDs are conferred with the authority to perform functions that are equivalent to those of national HoMs. Moreover, HoDs are accredited to the head of state. Whether that also means that an HoD can assume the title of ambassador—even with Article 14 VCDR applying in principle—has long been disputed. The term 'ambassador' was in common usage long before 1961 and carries great weight as it is the title used for the representative of the highest rank appointed by a state in a particular country. Moreover, rituals and etiquettes have accumulated since recorded history to endow the title with distinction and even glamour and a touch of mystique.[246]

There is a long-standing practice of informing the receiving state of the title that the Union wishes to see granted to its HoDs. As the Commission has explained:

> [i]t is in the nature of diplomatic practice that the accrediting State requests from the host State the level of accreditation it wishes for its diplomatic agents there. It is in this sense that the accrediting state grants the title to the official. This rule also applies to heads of the Commission's delegation, representation or office who are accredited at head of state level.[247]

In 1983, the Commission started referring explicitly to a 'Courtesy Title of Ambassador' in its letters of credence.[248] By 1999, it was customary for the accrediting state to accord the head of delegation the rank, and courtesy title, of ambassador.[249] However, the EU's envoys have always been cautious to actively utilize the ambassadorial title externally—even to the extent that the Protocol Service suggested that it should be avoided when it would ventilate

[246] Andrew F Cooper, Jorge Heine, and Ramesh Thakur, 'The Challenges of 21st-Century Diplomacy' in Cooper, Heine, and Thakur (n 49) 3.

[247] Answer given by the Commission to parliamentary question E-0328/2000, 11 February 2000.

[248] Véronique Dimier and Mike McGeever, 'Diplomats without a Flag: The Institutionalization of the Delegations of the Commission in African, Caribbean and Pacific Countries' (2006) 44 JCMS 483, 496; Philippe De Schoutheete and Sami Andoura, 'The Legal Personality of the European Union' (2007) LX Studia Diplomatica 7.

[249] Answer given by the Commission to parliamentary question P-0224/1999, 3 February 1999.

diplomatic sensitivities either in member states or third countries. As a result, there was a common understanding that, in regards to the EU, the ambassadorial title reflected a courtesy title only and not a function.

Internally, references to 'EU ambassadors' are more common and the term has been used since the 1960s. The EEAS uses its own classification system within delegations and employs a table setting out the equivalence between those administrative grades and diplomatic titles under the VCDR for staff posted to EUDELs.[250] However, the title has never appeared in legal texts issues by the Union. This did not change with the Lisbon reform: neither the Treaties nor the EEAS Council Decision allude to any diplomatic titles. In contrast, practices have evolved since 2009. The EEAS's establishment and the role of the local EU presidency largely entrusted to the EUDEL have put the missions under a greater spotlight and HoDs are increasingly called 'ambassador' or even 'ambassador of the EU' in their country of posting. Within the EU setting, diplomatic titles are never used in communications with Headquarters and have meaning and value only during the posting and in the receiving state (which has granted them); they do not confer rights of any sort to particular status during a subsequent posting or return to the EEAS Headquarters.

According to Belgian protocol, the title of ambassador is only to be used for heads of bilateral missions (embassies) who have presented their credentials to the king. Most heads of missions to the EU have done so as a consequence of their double accreditation. If not, their use of the ambassadorial title too, strictly speaking, is a courtesy title granted by their sending state. The same goes for the few heads of liaison offices and missions or IOs to the EU, which are not considered ambassadors for Belgian protocol purposes but may carry the title as a courtesy from their sending organization. Within the Union setting, the institutions will address a head of a third state's mission according to their ambassadorial and courtesy title.

### 4.3.3 Diplomatic Precedence

The precedence of heads of mission in a local diplomatic corps is a delicate topic in diplomacy because it ties in with the idea of equality of states in the international legal order.[251] The Vienna Convention has established a system based on seniority to rank diplomats present in a capital city. Important in terms of etiquette during official ceremonies, the *ordre protocolaire* is determined in accordance with Article 16(1) VCDR, according to which:

> [h]eads of mission shall take precedence in their respective classes in the order of the date and time of taking up their functions in accordance with article 13.

Depending on local custom, the ambassador's diplomatic status and period of service commence as soon as the true copies of their credentials are presented to the ministry of foreign affairs or from the point of accreditation to the head of state. The name of the HoM, however, will appear on the diplomatic list with the time and date on which the credentials were presented. Practice has refined the system and prescribes the drawing up of a *diplomatic list*, which contains all HoMs.[252] Custom further prescribes that representatives of

[250] See Appendix 8.

[251] Jan Wouters and Sanderijn Duquet, 'Unus Inter Plures? The EEAS, the Vienna Convention and International Diplomatic Practice' in Spence and Bátora (n 38).

[252] Chatterjee (n 145) 143.

states are listed first; part two of the classification comprises the representatives of IOs.[253] In addition to ceremonial considerations, the list of diplomats also serves a political purpose. It allows for the designation of a doyen or a dean of the corps (ie the most senior ambassador). Although not discussed in the Vienna Convention, the functions of a doyen include a role as spokesperson and representative of the corps to the government of the host state in the defence of common interests.[254] The dean also performs advisory functions within the corps on local protocol and etiquette. In countries having a Roman Catholic tradition, it was common practice for the diplomatic representative of the Holy See, the nuntius, to assume the status of doyen and taking precedence over the other HoMs, regardless of their seniority in the diplomatic corps. The tradition is referred to and approved in Article 16(3) VCDR, although, since 1994, the Holy See indicates that it no longer expects a de jure entitlement to the post of doyen.[255] In Belgium, the ceremonial tradition is still adhered to.[256]

In the EU's passive legation practice, the order of precedence is determined, exactly like in national practices, by the date and time at which the HoMs presented their credentials to the presidents (Art 16(1–2) VCDR). Precedence among the diplomatic staff of the mission is determined by the mission itself (Artis 13–14 and 17 VCDR). A list of ambassadors of third states accredited to the Union, in order of precedence, is available on the website of the Commission's Protocol Service;[257] there is no similar list for representatives of the member states or IOs and non-state entities. This entails that the ambassador of, among others, Palestine, the Order of Malta, and the African Union are not part of the EU's list of heads of mission.[258] In accordance with the former Catholic tradition, the EU opted to preserve the papal nuntius as the doyen of the diplomatic corps accredited to the Union. The accredited ambassador of longest standing assists the papal nuncio as vice-doyen and replaces them in their absence.[259] Ambassadors accredited to Belgium take precedence over the permanent representatives and HoMs accredited to the EU; those permanent representatives and HoMs to the EU in turn take precedence over their colleagues accredited to NATO. However, for an event primarily of interest to the Union (eg Europe Day) or for a ceremony where the invitations are issued by an HoM accredited to the Union permanent representatives to the Union will take precedence over the HoMs accredited to Belgium.[260]

In the Union's active legation practice, the application of Article 16 VCDR and accompanying rules of protocol have caused more ripples. EU HoDs are considered heads of mission of equivalent rank to ambassadors or nuncios in accordance with Article 14(1) VCDR. Yet, their precedence is established in accordance with the protocol rules of the host country. By its very nature, the system of diplomatic precedence creates competition between diplomatic missions and claiming a place on the diplomatic list has consequences for the remainder of the list. If the EU HoD were to be listed among state representatives, other ambassadors (possibly including those of the EU's own member states) who arrived later would be ranked lower. The Commission traditionally approached the matter with great care. On the one hand, it was reluctant to be listed in the second part of the diplomatic

[253] Salmon, *Droit Diplomatique* (n 5) 97; Plantey (n 30) 254.
[254] Denza, *Diplomatic Law* (n 15) 97; Roberts, *Satow* (n 28) 198.
[255] Denza, *Diplomatic Law* (n 15) 91–92.
[256] Roberts, *Satow* (n 28) 91; Circular note [BE] on 'The accreditation of a diplomatic head of mission in Belgium', 15 April 2011.
[257] See, for an analysis in 1962, Ehrhardt (n 87) 663.
[258] EEAS, 'Order of precedence of Heads of Mission', <https://www.eeas.europa.eu/eeas/order-precedence-heads-mission_en> accessed 3 June 2022.
[259] EEAS, 'Vade-Mecum for the Use of the Diplomatic Corps' (n 90) para V.
[260] Dopagne, Duquet, and Theeuwes (n 88) 34.

list, alongside representatives of IOs. On the other, it also deliberately avoided an apparent pleading to be equal to states.[261] The pragmatic solution was to ask for HoDs to be registered at the end of the first part of the list comprising of the heads of state missions holding the rank of ambassador but before heads of mission of lower rank. Translating this into legal terms, the self-imposed 'freezing of seniority' boils down to a voluntary derogation from the seniority rules laid down in Articles 13 and 16 VCDR. The practice further implied that the non-discrimination principle stipulated in Article 47 VCDR would not be invoked by EUDELs in relation to this issue.

Following Lisbon, the EEAS altered this policy and asked, in the spirit of the VCDR, for the EUDELs to be treated like national embassies. This was motivated by external reasons and the place the EU occupies in the world, as well as by functional reasons. The position of the EU HoD within the group of EU ambassadors represented locally had become difficult: it was considered counter-intuitive for the EU HoD to be chairing meetings of the member states' HoM while permanently being of lower rank. The EEAS instructed its delegations to make it known to the host state through a démarche that there would be no more voluntary waiver of seniority since the EU would no longer derogate from Articles 13 and 16 VCDR. This made local rules on seniority (and, where relevant, the alphabetical listing) of represented states applicable to the Union insofar as the host states were willing to accept this.

Practice indeed shows that a number of states continue to apply the former system, listing the EU HoD at the end of the first part of the diplomatic list. The EEAS does not object to this either, counting on a slow but steady change over time. The change in EEAS policy has modified practice in other states, quite a number of which now include the HoD among state ambassadors. It even occurred that the EU HoD in Nepal was asked, on the basis of seniority, to take on the function of doyen of the local *corps diplomatique*. The EEAS authorized its representative to accept and confirm this important position on the understanding that it had not been actively pursued and did not face serious opposition from the locally represented member states. Depending on comparable invitations by other receiving states, this mixed practice may lead to wider acceptance in future, thus adding to broader complete recognition of EUDELs in diplomatic corps. At the same time, the fragility of the EEAS's claims were exposed in 2019, when the Trump administration downgraded for a brief while the diplomatic status of the EU HoD to that of an IO without notice. In 2016, the Obama administration had accepted the EEAS démarche to change the Diplomatic Corps Order of Precedence to recognize the protocol status of the EU Ambassador to the United States as being equivalent to national ambassadors. The EU Ambassador, who had served since 2014 in Washington DC, had to find out he was downgraded from protocol position 20 to number 150 during President George H.W. Bush's state funeral without prior notice by the Trump administration, which was uncomfortable to say the least. Importantly, neither the VCDR, nor the personal immunities of the HoD, nor those of the delegation were put into question by the United States; the spat concerned a protocol discussion rather than a legal discussion. After discovering the downgrade, the Union and member states' diplomats in Washington reached out to the State Department. The matter was ultimately settled over a number of weeks in March 2019, when the United States decided to annul its decision amidst important EU–US trade negotiations. The EU foreign affairs spokesperson said in this regard that the EU was 'pleased that the United States took the decision to revert to usual practice'.

[261] Wouters and Duquet, 'New Horizons?' (n 33) 43.

### 4.3.4 Diplomatic Symbolism: Flags, Emblems, and Anthems

One of the functions of a diplomatic mission is to represent the sending state in the receiving state (Art 3(1)(*a*) VCDR). A diplomatic practice crucial to this is the use of symbols—a national flag, an emblem, a plaque, or the national anthem—as a practical means of representation abroad.[262] Article 20 VCDR sets out the basic right of a diplomatic mission to display the flag and emblem of the sending state on the premises of the mission and on the residence of its head as well as on the mission's means of transport.[263] Beyond the firmly established right to fly a flag in the Vienna Convention, the reciprocity principle regulates the specific conduct of flag-flying privileges. As such, diverse bilateral practices were established across the globe.[264] The right to play the national anthem does not even have a treaty basis.[265] Unlike the privilege of flying the national flag publicly, international usage limits the privilege to perform the national anthem to private occasions.

In 1985, the EU heads of state and government adopted the recommendations made by the ad hoc Committee on a People's Europe on symbols of Europe. The Committee, chaired by Pietro Adonnino, formalized the use of the European flag (a blue rectangle with a circle of 12 five-pointed gold stars in the centre) and the European anthem (the fourth movement of Beethoven's Ninth Symphony—Ode to Joy—as arranged by Herbert von Karajan).[266] Ever since, the Commission, and later the EEAS, have made use of their rights under the VCDR and the international custom to display the European flag and to play the European anthem in the diplomatic context. Therefore, it is an example of diplomatic symbolism and conduct in relation to which the EEAS generally does not encounter many complications abroad. This has not always been the case. Before the Lisbon Treaty, Dimier and McGeever referred to Commission delegations as 'diplomats without a flag' and it was generally known that the Commission had to approach flag flying with caution due to sensitivities of the member states and their respective diplomatic services. As the authors put it, 'various moves were made tending to introduce the use of the emblem in this context "selectively" or "progressively" or even "discreetly" which all came up against the difficulty that flags and pennants are not instruments of discretion but are meant to be noticed'.[267] Moreover, in the international arena, flag flying was traditionally considered a state's prerogative, which brought about rights and obligations under international law. This is probably one of the reasons the right to fly a flag was discussed in the 1959 van der Goes van Naters report on the Communities' right of legation:

> Le pavillon est propre à un État ou à un autre sujet de droit international. Arborer un pavillon a des conséquences juridiques, basées ou sur la coutume internationale, ou sur des conventions navales ou aériennes. Il implique des droits et des devoirs.[268]

[262] Eileen Young (Denza), 'The Development of the Law of Diplomatic Relations' (1964) 40 BYIL 141, 170.
[263] Salmon, *Droit Diplomatique* (n 5) 133.
[264] Pancracio (n 116) 220.
[265] Michael JL Hardy, *Modern Diplomatic Law* (Manchester UP 1968) 42.
[266] Conclusions of the Milan European Council [1985] Bull EC 6/1985.
[267] Dimier and McGeever (n 248) 497.
[268] Commission des Affaires Politiques et des Questions Institutionnelles de l'Assemblée Parlementaire Européenne (APE), Rapport sur les problèmes que posent les relations des Communautés européennes avec l'extérieur, en particulier le droit de légation et de pavillon (Rapporteur: Marinus van der Goes van Naters) 9 November 1959, Doc 87/1959, and Rapport complémentaire, 17 November 1960, Doc 88/1960–61, para 16: 'A flag is specific to a state or another subject of international law. Flying a flag has legal consequences, based either on international custom or on naval or air conventions. It implies rights and duties' [own translation].

Under the VCDR, host states may still restrict usage to special occasions to avoid violent reactions in the host state.[269] The counterpart to the display of a national flag on an embassy is in fact the obligation of the receiving state under diplomatic law to protect those premises. Where a flag is flown, international law imposes a particularly high duty of protection on host states. Denza argues in this respect that the existence and rationale for the greater duty imposed on the receiving state to protect an embassy flying its flag stems from the symbolic character of that flag since it has 'long made it an attractive target for demonstrators'.[270] The VCDR creates a positive obligation for the receiving state to take all appropriate steps to protect diplomatic premises against 'any intrusion or damage' and 'to prevent any disturbance of the peace of the premises or impairment of their dignity' (Art 22(2) VCDR). One may thus conclude that the acceptance by receiving states of the Union flying its own flag is not legally insignificant. On the contrary, it is closely linked to the manner in which host states observe other provisions of the Vienna Convention, in particular those on the inviolability of diplomatic premises. If the receiving state does not provide appropriate protection against intrusion on diplomatic premises or the occurrence of damage, it must make reparations for the injury caused.[271]

How much weight still should be accorded to international sensitivities is a moot point. Flying a national flag in a foreign territory is probably less sensitive now than in the past, and a legal explanation for the smooth acceptance of EU flag flying in receiving states may be the assumption that the right to fly the European flag does not exclude similar exercise of this right by other missions. Since all missions may simultaneously fly their own flag, it is unlikely that one of them should protest against similar usage by EUDELs. Member states too seem to have adjusted to the idea that the EU presents itself as a diplomatic actor abroad—including the visualization of the practice. Since the Lisbon reform, which resulted in the delegations representing the Union and no longer just one institution, it is easier for delegations to use the EU's common symbols. As a counterpart, states are guaranteed, on a reciprocal basis, the right to fly a flag in Brussels on the premises of their mission to the EU.

Delegations representing the EU are specifically instructed by the EEAS Headquarters on the use of the European flag and anthem, which are adapted in line with local custom. For instance, during an official ceremony organized by the EUDEL in a host country, the anthem of the host country is always played before the European anthem. The EEAS also accepts that EUDELs are subject to the general duty laid down in Article 41 VCDR to respect the laws and regulations of the receiving state when doing so. As such, they have to comply with regulations and modalities promulgated by the receiving country on the use of symbols by (national) diplomats. Most flags are flown all year long. Other appropriate occasions to fly flags are the national days of the sending and receiving states, principal public holidays, or even the birthday of the head of the receiving state. The flag may be flown at half-mast in the event of the death of a head of state or a disaster.[272] In its capacity as a receiving diplomatic actor, the EU, in turn, requests diplomatic missions accredited to the Union to fly their national flag over their chancellery building and, if they so wish, over the residence of their HoM, at least on Europe Day (9 May, marking the anniversary of the declaration by Robert Schuman on the establishment of the European Coal and Steel Community (ECSC)

[269] Denza, *Diplomatic Law* (n 15) 102.

[270] ibid. In the same sense: Roberts, *Satow* (n 28) 201.

[271] *Tehran Hostage* case (n 6) para 95; Jan Wouters, Sanderijn Duquet, and Katrien Meuwissen, 'The Vienna Conventions on Diplomatic and Consular Relations' in Cooper, Heine, and Thakur (n 49) 519.

[272] Roberts, *Satow* (n 28) 201.

in 1950). In Belgium, the practice of flying the flag of the sending state on the premises of the mission throughout the year is accepted and relatively widespread. That being said, the sending state is invited to fly its flag at the very least on the Belgian national day (21 July), the Belgian Feast of the dynasty (15 November), and during special ceremonies as determined by the host state's domestic regulation. Embassies and permanent missions of EU member states can hoist the European flag together with the national flag on the premises of its mission in Belgium.[273] Appropriate occasions to play the European anthem are official ceremonies organized by the EU (for instance, at the occasion of special celebrations such as Europe Day or 25 March, a date that marks the anniversary of the signing of the Treaty of Rome in 1957) and—depending on the protocol of each host country—during official visits or when HoDs present their credentials.

## 4.4 Diplomatic Law Not Covered by the VCDR

The EU's confidence in the 1961 Vienna Convention as the appropriate legal framework for its diplomatic endeavours was an instant hit. Through specific agreements with the host country, the Union shared in the successes of bilateral diplomacy and its constricted legal regime. This system also has its limits. While the VCDR comprehensively governs most aspects of diplomatic life, it is not all-encompassing: the body of law on international diplomatic relations also goes above and beyond the 1961 Convention. This section addresses two such topics that, for various reason, have not been codified: the use of diplomatic passports, the issuance of visa to diplomats and their family, and the practice of diplomatic asylum.

### 4.4.1 Diplomatic Passports

#### 4.4.1.1 Legal Value

A diplomatic passport is a travel document that certifies the identity and nationality of its holder as well as their mandate to travel on official government business. It is issued at the discretion of the issuing country primarily—but not exclusively—to those on diplomatic assignment and their accompanying dependents. Member states also issue diplomatic passports to citizens that are high-ranking EU officials such as the Presidents of the Commission, the European Council, and the CJEU. The main purpose is to communicate the diplomatic rank of the passport's holder and facilitate their international travel: among its benefits are the easy passage at borders (separate immigration queues at security, immigration, and custom controls) and simplified procedures to obtain a visa.[274] Beyond these facilities, which remain at the discretion of the foreign country, the diplomatic passport brings about few legal obligations under international law. US case law famously holds that a diplomatic passport might secure certain courtesies in international travel but is 'without significance in international law'.[275] Moreover, although the diplomatic passport is a globally accepted

[273] Response of the Minister of Foreign Affairs [BE] to the question of Member Lagasse, 20 February 1990 [1989–90] Bull QR, No 98.

[274] Ralph G Feltham, *Diplomatic Handbook* (8th edn, Martinus Nijhoff 2004) 42.

[275] Denza, *Diplomatic Law* (n 15) 258; US District Court, Southern District of Florida [US] 8 June 1990, 99 ILR 143, 165–67.

instrument, its use is not regulated by the VCDR. The Convention merely spells out that a general right to passage exists to take up or return to a diplomatic post, or when returning to their own country (Art 40). While in transit, a diplomatic agent receives 'inviolability and such other immunities as may be required to ensure his transit or return'.

The consequences are twofold. First, despite the fact that a diplomatic passport assists diplomatic agents in demonstrating their diplomatic status vis-à-vis foreign authorities in order to effectively claim the benefits of their privileges and immunities, it is not necessarily sufficient to prove diplomatic status.[276] It is a receiving state's prerogative to accredit diplomats as well as to issue a document that evidences for internal purposes that the holder is entitled to diplomatic treatment, privileges, and immunities. Most receiving states attest diplomatic accreditation by issuing their own diplomatic identity card to foreign diplomats. In Belgium, the diplomatic identity card serves as proof of the diplomatic status of its holder, including with respect to local courts and tribunals, which are therefore required to accord the person concerned the privileges and immunities associated with that status.[277] The diplomatic identity card issued by the host state is often seen as the only authoritative identity document of a foreign diplomat.[278] However, in the period before accreditation and during travel, the production of a diplomatic passport ought to be sufficient to demonstrate diplomatic status and rank, even though local authorities can always ask for additional evidence. It is generally accepted as sufficient evidence of status in order for diplomats to enjoy privileges as 'diplomats in transit' (Art 40 VCDR), to enjoy the exemption from personal baggage inspection at the border (Art 36(2) VCDR), and to enjoy their privileges and immunities from the moment they enter the receiving state's territory (Art 39(1) VCDR). Second, the issuance of a diplomatic passport by a sending state does not exempt the holder from obtaining, where relevant, the necessary visa that regulate their stay in a receiving state. Typically, states have a special visa category reserved for foreign diplomats, which can be obtained after a simplified procedure.

#### 4.4.1.2 The Belgian Practice

Belgian practices with regard to diplomatic missions to the EU and their staff correspond with what has been explained above. In order to enter Belgian territory with a view to taking up their duties, foreign diplomatic staff must be issued with a valid passport (usually a diplomatic passport) mentioning, where relevant, the diplomatic grade of its holder, and carrying an appropriate visa (type D) issued by a diplomatic or consular post located or accredited to the sending state. Visa waivers are granted to certain foreign diplomats in accordance with *(a)* EU law principles on the free movement of citizens (Art 21 TFEU), *(b)* agreements concluded between Belgium (or the Benelux countries) and third countries,[279] and *(c)* agreements concluded between the EU and third countries. Bilateral treaties of this last kind have been signed which give the parties reciprocal access to short-stay visa-free travel for holders of diplomatic passports. An EU–China agreement explicitly grants holders of European laissez-passer documents the same rights on the basis of

[276] Salmon, *Droit Diplomatique* (n 5) 167.

[277] Circular note [BE], 'Administrative procedure for the accreditation of members of diplomatic staff and administrative and technical staff of diplomatic missions in Belgium and their family members', 10 June 2012.

[278] See also: State Department (US), 'Diplomatic and Consular Immunity: Guidance for Law Enforcement and Judicial Authorities', 17, <https://2009-2017.state.gov/documents/organization/149734.pdf> accessed 4 May 2022.

[279] Dopagne, Duquet, and Theeuwes (n 88) 30.

reciprocity.[280] In relation to diplomats of African, Caribbean, and Pacific (ACP) countries accredited to the Union, the EU member states have pledged to facilitate the issuance of visa.[281]

#### 4.4.1.3 The EU Laissez-Passer

##### *4.4.1.3.1 EU diplomatic travel documents*

When the EU sends out its diplomats, their use of diplomatic passports is not obvious. Not being a state, the Union is prevented under PIL from issuing (diplomatic) passports. This situation complicates EU diplomats' international travel. The problem is less stringent for seconded national experts (SNEs) working for the EEAS, as they are likely to already have a diplomatic passport issued by their national governments. Moreover, some member states (eg Belgium) deliver a national diplomatic passport to EU officials of their nationality working in delegations as a matter of principle. But precisely this situation—factual and legal inequalities within the EU's diplomatic service—can give rise to tensions within EUDELs.

An EU alternative has been found for those diplomatic agents that do not receive a national diplomatic passport: the EU issues them a laissez-passer (EULP) document. The notion of *laissez-passer* has a long and interesting account in international relations.[282] The etymology of the phrase can be traced back to Biblical Hebrew, where it was defined as the act of a sovereign allowing a group of people to pass on their territory: the expression, meaning 'let pass', is referred to in the Old Testament where the king of Edom refuses to grant permission to civilians to pass through his land. A 'grant of passage' has been used in situations of warrant in relation to refugees. Both the Covenant of the League of Nations (Art 16) and the UN Charter (Art 43) refer to the right of passage for military forces for the purpose of maintaining international peace and security. At the outbreak of the First World War in 1914, the neutral Kingdom of Belgium was requested to grant 'free passage of German troops through her territory', which provoked the question whether this could be done without violating PIL.[283] In international refugee law, the concept of laissez-passer refers to a grant of passage by a state to individual asylum seekers or stateless persons enabling a safe return.

The use of the term 'laissez-passer' in the world of IOs has its origins in UN practices. Before the adoption of the system of international LPs, it was advocated that IOs should be granted to right to issue fully fledged diplomatic passports to their agents.[284] Article VII, section 24 of the 1946 Convention on the Privileges and Immunities of the United Nations (CPIUN), however, tasks UN member states' authorities to recognize and accept the UNLP as a valid travel document. The original European Community comprising six member states adopted the UN system and some of the language in the CPIUN when it started to produce its own travel document to high officials.

[280] See, for instance, the Agreement between the European Union and the Federative Republic of Brazil on short-stay visa waiver for holders of diplomatic, service or official passports [2011] OJ L66/2; Art 3(1) of the Agreement between the European Union and the Republic of Peru on the short-stay visa waiver [2016] OJ L78/4; Agreement between the European Union and the People's Republic of China on the short-stay visa waiver for holders of diplomatic passports [2016] OJ L76/19. The Chinese agreement explicitly grants holders of EULPs the same rights on the basis of reciprocity.

[281] ACP–EEC Cooperation Agreements, Annex LXXII, Declaration by the member states relating to Protocol 3.

[282] No 20:21, 21:23, Judg 3:28, as referred to by Richard C Steiner, 'A Jewish Aramaic (or Hebrew) Laissez-Passer from the Egyptian Port of Berenike' (2004) 63 J Near East Studs 277, 279.

[283] James W Garner, 'Some Questions of International Law in the European War' (1916) 10 AJIL 12.

[284] Josef L Kunz, 'Privileges and Immunities of International Organizations' (1947) 41 AJIL 828, 856; Anthony J Miller, 'Privileges and Immunities of United Nations Officials' (2007) 4 IOLR 169, 178.

The use of the EULP has expanded greatly over time. The laissez-passer may be issued to members and servants of all Union institutions by their presidents, as well as to EEAS officials. The categories allowed to apply are officials in grade AD 12–AD 16, officials serving outside the EU, and other officials for whom the use of the EULP is required in the interest of the EEAS.[285] Since Article 6(7) of the EEAS Decision states that officials of the Union and temporary agents coming from the diplomatic services of the member states have the same rights and obligations and should be treated equally, they can also be issued an EULP.[286]

Much like a diplomatic passport, the EULP does not grant diplomatic status but determines its holder's quality as an EU official and their rank and title when residing outside the EU. Likewise, it does not replace a national passport or identity card. As explained earlier, according to the EU Treaties, the Commission concludes agreements for these laissez-passer to be recognized as valid travel documents within the territory of third states.[287] In practice, however, EULP clauses now feature in the EAs concluded by the HR.[288] As regards the number of EULPs issued, figures show that the impact of the creation of the EEAS did not lead to a major increase in the number of LPs issued.

*4.4.1.3.2 Continued problems with the EULP*

The EULP provokes a number of problems. It remains unclear whether all foreign authorities at border crossings acknowledge the laissez-passer documents. Unlike the UN, which is dealing with its own member states only, the EU has to convince third states to recognize the EULP. There is the practical issue that an immigration officer in a local airport may not know of the existence of an EULP. As only about 10,000 EULPs have been issued to date, the documents do not frequently pass an officer's desk. Even member states' border police are not always aware of the EULP.[289] While its goal is to testify of diplomatic privileges and immunities there is no legal guarantee that Vienna Convention rules will be accordingly applied to travelling EU envoys. The situation is further complicated in cases when an EU diplomatic agent is not travelling directly to the country of destination—that is, the state where they are accredited—but instead passes through a third country while proceeding to take up or to return to their post or when returning to their own country. In this situation, it is hard to predict to what extent foreign authorities will accept the laissez-passer document as an alternative diplomatic passport or how they will apply inviolability and such immunities as may be required to ensure the EU diplomat's transit or return, as provided for in Article 40 VCDR dealing with the passage of a diplomatic agent through or stay in the territory of a third state. In practice, some EU diplomats rather use their receiving state-issued diplomatic identity card to smoothen a re-entry in the country of posting when that diplomat has not been issued a diplomatic passport by the member states of nationality.

More fundamental is the problem of the EULP's legal basis. A provision on the EULP has been inserted in the EAs only in the past twenty-five years, which means that recognition in some countries with older EAs lacking such clause is customary. Moreover, the network of EAs is not complete: countries that did not enter into an EA but opted to unilaterally

285 Article 23 EU Staff Regulations.

286 Answer to written parliamentary question E-5691/2010, 22 July 2010.

287 Article 6 of Protocol No 7 on the Privileges and Immunities of the European Union, attached to the EU Treaties [2012] OJ C326/266 (hereafter Protocol No 7).

288 See Chapter 3 for a discussion on the EAs.

289 Answer by the Commission to written parliamentary question E-002396/2011, 18 April 2011

recognize the right of legation of the EU also recognize the EULP in practice without legal agreement.[290]

There are also security concerns. Some third states do not (or until recently did not) recognize the EULP in its pre-2013 form as a valid travel document. Many point out that compared to a diplomatic passport, the EULP had outmoded security features and form. Explicit requests to update the EULP were made by the United States, Canada, and Japan, as well as by the UN Headquarters in New York. Other countries that did not recognize the EULP were: Antigua and Barbuda, the Bahamas, Bahrain, Iceland, Israel,; Jordan, Kuwait, Lebanon, Liberia, Malaysia, Montenegro, Netherlands Antilles, New Caledonia, Panama, Qatar, São Tomé and Príncipe,; Serbia, Somalia, Taiwan—Republic of China, Thailand, Tunisia, Tuvalu, Uzbekistan, and Palestine. Moreover, Russia, India, Saudi Arabia, and some major African countries also indicated that they would start requiring additional security guarantees.[291] Indeed, the laissez-passer for a long time was not compliant with international standards of the International Civil Aviation Organization (ICAO).[292]

Given the EULP's widespread use and importance, the Commission presented a Communication to the Council in 2007 in which it underlined the urgency of reviewing its form.[293] According to Article 6 Protocol No 7 on Privileges and Immunities, the form of the EULP should be 'prescribed by the Council, acting by a simple majority'. While the provision does not envisage a formal initiative by the Commission, it included a 'Draft Council Regulation' in its Communication in a spirit of mutual aid between the institutions. In addition to the outlined international complexities, five problems were identified as stumbling blocks: the EULP's *(a)* security, including with regard to the introduction of biometrical features (face- and fingerprints); *(b)* content; *(c)* layout and cover page; *(d)* use of language; and *(e)* period of validity. Due to international pressure, stress was mainly on the development of an EULP that is up to international standards concerning both security and ease of use rather than questions of diplomatic law. The EULP's physical quality needed to improve and be made machine readable, while it had to become possible for biometric data to be inserted.

Following prolonged discussions, it was the establishment of the EEAS that put the EULP's modernization back on the agenda. In the second half of 2013, the Lithuanian Presidency, assisted by a concerted Commission/EEAS effort, made it a priority topic. This resulted in the adoption of the 2013 Council Regulation defining the form of laissez-passer issued by the Union.[294] The document is now produced in all official EU languages—against the ICAO's recommendation of a three-language regime, which would have increased readability (Art 3). It is valid for a maximum period of six years, which can be adapted to the length stay or of posting (Art 4). The Council further took the security standards and biometrics for passports and other travel documents issued by member states (as provided for by Council Regulation 2252/2004)[295] as a basis for establishing the security standards of the EULP (Art 6).

[290] Internal survey (2013), conducted by the EEAS, in all its EUDELs (reported to the author in a letter dated 1 April 2014).

[291] Council, Presidency paper on the Laissez-Passer—document partially accessible to the public, 7 October 2013, 22–26.

[292] ICAO, Doc 9303: 'Machine Readable Travel Documents' (7th edn 2015).

[293] Commission, 'Communication on the Draft Council Regulation laying down the form of the laissez-passer issued to members and servants of the institutions', COM 2007/0849 final.

[294] Council Regulation 1417/2013 laying down the form of the laissez-passer issued by the European Union [2013] OJ L353/26. See also Council Decision 2015/2020 delegating to the Secretary-General of the Council the power to issue laissez-passer to members, officials and other servants of the European Council and of the Council [2015] OJ L295/42.

[295] Council Regulation 2252/2004 on standards for security features and biometrics in passports and travel documents issued by member states [2004] OJ L385/1.

During and following the introduction of the new EULP in 2015, the Union started a campaign to make the document publicly known: specimen kits for local governments were distributed through the EUDELs, the EULP was included in document databases, and the website <www.laissez-passer.eu> was launched.

Another issue is that the EU Treaties do not make reference to the use of the EULP by members of the household of an EU diplomat. It is the sending state that defines who forms part of the household of a diplomat, which can either be refused or accepted by the receiving state.[296] The EULP is only issued to family members of Union agents working in EUDELs in exceptional circumstances, 'when so required', and upon due motivation. Family members qualify as 'special applicants' in the sense of Article 1(1) of the Council Regulation, when they are family members of *(a)* a member of an EU institution, *(b)* other servants of the Union who fulfil the conditions laid down in Article 23 of the Staff Regulations (eg EEAS officials); *(c)* SNEs; and *(d)* junior professionals (Art 1, Annex II). The term 'family member' is further defined in Annex II of the Regulation as 'spouse or registered partner, the unmarried partner, the dependent children'. This definition does not exclude same-sex partners of diplomats from applying for an EULP, even when the member state of nationality does not recognize same-sex marriage or partnerships.

Despite its shortcomings, the EULP remains a crucial instrument of EU diplomacy. In fact, it is the only internationally recognized document that directly links the holder with the EU institutions. In diplomatic practice, the EULP facilitates the application process installed by third states for obtaining visas. Moreover, it eases the delivery of visas in third countries, including special diplomatic entry and residence visas, which can be attached to this document. This is crucial since most countries do not deliver diplomatic visas on normal national passports. In that sense, the EULP's upgraded security features ensure its complete reliability, in particular in order to match host third countries' increasingly sophisticated machine-assisted document-reading systems. In 2019, the International Organization for Standardization (ISO) assigned a new three-letter-code 'EUE' for the EULP; since 2017, the EU is a member of the ICAO Public Key Directory (PKD).

### 4.4.2 Diplomatic Visa and Same-Sex Relationships

In the autumn of 2015, the EUDEL in a third state (which will remain undisclosed but which has entered into an EA with the Union) received, together with all other embassies and missions present in the country, a note verbale from the local MFA. The note clarified the receiving state's position with regard to same-sex partners of diplomatic agents, stating that it would not issue family visas or residence permits to same-sex partners of accredited diplomats. The partners would still be allowed to apply for 'guest visas' that do not give access to the same level of immunities and protection. This is, unfortunately, not an isolated case: while LGBTQ+ rights have made considerable progress, many countries do not recognize same-sex relationships. According to Human Rights Watch, in 2021, at least sixty-nine countries had national laws criminalizing same-sex relations between consenting adults. Some, but not all, of these third countries reflect these approaches in their policies vis-à-vis foreign diplomats.

[296] Eileen Denza, 'Le Passeport Européen' (1982) *25* Rev du Marché Commun 489.

The VCDR does not directly address diplomats and their families' visa duty. Although a diplomatic agent is not exempt from the obligation to obtain a visa, as soon as the *agrément* is given, the visa application should be a formality. Article 7 VCDR permits the sending state to freely appoint the members of the staff of the mission, but this entitlement, quite obviously, does not say much of diplomatic agents' family members' situation. What is more, the VCDR fully subscribes to principles of state sovereignty, including the idea that state exercises control over the territory (including the access to it) and all persons and goods therein. The second recital of the VCDR's preamble refers to the principle of sovereign equality of state as laid down in the Article 2(1) UN Charter. Moreover, within its territory, a state exercises judicial, legislative, and executive jurisdiction. The enjoyment of VCDR immunities and privileges should be seen as an exceptional and voluntary restriction by states on their exclusive jurisdiction. Consequently, although it does not say as much, the Vienna Convention leaves the receiving state to regulate visa and residence permits of diplomats, including visa of family members joining the agent. The Convention's travaux préparatoires explicate that the 'free choice of staff mentioned in [Art 7 VCDR] does not imply exemption from visa formalities, where these are required by the receiving state'.[297] Moreover, while the receiving state may not discriminate 'as between States' (Art 47 VCDR), nothing in the Convention oppose visa practices that are discriminatory on a personal level, within a mission. Yet, the receiving state's refusal to grant a visa and/or privileges and immunities to a fully accredited diplomatic agent's family members conflicts with general principles of diplomatic law.

Discriminatory practices affect the Union too. Article 3(1) of the bilateral EA specifically accords the 'members of the families forming part of their respective households' the VCDR 'rights, privileges and immunities'. Visas and residence permits are not 'rights, privileges and immunities' as contained in the VCDR because there is no entitlement to them under diplomatic law. Yet, the refusal of a visa has the sole objective of barring same-sex partners from enjoying privileges and immunities; it constitutes an improper use of a receiving state's rights. The VCDR draws on a strong functional necessity rationale.[298] Diplomatic privileges and immunities are accorded to diplomatic agents *and* their family members out of a functional need: the special status in the receiving states allows diplomats to effectively perform their task without having to fear threats by the host state's government. There is, moreover, a positive duty to make sure diplomats can effectively perform their tasks. Article 25 VCDR obliges the receiving state to 'accord full facilities for the performance of the functions of the mission' and Article 21 demands receiving states to facilitate 'the acquisition on its territory, in accordance with its laws, by the sending State of premises necessary for its mission or assist the latter in obtaining accommodation in some other way'. Diplomatic immunity prevents the receiving states from prosecuting diplomats and their families or issuing threats in that regard. Especially in a country that has fundamentally different views on what constitutes a relationship than a sending state, such protection is much needed. Moreover, in subsidiary order, an argument can be made on the basis of Article 26 VCDR on the freedom of movement of diplomatic agents. Although the provision concerns the free movement *within* the receiving state and is therefore not applicable directly to visa applications, Salmon argues that it entails that diplomatic agents should benefit from a preferential treatment to enter and reside in the receiving state compared to 'normal foreigners'.[299] A final argument concerns the reciprocity of immunities and privileges. Since Belgium accords diplomatic family status

297 ILC, 'Draft Articles on Diplomatic Intercourse' (n 29) 92.
298 ibid 95.
299 Salmon, *Droit Diplomatique* (n 5) 353–54.

to same-sex spouses and partners of the third state's mission to the EU, one may expect the third state to reciprocate the treatment. Legally, this argument would boil down to an application of Article 47(2)(*b*). The third state could argue that by recognizing same-sex couples, Belgium is giving something 'extra'; an additional privilege that it is not legally obliged to give under the VCDR. If that is the case, the third state is under no obligation to reciprocate the 'additional' privilege.

This dossier confronts the EU with a dilemma of law and diplomacy. The EEAS faces two paths. A first option would be to immediately oppose third state policies on the basis of legal or political arguments. If the third state persists, the EU could opt to enter into consultations. More than half of the EAs between the Union and third states provide that parties resort to such talks in the event of disputes concerning the interpretation of the Agreement. This is in line with diplomatic law, which indicates that sending and receiving states have to try to mutually agree on a definition of the term 'family members' through negotiations. A second option would be for the EEAS to adapt its own policies and stop sending diplomats to a third country that does not recognize their partner. The legitimation is that, without a special status in the receiving state, the diplomatic agent and their partner's safety cannot be guaranteed. While a direct confrontation with the third country will be avoided, this, of course, risks being perceived as a de facto acceptance of a host state policy that goes against the EU's general stance on human rights and the protection of individual rights of its officials.

## 4.4.3 Diplomatic Asylum

### 4.4.3.1 Seeking Refuge at a Diplomatic Mission

Urgent requirements of humanity every so often cause diplomats to take unusual measures. One such possibility is the granting of diplomatic asylum in order to help an individual escape persecution by the host state. In certain cases, a temporary stay at the mission may be warranted, when a person is fleeing from an imminent danger (eg a violent mob). Occasionally, diplomatic premises of EU member states have served this purpose. The granting of refuge for humanitarian reasons is accepted by at least Belgium, France, the Netherlands, Spain, and Sweden in their practices as sending states.[300] Although the nature and scope of such sanctuary are debated, it is often stressed that its character is humanitarian rather than political—drawing a distinction with the traditional conception of diplomatic asylum, which has political undertones.

The practical viability of refuge in a diplomatic mission is facilitated by diplomatic law. Under the VCDR, states can apply their rights in a way that allows for the temporary guarding of an individual. Article 22(1) VCDR, conferring inviolability on the premises of the diplomatic mission, prevents the removal of an individual by local authorities without due consent. At the same time, Article 41(3) VCDR promulgates that a mission's premises may not be used 'in any manner incompatible with [diplomatic] functions'. Article 41(1) VCDR simultaneously imposes an obligation on the sending state and its diplomats not to interfere in the internal affairs of the receiving state and to abide by local laws. Because of their subjection to diplomatic law, EUDELs are able to grant refuge in a manner similar to national missions by means of the general inviolability rules. Both the EUDEL's premises and

[300] See, for examples by member states, ibid 236; Chatterjee (n 145) 233; Susanne Riveles, 'Diplomatic Asylum as a Human Right: The Case of the Durban Six' (1989) 11 HRQ 139.

the residence of its HoD fall under the scope of the VCDR (Article 1(*i*) VCDR). Unlike the UN Headquarters Agreement, which explicitly prohibits refuge, EAs concluded by the EU do not encompass a derogation from the VCDR.[301]

Diplomatic asylum remains a particularly controversial issue. The ICJ specified that a right of diplomatic asylum is not recognized under general international law. The topic was studied by the UNGA and the ILC at various sessions without an agreement being reached.[302] However, humanitarian shelter in diplomatic premises is broadly accepted for persons fleeing from imminent danger.[303] The extraterritorial application of the non-refoulement principle, with references to embassies and consulates, has been addressed by the ECtHR.[304] Moreover, a general obligation not to push back individuals into the arms of their persecutors can be derived from general human rights law as well as from the Charter, which has been accorded the status of primary Union law by the Treaty of Lisbon.[305] The Charter's Article 19(2) reflects the fundamental principle of non-refoulement, entrenched in international refugee and human rights law, and expands it explicitly to all cases of removal, expulsion, or extradition.

While requests for refuge in EUDELs have not yet been reported, individuals have already found their way to the EU's diplomatic missions to call for other forms of assistance.[306] In light of the ever-growing visibility of the EU in third countries and its assistance to human rights defenders, it is conceivable that such requests will continue to occur in the future and that one day there may be an appeal for shelter. The EU is quite outspoken about its human rights commitment, also in external relations and on an individual level. 2015 EU Action Plan on Human Rights and Democracy (HRD), for instance, embraces the intention to streamline shelter schemes for human rights defenders, where it commits to '[s]tep up consistent support to HRD by [ . . . ] increasing burden-sharing and co-ordination between Delegations and Member State Embassies on HRD protection activities' and to 'sharing best practices on relevant mechanisms including temporary shelter schemes and emergency visas'.[307]

### 4.4.3.2 Guidance for EUDELs

Diplomatic asylum in EUDELs has been addressed proactively by the Union, which has resulted in a set of internal guidelines on the matter. These guidelines were first introduced by the Commission's DG Relex and were later updated by the EEAS. The internal guidance shows a certain reluctance to deal with diplomatic asylum cases and a preference to work closely with member state missions in individual cases. The EU may have a number of reasons for not having its missions become safe havens: the lack of in-delegation expertise,

[301] Article 3(9(*b*)) of the Agreement regarding the Headquarters of the United Nations, signed at Lake Success on 26 June 1947, 11 UNTS 11.

[302] *Colombia v Peru* (n 36) paras 274–77.

[303] See already cases before the European Commission on Human Rights: *M v Denmark*, App No 17392/90, 14 October 1992; *X v Federal Republic of Germany*, App No 1611/62, 25 September 1965.

[304] *Banković and others v Belgium and others*, App No 52207/99, 12 December 2001, para 79; *Medvedyev and others v France*, App No 3394/03, 29 March 2010, para 65; *Hirsi Jamaa and others v Italy*, App No 27765/09, 23 February 2012, para 75. For a UK case, see *B and others* [2004] EWCA Civ 1344; [2005] QB 643.

[305] Violeta Moreno-Lax and Cathryn Costello, 'The Extraterritorial Application of the EU Charter of Fundamental Rights: From Territoriality to Facticity, the Effectiveness Model' in S Peers and others (n 143) 547; Jan Wouters, 'The EU Charter of Fundamental Rights—Some Reflections on Its External Dimension' (2001) 8 MJECL 3.

[306] Sanderijn Duquet and Jan Wouters, 'Seeking Refuge in EU Delegations Abroad: A Legal Imbroglio Explored' (2015) 40 ELR 723.

[307] Council, 'The EU Action Plan on Human Rights and Democracy' (2015), section 9(a).

political weight, or physical space to lodge someone, to name just a few. The main gain of having a member state's embassy accommodating the refuge rather than the EUDEL relates to the fact that the EU does not have the legal competence to grant territorial asylum since it is not a state. While this is not a prerequisite for providing temporary refuge, the lack of such competence may bring about additional complications when the Union has to negotiate the safe departure of the protected civilian from the third country to the EU.

EUDELs are encouraged to set up cooperative arrangements in third countries. These can mirror other institutionalized forms of human rights coordination between HoDs and member states' ambassadors. Specific measures can take the form of an informal agreement on the member state most suitable to grant temporary refuge. This can be the 'lead state' in the third country, that is, the member state already responsible for coordinating emergencies or a member states accomplished in assisting individuals in death penalty or torture cases. The EEAS acknowledges that, in cases where the HoD is informed in advance that an individual will seek refuge in the delegation, the individual should be referred to the lead state's embassy. When this is not possible (eg for safety reasons), as well as in cases where there is no agreement between the Union and locally represented member states, the EUDEL's staff (in consultation with EEAS Headquarters) will have to decide whether they want to provide shelter. The HoD has to report a refuge situation immediately to the EEAS Headquarters.

A decision whether or not to assist the refuge-seeker requires practical benchmarks. The EEAS commits to using standards developed by international tribunals to judge an individual situation. These could be, but are not limited to *(a)* the situation in the host country (such as the political situation, the human rights situation, and the respect for the rule of law) and *(b)* the particular case of the refuge-seeker (such as the reasons for persecution, activities exercised by the person(s) concerned, repression/persecution committed by the government). The basic assumption is that an EUDEL has to respect its obligation under PIL to surrender refuge-seekers convicted for ordinary crimes when the receiving state so requests, while not excluding that, exceptionally, the EEAS may be required to decide otherwise given the immediateness and seriousness of the risks faced.

ECtHR case law in refoulement cases provides guidance with regard to the type of circumstances that may warrant granting a refuge. The Court consistently holds that state parties need to assess whether '*substantial grounds* have been shown for believing that the individual concerned, if deported, faces a *real risk* of being subjected to treatment contrary to Article 3'.[308] In a (non-diplomatic) extraterritorial context, the ECtHR found a violation of Article 3 ECHR in a case concerning the transfer of two Iraqi nationals by UK troops in Iraq to the local authorities when there was a serious risk of them being subjected to the death penalty.[309] Exceptionally, cases in which the refuge-seeker is manifestly denied a fair trial may qualify as well.[310]

International case law accepts that not all risks are foreseeable, for example, in the case of a refuge applicant who leaves a diplomatic mission voluntarily.[311] The test for determining

[308] *Akram Karimov v Russia*, App No 62892/12, 28 May 2014, para 117 (emphasis added) and case law cited therein. See also *Mamatkulov and Askarov v Turkey*, App No 46827/99, 4 February 2005, para 67.

[309] *Al-Saadoon and Mufdhi v United Kingdom*, App No 61498/08, 2 March 2010, paras 143–44.

[310] *Soering v United Kingdom*, App No 14038/88, 7 July 1989; Hemme Battjes, 'The Soering Threshold: Why Only Fundamental Values Prohibit Refoulement in ECHR Case Law' (2009) 11 Eur J Migr Law 205, 206.

[311] Human Rights Committee (HRC) Decision 1539/2006, *Munaf v Romania* [2009] CCPR/C/96/D/1539/2006, para 14.6.

whether substantial grounds exist necessitates an examination of both the general human rights conditions in the receiving state and the individual case at hand.[312] EUDELs are accustomed to conduct human rights assessments and tools, ranging from human rights indicators, dialogues, proactive human rights monitoring, coming to the defence of human rights defenders, to country strategies.[313] Another factor, which perhaps is more controversial, is an evaluation of the security consequences for the delegation staff or premises, that is, the existence of possible threats from the persons requesting refuge as well as from the local authorities. In any event, the individual protection granted by an EUDEL is temporary and relative: it has to be granted for the period of time strictly necessary and only if the safety of the individual cannot be guaranteed in any other way.

In the hypothesis that a decision on refuge would be made, the EEAS commits to reach out to the member states represented locally and at the Council level. This not only serves the goal of informing member states but also facilitates the taking of a common EU position on the individual case, providing the EUDEL with the necessary mandate and legitimacy for further actions. If, in light of all information available, it is deemed that no substantial grounds exist for believing that the individual faces a real risk in the receiving state, the refuge-seeker will be asked to leave the EUDEL's premises. If they refuse, the HoD may, with the consent of Headquarters, invite the local authorities to enter the diplomatic premises and remove the asylum seeker. In practice, the EUDEL will draw up a 'consent' to temporarily defer from the rights in Article 22 VCDR for this specific action. Such consent should be detailed and, among other things, spell out the number of police officers that can be involved in the operation and the obligation for them not to touch, read, or take with them any EU property.

However, if the individual is granted EU protection, it can be necessary for the EUDEL to obtain diplomatic assurances from the territorial state, possibly including credible assurances that the sheltered individual will be allowed a safe departure.[314] Pledges by a local government of the receiving state, commonly formulated in legally non-binding notes verbales, should be examined in their practical application. Diplomats have a role to play here: from the Strasbourg case law, it transpires that the track record and intensity of the diplomatic relations between an extraditing state and a third state are important criteria for the trust that can be put in diplomatic assurances.[315] By way of comparison, the Human Rights Committee (HRC) monitoring the implementation of the International Covenant on Civil and Political Rights (ICCPR) found that a visit by the Swedish ambassador five weeks after the return of an expelled individual was insufficient. In its slow follow-up of the diplomatic assurances, Sweden had neglected a considerable period of maximum exposure to risk of harm.[316]

312 *Othman (Abu Qatada) v United Kingdom*, App No 8139/09, 17 January 2012, para 187.

313 See the 2015 EU Action Plan on Human Rights and Democracy (n 307) and the 'Guidelines to EU Policy towards third countries on torture and other cruel, inhuman or degrading treatment or punishment' (2012) 4. For further reading, see Rosa Balfour, *The Role of EU Delegations in EU Human Rights Policy* (European Parliament 2013).

314 Richtsteig (n 42) 47.

315 *MG v Bulgaria*, App No 59297/12, 25 March 2014; *Chahal v the United Kingdom*, App No 22414/93, 15 November 1996, para 105; *MSS v Belgium and Greece*, App No 30696/09, 21 January 2011 para 354.

316 *Alzery v Sweden*, Decision No 1416/2005 [2006] CCPR/C/88/D/1416/2005, para 11.5.

## 4.5 Customary Diplomatic Law

### 4.5.1 Introduction

EU diplomacy's connection with customary diplomatic law, a key source of international diplomatic law, is unclear and somewhat controversial. The EAs do not explicitly refer to CIL as a source of binding law in the relations between the EU and third states, although Protocol No 7 contains such a reference. As a complicating factor, rather than IOs, states are the main actors in the formation and application of CIL: to establish a rule of CIL, one needs to find a general state practice accepted as law by states.[317]

This section examines if and how CIL comes into play when the Union exercises its right of legation. Following a general introduction to CIL as a source of diplomatic law, two different aspects of the relationship between EU diplomacy and CIL are looked at. First, the chapter researches whether established CIL applies to the EU. This concerns the question whether, in their diplomatic activities, EU actors adopt legal acts and modify their behaviour in execution of customary norms, as well as whether these actors can enforce customary norms in their relations with third states. Second, it is investigated whether the EU contributes to the creation of CIL through its diplomatic practices.

### 4.5.2 A Source of Uncertainty

#### 4.5.2.1 The Finding of CIL

Before entering into the discussion regarding the EU's application of and contribution to CIL, it may be useful to revisit general understandings about this source of law. CIL has been the object of extensive scholarly debates throughout the years and still features as a topic in the ILC's long-term programme of work. ILC Special Rapporteur Sir Michael Wood has submitted no less than five reports on the 'identification of customary international law'. Yet, as Jan Klabbers stated, 'although customary law has always been plagued with controversial elements, at least one thing was certain: customary law is, almost by definition, law'.[318] However, despite its legal status and without denigrating the considerable utility of CIL in a great many of circumstances, including in diplomatic law, it must be taken into account that CIL also brings about uncertainty.[319] Rules of customary law require the establishment of evidence of 'a usage felt by those who follow it to be an obligatory one'.[320] Broadly speaking, there are three differing approaches to identifying this obligatory usage.[321] The *traditional approach* is cautious and requires widespread material practice by individual states as well

[317] Article 38(1)(*b*) Statute of the International Court of Justice (18 April 1946) 33 UNTS 993. See generally, David J Bederman, *Custom as a Source of Law* (CUP 2010); Alan Boyle and Christine Chinkin, *The Making of International Law* (OUP 2007); Jean d'Aspremont, *Formalism and the Sources of International Law* (OUP 2011).

[318] Jan Klabbers, *The Concept of Treaty in International Law* (Kluwer 1996) 4.

[319] Jörg Kammerhofer, 'Uncertainty in the Formal Sources of International Law: Customary International Law and Some of Its Problems' (2004) 15 EJIL 523.

[320] James L Brierly, *The Law of Nations: An Introduction to the International Law of Peace* (7th edn, OUP 2016) 57.

[321] See the assessments of Anthony D'Amato, 'The Theory of Customary International Law' (1988) 82 ASILPROC 242; Eric A Posner and Jack L Goldsmith, 'A Theory of Customary International Law' (1999) 66 UCLR 1113. For a critical account, see Andrew T Guzman and Jerome Hsiang, 'Some Ways That Theories on Customary International Law Fail: A Reply to Laszlo Blutman' (2014) 25 EJIL 553.

as proof that this practice is accepted as law. This places high demands on the finding of CIL, which factually puts this source of law in a secondary position when compared to treaty law.[322] A more *negative and critical view* holds that it is difficult to identify in a reliable way the actual practice and motives of states. This makes CIL susceptible to political abuse. For that reason, a customary rule requires a solid, if not uniform, basis in state practice. The *positive and dynamic approach* accepts that PIL has to recognize and even adjust to changes taking place. It argues that the international legal regime has to be both realistic and grounded in collective practice. This may include the tailoring of the criteria for CIL to specific circumstances, something that is not per se excluded by the ICJ.[323] Quite obviously, leaning on the third view, it will be easier to recognize that the EU, a new actor in diplomacy, applies and contributes to diplomacy. This section, however, will also take into account more conservative viewpoints.

#### 4.5.2.2 CIL in Diplomatic Relations

Customary rules arise out of social interactions over generations that establish behaviours, which are first thought acceptable, later on desirable, and are eventually viewed as obligatory. General diplomatic law emanates from such interactions and facilitates them: its rules originate from peaceful interactions developed from common usages from the Greek city states, over the Byzantine Empire, to medieval times. In early times, CIL seemed the natural vehicle for an international standard of treatment of privileges and immunities, which were the result of reciprocity between diplomatic actors. By the sixteenth and seventeenth centuries, usages received a high degree of international consensus. Later, attempts to codify the rules were made in order for them not to evaporate—for example, by scholars in draft codes, by the Congress of Vienna in 1815, and by the Vienna Conference in 1961.

For most of diplomacy's existence, it was CIL rather than treaty law that determined norms. The VCDR is based on custom and its text in direct words refers to the continuing application of custom to fill gaps left by the treaty. The preamble of the VCDR affirms in that regard that CIL 'should continue to govern questions not expressly regulated by the provisions of the present Convention'. In diplomacy, as in other legal domains, codification is part of the field's natural evolution. CIL ultimately revolves around the finding of agreement about the applicability of rules; the existence of such agreement is often put in writing for the rule to be reflected in a certain pattern that is easy to recognize. The VCDR unmistakeably reflects rules of law in a more advanced and detailed way than CIL ever could.

Diplomatic law's codification process brought about two consequences: *(a)* many diplomatic rules lost their connection to bilateral reciprocity by becoming part of a multilateral system and, even more so, *(b)* most rules of diplomatic law now have a basis both in treaty law and CIL. In diplomacy, the overlap between the two sources of international law is significant. In the meantime, newer rules that came out of the 1961 codification became CIL themselves.

[322] David P Fidler, 'Challenging the Classical Concept of Custom: Perspectives on the Future of Customary International Law' (1996) 39 Ger Yearb Int Law 198.

[323] *Military and Paramilitary Activities in and against Nicaragua (Nicaragua v United States of America)* (Judgment) [1986] ICJ Rep 14, paras 183–86; *North Sea Continental Shelf (Federal Republic of Germany v Denmark and Federal Republic of Germany v Netherlands)* (Judgment) [1969] ICJ Rep 4, paras 73–74. In their essay 'International Law on a Given Day', James Crawford and Thomas Viles evidence CIL's dynamism (originally published in Konrad Ginther and Karl Zemanek (eds), *Völkerrecht zwischen Normativen Anspruch und Politischer Realität: Festschrift für K. Zemanek* (Duncker & Humblot 1994).

Nevertheless, especially with regard to the social dynamics of the diplomatic setting, it is still not unusual for norms not to be written down in an organized way. Moreover, bilateral and regional custom still exists, for example, customs agreements in bilateral reciprocal relations between states or the topic of diplomatic asylum in the Latin-American practice. CIL regulates specific aspects of diplomatic law, which do not feature in the VCDR; it keeps diplomatic law up to date and allows states to adapt practices and have these general practices recognized as law. Importantly for the EU, diplomatic CIL contributes to the stability of norms and the emergence of rights. If the application of diplomatic law in the relation between the Union and states were to be grounded exclusively in the EAs, the denunciation of an EA would not just terminate the diplomatic relations between the Union and the third state but also the application of diplomatic law, even though one could also say that in practical terms the denunciation of the EAs is unlikely, as the diplomatic price would be too high for the receiving state.

Resultantly, the EU partakes in a system that is a construct of organized and reciprocal social interactions, in which custom provides a source of law. Before assessing whether the EU can create diplomatic custom, this chapter discusses the Union's passive, more receptive, role. Thereto, it seeks to establish that all participants in the diplomatic system are bound by the same legal rules. More concretely, it argues that the EU has a legal obligation to apply CIL and that, reversely, the Union is also able to invoke CIL vis-à-vis states.

### 4.5.3 The Application of CIL

The application of CIL by non-states has been a topic of interest in human rights law and international humanitarian law.[324] For obvious reasons, it has been much less of an issue in the state-based diplomatic regime—at least until the EU came along. It is worth considering that the EU increasingly acts like a state in the area of diplomatic relations. As a result, it is in its own interest to be subject to the same legal framework as its diplomatic partners and to have the same tools at hand to force them into compliance. However, proving that the EU is subject to diplomatic custom is not without complications as there is an absence of international instruments confirming the enactment of CIL in the diplomatic relations between the Union and third states. While the VCDR is being applied to the widest extent possible in the EU's bilateral diplomatic relations via the EAs, these instruments do not say if and how uncodified diplomatic law applies. Likewise, the HR's mandate to conclude the 'necessary practical arrangements' with receiving states in Article 5(6) of the EEAS Decision is silent on whether that includes making arrangements about the applicability of CIL. The above, however, does not mean that CIL does not apply. Generally speaking, customary law is binding on all subjects of international law, including IOs such as the EU.[325] This was

[324] See, among others, Daragh Murray, *Human Rights Obligations of Non-State Armed Groups* (Hart 2016); Marco Sassòli, 'The Implementation of International Humanitarian Law: Current and Inherent Challenges' (2007) 10 Y Intl HL 45, 63; Sandesh Sivakumaran, 'Binding Armed Opposition Groups' (2006) 55 ICLQ 369, 381; Antonio Cassese, 'The Status of Rebels under the 1977 Geneva Protocol on Non-International Armed Conflicts' (1981) 30 ICLQ 416, 429. See, for a more general assessment, Cedric Ryngaert, 'Imposing International Duties on Non-State Actors and the Legitimacy of International Law' in Math Noortmann and Cedric Ryngaert (eds), *Non-State Actor Dynamics in International Law: From Law-Takers to Law-Makers* (Ashgate 2013).

[325] *Interpretation of the Agreement of 25 March 1951 between the WHO and Egypt* (Advisory Opinion) [1980] ICJ Rep 73, para 37; Henry G Schermers and Niels M Blokker, *International Institutional Law: Unity within Diversity* (5th edn, Martinus Nijhoff 2011) 835; Jan Wouters and Dries Van Eeckhoutte, 'Giving Effect to

confirmed by the CJEU, which has held on various occasions that the EU is bound to respect CIL.[326]

This handbook argues that customary diplomatic law applies through the EAs. This is certainly the case for *codified diplomatic CIL*, which applies through the EAs' reference to the VCDR. The EU is bound by aspects of the VCDR that have been considered a mere reflection of pre-dating customs and usages as well by those provisions that reflect the progressive development of rules.[327] The reason should be simple; the VCDR is considered CIL in its entirety.[328] Moreover, it is maintained that all customs and usages relating to the implementation and interpretation of the 1961 Convention are applicable to the EU; these have become an integral part of the Convention itself and the diplomatic system it instigates. The normative value of the rules expressed in the EAs is similar to those contained in the VCDR, which has an impact on their being capable of reflecting CIL.[329]

In the diplomatic world, norms and practices are applied that do not—or do not comprehensively—feature in the VCDR. Whether CIL applies to the EU *beyond the Vienna Convention* is unconfirmed in legal scholarship. The analysis carried out in this handbook nevertheless shows that decades of intense and consistent diplomatic practice have given rise to the application of custom in the EU's bilateral relations with third states. Host states do not differentiate between rules stemming from treaty or general international law. It is doubtful, given the interwovenness of the sources, that this would even be possible. When a rule of CIL coincides with a rule captured in the VCDR, it is impossible to discern the intention of third countries when interacting with the EU; the receiving government may be acting in a particular way out of *opinio juris sive necessitates* but may just as well be implementing the EA in good faith. What is observed in practice is that, following the entering into diplomatic relations with the Union, states apply the entire body of diplomatic law to the EU—thus, without distinguishing between CIL and treaty law. Likewise, the EU conforms to and complies with (all) rules applicable to states. What is more, both parties do so pursuant to a legal obligation. Following the ratification of the EA, receiving states started applying diplomatic law in a similar manner to all accredited missions; it is in their interest to keep the diplomatic system as simple and closed as possible.

The above assumptions are supported by the reading of EAs as reciprocal instruments. Article 16 of Protocol 7 on Privileges and Immunities provides that Belgium 'shall accord the *customary* diplomatic immunities and privileges to missions of third countries accredited to the Union'. In principle, Protocol 7 applies in internal EU relations only. However, when read in conjunction with the EAs, Protocol 7 encompasses the most formal reference to the CIL's enactment in the relations between the EU and third states. Article 3(3) of the model EA spells out that:

Customary International Law through European Community Law' in Jolande M Prinssen and Annette Schrauwen (eds), *Direct Effect: Rethinking a Classic of EC Legal Doctrine* (Europa Law Publishing 2004) 181.

[326] *Air Transport Association of America (ATAA) and others v Secretary of State for Energy and Climate Change* [2011] ECLI:EU:C:2011:864, para 101 and *Racke GmbH & Co v Hauptzollamt Mainz* [1998] ECLI:EU:C:1998:293, paras 45–46.

[327] Kai Bruns, *A Cornerstone of Modern Diplomacy: Britain and the Negotiation of the 1961 Vienna Convention on Diplomatic Relations* (Bloomsbury Academic 2014) 127.

[328] *Tehran Hostage* case (n 6) para 62 *in fine*. See also Denza, *Diplomatic Law* (n 15) 2–5; Berridge (n 47) 109–10; Verhoeven (n 20) 106.

[329] On the characteristics of treaties conducive to CIL, see Jonathan Charney, 'International Agreements and the Development of Customary International Law' (1986) 61 Wash L Rev 971, 983.

> [the VCDR] rights and privileges and immunities shall be accorded *on condition that*, in conformity with the provisions of article 16 of the Protocol 7 on the privileges and immunities of the European Union annexed to the Treaty on the European Union and the Treaty on the Functioning of the European Union, the Member States of the European Union accord the same rights and privileges and immunities to the Mission of [XXX], to its Head and to its members, as well as to the members of their families forming part of their respective households [own emphasis] [330]

This shows how the EAs make the application of the VCDR rights to the EUDEL by the third country conditional to the EU's application of the same rights to the third country's mission. The reciprocity clause refers to Protocol No 7 containing a reference to CIL and not the Vienna Convention, which it predates.

It follows that the EAs are the contractual expression of the third states' intent to recognize participation by the EU, something which they would have failed to achieve through the long and windy CIL process. The EA technique facilitates the application of treaty *and* customary law. Moreover, from general observations, there is nothing to indicate that receiving countries are *not* applying CIL in their diplomatic relations with the Union. This assessment raises the issue of equivalence between states and the EU for the purpose of the application of CIL in diplomatic domain. Because the EU acts like a state in its diplomatic relations, it is a reasonable expectation of its diplomatic partners that the Union's institutions are accountable according to the rules applicable to states. Those partners, in turn, are bound by the CIL that has emerged in the interstate context now that they have accepted that the EU enjoys similar rights as do states in their territories.

In conclusion, the EAs make both codified CIL (reference to the VCDR) and uncodified CIL (reference to the CIL's reciprocal application in Protocol 7) applicable to the EU's diplomatic relations. These agreements prove to be a reliable source of law and are therefore preferred over a legal regime grounded solely in custom, which typically would be less definite in its formulation and less easy to identify and accordingly more often subject to doubt in practice. Nonetheless, the EU's diplomatic practice could be even better aligned with CIL. An explicit confirmation of the application of CIL would put the EU in an even better legal position. The finding of CIL in EU–third state relations, and the explicit confirmation thereof by the receiving state, for that reason remains crucial.

### 4.5.4 The Effect of EU Diplomacy on CIL

Now that it is established that the EU *applies* diplomatic treaty law and diplomatic customary law, and that these regimes are also *applied to* the EU missions by receiving governments, the analysis is taken a step further. It must be researched whether the EU's actions in diplomatic affairs have also resulted in the growth of new rules of CIL with regard to *(a)* the Union's partaking in diplomatic relations and *(b)* diplomatic practice.

#### 4.5.4.1 Participation Rules in Diplomacy

In Chapter 2, this handbook confirmed that the overwhelming recognition by states has resulted in the emergence of a customary right of legation for the EU. Recognition by third

[330] See Appendix 2 for the model EA and Chapter 3 for a discussion on the EA practice.

states has been an important subjective factor in this process of determining the existence of a right of legation. Recognition is expressed in a pattern of almost identical treaties, the EAs—a pattern that evidences a 'material source of custom'. According to James Crawford, such material sources of custom 'are manifold and include: diplomatic correspondence [ . . . ] and extensive pattern of treaties in the same terms'.[331] It can be inferred that the EA network now represents the state of CIL with regard to the EU's participation in diplomatic relations.

The following arguments can be advanced in support of such affirmation. As treaty-making is a form of *state practice* relevant for identifying norms of CIL, it is submitted that the phenomenon of EAs is so widespread and the content of these treaties so similar that a consensus among EA-signatory nations can be found to exist.[332] On the basis of the EA practice, a more than significant number of states engage in a consistent and uniform practice that indicates that the Union is viewed as having the right of legation. According to the ICJ, for CIL to emerge practice must be 'extensive and virtually uniform'. However, the application of the rules in question does not have to be perfect.[333] Through recurrence and repetition, a common behaviour has emerged with regard to the EU's status in the diplomatic corps. As the ILC articulated in the context of the customary law of consular relations:

> [a]n international convention admittedly establishes rules binding the contracting parties only, and based on reciprocity; but it must be remembered that these rules become generalized through the conclusion of other similar conventions containing identical or similar provisions, and also through the operation of the most-favoured-nation clause.[334]

But mere mimicry does not make custom. There are plenty of examples of legal fields in which similar treaties were signed without giving rise to the creation of CIL such as extradition law, air law, etc.[335] One also needs to assess the existence of opinio juris on the part of states. As Oscar Schachter underlines, opinio juris serves to distinguish custom from standardized patterns of practice which are not binding on state parties.[336] Such opinio juris derives from the conviction of states of being bound by a general obligation. The EA practice already signposts that an impressive number of states finds it desirable, and perhaps even necessary, that the EU participates in the diplomatic system. The reasons underlying the conclusion of the (large number of) recognitions of the EU's right of legation, as formalized in EAs (and in national laws), should also be considered. It may very well be true that, at the time of entering into relations with the EU, states did not share a conviction that their recognition was required by PIL. Some countries may have entered into diplomatic relations with the Union out of courtesy or, more realistically, for reasons of economic or political expediency. The question should be posed whether this matters. Diplomatic relations between states are also often entered into after parties consider mutual benefits.

Time also is a decisive factor in the finding of CIL and opinio juris. It takes a certain time to construct customary law and, by definition, CIL is an ex post facto construct. Crawford

[331] Crawford, *Brownlie's Principles* (n 27) 24.

[332] Boyle and Chinkin, *The Making of International Law* (n 317) 236–37.

[333] *North Sea Continental Shelf* (n 323) and *Military and Paramilitary Activities in and against Nicaragua* (n 323) para 98.

[334] ILC Report covering the work of its 12th session, UN Doc A/4425, YBILC [1960] para 21, 145.

[335] Jan Wouters, Sanderijn Duquet, and Nicolas Hachez, 'International Investment Law: The Perpetual Search for Consensus' in Olivier De Schutter, Johan Swinnen, and Jan Wouters (eds), *Foreign Direct Investment and Human Development: The Law and Economics of International Investment Agreements* (Routledge 2012) 39.

[336] Oscar Schachter, 'Entangled Treaty and Custom' in Yoram Dingtein and Mala Tabory (eds), *International Law in a Time of Perplexity: Essays in Honour of Shabtai Rosenne* (Martinus Nijhoff 1989) 732.

and Viles famously argued that it is impossible to tell what all of international law is on a given day: '[l]ike good coffee, international law has to be brewed'.[337] Here, it is observed that, over the years, a uniform practice was born out of the EAs and state behaviour that surpasses the original parties' intent. Indeed, through repeated practices, the EU's diplomatic presence has provoked a sense of obligation; an obligation that results in states inviting the EU diplomats to the negotiation table, treating them according to diplomatic protocol, granting them privileges according to local custom, . . . all of which are obligations that do not directly result from the VCDR. Further, a sense of legal obligation also stems from the reciprocal nature of the EAs.

Resultantly, the network of EAs and national clauses on the Union's participation in diplomacy, combined with daily practices all over the world and the absence of states refusing to entertain diplomatic relations with the EU, have ripened into new CIL with regard to the EU's right of legation. What is observed here is a contemporary formation of CIL, in which the collective factor plays a role. The contracting states and the EU have strong mutual interests, which resulted in consolidated practice, considered by some as *opinio juris communis*.[338]

However, this should not lead to the conclusion that the EU's participation in diplomacy has changed CIL on membership of the diplomatic community; states still apply a strict set of criteria to recognize diplomatic counterparts. Neither does this entail that states are not at liberty to break off diplomatic relations with the EU—much like interstate relations, this is still a perfectly legal possibility which, however, by itself, does not undermine the claim to a right of legation.

#### 4.5.4.2 The Content of Diplomatic Customary Law

CIL is the harvest of *state* practice and opinion. At the same time, changing global governance structures have altered the role of IOs in international law-making. IOs are no longer mere repositories of state practices; their actions have normative consequences beyond those explicitly delegated to them by states.[339] José Alvarez is one of those authors that challenges the traditional account of modern international law-making. According to Alvarez, the introduction of IOs to the international scene, their significant expansion in quality and quantity, and their penetration of international law has fundamentally changed the traditional sources of PIL. This has altered *(a)* the specific content of rules, *(b)* where to look in order to find law, and *(c)* the character and procedures of traditional sources. In light of these developments, can CIL be gathered from IO practice as well as from state practice?[340] More concretely, does the Union's behaviour in diplomacy influence the interpretation and future application of rules originally developed between states in their mutual diplomatic relations?

To know whether EU practice in diplomatic relations is capable of contributing to the emergence of diplomatic customary rules in terms of their content, this section relies on recent work done for the ILC by Sir Michael Wood on the identification of CIL. In his reports, which are generally cautious with regard to the taking into account IO practice and opinio

337 Crawford and Viles (n 323).

338 Lauri Hannikainen, 'The Collective Factor as a Promoter of Customary International Law' (2006) 6 Bal YIL 124, 139.

339 Jose E Alvarez, 'Governing the World: International Organizations as Lawmakers' (2008) 31 Suffolk Transnat'l L Rev 591, 593. In the same sense, José E Alvarez, *International Organizations as Law-Makers* (OUP 2005).

340 This debate is not new: see *Military and Paramilitary Activities in and against Nicaragua* (n 323); Krzysztof Skubiszewski, 'Forms of Participation of International Organizations in the Lawmaking Processes' (1964) 18 IO 790; Rosalyn Higgins, *The Development of International Law through the Political Organs of the United Nations* (OUP 1963).

juris to identify rules of CIL, the EU is singled out as a case for which it is difficult to deny that it contributes to the finding of relevant practice. In his own words, the Special Rapporteur:

> continues to consider that the practice of international (intergovernmental) organizations as such, in certain cases, may contribute to the creation, or expression, of customary international law. The relevance of such practice is difficult to deny in the case of the European Union or, in fact, in any case where member States may direct an international organization to execute on their behalf actions falling within their own competences.[341]

Earlier, in his second report the Special Rapporteur stated:

> the acts of international organizations on which States have conferred authority may also contribute or attest to the formation of a general practice in the fields in which those organizations operate.[342]

The most compelling reason to accept that the EU can contribute to diplomatic custom is the fact that it is authorized by its member states to exercise competences in the same way that they do. In the 2014 UNGA Sixth Committee debate, the EU representative stressed that:

> in areas where, according to the rules of the EU Treaties, only the Union can act it is the practice of the Union that should be taken into account with regard to the formation of customary international law alongside the implementation by the Member States of the EU legislation [343]

Although it does not replace the member states in diplomacy, the Union is mandated by them to diplomatically represent competences attributed to it in its international relations—a mandate that is recognized by third states in the EAs. Moreover, in its diplomatic relations, the EU vigorously tries to assimilate as much as possible to states: it copies state-like behaviour, subjects itself to rules created in a state-dominated context, and adopt titles and functions previously reserved to states. In essence, its practices in diplomatic relations may be equated with the practice of states. In any event, it is always recommended for the EU to take into account the position of member states in its interpretation of international law.[344] A major concern for the international community has been that the acceptance of IO practice and opinion of law or necessity would give rise to a decline in states' sovereign powers to find and create CIL. In diplomatic relations, such fear stands unsubstantiated. The Union does not replace its member states; it acts in addition to them. Accordingly, the weight of the Union's view on matters remains minimal at the global level. Whatever the EU says or does becomes one of the (close to) 200 practices of diplomatic actors. There is no indication of EU dominance in global diplomatic affairs, not even in combination with its member states'

[341] Sir Michael Wood, Fourth Report on the Identification of Customary International Law (2016) A/CN.4/695, para 20.

[342] Sir Michael Wood, Second Report on the Identification of Customary International Law (2014) A/CN.4/695, para 43.

[343] Quoted in Jan Vanhamme, 'Formation and Enforcement of Customary International Law: The European Union's Contribution' (2008) 39 Neth Yearb Int Law 127, 130. See also Sir Michael Wood, Third Report on the Identification of CIL (2015) A/CN.4/682 and Jed Odermatt, 'The Development of Customary International Law by International Organizations' (2017) 66 ICLQ 491.

[344] The Queen, on the application of International Association of Independent Tanker Owners (Intertanko) and others v Secretary of State for Transport [2008] ECLI:EU:C:2008:312, para 52.

actions, which may in fact also very well differ from the Union's practice.[345] In addition, accepting that EU practices contribute to the development of customary norms should not be too controversial since these practices exclusively emerge in the Union's relations with states. In other words, states are not unrelated to the contribution to custom by the EU. Moreover, they have the opportunity to object to the emergence of a new rule if desired.

#### 4.5.4.3 The Contribution of the Union to CIL

As a diplomatic actor, the EU interacts with and likely contributes to rules of diplomatic CIL. The actual measurement thereof faces methodological obstacles. There are virtually no (court) cases or government papers involving an inquiry into the effects of EU actions on customary rules in diplomacy. This section nevertheless illustrates where contributions are and could be made by showing how EU institutions have interpreted, applied, and modified CIL.

The most tangible way that the EU *contributes to CIL is through its application of diplomatic CIL*. The Union confirms existing CIL in its practices. On occasion, the Union goes beyond a faithful contribution and moves on to a *contribution by giving a rule its own interpretation*. For instance, Article 3 Protocol on Privileges and Immunities on tax privileges is grounded in diplomatic CIL but at the same time has been given a broader scope in the Union.[346] The EU also *contributes to CIL in its bilateral relations*. CIL developed in a bilateral context is mostly relied on to fill gaps, to provide appropriate rules of construction of the applicable instruments, and to determine the relation between instruments of national and international law. As a result, when a usage emerges with regard to the EU in a third country that is consistent, and applied out of a sense of legal obligation, it may give rise to a customary rule in the relation between the EU and that state.[347] Finally, the EU contributes to CIL *through* the execution of diplomatic relations. When finding CIL, one should look at state practice 'ordinarily by reference to official documents and other indications of governmental action.[348] Diplomatic correspondence, for instance, is broadly regarded as a primary source of elements of state practice and opinio juris.[349] Ample illustrations exist of such correspondence between the EU and states.

As a concluding remark, it must be noted that often in the passive legation practice the Union is effectively barred from making a contribution to CIL rules. It is host state Belgium that applies diplomatic law for the Union. Consequently, in the reception of diplomats, Belgium and the other member states are still the main contributors to CIL. Here, it becomes difficult to see how the Union can even assume a position that is different from the member state(s). The Council's approval of new ambassadors and the taking of a decision on a declaration persona non grata exemplifies this.

345 Vaughan Lowe, 'Can the European Community Bind the Member States on Questions of Customary International Law?' in Martti Koskenniemi (ed), *International Law Aspects of the European Union* (Kluwer 1998).

346 See Opinion of AG Stix-Hackl, *Commission v Belgium* [2007] ECLI:EU:C:2006:434, para 20, discussed in Chapter 5.

347 The existence of bilateral CIL was recognized by the ICJ *Right of Passage over Indian Territory (Portugal v India)* (Judgment) [1960] ICJ Rep 6.

348 American Law Institute, 'Restatement of the Law, Third, the Foreign Relations Law of the United States' [1987] para 103, comment (a).

349 Crawford, *Brownlie's Principles* (n 27) 24.

### 4.5.5 Conclusion

There is a fog of uncertainty shrouding the literature on the relationship between EU diplomacy and CIL. This section has revealed their interplay and discovered that (part of) the controversy is unnecessary. In its early days, the diplomatic presence of the EU in third countries may have been negotiable, but it is doubtful this still is the case. The Union's diplomatic relations are executed in a standardized global practice and anchored in legal obligation. Moreover, the EU—when acting similarly to a state—contributes to the shaping, content, and evolution of the customary legal regime on diplomatic relations. This is because practices and convictions of the EU and third states are well aligned and reciprocal. Now that the great majority of third states has become both host state to an EUDEL and sends its own mission to Brussels, a common interest emerges in forming a general regime for diplomatic relations. The agreeable solution has been to assimilate rights and obligations between the EU and third states as far as possible with those applying to states.

## 4.6 General Appraisal

This chapter discussed the application of diplomatic law and practices by the EU. It covered a selection of topics ordered not thematically but according to the legal source in which they can be found. At the beginning of this chapter, a number of principles were introduced that are considered fundamental in the diplomatic system but pose specific challenges to the EU. It was found that the EU has the minimum number of the relevant trappings of the right of legation so as to allow it (indirectly) to apply the 1961 VCDR and diplomatic norms not or only partly covered by the Convention (eg rules of protocol), rules developed in bilateral contexts (eg visa requirements), and CIL. Moreover, through the development of day-to-day routines that mimic those of national embassies, the practices of the EUDELs are easily recognizable for diplomatic partners. In itself, this makes for an original contribution to international diplomatic law.

Not all queries are solved, however. As it stands, the international diplomatic system requires the EU, in particular the EEAS, to take a creative approach to overcome legal burdens inherent to PIL. This makes the EEAS a 'diplomatic entrepreneur', its primary task being to ensure that EUDELs are treated according to international diplomatic standards. *Internally*, the EEAS cooperates with the other institutions and bodies to develop EU legislation implementing conditions that enable the enjoyment of diplomatic status by EUDELs and their recognition by third states. This was shown in the examples of the EULP, diplomatic asylum, and the issuing of letters of credence. The EEAS therefore plays—and will likely continue to play—a constructive role in ensuring that the EU and its delegations are given the tools to respond to challenges presented by international diplomatic law. *Externally*, the EEAS enforces the application of the bilateral agreements entered into with host states. Concretely, it demands that EUDELs are granted appropriate diplomatic status, that diplomats can exercise their functions, and that HoDs are entered on the diplomatic list but also that EUDELs may fly the European flag. This role, carried out primarily by the EEAS Protocol Unit, is analogous to that of a protocol service in a state's MFA. A particular feature of these appeals to host states is that the EEAS does not require one type or model treatment for its delegations. It asks for equal treatment. This approach evidences the primary concern of the EEAS, that is, recognition on the basis that it is 'one of the others', with all the others being states. It is here that an international legal impasse continues to exist and that creativity is called for.

European diplomatic practice is no longer outside but not yet equal. Because the EU remains a legally ambiguous actor in the diplomatic world, norms are twisted and stretched and innovative practices developed to fit in. This overview shows that the EU brings about improvements in the quality of diplomatic interactions and the architecture of institutions as well as in the interpretation of and emergence of (new) rules and norms in diplomacy. The debate about legal niceties may not be settled, but in practice the everyday life of EUDELs is unaffected. Indeed, as the examples demonstrated, the EEAS adopts a pragmatic attitude to the precarious balances that exist in the diplomatic order and local customs, striking a fine equilibrium in the delegations' use of diplomatic démarches, diplomatic symbols, and the respect of conventions related to diplomatic precedence. By treading both carefully and creatively, the EEAS effectively contributes to the ever-stronger participation of delegations in corps diplomatiques around the world, and this is no minor achievement.

# 5

# The Interplay between the EU and Its Member States

## 5.1 Diplomacy in the EU Legal Order

### 5.1.1 Defining Challenges

The diplomatic field challenges the interactions between the European Union (EU, or Union) and its member states. There is no fixed set of norms governing the EU/member state diplomatic ratio. Diplomacy is subject to a triangular relationship between the international, national, and EU legal systems. Norms stemming from each level shape and influence the following five interactions: *(a)* diplomatic and consular relations member states conduct with one another, *(b)* diplomatic and consular relations member states conduct with third states, *(c)* diplomatic and consular relations the EU conducts with third states, *(d)* diplomatic relations the EU conducts with member states, and *(e)* relations between the EU and the member states that host either EU institutions or EU delegations (EUDELs) accredited to international organizations (IOs). Relationships a and b predate and exist parallel to the internal interactions of the EU, whereas c, d, and e are more recent phenomena that are the direct result of the Union's exercise of the right of legation.

A first challenge relates to the coincidence of norms. In the EU, regulatory and executive actions in the diplomatic or consular spheres are governed by three different sets of rules: EU law, public international law (PIL), and national laws of member states. A conflict between these norms can invoke opposite obligations arising from the EU Treaties and diplomatic and consular law—regardless of whether transposed by national systems. A potential conflict also exists where EU law impacts the policy space of states. A second challenge relates to the coexistence of diplomatic activities. Each of the twenty-eight (twenty-seven member states plus the Union) European actors expresses an authentic *ius legationis*. This concurrent exercise of multiple and often overlapping rights of legation is an innovative phenomenon in the international arena that gives rise to a looming risk of competition between diplomatic actors but also offers tremendous opportunities for cooperation and integration.

To properly qualify the multidimensional relationship between the EU and the member states in diplomacy, it is necessary to first determine the bigger picture. This section therefore briefly revisits the broader context of European diplomatic integration and the relationship between international and EU law.

*EU Diplomatic Law.* Sanderijn Duquet, Oxford University Press. © Sanderijn Duquet 2022.
DOI: 10.1093/oso/9780192844552.003.0005

## 5.1.2 Diplomacy as a Competence

### 5.1.2.1 Qualifying Diplomacy

#### *5.1.2.1.1 Not a competence...*

Fundamentally the Union is an organization of attributed competences (Art 5(1)–(2) TEU). Actions taken by the EU need to find a legal basis as well as a corresponding objective in the Treaties.[1] Such legal base is indispensable for any commitment of money, human resources, or equipment but is probably a less compelling requirement for informal conduct or inactivity.

As explained in Chapter 2, there is no reference in the Treaties to an overall EU competence to engage in or conduct diplomatic and/or consular relations, nor is there an umbrella provision on diplomacy. The Treaties merely foresee a specific legal basis for the right to consular protection to be implemented by member states with the EU's support. This competence is found in the articles on EU citizenship, most prominently Article 20 of the Treaty on European Union (hereafter TEU) and Article 23 of the Treaty on the Functioning of the European Union (hereafter TFEU).[2]

It follows that for every EU action in diplomacy, a specific legal basis needs to exist in other provisions. Even this observation comes with its own challenges since diplomacy cannot be pinned down to one, two, or even three policy fields. Influence and authority are exercised in all sorts of thematic domains via diplomacy, ranging from those where the Union has extensive competences to those in which its role is minimal or absent.

#### *5.1.2.1.2 ... but an instrument*

If diplomatic and consular relations are not competences, how do they classify? The answer, it is suggested here, should be deduced from the traditional qualification of diplomacy as a tool for states to manage their relations and communication with the outside world. Diplomacy is an instrument through which states realize their international representation, communication, and negotiation. Similarly, EU diplomacy serves such instrumental and functional ends. Like states, the Union uses diplomacy as a means to realize other (specifically allocated) competences, to secure its interests and rights, and to influence power.[3] Diplomacy should consequently be qualified as an instrumental competence or, in other words, as a vehicle that emerges in connection with substantive powers properly allocated to the EU. The qualification as an instrumental competence also explains the lack of a direct reference to diplomacy in the Treaties. Its exercise is simply implied in the mandate—more concretely, in the corresponding discretion to choose the tools to execute that mandate—granted by member states in relation to the totality of the Union's interests and competences.

The above qualification brings about (at least) three consequences. First, diplomacy does not appear to induce changes to the normal application of the vertical division of competences as conceived in EU law. Consequently, the EU and its member states are entitled to use diplomatic means intersecting their respective fields of internal competences, whilst the division of competences curtails their respective capacities. Second, with a thematic focus that

[1] Allan Rosas and Lorna Armati, *EU Constitutional Law: An Introduction* (Bloomsbury Publishing 2012) 198.

[2] Consolidated Version of the Treaty on European Union [2012] OJ C326/01 (hereafter TEU); Consolidated Version of the Treaty on the Functioning of the European Union [2012] OJ C326/47 (hereafter TFEU).

[3] See chapter 2 Art 216(1) TFEU and the case law on implied powers: *Fédération Charbonnière de Belgique v High Authority of the European Coal and Steel Community* [1956] ECLI:EU:C:1956:11, 299; *Commission v Council* ('ERTA') [1971] ECLI:EU:C:1971:32; and *Cornelius Kramer and others* [1976] ECLI:EU:C:1976:114.

is neither static nor predefined, there is no definite and thorough answer as to whether EU or member state action in the diplomatic or consular sphere falls within their respective competences. Third, diplomacy remains subject to the legal framework underpinning the complex system of Union competences. Therefore, because decision-making rules and the role of EU institutions differ, the exercise of diplomacy between those fields also varies.[4] Moreover, where certain competences are not conferred to the Union, the EU will be prevented from taking diplomatic measures or measures impacting the diplomatic prerogatives of member states. Likewise, the member states' execution of their own right of legation will be impacted because of the transfer of competences to the Union.

*5.1.2.1.3 Division of competences*

The EU's division of competences, introduced in Article 2 TFEU, reveals ample links with diplomacy. The fourth paragraph of Article 2 TFEU lays down the Union's general competence to define and implement the Common Foreign and Security Policy (CFSP) and to progressively frame common defence policies (CSDP). A major part of the Union's active right of legation is put to practice through CFSP mechanisms and instruments, which are subject to specific rules and procedures (Art 24(1) TEU). In itself, the Union's external relations have a diffuse status: the CFSP can be branded a sui generis competence outside the area of simple shared competences.[5] The Union's designated diplomatic players (the High Representative (HR), the European External Action Service (EEAS), and the EU delegations (EUDELs)) are provided with a legal basis within Title V, Chapter 2 of the TEU. What is also special about the CFSP is that, while the Treaties set out a number of provisions on the basis of which the Union's policy positions are defined in the form of legal acts, there is also a long-standing practice in CFSP to use non-legal instruments such as action plans, guidelines, roadmaps, lines to take, declarations, statements, démarches, and interventions delivered in international fora. However, such EU non-binding acts may bring about legal consequences on the international level that bind the Union.

The CFSP competences are not designed to cover economic and technical aspects of external relations such as trade, finance, and technical cooperation, which have separate legal bases. To identify the appropriate legal basis of a particular action undertaken by the EUDELs, one has to scrutinize the substance of the work carried out by EU diplomats and the nature of the specific EU instruments upon which the action is based. Delegations represent many Union policies and each requires a legal basis under the Treaties including in non-CFSP domains. For instance, EUDELs are involved in the realization of exclusive EU competences abroad (Art 2(1) TFEU). Article 3 TFEU lists trade, competition, monetary policies, and the conservation of marine biological resources as being exclusive. The focus on these thematic domains comes naturally to EUDELs. Pre-2010, Commission delegations mainly represented such exclusive competences of the European Commission. Other exclusive external competences were recognized in case law and Treaties, including the possibility of dynamic growth of exclusive competences in the external spheres. Both explicit and implied external competences can become exclusive through the exercise of the Union's competences.[6] Over time, EUDELs have become increasingly involved in the execution of shared competences as defined in Article 2(2) TFEU. Article 4 lists inter alia agriculture and

[4] Bart Van Vooren and Ramses A Wessel, *EU External Relations Law: Text, Cases and Materials* (CUP 2014).

[5] Marise Cremona, 'EU External Relations: Unity and Conferral of Powers' in Loïc Azouli (ed), *The Question of Competence in the European Union* (OUP 2014) 66.

[6] Robert Schütze, *European Constitutional Law* (2nd edn, CUP 2015) 270–73.

fisheries, environment, consumer protection, and energy, all of which require external and sometimes diplomatic action. Delegations have been involved in the execution of environmental programmes and mobility partnerships where they often assume the first point of entry for local authorities and partners.[7] For example, the EUDEL in Moldova implements Commission projects on agriculture and rural development and the EUDEL in Algeria locally coordinates bilateral cooperation in the context of energy security. Furthermore, diplomatic action can be required for the execution of supporting or complementary competences (Arts 2(5) and 6 TFEU). On their own initiative, EUDELs can set up projects to inform foreign public of European science and culture.[8] Ventures of the EU into areas where it is not the primary actor are increasingly observed such as in economic policies (Art 5 TFEU), culture, tourism, and education (Art 6 TFEU). However, the actual EU involvement in third countries under the competence to support, coordinate, or supplement actions of member states depends on arrangements made with member states represented on the ground. For example, discussions with EU member states in the framework of 'division of labour' in Ethiopia have come to a clear conclusion that EU presence in the health sector is preferred over its presence in the education sector during the programming period that started in 2015. Additionally, Commission operations as executed by the EUDEL are also aligned to the Ethiopian Government's priorities and sector strategies.[9] Finally, Union competences in areas listed by Articles 2(3) and 5 TFEU are significantly weaker, as also reflected by the reduced vigour to address these issues through diplomatic means.

Most external policy is non-exclusive, whereby competences are either shared or fall within the CFSP. Likewise, diplomacy can be defined as a cooperatively mixed policy model, in which activities are exercised in parallel by the EU and its member states. The HR works with the mandate provided by the member states. In practical terms, this means that when consensus results in a CFSP policy, it will affect how national ministries of foreign affairs (MFAs) and their missions operate in third countries. Not all discussions as to how the CFSP competence should be exercised are settled. For instance, it is undetermined whether the CFSP falls under the general 'pre-emption' rule on shared competences, pursuant to which the member states can exercise their competence to the extent that the Union has not exercised them, or has decided to cease exercising its competences.[10] With regard to diplomacy however, pre-emption should not be applicable any more than it should have general application in regard to, for instance, the observance of human rights. The entire concept of pre-emption is based on the undesirability or the impossibility of having two sources of legislative power. Diplomatic functions do not involve the exercise of legislative powers.

### 5.1.2.2 Demarcation Issues

#### *5.1.2.2.1 General principles of EU law*

A key question that emerges is whether EU law provides sufficient tools to deal with 'diplomatic trespassing', that is, the exercise of diplomacy by the Union or the member states in areas considered to be part of the other actor's diplomatic turf. Generally, the division of

[7] Ane Kristine Djupedal, 'Recent Developments in the EU Migration Management Policy EU–Cape Verde Mobility Partnership, Frontex and the Management of the European Borders' (2011) 7(11) ARENA 39.

[8] Commission, 'Communication on a European agenda for culture in a globalizing world', 10 May 2007, COM(2007) 242.

[9] Answer given by the Commission to parliamentary question E-003750-2014, 26 March 2014.

[10] Christophe Hillion and Ramses A Wessel, 'Restraining External Competences of EU Member States under CFSP' in Marise Cremona and Bruno de Witte (eds), *EU Foreign Relations Law: Constitutional Fundamentals* (Hart 2008).

competences is governed by general principles of EU law, with numerous principles protecting the residuum of member states' powers. First, EU authority is contained by the principle of conferral (Art 4(1) TEU; also Art 5(1)–(2) TEU). This principle provides that the competences not allocated to the Union in the Treaties remain with the member states. Even when the EU is permitted to exercise a competence that incidentally or fundamentally affects national diplomacy, the EU institutions and bodies must behave prudently whilst adhering to the principles of subsidiarity and proportionality (Art 5(3)–(4) TEU). These two principles are logical extensions of the principle of conferral,[11] whereby subsidiarity requires public powers to be located at the lowest relevant tier of government where they can be exercised effectively. The principle of proportionality ascertains that the means employed by an authority are suitable without going beyond what is necessary to achieve a legitimate objective.[12] EU law provides a further constitutional safeguard to protect EU and member states' interests.[13] To assist the harmonious coexistence of multiple regulators, the Treaties contain an obligation of loyalty known as the principle of sincere cooperation (Art 4(3) TEU). This obligation installs a duty of good faith providing that the Union and member states are to refrain from taking any measures that could jeopardize the Treaty objectives' attainment. The duty is general and shared, given that it applies regardless of whether EU competences are exclusive or shared, with EU institutions as well as member states.[14] The Lisbon Treaty made it explicit that the principle of loyalty works both ways and that it requires cooperation and mutual respect.[15] Consequently, the principle of sincere cooperation is one of the few mechanisms for the EU to challenge a member state's efforts to block EU diplomatic action on the pretext of 'protectionism'. The principle's application is discussed in more detail in section 5.3 in this chapter.

##### *5.1.2.2.2 The national identity clause*

**Article 4(2) TEU's basic features** A question that deserves close scrutiny is whether member states' diplomatic and consular relations receive a special protection in EU law, which somehow outplays other more general principles related to the vertical division of competences. In other words, does EU law provide an ultimate 'sovereignty brake' protecting national claims in diplomacy?

Conveniently situated between the principles of conferral and sincere cooperation, one finds a provision demanding the EU to protect the very being of member states as well as the rights and functions allocated to it under PIL. The provision is referred to as the 'national identity clause', consisting of two different obligations. In its current form, Article 4(2) reads:

> [t]he Union shall respect the equality of Member States before the Treaties as well as their national identities, inherent in their fundamental structures, political and constitutional, inclusive of regional and local self-government. It shall respect their essential State functions, including ensuring the territorial integrity of the State, maintaining law and order

[11] Stephen C Sieberson, *Dividing Lines between the European Union and Its Member States: The Impact of the Treaty of Lisbon* (TMC Asser Press 2008) 142.

[12] *Netherlands v Parliament and Council* [2001] ECLI:EU:C:2001:523.

[13] Geert De Baere and Timothy Roes, 'EU Loyalty as Good Faith' (2015) 64 ICLQ 829.

[14] *Commission v Luxembourg* [2005] ECLI:EU:C:2005:341, para 58; *Commission v Germany* [2005] ECLI:EU:C:2005:462, para 64.

[15] Matej Avbelj, 'The Treaty of Lisbon: An Ongoing Search for Structural Equilibrium' (2010) 16 Colum J Eur L 521, 527.

and safeguarding national security. In particular, national security remains the sole responsibility of each Member State.

The first sentence of Article 4(2) TEU protects different elements of the member states' identity. While in common language, 'identity' evokes a broad meaning, EU law conceives it to encompass a political and institutional meaning only.[16] A second obligation concerns the protection of the essential functions of member states. This obligation finds its origins in the 'Christophersen clause', named after the chair of a working group at the Constitutional Convention.[17] The Lisbon Treaty's drafters decided not to include a list of essential functions constituting the elements of national identity.[18] Any inventory would risk being interpreted narrowly and therefore limit the autonomous execution of state sovereignty. The differences between these two obligations are significant.[19] The former obligation is an internal and subjective safeguard protecting constitutional traditions against an 'omnipresent' EU. The latter obligation, in contrast, is an objective guarantee the origin of which finds its root in PIL's definition of statehood. As Blanke and Mangiameli argue, what is comprised in Article 4(2) TEU's second sentence is the 'very identity as a state' as opposed to its 'constitutional identity' protected in the first sentence.[20] It is also observed that the Court of Justice of the EU (CJEU) displays some reluctance to engage with the national identity clause. The Court often considers arguments based on national identity being part of other more commonly used tests in EU law (eg the proportionality test).[21]

Article 4(2) TEU is an expression of the member states' will to incorporate certain safeguards to protect the main features of statehood. It serves four important functions. First, Article 4(2) anticipates the fear of an overly powerful Union that would neglect the autonomy of nations in the international legal order or one that would deprive them of their fundamental functions.[22] In that sense, it is an extra-constitutional check against an unlimited expansion of EU competences. Similarly, Article 352(4) TFEU can be conceived as a safeguard clause against progressive interpretation techniques used by the Union. It stipulates that the general 'residual' legal basis laid down in the article cannot be used to pursue CFSP objectives. Second, the clause is the closest codified definition of areas of national sovereignty in EU constitutional law.[23] The Treaties do not contain a list of exclusive member state powers but leave the matter to customary international law (CIL). Third, the national identity clause recognizes the diversity of member states in laws and practices. In combination with the rest of Article 4 TEU, the provision facilitates a concrete meaning to the EU's motto 'united in diversity'. Fourth, from a multilevel legal perspective, it is interesting to see how the provision defines both the relationship of EU law with national

[16] Wouter Devroe and Jan Wouters, *De Europese Unie: Het Verdrag van Maastricht en zijn Uitvoering: Analyse en Perspectieven* (Peeters 1996) 91.

[17] Henning Christophersen, 'Highlighting the Limits of EU Competence', Working Group V on 'complementary competence', Working Document 5, 11 July 2002 and Armin von Bogdandy and Stephan Schill, 'Overcoming Absolute Primacy: Respect for National Identity under the Lisbon Treaty' (2011) 48 CML Rev 1417, 1426.

[18] The European Convention, 'Note', 9 September 2002, Doc 2002CONV 251/02, 3.

[19] Partly different: Denis Preshova, 'Battleground or Meeting Point?: The Respect for National Identities in the European Union—Article 4(2) The Treaty on European Union' (2012) 8 CYELP 267, 283.

[20] Hermann-Josef Blanke and Stelio Mangiameli, 'Article 4 [The Relations between the EU and the Member States]' in Hermann-Josef Blanke and Stelio Mangiameli (eds), *The Treaty on European Union* (Springer 2013) 228.

[21] Elke Cloots, *National Identity in EU Law* (OUP 2015) 5–6; *Sayn-Wittgenstein v Landeshauptmann von Wien* [2011] ECLI:EU:C:2010:806, para 83; *Runevič-Vardyn and Wardyn* [2011] ECLI:EU:C:2011:291.

[22] European Parliament, Report on the Treaty of Lisbon (2007/2286(INI)), Committee on Constitutional Affairs, A6-0013/2008, 29 January 2008.

[23] Barbara Guastaferro, 'Beyond the Exceptionalism of Constitutional Conflicts: The Ordinary Functions of the Identity Clause' (2012) 31 Yearb Eur Law 263, 271.

law ('national identities') and PIL ('essential state functions'). The result is that it preserves the essence of the national right to self-determination and self-organization internally as well as its rights to position itself in relations with other nations.

The diplomatic domain serves as an interesting testing ground for the meaning of the national identities and essential state functions clauses. Article 4(2) TEU protects the right of legation, albeit in a qualified way, and therefore bridges PIL with EU law.

**Diplomacy as a component of national identity** One must be careful not to overstate the practical meaning of the protection of national identity. Under EU law, national identity constitutes far less than PIL's conception of national sovereignty.[24] In three instances, however, there is some effect as regards the diplomatic services of the member states.

A first effect is that Article 4(2), first sentence, TEU protects the way in which member states structure their (diplomatic) services. In the context of EU rules on public procurement, Advocate-General Mengozzi argued that: '[EU secondary law] cannot be interpreted as permitting interference in the institutional structure of Member States. Accordingly, acts of internal reorganisations of the powers of States remain outside the scope of EU law.'[25] A member state's organization of the right of legation can be considered as part of a state's fundamental structure in the sense of the first sentence of Article 4(2) TEU. To make it more concrete: the EU is barred from making decisions that would interfere with the member states' right to take decisions to open and close embassies, to opt for a particular type of representation whether permanent or ad hoc, and to determine their diplomatic service's organizational structure.[26] Moreover, member states enjoy a monopoly over the recruitment and appointment of national diplomatic agents, functions that they can (and effectively do) reserve to nationals in accordance with EU law. A number of EU states even have constitutional provisions on the recruitment of diplomats, including on the organization of the selection process.[27] One can point to Article 13 of the French Constitution, Articles 107 and 167 of the Belgian Constitution, Chapter 11 of the Finnish Constitution, and Article 41 of the Latvian Constitution, all of which discuss the nomination of diplomats. Constitutional provisions that grant a head of state the right to accredit and receive foreign ambassadors are also common among member states; see, for instance, Article 14 of the French Constitution, Article 9(4) of the Hungarian Constitution, and section 63 of the Spanish Constitution.[28]

A second effect of the national identity guarantee is the protection of the devolution of member state powers to sub-state entities. Article 4(2) TEU indeed safeguards the horizontal relationship between the regions having their own powers within a member state having a federal structure.[29] This entails that, the Union is obliged to respect the choice of the member states to grant external competences or a form of representational rights to sub-federal or even local authorities. As a result, EU law indirectly acknowledges a second form of non-traditional diplomacy in addition to introducing the Union's own diplomatic capacity. This makes EU Treaties one of the few if not the only international instrument to confirm the

[24] Jens Bartelson, 'The Concept of Sovereignty Revisited' (2006) 17 EJIL 463.

[25] Opinion of AG Mengozzi of 30 June 2016 in *Remondis GmbH & Co, KG Region Nord v Region Hannover* [2016] ECLI:EU:C:2016:504, para 41.

[26] Ronald P Barston, *Modern Diplomacy* (4th edn, Pearson 2013) 16.

[27] For further reading, see Biswanath Sen, *A Diplomat's Handbook of International Law and Practice* (3rd edn, Martinus Nijhoff 1988) 34; Ivor Roberts (ed), *Satow's Diplomatic Practice* (6th edn, OUP 2011) 84; Malcolm N Shaw, *International Law* (CUP 2014) 547.

[28] Eileen Denza, *Diplomatic Law: Commentary on the Vienna Convention on Diplomatic Relations* (4th edn, OUP 2016) 49.

[29] *Digibet and Albers v Westdeutsche Lotterie* [2014] ECLI:EU:C:2014:1756, paras 34–35.

existence of multilevel diplomacy. This is particularly relevant as several EU member states are ahead in terms of allocating sub-state entities the means and competences to establish permanent representations in foreign countries. Such structures are nothing less than expressions of regional and local self-government provided for in Article 4(2) TEU. Prime examples include the Belgian and Spanish regional actors, who are tasked to represent, defend, and promote the general interests of the region and maintain relations with the EU's institutions.[30] However, the concrete consequences of the protection of sub-state diplomacy in EU law seems to be relative. The CJEU held prior that member states do not enjoy an absolute claim under Article 4(2) TEU based on regional self-government. Without delving into the discussion whether or not the Union is *landesblind*, it is interesting to note that the Court did not accept the following party arguments based on Article 4(2) TEU: *(a)* the submission by Spain that the Court had no jurisdiction to adjudicate on the regional exercise of powers in tax matters (enshrined in Spanish constitutional law);[31] *(b)* the argument advanced by the Northern Ireland Assembly that the lack of locus standi of the regional legislative power went against the obligation to respect the United Kingdom's national identity, including its regional self-government—the General Court found that the Northern Ireland Assembly did not satisfy the condition that it be directly affected, a condition for admissibility laid down in Article 263 TFEU;[32] and *(c)* the observation by the German Federal Government that the *Länder* should be free to determine whether, and to what extent, they must create and manage specialized detention facilities, granted that they enjoy administrative sovereignty in this area according to the German Basic Law.[33]

Neither does Article 4(2) TEU in itself confer special privileges to the regional representatives of member states in the international sphere. This is observed in the diplomatic relations between the Union and member states, whereby the Union only accredits diplomats of member states and not those of regions. The Commission confirmed that 'all official contacts with the authorities of a Member State, whether national, regional or local, must be conducted via the Permanent Representation of that Member State', when asked whether the Commission would speak directly to the Catalan Regional Government's Representative to the EU on matters concerning Catalonia.[34] Further, the obligation to respect national fundamental structures under Article 4(2) TEU has been framed as a passive EU legal obligation of non-interference in national arrangements in diplomacy rather than as an active international legal recognition of sub-state diplomatic actors. Commission Vice-President Timmermans confirmed this view when stating in the Catalonian case that 'it is not for the Commission to comment on the creation of administrative structures in a Member State'. Much like the previous section, what is protected under the phrase protecting sub-state entities seems to be limited to the architecture and organization of national diplomatic services.[35]

A third issue requiring consideration is the extent to which the historical, sociological, political, and symbolic aspects of member states' diplomatic relations are protected under Article 4(2) TEU. The obligation under Article 4(2) is different from the respect the Union should display for member states' history, culture, and tradition as laid down in the preamble

[30] Introduction to Decree 170/2014 [ES] 23 December 2014 on the structure of the ministry of foreign affairs and the EU.
[31] *Commission v Spain* [2014] ECLI:EU:C:2014:2130, para 42.
[32] Order in *Northern Ireland Department of Agriculture v Commission* [2012] ECLI:EU:T:2012:106, para 65.
[33] *Bero* [2014] ECLI:EU:C:2014:2095.
[34] Answer given by the Commission to parliamentary question P-000302/2015, 19 March 2015.
[35] Cloots (n 21) 234 et seq.

of the TEU; the latter's coverage is substantially smaller.[36] Despite the lack of a direct reference to cultural aspects, the CJEU has used the provision to reinforce a respectful attitude to cultures and traditions of member states as a recognition of the respect for national identities. Even more so, language has long been considered as a legitimate objective and part of the national identity.[37] As Advocate-General Kokott argued:

> [r]espect for and promotion of the diversity of its cultures constitutes one of the Community's main preoccupations in all areas [ ... ] it is ultimately an expression of the European Union's respect for the national identities of its Member States. [38]

Surely, every member state possesses certain preferences on how to conduct foreign affairs and how to influence geopolitical patterns; some may even be considered to have evolved into a diplomatic culture.[39] However, proving EU infringements on the basis of Article 4(2) TEU is conditional on national diplomatic practices and patterns having become part of the state's fundamental structures. Therefore, to qualify under the test, member states must evidence that such practice is constitutionally essential.

Other aspects of the diplomatic culture are more likely to fall under Article 4(2) TEU. First, the protection of symbols in diplomacy such as the national flag or anthem used by the missions of member states can be seen as an expression of national identity. Under PIL, the use of symbols is conceived as an entitlement of diplomatic missions, given that these contribute to the visibility and promotion of the identity of nations. Article 20 of the Vienna Convention on Diplomatic Relations (VCDR) 1961, for instance, includes a reference to the right to use the flag and emblem in diplomatic relations.[40] Much like the appointment of diplomats, diplomatic symbols often feature in member states' constitutions. Article 22 of the Basic Law for the Federal Republic of Germany (flag) and Article 193 of the Belgian Constitution (national colours and motto) are two examples.

**Diplomacy as an essential state function** It must be determined whether the right of legation is, in fact, an essential function of a state. In the ordinary meaning of the word, a 'function' is something a state does whilst a right may be but is not necessarily exercised. In international law, the concept struggles with occasional vagueness. Article 3 of the 1933 Montevideo Convention considers it a state's right to defend its integrity and independence, to organize itself as it sees fit, to legislate upon its interests, and to define the jurisdiction and competence of its courts.[41] Shaw considered the following three rights as being the most fundamental: independence, equality, and peaceful coexistence. None of these categorizations are free from overlaps and ambiguities.[42] On a plain reading, it appears that the adjective 'essential' suggests that Article 4(2) TEU only targets the absolute core of the many functions at the disposal of states. The article provides three non-exhaustive examples that seem to suggest otherwise: *(a)* ensuring the state's territorial integrity, *(b)* maintaining law and

[36] See also the preamble to the EU Charter on Fundamental Rights.
[37] *Commission v Luxembourg* [2011] ECLI:EU:C:2011:336, para 124; *Las v PSA Antwerp NV* [2013] ECLI:EU:C:2013:239.
[38] Opinion of AG Kokott of 4 September 2008 in *Unión de Televisiones Comerciales Asociadas ('UTECA')* [2009] ECLI:EU:C:2008:468, para 93.
[39] Wilfried Bolewski, *Diplomacy and International Law in Globalized Relations* (Springer 2007) 75.
[40] Jean Salmon, *Manuel de Droit Diplomatique* (Bruylant 1994) 193.
[41] Convention on Rights and Duties of States, signed on 26 December 1933, entered into force 26 December 1934, 165 LNTS 20.
[42] Shaw (n 27) 153.

order, and *(c)* safeguarding national security. This enumeration strongly relates to the concepts of territorial sovereignty, the protection of which is subject to a number of conditions, and self-defence.[43] The concept of *state functions* in EU law therefore seems to overlap with that of *state rights* in international law. Moreover, it seems that the Treaties' drafters did not seek to attribute to the term 'essential' the meaning of 'absolute'. States have a wide discretion with regard to the exact means they can use to ensure territorial integrity. In the EU context, member states have even set up cooperation and coordination schemes to protect their territories and security. In spite of the sensitivity of the topic of internal security in terms of essential state functions, and the explicit reference to national sovereignty, a common governance framework with specific characteristics has emerged in the counter-terrorism field.[44] The solidarity clause in Article 222 TFEU is but one example.

National courts of member states have hinted at diplomatic relations being an essential state function.[45] In a post-Lisbon judgment, the German Federal Constitutional Court held that the European project has already reached into the traditional core areas of states' areas of competences.[46] The *Bundesverfassungsgericht* observed a growing EU involvement in external relations, including in representational activities, concluding that this impacts the external relations of member states. However, the Lisbon Treaty was not interpreted to mean that the member states' legal personality, functions, and competences in external relations and diplomacy have deteriorated.

In turn, a 2010 judgment by the Polish Constitutional Tribunal identified an actual list of what it considered to be state competences.[47] It thereto conducted an assessment of the concept of sovereignty, which it considered to include the maintenance of diplomatic relations.[48] The Court, however, did not list diplomatic relations within those functions that it considered inalienable and therefore excluded from ever being the subject of a conferral to the Union. Such transfer would not mean that states have lost such rights indefinitely, which they retain by virtue of their constitutions.

PIL has its own take on matters, viewing diplomacy largely as a state business. Although exceptions are noted, the right of legation is a direct consequence of statehood. In the 1933 Montevideo Convention, the capability to enter into relations with other states is even considered a criterion of statehood.[49] It was later omitted, however, by the Arbitration Commission of the Conference on Yugoslavia (the 'Badinter Arbitration Commission').[50] Crawford also refers to the case of the Free City of Danzig, which had the legal marks of statehood when created by the 1919 Treaty of Versailles in spite of the fact that Poland held the power to conduct its external relations.[51]

[43] Olivier Corten, *The Law against War: The Prohibition on the Use of Force in Contemporary International Law* (Hart 2010) 401.

[44] Jörg Monar, 'EU Internal Security Governance: The Case of Counter-Terrorism' (2013) 23 European Security 195.

[45] Armin Steinbach, 'The Lisbon Judgment of the German Federal Constitutional Court—New Guidance on the Limits of European Integration?' (2010) 11 Ger Law J 367, 373–74.

[46] Bundesverfassungsgericht [DE] Judgment of 30 June 2009 concerning the Treaty of Lisbon, paras 248 and 297 (hereafter *Lisbon Judgment*).

[47] Constitutional Tribunal [PL] Judgment of 24 November 2010 concerning the Treaty of Lisbon, No K 32/09.

[48] ibid 280, para 2.1.

[49] Article 1 Convention on Rights and Duties of States, signed on 26 December 1933, entered into force 26 December 1934, 165 LNTS 20. See, for further reading, Matthew Craven, 'Statehood, Self-Determination, and Recognition' in Malcolm D Evans (ed), *International Law* (4th edn, OUP 2014) 217.

[50] Consideration 1(*b*) of Opinion No 1 of the Arbitration Commission of the Conference on Yugoslavia (the 'Badinter Arbitration Commission'), 29 November 1991, reprinted in Alain Pellet, 'The Opinions of the Badinter Arbitration Committee: A Second Breath for the Self-Determination of Peoples' (1992) 3 EJIL 178, 182.

[51] James Crawford, *The Creation of States in International Law* (2nd edn, OUP 2006) 236–41.

Diplomacy is a vehicle for states to create and maintain mutual relations, communicate, collect information, negotiate, and exercise influence to enable the preservation of other state functions including those listed in the EU Treaties. Permanent diplomatic relations ensure states' territorial integrity by peacefully settling interstate disputes before they lead to acts of aggression, the use of force, or other violations of territorial sovereignty—examples of essential state functions as listed in Article 4(2) TEU. Formal diplomatic channels may be employed by states to inform that it considers its core functions threatened by another state's acts. An example is French President Hollande's summoning the US ambassador in June 2015, following WikiLeaks revelations that the National Security Agency had spied on the past three French presidents. The official statement on the convocation read that 'France will not tolerate actions that threaten its security and the protection of its interests.' These 'all-round' and instrumental features of diplomacy render it fundamental to the functioning of states.[52] As such, the very core of national diplomatic relations seems to be protected by the second sentence of Article 4(2) TEU.

*5.1.2.2.3 Declarations 13 and 14 attached to the EU Treaties*

A final element in determining demarcation issues between the Union's and member states' competences in diplomacy targets the exercise of diplomatic and consular relations proper. In two declarations (Declarations 13 and 14 attached to the Final Act of the Intergovernmental Conference which adopted the Treaty of Lisbon), the member states quite clearly provided such demarcations at the occasion of the introduction of modifications to the EU institutional and legal landscape that came with the Lisbon Treaty.[53] The Declarations primarily target the Lisbon Treaty's most prominent novelty: the establishment of the EEAS, the Union's foreign service.

The EEAS's mandate is minimally defined—Article 27(3) TEU is the only primary law clause dealing with the Service—as the Treaties left it for the Council to elaborate its organization and functioning.[54] However, at the time of establishment it was already apparent that the Service was not an MFA and that it did not have the mandate or a presupposed intention to replace national ministries. Moreover, the EEAS would not significantly impact the EU's vertical division of competences. Despite these guarantees, the member states seemed slightly uncomfortable with the changes instigated. There was a perceived fear that the Lisbon Treaty had created an invigorated entity that did not seek to assert itself only in the world but also among its members. In that sense, Declarations 13 and 14 serve as reminders of the CFSP's specific nature, a domain known for member state dominance.[55]

Both Declarations contain references to the diplomatic relations of member states. The first paragraph of Declaration 13 expresses that the newly defined CFSP, will:

> not affect the responsibilities of the Member States, as they currently exist, for the formulation and conduct of their foreign policy nor of their national representation in third countries and international organisations.

[52] James Crawford, *Brownlie's Principles of Public International Law* (OUP 2012) 395.

[53] Declarations 13 and 14 concerning the Common Foreign and Security Policy attached to the Final Act of the Intergovernmental Conference adopting the Treaty of Lisbon [2012] OJ C326/01 (hereafter Declarations 13 and 14 concerning the CFSP).

[54] This was done in Council Decision 2010/427/EU establishing the organization and functioning of the European External Action Service [2010] OJ L201/30 (hereafter 'EEAS Decision').

[55] Federica Bindi, 'One Year On: Assessing the European Foreign Policy and the European External Action Service' (2010) 17 BJWA 125, 126.

Declaration 14 can be perceived as a manifestation of the member states' quest to protect their competences in the internal organization of diplomatic services in the context of an emerging European diplomacy. The Declaration provides that the Lisbon Treaty:

> will not affect the existing legal basis, responsibilities, and powers of each Member State in relation to the formulation and conduct of its foreign policy, its national diplomatic service, relations with third countries and participation in international organisations, including a Member State's membership of the Security Council of the United Nations.

The Declarations encompass two distinct notions. The first relates to the formulation of an independent foreign policy and the safeguarding of competences to determine national interests and external strategies. The phrasing targets the content of policymaking in the external domain and its execution by national diplomatic missions. The Declarations therefore counterbalance the right of initiative that the HR holds jointly with member states in the CFSP (Art 30(1) TEU). The second notion exemplifies an institutional finality and comprises the will to protect national diplomatic services' legal basis and powers.

With the introduction of the EEAS Decision in 2010, setting out the nature and scope of action of the Service, came the legal confirmation that national representations are outside its ambit (Art 1). However, the Declarations remain relevant. At the very least, they serve as reminders of the sensitivities in the field of diplomatic representation. Even as the Declarations are not legally binding instruments, they constitute useful interpretive tools of the will of the member states.[56] Moreover, the relation of the Declarations with the national identity clause is obvious. Although the Declarations refer to member states' *responsibilities* rather than their essential state *functions,* the terms overlap and therefore can be substitutable. Admittedly, the Declarations' scope is more limited than Article 4(2) TEU now that the Declarations only target three specific aspects of the right of legation, namely, external, representational, and organizational elements. Therefore, perhaps the most important effects of the Declarations are that they form express reflections of the member states' will to protect their core functions, a final halt against their consideration of a diplomatic competence appropriation.

#### *5.1.2.2.4 Diplomacy as a domaine réservé?*

On the basis of EU law principles, the national identity clause, and Declarations 13 and 14, some member states have argued that the bilateral diplomatic relations of or between member states are excluded from the ambit of EU law.[57] In *Hungary v Slovak Republic*, the Slovak Republic expressed the view that:

> [t]he principle of the conferral of competences under Article 3 TEU, Article 4(1) TEU and Article 5 TEU excludes bilateral diplomatic relations between Member States from the ambit of EU law.

Such a broad claim does not hold up. The sphere of national diplomatic and consular relations in the EU context is no longer exclusively governed by CIL and otherwise applicable international conventions. It is, however, correct to state that particular aspects of member

[56] Jacqueline Dutheil de la Rochere, 'The Lisbon Compromise: A Synthesis between Community Method and Union Acquis' (2007) 31 Fordham Intl L J 1143, 1146–47.
[57] *Hungary v Slovak Republic* [2012] ECLI:EU:C:2012:630, para 34.

states' diplomacy remain untouched by EU law. The following sections argue that this is the case for most of the formal aspects of diplomatic and consular relations and only some of the many substantive fields affected by diplomacy.

Procedural features of national diplomatic and consular relations are part of the domaine réservé of the member states and the EU. First, exclusively technical aspects of the application of the international legal framework on national diplomacy relations are each diplomatic actor's own concern. Much of the VCDR[58] and the 1963 Vienna Convention on Consular Relations' (VCCR)[59] concrete application firmly rests in the hands of states, including the granting of privileges and immunities, the issuing of diplomatic licence plates or identity cards, and the accreditation and receiving of the notification on diplomatic and consular agents' arrival and final departure.[60] In principle, in the course of its own diplomatic practice, the EU enjoys the same competences in the application of the VCDR. However, as explained earlier, this internal competence is not (always) matched perfectly with a corresponding international capacity.

The second formal domaine réservé in diplomacy concerns the management of representations and the appointment and accreditation of diplomatic and consular agents. An example concerns any decision regarding the size of a foreign mission and composition of staff. This was recognized by the Council when it stated that the 'question of the presence of national diplomats in Member States' embassies abroad is a purely national competence and is not a matter for the Council'.[61] A further example concerns the decisions on the geographic spread and the opening and closing of permanent missions, embassies, and consulates. The HR explained that it 'is the prerogative of each Member State to decide on the size of its diplomatic service and on its geographic presence in the world'.[62] These competences, however, can be exercised by the Union and member states in parallel. Acting as the manager of the EU's diplomatic network, the HR can decide without the direct involvement of member states on the appointment of Heads of Delegation (HoDs) and decisions on the opening and closing of EUDELs.[63]

Where diplomacy is used to deal with a substantive area subject to the ordinary division between the EU and the member states, the situation is more complex. The principles of EU law, the national identity clause, and Declarations 13 and 14 hardly offer any guidance with regard to that situation. It is certain that member states wished to retain competences to formulate own foreign policy, protect the most fundamental aspects of their identities, and pursue own national interests through diplomacy. Yet, the de facto retention of competences proves difficult to ascertain. The starting point should be that the representation of national interests in domains not conferred to the Union remains the primary concern of the member states. However, when the diplomatic representation concerns a domain strongly influenced by EU law (eg trade negotiations), member states must respect the overarching EU rules on the division of competences. A model to deal with this type of questions is presented in part 5.3 of this chapter.

[58] Vienna Convention on Diplomatic Relations, opened for signature on 18 April 1961, entered into force 24 April 1964, 500 UNTS 95 (hereafter VCDR).

[59] Vienna Convention on Consular Relations (opened for signature 24 April 1963, entered into force 19 March 1967) 596 UNTS 261 (hereafter VCCR).

[60] See also *Commission v Belgium* [2007] ECLI:EU:C:2007:178, para 33.

[61] Answer given by the Council to parliamentary question E-3445/2010, 14 May 2010. The Council's answer also refers to Declaration 13, attached to the Treaties and discussed in section 5.1.2.2.3.

[62] Answer given by High Representative to parliamentary question E-3446/2010, 14 May 2010.

[63] Article 5(1) EEAS Decision (n 54). See Chapter 4 on the appointment of EU HoDs.

### 5.1.3 Diplomacy as a Source of Law

#### 5.1.3.1 Incorporating International Legal Norms

In its relations with the wider world, the Union set an objective to contribute to 'the strict observance and development of international law, including respect for the principles of the United Nations Charter' (Arts 3(5), 21(1)(2)(*b*) TEU). Moreover, the Union is legally required by its own constitutional principles to comply with principles of international law in humanitarian aid operations (Art 214(2) TFEU) and in the CSDP (Art 42(1–2) TEU). However, the Treaties do not extensively cover the topic of international law's incorporation into the EU legal order. The actual modalities of the incorporation therefore rest in the CJEU's hands.

The Court has displayed a generally receptive attitude towards PIL. Early case law specifically demonstrates the CJEU's conception of *Völkerrechtsfreundlichkeit*.[64] In its 1992 *Poulsen* judgment, the Court stressed that the Union 'must respect international law in the exercise of its powers'.[65] There are numerous cases repeating this principle, thereby substantiating what can now be considered a settled principle of EU law. The Court subsequently specified that the totality of international law (including CIL and, in certain cases, agreements that the EU is not a party to) is part of the EU legal order.[66] Later on, the Court stressed more explicitly the autonomy of the EU legal order from the member states' orders but also from the international legal order.[67] Recent case law increasingly demonstrates that the debate on internalization does not boil down to a black-and-white choice between upholding a receptive attitude towards international law and managing protective tendencies.[68] PIL can equally be used to protect the EU legal order in the same way that, through the application of EU law, international legal principles can be given concrete meaning in the Union. In 2015, the General Court relied on international law to find that there is no absolute prohibition for the EU institutions to conclude treaties applied to disputed areas.[69] In the appeal judgment, the ECJ Grand Chamber accepted that the people of the Western Sahara have an international right to self-determination. However, because the Agreement does not apply—although it is de facto applied by the Moroccan authorities—to the Western Sahara, its representatives had no standing to challenge the EU decision.[70]

#### 5.1.3.2 Diplomatic and Consular Law as Part of the EU Legal Order

This section looks at the reception of two specific international instruments in the EU legal order, namely, the 1961 and 1963 Vienna Conventions. Since the Union is not a signatory to either, the Treaties are not binding upon the Union via Article 216 TFEU. However, the EU is confronted with the rules of VCDR and VCCR in at least the following four ways: as a result

[64] *Haegeman v Belgium* [1973] ECLI:EU:C:1974:41; *Hauptzollamt Mainz v CA Kupferberg & Cie KG aA* [1982] ECLI:EU:C:1982:362.

[65] *Poulsen and Diva Navigation Corp* [1992] ECLI:EU:C:1992:453, para 9.

[66] See *Racke GmbH&Co v Hauptzollamt Mainz* [1998] ECLI:EU:C:1998:293, paras 45–46; *The Queen, on the application of International Association of Independent Tanker Owners and others v Secretary of State for Transport* [2008] ECLI:EU:C:2008:312 (hereafter *Intertanko*); and *Kadi and Al Barakaat International Foundation v Council* [2008] ECLI:EU:C:2008:461, para 291 (hereafter *Kadi I*).

[67] *Commission v Ireland ('Mox Plant')* [2006] ECLI:EU:C:2006:345, para 123.

[68] See, for a recent protectionist spasm of the CJEU, *Opinion 2/13 pursuant to Article 218(11) TFEU* [2014] ECLI:EU:C:2014:2454.

[69] *Front Polisario v Council* [2015] ECLI:EU:T:2015:953, para 205.

[70] *Council v Front Polisario* [2016] ECLI:EU:C:2016:973, paras 132–33.

of *(a)* the accession of all member states to both Conventions, *(b)* the CIL status of the rules in the Conventions, and as regards *(c)* the references made to the VCDR in bilateral agreements concluded with third countries and *(d)* the references to customary diplomatic law in Protocol No 7 attached to the Treaties.[71] This section looks at how the incorporation of diplomatic and consular law takes place in the above scenarios and tries to define their limits.

*5.1.3.2.1 Functional succession*

In extraordinary cases, the CJEU accepted the application of an international treaty in the EU legal order where all member states have acceded to it. In *International Fruit Company*, it was decided that, although the European Community was not a signatory to the 1947 General Agreement on Tariffs and Trade (GATT), the Community should have considered itself bound by the Agreement observing an exclusive competence over the common commercial policy.[72] As such, the CJEU ruled that a treaty can become binding on the EU where it exercises competences previously held by member states and is, for that reason, considered as their functional successor.[73] In practice, however, the benchmark for functional succession set by the Court is high and therefore rarely observed.[74]

Neither the VCDR nor the VCCR comply with the jurisprudential criteria for functional succession. The requirements for the EU to be bound are that 'it must have assumed, and thus had transferred to it, *all* the powers previously exercised by the member states that fall within the convention in question' [own emphasis].[75] Even when this would be generously interpreted in the sense that this does not mean that the EU's competences must be exclusive, the diplomatic domain does not fulfil the criterion. The member states retained the right to conduct diplomacy and the Union develops its own diplomatic relations by definition in limited domains—a *full* transfer therefore never occurred.[76] In the *Intertanko* judgment, the Court also held that the Union 'cannot, simply because all those States are parties to Marpol 73/78, be bound by the rules set out therein, which it has not itself approved'. Likewise, the EU cannot be considered the member states' functional successor in diplomatic or consular relations.

*5.1.3.2.2 Customary international law status*

CIL binds the Union and can be given effect within the EU legal order.[77] Consequently, provisions in international agreements the Union is not party to can become binding insofar as they codify customary rules or have become CIL in the meantime. This process was observed in the context of the Convention on the Law of the Sea (UNCLOS), which was recognized by the CJEU as an expression of CIL prior to its entry into force.[78]

[71] Protocol No 7 on the Privileges and Immunities of the European Union, attached to the EU Treaties [2012] OJ C326/266 (hereafter Protocol No 7).

[72] *International Fruit Company NV and others v Produktschap voor Groenten en Fruit* [1972] ECLI:EU:C:1972:115, para 18.

[73] *Air Transport Association of America and others v Secretary of State for Energy and Climate Change* [2011] ECLI:EU:C:2011:864, para 62 (hereafter *ATAA*).

[74] *Nederlandse Spoorwegen v Inspecteur der invoerrechten en accijnzen* [1975] ECLI:EU:C:1975:154; *Societa Petrolifera Italiana and Michelin Italiana* [1983] ECLI:EU:C:1983:78, para 17.

[75] *ATAA* (n 73) para 63.

[76] *Intertanko* (n 66) para 49; *ATAA* (n 73) paras 63–65; *Bogiatzi v Deutscher Luftpool and others* [2009] ECLI:EU:C:2009:649, paras 29–30.

[77] *ATAA* (n 73) para 101; *Racke* (n 66) paras 45–46.

[78] *Poulsen* (n 65) paras 9–10; *Intertanko* (n 66) para 39.

Similarly, the CJEU unequivocally confirmed the CIL status of the VCCR in its 2015 *Evans* judgment.[79] In this consular case, the Court accepted that the 1963 VCCR had obtained CIL status in its entirety. It stated that secondary law:

> ought to be interpreted in the light of the relevant rules of customary international law [ . . . ], namely the Vienna Convention of 1963, which codifies the law of consular relations and states principles and rules essential for the maintenance of peaceful relations between States and accepted throughout the world by nations of all creeds, cultures and political complexions [ . . . ].[80]

It is interesting to reflect on how the Court reached its decision. To determine CIL status, the CJEU reproduced a single (and fairly general) reference to both Vienna Conventions in the 1980 International Court of Justice's (ICJ) *Tehran Hostages* case.[81] Referring to the international Court's judgment exemplifies the CJEU's openness to international law but is not beyond reproach.[82] De Baere and Ryngaert explain that the Court's reliance on the ICJ's case law has often become habitual and 'is a notable example of deference towards the ICJ and international law more broadly' but also 'arguably a technique to mitigate the risk of diverging interpretations threatening the consistency of international law'.[83]

First, in *Tehran Hostages* the Court primarily dealt with receiving states' specific obligation to protect diplomatic and consular premises and staff as stipulated in the VCDR and VCCR.[84] Although tempting, one must be careful not to readily draw general conclusions from a case that deals with specific aspects of diplomatic life. Second, the referred-to paragraph 45 does not directly refer to CIL:

> [t]he Vienna Conventions, which codify the law of diplomatic and consular relations, state principles and rules essential for the maintenance of peaceful relations between States and accepted throughout the world by nations of all creeds, cultures and political complexions.

As Advocate-General (AG) Wahl also observed, in *Tehran Hostages* the ICJ has fallen short of 'an actual statement that the VCCR amounts to a codification of the rules under customary international law'.[85] Indeed, the fact that the rules were codified at one point does not necessarily imply that they form part of general customary law over fifty years later. Moreover, it is a bit of a mystery as to why the CJEU did not refer to *Tehran Hostages*' paragraph 62 *in fine*, the more often quoted one in literature to prove customary status of certain provisions of both Vienna Conventions:[86]

> [i]n the view of the Court, the obligations of the Iranian Government here in question [pertaining to the protection of diplomatic and consular premises and staff] are not merely

[79] *Raad van bestuur van de Sociale verzekeringsbank v LF Evans* [2015] ECLI:EU:C:2015:12, paras 35–36 (hereafter *Evans*).

[80] ibid, para 36.

[81] *Case Concerning United States Diplomatic and Consular Staff in Tehran (United States of America v Iran)* (Judgment) [1980] ICJ Rep 3, para 45 (hereafter *Tehran Hostage* case).

[82] A proven technique, also used by the Court in *ATAA* (n 73) para 104 and *Racke* (n 66) para 50.

[83] Geert De Baere and Cedric Ryngaert, 'The ECJ's Judgment in Air Transport Association of America and the International Legal Context of the EU's Climate Change Policy' (2013) 18 EFAR 389, 393.

[84] *Tehran Hostage* case (n 81) para 95.

[85] Opinion of AG Wahl in *Evans* [2015] ECLI:EU:C:2014:2015, para 36.

[86] *Tehran Hostage* case (n 81) para 62.

contractual obligations established by the Vienna Conventions of 1961 and 1963, but also obligations under general international law.

The Court could have also referred to the 2002 *Arrest Warrant* case in which the ICJ confirmed the customary nature of immunities of diplomatic and consular.[87]

The *Evans* judgment is liable to criticism for referring pro forma to the ICJ's judgment without substantiation the finding by legal analysis.[88] This has happened in other cases too: when the CJEU determined that privileges and immunities enjoyed by heads of state were part of CIL, it did so without support of any evidence. Privileges and immunities seem to be considered a given or a fact of international law, which in itself tells something about their legal status. It is somewhat unfortunate that the CJEU did not seize the opportunity to properly analyse the VCCR (or the VCDR, although this was not the main subject in the case); neither did the Court look at the Conventions' negotiation history and specific function in international relations.[89]

The practical consequences of the CJEU's reluctance to conduct an enquiry regarding the existence of CIL are different for the VCDR than for the VCCR. With regard to diplomatic law, the situation is not overly problematic. Although the VCDR's customary status was not directly at issue in *Evans*, it is legitimately assumable that the Court a fortiori recognized the CIL status of VCDR rules; it even makes reference to both Conventions. Moreover, the finding that the 1961 Vienna Convention has customary law status in its entirety is valid and uncontroversial. To a large extent, the VCDR has indeed codified the customary rules on bilateral diplomatic relations between states.[90] Although the 1961 codification also contained new rules and progressive interpretations of existing rules, all provisions have become part of general international law over time. Sir Francis Vallat, head of the British delegation to the 1961 Vienna Conference referred to the VCDR as a 'fair codification of existing law and practice with some significant changes'.[91] The exaggeratedly careful approach of the 1992 opinion of AG Jacobs, who observed that the '1961 Vienna Convention on Diplomatic Relations [ … ] *broadly reflects* the position under customary international law' should be rejected for these reasons.[92]

In contrast to the VCDR, the question whether *all* VCCR provisions are recognized as CIL is still a matter of academic dispute, one that is not reflected in the *Evans* judgment. Rather, the CJEU relied on the general understandings of diplomatic law and considered these also applicable to consular law. This might have been an outright generalization. As noted by the ICJ, the VCCR and VCDR share much of the same pedigree: both originated from the early 1960 UN agenda to codify international law. In addition, the Conventions foresee the possibility of consular functions being performed by diplomatic agents and diplomatic functions performed by consular mission, respectively.[93] Contrarily to its diplomatic counterpart, however, the VCCR cannot be considered a simple codification of CIL. In 1963,

[87] Arrest Warrant of 11 April 2000 *(Democratic Republic of the Congo v Belgium)* (Judgment) [2002] ICJ Rep 3, para 52.

[88] *Hungary v Slovak Republic* (n 57) para 46.

[89] See also Sanderijn Duquet, 'Raad van Bestuur van de Sociale Verzekeringsbank v LF Evans, Judgment, Case C-179/13' 078 ILEC, Oxford Reports on International Law (CJEU 2015).

[90] Geoff R Berridge, *Diplomacy: Theory and Practice* (5th edn, Palgrave Macmillan 2015) 109–10; Denza, *Diplomatic Law* (n 28) 2–5; Joe Verhoeven, *Droit International Public* (Larcier 2000) 106.

[91] Quoted in Kai Bruns, *A Cornerstone of Modern Diplomacy: Britain and the Negotiation of the 1961 Vienna Convention on Diplomatic Relations* (Bloomsbury Academic 2014) 133.

[92] *Bestuur van de Sociale Verzekeringsbank v A de Wit* [1992] ECLI:EU:C:1992:463, para 19 [own emphasis].

[93] Article 3(2) VCDR; Art 17(1) VCCR.

agreement had to be found among delegates on a larger number of disputed issues than had been the case in 1961 for diplomatic law.[94] The VCCR embodies a general framework of minimum standards; Article 73 VCCR recognizes the validity of other agreements, bilateral or regional, in existence before the VCCR came into force. The answer to the question of whether the VCCR in the meantime has become part of general international law is therefore somewhat (though arguably less and less) contested. In *Tehran Hostages*, the ICJ only confirmed the customary status of particular provisions, that is, those related to the protection of consular premises and staff. When granted the opportunity in more recent cases on the 1963 Convention, the ICJ did not make similar statements regarding other VCCR provisions.[95] One reason for this could be that states observe a continuous interest in bilateral consular agreements that cover issues dealt with by the VCCR. Such consular treaties that sometimes derogate from and sometimes paraphrase the VCCR continue to exist in great numbers. Hesitations are also present in literature, while some merely note that the 'main principles of consular law' are applied uniformly.[96] Was the CJEU's conclusion to mark the whole Convention as customary in nature unjustifiable? Probably not. In light of the longstanding close relationship between the two sister Conventions, the increased state participation to the VCCR and increased generalization of consular practices all over the world, the argument can be made that the VCCR largely, if not entirely, has become CIL. If anything, the CJEU missed an opportunity to more extensively shine its light on the above discussion.

##### 5.1.3.2.3 *Direct references to diplomatic law*

As extensively discussed in Chapter 3, whilst not a signatory to the 1961 VCDR, the EU is subject to its legal regime through the means of multiple bilateral establishment agreements (EAs) with receiving states. Due to the reciprocity clause and reference to Article 16 of Protocol No 7 on the Privileges and Immunities of EU, the VCDR applies to Brussels-based missions of third states; due to Article 10 Protocol No 7, missions of member states too are granted customary privileges, immunities, and facilities. Practice indicates that the differences between missions of third states and member states and those accredited to the Union or Belgium are insignificant. Therefore, it can be concluded that, in its conventional and customary forms, diplomatic law has entered the EU legal order as the applicable law to deal with the Union's active and passive diplomatic relations by virtue of the EAs and Protocol No 7. This important finding brings diplomatic law directly into the EU legal order, making it binding on the Union when exercising the right of legation.

Nevertheless, caution should be exercised with regard to this finding. The mechanism only makes diplomatic law directly applicable to the Union's diplomatic relations. As a result, it is uncertain whether the interpretation of EAs *j* Protocol No 7 should go as far as to recognize that the Union is bound to respect the VCDR when promulgating other norms. In such cases, it is more likely that diplomatic law applies to the Union because of its CIL status. Since the Union does not send or accredit consular missions, the VCCR is not directly (made) applicable to the EU. There is one notable exception: the EA entered into with Hong Kong refers to the VCCR as the applicable legal framework for EU's mission. However, the text of Article 16 Protocol No 7 referring only to 'diplomatic' customary rules is not favourable to the reciprocal application of consular rights and privileges.

[94] Luke T Lee and John B Quigley, *Consular Law and Practice* (3rd edn, OUP 2008) 21–23.
[95] *LaGrand (Germany v United States of America)* (Judgment) [2001] ICJ Rep 466); *Avena and other Mexican Nationals (Mexico v United States of America)* [2004] ICJ Rep 12.
[96] Roberts (n 27) 251.

### 5.1.3.3 Consequences

#### *5.1.3.3.1 Member states' law*

The fact that diplomatic and consular law are part of the law of the EU leads to various consequences for the member states.[97] Diplomatic and consular law are now binding on member states not just due to having acceded the Vienna Conventions but as an obligation deriving from the EU legal order.[98] As part of EU law, customary diplomatic and consular law automatically takes primacy over any conflicting national laws. The status of diplomatic and consular law in the national legal orders is also no longer exclusively in the hands of the member states.[99] Moreover, the CJEU's finding that the VCCR became CIL in its entirety impacts the status of particular norms of consular law in the member states, over which confusion still persists.[100] Finally, the interpretation of the rights and obligations stemming from the diplomatic and consular regimes are no longer exclusively matters for the national courts of member states.[101] In its striving for a uniform application of the law, the CJEU can determine the reach and substance of rules. Evidently, this discussion is largely theoretical since member states show high compliance with diplomatic and consular norms.

#### *5.1.3.3.2 EU law*

Similarly to international agreements that the EU is a party to, CIL binds the Union and may be used to review the validity of its acts. As to the more concrete effects, a distinction must be made between primary and secondary law. In the EU hierarchy of norms, PIL takes primacy over instruments of secondary Union law. Under Article 3(5) TEU, the Union is to contribute to the strict observance and the development of international law. When it adopts an act, it is bound to observe international law in its entirety, including CIL, which is binding upon the institutions of the EU.[102] Consequently, when adopting legislative acts or individual measures, it is required for EU institutions to comply with customary diplomatic and consular international law.[103] When conflicts arise, the CJEU favours an integrative reading of the two bodies of law: 'provisions must so far as possible, be interpreted in a manner that is consistent with [international] agreements'.[104] This is different regarding primary law. Neither diplomatic or consular law nor EU primary law are by definition superior to the other due to lack of a hierarchy of norms. As such, the Court retains an important leeway to determine the effects of diplomatic and consular law within the European legal order. However, even in the absence of a hierarchy, EU law must be interpreted in light of the international obligations entered into by member states and CIL.[105]

In different domains, EU law has given effect to principles of diplomatic and consular law. Quite evidently, this phenomenon arises when legislation is promulgated in the diplomatic sphere. For instance, the 2015 Council Directive on consular protection for unrepresented citizens makes it clear that it:

[97] See generally, Jan Wouters, André Nollkaemper, and Erika De Wet (eds), *The Europeanisation of International Law: The Status of International Law in the EU and Its Member States* (TMC Asser Press 2008).

[98] Koen Lenaerts and Tim Corthaut, 'Of Birds and Hedges: The Role of Primacy in Invoking Norms of EU Law' (2006) 31 ELR 287, 289.

[99] *Flaminio Costa v ENEL* [1964] ECLI:EU:C:1964:66; Geert De Baere, *Constitutional Principles of EU External Relations* (OUP 2008) 36.

[100] See the discussion of *Evans* (n 79) in section 5.2.

[101] *Hermès International v FHT Marketing Choice* [1998] ECLI:EU:C:1998:292, para 28 on the application of the TRIPS agreement by national courts.

[102] *ATAA* (n 73) para 101.

[103] *Racke* (n 66) para 45.

[104] *Commission v Germany* [1996] ECLI:EU:C:1996:313, para 52; *Kadi I* (n 66) para 291.

[105] *Poulsen* (n 65) para 9; *Defrenne v Sabena* [1976] ECLI:EU:C:1976:56, para 37.

> does not affect consular relations between Member States and third countries, in particular their rights and obligations arising from international customs and agreements, in particular from the Convention of 24 April 1963 on Consular Relations (the Vienna Convention), that Member States apply in compliance with Union law. Under Article 8 of the Vienna Convention, Member States may provide consular protection on behalf of another Member State upon appropriate notification and unless the third country concerned objects.[106]

In an increasing number of cases, diplomatic (and sometimes consular) law is also referred to in other contexts. First, EU instruments may refer to these bodies of law when defining the scope ratione materiae of a rule. For instance, the imposition of restrictive measures against third states does not commonly target payments:

> to be paid into or from an account of a diplomatic mission or consular post or an international organization enjoying immunities in accordance with international law, in so far as such payments are intended to be used for official purposes of the diplomatic mission or consular post or international organization.[107]

The Council Guidelines on sanctions in the CFSP framework mention that, where restrictive measures might have an effect on diplomatic missions and members of their staff enjoying privileges and immunities, the necessary steps must be taken to ensure that such missions and their staff members are not hindered as a consequence in the performance of their official functions in accordance with Article 25 VCDR.[108]

Similarly, diplomatic and/or consular status can be an excluding factor when EU legislation defines its scope ratione personae. For instance, directives on the status of third-country nationals legally residing in the Union commonly do not apply to those who enjoy diplomatic or consular status. For example, Directive 2003/109/EC concerning the status of third-country nationals who are long-term residents excludes from its scope third-country nationals who:

> enjoy a legal status governed by the Vienna Convention on Diplomatic Relations of 1961, the Vienna Convention on Consular Relations of 1963, the Convention of 1969 on Special Missions or the Vienna Convention on the Representation of States in their Relations with International Organisations of a Universal Character of 1975.[109]

Finally, diplomatic and consular law may also serve as the reason why member states retain a margin of appreciation in a given policy domain. An example concerns the harmonized legislation on aviation security standards. The applicable Commission Regulation provides

[106] Consideration 6 of Council Directive 2015/637 on the coordination and cooperation measures to facilitate consular protection for unrepresented citizens of the Union in third countries [2015] OJ L106/1 (hereafter Council Directive 2015/637 on consular protection).

[107] See, among others, Art 1 Council Decision 2012/212/CFSP concerning restrictive measures against Belarus [2012] OJ L113/11 and Art 27 of Council Regulation (EU) 2015/1861 concerning restrictive measures against Iran [2015] OJ L274/1.

[108] Council, 'Guidelines on implementation and evaluation of restrictive measures (sanctions) in the framework of the EU Common Foreign and Security Policy', Brussels, 15 June 2012, 35.

[109] See, for instance, Council Directive 2003/109/EC concerning the status of third-country nationals who are long-term residents [2003] OJ L16/44.

that member states are entitled to policy space with regard to the scanning of diplomatic and consular bags (Art 27(4) VCDR; Art 35(4) VCCR). More concretely, a national authority:

> may allow a diplomatic bag to be exempted from screening or to be subjected to special security procedures provided that the requirements of the Vienna Convention on Diplomatic Relations are met.[110]

The above examples show that EU legislation can preclude its own enforcement (*negative effect*) to the benefit of the advancement of member states' compliance with international diplomatic and consular law (*positive effect*). References to PIL avoid collisions between EU law and the member states' international commitments. The inclusion of diplomatic and consular law clauses in EU law therefore also has a preventive purpose. However, EU law is not standardly checked for possible violations. Frequently, EU legislation is only adapted following a diplomatic incident or a third state's request. Any further screening of EU legislation for incompatibilities is therefore encouraged. An example of the opposite are the Council Guidelines on CFSP sanctions, which propose a standard exemption for diplomatic bank accounts.[111]

*5.1.3.3.3 Legal enforcement*

A final consequence is that diplomatic and consular norms and rules can be invoked to review the legality of an EU act or its implementation by member states. This includes infringement procedures initiated by the Commission against member states (Art 258 TFEU), actions brought by member states against one another (Art 259 TFEU), and actions brought against the acts of EU institutions, bodies, offices, or agencies (Arts 263 and 265 TFEU). Moreover, under Article 267 TFEU, a question involving the diplomatic and consular law may be the object of a preliminary ruling.

In practice, despite the theoretical avenues for judicial review, very few diplomatic and/or consular law cases actually end up in Luxembourg. There are at least four reasons for this, relating to *(a)* the Court's limited jurisdiction in the CFSP, *(b)* the Court's lack of jurisdiction to rule on the interpretation of international law provisions within the member states' exclusive competences, *(c)* preferences by states to deal with diplomatic incidents via diplomatic rather than judicial means, and *(d)* the limited direct effect of rules of customary diplomatic and consular law.

The first obstacle is that, in practice, many topics related to the EU's own diplomatic and consular relations have a legal basis that falls within the CFSP. Conflicts arising in the sphere of the EU's right of legation must be considered as subject to the jurisdictional restrictions the CFSP gives rise to: Article 275 TFEU rules out the CJEU's jurisdiction as regards the CFSP provisions of the Treaties, known as Title V, except in a direct action for annulment regarding sanctions imposed on individuals or in 'legal basis' cases. Importantly for the diplomatic domain, however, the Court has confirmed that the limitations to its jurisdiction in the CFSP must be interpreted narrowly in a case concerning *(a)* a staff dispute raised by an official serving the (CFSP) EU Police Mission in Bosnia and Herzegovina (*H v Council*) and *(b)* in

[110] Commission Regulation (EU) No 185/2010 of 4 March 2010 laid down detailed measures for the implementation of common basic standards on aviation security [2010] OJ L55/1, Annex, 4.1.2.11.

[111] Council Guidelines on implementation and evaluation of restrictive measures in the framework of the EU Common Foreign and Security Policy, 15 June 2012, 34–35.

a case on restrictive measures against natural and legal persons in a procedure other than a direct action for annulment (*Rosneft*).[112]

The CFSP issue is only one hurdle. A second assumption that the Court would be careful not to rule on the interpretation of VCDR or VCCR provisions when applied in cases outside the confines of EU law.[113] This would primarily concern cases on Vienna Conventions' provisions established entirely within the exclusive domains of member states such as 'technical' rules on the application of privileges, immunities, inviolabilities, the management of missions, or issues concerning the accreditation and appointment of diplomats. In contrast, the Court's stance on interpretations of the same rules should not be ruled out when concerning the Union's diplomatic activities or when affecting EU law.

The third observation is that cases on the application of diplomatic and consular law rarely end up before the CJEU. States tend to prefer to solve diplomatic issues outside of courts. For many centuries, soft diplomacy and political pressure have proven to be more popular than court proceedings; the effect is even reinforced by the general European context, where the member states rarely initiate infringement procedures against one another under the Article 259 TFEU procedure.

The limited direct effect of diplomatic and consular law is a final obstacle. The origins of the notion of direct effect lie in the seminal *Van Gend & Loos* case. Subsequently, its meaning has been clarified—and narrowed—in the CJEU's case law.[114] In the early days, the existence of an international norm in the EU legal order may have seemed to entail that an individual could invoke that rule in Court. Case law on direct effect has significantly narrowed the applicability of such claims.[115] The CJEU established that an individual cannot invoke norms of the World Trade Organization (WTO)[116] agreements and the UN Convention on the Law of the Sea (UNCLOS) in light of the assumed nature and broad logic of those regimes. In a string of case law, the Court observed that the aforementioned bodies of international law do 'not establish rules intended to apply directly and immediately to individuals and confer upon them rights and freedoms capable of being relied upon against States [ … ]'.[117] In *Van Parys*, the Court viewed the 'nature and structure' of WTO law as a reason to deny it direct effect.[118] In *Intertanko*, the Court deals with Marpol 73/78, to which the Union is not a party but all member states are. The Court denied the instrument direct effect after an analysis of the obligations flowing from the agreement. The fact that the Union was not a signatory was not a decisive factor, although it did weigh in as a reason as to why the Union had not assumed binding obligations.[119] However, the Court did not rule out that a single international agreement may contain provisions having both direct and indirect effect.[120]

[112] *H v Council* [2016] ECLI:EU:C:2016:569 and *Rosneft* [2017] ECLI:EU:C:2017:236. See Marise Cremona and Anne Thies (eds), *The European Court of Justice and External Relations Law: Constitutional Challenges* (Hart 2014).

[113] *Vandeweghe and others v Berufsgenossenschaft für die Chemische Industrie* [1973] ECLI:EU:C:1973:131, para 2; *Hurd v Her Majesty's Inspector of Taxes* [1986] ECLI:EU:C:1986:2, para 20.

[114] *Van Gend & Loos v Administratie der Belastingen* [1963] ECLI:EU:C:1963:1.

[115] Ramses A Wessel, 'Reconsidering the Relationship between International and EU Law: Towards a Content-Based Approach?' in Enzo Cannizzaro, Paulo Palchetti, and Ramses A Wessel (eds), *International Law as Law of the European Union* (Martinus Nijhoff 2011) 13.

[116] *International Fruit Company* (n 72); see also *Portugal v Council* [1999] ECLI:EU:C:1999:574.

[117] *Intertanko* (n 66) para 64.

[118] *Van Parys NV v Belgische Interventie- en Restitutiebureau* [2005] ECLI:EU:C:2005:121, para 39.

[119] *Intertanko* (n 66) paras 47–49.

[120] *Simutenkov v Ministerio de Educación y Cultura and Real Federación Española de Fútbol* [2005] ECLI:EU:C:2005:213, para 28.

Under these criteria, the international diplomatic and consular regimes do not easily lend themselves to direct application, perhaps even less so than other international regimes. Diplomatic and consular law operate predominantly in interstate relations, and have as their ultimate aim to facilitate interactions between states. The VCDR's preamble, third recital, clearly states in this regard that the Convention will contribute 'to the development of friendly relations among nations, irrespective of their differing constitutional and social systems'.[121] The rules are designed to protect states and their international relations, whereas the purpose and nature of the diplomatic and consular regimes do not provide for extensive individual rights. An important part of the diplomatic and consular cases that end up before national courts concern individuals who, often without success, attempt to invoke arguments based on the right to access to courts and justice to try to limit immunities and inviolabilities granted by diplomatic and consular law. Even the immunities enjoyed by diplomatic and consular agents and their family members in receiving states cannot be qualified as with individual rights. Article 25 VCDR, Article 28 VCCR, and the preambles of both Vienna Conventions explain that the 'purpose of such privileges and immunities is not to benefit individuals but to ensure the efficient performance of the functions' of 'diplomatic missions as representing States' (VCDR) and by 'consular posts on behalf of their respective States' (VCCR). Their privileged status is a direct result of the appointment of the agent by the sending state to represent its sovereign character abroad; the immunities do not serve to benefit the agent in a personal capacity. The rights resulting from the diplomatic or consular status are to be invoked and waived by that sending state, not the individual agent (Art 32 VCDR and Art 45 VCCR). The state may waive the immunity of a (former) agent even if such a waiver would be contrary to their personal interests. In such circumstances, it must be found that the Vienna Conventions do not contain individual rights as they do not confer individual rights or freedoms that can be relied upon against the sending state's will.

One clause, however, requires more scrutiny: Article 36 VCCR codifies the 'right to consul', a provision of the rights of an individual when arrested, in custody, or otherwise detained in a foreign country, to request the receiving state's authorities to inform the sending state's consular post without delay (Art 36(1)(*b*) VCCR). Subsequently, the sending state has the right to correspond with its national and arrange for legal representation (Art 36(1)(*c*) VCCR). In 1999, the Inter-American Court on Human Rights was the first international adjudicating body to issue an advisory opinion recognizing that Article 36 VCCR created individual rights.[122] In the 2001 *LaGrand*[123] and the 2004 *Avena and Other Mexican Nationals* judgments,[124] the ICJ identified that Article 36 VCCR provides a rare instance where a treaty obligation affects both the rights of the sending state and individual rights of the national concerned. Moreover, the Court deemed both fit for international adjudication.[125] The *Avena* case concerned fifty-two Mexican nationals facing the death penalty in the United States who were unable to or not told that they could communicate with the Mexican consulate. The United States was found to be in violation of the VCCR's information duty with

[121] See, similarly, the fourth recital of the VCCR.

[122] Advisory opinion of the Inter-American Court of Human Rights [1999] Ser A No 16, para 87.

[123] *LaGrand* (n 95). See Joan Fitzpatrick, 'The Unreality of International Law in the United States and the LaGrand Case' (2002) 27 Yale J Intl L 427; John B Quigley, 'LaGrand: A Challenge to the US Judiciary' (2002) 27 Yale J Intl L 435.

[124] *Avena* (n 95) and the Request for Interpretation of the Judgment of 31 March 2004, dated 9 January 2009. See Nathalie Klein, 'Avena and Other Mexican Nationals (Mexico v United States of America)' (2004) 11 Aust Int Law J 143. See also the *Case Concerning the Vienna Convention on Consular Relations* (*Paraguay v United States of America*) (Order) [1998] ICJ Rep 426.

[125] *LaGrand* (n 95) paras 77, 125.

respect to fifty-one of those cases. The influence of the *Avena* decision was soon measured in the United States' domestic legal order when one of the nationals involved in the case, Mr Medellin, was denied relief by a federal appellate court following the ICJ's ruling. The holding of the *Avena* case was not considered binding by US federal courts as was later confirmed by the US Supreme Court.[126]

The ICJ's qualification evokes questions with regard to the EU legal order and direct effect. The CJEU has not yet ruled on Article 36 VCCR. However, AG Kokott, in her opinion in the *ATAA* case, paraphrased the ICJ by stating that Article 36 VCCR 'creates immutable individual rights, as opposed to individual rights derivative of the rights of states'.[127] Knowing that both the member states and the EU have constitutional, though specific, obligations to assist EU citizens abroad, the discussion could arise in the future. Indeed, member states must ensure that their consular protection measures are compatible with Article 20(1)(*c*) TEU on the entitlement of EU citizens to consular protection on a non-discriminatory basis. In that context, Article 36 VCCR theoretically could be relied upon by individuals for the purpose of the Court's examination of other rights, 'which the individual derives from European Union law or to create obligations under European Union law in this regard'.[128]

### 5.1.4 Observations

This section analysed the triangular relationship between EU law, PIL, and domestic law in diplomatic and consular affairs. It was found that EU law often serves as the *law of reference*: it defines which diplomatic actor is competent to act, that is, the Union, the member states, or both. While this distribution of powers occurs internally, it has obvious consequences externally. PIL, for its part, generally functions as the *law of procedure*. It deals with the formal rules on diplomatic and consular intercourse and accordingly directly binds the member states as well as the EU when exercising their rights of legation. The more detailed regulation and codes of conduct are to be found at the national level and include, for example, the exact privileges granted to accredited diplomats. Those national codes must respect both international and EU law. Indeed, when it comes to the *law of substance,* all three levels profoundly affect diplomatic and consular relations.

## 5.2 Coexisting Norms

In executing its tasks, the Court is bound by two distinct legal obligations: a duty to ensure the interpretation and application of the EU Treaties (Art 19 TEU) and, as an EU institution, a duty to contribute to the strict observance of international law (Art 3(5) TEU). In domains other than diplomacy, it has been have observed that the Court fulfils both obligations by

[126] See Court of Appeals, *Medellín v Dretke* [US] 371 F3d 270 (5th Cir 2004); Supreme Court [US] in *Medellín v Texas*, 552 [US] 491 (2008); and Supreme Court [US] *Sánchez-Llamas v Oregon*, 548 [US] 331 (2006), ILDC 697; and the discussion in Steve Charnovitz, 'Correcting America's Continuing Failure to Comply with the Avena Judgment' (2012) 106 AJIL 572; Mark J Kadish, 'Article 36 of the Vienna Convention on Consular Relations: The International Court of Justice in Mexico v United States (Avena) Speaks Emphatically to the Supreme Court of the United States about Fundamental Nature of the Right to Consul' (2004) 36 Georget J Int Law 1; John B Quigley, 'The United States' Withdrawal from International Court of Justice Jurisdiction in Consular Cases: Reasons and Consequences' (2008) 19 Duke J Comp & Intl L 263.

[127] Opinion of AG Kokott in *ATAA* [2011] ECLI:EU:C:2011:637, n 89.

[128] *ATAA* (n 73) para 107.

expressing a desire for integrated interpretation methods and an aversion to interpretations that put the Union in a position of non-compliance with PIL.[129] Moreover, scholarship distinguishes two roles assumed by the Court when dealing with PIL. The CJEU is perceived as a *gatekeeper* when considering how effect is given to international law within the EU legal order and as an *enforcer* when considering the content of international norms.[130] The following sections research whether, when considering diplomatic and consular law, the Court lives up to these constitutional obligation roles.

### 5.2.1 Applying EU Law or Diplomatic and Consular Law

#### 5.2.1.1 The Internal Market

The freedom of movement of goods, persons, services, and capital underpins the Union. Ultimately, these four freedoms promote EU citizens' ability to move and function within the common market and protect market participants from any potential unequal treatment. EU law is susceptible to interaction with diplomatic and consular law since these branches of law also contain rules on the international movement of people and goods.

In diplomatic and consular law, rules on the movement of goods are often framed as privileges. A typical example would be whether and in what quantities luxury products such as spirits, tobacco, cars, and fuel are exempted from customs duties or subject to import quotas. Some of these predate the VCDR, as is the case for some specific Belgian exemptions for Luxembourg and the Netherlands.[131] This type of measure is often subject to reciprocity (Art 36(1)(*b*) VCDR; Art 50(1)(*b*) VCCR) and therefore governed by arrangements between sending and receiving states. Rules that facilitate the import of goods by diplomats can potentially collide with either the common commercial policy or rules on freedom of movement of goods.

The following sections focus on the freedom of movement in the internal market of persons having diplomatic status. In general diplomatic law, states are at liberty to grant agrément or exequatur and accredit a foreign envoy (Art 4 VCDR; Art 12 VCCR), to declare an envoy persona non grata (Art 9 VCDR; Art 23 VCCR), or to request the sending state to downsize the mission (Art 11 VCDR; Art 20 VCCR). One exception is Article 40(2) VCDR, providing that third states *shall not hinder* the passage of members of the administrative and technical or service staff of missions and members of their families through their territories. Articles 40(1) VCDR and 54 VCCR leave open the possibility that diplomatic agents passing through or being in the territory of a third states are subjected to visa duties. The Vienna Conventions effectively provide the receiving states with tools to decide whether a foreign diplomat is prohibited from entering or forced to leave the state's territory. Other customary practices also give host states considerable discretion to regulate access, suffice it to point to national policies related to the issuance of diplomatic identity cards and diplomatic visas. The question becomes how these rules and, most interestingly, the restrictions that follow

[129] Jan Wouters, Jed Odermatt, and Thomas Ramopoulos, 'Worlds Apart? Comparing the Approaches of the European Court of Justice and the EU Legislature to International Law' in Marise Cremona and Anne Thies (eds), *The European Court of Justice and External Relations Law: Constitutional Challenges* (Hart 2014) 267.

[130] Jed Odermatt, *International Law and the European Union* (CUP 2021) 170.

[131] Circular note [BE] on the Annual duty-free quotas for diplomatic purchases, 1 September 2013, and Art 33(2) of the Ministerial Decree of 17 February 1960 (published in the Belgian State Gazette on 18 February 1960).

from them play out in a context where people may enjoy rights to move from one member state to another on the basis of their status as an EU citizen.

### 5.2.1.2 Freedom of Movement of EU Citizens

One of the most memorable cases on diplomatic law in an EU context is the 2012 *Hungary v Slovak Republic* case, which resulted from a diplomatic incident that happened between two EU member states.[132] At stake was the freedom of movement of a head of state, equally an EU citizen. In 2009, the President of Hungary László Sólyom was scheduled to attend a ceremony in the Slovak town of Komárno to inaugurate a statue of Saint Stephen, the first king and founder of Hungary. The Slovakian authorities considered this trip a provocation for three reasons. First, the visit was set to take place on a sensitive date. There is a national holiday on 20 August in Hungary to celebrate Saint Stephen, but the following day commemorates the 1968 invasion of the Czechoslovak Socialist Republic by armed forces of Warsaw Pact countries, including Hungary. Second, the location of the ceremony was of a delicate nature. The South of Slovakia is an area populated by minority ethnic Hungarians. Third, the Hungarian President did not intent to meet any Slovakian officials during his stay in Slovakia, suggesting that the visit was in a private capacity.

Before it took place, Hungary and Slovakia discussed the scheduled visit via diplomatic exchange. Since an understanding was not reached, Slovakia prohibited the Hungarian President from entering its territory, seeking a legal justification in the exceptions of Directive 2004/38/EC relating to the freedom of movement of EU citizens.[133] The message was communicated in a note verbale sent to the Ambassador of Hungary in Bratislava. Mr Sólyom, already on his way to the ceremony, acknowledged receipt of the note and refrained from accessing Slovakia.

The Hungarian authorities subsequently sought the Commission's position on the matter. The Commission expressed the view that any restriction of the right of free movement must observe the principle of proportionality and that a restriction under Article 27(2) of Directive 2004/38/EC must comply with three requirements. First, it has to be based on the personal conduct of the individual concerned. Second, the person must be notified of the decision in the manner prescribed in Article 30 Directive 2004/38/EC. Third, the person must be given a full and precise explanation of the reasons for the restriction.[134] Although the Commission concluded that Slovakia had wrongly relied on Directive 2004/38/EC, the Commission did not observe a breach of EU law in the denial. The Commission pointed to the principle of conferral (Arts 4(1) and 5 TEU) by recalling the member states' 'right to control the access of a foreign Head of State to their territory, regardless of whether that Head of State is a Union citizen'. It concluded that EU law on the movement of citizens between member states does not apply to heads of member states' visits to another state's territory. Interestingly, the Commission distinguished between official and unofficial visits. The arrangement of an official visit is a matter dealt with through bilateral diplomatic arrangements and, as such, does not happen in the sphere of EU law application. In contrast, where a head of state visits another member state in a private capacity, Article 21 TFEU and Directive 2004/38/EC apply.

[132] *Hungary v Slovak Republic* (n 57). See Sanderijn Duquet, 'Hungary v Slovak Republic, Judgment, Case C-364/10 [2012] ECLI:EU:C:2012:630' 024 ILEC, Oxford Reports on International Law (CJEU 2012); Lucia Serena Rossi, 'EU Citizenship and the Free Movement of Heads of State: Hungary v Slovak Republic' (2013) 50 CML Rev 1451.

[133] Directive 2004/38/EC of the European Parliament and of the Council on the right of citizens of the Union and their family members to move and reside freely within the territory of the member states [2004] OJ L158/77.

[134] *Hungary v Slovak Republic* (n 57) para 13.

Advocate-General Bot later largely joined the Commission in its reasoning. The AG explicitly excluded the diplomatic visits of the head of state of one member state to another from the ambit of EU law on the basis of the principle of conferral.[135]

Lacking the Commission's support, Hungary initiated direct proceedings against Slovakia under Article 259 TFEU. The present case was only the fourth time that the Court had been asked to rule on the applicability and the possible failure to comply with EU law in a case initiated by one member state against another.[136] Having established its jurisdiction, the Court categorized the dispute as concerning the interpretation of EU law.[137] The main issue was therefore whether an EU head of state should be regarded as a citizen of the Union, thereby enjoying the freedom of movement, or whether international law was applicable regarding the right to control the access to territory vis-à-vis the visits of EU heads of state. The first hypothesis would entail the application of EU law as pleaded by Hungary, the second approach would require the application of CIL as pleaded by Slovakia.

The Court disagreed with both contentions, subsequently adopting a compromise solution recalling the idea that EU law must be interpreted in the light of relevant rules of international law, as firmly established in case law. First, it was specified that the starting point of the analysis was EU law on citizenship, whereby the principle of conferral was deemed not at issue. There was no direct conflict between the freedom of movement and CIL on bilateral diplomatic relations in the case at hand. Conveniently, this allowed the Court not to have to dismiss long-standing case law on the fundamental character of citizenship for 'every person holding the nationality of a member state'.[138] Hungarian president Sólyom unquestionably enjoyed citizenship and the rights and freedoms that accompany it by virtue of being a Hungarian national. This includes the primary and individual right to move and reside freely within the territory of the member states as laid down in Article 21 TFEU.[139]

Second, the Court qualified international law as an exception to the general rule that every EU citizen enjoys freedom of movement. Notwithstanding the Court's emphasis on its fundamental character and additional legal basis in Article 45 of the Charter of Fundamental Rights of the EU, it was nevertheless deemed as containing exceptions. Consequently, the privileged status enjoyed by the heads of states under PIL legitimizes an approach distinct from that of other Union citizens. This means that international law on privileges and immunities can limit the application of the right of free movement, a fundamental EU principle irrespective of the official or private nature of visits by persons who enjoy a privileged status by virtue of international law.

The Court assessed Slovakia's argument that the VCDR applied, concluding that since the Vienna Convention's purpose is to govern the presence of *permanent* diplomatic posts and travels of diplomats between such posts rather than short-term stays of foreign heads of states, it did not. The CJEU resorted to the codified and customary international legal framework on the temporary presence of diplomats and heads of states such as the New York Convention on the Prevention and Punishment of Crimes against Internationally Protected

[135] Opinion of AG Bot of 6 March 2012 in *Hungary v Slovak Republic* [2012] ECLI:EU:C:2012:124, paras 50–57. In para 52, the AG relies on para 33 of *Commission v Belgium* (n 60).

[136] Timothy Roes, 'Case Note: Hof van Justitie—16 Oktober 2012' (2014) 77 RW 518.

[137] *Hungary v Slovak Republic* (n 57) para 26.

[138] *Janko Rottman v Freistaat Bayern* [2010] ECLI:EU:C:2010:104 and *Murat Dereci and others v Bundesministerium für Inneres* [2011] ECLI:EU:C:2011:734.

[139] *Hungary v Slovak Republic* (n 57) paras 40–43.

Persons.[140] It has been considered problematic that the Court 'did not exactly define where this derogation of international law comes from (exact provisions), nor its extent'.[141]

To come to its conclusion, the Court did not engage in an analysis based on the principle of conferral as proposed by the Commission and the AG. Neither did the Court lean towards an interpretation of Article 4(2) TEU, which, as explained earlier, preserves the member states' territorial organization. *Hungary v Slovak Republic* therefore can be seen as confirmation that the territorial organization of diplomatic relations remain in the hands of member states.[142] Conversely, the CJEU incorporated the sovereign competences of states to regulate the access to their territories of foreign heads of state as an exception to the freedom of movement. The Court used this technique in other cases when defining the scope of the four freedoms.[143] In practice, however, both techniques are likely to yield the same result, that is, the prevalence of international law on privileges and immunities. The most important conclusion, therefore, may be the Court's reminder of the continued relevance of EU law in the broader diplomatic domain as a matter of principle, even when member states execute their sovereign powers under PIL.

The principles on the right of free movement set out in *Hungary v Slovak Republic* can be applied to diplomatic and consular agents.[144] This application is justified, first, as there are apparent similarities between the legal framework on the immunities of heads of state and diplomatic and consular agents. Second, in other cases, the CJEU has already applied general principles of PIL with regard to (access) to the territory as exceptions to EU law.[145] A question that has not yet been addressed by the Court is whether an EU citizen, who is also a diplomat, enjoys a right of residence in the receiving state in addition to a freedom of movement either during or at the end of a diplomatic or consular posting. In other words, can the diplomatic or consular agent legally argue that they have sufficient resources for themselves and their family members not to become a burden on the social assistance system of the host member state in the sense of Article 7 of Directive 2004/38/EC? Even more so, can they make the years they spend in the host country as a diplomat or consul count in order to acquire a right of permanent residence, which requires a five-year period of uninterrupted legal residence as defined in Article 16 of Directive 2004/38/EC? While Directive 2003/109/EC on third-country nationals who are long-term residents explicitly excludes those enjoying a legal status governed by the VCDR and VCCR, Directive 2004/38/EC is silent on the matter.[146] The legal issue is whether the diplomat or consul 'resides' in the sending state in the sense of EU law, which is a necessary criterion to be able to apply for a stay of more than three months or to claim permanent residency. The agent is part of an official mission rather than having moved in the EU in personal name, with the single goal of performing a specific function well defined by international law. International law is rather clear on the topic: there is no right to residence for a diplomat and consul, only a right to move freely

[140] Article 1 New York Convention on the Prevention and Punishment of Crimes against Internationally Protected Persons, including Diplomatic Agents, done on 14 December 1973, entered into force 20 February 1977, 1035 UNTS 167; *Hungary v Slovak Republic* (n 57) paras 44–49.

[141] Mattia Filippini, 'A Change for Future Intra-European Diplomatic Relations? Case C-364/10 Hungary v Slovakia' (2013) 20 MJECL 120, 126.

[142] See the discussion on the national identity clause above.

[143] Pedro Caro de Sousa, *The European Fundamental Freedoms: A Contextual Approach* (OUP 2015) 156,166.

[144] *Hungary v Slovak Republic* (n 57) paras 44–52.

[145] *Van Duyn v Home Office* [1974] ECLI:EU:C:1974:133, para 22; *Ahlström Osakeyhtiö v Commission* [1988] ECLI:EU:C:1988:447.

[146] Article 1 Directive 2003/109/EC concerning the status of third-country nationals who are long-term residents [2004] OJ L16/44.

within the territory of the receiving state and to travel to and back from the posting (Art 26 VCDR; Art 34 VCCR). Moreover, the Vienna Conventions very explicitly limit the immunities and privileges of agents (Art 38 VCDR; Art 71 VCCR) who are permanent residents in the host state. The underlying assumption is that diplomats and consuls should not have too much of a personal connection to the state in which they will perform official functions. Finally, in member state practice, receiving states do not issue 'EU citizen' identity documents to diplomats or consuls from fellow member states but provide them with a special diplomatic identity card and, as such, do not register them as an EU citizen in the national registers either. The above shows a national preference for having two different systems in place: one for diplomats and consuls (and their family members) and one for EU citizens. EU citizens registered under the former may therefore see the rights they would otherwise enjoy as EU citizens curtailed when in contradiction to their diplomatic or consular status.

The CJEU has had one other occasion to clarify the right of an EU citizen to reside in another member state in a consular context. *Radiom* concerned a dual Iranian–Irish citizen who worked for the Iranian consulate in Manchester at a time when diplomatic relations between the United Kingdom and Iran had severed.[147] As a retaliation, the Home Office had requested Iran to downsize its mission and informed Mr Radiom that he would be detained and deported if he did not leave the United Kingdom. The Court did not comment on the United Kingdom's decision to downsize the mission since a request that the size of the staff be kept within limits is lawful under the VCCR's Article 20. More problematic is that, on the basis of EU law, EU citizens should have access to legal remedies in respect of any decision ordering expulsion from the territory, even when that decision is a public security measure. Mr Radiom therefore challenged the interpretations of Articles 8 and 9 Council's Directive 64/221/EEC.[148] In its prejudicial judgment, the CJEU affirmed that a national of a member state against whom an initial decision refusing entry into another member state has been made on grounds of public order or public security has a right of appeal under Article 8 of the directive and, if appropriate, a right to obtain the opinion of an independent competent authority in accordance with Article 9 of the Directive. Such a right does not exist on the basis of PIL.

### 5.2.1.3 Freedom of Movement of EU Workers

The question arises whether diplomatic and consular agents that are nationals of one of the members states can be considered 'workers' as defined in Article 45 TFEU and, as such, be entitled in the receiving state to the rights the Treaty provision brings about for EU citizens working in other member states. The very nature of the diplomatic and consular function seems to preclude this, as paragraph 4 states that the provisions of Article 45 do not apply to those employed in public service. A diplomat or consul clearly exercises government authority since they can legally act on behalf of the sending state. These officials are the direct representatives—quite literally the face—of their home state in a receiving state. A diplomat or consul also does not enter the labour market when posted abroad; their presence is limited to a well-defined and, by definition, temporary mission. What is more, member states may lawfully limit the access to diplomatic and consular jobs to nationals only. As a result, Article

[147] *Queen v Secretary of State for the Home Department, ex parte Mann Singh Shingara and Abbas Radiom* [1997] ECLI:EU:C:1997:300.

[148] Council Directive 64/221/EEC on the coordination of special measures concerning the movement and residence of foreign nationals justified on grounds of public policy, public security or public health [1964] OJ L56/850.

45 does not seem to apply to diplomats and consuls to determine their legal status in another member state (in this case, the receiving state).

This being said, Article 45 TFEU may come into play to conclude that the agent enjoys certain rights vis-à-vis their own member state (in this case, the sending state) when returning from a posting abroad—regardless of the finality of that posting. In *Alevizos*, a 2005 case concerning an officer in the Greek Air Force deployed in an EU member state under the North Atlantic Treaty Organization (NATO) Status of Forces Agreement, the Court considered said military officer a worker for the purposes of a tax exemption he wanted to obtain when returning to his home member state.[149]

Article 45 TFEU is also relevant in cases of EU citizens working in embassies of consulates but not executing diplomatic or consular jobs. One of the more popular topics in general case law on the broader topic of diplomacy concerns the employment relationships between diplomatic and consular missions and their locally hired staff members. Typically, disputes arise on the dismissal conditions or the remuneration of such (former) employees. If sued, it is common for a sending state to invoke its immunity from jurisdiction. National case law has been relatively unclear on this point, for three reasons. First, there has been confusion in regard to the identification of immunity in question: some judges make references to the individual immunity of the member of the mission, whereas it is the immunity of the sending state that was relevant. Second, there exists confusion regarding the characterization of acts as either non-sovereign (*acta iure gestionis*), falling outside the sending state's immunity from jurisdiction, or as sovereign (*acta iure imperii*) and therefore subject to such immunity. Third, there is discussion on whether the immunity disproportionally restricts the individual's right of access to court. Against such a backdrop, the conclusion of the UN Convention on Jurisdictional Immunities of States and Their Property is interesting and helps to ensure greater certainty in case law. Indeed, applicants frequently invoke their right to access to court under Article 6 European Convention for the Protection of Human Rights and Fundamental Freedoms (ECHR);[150] in some cases, the matter has even ended up before the European Court of Human Rights (ECtHR).[151] The question whether EU citizens employed by a Union member state can invoke EU law principles to overcome the protection that PIL grants sending states and their diplomatic missions has been subject to a limited legal review.[152] According to the European Commission:

> [w]orkers performing their activity in diplomatic representations of EU Member States are not excluded from the scope of EC law, including labour legislation. EU labour law usually covers employees as defined according to national legislation or practices on employment contracts or relationships. It follows that Member States may decide to exclude certain situations from the definition of employment contracts or relationships (for example, civil servants, the police or the army). This may affect employees of diplomatic representations of EU Member States.[153]

[149] *Georgios Alevizos v Ipourgos Ikonomikon* [2005] ECLI:EU:C:2007:251.

[150] European Convention for the Protection of Human Rights and Fundamental Freedoms, signed on 4 November 1950, entered into force 3 September 1953, 213 UNTS 222.

[151] *Cudak v Lithuania*, App No 15869/02, 23 March 2010 and *Sabeh El Leil v France*, App No 34869/05, 29 June 2011. See generally, Jean Salmon, 'Les Immunités Diplomatiques dans la Tourmente' in *Liber Amicorum Jean-Pierre Cot: Le Procès International* (Bruylant 2009).

[152] Richard Garnett, 'State and Diplomatic Immunity and Employment Rights: European Law to the Rescue?' (2015) 64 ICLQ 783.

[153] Answer given by the Commission to parliamentary question E-2112/2007, 19 April 2007.

This section assesses two such cases brought before the CJEU, one where the member state operated as a receiving state of a third state's mission employing an EU citizen and one where the member state operated as a sending state employing an EU citizen in a third country.

The first case, the 2015 *Evans* judgment, has been introduced before because it confirms the VCCR's CIL status. It is also one of the few consular law cases to have reached the Luxembourg judges. The case concerned a UK citizen, Ms Evans, who had exercised her freedom of movement for workers when employed by the US consulate in the Netherlands. At the time of retirement, Ms Evans was dissatisfied with the calculation of pension benefits proposed by the Netherlands. The Dutch Government had excluded the times of employment when Ms Evans worked at the US consulate on the grounds that customary consular law applied during such periods. Because consular law does not require receiving states to grant pension to workers, she was de facto denied a pension. Before the Dutch court, Ms Evans invoked Regulation 1408/71, which coordinates the national social security legislation and protects the social security rights of persons who move within the EU to claim equal treatment to national citizens.[154] In a preliminary ruling, the CJEU concluded that Regulation 1408/71 did not apply in the case of permanent residents working at a consular mission of a third state.

The Court applied the EU's division of competences when ruling that it is for the member states to determine the conditions for permanent residents to become affiliated to pension schemes in the absence of harmonization at EU level. The Court referred to rulings in similar Dutch social security cases in a non-consular context.[155] Since Regulation 1408/71 did not set up a common scheme of social security across the EU, member states remain the sole competent actors in the field. The judgment confirms that social policies, including the Regulation at hand, form part of the competences shared between the EU and the member states as well as that the EU's role is limited in this area. The *Evans* judgment recalls that 'EU law does not, in principle, affect the competence of the Member States to regulate their social security systems'.[156]

PIL was taken into account only during a second step in the Court's reasoning. When determining the member state's de facto legal obligations, the Court interpreted consular law, leading to the finding that this body of law does not require receiving states to include consular employees in their social security schemes. Indeed, in this case, the phrase of Article 2 of Regulation 1408/71 'subject to the legislation of a Member State' had to be read in light of the VCCR. Consular law is fairly clear on this point: Article 48 VCCR provides a general exemption from social security provisions of the receiving state for members of consular posts, whilst Article 71 VCCR foresees an exception for permanent residents in the receiving state. Under international law, permanent citizens only enjoy social security privileges insofar as these were granted by the receiving state, whereby the 1963 Convention does not require a compulsory affiliation of permanently resided members of consular posts in a receiving state to a social security scheme. Under PIL, therefore, the Netherlands has a discretion to decide whether to affiliate consular employees residing in their territory to the national social security schemes and, if so, under what circumstances.[157] Although, in *Evans*, member states were the competent actors in the field, the Court concluded that when calculating pensions,

[154] Regulation 1408/71 of the Council on the application of social security schemes to employed persons and their families when moving within the Community [1971] OJ L149/2.

[155] *AJ van Pommeren-Bourgondiën v Raad van bestuur van de Sociale Verzekeringsbank* [2005] ECLI:EU:C:2005:431; *MJ Bakker v Minister van Financiën* [2012] ECLI:EU:C:2012:328.

[156] *Evans* (n 79) para 33.

[157] ibid, para 48.

the states ought to abide by customary consular law. In that regard, the judgment's paragraph 44 confirmed that '[a]lthough Member States retain the power to organise the conditions of affiliation to their social security schemes, they must none the less, when exercising that power, comply with EU law'. Moreover, paragraph 36 reads that EU law (*in casu*, Art 2 of Regulation 1408/71) 'ought to be interpreted in the light of the relevant rules of customary international law [ ... ] namely the Vienna Convention of 1963'.

The second employment dispute, *Boukhalfa v Germany*, displays a different set of facts. It takes place in the diplomatic sphere and discusses the application of EU law by member states in their role as sending states.[158] Ms Boukhalfa, a Belgian-Algerian national, was employed by the German Embassy in Algiers, where she also permanently resided. Ms Boukhalfa's legal position in the embassy differed from the previous case as the conditions of her employment were governed by Algerian law, whereas the legal status of local staff, having German nationality, was determined by German law.[159] Ms Boukhalfa invoked Article 45(2) TEU[160] and Article 7(1)–(4) of Regulation 1612/68; these prohibit any discrimination based on nationality between workers who are nationals of EU member states. The German Government argued that Community law was geographically inapplicable. The CJEU disagreed and deemed Ms Boukhalfa's situation to be subject to EU law's non-discrimination provisions. Multiple facts were taken into account to reach this conclusion: the applicant's employment contract was governed by German law, contained a jurisdiction clause giving jurisdiction over any dispute to German courts in Bonn, and spelled out an affiliation to the German national social security system with a subjection to the German income tax authorities.[161]

The Court furthermore confirmed that member states cannot discriminate based on nationality in cases where a permanently residing national is in a non-member country where they are employed by another member state's embassy. To come to this conclusion, the CJEU relied exclusively on principles related to the extraterritorial application of EU law. Rightfully, diplomatic law was treated as an incidental factor that required no substantial analysis or application. The employment relations between sending states and its staff posted to missions abroad do not concern PIL and therefore do not feature in the Vienna Conventions.

#### 5.2.1.4 Analysis

The CJEU has considerable discretion in qualifying a conflict as falling within its jurisdiction. In the above cases, the Court used this discretion to successfully bring international law within the scheme of EU law. The Court concluded in two cases that international law applied, either as an exception to an EU rule (*Hungary v Slovakia*) or as the applicable rule in cases where the EU did not yet regulate (*Evans*). The CJEU demonstrates a guarded approach towards issues of diplomatic and consular law first brought in the general EU scheme, then treated as an excluding factor for the application of substantive rules of EU law. The two-step reasoning shows that the Court is worthy of the name of 'supreme guardian of Union law'. However, it also confirms that the Court considers international law only *because* EU law demands it. *Boukhalfa* and *Radiom* are not in contrast with the above findings. The facts of these cases may have operated in the diplomatic and consular spheres, but they ultimately

[158] *Boukhalfa v Germany* [1996] ECLI:EU:C:1996:174.
[159] ibid, para 4.
[160] Originally Art 48(2) EC Treaty.
[161] *Boukhalfa* (n 158) paras 16, 19.

did not raise questions of diplomatic and consular law. They did, however, grant citizens their rights under EU law in a diplomatic and consular context.

Even as in *Hungary v Slovakia* and *Evans* it was decided that it was up to the member states to apply PIL, from time to time, the Court also ventures into the interpretation of diplomatic and consular law. The conclusions reached by the Court in the above cases are generally in line with PIL. However, it is remarkable that the level of analysis in both *Evans* and *Hungary v Slovakia* lacks depth in regards to the actual customary nature of the international norms invoked. It was also observed that the Court did not take an obstacle-based approach but rather brought a new conflict to the EU system while, at the same time, flirting with the limits of the rules of the four freedoms. A highly relevant consideration to be deduced from *Hungary v Slovakia* and *Evans* is that diplomatic and consular international law can provide such limitations while *Boukhalfa* and *Radiom* show that, where possible, EU law should still be applied to the widest extent possible. When it comes to diplomatic and consular law, the CJEU adopts a monist approach, promoting the idea that the European and international legal systems are intertwined. *Hungary v Slovakia* can even be seen as a derogation from the dualist views expressed in the *Kadi I* case according to which EU and international law are separate and distinct.[162]

## 5.2.2 Interpreting EU Law in Light of Diplomatic and Consular Law

### 5.2.2.1 Privileges and Immunities

Similarly to most IOs, the EU has its own body of law dealing with the organization's privileges and immunities, staff, and accredited representatives. Although international law on diplomatic privileges and immunities clearly inspired Protocol No 7 on the Privileges and Immunities of EU, the two schemes should be distinguished. Rules of international institutional law (such as Protocol No 7) generally serve to ensure that the organization functions independently in and from host or member states. The ECtHR confirmed in *Waite and Kennedy* that 'the attribution of privileges and immunities to international organisations is an essential means of ensuring the proper functioning of such organisations free from unilateral interference by individual governments'.[163] Diplomatic law is a bit different as it protects the 'efficient performance of the functions of diplomatic missions as representing States' (*ne impediatur legatio*).[164] While distinct, the two bodies of law also clearly overlap, fuelling the temptation to use the concepts developed in diplomatic law in international institutional law and thereby potentially in EU law as well. In the 1996 Opinion in the *OH v ID* case, for example, it is argued that the 'interpretation of Article 11 of Protocol No 7 is also consistent with Article 31(1) of the Vienna Convention on Diplomatic Relations'. While the comparison was not per se wrong to define the scope of the immunity in this case, Article 11 of Protocol No 7 concerns the functional immunity of EU staff only, while Article 31(1) VCDR concerns the absolute immunity of diplomats.[165] Protocol No 7 attached to the EU Treaties contains a direct reference to customary diplomatic law. Its Article 16 promulgates that the permanent representations of member states and the missions of third countries enjoy customary privileges, immunities, and facilities. Since the Union aims to grant its

[162] *Kadi I* (n 66).
[163] *Waite and Kennedy v Germany*, App No 26083/94, 18 February 1999, para 63.
[164] Recital 4 VCDR.
[165] Opinion in *OH v ID* [1996] ECLI:ECLI:EU:C:2021:86, para 70.

accredited diplomatic representations the same privileges and immunities enjoyed by bilateral diplomatic missions, it may be assumed that the interpretation of these concepts corresponds. Whether customary diplomatic law can also be used to interpret the Union's institutional immunities and privileges, and those granted to its officials and assets, is less obvious. This section assesses two cases decided on the basis of the Protocol on Privileges and Immunities that refer to diplomatic law.

The first case concerns a dispute between the Commission and Belgium in its role as a host state of the then European Communities. The Court had to consider the compatibility of a tax imposing order issued by the regional government of Brussels installing a regional tax on occupiers and owners of buildings in Brussels with the Union's fiscal immunity as provided in EU law. As a reminder, Article 3 of Protocol 7 attached to the Treaties reads:

> [t]he Union, its assets, revenues and other property shall be exempt from all direct taxes.
>
> The governments of the Member States shall, wherever possible, take the appropriate measures to remit or refund the amount of indirect taxes or sales taxes included in the price of movable or immovable property, where the Union makes, for its official use, substantial purchases the price of which includes taxes of this kind. These provisions shall not be applied, however, so as to have the effect of distorting competition within the Union.
>
> No exemption shall be granted in respect of taxes and dues which amount merely to charges for public utility services.

Although the disputed tax was charged to the owners of office spaces and not to the EU institutions that rented them, the tax burden nevertheless passed to the occupier indirectly through elevated rental payments. The Commission argued that the Brussels order had a de facto effect of what amounted to taxing the Commission and the Council in respect to buildings that the institutions rented. The Commission and Council argued that the tax made leasing the buildings to the Communities particularly advantageous from a fiscal point of view for Belgium since it received tax on the rent—collected by the landlord from the Communities—without having to grant tax deductions to the tenant as would be the case for corporations renting buildings in Brussels. The CJEU did not accept this argument because 'the institutions of the Communities do not operate on a profit-making basis and are completely different in nature from undertakings subject to corporation tax'.[166]

In the proceedings, the parties sought to clarify the term 'direct tax' for purposes of the Treaties. Belgium argued that it had not circumvented EU law by indirectly making the Communities bear the burden of the property tax. The reading of Article 3 Protocol No 7 was proposed by Belgium to be in conjunction with the VCDR because Protocol No 7 'was based on that convention and [ … ] must be interpreted having regard to general public international law'.[167] Further, to justify its actions, Belgium's arguments referred to Article 23 VCDR, which exempts sending states from taxes in receiving states. The provision's second paragraph specifies that the exemption from taxation does not apply if the sending state is a tenant and the tax is payable by the landlord.

The Court rejected the Belgian arguments, including the attempted reliance on the VCDR to interpret Article 3 Protocol No 7. Without excluding the theoretical possibility of explaining Protocol No 7 in light of the VCDR, the Court noted that Article 23 VCDR is

[166] *Commission v Belgium* (n 60) paras 19–20, 62.
[167] ibid, para 27.

worded differently from Article 3 Protocol No 7. The VCDR provides a minimal principle of fiscal immunity, whereas EU law foresees the exemption of *all* direct taxes. In 1996, in *AGF Belgium v EEC and others,* the Court observed that Article 3 Protocol No 7 provides:

> not only that the Communities, their assets, revenues and other property shall be exempt from all direct taxes, but also that the Member States are to remit or refund the amount of indirect taxes or sales taxes included in the price of substantial purchases made by the Communities for their official use.[168]

AG Stix-Hackl had stated that the Vienna Convention may fulfil the role of a useful point of reference without implying that it may be legally relevant to the particular case. This was not the first case where the VCDR served as a direct point of reference in an AG's opinion.[169] First, in a case on the terms of current Article 12 Protocol No 7 exempting from national taxation salaries and emoluments paid by the Union, AG Gand referred to Article 33 VCDR.[170] Second, in a case on current Article 12 Protocol No 7, AG Roemer referred to Article 34 VCDR.[171] Third, in a case concerning the waiver of inviolability of premises and buildings of the Union, AG Lenz compared Article 1 of Protocol No 7 to Article 22(1) VCDR.[172] In all three cases, the Court considered Protocol No 7 to be sufficiently clear and omitted any reference to the diplomatic system.

AG Stix-Hackl also argued that in principle the Convention only applied to the member state's bilateral relations and not to the EU's institutional immunities:

> [i]n principle, the Vienna Convention concerns bilateral relationships between States (sending and receiving States) and not, as in the present case, the relations between the Community (an international organisation) and the country in which an institution of that organisation has its seat (Belgium).[173]

The Court followed the reasoning. In the judgment's paragraph 33, it held that:

> [a]s regards Article 23 of the Vienna Convention, to which the parties refer, it should be noted that that convention is a public international law convention concluded by the Member States and non-Member States acting in the exercise of their powers as regards diplomatic relations. In principle it concerns bilateral relations between States and not relations between the Community, which is, moreover, not a party to that convention, and the State where an institution of the Communities has its seat, in this case the Kingdom of Belgium.

Without undermining the idea that the Communities should observe PIL in the exercise of their powers, the Court referred to the VCDR as 'not of decisive importance in this case'.[174] EU law governing the fiscal immunities was found to be sufficiently clear and more specific

[168] *AGF Belgium v EEC and others* [1996] ECLI:EU:C:1996:144, para 19. See also the arguments of the Council in *Commission v Belgium* (n 60) para 23.

[169] Sam Muller's *International Organizations and Their Host States: Aspects of Their Legal Relationship* (Martinus Nijhoff 1995) 32.

[170] Opinion in *Klomp v Inspektie der Belastingen* [1969] ECLI:EU:C:1969:2, 58.

[171] Opinion in *Van Leeuwen v City of Rotterdam* [1968] ECLI:EU:C:1968:2, 51.

[172] Opinion in *Forafrique Burkinabe* [1993] ECLI:EU:C:1993:28, para 41.

[173] Opinion of AG Stix-Hackl in *Commission v Belgium* [2007] ECLI:EU:C:2006:434, para 36.

[174] *Commission v Belgium* (n 60) para 34.

than the VCDR in determining the scope of the Communities' fiscal immunities.[175] The outcome would probably not have differed if the VCDR had been applied.

In the end, the regional tax was not considered contrary to the wording or the objectives of Article 3 Protocol No 7.[176] Insofar as there was no infringement of Community law, the member states' competence in taxation allowed them 'to introduce new taxes, specify taxpayers and exemptions other than those in earlier analogous legislation, or to increase the rate of taxation'.[177] The Commission had not conclusively evidenced that the passing of the tax had adversely affected the Communities' independence or hindered its proper functioning.[178] In other words, the Court took the underlying rationale of immunities in international institutional law and turned it into a criterion to examine an infringement of Article 3 Protocol No 7 by the member states.

The CJEU's 1983 *Depoortere* judgment provides a second example of an interaction between Protocol No 7 and the VCDR. Mr Depoortere was a Belgian Commission official who worked in Brussels and who had invoked a violation of his rights under Protocol No 7.[179] His application related to the Belgian–Luxembourgish rules on exchange transactions. As a Belgian national, Luxembourg excluded him from using the rules on special foreign convertible accounts; however, as a Commission official he was entitled to a special beneficial status on the basis of Article 11(*c*) Protocol No 7 (Art 12(*c*)). This provision reads:

> [i]n the territory of each Member State and whatever their nationality, officials and other servants of the Union shall:
>
> (*c*) in respect of currency or exchange regulations, be accorded the same facilities as are customarily accorded to officials of international organisations.

The reference of Protocol No 7 talks about the customary practices in IOs. However, the Commission submitted that institutional practices were largely based on customary and conventional diplomatic law and therefore equivalent. The Commission therefore pointed to a comparative study which found similar provisions of numerous Western European organizations such as the Council of Europe, the Organization for Economic Cooperation and Development, the Western European Union, and the European Space Agency. One indeed finds that section 18 of Article 5 of the Convention on the Privileges and Immunities of the United Nations (CPIUN) and Article 6 of the Convention on the Privileges and Immunities of the Specialized Agencies of the United Nations (CPIUN-SA), as well as numerous other constitutions and headquarters agreements of IOs, refer to customary diplomatic law. In that regard, Article 38 VCDR was deemed of relevance, a provision that establishes that receiving states are under no obligation to accord exchange facilities to diplomatic servants who are nationals or permanent residents of the state. The Commission argued that it is international diplomatic practice not to accord exchange facilities to officials who are nationals of the state where they are employed. The argument is interesting as it exemplifies the potential of customary diplomatic law to influence EU law in an indirect manner as the general law of immunities by virtue of the reference to international practice of IOs in EU law. Through the double cross-reference, diplomatic law has thus become the relevant standard

175 ibid, para 35.
176 ibid, para 63.
177 ibid, para 57.
178 ibid, para 56.
179 *Depoortere v Commission* [1983] ECLI:EU:C:1983:359.

of interpretation. In light of the above, it is all the more disappointing that the Court never addressed the points raised by the Commission. The claim was dismissed on different grounds: Mr Depoortere had not established a chain of causation between the Commission's allegedly unlawful conduct and the damage suffered.[180]

### 5.2.2.2 Diplomatic Concepts

The reach of diplomatic and consular law surpasses Protocol No 7 cases. In a few other cases, the Court was asked to interpret a diplomatic term featuring in EU law and policy. Staff disputes that arose before the former Civil Service Tribunal featured a discussion on the interpretation of the notions 'chargé d'affaires' and 'diplomatic notification and protocol'.

*Skareby v Commission* concerned the case of an employee of the Directorate General for External Relations (DG RELEX).[181] Between 2004 and 2007, Ms Skareby had been appointed to the Commission delegation in Almaty (Kazakhstan) whilst also occupying the position of 'Head of Section with the rank of Chargé d'Affaires ad interim in absence of the Head of Delegation' in Kyrgyzstan. Ms Skareby sought an annulment of the Commission's decision rejecting her request for assistance in respect to a complaint of psychological harassment allegedly suffered during her post due to the acts of two successive HoDs in Kazakhstan.[182] Ms Skareby stated that the HoDs 'had systematically undermined and minimised her role within the Almaty and Bichkek delegations which, she claimed, had discredited and humiliated her vis-à-vis her counterparts in the Governments of Kazakhstan and Kyrgyzstan, the embassies of Member States of the European Union and international organisations and non-governmental organisations present in those countries'. The Commission's decision not to grant such assistance was partly based on the assessment that Ms Skareby formed part of the 'middle management', whereas only officials higher up in the Commission's hierarchy were entitled to the requested psychological assistance. Ms Skareby invoked the VCDR's job description of a chargé d'affaires ad interim (ai), to claim that she had been accorded a greater level of responsibility. In diplomatic law, the chargé d'affaires position is indeed a well-established and respected function. Under Article 5(2) VCDR, the sending state may 'establish a diplomatic mission headed by a chargé d'affaires ad interim in each state, where the head of mission does not have his permanent seat'. International practice is familiar both with the concepts of chargé d'affaires *titular* and the chargé d'affaires *en pied*. Both can be appointed *ad interim* or *en titre*. The rules with regards to the presentation of credentials apply to a *chargé d'affaires en titre*.[183]

Surprisingly, the Tribunal did not see the need to examine the status of chargés d'affaires under international law. The assessment focused exclusively on the applicant's personal rank as established by the Commission for internal purposes. The Tribunal's statement that the VCDR 'only governs the relations of diplomatic missions with the receiving *states*' [own emphasis] was striking.[184] There was no mention in the proceedings of the establishment agreement signed between the Commission and the Kyrgyz Republic one month prior to the accreditation of Ms Skareby, an agreement that expressly stated that it governed the relations between the Commission and the third state. As is common, this specific EA contains an Article 3 that makes the Vienna Convention applicable to the mutual relations, including

180 ibid, paras 7–8, 11–12.
181 *Skareby v Commission* [2012] ECLI:EU:F:2012:64.
182 ibid, para 7.
183 Charles Chatterjee, *International Law and Diplomacy* (Routledge 2007) 161.
184 *Skareby* (n 181) para 83.

rules on the position of the chargé d'affaires.[185] This does not mean that the agreement governed the relationship between the Commission and its staff too. However, the Commission's active use of VCDR titles and ranking is at least indicative of the applicant's actual responsibilities. Although a chargé d'affaires *ad interim* does not hold the rank of the head of mission (as opposed to a chargé d'affaires *en titre;* see Arts 14 and 19 VCDR), the attributed responsibilities are extensive. For instance, the designated person is entitled to represent the diplomatic mission in the receiving state in all external contacts; a job description that also features in the internal EU diplomatic staff manual.[186] As the chargé d'affaires, Ms Skareby was empowered under the Vienna Convention to represent the Commission in the absence of the HoD, a task she executed for numerous years. The Tribunal nevertheless upheld the Commission's decision.[187]

In two cases heard in the post-Lisbon era, the Civil Service Tribunal examined the commencement and ending of diplomatic functions of EEAS officials. In *Delcroix*, the former head of delegation in Djibouti sought an annulment of the decision to transfer him back to the EEAS, thereby terminating his posting early. Here, the Tribunal concluded that diplomatic law does not govern the employment relationship between the EU and staff and was therefore not decisive to the outcome of the case.[188]

In another 2014 case, *De Loecker v EEAS*, the Tribunal examined the term 'notification of arrival and final departure of the Head of Mission' (Art 10 VCDR) in the course of an internal dispute.[189] Mr De Loecker sought an annulment of the EEAS's decision to reassign him from his post as HoD in Bujumbura (Burundi) to the Brussels Headquarters. This decision will not be assessed as such: the EU institutions and bodies have a wide discretion to organize their departments and reassign temporary staff in accordance with the equivalence of post principle. More interesting is Mr De Loecker's claim that the immediate nature of his reassignment violated the Vienna Convention. By not informing or requesting a farewell audience with the Burundi President, he claimed that the EEAS had acted contrary to common courtesy rules, diplomatic practices in force in Burundi, and to Articles 10 and 19(1) VCDR.[190] In its argument, the EEAS itself surprisingly used the incorrect finding of the Tribunal in *Skareby* to claim that the Union is not bound by the Vienna Convention. A better argument would have been that the EU is not bound by the VCDR vis-à-vis its officials.

The Tribunal rightfully disagreed, not by referring to the EA between the Commission and Burundi but by citing the Treaties' provisions on the EEAS:

> [t]outefois, il ressort de l'article 221 TFUE et de l'article 5 de la décision 2010/427/UE du Conseil, du 26 juillet 2010, fixant l'organisation et le fonctionnement du SEAE [ . . . ] que les délégations assurent la représentation diplomatique de l'Union conformément à la convention de Vienne.[191]

[185] Agreement between the Commission of the European Communities and the Government of the Kyrgyz Republic on the Establishment and Privileges and Immunities of the Delegation of the Commission of the European Communities in the Kyrgyz Republic, 17 March 2003.

[186] Denza, *Diplomatic Law* (n 28) 100–01.

[187] *Skareby* (n 181) para 81.

[188] *Delcroix v EEAS* [2014] ECLI:EU:F:2014:9.

[189] *De Loecker v EEAS* [2014] ECLI:EU:F:2014:246.

[190] ibid, para 101.

[191] ibid, para 103: '[h]owever, it is clear from Article 221 TFEU and from Article 5 of Council Decision 2010/427/EU of 26 July 2010 laying down the organization and functioning of the EEAS [ . . . ] that delegations shall

The Tribunal restated the applicable diplomatic law on the matter: even though Articles 10(1) and 19(1) VCDR make the notification of changes in the diplomatic staff to the ministry of foreign affairs of the receiving country obligatory, there is no requirement to send a formal notification to the head of state. The Tribunal pointed out that prior notification of a final departure is to be given only 'where possible'.[192] The claim that there existed a customary practice with regards to farewell audiences in Burundi proved more difficult to judge. Diplomatic law certainly does not require it, but some countries abide by the practice even in the absence of being mentioned in the VCDR. For example, in Belgium, the King organizes a farewell audience *where appropriate*.[193] The Tribunal found that the applicant failed to provide evidence of the customary nature of the courtesy visit practises in Burundi. Following a careful analysis of codified law, the Tribunal ruled that the EEAS had therefore acted in conformity with international diplomatic law. In the facts, the EEAS complied with all formalities as described in the VCDR: it had notified the MFA of the termination of applicant's duties and the appointment of a chargé d'affaires ai.

As a result, the Tribunal in one case (*De Loecker)* referred to the meaning of diplomatic concepts attributed to the terms by international diplomatic law, while in the other (*Skareby)* it refrained from doing so. While one should abstain from making overly broad generalizations on this thin basis, it is interesting to note that, in exceptional cases, the CJEU indirectly does rule on cases about the EU's role as a diplomatic actor.

### 5.2.2.3 Non-Diplomatic Concepts

In its interpretation of EU law, the CJEU regularly goes beyond the literal readings of concepts and provisions to explore their purposes and contexts.[194] Occasionally, the Court or parties appearing before it sail to the wider seas of international diplomatic and consular law to provide a contextual reading of EU law. The following interpretative cases concern the notions of *(a)* an 'entry visa' in Council Directive 68/360, *(b)* 'non-discrimination' in Article 62 Lomé Convention, *(c)* a 'branch' in the Brussels I Regulation, *(d)* the 'interest of the service', and *(e)* the 'working for a State' in the EU Staff Regulations.

In 1980, the Welsh Pontypridd Magistrates' Court referred to the CJEU an interpretation request on the meaning of 'entry visa or equivalent requirement' as used in Article 3(2) of Council Directive 68/360, the current Citizenship Directive.[195] This provision states that member states may not demand an entry visa or equivalent document from workers of other member states. The case concerned Mr Pieck, a Dutch national who first entered the United Kingdom in 1973 and subsequently resided and worked there. His passport was renewed at the Netherlands' Consulate in London in 1976. On each occasion, when entering the United Kingdom, the immigration authorities noted in his passport the date and place of entry followed by the words 'given leave to enter the UK for six months'. In 1979, Mr Pieck left the United Kingdom for more than six months and subsequently was charged with an offence

ensure the representation of the Union in accordance with the Vienna Convention' [own translation]. The same phrase is used in *Delcroix* (n 188) para 25.

[192] *De Loecker* (n 189) para 104.

[193] Circular notes [BE] of 10 June 2012 ('Administrative procedure for the accreditation of members of diplomatic staff and administrative and technical staff of diplomatic missions in Belgium and their family members') and 15 April 2011 ('The accreditation of a diplomatic head of mission in Belgium').

[194] Koen Lenaerts and José Antonio Gutiérrez-Fons, 'To Say What the Law of the EU Is: Methods of Interpretation and the European Court of Justice' (2014) 20 Colum J Eur L 3; Nial Fennelly, 'Legal Interpretation at the European Court of Justice' (1996) 20 Fordham Int Law J 656.

[195] Council Directive 68/360/EEC on the abolition of restrictions on movement and residence within the Community for workers of member states and their families [1968] OJ L257/13.

for having acted contrary to the United Kingdom's 1971 Immigration Act. Appearing before the national court, Mr Pieck did not contest the evidence but instead relied on Directive 68/360 to show that the initial grant of six months' leave to enter the United Kingdom and the requirement to extend it were incompatible with the Community law.

In its submissions, the Commission sought to find the ordinary meaning of the term 'entry visa' in the consular practice. It argued that in consulates, an entry visa is given a broad meaning 'to denote a document or stamp issued to an alien before he presents himself to an immigration officer as a prerequisite to his admission to a State'. The Commission further pointed out that the VCCR authorizes consular agents to issue such entry visa by virtue of Article 5 VCCR. This provision lists the consular functions, one of which is (f) 'issuing passports and travel documents to nationals of the sending State, and visas or appropriate documents to persons wishing to travel to the sending State'. On the basis of the broad conception of consular tasks, the Commission considered it feasible to construe the term 'visa' in Directive 68/360 more generally so as to encompass all kinds of written formats to enable entry into a state. The Commission also referred to the relevant literature on consular relations to display the many forms of entry visa used in the consular practice, including a simple note in a passport, a certificate, or another official document made by the consular officer.[196] The British Government attributed a narrower meaning to the term 'entry visa', arguing that it is 'a documentary clearance issued before the traveller arrives at the frontier in the form of an endorsement on his passport or of a separate document'.[197] The Court favoured the Commission's contention. The phrase 'entry visa or equivalent requirement' covers any formality for the purpose of granting leave to enter territory of a member state coupled with a passport or identity card check at the frontier, 'whatever may be the place or time at which that leave is granted' and in whatever form it may be granted.[198] Without referring to consular law, the Court thus indirectly permitted harmonization at the EU level in such a way that it respects the multitude of member states' consular practices.

Consular law also inspired a preliminary ruling in 1977 on the reach of a non-discrimination provision in the 1975 Lomé Convention between the African, Caribbean, and Pacific States (ACP) and the European Economic Community (EEC).[199] In *Razanatsimba*, the CJEU decided that a member state is allowed to reserve a more favourable treatment to the ACP states so long as such treatment results from a provision of an international agreement comprising reciprocal rights and advantages.[200] The Court reached this conclusion after the French Government based an argument on the legal-technical parallels between the ACP and the consular regimes.[201] As to the facts, France had concluded with a small number of ACP states establishment conventions or judicial conventions installing the reciprocal application of national treatment. The VCCR permits the continued existence of special agreements with reciprocal obligations between sending and receiving states. Such agreements are not considered discriminatory when in accordance with the VCCR: Article 72 VCCR targets non-discrimination in the application of VCCR provisions; Article 73 VCCR deals with the relationship between the Convention and other international agreements. According to the

[196] *Regina v Pieck* [1980] ECLI:EU:C:1980:179, n 3 (hereafter *Pieck*) refers to Luke T Lee, *Consular Law and Practice* (Praeger 1961).

[197] *Pieck* (n 196) para 2.

[198] ibid, para 10.

[199] ACP–EEC Convention signed at Lomé on 28 February 1975 between the African, Caribbean and Pacific States of the one part and the European Economic Community of the other part [1976] OJ L25/2.

[200] *Razanatsimba* [1977] ECLI:EU:C:1977:193, para 19.

[201] Opinion of AG Reischl in *Razanatsimba* [1977] ECLI:EU:C:1977:179, 2247.

French, the Lomé Convention put in place a system similar to the VCCR that tolerates bilateral agreements supplementing it. The influence of consular law in *Razanatsimba* therefore did not relate to transposing substantive parts of the VCCR to the Lomé Convention. Rather, it introduced the consular system's legal design and techniques of multilateralism to a Treaty regime in a different context. Consequently, albeit indirectly, a parallelism was established between the VCCR and the Lomé Convention.

This is not the only time that diplomatic and/or consular regimes have served as an inspiration. In the 1998 *Gilly* case, the Court had to interpret Article 19 of the 1992 version of the OECD model's Double Taxation Convention on Income and Capital, which formed the basis of a double taxation treaty between Germany and France.[202] Both states submitted in their written observations that the provision is based on the comity of nations and sovereignty. Moreover, they pointed out that the commentary on Article 19 of the Model Convention provided that the taxation system originates from the VCDR and VCCR, whereby the receiving state has the right to tax the remuneration of members of certain categories of staff of foreign consular and diplomatic missions who reside permanently in that state or who are nationals thereof.[203] Without referring to it directly in its judgment, the Court accepted the reading of the Model Convention in a manner that resembles the diplomatic/consular taxation regime.

A third case concerns another employment law dispute, with a member state adopting the role of forum state to a third state's embassy. In *Mahamdia v Algeria*, the driver of the Algerian mission in Germany sought a review of the validity of his dismissal by the German courts, despite his employment contract's conferral of jurisdiction to the Algerian courts.[204] In a preliminary ruling, the CJEU was asked to determine whether the notions of 'agency', 'branch', or 'other establishment' within the meaning of the Brussels I Regulation containing a jurisdictional regime in civil and commercial matters cover a third-state embassy located in one of the member states.[205] Although Brussels I typically extends to entities that operate as private actors only, AG Mengozzi did not seek to exclude diplomatic missions. Following a brief enumeration of the diplomatic tasks as reflected in Article 3 VCDR, he concluded that although 'the functions of an embassy cannot be described as 'commercial', [ ... ] their commercial implications cannot be completely ignored either'.[206] In another instance, he even referred to the embassy as a 'place of business'.[207] In comparison, the Court's reasoning corresponded more truthfully to diplomacy's finalities and objectives. The Court acknowledged that the functions of an embassy as stated in Article 3 VCDR comprise essentially a representational function and that this is, by definition, a non-commercial activity.[208] The CJEU nevertheless held that an embassy can also fall under the notion of 'other establishment' for the purposes of the Brussels I Regulation in cases where it does not act as a public entity. As such, the Court used the distinction between *acta jure imperii* and *acta iure gestionis*—well known in the law of sovereign immunity but not in diplomatic law—to rule on the qualification of an embassy in the context of European private law. This seems to result in an obligation for national courts to determine the precise nature of functions carried out by an

[202] *Gilly v Directeur des Services Fiscaux du Bas-Rhin* [1998] ECLI:EU:C:1998:221.
[203] Opinion of AG Ruiz-Jarabo Colomer in *Gilly* [1997] ECLI:EU:C:1997:556, para 41.
[204] *Mahamdia v Algeria* [2012] ECLI:EU:C:2012:491.
[205] Article 18(2) Council Regulation 44/2001 on the jurisdiction and the recognition and enforcement of judgments in civil and commercial matters [2001] OJ L12/1 (hereafter Brussels I).
[206] Opinion of AG Mengozzi in *Mahamdia* [2012] ECLI:EU:C:2012:309, para 45.
[207] ibid, para 48.
[208] *Mahamdia* (n 204) para 49.

employee of a foreign mission. *In casu*, the employee was found not to have exercised any public powers.[209] It follows from *Mahamdia* that for disputes relating to employment contracts, the sending state is considered as domiciled in a member state where it established a mission (Art 18(2) Brussels I), which entails the jurisdiction of member state courts (Art 19(1) Brussels I). In the same judgment, the CJEU also held that an agreement on jurisdiction inserted in the employment contract before the dispute arose, conferring jurisdiction upon the courts of the sending state not a member to the EU, fell within Article 21(2) of this Regulation provided that, ordinarily, the courts having jurisdiction under the Brussels I Regulation are not excluded.

*Ojha v Commission* concerned a Commission official assigned to the Commission delegation in Dacca (Bangladesh) in 1991 and recalled to Brussels a year later.[210] Mr Ojha's reassignment was a result of a human resources report stating that his capacities could be used better when working for the Commission in Brussels than for a delegation as his capacity to adapt to the diplomatic milieu was not as hoped following difficult interactions with diplomatic partners, an assessment Mr Ojha disagreed with. Rather than being a disciplinary measure, the reassignment decision was motivated on the grounds of the 'interests of the service' (Art 7(1) Staff Regulations). In the appeals case, the Court found that the evaluation of the official's failure to adapt to the diplomatic environment on the basis of external complaints did not constitute an infringement of the principles of legal certainty and sound administration.[211] The Court explained that in the context of diplomatic relations it may not even matter whether external complaints are unfounded. What matters is that it is in the interest of the Commission that a relationship of trust is maintained and that diplomatic tasks are performed with respect for diplomatic partners. The AG found that the facts proved that '[i]rrespective of whether each of the complaints considered in isolation was well founded, the situation created at the date of the contested decision was the very antithesis of the diplomatic function'.[212] At the time, the Court had already developed case law dealing with officials employed in Brussels, in which it had repeatedly held that where interpersonal difficulties are a source of tension that impair the proper functioning of the service, they justify the transfer of an official in the interests of the service under Article 7(1) Staff Regulations. The same reasoning:

> applies a fortiori in relation to the external relations of a department, especially where it is entrusted with diplomatic tasks. The essential element of diplomatic functions is, indeed, to prevent tensions from arising and to smooth out any which do. Such functions absolutely require the confidence of those involved. Once that is shaken, for whatever reason, the official in question is no longer able to carry out the functions.[213]

Extra weight was consequently attributed to the well functioning of the Union in a diplomatic environment. Because the official's behaviour threatened to result in an imminent breakdown of aspects of the Commission's external relations had a solution not been found, the Commission's decision was considered justified.

209 ibid, para 57.
210 *Ojha v Commission* [1996] ECLI:EU:C:1996:434.
211 ibid, para 43.
212 Opinion *Ojha* [1996] ECLI:EU:C:1996:277, 1997–99.
213 *Ojha* (n 210) para 42.

The final two cases can be dealt with together as they originate from a similar issue, namely, the Commission's refusal to pay an allowance fee to newly hired officials who had previously worked for their national diplomatic mission in Brussels. In *Pasqualetti v Commission* and *Commission v Hosman-Chevalier*, the applicants sought an annulment of the Commission's decision refusing to pay an allowance fee following recruitment.[214] The CJEU was asked to clarify whether one can be considered as working in Belgium under the Staff Regulations of EU Officials when employed by another member state's diplomatic mission.[215] The CJEU has ruled on similar issues, that is, the taking into account of periods of work done for embassies and consulates in staff cases to grant certain allowances or benefits.[216] These cases are not discussed here since neither international diplomatic law nor the diplomatic status of applicants played a role in determining the scope of application of EU law.

The 2015 *Pasqualetti* judgment concerned a Hungarian official of the Hungarian Ministry of Foreign Affairs temporarily seconded to his country's permanent representation (PR) to the EU before being seconded to the EEAS. The Commission argued that the entitlement to allowance fees of new officials intends to compensate for the fact that they can no longer live in their previous place of residence and is therefore linked with the act of relocating. Since Mr Pasqualetti and his family already lived in Brussels, they did not satisfy the basic conditions to receive the allowance fee under Article 20 of the Staff Regulations.[217] Invoking diplomatic law, Mr Pasqualetti argued that during these periods, he maintained his residence in Budapest and that, as a diplomat, the centre of his interests remained in Hungary.[218] Based on the general understandings of the diplomatic regime rather than arguments grounded in law, the Tribunal agreed that a diplomat's habitual residence is in his sending state. Officially, Mr Pasqualetti established residence in Brussels for the first time when recruited by the Union, thereby entitling him to the allowance.[219]

In the 2007 *Hosman-Chevalier* judgment, more complicated factors and reasons are prevalent. In an appeal from the Court of First Instance, the ECJ was required to rule on the status of regional representations associated with permanent representations accredited to the Union. At first glance, the facts corresponded to those in *Pasqualetti* in that Ms Hosman-Chevalier was refused an establishment fee when recruited by the Commission because she had lived in Belgium before; Article 4 of Annex VII of the Staff Regulations stipulates that the establishment allowance is not to be paid to an official who, during a five-year period before they entered the service, carried out a main occupation in Belgium. The discussion surrounded the interpretation of an exception to this rule for those who carried out work 'for another State or for an international organization' during the reference period. Interestingly, staff that enjoyed diplomatic status not because of the employment by a foreign mission but by virtue of their relationship with a diplomat (*in casu*, the wife of a diplomat being granted privileges and immunities under the VCDR) who resided in Belgium before taking up a function at the EU is not considered to have been working 'for another State or for an international organization' as defined in the Staff Regulations.

214 *Commission v Hosman-Chevalier* [2007] ECLI:EU:C:2007:367 (hereafter *Hosman-Chevalier*) and *Pasqualetti v Commission* [2016] ECLI:EU:F:2016:64.

215 Staff Regulations of Officials and the Conditions Employment of Other Servants of the European Communities, as laid down by Arts 2 and 3 of Council Regulation 259/68 [1968] OJ L56/1.

216 *Nunez v Commission* [1988] ECLI:EU:C:1988:275; *Atala-Palmerini v Commission* [1989] ECLI:EU:C:1989:365; *Olesen v Commission* [2005] ECLI:EU:T:2005:264.

217 See the arguments put forward by the Commission in *Pasqualetti* (n 214) paras 26–27.

218 ibid, paras 19–20.

219 ibid, para 64.

The Commission submitted that this was not the case for Ms Hosman-Chevalier: her employment at the liaison office for the *Land* Tyrol, and at the *Verbindungsstelle der Bundesländer*, the *Länder* Liaison Office and then, for the *Österreichischer Gewerkschaftsbund* (the Austrian Federation of Trade Unions), could not be considered as 'work done for another State'.[220] Ms Hosman-Chevalier argued that the regional offices were integrated in Austria's permanent representation to the EU in Brussels; she was fully accredited to the Belgian Government as a member of the PR's technical and administrative staff (Art 1(*f*) VCDR), received privileges and immunities (Art 37(2) VCDR), and worked under the Austrian Ambassador's authority.[221]

In its ruling, the Court first equated EU member states' permanent representations with their embassies as in both places representational work is conducted in the meaning of the Staff Regulations:

> [i]n the country to which the official concerned was posted, the other States are represented by embassies or diplomatic missions and by permanent representations to international organisations, as follows from the rules of customary international law, codified in particular by the Vienna Convention of 18 April 1961 on Diplomatic Relations and the Vienna Convention of 14 March 1975 on the Representation of States in their Relations with International Organisations of a Universal Character.[222]

Permanent representations thus broadly fulfil the same representational role as bilateral diplomatic missions.[223] Second, the Court interpreted the concept of a state in the Staff Regulations as comprising the state as a legal person and unitary subject of international law, including all its government bodies regardless of their (internally defined) independent character. Consequently, all the PR's staff should be considered as working for the member state.[224] The ECJ confirmed the Court of First Instance's findings, indicating that although Ms Hosman-Chevalier was not employed by the Austrian central administration, due to her position in the representation and subjection to the supervisory authority of its ambassador she had to be regarded as having worked for the Austria.[225] The Court accepted the applicant's diplomatic status, confirmed by the Belgian Government, as an objective fact that evidences an official link to Austria. It was this privileged status that prevented her from forming a lasting tie linking her to Belgium.[226]

The Court clarified its position in four civil servant judgments, jointly issued on 29 November 2007. At first glance, the facts of these cases seem similar to those in *Hosman-Chevalier*.[227] All four cases concerned Spanish nationals who were employed by the representative office of the *Patronat Català Pro Europa* in Brussels, the body in charge of managing the interests of the Spanish Autonomous Community of Catalonia (*Comunidad Autónoma de Cataluña*) within the EU institutions in Brussels. Much like Ms Hosman-Chevalier, when

220 *Hosman-Chevalier* (n 214) paras 18–19.

221 ibid, paras 32, 45.

222 ibid, paras 39–40.

223 See also Opinion of AG Mengozzi in *Hosman-Chevalier* [2007] ECLI:EU:C:2007:169, para 82 (hereafter Opinion in *Hosman-Chevalier*).

224 *Hosman-Chevalier* (n 214) para 41.

225 ibid, para 42.

226 ibid, para 43.

227 All four cases confirm the principles established in *Hosman-Chevalier* (n 214): *Salvador García v Commission* [2007] ECLI:EU:C:2007:724; *Herrero Romeu v Commission* [2007] ECLI:EU:C:2007:725; *Salazar Brier v Commission* [2007] ECLI:EU:C:2007:726; *De Bustamente Tello v Council* [2007] ECLI:EU:C:2007:727.

the applicants were recruited by the Council or Commission they were denied an expatriation allowance because they had previously worked in Belgium. Once again, according to the institutions, the work carried out for the Patronat in Brussels did not qualify as 'work done for another State' within the meaning of Article 4(1) of Annex VII to the Staff Regulations. Unlike Ms Hosman-Chevalier, none of the Spanish applicants had been formally integrated in Spain's permanent representation to the EU; they did not enjoy a privileged status in the sense of VCDR, nor were they accredited to the Belgian Government. The applicants contended that there was a discrimination between officials who worked for the state 'through the intermediary of the central administration in a permanent representation, whose entitlement to the expatriation allowance is recognized and those who worked through the intermediary of the administration of an autonomous community'.[228] The Court disagreed. In staff cases, the question is not whether work was done for the state through a central administration or an autonomous community; Ms Hosman-Chevalier also worked for a sub-state entity. Rather, the relevant criterion is whether a person is formally integrated into the national permanent representation.[229] In the Spanish cases, this was not the case.[230]

A final remark relates to the discussion on EU interference in the member states' choices in diplomacy. In *Hosman-Chevalier*, before Declarations 13 and 14 to the Treaties had even seen the light of day, and without quoting the national identity clause, the Court proved sensitive to some of the core concerns of member states related to the Union overreaching in the way they organize their national diplomatic missions. The Court confirmed that a member state should be represented by a single diplomatic representation at the international level.[231] However, it decided, as the AG suggested,[232] that it is for the member state to determine which coexisting bodies form part of this mission and to safeguard the different public interests they promote. In *Commission v Hosman-Chevalier*, the CJEU expressly confirmed the protection of national autonomy in organizing diplomatic structures. The Spanish cases left this principle untouched.

### 5.2.2.4 Analysis

One of the most direct ways the CJEU gives effect to international law in the EU legal system is by using international law to clarify provisions of EU law. The technique of interpretation in conformity is a conflict avoidance tool, which benefits the harmonious relationship between EU law and PIL.[233] The Court invoked and drew on diplomatic and consular law to support an interpretation of EU law in cases concerning Article 10 VCDR (*De Loecker*), Article 3 VCDR (*Mahamdia*), and Articles 1(*f*) and 37(2) VCDR (*Hosman-Chevalier*). In three further cases of *Pieck*, *Pasqualetti*, and *Razanatsimb*, the CJEU withheld the argument made by parties comprising of diplomatic and consular principles, albeit without explicitly acknowledging it. In *Razanatsimba*, it was the architecture of VCCR that provided a source of inspiration to interpret another international law instrument. In contrast, in *Pasqualetti* and *Ohja*, the diplomatic regime's general understandings were relied upon. In the *Ohja* judgment, the Court acknowledged that the diplomatic scene is a distinctive environment, characterized

228 *Romeu* (n 227) para 48.
229 *De Bustamente Tello* (n 227) para 40.
230 See *Salazar Brier* (n 227) para 49; *De Bustamente Tello* (n 227) para 41. This has been the case for other officials working for the autonomous communities, *Romeu* (n 227) para 53; *García* (n 227) para 59.
231 *De Bustamente Tello* (n 227) para 39.
232 *Hosman-Chevalier* (n 214) para 46; Opinion in *Hosman-Chevalier* (n 223) paras 82, 89.
233 Katja S Ziegler, 'Beyond Pluralism and Autonomy: Systemic Harmonization as a Paradigm for the Interaction of EU Law and International Law' (2016) 35 Yearb Eur Law 667, 676.

by particular rules and practices. The Court honoured this by applying a fortiori settled case law in relation to the Union's diplomatic relations. In two cases, diplomatic and consular law were deemed irrelevant. In *Commission v Belgium*, the Court correctly ruled that another set of international rules applied instead, that is, international institutional law. Conversely, the Tribunal erred in *Skareby* by considering the international diplomatic law as inapplicable in the Commission's relations with third countries.

In cases where the Court declared that it is a requirement for EU law to be construed in harmony with norms of diplomatic and consular law (ie where it allowed PIL to enter the EU legal order), it provided an analysis that came close to a text-book interpretation of norms of international diplomatic or consular law. As explained prior in the discussion on the judgments of *Pieck* and *Hosman-Chevalier*, the CJEU mirrored the original meaning of the diplomatic terms when interpreting the Vienna Conventions. Therefore, the Court may not always accept diplomatic and consular law as the legal framework against which to measure acts, but when the answer is positive, the Court has a good record on interpreting the relevant international norms.

### 5.2.3 Interpreting EU Law in Light of Diplomatic and Consular Interests

Diplomatic and consular relations are instruments to exercise power and to protect interests. *Commission v Portugal* presents a case where a member state's diplomatic interests were opposite to those of the EU.[234] In the 1990s, the Commission initiated an action against Portugal claiming that the country had not fulfilled its obligations under Articles 3 and 4(1) of Council Regulation (EEC) No 4055/86 by failing to denounce or adjust a bilateral pre-Community merchant shipping agreement it had concluded with Angola.[235] Portugal agreed that the contested bilateral agreement required a revision to eliminate incompatibilities with the EC Treaty and the Commission's shipping policy. The reason it had not yet done so related to 'diplomatic savoir-faire'. Portugal claimed it had encouraged, without success, the Angolan authorities to accept an adjustment. However, it found the time diplomatically unfeasible to put more pressure on the third state to force it to renegotiate the bilateral agreement. The Commission's time frame did not match the particularities and dimensions of the Portuguese–Angolan diplomatic relations and would cause a disproportional harm to the Portuguese foreign-policy interests. The state of war and constant tension prevailing in Angola considerably complicated the normal conduct of diplomatic relations.

Portugal's arguments were dismissed by the Court—according to Jan Klabbers 'perhaps somewhat harshly'.[236] The Court held that the existence of a difficult political situation in a third state cannot justify a continuing failure on the part of a member state to fulfil its EU law obligations. Insofar as the denunciation of a Treaty agreement is possible under international law, it is incumbent on the member state concerned to actually denounce it.[237] Obviously, member states are legally obliged to take appropriate steps to eliminate any incompatibilities with the Treaties. *Commission v Portugal* confirms that this is no different when diplomatic

[234] *Commission v Portugal* [2000] ECLI:EU:C:2000:358.

[235] Council Regulation 4055/86 applying the principle of freedom to provide services to maritime transport between member states and between member states and third countries [1986] OJ 1986 L378/1.

[236] Jan Klabbers, *Treaty Conflict and the European Union* (CUP 2009) 138.

[237] *Commission v Portugal* (n 234) para 39, referring to *Commission v Belgium* (n 60) para 42.

interests are in play. As such, the CJEU confirmed that it attaches more value to the respect for EU law than the form or process through which this result should be obtained.[238] This legalistic approach may dissatisfy the member states, especially in diplomatic domains where political considerations sometimes tend to trump the legal ones.

### 5.2.4 Observations

International law and practices pervade the European legal order in different ways and to varying degrees. This section discussed instances where the CJEU accepted and denied diplomatic and consular law's influence on the basis of a study sample comprising of twenty cases. Due to the limited quantity of available data, this conclusion does not claim to offer a full and final theory on the reception and application of diplomatic and consular law and probably raises more questions on the interactions between EU law and diplomatic and consular law than it solves.

Prior to engaging in the application of diplomatic and consular law, it is interesting to recall which types of cases end up in Luxembourg. The Court deals with diplomatic and consular law cases through preliminary rulings (Art 267 TFEU) and somewhat fewer via direct actions (Arts 258 and 259 TFEU). Cases deal with the Union's passive and active right of legation but quite prominently also with staff disputes (Art 270 TFEU). The increase in civil servant disputes is a logical consequence of the rise of the EU's diplomatic actorness accompanied by an increase in the recruitment of diplomatic staff. These cases constitute an autonomous way by which international law enters the EU legal system. However, one must be methodologically careful not to overstate the observations flowing therefrom. Administrative cases are susceptible to a particular flavour and especially the former Civil Service Tribunal's findings may not accurately reflect the latest CJEU approaches towards international law. Moreover, there was some variety regarding the quality of staff cases and the level of analysis they contained.

The Court permitted diplomatic and consular principles to influence the outcomes of thirteen cases, either directly (ten cases) or indirectly (three cases). These numbers indicate a general friendliness and openness of the Court to engage with diplomatic and consular law. Further, the Court decided in six cases that it did not have to take into account principles stemming from the international level because another international legal framework applied, diplomatic law did not govern the conflict, or EU law was deemed to be sufficiently clear. One case did not reach a final judgment.

When invited to rule on matters of diplomatic and consular law, the Court reiterated its roles as an enforcer of international law and a gatekeeper of the application of international law to the EU legal system. In pursuing its *gatekeeping role*, the Court retains control of how diplomatic and consular law translate into the EU legal order. The Court exemplifies a predominant concern for internal and constitutional questions and attempts to fit diplomatic and consular law in the general EU legal framework before adjudicating the underlying conflict. Similarly to when dealing with international law in general, the Court most likely applies such technique of legal reasoning to maintain the autonomy of EU legal order and integrity of EU law. The CJEU also actively *enforces diplomatic and consular law*. First, the international regime certainly influences the interpretation of norms across the EU spectrum

[238] *Commission v Portugal* (n 234) para 50.

whereby the CJEU engages in both substantive borrowing (by reference to VCDR and VCCR articles) and contextual borrowing from the international level. Second, the international regime is used to delimit the competences between the member states and the Union (*Hungary v Slovakia* and *Evans*). Third, the diplomatic and consular regimes were also invoked as gap-fillers in the absence of explicit provisions. One may have expected that, due to the overlaps between the Protocol No 7 on privileges and immunities and customary diplomatic law, this would occur in cases related to the Protocol. However, it is rather in cases comprising an analysis of the general international practices (eg *Ojha* and *Hosman-Chevalier*) that gap-filling is observed.

The CJEU does not commonly refer to diplomatic and consular law as a *special* kind of PIL. There are only few references to the singularity of the diplomatic craft, profession, or premises. For instance, in *Ojha*, the Court took into account arguments based on the rationale of diplomatic relations by permitting the Commission to make staff-related decisions in the interest of the efficient conduct of diplomatic relations. This contrasts significantly with the special and sometimes quasi-sacred status attributed to diplomatic and consular relations in PIL. However, despite the fact that it only occasionally refers to diplomatic and consular relations directly (in *Hosmans-Chevalier* and follow-up cases), the Court accepted that diplomatic and consular relations remain within the ambit of member state sovereignty in an increasingly integrated EU. As such, the Court confirmed that member states remain at liberty to determine the Vienna Conventions' application (as seen in *Evans* and *Pieck*) and to tax the Union when in accordance with the norms of PIL (as seen in *Commission v Belgium*).

When they collide with rules of EU law, sovereign decisions can be subject to *judicial scrutiny*. The Court does not shy away from reviewing national choices in diplomacy from the vantage point of EU law. This finding, however, does not say much about the intensity of the review carried out. From the sample of cases at our disposal, it is deduced that the Court assesses the member states' autonomous application of the right to legation through a marginal standard of review. Indeed, the CJEU generally accepts that it is ultimately for the member states to decide on the Vienna Conventions' specific application. The Court has conducted more intense evaluations in civil servant cases. In such a context, the Court tends to defer to the prerogatives and discretion of the EU executive to manage its diplomatic staff and relations, as most national administrative courts would do.

In light of the many roles played by the CJEU and the different standards of review, it is uncontested that discussions are far from settled. The internal effect of diplomatic and consular law in the EU legal system is not governed by a principled approach but is rather handled on an ad hoc basis. This brings about a positive effect: the incorporation of rules of diplomatic and consular law in the EU legal order and their enforcement by the CJEU makes the Vienna Conventions truly living instruments.

## 5.3 Coexisting Rights of Legation

### 5.3.1 Between Interaction and Parallelism

European diplomacy hinges on two seemingly contradictory concepts of integration and protectionism. By splitting the right of legation among plural entities, sovereign member states enabled the Union to develop its diplomatic network without giving up their sovereign rights to equally do so. This section researches how these dynamics between the Union and member states play out in real diplomatic life. This requires a contextualized analysis of rights, duties, and practices that directly or indirectly refer to the way the Union's and member states' rights of legation are or should be exercised. A specific theoretical model—from here on referred to as the *model of coexisting rights of legation*—is introduced to carry out this analysis. The model builds on a twin-track approach to diplomacy observed earlier, namely, that EU law encompasses and promotes ideas of parallelism and interaction. It essentially boils down to what in the post-Lisbon ruling of the *Bundesverfassungsgericht* was qualified as the cooperatively mixed policy model of the EU's foreign relations, in which diplomatic activities are exercised both separately and together by the EU and its member states.[239]

### 5.3.2 Parallel Diplomacy

According to the model of coexisting rights in diplomacy, the Union and its member states enjoy separate legal entitlements to diplomacy. Executing those entitlements, European actors operate side by side in the international arena. For both the Union and the member states, conducting diplomacy is a means to ensure the meaningful exercise of competences and powers. Moreover, by conducting diplomatic and consular activities they each make a claim to international actorness and identity. The nexus between diplomacy and identity is quite logical. In the past, diplomats were considered to be direct representatives of the sovereign and, still, diplomacy facilitates the reflection of the identity of an actor abroad.[240] As will be shown, several legal provisions facilitate such diplomatic parallelism.

#### 5.3.2.1 National Prerogatives in Diplomacy

Through the conduct of foreign policy and diplomatic relations, domestic views can be defended externally. Over the centuries, Europe has produced world-class diplomatic services, each with their own preferences, strengths, diplomatic culture, and being capable of projecting the national identity in the wider world. A direct reference to the member states' right of legation does not feature in EU primary law. Yet, general principles of EU law certainly protect the member states' diplomatic and consular activities. Most notably, the principle of conferral and the national identity clause, as well as Declarations 13 and 14 attached to the Treaties, secure national prerogatives in diplomacy.[241] Evidently, the general capacity to represent the nation, the diplomatic representation of competences not transferred to the Union, and the representation of the national persona all rest with the member states, both within and outside the common borders. Especially in external relations, the identity of the member states is far from being subsumed by the emergence of a European identity.[242] Moreover, in the context of Article 4(2) TEU, the EU Treaties have brought the protection of the identity of member states into the legal sphere.[243]

239 *Lisbon Judgment* (n 46) para 375.
240 von Bogdandy and Schill (n 17) 4128.
241 Declarations 13 and 14 concerning the CFSP (n 53).
242 Pierre-Étienne Lehmann, 'Le Respect de l'Identité Nationale des États Membres' in Jean-Christophe Barbato and Yves Petit (eds), *L'Union Européenne, Fédération Plurinationale en Devenir?* (Bruylant 2015) 158–59.
243 Anne Levade, 'Identité Nationale ou Constitutionelle?' in Marthe Fatin-Rouge Stéfanini and others (eds), *L'Identité la Croisée des Etats et de l'Europe: Quel Sens? Quelles Fonctions?* (Bruylant 2015) 189.

### 5.3.2.2 The Union's Prerogatives in Diplomacy

Since the early days of European integration, there has been debate as to whether the EU created, or ought to create, a common identity.[244] These discussions are mostly linked to those on the rhetoric of the EU's foundations. In 1973, the then nine member states attempted to define a European identity to enable the Communities to achieve a 'better definition of their relations with other countries and of their responsibilities and place which they occupy in world affairs'.[245] This makes the EU's relations with the world a fundamental element in the construction of a European identity. The diplomacy–identity nexus is also revealed in the eighth recital of the TEU's preamble. In what probably is the closest approximation to a self-definition of the Union's diplomatic identity in a legal document, the Treaty drafters indicated that they were:

> [r]esolved to implement a common foreign and security policy [ ... ] thereby *reinforcing the European identity* and its independence in order to promote peace, security and progress in Europe and in the world [own emphasis]

This language discloses that the strengthening of the European identity is a desirable consequence of the implementation of CFSP, therefore indicating that the concept requires CFSP action amid further development. Furthermore, the provision stresses the Union's independent persona. Similarly, Article 21(2)(*a*) TEU (on the Union's objectives) emphasizes that it is a goal of EU foreign policy to achieve the EU's independent character in engaging in international relations. Changes instigated by the Lisbon Treaty further underscore the EU's (diplomatic) identity. EUDELs now represent the Union and not only one institution, whereby they are specifically mandated to enhance the Union's visibility, understanding, and to strengthen the consistency in external relations (Art 18(4) TEU). This in turn contributes to the construction of a single identity in the international arena.[246] Nowadays, the receiving state and locally represented missions easily recognize the EU delegation, characterized by its own diplomatic culture and traditions, and distinguish it from other diplomatic actors.[247] When representing the Union, the EUDELs actively use common symbols and rhetoric developed to contribute to invigorating the European identity.[248]

It has been explained in Chapter 2 that there is no direct reference to the Union's right of legation in EU primary law. However, EU constitutional law contains a blueprint for the structures and responsibilities of the EU's diplomatic service, comprising an isolable set of rules and resources, which—at least for social constructivist thinkers—adds to the idea of the construction of a distinguishable diplomatic identity.[249] Articles 18 and 27 TEU describe the HR's functions in relatively clear terms. The Treaties also adopt a brief stance on the EEAS, mentioning the Service's name, basic composition, and essential functions (Art 27(3)

[244] Armin von Bogdandy, 'The European Constitution and European Identity: Text and Subtext of the Treaty Establishing a Constitution for Europe' (2005) 3 ICON 295, 295.

[245] See the 'Declaration on European Identity' of the Copenhagen European Summit [1973] Bull EC No 12, 118–22.

[246] Ingolf Pernice, 'The Treaty of Lisbon: Multilevel Constitutionalism in Action' (2008) 15 Colum J Eur L 349, 398.

[247] Maureen Benson-Rea and Cris Shore, 'Representing Europe: The Emerging "Culture" of EU Diplomacy' (2012) 90 PA 480; Caterina Carta, *The European Union Diplomatic Service: Ideas, Preferences and Identities* (Routledge 2012).

[248] Manfred Kohler, *European Identity* (Neuer Wissenschaftlicher Verlag 2012) 94 et seq. See, on the symbols of the Union, Chapter 4, section 4.3.4.

[249] See Anthony Giddens, *The Constitution of Society: Outline of the Theory of Structuration* (University of California Press 1984) 17.

TEU). The 2010 EEAS Decision provides more details on the organizational aspects of EU diplomacy. Its Article 5 provides the responsibilities, powers, and hierarchal organization of EUDELs. These 'organizational' provisions are the counterpart of the member states' laws on structures and functions in diplomacy, as protected by the national identity clause (Art 4(2) TEU). As such, the articles on the organization and structure of the EEAS and the delegations strongly testify of the Union's diplomatic identity.

The EU's Staff Regulations also contain rules that protect the Union's independent character: officials ought to perform diplomatic functions with only the Union's interests in mind. Deploying national diplomats (known as seconded national experts or SNEs) in EUDELs potentially impacts the Union's diplomatic identity and threatens its independence. The HR sought to address this issue in a 2011 Decision intended to ensure that SNEs carry out their duties respecting the interests of the EEAS (Recital 6).[250] It spells out that, during secondments, SNEs have to report to the EU HoD rather than to the member states of their nationality (Art 23(2) Decision). The duty of loyalty observed here aims to positively influence the common esprit de corps.[251]

#### 5.3.2.3 The Parallel Exercise of Rights of Legation

The first main feature of the model of coexisting rights of legation relates to the rights' parallel exercise. The EU and the member states maintain their own courses of diplomatic action, whereby an interference by either entity in one another's diplomatic conduct is in principle prohibited as decisions are taken autonomously, policies defined independently, and diplomatic instruments issued by diplomatic staff loyal to singular actors only. Parallel diplomacy allows the Union to act alongside member states and the member states to act alongside one another and the EUDEL.

The parallel execution of different rights of legation is observed in both the EU's passive and active legation practices. In the *passive practice*, one observes that the corps diplomatique accredited to the Union has not merged with the corps diplomatique accredited to the Kingdom of Belgium, or that of any other member state for that matter. Both organizational structures function under a different doyen and have a unique composition, despite many third-state ambassadors enjoying a double accreditation. Parallelism also means that the Union autonomously decides whom it accredits or declares persona non grata, leaving the role of Belgium as purely instrumental.

A maximum of twenty-eight (twenty-seven plus one) European diplomatic representations can appear in third states to execute an *active right of legation*, whereas the number of European missions can reach up to twenty-six (member state) representations in another member state. Parallel diplomacy is probably most visible when the EU and its member states assume international obligations that require conduct falling within the ambit of competence of both entities simultaneously or when common principles and values are defended. There seems to be a general understanding that a number of goals pursued through diplomacy (such as the promotion of peace, security, international cooperation, democracy, human rights, and the rule of law—Art 3(5) TEU subjects) are shared between the member states and the Union. According to Joseph Weiler, these values are part of the Union's constitutional development and represent its collective identity.[252] In practice, the EUDEL and

[250] Decision of the High Representative establishing the rules applicable to National Experts Seconded to the European External Action Service [2012] OJ C12/8.

[251] Kohler (n 248) 119.

[252] Joseph HH Weiler, 'A Constitution for Europe? Some Hard Choices' (2002) 40 JCMS 563, 569. See also Marise Cremona, 'The Union as a Global Actor: Roles, Models and Identity' (2004) 41 CML Rev 553, 559.

member state missions frequently respond individually to single events and accordingly take measures that encompass their own diplomatic competences. All European missions can issue statements, send notes verbales, summon foreign diplomatic representatives, and exert diplomatic pressure. When such diplomatic means address policy domains of the Union and member states alike (eg issues of human rights and rule of law), instruments are often promulgated in parallel. For example, prior to the 2010 inauguration of the Sudanese President Omar al-Bashir, the EU delegation issued a statement recalling the EU's continuous commitment to the country's full and timely implementation of the Comprehensive Peace Agreement, in parallel to other statements containing a similar message issued by member state missions. The EU was represented at the level of chargé d'affaires at al-Bashir's inauguration, among representatives of the member states that attended in their bilateral capacities.[253] Another example concerns the monitoring of trials in human rights cases abroad: it has happened that both the EUDEL and member state missions send their own representative to attend court cases of imprisoned opposition leaders. This was the case in Venezuela, where the EUDEL and member states' embassies sent representatives to observe the presumably political 2015 trial of Venezuelan opposition leader Leopoldo López and the student activists detained with him.[254]

Parallel diplomacy works best where there is a clear marking of territories or when there is no competition between thematic fields. Sometimes, parallelism is partly illusory. It is, for instance, well established that the HR and the EUDELs do not need a separate member state approval to voice positions that have been previously coordinated within the Council organs—and as such reflecting member states' opinions.[255]

This model is also particularly attractive to represent diplomatic actors' individual identities in the international sphere. Consequently, parallelism enhances principles of independence and equality, therefore relating to many core ideas of diplomacy as traditionally conceived in PIL. The parallel exercise of diplomatic activities also has its drawbacks. First, there is an economies-of-scale argument: strict parallelism may obstruct the finding of more efficient and synergetic solutions. Second, sometimes a need for more uniformity arises. When diplomacy requires conduct that simultaneously falls within the competence of the EU and the member states, reactions of European missions require coordination. The model of parallel diplomacy draws on the ideology that competences are split between European actors, an idea that presupposes a perfect compartmentalization of powers. When considered individually, the plurality of diplomatic actors certainly possesses diplomatic means related to their own competences and identities. Yet, the EU's distribution of competences is not symmetric, even to the extent that it leads to the overlap, sometimes even the merge, of activities and identities. Therefore, the idea of parallel diplomacy ought to be counterbalanced with ideas of a more interactive diplomacy.

### 5.3.3 Interactive Diplomacy

While the previous section explained how different European actors can use their right of legation to their likening, this section considers how EU law prompts their interactions, either incidentally or purposefully. These exchanges too are captured by different legal obligations.

[253] Answer by the Council to parliamentary question E-4095/2010, 11 June 2010.
[254] Answer by High Representative to parliamentary question E-003350/2015, 27 February 2015.
[255] Article 27 TEU; Art 221 TFEU; and Art 6(4) 2010 Council Decision.

#### 5.3.3.1 General Obligations

##### *5.3.3.1.1 Member states*

An important set of legal obligations for member states stems from the notions of sincere cooperation and loyalty (Art 4(3) TEU). Sincere cooperation is a container principle requiring member states to behave in a manner that does not harm and is loyal to the Union. The desired behaviour is concretized in different other Treaty provisions, for instance, those on non-discrimination (Arts 20 and 21 TFEU), including explicitly in the consular (Art 23 TFEU) and diplomatic practices (Art 32, third paragraph, TEU).

Loyalty to the Union, among other things, implies that member states in their diplomatic practice should exercise powers consistently with EU law. This principle is 'of general application' to the Union's external actions and does not depend on competences exercised.[256] Even where member states have retained competences, these must be conducted consistently with the objectives and law of the Union. When those national competences affect the Union's functioning, they may even be subject to judicial review. The CJEU confirmed this principle in cases concerning nationality law,[257] direct taxation,[258] and the registration of vessels.[259] Similarly to diplomacy, these domains comprise powers traditionally considered sovereign prerogatives. Of those examples, the discussion on national/European citizenship probably shares most obvious resemblances to that on nationality/European diplomacy. In both cases, national competences flow from international law directly: PIL allows member states to lay down the conditions for the acquisition and loss of nationality, just like it is for each nation to decide how to exercise its right of legation. Moreover, while neither diplomacy nor nationality falls within the purview of the Union, the EU created its own version of both concepts. Corresponding to EU citizenship, which is additional to and does not replace national citizenship, EU diplomacy creates an additional layer of representation that does not seek to replace the national conceptions of a right of legation. The phrase 'additional to' does not install a hierarchy, which would imply that EU diplomacy is subsidiary to national diplomacy.

Two concrete obligations can be distilled from the duty to exercise powers consistently with EU law. First, there is a duty for member states not to harm other member states' or the Union's simultaneous exercise of rights. For instance, the CJEU deemed it impermissible for a member state to restrict the effects of a nationality granted by another member state by imposing additional conditions for the recognition of that nationality.[260] Based on this case law, it is submitted that a member state's exercise of diplomatic and consular relations similarly cannot restrict other member states' exercise of the right of legation.

Second, as indicated, there is a duty for member states to not engage in the overt or covert discrimination of EU citizens, even in those domains not regulated by the Union. This individual dimension of the obligation to exercise powers consistently with EU law is evident in cases of EU citizenship and direct taxation.[261] As the Court stated in *Asscher*, 'although

[256] *Commission v Sweden* [2010] ECLI:EU:C:2010:203, para 71 (hereafter *PFOS*).

[257] *Micheletti v Delegación del Gobierno en Cantabria* [1992] ECLI:EU:C:1992:295, para 10; *Garcia Avello v Belgium* [2003] ECLI:EU:C:2003:539, para 28; *Zhu and Chen v Secretary of State for the Home Department* [2004] ECLI:EU:C:2004:639, paras 37, 39.

[258] *Finanzamt Koeln-Altstadt v Schumacker* [1995] ECLI:EU:C:1995:31, paras 21–26; *Wielockx v Inspecteur der Directe Belastingen* [1995] ECLI:EU:C:1995:271, para 16; *Asscher v Staatssecretaris van Financiën* [1996] ECLI:EU:C:1996:251, para 36.

[259] *The Queen v The Secretary of State for Transport, ex parte Factortame LTD and others* [1991] ECLI:EU:C:1991:320, para 17 ('*Factortame II*'); *Commission v Greece* [1997] ECLI:EU:C:1997:565, para 22.

[260] See, for a confirmation of this principle, *Rottman* (n 138) para 33.

[261] See Art 61 TFEU.

direct taxation falls within the competences of Member States, the latter must nonetheless exercise that competence consistently with Community law and therefore avoid any overt or covert discrimination by reason of nationality'.[262] Transposing the non-discrimination principle to the diplomatic domain is less obvious: since the diplomatic context does not generally provide for individual rights, the principle does not seem to add additional duties on governments. This is different for the consular field, where the Treaties require member states to grant unrepresented Union citizens in third countries consular protection on a non-discriminatory basis.[263]

The application of Article 4(3) TEU in the external context is confirmed in the Treaties and relevant jurisprudence. The CFSP-specific duty of cooperation (Art 24(3) TEU) states that:

> [t]he Member States shall support the Union's external and security policy actively and unreservedly in a spirit of loyalty and mutual solidarity and shall comply with the Union's action in this area. The Member States shall work together to enhance and develop their mutual political solidarity. They shall refrain from any action which is contrary to the interests of the Union or likely to impair its effectiveness as a cohesive force in international relations. The Council and the High Representative shall ensure compliance with these principles.

This article establishes that the requirements to comply with the Union's action and to uphold the Union's positions in international fora are legal obligations. However, the scope of the terms action and position (although a reference exists in Art 29 TEU) are not defined.

The sincere cooperation principle's practical application has been explored in the broader diplomatic context by the CJEU.[264] Case law focuses mostly on ensuring that member states respect EU law and objectives in multilateral fora. In IOs that only recognize states as participating members or in which the EU is not represented, it is fairly well established that the represented EU member states must give due regard to the interests of EU while exercising their functions.[265] In the *PFOS* case, the Court clarified that this may require member states to abstain from acting when their action could jeopardize the attainment of Treaty objectives.[266] In the *Inland Waterways* cases, the CJEU reflected on the specific duties for member states, by stating that:

> [t]he adoption of a decision authorising the Commission to negotiate a multilateral agreement on behalf of the Community marks the start of a concerted Community action at international level and requires for that purpose, if not a duty of abstention on the part of the Member States, at the very least a duty of close cooperation between the latter and the Community institutions in order to facilitate the achievement of the Community tasks and to ensure the coherence and consistency of the action and its international representation.[267]

[262] *Asscher* (n 258) para 36.

[263] Article 35 TEU; Art 20(2)(*c*) TFEU; Art 46 Charter of the Fundamental Rights of the EU.

[264] In both *Commission v Greece* [2009] ECLI:EU:C:2009:81 in the context of the International Maritime Organization (IMO) and *PFOS* (n 256) concerning the Stockholm Convention on Persistent Organic Pollutants, the member state was found to have failed to fulfil its EU law obligations.

[265] *Opinion 2/91 on the ILO Convention* [1993] ECLI:EU:C:1993:106.

[266] *PFOS* (n 256) para 103.

[267] *Commission v Luxembourg* [2005] ECLI:EU:C:2005:341, para 60.

Unilateral external actions of member states may not be permitted in order to preserve the unity of EU external representation. Two principles, codified in Article 34 TEU, must be recalled. First, when coordination has taken place, member states are under a specific duty to uphold the coordinated Union position, even when not specifically engaged. Second, in the absence of an EU coordinated position or action, permanent representations of member states can act unilaterally, subject to defined limits. The criterion to determine the scope of member state action is not whether a coordinated position exists; rather, one has to determine the potential impact of member states' actions regarding an existing *or* prospectively coordinated position.

In the diplomatic context of third states, the principle of loyalty could be attributed the meaning that member states must also act as 'trustees of the Union interest' in meetings where the EU delegation is not present.[268] In such circumstances, a positive obligation for embassies of member states exists to operate as the representative of the Union's interests as well as the negative obligation not to undermine the unity of the EU's representation.[269]

The principle of sincere cooperation comprises a horizontal dimension, binding member states in their mutual diplomatic and consular relations.[270] The application of Article 4(3) TEU in the 'internal' EU context is, however, more controversial. As outlined earlier, EU institutions do not commonly review or engage with inter-member state diplomacy. However, this does not mean that the principle of sincere cooperation does not apply; rather, it is more a question of *how* the principle ought to be constructed when member states engage in diplomatic or consular relations with one another.

A lead can be found in the opinion of AG Bot in the 2012 *Hungary v Slovak Republic* case.[271] In paragraph 58, AG Bot argued that:

> as in the case of any competence reserved for them, the Member States should not exercise their diplomatic competence in a manner that might lead to a lasting break in diplomatic relations between two Member States. Such a break would, in fact, be incompatible with the integration process aimed at creating, in the words of the preamble to the EU Treaty, 'an ever closer union among the peoples of Europe' and would constitute a barrier to the attainment of the essential objectives of the Union, including the aim of promoting peace.

This opinion supports the view that even in the conduct of diplomatic relations among themselves, member states must abide by the core EU principles and objectives. The AG highlights two of those objectives, namely, the creation of an ever-closer Union and the promotion of peace. It need not be recalled that these are among the integration project's oldest and most fundamental principles enshrined in the preamble of the 1957 Treaty of Rome. The concept of an ever-closer Union is often thought to be of symbolic impact, whereby the deliberate ambiguity defines a journey and not a destination. The AG attempted to convert the notion into enforceable EU law language by rephrasing the criterion in legal terms whilst adding a new element of intensity. He stated that:

[268] Marise Cremona, 'Member States as Trustees of the Union Interest: Participating in International Agreements on Behalf of the European Union' in Anthony Arnull and others (eds), *A Constitutional Order of States? Essays in EU Law in Honour of Alan Dashwood* (Hart 2011).

[269] *Opinion 2/91* (n 265) para 37. See also Peter Van Elsuwege and Hans Merket, 'The Role of the Court of Justice in Ensuring the Unity of the EU's External Representation' (2012) Cleer Working Paper No 5.

[270] Rossi (n 132) 1462, points to the EU version of *Bundesfreundliches Verhalten.*

[271] *Hungary v Slovak Republic* (n 57).

> [o]nly a situation of persistent paralysis in diplomatic relations between two Member States, contrary to their commitment to maintain good-neighbourly relations consubstantial with their decision to join the Union, would be covered by EU law, if only because, in accordance with the last paragraph of Article 4(3) TEU, Member States must refrain from any measure that could jeopardise the attainment of the Union's objectives.

Through this argument, member states' bilateral diplomatic relations emerge within the sphere of EU law. The AG's point of view implies that in addition to a vertical division of competences that uses material criteria to determine whether EU law applies, a situation could be considered where EU law impacts national competences on the basis of qualitative criteria. The implication is that any diplomatic conflict between member states serious enough to threaten the EU's continued cooperation can violate the principle of sincere cooperation. The above has consequences for bilateral diplomacy. For one thing, the AG reading seems to imply that EU law does not permit member states to use their powers under PIL to suspend or terminate bilateral diplomatic relations as between one another. From the point of view of PIL, this statement is incorrect as the termination of diplomatic relations clearly is a right under international law, as confirmed by the Eritrea–Ethiopia Claims Commission: 'Ethiopia was at all times free to terminate diplomatic relations with Eritrea and hence to close its mission'.[272] Furthermore, the AG suggests that the member states' power to determine diplomatic sanctions (eg a declaration persona non grata) or countermeasures in the diplomatic context can be curtailed by EU law when jeopardizing good-neighbourly relations.

Surely, the potential of Union law to limit the exercise of the right of legation as conceptualized in the Vienna Conventions and CIL is significant. However, the proposition that EU law prohibits member states from breaking relations with one another, to refuse an ambassador, or declare a diplomat persona non grata is questionable. Their membership of the Union ought not to lead to the conclusion that the member states have lost their sovereign decision-making power to suspend or terminate diplomatic relations with one another; although it seems politically not done, circumstances where it might happen are also not unthinkable.

*5.3.3.1.2 The Union*

The EU too is legally obliged to exercise its diplomatic powers in a certain way. First, there exists an obligation for the Union to exercise its powers consistently with PIL and, as such, to respect the member states' prerogatives under international law. The 1976 Kramer judgment[273] illustrates how international law impacts the Union's scope of action, a principle later refined in cases on fisheries,[274] competition law,[275] and trade concessions.[276] It is persuasively assumable that as a general principle, the limits of EU diplomacy must be defined in light of the relevant rules of international diplomatic and consular law. Moreover, this handbook has established that the exercise of the Union's powers must respect the member states' constitutional identity and essential state functions.[277] The German Federal Constitutional Court held that even when EU diplomats represent exclusive competences, member states

[272] Eritrea–Ethiopia Claims Commission, Partial Award: Diplomatic Claim—Eritrea's Claim 20 [2005] Report vol XXVI 381, paras 46–47.

[273] *Kramer* (n 3) paras 30–33.

[274] *Commission v Ireland* [1978] ECLI:EU:C:1978:29, para 63; *Commission v Council* [1996] ECLI:EU:C:1996:114, para 44; *Poulsen* (n 65) para 9.

[275] *Ahlström Osakeyhtiö and others v Commission ('Woodpulp')* [1988] ECLI:EU:C:1994:12, para 18.

[276] *Racke* (n 66) para 45.

[277] Jean Denis Mouton, 'L'Identité, un Concept Pertinent au Regard du Droit International?' (2014) 118 RGDIP 501.

can decide that their diplomatic presence is required to facilitate their participation in discourses on the socio-political and economic policy issues fundamental to their state.[278] Such diplomatic involvement will enable member states to discuss the arguments and results of international negotiations at the national level. The above observation was made by the Constitutional Court in the specific context of the WTO, where the Commission represents the EU. Article 4(2) TEU is conceived as more than a basic principle of parallel diplomacy that protects the member states' right of legation; it also functions to pose limits on the Union's independent exercise of the right of legation, emphasizing the autonomous and parallel exercise of diplomacy in the EU context.

This book also observed that when the Union exercises diplomatic functions, there is a thematic predominance of matters where the EU enjoys exclusive, shared, and parallel competences (Arts 3–4 TFEU).[279] To a certain extent, curbs are self-imposed: there is a tendency to avoid running into competence battles with member states on the ground.[280] As a result, in domains where EUDELs' activities risk causing discussions on the delimitation of competences, a lower activity level is observed. Additional curbs originate from the subsidiarity principle (Art 5(3) TEU): EUDELs prefer to take new initiatives in areas that are dealt with at the European rather than the national level. When defining functions, EUDELs also avoid duplicating locally represented embassies' activities. This can be considered as an application of the principles of complementarity and efficiency.

Much like its member states, the Union must respect the principle of sincere cooperation (Art 4(3) TEU) in all circumstances, including when exercising exclusive competences via diplomatic means. The principle of sincere cooperation also comprises a horizontal meaning in the sense that the EEAS, the Commission, and the Council must abide by it and inform and consult one another on all matters of external action, a specific application contained in Article 13(2) TEU.[281] The principle surfaces in the two following situations. First, it can be invoked to limit the exercise of EU powers. A typical example would be the situation where an EU diplomat presents a statement on behalf of the Commission or the Union in a multilateral forum. The principle of sincere cooperation requires the EU diplomat not to jeopardize the position of member states in those fora. Moreover, member states can 'supplement' Union statements in view of protecting their interests.[282] Second, the EU has to take into account the position of member states in its interpretation of diplomatic and consular law.[283] This occurs specifically when the Union, in its own diplomatic relations, has to determine the scope of VCDR provisions or these provisions' evolution in customary practice. Legal support for this can be found in *Intertanko*, where the CJEU found that the good faith (PIL) and sincere cooperation (EU law) principles require the Union to interpret

[278] Such concerns are less present in Opinion 1/94 on the *Competence of the Community to conclude international agreements concerning services and the protection of intellectual property* [1994] ECLI:EU:C:1994:384, paras 106–10 (hereafter Opinion 1/94).

[279] Michael H Smith, 'Does the Flag Still Follow Trade? Implications for European Union Diplomatic Practices in Third Countries' (2018) 13 HJD 41.

[280] Sanderijn Duquet, 'Bound or Unbridled? A Legal Perspective on the Diplomatic Functions of European Union Delegations' (2018) 13 HJD 21.

[281] For further reading, Geert De Baere and Ramses A Wessel, 'EU Law and the EEAS: Of Complex Competences and Constitutional Consequences' in David Spence and Jozef Bátora (eds), *The European External Action Service: European Diplomacy Post-Westphalia* (Palgrave Macmillan 2015) 178.

[282] Council, 'General arrangements for EU statements in multilateral organisations', Brussels, 24 October 2011, 16901/11, 3. See also Ramses A Wessel and Bart Van Vooren, 'The EEAS's Diplomatic Dreams and the Reality of European and International Law' (2013) 20 J Eur Public Policy 1350, 1354.

[283] Alessandra Gianelli, 'Customary International Law in the European Union' in Cannizzaro, Palchetti, and Wessel (n 115) 109.

directives taking into consideration a treaty to which the member states were parties and the Union was not.[284] Whenever the Union would adopt a decision on the interpretation of the Convention that contradicts general practices, it is recommended that it informally asks its member states—parties to the treaties—how they have dealt with similar issues in their bilateral relations.

### 5.3.3.2 Specific Obligations

#### *5.3.3.2.1 The obligation to (sincerely) cooperate*

In addition to the duties derived from general EU law, more specific legal obligations to respect, inform, and cooperate exist for both the member states and the Union.[285] Such interactions in diplomacy are often desired and in some cases even legally obliged by way of the EU Treaties. In fact, legal clauses on the fostering of close cooperation between delegations and member states' diplomatic and consular missions significantly outnumber other constitutional provisions on European diplomacy. The most general formulation of the mutual duty to cooperate in diplomatic and consular affairs is found in the third paragraph of Article 32 TEU:

> [t]he diplomatic missions of the Member States and the Union delegations in third countries and at international organisations shall cooperate and shall contribute to formulating and implementing the common approach.

Obligations are also targeted specifically to member state missions, which must 'cooperate in ensuring that decisions defining Union positions and actions adopted pursuant to [the CFSP] are complied with and implemented' (Art 35, para 1 TEU). In addition, Article 26 TEU introduces a more general obligation for the Council and the HR to 'ensure the unity, consistency and effectiveness of action by the Union'. The second sentence of Article 221(2) TFEU repeats these principles, this time written from the EUDELs' perspective, obliging them to 'act in close cooperation with member states' diplomatic and consular missions. A similar, general, obligation can be read in Article 24(3) TEU, which states that the member states have to support the Union's external and security policy 'actively and unreservedly in a spirit of loyalty and mutual solidarity'.

Arguably, the above is merely a practical application of the principle of sincere cooperation—a duty comprising different gradations of legal obligation. In diplomacy, it entails a duty to inform, a duty to coordinate, and sometimes a duty to collaborate. In addition, informal cooperation between member states' missions and with the EUDEL in foreign capitals has grown, mostly in parallel with the gradual expansion of CFSP policies.[286]

#### *5.3.3.2.2 The obligation to exchange information*

Exchanges of information are often seen as the first step towards forming a community of action. De Schoutheete submitted in this sense that, to construct a common external policy:[287]

[284] *Intertanko* (n 66) para 52.

[285] Christophe Hillion, 'Mixity and Coherence in EU External Relations: The Significance of the Duty of Cooperation' (2009) CLEER Working Paper No 2; Rosa Balfour, Caterina Carta, and Katri Raik, *The European External Action Service and National Foreign Ministries: Convergence or Divergence?* (Ashgate 2015).

[286] Roberts (n 27) 49.

[287] Philippe De Schoutheete, *La Coopération Politique Européene* (2nd edn, Nathan 1980) 45: 'it is first of all a question of creating, through a series of organic links and agreed practices, a community of information: shared information being, in foreign policy as elsewhere, the basis for any common analysis of problems' [own translation].

> [i]l s'agit en premier lieu de créer, par une série de liaisons organiques et de pratiques convenues, une communauté d'information: l'information partagée étant, en politique extérieure comme ailleurs, la base de toute analyse commune des problèmes.

In the diplomatic sphere, Article 35(2) TEU confirms that national missions and the EUDELs 'shall step up cooperation by exchanging information'. The Treaties' choice of lexis reveals that information sharing is indeed seen as a method to boost cooperation between European missions. The obligation's scope is not further defined, but general understandings of the duty of sincere cooperation are applicable. This means that relevant information ought to be shared in good faith and in a timely fashion. Furthermore, it is assumed that Article 35 comprises an obligation to transmit separable information (addressed to a single mission because it concerns an issue affecting a particular member state) as well as general information (comprising the interest of all locally represented missions).

Somewhat confusingly, Article 5(9) EEAS Decision introduced a similar obligation to transfer information but defined it in a non-mutual way. The Decision transferred the burden onto the EUDELs, by stipulating that:

> [t]he Union delegations shall [ ... ] share information with the diplomatic services of the Member States.

The EEAS Decision's phrasing also does not challenge the constitutional principle that the sharing of information is supposed to be reciprocal. The EU hierarchy of norms and the logic of the principle of sincere cooperation support the view that, indeed, this obligation should be read as a mutual one.[288] The initial draft of the Decision even contained a reciprocal obligation and it remains unclear why exactly it has disappeared.[289] One possibility is that it may be the result of the Decision's focus on the EEAS rather than on the member states. In practice, it is also simply established that information predominantly flows in one direction.[290] This must not necessarily be judged negatively. First, the EUDELs enjoy a bigger capacity and often more manpower to process information than most member states. In that sense, it is but normal that they share information with smaller missions of the member states, if at all represented. Second, the EU has a strategic interest in sharing information since the practice of collecting and sharing information also provides the Union with control over the information flow. This entails the power to encourage unified views of member states. Third, EU diplomats have indicated that they consider information flowing from member states to EUDELs only pertinent when it concerns issues EU diplomats are not yet aware of and which are relevant to the EU. In practice, a constant information flow from the member states to the EUDEL could even be judged negatively by EU diplomats: when member states share information, they often simultaneously start expressing their national views on matters, creating a burden on the EUDEL.

In 2011, the Council drew up Guidelines for EU cooperation in third countries, confirming the EUDELs' role in gathering and diffusing information.[291] In the information

[288] Jan Wouters and others, *The Organisation and Functioning of the European External Action Service: Achievements, Challenges and Opportunities* (European Parliament 2013) (hereafter Wouters and others, *2013 EEAS Study*).

[289] De Baere and Wessel (n 281) 181.

[290] Steven Blockmans and Christophe Hillion (eds), *EEAS 2.0: A Legal Commentary on Council Decision 2010/427/EU Establishing the Organisation and Functioning of the European External Action Service* (Swedish Institute for European Policy Studies 2013) 35.

[291] Council, Guidelines for EU cooperation in third countries (2011) ARES(195311).

process it describes, the EUDEL gathers information and produces reports and advices. If the desired outcome is a joint EU report, a coordination is organized with member states locally represented. Mutual information exchanges are also foreseen in the Guidelines: the EUDEL and member state missions jointly draw up a calendar of important local events and inform one another on high-level visits to the country. Member states are encouraged to share their own reports. Those member states not represented in a certain country can inform the EEAS on how they want to be kept up to date.

The means used to transfer information range between oral presentations during coordination meetings to traditional diplomatic cables and information exchanges over the EU's Coreu system (French: Correspondance Européenne).[292] The sharing of sensitive information via mail can only take place via (national or EU) secure communications. The EU disposes of its proper systems, called SECEM, REU, and CIMS, to be used according to the level of classification of the report.

Delegations draw up two types of reports. The first are sent to the Brussels-based EEAS Headquarters and the relevant Commission DGs (Brussels only);[293] the second type is shared with missions on the ground and MFAs of member states not locally represented. EUDELs and locally represented missions also engage in the collective gathering of and reporting upon local events to the benefit of the EEAS/EC and member states' MFAs. In local settings, transcripts of heads of missions' (HoMs) meetings are summarized in 'HoM reports' and shared with relevant European capitals, reaching the EEAS and national officials in the Council working parties. Therefore, the reports qualify as 'joint assessments' in the sense of Article 35 TEU. At Council level, local HoM reports are welcomed and used to feed discussions on new policy guidelines; this makes them essential political tools to strengthen interactions between the delegations, the Brussels Headquarters, and member states. Information sharing also takes place in foreign countries' thematic working groups. For example, when the Ambassadors of Germany and France visited the Peace Community of San José de Apartadó in Colombia, they shared their report on the visit in the local EU Working Group on Human Rights, where the EUDEL and member states' embassies participate.[294] Data collected between 1998 and 2010 shows that HoM reports provide detailed information, especially on countries where the diplomatic network of most member states are thin or non-existent.[295] The HoMs reports assimilate diplomatic cables between embassies and capitals and combine information and knowledge but are characterized by being shorter and sent more frequently—often daily.[296] The EUDEL and the member states may also decide to send a common observer, for instance, to attend and report on a human rights trial. This was the case in Ethiopia, when seventy-six prisoners, including elected MPs, journalists, and human rights defenders, were prosecuted in May 2006, having contested the outcome of the local elections. Funded by a joint EU initiative, an independent lawyer-observer followed the trial on behalf of the EU and the member states. The observer reported to the EU HoMs in Addis Ababa; a report drawn on this basis was subsequently delivered to the Ethiopian Government.[297]

[292] Federica Bicchi and Catarina Carta, 'The COREU/CORTESY Network and the Circulation of Information within EU Foreign Policy' (2010) 34 J Eur Integr 1.

[293] See the research of Damien Helly, Anna Knoll and Greta Galeazzi, 'A Closer Look into EU's External Action Frontline: Framing the Challenges Ahead for EU Delegations' [2014] No 62 ECDPM Briefing Note.

[294] Answer given by the High Representative to parliamentary question E-011487/2015, 17 July 2015.

[295] Federica Bicchi, 'Information Exchanges, Diplomatic Networks and the Construction of European Knowledge in European Union Foreign Policy' (2014) 49 Coop Confl 239, 241.

[296] ibid 246.

[297] Answer of the Commission to parliamentary question E-1075/2007, 6 March 2007.

EU missions also consult each other on different practical questions. For example, in 2005, Italy consulted fellow member states concerning the granting of a visa to Zimbabwean President Robert Mugabe to attend the funeral of Pope John Paul II. At the time, the President was barred from entry into, or transit through, the territories of member states.[298] Similar consultations occur when the Union or the member states have doubts as to the appropriate treatment and protocol when receiving a (former) head of state, or a member of a foreign (unrecognized) government, or as to the appropriateness of sending an official message of congratulations, condolences, or support to third-state authorities.

The added value of European reporting and information sharing should not be underestimated, particularly for smaller and unrepresented member states, as it gives them access to information and strategic analysis otherwise not available to them. It therefore permits them to reallocate resources to other diplomatic tasks than information gathering or reporting. Federica Bicchi noticed that the geographical reach of national diplomatic networks is limited. She shows that most member states have large gaps in their outreach and often do not possess the necessary information (or knowledge, for that matter) when faced with the need to take a decision at EU level.[299] Because the risk of observational functions undermining national prerogatives in diplomacy is low, this function is one of the most used and tangible modes of cooperation between the EU and the member states. Moreover, the practice is said to have resulted in a 'better institutional memory', allowing the EUDELs to 'emerge as true information and coordination hubs'.[300] The practice is also what sets European diplomatic missions apart from other actors in diplomacy, who generally exemplify the propensity to guard rather than to share information.

*5.3.3.2.3 The obligation to coordinate*

The obligation to cooperate in diplomacy demands EUDELs and member state missions to coordinate their actions. The duty of coordination is not new. In 1981, a report that later formed the basis of the European Political Cooperation (EPC) was drawn up in London by the foreign ministers of the then ten member states exactly on that topic. The London report pushed for the increased synchronization of actions and information exchanges in diplomacy by stating:

> that the Heads of Mission of the Ten [must maintain] the practice of meeting regularly in order to exchange information and coordinate views. In considering their response to significant developments in the country to which they are accredited, their first instinct should be to coordinate with their colleagues of the Ten.[301]

The above expression of the member states' desire to coordinate practices in third countries leaves out a role for the delegations.[302] However, Commission delegations informally joined coordination exercises since the early days, a practice layer confirmed in the EU Treaties. The

[298] Answer of the Council to parliamentary question P-1489/2005, 14 April 2005.

[299] Bicchi (n 295).

[300] Frauke Austermann, 'Towards Embassies for Europe? EU Delegations in the Union's Diplomatic System' (2012) Jean Monnet Multilateral Research Network Policy Paper 8, 5.

[301] Report on European Political Cooperation, adopted in London [1981] Bull EC Supp No 3, 14–17, para 8 (hereafter 1981 London Report).

[302] See, for an appraisal, Bernard R Bot, 'Co-operation between the Diplomatic Missions of the Ten in Third Countries and International Organisations' (2012) 10 LIEI 149.

obligation to coordinate has been extended to the EUDELs, in both multilateral and bilateral contexts. Article 35 TEU provides that:

> [t]he diplomatic and consular missions of the Member States and the Union delegations in third countries and international conferences, and their representations to international organisations, shall cooperate in ensuring that decisions defining Union positions and actions adopted pursuant to this Chapter are complied with and implemented.

The EU Treaties repeat this principle specifically as regards the coordination of actions in international organizations and at international conferences. Article 34(1) TEU stipulates that:

> Member States shall coordinate their action in international organisations and at international conferences. They shall uphold the Union's positions in such forums. The High Representative of the Union for Foreign Affairs and Security Policy shall organise this coordination.

Although the above obligation addresses member states, it is the HR who is entrusted with the management of such coordination. The HR can delegate its general coordinative role to the EUDEL in a third country. Discussing draft EU statements is done in a spirit of loyalty and mutual solidarity and with the aim of achieving a final result (Arts 24(3) and 35, para 1 TEU). While there is no obligation to reach a coordinated position, member states must ensure that they have made all reasonable efforts to arrive at this result. Where a coordinated position is established and presented by the EUDEL, an individual member state is allowed to support it, provided that the topic falls within its competences. Where there is no Union policy position approved by the Council, it is not possible for the HR, the EUDEL, the rotating presidency, or another actor representing the Union to make a statement on behalf of a group of member states. That same group of member states (even the one holding the rotating presidency) is, however, allowed to coordinate their position and jointly represent it, as long as they do not purport to do so on behalf of the Union or the rotating presidency. There is also the possibility for the HR to issue statements in its own name as part of its general responsibility to represent the Union. In the absence of a coordinated position, member states are required in the expression of their national positions to uphold the policies of the Union in accordance with the principle of sincere cooperation. Previously agreed positions at the level of the Council cannot be put into question or be renegotiated, and national policies should be adopted to conform to these Union positions (Art 29 TEU).

The duty to coordinate demands an active participation from diplomats. It is unsurprising that coordination often takes place during meetings that are organized on the ground, either at the HoM level or in thematic meetings attended by counsellors, although it may also take place in Brussels.[303] Until the Lisbon reform, the embassy of the member state that held the rotating presidency was responsible for chairing coordination meetings and functioned as the voice of the locally represented member states. This happened sometimes in a troika constituency.[304] In the course of implementing the Lisbon Treaty, delegations took over most

[303] Geert De Baere and Esa Paasivirta, 'Identity and Difference: The EU and the UN as Part of Each Other' in Henri de Waele and Jan-Jaap Kuipers (eds), *The European Union's Emerging International Identity: Views from the Global Arena* (Martinus Nijhoff 2013) 28; Wouters and others, *2013 EEAS Study* (n 288) 37–45.

[304] 1981 London Report (n 301) para 7.

coordinative roles and functions.[305] Additionally, as of 2009, the EUDELs are responsible for representing coordinated positions to the local government and corps diplomatique.[306] Most coordination meetings are now instigated by the EUDEL and organized in the delegation. Practical concerns are also relevant. Delegations usually have a meeting room with enough space to sit the representatives of member states (up to twenty-seven) and EUDEL officials, to hang flags of all these actors, and to provide even translation equipment. Member state missions tend to be smaller and do not always accommodate large meeting rooms. However, exceptions continue to exist and the role played by the EUDEL varies between meetings, depending on what is on the agenda. When discussing intergovernmental topics such as consular affairs, member state representatives will take the lead and assume the chair. In the majority of other cases, the EUDEL's representative chairs the meeting. When a position is determined 'on the spot' (eg during an international conference), it is not legally required to secure the Council's approval beforehand as long as the statement is in line with agreed Union policy. The EEAS has also progressively taken up chairmanship tasks of the relevant meetings taking place in Brussels.

It is particularly interesting to look back on what was agreed in the 1981 London Report and to see how it has shaped practices over the years. First, the report insisted on the confidential character of European meetings—a principle still observed. Second, the report established the mandatory participation of the head of mission, guaranteeing that coordination takes place at the highest level. A member of the mission was only allowed to replace the ambassador in extraordinary instances.[307] Currently, coordination has grown so exponentially that HoMs no longer take part in every element. Thematic groups gather to focus on human rights, consular protection, economic affairs, and so on. Meetings are subject to regular intervals; those organized at the level of HoMs usually take place on a biweekly or monthly basis. Depending on the needs of relevant countries, technical and thematic coordination meetings can take place weekly or more frequently in international organizations.[308] In 2015, the EUDEL in New York hosted more than 1,300 coordination meetings and delivered more than 220 statements, including 31 at the UNSC.[309]

Coordination meetings generally result in *(a)* a *technical report or HoM report,* sometimes comprising *a joint assessment* (sent to European capitals, the EEAS, relevant DGs, and/or working parties in the Council); *(b)* a *common position or statement* of the EU and the member states (transmitted to the local government or corps diplomatique); or *(c)* a *joint démarche.* Démarches are delivered by the EUDEL or the members states. Every six months, the EEAS draws up a list of all the démarches carried out locally, identifying the member states, if any, that signed up to them.[310] Interestingly, the 2011 Guidelines on political démarches spell out that the participation of member states in an EU démarche may be considered only in 'duly justified circumstances' and should not be a systematic practice. This reflects the idea of the parallel diplomacy model discussed in section 5.3.2. The EU or member states sometimes team up with third states and/or international organizations to

[305] Michael Emerson and others, *Upgrading the EU's Role as Global Actor* (Centre for European Policy Studies 2011) 52.

[306] EEAS, Report by the High Representative of 22 December 2011, para 16.

[307] 1981 London Report (n 301) para 8.

[308] The HR's report on the EEAS Review pursuant to Art 13(3) of Council Decision 2010/427/EU [2016] 12 (hereafter EEAS Review).

[309] Jan Wouters and Marta Hermez, 'The EU's Contribution to the Strict Observance and the Development of International Law at the UNGA Sixth Committee' [2016] GGS Working Paper No 177, 5.

[310] EEAS, 'Guidelines for Political Démarches', EEAS/D(2011)1195321.

produce joint diplomatic messages. Subsequent to violent incidents in Kumanovo (Republic of North Macedonia) in 2015 between police and armed extremists, a joint statement was issued by the EU, United States, OSCE, and NATO missions to the country.[311] In some circumstances, coordination can result in *(d) practical or quasi-legal agreements*. For example, in the context of international organizations, permanent missions of the EU and the member states coordinate the co-sponsoring of draft resolutions.[312] In the bilateral context, separate agreements can be drawn up to specify the modus operandi between the Union and member states. For instance, in 1994, the Commission and ten member states signed a Memorandum of Understanding (MoU) concerning the construction of a joint complex of embassies in Abuja, Nigeria. The parties to the MoU acted in accordance with Article J.6 TEC of the 1992 Maastricht Treaty. Participating member states included Belgium, Denmark, Germany, Greece, Spain, France, Ireland, Italy, the Netherlands, and Portugal. The initial memorandum was supplemented by an accession protocol following the accession of Austria, Finland, and Sweden. Article 1 of the MoU emphasized that embassies of the participating member states and the Commission delegation were distinct diplomatic missions subject to the VCDR and also the VCCR as regards the member states. By virtue of Article 10 of the Memorandum, the Commission was mandated to act as the coordinator of the Abuja II project 'on behalf of' the other partners. With this authorization, the Commission was mandated to undertake architectural feasibility studies and initial decisions regarding costs and design (Art 11 MoU). The MoU installed a permanent Steering Committee, comprising representatives of all participating member states and chaired by the Commission. The project was financed by contributions from participating member states and the Commission, calculated based on each partner's individual part in the project. It was the Commission that made the payments to third parties. The Memorandum later gave rise to an action dispute between Greece and the Commission. The member state's claim that the Commission had made errors regarding financial obligations were dismissed by the CJEU.[313] A coordination may finally result in *(e) a common action*. In 2011, the arbitrary sentencing of Biram Dah Abeid, the leader of an anti-slavery movement in Mauritania, and two fellow human rights defenders was extensively discussed by EU HoMs. Mandated by the member states, the EUDEL subsequently inquired into the conditions of Mr Biram's arrest and detention; it also engaged with several civil society activists, human rights defenders, and political personalities in Mauritania.[314]

The literature is divided on the question as to whether the intense coordination activities between EU actors have altered international diplomacy.[315] Some have argued to the positive, as coordination meetings and agreements between European missions tend to lead to premeditated international negotiations. Undeniably, the dynamics of international negotiations change when European diplomats present a coordinated position. Empirical scholarship on decision-making in the UNSC noted—well before Brexit—that if the United States, China, and Russia sit at the UNSC table with Europeans presenting such a coordinated position, bargaining resembles 'bilateral cooperation between the EU and these countries in a

[311] Answer by the High Representative to parliamentary question E-007580/2015, 11 May 2015.

[312] Frank Hoffmeister and Pieter Jan Kuijper, 'The Status of the European Union at the United Nations' in Jan Wouters, Frank Hoffmeister, and Tom Ruys (eds), *The United Nations and the European Union: An Ever Stronger Partnership* (TMC Asser Press 2006) 17.

[313] *Greece v Commission* [2008] ECLI:EU:C:2008:606.

[314] Answer given by the High Representative to parliamentary question E-000097/2011, 20 January 2011.

[315] Knud Erik Jørgensen and Ramses A Wessel, 'The Position of the European Union in (Other) International Organizations: Confronting Legal and Political Approaches' in Panos Koutrakos (ed), *European Foreign Policy* (Edward Elgar 2011) 282–83.

multilateral context'.[316] Coordination also altered the art of diplomacy. In the individual relations between European missions and third countries, informal diplomacy and the exercise of personal contacts reportedly are lowered to the advantage of formal contacts. Finally, a natural effect of EU coordination is that the end result of international negotiations increasingly resembles an EU-style compromise, in which different views of different power blocs are reflected. A side effect of EU coordination in diplomacy therefore is the introduction of the EU's internal compromise-seeking system to the international arena.

*5.3.3.2.4 Obligations related to consular services rendered to EU citizens*

Since the 1992 Treaty of Maastricht, any person who holds the nationality of an EU country is automatically also granted EU citizenship.[317] As an EU citizen, a person is entitled to a number of rights spelled out in the EU Treaties. One of these entitlements listed in the EU Treaties has a purely external dimension: it grants citizens travelling or working abroad the right to be protected by the diplomatic and consular authorities of any other EU member state.[318] The entitlement to consular protection is enshrined in paragraph 1 of Article 23 TFEU and Article 20(2)(c) and echoed by Article 46 of the EU Charter:

> [e]very citizen of the Union shall, in the territory of a third country in which the Member State of which he is a national is not represented, be entitled to protection by the diplomatic or consular authorities of any Member State, on the same conditions as the nationals of that State [ ... ][319]

The title of Article 46 refers to 'diplomatic and consular protection'. However, the drafters only intended to regulate the notion of 'consular protection', which can be delivered by either the diplomatic or the consular authorities of member states.[320]

Since 1992, the EU has been working on practical guidelines for the member states whose missions abroad had to put the right to consular protection into practice.[321] For a long time, there was no clear consensus in Europe on the right's content, nor on the responsibilities it entailed. Due to the changing social and economic patterns, making it easier and cheaper for citizens to travel the world and more attractive to work or study abroad, mobility has only increased. In practical terms, this can lead to a situation where an EU citizen requiring (medical, legal, administrative) assistance in a foreign country following a personal (eg an accident or a detention) or general crisis (eg a war, tsunami, or earthquake) may be left with consular representation by their own member state.

When the right to consular protection was first enshrined in the Treaty of Maastricht, the EU's contribution centred on coordinating member state actions. The Union facilitated a forum for talks between member states on how to implement the obligation to provide consular assistance. In the mid-1990s, negotiations among member states resulted in two

[316] Sven Biscop and Edith Drieskens, 'Effective Multilateralism and Collective Security: Empowering the UN' in Katie Verlin Laatikainen and Karen Elizabeth Smith (eds), *The European Union at the United Nations: Intersecting Multilateralisms* (Palgrave Macmillan 2006) 120.

[317] Dimitry Kochenov, 'The Right to Have What Rights? EU Citizenship in Need of Clarification' (2013) 19 ELJ 502.

[318] Claude Blumann, 'Citoyenneté Européenne et Droits Fondamentaux' (2006) 1 Rev Aff Eur 73, 80.

[319] Originally Art 8(*c*) TEC (1992 Maastricht Treaty), subsequently Art 20 TEC (1997 Amsterdam Treaty).

[320] Jean Weyland, 'La Protection Diplomatique et Consulaire des Citoyens de l'Union Européenne' in Epaminondas A Marias (ed) *European Citizenship* (EIPA 1994) 67.

[321] Jan Wouters, Sanderijn Duquet, and Katrien Meuwissen, 'Caring for Citizens Abroad: The European Union and Consular Tasks' (2014) 19 EFAR 563.

Council Decisions clarifying the rules on exercising consular protection and the methods of offering assistance.[322] Meanwhile, to informally coordinate their practices, the Commission distributed a brochure, 'Consular Protection for the Citizens of the European Union', among national embassies and consulates.[323] In the mid-2000s, the Commission repeatedly asked to increase its tasks in consular protection, foreseeing a more active role for its worldwide network of delegations.[324] Member states (particularly the larger ones) traditionally argue for an intergovernmentally steered cooperation.[325]

Finally, in 2015, a Directive operationalized the entitlement to consular protection, repealing a 1995 Decision on the subject.[326] The Directive lays down when and how unrepresented EU citizens can receive consular assistance from other EU countries' embassies or consulates. Similarly to the relationship between nationality and EU citizenship, EU involvement in consular protection is supplementary to and does not replace national rights to protection (Art 9 TEU); member states bear the responsibility to define the recipients, scope, and content of the consular assistance whereby the EUDELs' obligations to implement the right of consular protection are of a secondary nature. The 2015 Directive focuses on the EU's coordination duties rather than defining the Union's direct responsibilities or establishing direct contacts between the Union and its citizens. In practice, the EUDEL's role is largely limited to the coordination of local crisis cooperation and the provision of logistical support.[327] The discussion is far from settled, as was shown in the aftermath of the 2021 Afghanistan evacuations, when (often smaller and medium-sized) member states asked to have the debate on greater European consular involvement to be put back on the political agenda.

**Consular protection to unrepresented EU citizens** Member states are the addressees of two different sets of constitutional obligations on consular matters. The first obligation is the duty to grant unrepresented citizens consular protection. This obligation has been subject to political sensitivities of member states. The specific content of Article 23 TFEU was unclear, resulting in diverging and ad hoc implementations. Some member states argued that Article 23 TFEU set out an obligation of non-discrimination for the member states without creating a self-standing right to assistance for the individual. As the UK House of Commons argued in 2007:

> [i]n relation to EU law, Article 20 TEC [now Art 23 TFEU] sets out an obligation of non-discrimination. It requires Member States to treat requests for consular assistance by unrepresented nationals of Member States on the same basis as requests by their own nationals. In compliance with this, the UK provides consular assistance to significant

[322] See Council Decision 95/553/EC regarding protection for citizens of the European Union by diplomatic and consular representations [1995] OJ L106/1 (hereafter Decision 95/553/EC on the protection of EU citizens) and Council Decision 96/409/CSFP on the establishment of an emergency travel document [1996] OJ L168/4 (hereafter Decision 96/409/CSFP on the ETD).

[323] Stelios Stavridis and Colleen Thouez, 'The International Protection of the EU Citizen: Problems and Prospects' in Richard Bellamy and Alex Warleigh (eds) *Citizenship and Governance in the European Union* (Continuum 2005) 169.

[324] Commission, 'Green Paper on Diplomatic and Consular Protection', 28 November 2006 (COM(2006)712 final), paras 1.4, 2.2, 3.1, 4.1 (hereafter Commission, 'Green Paper on Consular Protection').

[325] See the critique of France, the United Kingdom, and Portugal on the Commission's Green Paper: Commission, 'Summary Report of Public Hearing of 29 May 2007 on the Green Paper on Diplomatic and Consular Protection', 5.

[326] Council Directive 2015/637 on consular protection (n 106); Decision 95/553/EC on the protection of EU citizens (n 322).

[327] Article 11 Council Directive 2015/637 on consular protection (n 106).

> numbers of unrepresented Member States' nationals. But Article 20 TEC does not create any right to assistance beyond this. Decisions 95/553/EC and 96/409/CFSP do not affect this position or broaden the basic legal principle set out in Article 20.[328]

Most member states lack a law granting citizens the right to consular protection and merely offer assistance as a favour, based on standards such as 'appropriateness' or 'reasonableness'.[329] In the past, nationals have challenged such states without success in court for a perceived lack of assistance.[330] Those states, quite obviously, did not want to be obliged to grant a protection to unrepresented EU citizens they may not have had to grant to their own. A second group of member states is legally obliged to provide consular assistance to their nationals.[331] This means that these states would have to grant protection to unrepresented EU citizens on the basis of their own laws.[332] Yet other member states had already entered into bilateral or multilateral agreements granting consular protection to each other's or third-state citizens. The Nordic countries, for instance, had systems in place that allowed for this.

At the time of adoption of the Directive, member states were sensitive to the argument that the difference in domestic laws may facilitate 'consular shopping', with unrepresented Union citizens being free to visit different consular posts to find the best service. (Bigger) member states have been even more aware of the 'risk' that large numbers of EU citizens from smaller member states could place a disproportionate burden on their finances and resources.[333] Further, member states with limited representations would benefit from the large representational networks of other member states throughout the world. Unlike in many other international legal arrangements, reciprocity in consular assistance is unequal: states with more representations often need less assistance for their nationals. Moreover, this led to legal uncertainty whereby citizens were often inadequately informed of their rights.[334]

The problem of under-regulation was addressed in 2015, when the legal principles contained in Article 23 TFEU were operationalized in Council Directive 2015/637. First, the Directive delineates the concept of an 'unrepresented citizen' through accessibility criteria.[335] Article 4 defines it as 'every citizen holding the nationality of a Member State which is not represented in a third country as set out in Article 6'. Article 6, in turn, stipulates that 'a Member State is not represented in a third country if it has no embassy or consulate established there on a permanent basis, or if it has no embassy, consulate or honorary consul there which is effectively in a position to provide consular protection in a given case'. This does not include the situation were a citizen's state is represented but is unwilling to assist their national. This citizen will be considered 'represented' for the purposes of EU law. The original

[328] See House of Commons, European Scrutiny Committee, Sixteenth Report, Annex 1, March 2007, para 1.8.

[329] See, regarding the United Kingdom, ibid, para 1.7.

[330] See, eg Court of Appeal of The Hague (Civil Law Section) [NL] *Van Dam v The Netherlands*, 25 November 2004, LJN AR7484; Conseil d'Etat (Section Premier ressort) [FR], Rejet No 11946, 111949, No de rôle 015, 29 January 1993, Recueil des décisions du Conseil d'État—Lebon 1993.

[331] See the Constitutions of Bulgaria (Art 25 (5), Constitution of 13 July 1991), Croatia (Art 10, Constitution of 6 July 2010), Estonia (Chapter 1, para 13, Constitution of 3 July 1992), Hungary (Art 69 (3), Constitution of 18 October 1989), Latvia (Art 98, Constitution of 15 February1922), Lithuania (Art 13, Constitution of 2 November 1992), Poland (Art 36, Constitution of 2 April 1997) and Romania (Art 17, Constitution of 21 November 1991).

[332] See the Care Project, 'Consular and Diplomatic Protection Legal Framework in the EU Member States' (2010) 198–99, <www.careproject.eu/images/stories/ConsularAndDiplomaticProtection.pdf> accessed 5 May 2022 (hereafter Care Project Final Report); Matthias Ruffert, 'Diplomatischer und Konsularischer Schutz zwischen Völker- und Europarecht' (1997) 35 ADV 459, 470–71.

[333] Care Project (n 332) 552.

[334] Ruffert (n 332) 680.

[335] Council Directive 2015/637 on consular protection (n 106).

proposal was a bit more detailed on the matter and contained a clause that considered Union citizens as unrepresented if it was impossible for them to reach the embassy or consulate of their nationality and return to the place of departure via means of transport commonly used in the third country at least the same day.

Second, it has become clear that the consular protection legally qualifies as an obligation not to discriminate,[336] requiring member states to treat requests for consular assistance by unrepresented nationals of other member states on the same basis as requests by its own nationals. As a result, a general obligation for member states to grant consular protection cannot be discerned; the obligation can be better understood as a national treatment clause. Article 5 of the Directive explicitly affirms that third-country family members of Union citizens can benefit from European consular protection. This is no more than a practical application of the principle (held by the CJEU on numerous occasions) that the main rights granted to Union citizens are also extended to their family members.[337] Non-discriminatory treatment also comprises the principle that consular protection of EU citizens meets the same conditions, as stipulated in Article 23 TFEU. Finally, Chapter 3 of the 2015 Directive provides the financial procedures for reimbursing costs of consular protection from the unrepresented citizens or their home member states.

The second obligation flowing from the EU Treaties requires member states to take action at the international level. Article 23, paragraph 1, *in fine* provides that the:

> Member States shall adopt the necessary provisions and start the international negotiations required to secure [consular] protection.

The provision aims to bring the EU legal framework on consular protection, a *res inter alios acta*, in line with international consular law. The issue has received scant attention thus far. Article 8 VCCR permits the exercise of consular functions by third states unless the receiving state objects:

> [u]pon appropriate notification to the receiving State, a consular post of the sending State may, unless the receiving State objects, can exercise consular functions in the receiving State on behalf of a third State.

Article 23 TFEU therefore tasks the member states to enter into legal agreements with third states that stipulate that the latter will not object to consular services being rendered to EU citizens by different European consulates. Such agreements can either take the form of *(a)* a bilateral agreement between EU member state and a third state for the protection of non-nationals; *(b)* a multilateral agreement between EU member states and a third state; or *(c)* a mixed agreement between third states, the EU, and the member states. Because it is difficult to imagine member states individually reaching out to some 160 third states, the Commission's 2006 Green Paper proposed to insert a model consent clause in mixed agreements concluded with third countries.[338] Nowadays, the Commission seems to be of the

[336] Wouters, Duquet, and Meuwissen (n 321) 576; Eileen Denza, 'Art 46—Diplomatic and Consular Protection' in Steve Peers and others (eds), *The EU Charter of Fundamental Rights: A Commentary* (2014) 1182.

[337] *Mary Carpenter v Secretary of State for the Home Department* [2002] ECLI:EU:C:2002:434, para 38; *Blaise Baheten Metock and others v Minister for Justice, Equality and Law Reform* [2008] ECLI:EU:C:2008:449, paras 83, 90; *Giersch and others* [2013] ECLI:EU:C:2013:411, paras 36–40.

[338] Commission, 'Green Paper on Consular Protection' (n 324).

view that both the EU and member states should embark on such negotiations with non-member states to confirm the member states' entitlement to protect any EU citizen whose own member state is not represented. One can question whether such agreements are legally or practically required and would potentially not even be counterproductive.[339] Currently, few agreements exist with third states that rely upon Article 23 TFEU and in practice third states rarely invoke Article 8 VCCR to oppose European practices.[340] It is, moreover, uncertain whether bilateral agreements concluded between member states and third states can be generalized in the sense that other EU member states can benefit from them. Vermeer-Künzli illustrates this *problématique* as follows: in the case of a consular agreement between Portugal and Brazil, a consular officer of Brazil in a third country can be requested to assist Union citizens who are not Portuguese, whose own state of nationality is not represented in the relevant third country, and who invokes the bilateral agreement between Portugal and Brazil based on the non-discrimination principle. Whilst Brazil may argue that it is not bound by any agreement between Portugal and other EU member states, this argument does not apply to Portugal as the latter is obliged under EU law to offer consular assistance to non-represented Union citizens on the same conditions as its own nationals.[341] The present EU legal and policy framework fails to consider this problem.

The (more limited) role of Union delegations in providing consular protection is defined by EU law. The third sentence of Article 35 TEU provides that the EUDELs:

> shall contribute to the implementation of the right of citizens of the Union to protection in the territory of third countries [ . . . ]

The EEAS Decision specifies that upon request of a member state, Union delegations can support a member state in providing consular protection to EU citizens in third countries 'on a resource-neutral basis'.[342] These provisions indicate that the EU's role is subordinate, triggered only by a member state's request.[343]

**Crisis diplomacy** The EU is well placed to take the lead in cases of emergency that feature an EU citizen in distress. Past practices indicate that the EEAS is inclined to do so when a need arises and has done so successfully and without any resistance from member states or non-member states. EUDELs generally undertake three types of actions to support unrepresented citizens in urgent need of assistance. The delegation may *(a)* function as an intermediary to communicate between the Union citizen and local authorities; *(b)* bring the citizen in contact with the authorities of their home state; and *(c)* help the citizen to leave the country, for example by pre-financing the transport to their home state. These arrangements have no clear basis in law and are of a practical nature. When a crisis encompasses a 'European' dimension (ie when it concerns incidents involving citizens of two or more member states), the EEAS can also offer coordinating know-how. Following the 2012 attack on a group of European tourists in the remote region of Afar in Ethiopia that left five EU citizens killed, three injured, and two kidnapped, the EUDEL was 'in close contact with the relevant EU

339 Denza, 'Art 46' (n 336).

340 Care Project Final Report (n 332) 36–38; 592–603.

341 Annemarieke Vermeer-Künzli, 'Where the Law Becomes Irrelevant: Consular Assistance and the European Union' (2011) 60 ICLQ 965, 970–71.

342 Article 5(10) EEAS Decision (n 54).

343 See Elisabeth Tichy-Fisslberger, 'Der Schutz der EU-Bürger durch die Diplomatischen und Konsularischen Vertretungsbehörden' (2012) 13 Europarecht 217, 217.

Member States' embassies in Addis Ababa'.[344] When, in 2011, a nuclear disaster hit Japan and revolutionary protests broke out in Libya, the member states decided to jointly evacuate citizens, whereby Union delegations also automatically assumed a more active role. In critical situations or otherwise, nothing precludes the EU from offering assistance via other means, such as the Community Civil Protection Mechanism set up in 2001, pooling civil protection capabilities of member states and other participating countries. The Mechanism can be used to supply consular assistance to Union citizens in major emergencies in third countries for civil protection purposes when requested by the consular authorities of the member states.[345] Directed by the Commission, the mechanism meets two oft-heard criticisms related to the Union delegations taking a role in crisis management: first, it operates without a necessity of additional resources and, second, it operates without the pooling of sovereign decision-making from member states to the EU level. The consular domain is still developing, and much remains to be done in making European consular services more interoperable. A joint EU consular crisis preparedness framework was implemented in 2019 for ensuring enhanced cooperation and making coordination more efficient and effective in the event of a consular crisis.[346]

**Administrative and legal consular services** There is no obligation for the EU and the member states to offer common consular administrative and legal services abroad. Notarial and regulatory practices of states are insufficiently integrated and standardized to realize such undertaking. Many consular functions (eg registration of births and marriages and migration-related functions) can only be performed in practice by a consul with the nationality of the citizen seeking help.

However, in the field of travel documents, certain modes of cooperation have been set up.[347] The Council established a standard model for a European 'emergency travel document' (ETD) in as early as 1996.[348] ETDs can be issued to Union citizens in territories or countries where their home member state has no accessible diplomatic or consular representation with the capacity to issue such travel documents. The Schengen Visa Code defines common procedures and conditions for the issuance of visas for transit or intended stays in territories of member states not exceeding three months in any six-month period.[349] It created a legal framework obliging the delivery of uniform visas by consulates of member states to third country nationals travelling to EU.

The realization of a more integrated consular visa services is an option rather than a legal obligation under the current Treaty regime. First, although the common visa policy has a constitutional status through its inclusion in EU Treaties, it builds on the Schengen acquis whereby not all member states are participants. Second, European policies on the access to national territories remain a sensitive matter even for Schengen states. States prefer to maintain a certain level of control on the influx of migrants into their respective countries, especially with regard to long-term visa.[350] Another current practice is member state cooperation

[344] Answer given by the High Representative to parliamentary question E-001167/2012, 27 March 2012.
[345] Council Decision 2007/779/EC establishing a Community Civil Protection Mechanism [2009] OJ L314/9.
[346] Answer given by the High Representative to parliamentary question E-000972/2018, 26 June 2018.
[347] Ana Mar Fernández, 'Consular Affairs in the EU: Visa Policy as a Catalyst for Integration?' (2008) 3 HJD 21, 30; Blumann (n 318) 80.
[348] Decision 96/409/CSFP on the ETD (n 322).
[349] Regulation 810/2009 establishing a Community Code on Visas [2009] OJ L243/1.
[350] Ana Mar Fernández, 'Consular Affairs In An Integrated Europe' in Jan Melissen and Ana Mar Fernández (eds), *Consular Affairs and Diplomacy* (Brill Nijhoff 2011) 106; Annalisa Meloni, *Visa Policy within the European Union Structure* (Springer 2005).

in (commercial) 'Common Application Centres' (CACs).[351] In such centres, biometrics can be introduced and a visa application can be launched.[352] Essentially, CACs constitute a specific type of outsourcing and states participate at their own discretion. Sympathetic to existing collaborations, in 2009, the Commission specified that in the long term it envisioned the centres to become all-round common offices that perform consular functions, including issuing visas or legalizing documents.[353] However, further integration of consular functions was not captured as the object of supplementary legislations, minimizing any immediate possibility for the EU to play a more enhanced role in the field. Nevertheless, the European Parliament's Committee on Foreign Affairs stated that it 'believes that in the long term, Union delegations should have a leading coordination role in this respect and, in well-defined circumstances, even be entrusted with consular tasks'. Elsewhere, it 'expresses the view that the Commission proposal could have been much more ambitious and that it does not make use of all the possibilities offered by the Lisbon Treaty and especially the role of the EU Delegations highlighted in Article 35 TEU'.[354]

**The EUDELs' involvement in consular affairs** Four obstacles must be overcome for a more extensive EU involvement to materialize in consular affairs. First, a revision of primary law would be necessary since it is doubtful that the EEAS or the EUDELs have the necessary competences to issue visa or perform administrative tasks on behalf of citizens. These duties surpass 'supporting' roles in consular affairs. Additionally, 'consular *protection*' should probably be read narrowly in light of Article 23 TFEU and not include all forms of 'consular *assistance*'. Admittedly, such textual reading is tricky as the difference between consular protection and assistance is often not upheld in policy documents.[355] Second, from the EEAS viewpoint, the typical administrative tasks do not confer much added value to the current functions of EUDELs, which are mainly of a political nature ('high diplomacy'). Third, budgetary constraints obstruct a deeper engagement of the EEAS in consular affairs. No additional funding is foreseen for the EEAS in respect of consular training for staff or the practical implementation of the new tasks. HR Ashton explicitly referred to this lack of resources during the 2013 EEAS Review as a reason not to engage in consular affairs.[356] A final practical problem the EU encounters in its diplomatic relations is its limitation of having a maximum of one delegation per third state. In large or significant countries, member states often have one or more consular offices that can be used as local antennas of the embassy. In contrast, the EU's centre of power is by default situated in the capital city. Before the Lisbon Treaty's entry into force, the Commission's delegation would reach out to consulates of the rotating presidency, for example, when it needed a document delivered or an economic transaction covered in a distant area. Post-Lisbon, EUDELs saw teething troubles. A general political agreement on how to replace the former Commission practices has not yet been reached. Certain arrangements nevertheless emerged locally. In the United States, where the EUDEL is not properly

351 Mara Wesseling and Jérôme Boniface, 'New Trends in European Consular Services: Visa Policy in the EU Neighbourhood' in Melissen and Fernández (n 350) 126.

352 Consideration 14, Regulation 390/2009 amending the Common Consular Instructions on visas for diplomatic missions and consular posts in relation to the introduction of biometrics including provisions on the organisation of the reception and processing of visa applications [2009] OJ L131/1.

353 Commission, 'Green Paper on Consular Protection' (n 324) 11.

354 European Parliament, Opinion of the Committee on Foreign Affairs on the proposal for a Council Directive 2015/637 on the consular protection for unrepresented citizens, 38.

355 See, eg the Commission's 2006 Green Paper (n 324) on 'diplomatic and consular *protection* of Union citizens in third countries' [emphasis added] that dedicates a section to the issuing of visas.

356 Statement by the EU High Representative on EEAS Review, Strasbourg, 12 June 2013, 5.

represented beyond the Washington DC beltway, an informal and voluntary agreement was concluded with eleven member states. On the basis of the agreement, the EUDEL can instruct consulates of participating member states to take care of diplomatic business in the US states where those states are represented.

*5.3.3.2.5 The obligation to cooperate in the external representation of the Union*

Much has been written and said about the international representation of the EU and the member states, especially in multilateral fora.[357] Numerous legal principles apply to the question of whether permanent representations of member states or the EUDEL will take the floor to present a statement on behalf of the Union, the Union and member states, or the member states only. A document provided by the Council in 2011 somewhat clarified when and on whose behalf Union actors speak, but the issue remains contested in European diplomacy.[358]

As a general principle, both the EU and the member states represent competences allocated to them. European actors can make arrangements on their common representation whereby the Commission, the HR, and the member states can provide the EUDEL's staff with a mandate to negotiate on their behalf. This notion ought to be immediately clarified by pointing to the complicating factors that surface. There are internal factors since matters discussed in a third state or IOs often fall within the competence of both the Union and member states. External factors are equally relevant: the EU may be excluded from the negotiation table by reason of PIL restrictions.[359] Internal laws of IOs often envisage specific rules on the status of EU, the speaking rights, the application of the regional economic integration organization (REIO) technique and/or voting procedures.[360]

The CJEU clarified the legal duties for member states when factors external to EU law silence the Union. In such cases, the member states must use their international prerogatives to overcome the Union's lack of capacity. Even in *Kramer*, it confirmed that the member states are under a duty 'to use all the political and legal means under their disposal to ensure the participation of the [Union] in the Convention and in other similar agreements'.[361] Member state missions can be authorized by the EUDEL to act as the Union's agent in fields that fall within EU competences. As the Court observed in *Sweden v Commission*, in the context of an IO:

> [w]here it is apparent that the subject-matter of an agreement or convention falls partly within the competence of the Community and partly within that of its Member States, it is essential to ensure close cooperation between the Member States and the Community institutions, both in the process of negotiation and conclusion and in the fulfilment of the commitments entered into. That obligation to cooperate flows from the requirement of unity in the international representation of the Community.[362]

357 Ramses A Wessel, 'The Legal Framework for the Participation of the European Union in International Institutions' (2011) 33 LIEI 621; EEAS Review (n 308) paras 16–17.

358 Council, 'EU Statements in multilateral organisations—General Arrangements' (2011) Doc 15901/11.

359 Frank Hoffmeister, 'Outsider or Frontrunner? Recent Developments under International and European Law on the Status of the European Union in International Organizations and Treaty Bodies' (2007) 44 CML Rev 41.

360 Duncan B Hollis, 'Why State Consent Still Matters: Non-State Actors, Treaties, and the Changing Sources of International Law' (2005) 23 BJIL 137, 159.

361 *Kramer* (n 3) para 45.

362 *PFOS* (n 256) para 73. See also: *Opinion 2/91* (n 265) para 36; Opinion 1/94 (n 278) para 108.

Until now, case law has mainly emphasized the member states' obligation to permit the Union to participate in decision-making in IOs. There is no reason to deny that similar obligations exist in bilateral diplomatic relations with third states.

The UN Security Council (UNSC) exemplifies an interesting case study for cooperation. The UNSC is known for its strict rules on its composition and the confidentiality of its deliberations. Following Brexit, France is the only member state that permanently sits on the UNSC and enjoys a veto power. From the ten non-permanent members, up to three (theoretically even four) EU member states could also be elected. The EU itself is barred from taking part: at most, it can intervene during public UNSC sessions. Under the post-Lisbon arrangements of Article 34(2) TEU, member states sitting on the UNSC are required to keep the HR and fellow EU member states informed and to defend the Union's interest and positions. Where the EU defines a position on a subject on the UNSC agenda, its member states sitting in the UNSC are expected to request the Security Council to invite the HR to present that position, that is, under the proviso that the format permits non-UNSC member participation and that a common position exists for the purposes of Article 34(2) TEU. In such cases, typically, the EU HoD in New York takes the floor in the Council on the HR's behalf.

European cooperation can be a powerful instrument, especially in fora where the Union is not formally represented. Nevertheless, the realities of international fora that leave the steering of debates in the hands of the members may equally disadvantage common European interests. A lack of coordination and cooperation can have serious consequences for the Union and member states. A notorious and ill-fated episode occurred in the autumn of 2011, when the United Kingdom insisted on delivering a statement on behalf of the 'EU and its member states' rather than on behalf of the EU as a single entity in the UN General Assembly (UNGA). The UK action negatively impacted European diplomacy: the Union was barred from speaking up on well-prepared initiatives for which the political support seemed clear. A similar irritation is noticeable when Hungary blocks statements or positions in the domain of asylum and migration, something that has been increasingly witnessed over the past couple of years, to the displeasure of EU diplomats.

*5.3.3.2.6 The obligation to facilitate the EU's exercise of passive right of legation*

Article 16 of Protocol No 7 on Privileges and Immunities can be viewed as imposing a targeted duty of cooperation upon the member state where the Union has its seat. Belgium must accord customary diplomatic immunities and privileges to missions of third countries accredited to the Union. The obligation's modalities are discussed in Chapter 3 in more detail. It suffices here to briefly state that similarly to other duties of EU law, the obligation affects the international diplomatic system as traditionally conceived. Under CIL, the reception of foreign nationals and the granting privileges and immunities is a matter of discretion pertaining to the territorial sovereignties of states. The EU Treaties alter this idea, whereby the Union has the right to inform Belgium of diplomats that it will accredit; following such accreditation, Belgium is subsequently obliged to grant them privileges and immunities.

### 5.3.3.3 Cooperation Modes Not Explicitly Foreseen in EU Law

*5.3.3.3.1 The sharing of staff, housing, and security*

For some time now, member states have been experimenting with colocation projects on an ad hoc basis. In these projects, European missions share premises and sometimes administrative staff.[363] In European compounds, the missions can even jointly arrange security

[363] Article 27(1) VCCR enables this in the case of a severance of consular relations.

measures and hire local staff for certain functions (eg a driver or chef). Denza notes that there were eleven UK diplomatic missions in 2003 that shared facilities with other EU actors. In 2005, Germany had nine such projects.[364] Union delegations are also increasingly housing national diplomats, jointly renting premises or building a common complex of European embassies. The overall number of EUDEL colocation projects went from 20 in 2011 to 116 in 2020 (42 with member states and 74 with other EU partners). The way colocations are managed has also evolved from using local Memoranda of Understanding (eg with Luxembourg in Ethiopia and with Spain in Yemen) to centrally managed Framework Agreements with colocation partners.[365] Colocation opportunities are likely to be seized even more frequently in the future. It helps deal with difficult real estate markets abroad and budget cuts in national MFAs as the use of office space is optimized. Quite obviously, a positive side effect is that colocation also facilitates cooperation and coordination among European partners. Belgium even adapted its national law to this effect. According to Article 2 of the Belgian Consular Code, it can decide to establish a Belgian consular post in premises of a diplomatic or consular mission of a fellow member state. The Code omits a direct reference to the possible establishment in an EUDEL, which is probably an oversight of the legislator.[366]

In contrast to more integrative forms of cooperation, such as carrying out joint assessments or the absorption of diplomatic agents of member states in the EEAS (Art 27(3) TEU)), colocation projects do not entail the loss of independence. When multiple missions share premises, each maintains separate working methods, communications, and archives. Moreover, the respective emblems are shown on the premises; the missions often even have separate entrances. The non-integrative features are probably also the reason why some member states have also established colocation projects with non-EU states.

#### *5.3.3.3.2 The lead state concept*

A common European diplomatic culture is also entrenched through 'lead state' practices. This concept has proven useful in strengthening cooperation between member states when dealing with matters where the EU (delegation) lacks competences.[367] In many third countries, a specific member state can be designated that, for geographical, diplomatic, historic, or linguistic reasons, has a more intense alliance with the given country than fellow member states. The criteria for determining which member state will take the lead in any third country will be established by the member states on a case-by-case basis, depending, inter alia, on local conditions. Examples include Portugal in Brazil, Spain in Honduras, and France in Morocco. The member state does not only have an excellent knowledge of the area and the political regime, but its citizens will most likely also constitute the largest group of European nationals residing permanently or temporarily in the given third state. Such connection naturally generates a leading role for that member state, especially in handling unforeseen crises. The role of the lead state is always voluntary, requires the active support and participation of all member states, and does not exclude support by the EUDEL. Member

[364] Denza, *Diplomatic Law* (n 28) 59.

[365] See Press release, 'EEAS and Spain Sign Memorandum of Understanding to Establish Spanish Embassy on Premises of EU Delegation to Yemen', 10 December 2012, Brussels, A 568/12, <www.consilium.europa.eu/uedocs/cms_data/docs/pressdata/EN/foraff/134154.pdf> accessed 5 May 2022. Five more EUDELs (Bolivia, China, Fiji, Israel, and Thailand) welcomed co-location partners in 2016; see EEAS, Human Resources Report 2020, at 38, <https://www.eeas.europa.eu/sites/default/files/documents/eeas_hr_report_2020_8.pdf> accessed 5 May 2022.

[366] Law on the Consular Code of 21 December 2013 [BE] published in the Belgian State Gazette 30 April 2014 (hereafter Belgian Consular Code).

[367] Council, Stocktaking Report: measures to increase the effectiveness, coherence, and visibility of EU external policies, Doc 10612/08, 13 June 2008, 10.

states have to ensure that an appropriate share of the burden is allotted to each mission present in that third country.[368]

The lead state concept originates from NATO practices between allies in the event of crisis. In the EU, the concept was first introduced in consular matters as a feature in consular arrangements between member states as well as, more formally, in Article 6 Council Decision 95/553/EC on the protection of EU citizens.[369] It was implemented into practice for the first time in February 2008 during the crisis in Chad, where France assumed a leading role. The French Embassy in N'Djamena coordinated the evacuation of 1,200 EU citizens from 12 member states not represented.[370] Practical arrangements regarding lead states were installed in 2015 in 29 out of 146 third countries where at least one member state was represented.[371] However, the concept is not without criticism. When EU citizens in need of assistance are automatically directed to the lead state embassy or consulate, the concept undermines the spirit and wording of Article 23 TFEU, providing that citizens are 'entitled to protection by the diplomatic or consular authorities of *any* Member State'.[372]

Following the introduction of Council Directive 2015/637 installing consular protection for unrepresented citizens, the lead state concept received a legal base. The Directive defines a lead state as:

> one or more Member State(s) represented in a given third country [ . . . ] in charge of coordinating and leading the assistance of unrepresented citizens during crises.[373]

The Directive consequently limits the concept's use to crises only: member states may designate a lead state in preparatory crisis arrangements whereby a designated state assumes co-ordinating tasks and evacuation capacities on the basis of agreed arrangements as triggered by said crisis. Other represented member states and the EUDEL are obliged to offer the lead state support, whereas the unrepresented member states must provide it with all relevant information regarding their concerned citizens.[374] Certain member states incorporated legislation to deal with potential privacy concerns. Article 36 of the Belgian Consular Code, for instance, foresees that all data necessary for the evacuation of Belgians in need can be shared with consulates of fellow member states responsible for that evacuation. The Code does not mention data sharing with EUDELs.[375] The designated lead state may also request the Union's Civil Protection Mechanism and the EEAS's crisis management structures to assist the management of the consular protection of unrepresented citizens.[376] In 2004, when an earthquake and tsunami hit the Indian Ocean, the then Dutch Presidency, for instance, called on the EU's Civil Protection Mechanism to assist EU citizens in the affected area.[377]

368 Answer given by the Council to parliamentary question E-2865/2007, 27 September 2007.

369 European Council Guidelines on the implementation of the consular lead State concept [2008] OJ C317/6. See, for further reading, Sébastien Touzé, 'Aspects Récents (et Choisis) de la Protection Consulaire des Citoyens de l'Union Européenne' (2011) 1 Rev Aff Eur 79, 81; Tichy-Fisslberger (n 343) 223.

370 Federico Forni, 'The Consular Protection of EU Citizens during Emergencies in Third Countries' in Andrea de Guttry, Marco Gestri, and Gabriella Venturini (eds), *International Disaster Response Law* (TMC Asser Press 2012) 170.

371 See the explanatory notes to the Council Directive 2015/637 on consular protection (n 106) 5.

372 See the criticism of Vermeer-Künzli (n 341) 977.

373 Consideration 23, Council Directive 2015/637 on consular protection (n 106).

374 Article 13(3) Council Directive 2015/637 on consular protection (n 106) deals with crisis preparedness.

375 Belgian Consular Code (n 366).

376 Article 13(4) on crisis preparation and cooperation and Consideration 22, Council Directive 2015/637 on consular protection (n 106).

377 'European Commission mobilizes the Civil Protection Mechanism for victims of the earthquake and tsunami in South Asia', IP/04/1543, Brussels, 27 December 2004.

The lead state's role is significantly less than what the Commission had originally envisaged in its Directive proposal and differs even more from the path the European Parliament (EP) had chosen to follow: the Parliament had amended the Commission's proposal so to promote the Union delegations to a leading role. To prevent imposing an unbearably heavy burden on the lead state, or any member state present in the area, the Parliament argued that Union citizens should be given the choice to contact the consulate *or* the EUDEL to claim protection. The Parliament furthermore suggested that Union delegations ought to deal with coordination and cooperation activities, including the communication of contingency plans, evacuation, and the timely exchanges of information.[378] It is somewhat regrettable that this proposal was not signed into law since the Union delegations are already accustomed to the coordinative function. For example, the EUDEL in Japan spontaneously assumed a leading role when a nuclear disaster caused the official proclamation of an emergency situation in 2011. However, in 2015, the Council emphasized that consular protection remains a purely national competence.

*5.3.3.3.3 Ad hoc cooperation*

With all its twists and turns, the diplomatic practice also calls for unplanned cooperation. Ad hoc collaborations are difficult to capture by legal provisions as they are observed in many varieties. Coordination between the EU and the member states can be quickly set up and adjusted on the basis of mutual trust to cope with circumstances and needs on the ground. Because academic scholarship rarely reports on these practices, it is hard to determine trends or general practices. This subsection aims to counter this obstacle by looking at how cooperation played out in two concrete examples.

The first case involved the arrest of the Slovak Ambassador to Ethiopia in 2011.[379] The Ambassador was arbitrarily held by local Ethiopian security forces for two days without being given permission to notify the Slovak authorities. The European diplomatic machinery was immediately put in motion: EU and member state diplomats in Ethiopia collectively condemned the arrest as a textbook violation of the VCDR. Poland, as the then holder of the rotating presidency, and the EUDEL in Addis Ababa intervened on behalf of the Slovak Republic. HR Ashton called the Ethiopian Ambassador to the EU to discuss the incident and to express diplomatic discontent. Following the discussion, the EU obtained from the Ethiopian Government:

> a clear statement of regret and apology, a statement that this was an undesired incident, the commitment to investigate and to take measures to prevent such incidents in future, the assurance of re-establishment of H.E. [ . . . ] as a fully respected Ambassador, and the reassurance of the importance attached by Ethiopia to relations with Slovakia and with the EU.

The EEAS's brokering of this amicable solution resulted in the release of the Ambassador. Afterwards, Slovakia sent a letter of thanks to HR Ashton.

In a second example, a top-ranking police officer was arrested in Burundi in 2015, having disobeyed an order to open fire to unarmed protestors. While in custody, he was subjected to extreme torture.[380] The police officer possessed Burundi and Greek nationality. Because

[378] European Parliament, Report on the proposal for a Council Directive on consular protection for citizens of the Union abroad (COM(2011)0881), 25 October 2012.

[379] Answer given by the High Representative to parliamentary question E-010863/2011, 24 November 2011.

[380] Answer given by the High Representative to parliamentary question E-012182/2015, 27 August 2015.

Greece was not diplomatically represented in Burundi, its permanent representation in Brussels brought the case to the attention of the EU. Upon notification, the EEAS asked the EUDEL in Bujumbura to pursue the matter with local authorities in close cooperation with the Honorary Consul of Greece in Burundi and the Greek Embassy in Nairobi. In the following days, a representative of the delegation met the detainee's lawyer and members of his family. At the request of the Greek Embassy in Nairobi, a locally represented EU member state sent a note verbale to Burundi's MFA, demanding information about the situation and conditions of its eventually released national.

It follows from these examples that in many scenarios in the diplomatic/consular context there are no fixed cooperation mechanisms between the EU and individual member states. Despite this observation, the EU and member states (including via the rotating presidency) liaise at regular intervals without a predefined requirement to do so. The extent and type of assistance offered by the EUDEL to member states depends on the case at hand but can take the form of the sharing of contacts, the collective exercise of diplomatic pressure, and the exercise of diplomatic functions, either on behalf of an unrepresented state or in the Union's name.

#### 5.3.3.4 The Legal Status of the Obligations to Interact in Diplomacy

The principle of sincere cooperation is arguably the epitome of a context-specific duty. It can imply a best efforts obligation and be transformed into a duty of information and consultation or, in other cases, an obligation of result or a duty of abstention if required to ensure the coherence and consistency of the EU's international action and representation.[381] The obligations to share information, to conduct joint assessments, and to participate in coordination are substantive legal obligations that can be qualified as obligations as to means or conduct. These obligations want to alter member state behaviour towards a desired direction and promote collaborative conduct. Yet, diplomatic actors retain flexibility as to the working modes, leaving the actual outcomes uncertain. Moreover, diplomatic actors may invoke sovereign prerogatives and diplomatic priorities to be exempted from releasing information or from participating in joint European activities. The general duty to respect EU law and objectives, the duty to enter into negotiations with third countries permitting consular protection, and the duty to implement the entitlement to consular protection are more closely linked to obtaining a particular result.[382] Additionally, when the Union enjoys an exclusive competence to act, member states are often under distinct obligations to produce results and are thereby either obliged to follow the Union position or to refrain from acting altogether.

#### 5.3.3.5 The Interactive Exercise of Rights of Legation

The diplomatic and consular relations of European actors are imbued with principles of integration and interaction. Integrative diplomacy manifests in three constellations. First, there are the cases where the member states exercise their rights of legation collectively (*up to twenty-seven*). A typical example is intergovernmental cooperation reliant on the lead state concept or in consular affairs more generally. In a second scenario, the EU and the member states act together (*up to twenty-seven plus one*). Such a form of collective and pluralistic diplomacy allows the Union to exercise its right of legation alongside that of the member states. In the third sense, cooperation is so tight it merges the Union's and member states' distinctive

381 *Commission v Germany* [1996] (n 104) para 60.

382 Alessandro Ianniello Salicetti, 'The Protection of EU Citizens Abroad: Accountability, Rule of Law, Role of Consular and Diplomatic Services' (2011) 17 EPL 91, 101.

diplomatic identities (*into one*). In such case, the EUDEL assumes a blended identity representing the totality of the Union and the member states. Arguably, when so profound, cooperation results in integration. The scenario is hard to distinguish from the one where the Union independently acts along the lines of parallel diplomacy. In other words, interactions between the EU and the member states can lead to the creation of a new construct that works in isolation from the other interactions so much that the new construct's mechanism becomes invisible.

### 5.3.4 A European Diplomacy Model

The interactions of the EU and its member states in diplomacy are guided by mutual positive duties of cooperation, on the one hand, and mutual negative duties of respect for prerogatives held by other actors, on the other. Two behavioural patterns determine European diplomacy. First, the EU and its member states act as independent diplomatic powers and operate in distinct ways in situations that broadly fall within their sphere of competences. However, even when acting separately, European diplomatic actors act in complementary manners when to do so benefits their common interest or overcomes functional deficiencies derived from the division of competences (internal) or international participation rules (external). The EU and the member states *live apart together*. Second, European entities also behave as parts of a composite European actor. The model of European diplomacy strives for interaction and collaboration to the benefit of a diverse set of individual and common interests. The Union and its member states manage to increasingly handle diplomatic positions collectively without witnessing a decrease of identity and power. The EU and the member states *live together apart*.

Enjoying the right of legation but sharing powers, entities such as the Union and its member states challenge traditional conceptions of diplomacy that international law relied upon for centuries. Bilateral and multilateral diplomatic fora are mostly familiar with states as unified diplomatic actors that inherently enjoy sovereign powers and diplomatic prerogatives. The model of European diplomacy is a testimony to an alternative view on the exercise of the right of legation, capturing the effectiveness of diversity and association. When represented in diplomacy, the international identity of European diplomatic actors can be collective or individual and may be best defined as a heterogeneous construction with multiple parameters and—depending on the context—a certain adaptability.

# 6
# Concluding Thoughts

## 6.1 Introduction

For centuries, well-managed diplomatic and consular relations have advanced societies and political, commercial, scientific, and cultural understandings. Diplomacy is a coexistence mechanism that strives to maintain international order and communication, including between states whose structural differences and internal choices complicate interactions. In Europe, the birthplace of the right of legation, a new actor has arisen, one that incorporated and arguably altered this diplomatic tradition. Over the past sixty or so years, the European Union (EU, or Union) has gradually built its own permanent bilateral and multilateral diplomatic network, which functions as a flagship instrument of the Union's external relations policy. This handbook has presented evidence on this spectacular development. It has also found that EU diplomacy, despite its practices and wide recognition, gives rise to a considerable number of vexed legal problems and questions. The main findings of this study are summarized in the next sections.

## 6.2 The International Diplomatic System

The key to EU diplomacy is the international community's recognition of the Union's entrance into the diplomatic system. External actors have largely accepted the Union and member states' diplomatic conduct, taken individually and collectively, as an inevitable result of European integration. Likewise, the EU makes the case that because its needs are not essentially different from those of states, neither should its rights be different. This recognition, however, does not prevent legal friction. To overcome tensions between the EU and the international legal framework under which it operates, the EU has adopted coping mechanisms. The result thereof is that, to fit in, EU diplomacy largely conforms to the international diplomatic system.

When the Parliamentary Assembly first proclaimed the European right of legation in 1960, that right was not yet legally established. The Assembly was mistaken about two factors: the peculiar qualities a diplomatic actor must possess and the actual character of the international legal order. This combination resulted in misconceptions about the true nature of the Communities' early-stage diplomatic relations. In retrospect, the parliamentary declaration also had its merits: it created the idea of the Communities being worthy of conducting diplomatic relations. While this early projection was far from globally recognized at first, the image may have later influenced third countries' willingness to accept the EU's petitions to join the diplomatic system. External factors also play a role. The absence of similar claims by other international organizations strengthens the idea that the EU conveys exceptional qualities that justify its right of legation. There was and still is a strong belief that the Union's place in the world is unique, a conviction that easily seeps into EU rhetoric. The

*EU Diplomatic Law.* Sanderijn Duquet, Oxford University Press. © Sanderijn Duquet 2022.
DOI: 10.1093/oso/9780192844552.003.0006

EU's assertions that it is essentially different from other international organizations (IOs) is generally interpreted in terms of superiority: the EU may not be a state but it is surely much more than an 'ordinary' IO. The Union's claims for diplomatic treatment go back to this sui generis rationale. The EU's shift in terminology from 'Commission Delegations' to 'Union Delegations' and 'Head of Delegation' to 'EU Ambassador' also speaks volumes about European ambition, the member states' acceptance, and third states' recognition of the EU's role in the world.

Much more than a matter of prestige, however, EU diplomacy is grounded in sheer necessity. Throughout the European integration process, changing circumstances allowed the EU to live up to its goal of being a diplomatic actor. It is the Union's configuration and level of integration that has increasingly legitimated and facilitated the conduct of diplomatic activities. At the same time, third states have also actively looked to set up coordinated interactions with the Union that went beyond what would normally be the case for interactions with IOs. European diplomacy thus has become ever more accepted not for normative reasons but out of a functional need to interact on the global plane. In turn, this has smoothened the EU's demand for equal treatment. Much like for states, the purpose of the immunities and privileges granted to the Union is not to benefit the Union or the individuals representing it but to ensure the efficient performance of diplomatic functions by the EU delegations (EUDELs).

But how does the EU's propensity for conformism in diplomacy and diplomatic law work in practice? To influence its level of social categorization in the diplomatic arena, the Union adopts the technique of behavioural integration. Indeed, EU diplomacy has a preference for assimilation rather than divergence. There are two advantages to this. First, it helps the Union to keep a low profile and not to upset existing power balances. Second, by modelling its needs and requests on those of states, outcomes equally resemble those applied to states. As a result, in its day-to-day diplomatic relations, the EU contrasts with states in a less defining way than one may assume.

The EU's efforts to establish a legal framework that provides the EU's entry ticket in diplomacy should be distinguished from the concrete application of norms in a non-discriminatory way. There is little doubt or controversy about the fact that when dealing with third states or other IOs, the Union cannot impose its wishes or internal laws upon them. Rather, it must seek ways to participate in the diplomatic arena by agreement. In practice, the EU carefully studies how member states, third states, and—judging from the similarities between the language used in establishment agreements (EAs) and the UN Convention on Privileges and Immunities (CPIUN)—even other actors conduct diplomatic relations. To blend in with the international system, the Union adopts creative solutions that are both assimilative and result-orientated. Using EAs, agreements making the Vienna Convention on Diplomatic Relations (VCDR) (1961) the EU's choice of law and containing a reciprocity clause, the Union simply adopts diplomatic norms as they were conceived between states. As a result, with a minimum of efforts and backed by a firm belief in a diplomatic entitlement, the EU creates the optimal conditions to participate on fairly equal terms in the diplomatic system from which most non-states are excluded. Rather than attempting to untie the apparently intractable Gordian knot of the international diplomatic system, the Union establishes a mechanism that grants itself rights not directly inferred from diplomatic and consular law.

The presence of a legal framework that allows for the VCDR's application does not automatically bring about the non-discriminatory application of norms. Reconciling its needs, wants, and tools with diplomatic and consular law, the Union finds a set of well-established norms, tailor-made to the needs and wants of sovereign states. The Union has long resolved issues with regard to the application of the VCDR's core rules; norms imperative to the system's functioning (personal privileges and immunities, the inviolability of diplomatic premises and communication, etc) are copy/pasted. A more prudent approach is discerned in relation to rules that could be interpreted as the EU claiming a position equal to that of states (in protocol, during ceremonies, etc). It is clear that the Union avoids challenging sovereign dominance in diplomacy. Rather, it balances its needs against those of the system, an approach that evidences the EU's adaptation to the international system rather than the other way around. However, in recent years, a shift was observed in the Union's behaviour, with a much more active EEAS asking for equal protocol treatment when circumstances on the ground so allow. In other words, the EU's conformism results in assimilation tempered by pragmatism, functionalism, and even diplomatic savoir-faire.

The most difficult legal conflicts are provoked when the EU is subjected to simultaneous obligations from different international legal regimes. Diplomatic law shares uncertain boundaries with human rights law and international institutional law. In diplomatic asylum cases or when defining the EUDELs' functions, the Union must find clever legal and diplomatic solutions. Legally speaking, the EU needs to seek an appropriate balance between coexisting binding norms of diplomatic and other legal regimes by favouring either one or the other as the appropriate legal framework. Diplomatically speaking, the EU's solution should avoid disrupting friendly relations between the Union and an adversary state by all means possible. Fundamentally, however, this balancing exercise is not different from challenges (democratic) states are confronted with in their diplomatic practices.

The EU's own legal framework also occasionally struggles to adapt to diplomacy's demands. The Union's legal order, which is generally receptive towards international law, also tends to be protective of its own autonomy and the finely honed legal system it created. International and EU law keep one another intact, and the member states must simultaneously abide by international and EU norms. From time to time, controversy has surrounded the application of diplomatic and consular law to interactions between member states and interactions between the Union and (a) member state(s). All in all, the EU's right of legation is not considered to profoundly curtail the legal capacity of member states to establish and terminate diplomatic relations. More integration in diplomacy does not necessarily constitute a loss of national sovereignty but rather pools sovereignties across traditional nation-state boundaries. The effect, then, is the introduction of certain quantitative and qualitative conditions that dictate how the member states' right of legation is exercised (instrumental limitation) and what themes can be addressed (substantive limitation).

The result of the above is that EU diplomacy adheres to the existing diplomatic order without fundamentally changing it. While it had a profound impact on the traditional diplomatic system, EU involvement has not revolutionized it. Diplomatic law's content crystalized many years ago, and principles of tradition and continuity are embedded in diplomatic interactions. It is not the EU's intention to change those features. Quite to the contrary, by subjecting itself to the corpus of international rules and standards the EU maintains the precision and workability of the diplomatic and consular legal regimes. Perhaps more spectacular is how, internally, the EU challenges the existing diplomatic order. After having acceded to the Union, a more perfect interstate system of international relations, member states voluntarily limited the execution of the rights they have under international law. Between member states, preference is often given to means and methods developed in the EU to communicate and cope with conflict. In their external relations, cooperation schemes are set up between member states to share information and resources. Moreover, the EU has made it rather unlikely for its member states to suspend or terminate diplomatic or consular relations with one another. In that sense, the EU has revolutionized the way in which sovereign powers are executed in diplomacy.

A final conclusion is that public international law maintains a high degree of malleability. The EU diplomacy serves as an example of how public international law (PIL) can be modified, even perfected, and used to the wishes of its principal and engineering actors: nation states. Now, as was often the case in the past, when states want something to work, it will work, even when this requires using traditional PIL concepts in a different context or in relation to different subjects. The diplomatic realm is used for social purposes. States are capable of establishing social ties by applying international (diplomatic) law to other subjects of international law. This pragmatism allows diplomatic and consular law to modernize along the lines of demands of a changing global order.

## 6.3 The EU's Diplomatic Identity and the Perception Thereof

The Union is particularly prone to portray itself as a diplomatic actor. Because of the EU's long-standing diplomatic practices, it is tempted to conclude that it has been subsumed by the diplomatic system. Through its diplomatic participation, the Union has indeed adopted diplomacy-specific attitudes and language. However, the EU remains a unique diplomatic actor, one that possesses features distinctive from those of states. Its singularity, as will be argued below, stems from its structural collective characteristics and thematic preferences.

The EU differs from other diplomatic actors because it operates in the international system through a coordinated approach with its member states. Structurally, the Union's diplomatic identity originates from ideas of cooperation and interaction—framed as legal obligations for the EU and the member states—rather than from power. It is the product of the integration process between formerly independent diplomatic and consular actors, which evolved into a hybrid construct that allows the member states to continue to exercise their right of legation in ways that largely transcend Westphalian ideas. EU diplomacy finds its origins in patterns of coercion, accumulation of competences, and a distribution of rights between the Union and states. European diplomacy shows that competences do not necessarily need to be unitarily represented. Rather, the EU and its member states exemplify that diplomatic and consular powers, no less than other governmental powers, can be exercised in a system of institutional pluralism. European diplomacy is grounded in this compatibility rationale and the idea of mixed and cooperative diplomacy colours the projection of the EU's image to the world, perhaps unintendedly so.

The Union may be less unique when it comes to the content of its diplomatic practices. Like many of its member states, it uses diplomacy to pursue political and economic interests as well as to proclaim and promote common principles including peace, democracy, the rule of law, and human rights, as enshrined in the *acquis communautaire*. It leaves no doubt that the EU tries to accomplish both to maximize its own advantage: it seeks a position of (traditional, diplomatic) power to negotiate a solution beneficial for the Union and its citizens while also acting in accordance with the values and objectives in Article 3(5) TEU.[1] The Union is capable of positioning itself in a world of power, national interest, and foreign policy even to the extent that competition can and does emerge between the EU and

[1] Consolidated Version of the Treaty on European Union [2012] OJ C326/01 (hereafter TEU).

the member states. Like other diplomatic protagonists, the extent to which the EU actively endorses its values depends on the diplomatic context and the counterpart(s). Although the stress put on human rights protection is a distinctive (rhetorical) feature of the Union's diplomatic character, it cannot be said that the Union prioritizes one set of interests over the other.

In summary, six characteristics define how EU diplomacy is shaped. First, the Union's diplomacy is an original *construct*, erected to deal with internal and external challenges. It can therefore be deemed a consciously created by-product of the broader European integration process. Second, the diplomacy model the Union presents to the world is *asymmetric*, whereby the external representation of the Union and its member states may not always correspond with internal competences. Diplomatic powers moreover will depend on the entity's recognition as an international subject of law. This may provoke two discrepancies: the Union may possess an internal competence but be prevented from representing it diplomatically; conversely, it may happen that the lack of an internal mandate to represent a particular competence or interest hinders the member states, this despite their general right of legation. As a consequence of the original legal position, where the scope of international capacity does not fully coincide with the scope of internal competences, a certain unevenness is intrinsic to the European diplomatic model. Third, deviating from the rational picture scholars paint of the diplomatic domain and its participants, EU diplomacy is *variable, contextual, and rooted in experimentalism*. It does not represent a perfect division of labour and has only a few clear-cut obligations. Instead, its scope and shape depend on internal factors, such as the number of missions present, and external factors, including the bilateral or multilateral third-party-led context. This makes EU diplomacy subject to evolution. Fourth, there is a *built-in tension* because EU diplomacy allows for coexisting rights of legation. Principles of parallel diplomacy promote closeness and secrecy, whilst the principles of integrative diplomacy promote openness and interactions. EU diplomacy aims to reconcile the two positions. To deal with the contradictory process of autonomy and integration (fifth), *dialectic thinking* is required. European entities enjoying an autonomous right of legation establish and engage with a cooperative dialogue on the basis of reasoned arguments. This supports the acknowledgment of a perceived common interest against diverse national interests. Sixth, EU diplomacy presents a *hybrid global governance* model of diplomacy in that it is neither pre-Second World War bilateral nor post-Second World War multilateral.

The model of coexisting rights of legation as presented in this handbook is not perfectly polished. Problems occur when a (diplomatic) entity does not recognize the diplomatic capacities enjoyed by a(nother) European entity and a coordinated contribution via the respective legal capacities is denied. The model, based on separate yet integrated diplomatic identities, also falters when there are gaps between diplomatic actors' diplomatic interests. What is more, diplomatic counterparts are not necessarily knowledgeable about the subtleties of EU diplomacy. The EU is capable of actively representing one or more diplomatic entities, a duality that gives rise to (identity) confusion and demarcation issues. For example, diplomatic colleagues may perceive the Union as a unified actor representing all member states regardless of the topic at hand. Vice versa, third-state diplomats may reach out to member states' mission on topics within the Union's sphere of exclusive competences. As a result, from an external perspective, diplomatic identities risk being perceived as unnecessarily separated or blurred. Some confusion thus originates in the Union's diplomatic identity, which encompasses the independent identity of the EU, on the one hand, and the Union's identity as a collective diplomatic representative of the EU and the member states, on the other. These issues can and probably will be addressed when respect for the Union's diplomatic capacities and interests increases.

## 6.4 The Contribution of the EU to Diplomatic and Consular Law

This handbook sought to discern the EU's contribution to international diplomatic and consular law. This is no easy task. EU diplomacy only has a few decades of hindsight—most (member) states have a long history of diplomatic practice and recognized actorness that allow them to modify and interpret rules, norms, protocol, and PIL. Due to historical understandings and constraints posed by the international legal order, the EU is often not in the driver's seat when it comes to formulating international law in the state-dominated domain of diplomatic and consular relations. Furthermore, any actor's individual contribution to the development of a general body of law would be hard to measure as only international actors' collective will crystallizes into legal rules. Finally, the diplomatic context, in which interactions take place in secretive settings and public disclosures are rare, is especially challenging. Be that as it may, this book evidences that, while barely a little more than sixty years old, the Union has contributed to the field of diplomatic and consular law in at least the three following ways: *(a)* as an actor, *(b)* in a direct fashion, and *(c)* in an indirect fashion.

Probably the *biggest contribution* the Union makes to diplomacy is being a part of the international diplomatic and consular system. Through its existence as a diplomatic actor, the EU at the same time tests and confirms diplomatic participation rules. Further, the EU's participation impacts the reach and scope of international diplomatic law, which is now applied in a multiplicity of EU–state relations. With regard to consular law, the EU is much more modest, but it has changed the way member states treat each other's citizens. Moreover, the Union has a role in coordinating the cooperation of and between member states and, surely, in crisis situations.

The EU *directly shapes international diplomatic law*. Formally, the EU contributes to diplomatic law by applying it to its own relations with third states and IOs. Obvious examples are the establishment agreements and Protocol No 7 on Immunities and Privileges, as well as the inclusion of EU-specific clauses in headquarters agreements that deal with immunities of representatives. When applying diplomatic rules, the Union sometimes adopts small alterations or practices that put a twist on particular rules. EU ceremonies for the presentation of credentials and the signing of letters of credence by the Commission President and the President of the European Council are two such examples. The Union also makes substantive contributions to the evolutive interpretation of the VCDR through its practices in Brussels, in third states, and at IOs. For example, through its participation in the UN General Assembly's host state committee, the EU left its fingerprint on resolutions that contain modern interpretations of diplomatic law. Different instruments are used to exert influence: EU primary and secondary law, Treaty law, and customary international law. In contrast, the Court of Justice of the European Union (CJEU)—often seen as a driving force of integration—has played a more limited role in contributing to diplomatic and consular affairs. This is partly due to the limited number of cases on the topic that make it to Luxembourg.

The EU also *indirectly contributes to the diplomatic system*, although patterns may be difficult to see. The EU's behaviour on the international scene testifies to its preference for negotiated and non-violent solutions, thereby subscribing to the core values of diplomacy. This pattern can be observed in the EU's démarches and speeches held in third countries and at international fora. Indirectly, the EU also contributes to international law through its representation in treaty negotiations and when decisions are made. Finally, the EU indirectly promotes coalition-forming on the international scene. Because its powers lie in presenting carefully coordinated positions to partners, it may incidentally encourage third-state partners to also collectively present pre-negotiated solutions.

Finally, it must be noted that the reverse situation is also true: *international diplomatic and consular law make contributions to EU law and practice.* In other words, the Union's emergence as a diplomatic actor has its effects on EU law. The Union's rise in the international arena brings ever more pressure to bear on European governments to extend the EU's competences and to create new powers to be represented internationally. International law is more than a legal framework under which the Union operates. Diplomacy allows the EU to fulfill its (international) objectives. Through the application of international rules, political interests are defended and international legal rules created at bilateral and multilateral gatherings. Diplomacy also contributes to the Union's image: the permanent presence of the EU in third countries has improved the Union's visibility with local authorities as well as foreign publics.

APPENDIX 1

# Facts and Figures

## 1.1 List of Third Countries Where EU Representation is Exercised by the EUDEL

1. AFGHANISTAN (Kabul)
2. ALBANIA (Tirana)
3. ALGERIA (Algiers)
4. ANGOLA (Luanda)
5. ARGENTINA (Buenos-Aires)
6. ARMENIA (Yerevan)
7. AUSTRALIA (Canberra)
8. AZERBAIJAN (Baku)
9. BANGLADESH (Dhaka)
10. BARBADOS (Bridgetown), also accredited to the Eastern Caribbean States, the OECS and CARICOM
11. BELARUS (Minsk)
12. BENIN (Porto-Novo)
13. BOLIVIA (La Paz)
14. BOSNIA-HERZEGOVINA (Sarajevo)
15. BOTSWANA (Gaborone)
16. BRAZIL (Brasilia)
17. BURKINA FASO (Ouagadougou)
18. BURMA/MYANMAR (Yangon)
19. BURUNDI (Bujumbura)
20. CAMBODIA (Phnom Penh)
21. CAMEROON (Yaoundé)
22. CANADA (Ottawa)
23. CAP-VERT (Praia)
24. CENTRAL AFRICA (Republic) (Bangui)
25. CHAD (N'Djamena)
26. CHILE (Santiago)
27. CHINA (People's Republic) (Beijing)
28. COLOMBIA (Bogotá)
29. CONGO (DRC) (Kinshasa)
30. CONGO (Republic of) (Brazzaville)
31. CÔTE D'IVOIRE (Abidjan)
32. COSTA RICA (San José)
33. CUBA (Havana)
34. DJIBOUTI (Republic of) (Djibouti)
35. DOMINICAN REPUBLIC (Santo Domingo)
36. ECUADOR (Quito)
37. EGYPT (Cairo)
38. EL SALVADOR (San Salvador)
39. ERITREA (Asmara)
40. ESWATINI (Mbabane)
41. ETHIOPIA (Addis Ababa)
42. FIJI PACIFIC (Suva)

43. GABON, SAÕ TOMÉ AND PRÍNCIPE and ECCAS (Libreville)
44. GAMBIA (Banjul)
45. GEORGIA (Tbilisi)
46. GHANA (Accra)
47. GUATEMALA (Guatemala)
48. GUINEA (Conakry)
49. GUINEA-BISSAU (Bissau)
50. GUYANA (Georgetown)
51. HAITI (Port-au-Prince)
52. HONDURAS (Tegucigalpa)
53. ICELAND (Reykjavik)
54. INDIA (New Delhi)
55. INDONESIA (Jakarta)
56. IRAQ (Baghdad)
57. ISRAEL (Tel Aviv)
58. JAMAICA (Kingston)
59. JAPAN (Tokyo)
60. JORDAN (Amman)
61. KAZAKHSTAN (Astana)
62. KENYA (Nairobi)
63. KIRGHISTAN (Bishkek)
64. KOREA (Seoul)
65. KUWAIT (Kuwait)
66. LAO PEOPLE'S DEMOCRATIC REPUBLIC (Vientiane)
67. LEBANON (Beirut)
68. LESOTHO (Maseru)
69. LIBERIA (Monrovia)
70. LIBYA (Tripoli)
71. MADAGASCAR (Antananarivo)
72. MALAWI (Lilongwe)
73. MALAYSIA (Kuala Lumpur)
74. MALI (Bamako)
75. MAURITANIA (Nouakchott)
76. MAURITIUS (Port Louis)
77. MEXICO (Mexico)
78. MOLDOVA (Chisinau)
79. MONGOLIA (Ulaanbaatar)
80. MONTENEGRO (Podgorica)
81. MOROCCO (Rabat)
82. MOZAMBIQUE (Maputo)
83. NAMIBIA (Windhoek)
84. NEPAL (Kathmandu)
85. NEW ZEALAND (Wellington)
86. NICARAGUA (Managua)
87. NIGER (Niamey)
88. NIGERIA (Abuja)
89. NORTH MACEDONIA (Skopje)
90. NORWAY (Oslo)
91. PAKISTAN (Islamabad)
92. PANAMA (Panama City)
93. PAPUA NEW GUINEA (Port Moresby)
94. PARAGUAY (Asuncion)
95. PERU (Lima)
96. PHILIPPINES (Manila)
97. QATAR (Doha)—*to be opened in 2022*

98. RUSSIAN FEDERATION (Moscow)
99. RWANDA (Kigali)
100. SAUDI ARABIA (Riyadh)
101. SENEGAL (Dakar)
102. SERBIA (Belgrade)
103. SIERRA LEONE (Freetown)
104. SINGAPORE (Singapore)
105. SOMALIA (Mogadishu)[1]
106. SOUTH AFRICA (Pretoria)
107. SOUTH SUDAN (Juba)
108. SRI LANKA (Colombo)
109. SUDAN (Khartoum)
110. SWITZERLAND (Bern)
111. SYRIA (Damascus)
112. TAJIKISTAN (Dushanbe)
113. TANZANIA (Dar es-Salaam)
114. THAILAND (Bangkok)
115. TIMOR LESTE (Dili)
116. TOGO (Lomé)
117. TRINIDAD AND TOBAGO (Port of Spain)
118. TUNISIA (Tunis)
119. TURKEY (Ankara)
120. TURKMENISTAN (Ashgabat)
121. UGANDA (Kampala)
122. UKRAINE (Kiev)
123. UNITED ARAB EMIRATES (Abu Dhabi)
124. UNITED KINGDOM (London)
125. UNITED STATES OF AMERICA (Washington DC)
126. URUGUAY (Montevideo)
127. UZBEKISTAN (Tashkent)
128. VATICAN/HOLY SEE (Rome)-also accredited to the UN
129. VENEZUELA (Caracas)
130. VIETNAM (Hanoi)
131. YEMEN (Sanaa)
132. ZAMBIA and COMESA (Lusaka)
133. ZIMBABWE (Harare)

## 1.2 List of the EU's Special Representation Offices

1. TAIWAN (Taipei)
2. HONG KONG (Hong Kong)
3. OCCUPIED PALESTINIAN TERRITORY (Jerusalem)
4. KOSOVO (Pristina)

## 1.3 EU Representation by an EUDEL Accredited to the Country in Parentheses

1. ANTIGUA AND BARBUDA (St. Johns): EUDEL Barbados
2. BAHAMAS (Nassau): EUDEL Jamaica
3. BELIZE (Belmopan): EUDEL Jamaica

[1] Head of Delegation currently residing in Nairobi.

4. BHUTAN (Thimphu): EUDEL India
5. COOK ISLANDS (Avarua): EUDEL Fiji
6. DOMINICA (Roseau): EUDEL Barbados
7. GRENADA (St George's): EUDEL Barbados
8. KIRIBATI (South Tarawa): EUDEL Fiji
9. LIECHTENSTEIN (Vaduz): EUDEL Switzerland
10. MALDIVES (Male): EUDEL Sri Lanka
11. MARSHALL ISLANDS (Majuro): EUDEL Fiji
12. MICRONESIA (Palikir): EUDEL Fiji
13. NAURU (Yaren): EUDEL Fiji
14. NIUE (Alofi): EUDEL Fiji
15. PALAU (Koror): EUDEL Fiji
16. SAINT KITTS AND NEVIS (Basseterre): EUDEL Barbados
17. SAINT VINCENT AND GRENADINES (Kingstown): EUDEL Barbados
18. SAMOA (Apia): EUDEL Fiji
19. SOLOMON ISLANDS (Honiara): EUDEL Fiji
20. TONGA (Nuku'alofa): EUDEL Fiji
21. TUVALU (Funa-Futi): EUDEL Fiji

## 1.4 Third Countries Where EU Representation is Exercised by a Member State's Local Representative

1. ANDORRA (Andorra la Vella)
2. BAHRAIN (Manama)
3. BRUNEI (Bandar Seri Begawan)
4. COMOROS (Moroni)
5. GUINEA EQUATORIAL (Malabo)
6. IRAN (Tehran)
7. KOREA (DPRK) (Pyongyang)—*although at the time of writing diplomatic communication is only possible through DPRK embassies in member states.*
8. MONACO (Monaco)
9. OMAN (Muscat)
10. SAINT LUCIA (Castries)
11. SAN MARINO (San Marino)
12. SÃO TOMÉ E PRÍNCIPE (São Tomé)
13. SEYCHELLES (Victoria)
14. SURINAME (Paramaribo)
15. VANUATU (Port Vila)

## 1.5 List of EU Multilateral Representations

1. AUSTRIA (Vienna): UN, OSCE, IAEA
2. ETHIOPIA (Addis Ababa): African Union
3. FRANCE (Paris): UN, OECD, as well as the Principalities of Andorra and Monaco
4. FRANCE (Strasbourg): Council of Europe
5. INDONESIA (Jakarta): ASEAN
6. ITALY (Rome): UN, as well as the Holy See, the Republic of San Marino and the Order of Malta
7. SWITZERLAND (Geneva): UN and others
8. SWITZERLAND (Geneva): WTO
9. UNITED STATES OF AMERICA (New York City): UN Headquarters

APPENDIX 2

# Model Establishment Agreement (2010)

[Header: EU flag]

*Agreement between the Government of [the Kingdom/Republic of] XXX and the European Union on the Establishment and the Privileges and Immunities of the Delegation of the European Union in [the Kingdom/Republic of] XXX*

The Government of [*the Kingdom/Republic of*] XXX and the European Union,

Desirous of further strengthening and developing the friendly relations and co-operation between [*the Kingdom/Republic of*] XXX and the European Union,

Wishing to lay down terms concerning the establishment on the territory of [*the Kingdom/Republic of*] XXX of a Delegation of the European Union and concerning the privileges and immunities of that Delegation, have agreed as follows:

## Article 1

The Government of [*the Kingdom/Republic of*] XXX hereby agrees to the establishment on its territory of a Delegation of the European Union.

## Article 2

1. The European Union and the European Atomic Energy Community shall each have legal personality on the territory of [*the Kingdom/Republic of*] XXX.

2. The European Union and the EAEC shall have the capacity to conclude contracts, to acquire and dispose of immovable and movable property as necessary for the effective fulfilment of their duties, in accordance with the procedural and administrative requirements imposed by the law of [*the Kingdom/Republic of*] XXX, and to conduct legal proceedings, and shall be represented for that purpose by the European Commission.

## Article 3

1. The Delegation of the European Union, its Head and its members, as well as the members of their families forming part of their respective households, shall, on the territory of [*the Kingdom/Republic of*] XXX, enjoy such rights, privileges and immunities and be subject to such obligations as correspond to those laid down in the Vienna Convention on Diplomatic Relations of 18 April 1961 and respectively accorded to and assumed by Diplomatic Missions accredited to [*the Kingdom/Republic of*] XXX, the heads and members of those Missions, as well as the members of their families forming part of their respective households.

2. The other provisions of the Vienna Convention on Diplomatic Relations of 18 April 1961 shall be applicable *mutatis mutandis*.

3. Those rights and privileges and immunities shall be accorded on condition that in conformity with the provisions of article 16 of the Protocol 7 on the privileges and immunities of the European Union annexed to the Treaty on the European Union and the Treaty on the Functioning of the European Union, the Member States of the European Union accord the same rights and privileges and immunities to the Mission of [*the Kingdom/Republic of*] XXX, to its Head and to its members, as well as to the members of their families forming part of their respective households.

## Article 4

The Government of [*the Kingdom/Republic of*] XXX hereby recognises the *laissez-passer* issued by the European Union to officials and other servants of its institutions as valid travel documents.

## Article 5

Any dispute concerning the interpretation of this Agreement shall be settled by consultations between the two Contracting Parties with the aim of arriving at a conciliation.

## Article 6

Each Contracting Party shall notify the other of the completion of the respective procedures necessary for the approval of the present Agreement, which will enter into force on the date of reception of the second notification.

IN WITNESS WHEREOF, the undersigned, duly authorised to this effect, have signed this Agreement.

| | | |
|---|---|---|
| Done at | on | 20XX |
| ..................... | | .................. |
| For the Government of<br>[*the Kingdom/Republic of*] XXX | | For the European Union<br>The HR/VP |

APPENDIX 3

# Diplomatic Arrangements Entered Into by the EU

| Third state | Year |
|---|---|
| Afghanistan | 2004 |
| Albania | 1993 |
| Algeria | 1985 |
| Angola | 1992 |
| Argentina | 1991 |
| Armenia | 2004 |
| Australia | 1980 |
| Azerbaijan | 2008 |
| Bangladesh | 1989 |
| Barbados | 1995 |
| Belarus | 2008 |
| Belize | 1990 |
| Benin | 1989 |
| Bolivia | 1995 |
| Bosnia and Herzegovina | 1996 |
| Botswana | 1993 |
| Brazil | 1984 |
| Burkina Faso | 1986 |
| Burundi | 1988 |
| Cambodia | 2001 |
| Cameroon | 1989 |
| Canada | 1976 |
| Cap-Vert | 1990 |
| Central African Republic | 1992 |
| Chile | 1990 |
| China | 1987 |
| Colombia | 1982 |
| Comoros | 1990 |
| Congo (DRC) | 1987 |
| Congo (Republic of) | 1990 |
| Costa Rica | 1991 |
| Cuba | 2003 |
| Djibouti | 1988 |
| Dominican Republic | 1990 |

| Third state | Year |
|---|---|
| Ecuador | 2003 |
| Egypt | 1994 |
| El Salvador | 2005 |
| Equatorial Guinea | 1990 |
| Eritrea | 1994 |
| Ethiopia | 1991 |
| Fiji | 1989 |
| Gabon | 1992 |
| Gambia | 2004 |
| Georgia | 1992 |
| Ghana | 1989 |
| Grenade | 1986 |
| Guatemala | 1996 |
| Guinea | 1989 |
| Guinea-Bissau | 1992 |
| Guyana | 1991 |
| Haiti | 1990 |
| Honduras | 2004 |
| Hong Kong and Macau | 1997 |
| Holy See | 1970 |
| Iceland | 2009 |
| India | 1982 |
| Indonesia | 1988 |
| Iraq | 2005 |
| Israel | 1980 |
| Ivory Coast | 1987 |
| Jamaica | 1988 |
| Japan | 1974 |
| Jordan | 1980 |
| Kazakhstan | 1993 |
| Kenya | 1994 |
| Kuwait | 2019 |
| Kyrgyzstan | 2004 |
| Laos | 2003 |
| Lebanon | 1979 |
| Lesotho | 1997 |
| Liberia | 2009 |
| Madagascar | 1991 |
| Malawi | 1990 |
| Malaysia | 1991 |
| Mali | 1991 |

| Third state | Year |
|---|---|
| Mauritania | 1991 |
| Mauritius | 1991 |
| Mexico | 1988 |
| Moldova | 2005 |
| Mongolia | 2017 |
| Montenegro | 2007 |
| Morocco | 1979 |
| Mozambique | 1992 |
| Myanmar | 2012 |
| Namibia | 1991 |
| Nepal | 2002 |
| Libya | 2010 |
| New Zealand | 2004 |
| Nicaragua | 2005 |
| Niger | 1990 |
| Nigeria | 1992 |
| North Korea | 2002 |
| North Macedonia | 2000 |
| Occupied Palestinian Territory | 2001 |
| Pakistan | 1985 |
| Panama | 2003 |
| Papua New Guinea | 1991 |
| Paraguay | 2001 |
| Peru | 1990 |
| Philippines | 1990 |
| Qatar | 2022 |
| Russia | 1991 |
| Rwanda | 1991 |
| Samoa | 1989 |
| São Tomé e Príncipe | 1988 |
| Saudi Arabia | 2003 |
| Senegal | 1991 |
| Serbia | 1980 |
| Sierra Leone | 1989 |
| Singapore | 2002 |
| Solomon Islands | 1992 |
| Somalia | 2015 |
| South Africa | 1993 |
| South Korea | 1989 |
| South Sudan | 2011 |
| Sri Lanka | 1995 |

| Third state | Year |
|---|---|
| Sudan | 1985 |
| Suriname | 1989 |
| Swaziland | 1992 |
| Switzerland | 2005 |
| Syria | 1979 |
| Tajikistan | 2004 |
| Taiwan | 2002 |
| Tanzania | 1991 |
| Tchad | 1986 |
| Thailand | 1979 |
| Timor Leste | 2007 |
| Togo | 1987 |
| Tonga | 1989 |
| Trinidad and Tobago | 1993 |
| Tunisia | 1981 |
| Turkey | 1987 |
| Turkmenistan | 2013 |
| Uganda | 1990 |
| UK | 2021 |
| Ukraine | 1993 |
| United Arab Emirates | 2013 |
| United States of America | 1972 |
| Uruguay | 1989 |
| Uzbekistan | 2011 |
| Vanuatu | 1990 |
| Venezuela | 1977 |
| Vietnam | 1995 |
| Yemen | 2003 |
| Zambia | 1991 |
| Zimbabwe | 1988 |

APPENDIX 4

# List of Third State Arrangements

| | | |
|---|---|---|
| Albania | 11/01/1994 | Decision No 167 approving the Establishment Agreement, Official Gazette, 11 January 1994 |
| Algeria | 24/02/1987 | Décret No 87-53 portant ratification de l'accord entre le Gouvernement de la République Algérienne Démocratique et Populaire et la Commission des Communautés Européennes sur l'établissement ainsi que sur les privilèges et immunités de la délégation de la Commission des Communautés Européennes, signé à Alger le 9 décembre 1985, Journal Officiel de la République Algérienne, 25 February 1987, p 203 (Agreement published in full) |
| Argentina | 14/09/1992 | Law No 24.115, Boltín Oficial, 14 September 1992, 27.471 (Agreement published in full) |
| Australia | 10/04/1980 | Insertion of a new section 5A in the Diplomatic Privileges and Immunities Act No 16 of 1967, amended in 1980 |
| Azerbaijan | 2/06/2008 | Law of the Republic of Azerbaijan on the adoption of the agreement on the establishment and the privileges and immunities of the Delegation of the Commission of the European Communities in the Republic of Azerbaijan between the Government of the Republic of Azerbaijan and the Commission of the European Communities, Official Gazette, 29 June 2008 |
| Brazil | 30/10/1984 | Decreto Legislativo No 48 de 1984 aprova o texto do Acordo sobre o estabelecimento e os privilégios e imunidades da Delegação da Comissão das Comunidades Européias no Brasil, firmado entre o Governo da República Federativa do Brasil e a Comissão das Comunidades Européias e concluído em Bruxelas a 4 de abril de 1984, Diário do Congresso Nacional, ANO XXXIX, No 138, 30 October 1984, p 103 |
| Cabo Verde | 13/04/1991 | Decreto No 1 de 13 Abril 1991, Boletim Oficial da república de Cabo Verde, No 15, 13 April 1991, p 184 (Agreement published in full) |
| Canada | 29/12/1976 | European Communities Privileges and Immunities Order of 23 December 1976, Foreign Missions and International Organizations Act, Consolidated Regulations of Canada 1308, Canada Gazette Part II, Vol 111, No 1, 12 January 1977 |
| Costa Rica | 28/09/1998 | Leyes No 7821 Aprobación del acuerdo entre el Gobierno de Costa Rica y la Comisión de las Comunidades Europeas sobre el establecimiento de la Delegación de la Comisión en la República de Costa Rica, La Gaceta, Diaro Oficial, No 188, 28 September 1998 (Agreement published in full) |
| Ecuador | 23/12/2003 | Decreto Ejecutivo número 1233 de 23 de diciembre de 2003, mediante el cual ratificó el Acuerdo entre la Comisión de las Comunidades Europeas y el Gobierno de Ecuador sobre el Establecimiento de la Delegación |
| Egypt | 18/08/1994 | Résolution du président de la République Arabe d'Egypte No 149 de l'année 1994 portant sur l'approbation de la Convention signée au Caire le 4 Mars 1994 par la RAE et la Commission des Communautés Européennes sur la création de la Délégation de la CCE ainsi que les privilèges at immunités accordés à la délégation en RAE approuvé par l'assemblée du peuple le 13 juin 1994, Journal Officiel, 2236, No 33, 18 August 1994. See also Résolution du Ministre des Affaires Etrangères No 67 de l'année 1994. |

| | | |
|---|---|---|
| El Salvador | 9/02/2007 | Acuerdo Ejecutivo No 967 del Ramo de Relaciones Exteriores, aprobándolo y Decreto Legislativo No 209, ratificándolo Acuerdo entre la Comisión de las Comunidades Europeas y el Gobierno de la República de El Salvador sobre el Establecimiento y los Privilegios e Inmunidades de la Delegación de la Comisión de las Comunidades Europeas en la República de El Salvador, Diario Oficial, No 27, Tomo No 374, 9 February 2007, pp 41–45 |
| Grenada | 30/12/1986 | Commission of the European Communities (Privileges and Immunities) Act, Act No 45 of 1986, Official Gazette, 30 December 1986, pp 329–33 |
| Guinea-Bissau | 21/09/1992 | Resolução No 13/92 acordó entre o governó da República da Guinea-Bissau e a Comissão das Comunidades Europeias sobre o estabelecimento assim como os privilégios e imunidades da delegação da Comissão das Comunidades Europeias assinado ao 24 de Abril de 1992, Official Gazette, 29 September 2009, 2.5.4. |
| Israel | 20/10/1980 | Acceptance by the Government of the State of Israel, in accordance with the powers vested in it by law, of the Agreement between the Government of the State of Israel and the Commission of the European Communities (8 September 1980, inscribed in the Fifth Book of Protocol under No 1330) |
| Korea | 26/07/1989 | Agreement between the Government of the Republic of Korea and the Commission of the European Communities on the Establishment and the Privileges and Immunities of the Delegation of the Commission of the European Communities in the Republic of Korea, published in full in the National Treaty Series |
| Kyrgyzstan | 6/02/2009 | Law of the Kyrgyz Republic No 36 of 6 February 2009, as approved by Parliament and signed by the President |
| Madagascar | 18/07/2007 | Loi No 2007-002 du 11 juillet 2007 autorisant la ratification et Décret No 2007-709 du 18 juillet 2007 portant ratification de l'accord entre le Gouvernement de la république de Madagascar et la Commission Européenne sur l'établissement ainsi que les privilèges et immunités de la Délégation de la Commission Européenne, Journal officielle de la République, No 3178, 3 April 2008, p 2968 |
| Mexico | 31/5/1989 | Decreto de Promulgacion del Acuerdo entre los Estados Unidos Mexicanos y la Comision de las Communidades Europeas relativo al establecimiento de la Delegacion de la Comision en los Estados Unidos Mexicanos, Diario Oficial, 31 May 1989, Tomo CDXXVIII, No 22, p 12 |
| Morocco | 30/04/1987 | Dahir No 4-84-16 sur la ratification de l'accord entre le Gouvernement du Royaume du Maroc et la Commission des Communautés Européennes, 14 November 1986 |
| New Zealand | 2/03/2004 | Section 9AB on the Privileges and immunities of members, and of private servants of members, of EC delegations in the Diplomatic Privileges and Immunities Act 1968, inserted on 2 March 2004 by section 3 of the Diplomatic Privileges and Immunities Amendment Act 2004 (2004 No 1) |
| Nicaragua | 6/06/2006 | Decreto Presidencial Número 33-2006 del 22 de Mayo del 2006, el Acuerdo entre el Gobierno de la Republica de Nicaragua así como a los Privilegies e Inmunidades de la Delegación de la Comisión de las comunidades europeas en la República de Nicaragua, La Gaceta, Diario Oficial, Número 109 del 6 de junio del 2006, p 4216 |
| Niger | 15/05/1991 | Loi No 91-004 du 24 Avril 1991 autorisant la ratification de l'Accord entre le Gouvernement de la République du Niger et la Commission des Communautés Européennes sur l'établissement ainsi que les privilèges et immunités de la Délégation des Communautés Européennes signé à Niamey le 9 Novembre 1990, Journal Officiel de la République du Niger, 15 May 1991, p 298 |
| Norway | 26/10/1987 | Avtale mellom Norge og de Europeiske Fellesskaps Kommisjon om opprettelse i Norge av en delegasjon for de Europeiske Fellesskaps Kommisjon og dens privilegier og immunitet, Overenskomster 1987 (Norway Treaty Series), s 1326, No 1 Bilateral, 26 October 1987 (Agreement published in full, entry into force 27 October 1987) |

| | | |
|---|---|---|
| Paraguay | 21/10/2003 | Ley No 2250 promulgada por el Podor Ejecutivo el 21 de octobre de 2003 que aprueba el acuerdo entre la República del Paraguay y la Comisión de las Comunidades Europeas sobre el establecimiento de la delegación de la Comisión de las Comunidades Europeas en la República del Paraguay y sobre los privilegios e inmunidades de dicha delegación, Gaceta oficial, No 215, 7 November 2003, pp 1–2 (Agreement published in full) |
| Peru | 27/09/1995 | Resolución Legislativa No 26532 Aprueban acuerdo suscrito con la Comisión de las Comunidades Europeas relative al establecimiento, privilegios e inmunidades de la delegación de la Comisión en la República del Perú, entry into forcé, 20 October 1995, El Peruano, Diario Oficial, 28 September 1995, Ano XIV, No 5562, p 134443 |
| Rwanda | 12/12/1991 | Loi No 59/91 du 12 décembre 1991 portant approbation et ratification de l'accord entre le gouvernement de la République Rwandaise et la Commission des Communautés Européennes sur l'établissement ainsi que les privilèges et immunités de la Délégation des Communautés Européennes signé à Kigali le 26 avril 1991 et à Bruxelles le 8 Mai 1991 |
| Saudi Arabia | 13/10/2014 | Royal Decree No M/43 of 28/7/1425 (corresponding to 13 October 2004) |
| Sri Lanka | 12/12/1997 | Order under Section 4 of the Diplomatic Privileges Act No 9 of 1996 declaring that its provisions apply in respect of the Commission of the European Communities, 10 December 1997, Gazette of the Democratic Socialist Republic of Sri Lanka, No 1005/23 (Article 3 of the EA published) |
| Switzerland | 26/10/2005 | Décision du 26 Octobre 2005 du Conseil federal (autoriase la Commission à ouvrir une Délégation permanente à Berne); Decree of the Swiss Federal Council of 31 March 1948, as amended on 20 May 1958 and on 3 November 1967 and the declaration of the Swiss Federal Council of 20 May 1958 |
| Thailand | 19/03/1979 | Act protecting the operations of the European Economic Community and the European Economic Community Commission in Thailand, BE 2522 (1979), Government Gazette, Vol. 96, Special Issue, Part 42, 25 March 1979 |
| Trinidad and Tobago | 6/01/1995 | Legal Notice No 6 of 1995 on the Privileges and Immunities (Commission of the European Communities) Order inserted in the Privileges and Immunities Act, Chapter 17/01 (approved by Parliament), Official Gazette, Legal Supplement Part B, Vol 34, No 11, 17 January 1995 (Agreement published in full) |
| Tunisia | 21/02/1982 | Loi No 82-15 du 21 Février 1982 portant ratification de l'Accord conclu à Bruxelles le 24 juin 1981 entre le Gouvernement de la République Tunisienne et la Commission des Communautés Européennes sur l'établissement ainsi que sur les privilèges et immunités de la Délégation des Communautés Européennes, Journal Officiel de la République Tunisienne, 125ieme année, No 12, 23 February 1982, p 456 |
| Uruguay | 20/04/1993 | Poder Legislativo el 13 de Abril de 1993, mediante la Ley No 16.356, promulgada por al Poder Ejecutive el día 20 del mismo más y ano |
| United States of America | 18/10/1972 | Act to extend diplomatic privileges and immunities to the Mission to the United States of America of the Commission of the European Communities and to members thereof, P.L. 92-499 (18 October 1972, 86 STAT 815); Ex Ord No 11689, 5 December 1972, 37 FR 25987, issued by President Richard Nixon |
| Venezuela | 15/12/1977 | Resolución por la cual gozarán individualmente en el territorio nacional de personalidad jurídica y en consecuencia podrán celebrar los actos jurídicos que se requieran para el normal desarrollo de sus actividades, la Comunidad Europea del Carbón, del Acero y de la Energía Atómica, denominadas globalmente las Comunidades Europeas, Numero 104, Caracas, 15 de diciembre de 1977, 168° y 119°, Gaceta official de la Republica de Venezuela, 19 December 1977, No 31385, p 236337–236338. |

APPENDIX 5

# Missions of International Organizations and Other Non-State Entities

| International organization | Type of mission | Headed by | Legal regime |
|---|---|---|---|
| African Union | Permanent mission | Ambassador | Headquarters Agreement between the Kingdom of Belgium and the Organization of African Unity, signed in Brussels on 9 October 1985; Exchanges of Letters of 9 October 1985 and 29 June 1998 between the Kingdom of Belgium and the Organization of African Unity (adopted by Belgian law 21 February 2006: Belgian State Gazette, 21 February 2006) |
| Arab League | Permanent mission | Ambassador | Headquarters Agreement between the Kingdom of Belgium and the League of Arab States, signed in Brussels on 16 November 1995 (adopted by Belgian law 9 June 1999: Belgian State Gazette, 4 November 1999) |
| Council of Europe | Liaison office | Ambassador | General Agreement on Privileges and Immunities of the Council of Europe, ETS No 002, done at Paris on 2 September 1949, entered into force 10 September 1952 (adopted by Belgian law 13 April 1951: Belgian State Gazette, 17 May 1951); Supplementary Agreement between the Kingdom of Belgium and the Council of Europe, to the General Agreement on Privileges and Immunities of the Council of Europe, done at Strasbourg on 3 December 1974 (adopted by Belgian law 5 November 1990: Belgian State Gazette, 30 April 1991) |
| European Free Trade Association | Liaison office | Secretary General | Headquarters Agreement between the Kingdom of Belgium and the European Free Trade Association, done at Brussels on 27 January 1993 (adopted by Belgian law 9 February 1999: Belgian State Gazette, 20 March 1999) |
| European Patent Organisation | Liaison office | Head of the liaison office | Protocol on Privileges and Immunities of the European Patent Organisation to the Convention on the Grant of European Patents, done at Munich on 5 October 1973 (adopted by Belgian law 15 December 1975: Belgian State Gazette, 7 October 1977) |
| Food and Agriculture Organization | Liaison office | Head of the liaison office | Convention on the Privileges and Immunities of the UN Specialized Agencies, done at New York on 21 November 1947, entry into force 2 December 1948, 33 UNTS 261 [CPIUN-SA]; Constitution of the United Nations Food and Agriculture Organization, done at Quebec on 16 October 1945; Agreement between the Kingdom of Belgium and the Food and Agriculture Organization of the United Nations on the establishment in Belgium of a Liaison Office of the Organization, done at Brussels on 5 February 1997 (adopted by Belgian law 3 July 2000: Belgian State Gazette, 7 November 2002) |

| International organization | Type of mission | Headed by | Legal regime |
|---|---|---|---|
| Gulf Cooperation Council | Liaison office | Ambassador | Headquarters Agreement between the Kingdom of Belgium and the Cooperation Council of the Arab States of the Gulf, done at Brussels on 11 May 1993 (adopted by Belgian law 22 January 1999: Belgian State Gazette, 20 October 1999) |
| Inter-American Development Bank | Liaison office | Representative | Agreement Establishing the Inter-American Development Bank and Annexes A and B, signed in Washington on 8 April 1959, entered into force 30 December 1959 (adopted by Belgian law 6 July 1976: Belgian State Gazette, 31 July 1976) |
| International Labour Organization | Liaison office | Head of the liaison office | CPIUN-SA; Art 40 Constitution of the International Labour Organization, adopted by the Peace Conference in April 1919; Agreement between the Kingdom of Belgium and the International Labour Organization on the establishment in Belgium of the Office of the Organization and the exchange of letters, signed in Brussels on 4 November 1976 (adopted by Belgian law 31 July 1978: Belgian State Gazette, 28 October 1978) |
| International Monetary Fund | Liaison office | Head of the liaison office | CPIUN-SA; Art IX of the Articles of Agreement of the International Monetary Fund, done at Bretton Woods (New Hampshire) on 22 July 1944, entered into force 27 December 1945; Agreement between the Kingdom of Belgium and the International Monetary Fund on the establishment in Belgium of a Liaison Office of the Organization, done at Brussels on 16 March 2004 (adopted by Belgian law 29 July 2014: Belgian State Gazette, 22 October 2014) |
| International Organisation for Migration | Liaison office | Head of the liaison office | Constitution of 19 October 1953 of the Intergovernmental Committee for European Migration (former designation of the Organization), entered into force on 30 November 1954 (as amended); Agreement between the Kingdom of Belgium and the International Organization for Migration on the privileges and immunities of the organization in Belgium, signed at London on 4 December 1996 amending the Agreement between the Kingdom of Belgium and the Intergovernmental Committee for European Migration, done at Geneva on 2 July 1973 (adopted by Belgian law 2 July 1973: Belgian State Gazette, 9 June 1978 and 5 March 2002) |
| International Criminal Police Organization | Liaison office | Head of the liaison office | Headquarters Agreement (by exchange of letters) between the Kingdom of Belgium and the International Organization for Criminal Police (OICP—INTERPOL), done in Lyon on 14 October 2014 and in Brussels on 24 October 2014 (awaiting ratification by all federated entities and the federal government) |

| International organization | Type of mission | Headed by | Legal regime |
|---|---|---|---|
| Organisation internationale de la Francophonie | Permanent mission | Ambassador | Art 8 Convention portant création de l'Agence de Coopération Culturelle et Technique, done at Niamey on 20 March 1970; Headquarters Agreement between the Kingdom of Belgium and the Agency for Cultural and Technical Cooperation, done in Brussels on 16 November 1995 (adopted by Belgian law 5 June 1998: Belgian State Gazette, 11 December 1999) |
| Organisation of Islamic Cooperation | Permanent mission | Ambassador | Headquarters Agreement between the Kingdom of Belgium and the Organization of the Islamic Conference, done in Brussels on 4 February 2011 (adopted by Belgian law 16 January 2016: Belgian State Gazette, 16 February 2016) |
| United Nations | Liaison office | Head of the liaison office | Convention on the Privileges and Immunities of the United Nations, done at New York on 13 February 1946, entry into force 17 September 1946, 1 UNTS 15 [CPIUN]; Agreement between the Kingdom of Belgium and the United Nations Organisation on the Privileges to the General Agreement and immunities of the United Nations, signed in Brussels on 22 January 1976 (adopted by Belgian law 22 May 1978: Belgian State Gazette, 4 August 1978) and supplementary exchange of letters [Belgium–UN Agreement] |
| United Nations Children's Fund | Liaison office | Head of the liaison office | CPIUN; Belgium–UN Agreement |
| United Nations Development Programme | Liaison office | Head of the liaison office | CPIUN; Belgium–UN Agreement |
| United Nations Educational, Scientific and Cultural Organization | Liaison office | Head of the liaison office | CPIUN–SA; Art XII of the Constitution of the United Nations Educational, Scientific and Cultural Organization, done at London on 16 November 1945 |
| United Nations Entity for Gender Equality and the Empowerment of Women | Liaison office | Head of the liaison office | CPIUN; Belgium–UN Agreement |
| United Nations Environment Programme | Liaison office | Representative | CPIUN; Belgium–UN Agreement |
| United Nations High Commissioner for Refugees | Liaison office | Representative of the UNSG | CPIUN; Belgium–UN Agreement |
| United Nations Human Settlements Programme | Liaison office | Head of the liaison office | CPIUN; Belgium–UN Agreement |

| International organization | Type of mission | Headed by | Legal regime |
|---|---|---|---|
| United Nations Industrial Development Organization | Liaison office | Representative | CPIUN–SA; Art 21 Constitution of the United Nations Industrial Development Organization adopted on 8 April 1979 at Vienna Agreement between the Kingdom of Belgium and the United Nations Industrial Development concerning the establishment in Belgium of a Liaison Office of the Organization, done at Brussels on 20 February 2006 (adopted by Belgian law 29 June 2014: Belgian State Gazette, 24 October 2014) |
| United Nations Office for Project Services | Liaison office | Representative | CPIUN; Belgium–UN Agreement |
| United Nations Office for the Coordination of Humanitarian Affairs | Liaison office | Head of the liaison office | CPIUN; Belgium–UN Agreement |
| United Nations Office on Drugs and Crime | Information Centre | Head of the liaison office | CPIUN; Belgium–UN Agreement |
| United Nations Population Fund | Liaison office | Head of the liaison office | CPIUN; Belgium–UN Agreement |
| United Nations Regional Information Centre | Liaison office | Head of the liaison office | CPIUN; Belgium–UN Agreement |
| United Nations Relief and Works Agency for Palestine Refugees | Liaison office | Head of the liaison office | CPIUN; Belgium–UN Agreement |
| United Nations World Food Programme | Liaison office | Head of the liaison office | CPIUN; Belgium–UN Agreement |
| World Bank Group | Liaison office | Representative | CPIUN–SA; Art VII of the Articles of Agreement of the International Bank for Reconstruction and Development, done at Bretton Woods (New Hampshire) on 22 July 1944 and entered into force 27 December 1945; Agreement between the Kingdom of Belgium and the International Bank for Reconstruction and Development on the establishment in Belgium of a liaison office of this organization, signed in Brussels on 26 April 1999 (adopted by Belgian law 4 March 2002: Belgian State Gazette, 9 March 2005) and the Additional Protocol of 28 February 2005 (adopted by Belgian law 3 April 2013: Belgian State Gazette 25 October 2013) |

| International organization | Type of mission | Headed by | Legal regime |
|---|---|---|---|
| World Health Organization | Liaison office | Head of the liaison office | CPIUN–SA; Chapter XV of the Constitution of the World Health Organization, done at New York on 22 July 1946; Agreement between the Kingdom of Belgium and the World Health Organization concerning the establishment in Belgium of a liaison office of this organization, signed in Brussels on January 6, 1999 (adopted by Belgian law 24 January 2002: Belgian State Gazette 19 March 2003) |

| Other representations: Non-state entities | Type of mission | Headed by | Legal regime |
|---|---|---|---|
| General delegation of Palestine | Liaison office | Ambassador | Exchange of notes between the European Commission and the Government of Israel, dated 7 February 1992 and 14 November 1994 |
| Hong Kong | Economic and trade office | Representative | Exchange of letters between the European Commission and the Government of the People's Republic of China, dated 25 June 1997 and 1 July 1997 |
| Macao | Liaison office | Head of the liaison office | Exchange of letters between the European Commission and the Government of the People's Republic of China, dated 25 June 1997 and 1 July 1997 |
| Sovereign Order of Malta | Permanent Mission | Ambassador | Informal agreement |

| Other representations: Non-governmental/ private actors | Type of mission | Headed by | Legal regime |
|---|---|---|---|
| International Committee of the Red Cross | Liaison office | Head of the liaison office | Headquarters Agreement between the Kingdom of Belgium and the International Committee of the Red Cross, done at Brussels on 19 April 1999 (adopted by Belgian law 4 March 2002: Belgian State Gazette, 28 May 2004) |
| International IDEA | Liaison office | Head of the liaison office | Headquarters Agreement between the Kingdom of Belgium and the International Institute for Democracy and Electoral Assistance, signed in Brussels on 15 May 2014 (not yet entered into force) |
| Regional Cooperation Council | Liaison office | Head of the liaison office | Headquarters Agreement between the Kingdom of Belgium and the Secretariat of the Regional Cooperation Council, signed in Brussels on 29 August 2008 (not yet entered into force) |

APPENDIX 6

# Model Accreditation Letter (2010)

| **The President of the European Council** | **The President of the European Commission** |
| --- | --- |

**to**

**His/Her Majesty King/Queen xxxx**
**King/Queen of xxxx**

Your Majesty,

The European Union, desirous of maintaining and strengthening the harmonious relations which exist between the Kingdom of xxxx and the European Union, has decided to accredit to Your Majesty xxxx YYYY in the quality of Head of the Delegation of the European Union to the Kingdom of xxxx, with residence in the Kingdom of xxxx.

Mr/Ms xxxx YYYY will have the rank and courtesy title of Ambassador.

The personal qualities of Mr/Ms xxxx YYYY, and the zeal and devotion which he/she has constantly displayed in the discharge of the duties entrusted to him/her, have convinced us that he/she will fully merit Your Majesty's approbation and esteem.

In this confidence, we request that Your Majesty will receive Mr/Ms xxx YYYY favourably and will give entire credence to all that he/she will communicate to Your Majesty in accordance with the instructions of the European Union and especially when he/she will convey to Your Majesty the assurances of our highest consideration.

Brussels,

President of the European Council                President of the European Commission

APPENDIX 7

# Model Note Verbale

*[Header: EU flag]*

NOTE VERBALE

The Delegation of the European Union presents its compliments to the Embassy/Permanent Mission of [xxxx] and has the honour to [inform/advise/request etc]

The Delegation of the European Union avails itself of this opportunity to renew to the Ministry of Foreign Affairs/the Embassy/the Permanent Mission of [xxxx] the assurances of its highest consideration.

*[Stamp of the EUDEL, round (Ø 3 cm) and in blue ink]*

Name of city, date

APPENDIX 8

# Administrative Grades and Diplomatic Titles for EU Staff

| Administrative grade | Diplomatic title |
|---|---|
| Head of Delegation | Ambassador |
| AD16 (Deputy Head of Delegation) | Minister |
| AD16 | Minister Counsellor |
| AD15 (Deputy Head of Delegation) | Minister |
| AD15 | Minister Counsellor |
| AD14 (Deputy Head of Delegation) | Minister |
| AD14 | Minister Counsellor |
| AD13 (Deputy Head of Delegation) | Minister |
| AD13 | Minister Counsellor |
| AD12 (Deputy Head of Delegation) | Minister Counsellor |
| AD12 | First Counsellor |
| AD11 | First Counsellor |
| AD10 | Counsellor |
| AD9 | Counsellor |
| AD8 | First Secretary |
| AD7 | First Secretary |
| AD6 | Second Secretary |
| AD5 | Second Secretary |
| AST11 | Attaché |
| AST10 | Attaché |
| AST9 | Attaché |
| AST8 | Attaché |
| AST7 | Attaché |
| AST6 | Attaché |
| AST5 | Attaché |
| AST4 (Head of Administration) | Attaché |
| AST4 | Assistant Attaché |
| AST3 (Head of Administration) | Attaché |
| AST3 | Assistant Attaché |
| AST1 (Head of Administration) | Attaché |
| AST1 | Assistant Attaché |
| ACIV | Attaché |
| ACIII | Attaché |
| ACII | Assistant Attaché |

# Bibliography


Abbott KW and Snidal D, 'Why States Act through Formal International Organizations' (1998) 42 J Conflict Resolut 3

Addicott JF, 'The Status of the Diplomatic Bag: A Proposed United States Position' (1991) 13 Houst J Int Law 221

Agence France-Presse, 'EU Trying to "Resolve" Envoy Expulsion with Sudan', *Sudan Tribune*, 25 August 2007, <www.sudantribune.com/spip.php?article23432> accessed 4 May 2022

Alvarez JE, *International Organizations as Law-Makers* (OUP 2005)

Alvarez JE, 'Governing the World: International Organizations as Lawmakers' (2008) 31 Suffolk Transnat'l L Rev 591

Amador G, 'General Debate on Diplomatic Intercourse and Immunities' (1957) I YBILC, A/CN.4/91, 9

Ambast R and Tyagi V, 'Ambassadors of Europe' (2008) 61 Studia Diplomatica 173

Amerasinghe CF, *Principles of the Institutional Law of International Organizations* (2nd edn, CUP 2005)

Anderson MS, *The Rise of Modern Diplomacy, 1450–1919* (Routledge 2005)

Anzilotti D, *Cours de Droit International* (French trans of 3rd Italian edn, Recueil Sirey 1929)

Arnull A and Wyatt D (eds), *Wyatt and Dashwood's European Union Law* (6th edn, Hart 2011)

Aufricht H, 'Principles and Practices of Recognition by International Organizations' (1949) 43 AJIL 679

Aust A, *Modern Treaty Law and Practice* (3rd edn, CUP 2013)

Austermann F, 'Towards Embassies for Europe? EU Delegations in the Union's Diplomatic Service' Policy Paper 8 (Jean Monnet Multilateral Research Network 2012)

Austermann F, *European Union Delegations in EU Foreign Policy* (Palgrave Macmillan 2014)

Austermann F, 'Representing the EU in China: European Bilateral Diplomacy in a Competitive Diplomatic Environment' in D Spence and J Bátora (eds), *The European External Action Service: European Diplomacy Post-Westphalia* (Palgrave Macmillan 2015)

Avbelj M, 'The Treaty of Lisbon: An Ongoing Search for Structural Equilibrium' (2010) 16 Colum J Eur L 521

Balekijan WH, 'Rechtsstatus Permanenter Missionen von Nichtmitgliedstaaten bei Internationalen Organisationen' (1976) 27 ZöR 67

Balfour R, *The Role of EU Delegations in EU Human Rights Policy* (European Parliament 2013)

Balfour R and Raik K, *National Diplomacies, the European External Action Service and the Making of EU Foreign Policy* (Finnish Institute of International Affairs 2013)

Balfour R, Carta C, and Raik K, *The European External Action Service and National Foreign Ministries: Convergence or Divergence?* (Ashgate 2015)

Barbero JR, 'The Relationship of the Member States' International Agreements with the EU' in P Eeckhout and M Lopez-Escudero (eds), *The European Union's External Action in Times of Crisis* (Bloomsbury 2016)

Barder B, 'Diplomacy, Ethics, and the National Interest: What Are Diplomats For?' (2010) 5 HJD 289

Barents R, *Het Verdrag van Lissabon: Achtergronden en Commentaar* (Kluwer 2008)

Barker JC, *International Law and International Relations* (Continuum 2000)

Barker JC, 'The Function of Diplomatic Missions in Times of Armed Conflict or Foreign Armed Intervention' (2012) 81 Nord J Int Law 387

Barnhoorn L, 'Diplomatic Law and Unilateral Remedies' (1994) 25 Neth Yearb Int Law 39

Baroncini E, 'The Treaty Making Power of the European Commission' in M Dony and LS Rossi (eds), *Démocratie, Coherence et Transparence: Principes Constitutionnels de l'Union Européenne* (Éditions ULB 2008)

Baroncini E, 'Le Delegazioni dell' Unione Europea Dopo il Trattato di Lisbona. Struttura, Status e Funzioni' (2014) 6 CDT 68
Barston RP, *Modern Diplomacy* (4th edn, Pearson 2013)
Bartelson J, *A Genealogy of Sovereignty* (CUP 1995)
Bartelson J, 'The Concept of Sovereignty Revisited' (2006) 17 EJIL 463
Bátora J, 'The "Mitrailleuse Effect": The EEAS as an Interstitial Organization and the Dynamics of Innovation in Diplomacy' (2013) 51 JCMS 598
Bátora J and Spence D, 'The EEAS as a Catalyst of Diplomatic Innovation' in D Spence and J Bátora (eds), *The European External Action Service: European Diplomacy Post-Westphalia* (Palgrave Macmillan 2015)
Battjes H, 'The Soering Threshold: Why Only Fundamental Values Prohibit Refoulement in ECHR Case Law' (2009) 11 Eur J Migr Law 205
BBC News, 'Malaysia Fury at EU Envoy Remarks', 25 June 2007, <http://news.bbc.co.uk/1/hi/world/asia-pacific/6237328.stm> accessed 4 May 2022
Bederman DJ, *Custom as a Source of Law* (CUP 2010)
Behrens P, 'None of Their Business?: Diplomatic Involvement in Human Rights' (2014) 15 Melb J Int Law 190
Behrens P, 'The Law of Diplomatic Asylum—A Contextual Approach' (2014) 35 Mich J Int Law 319
Behrens P, *Diplomatic Interference and the Law* (Hart 2016)
Beirlaen A, 'Répresentation Diplomatique et Consulaire' in SBDI (ed), *Les Etats Fédéraux dans les Relations Internationales* (Bruylant 1984)
Benlolo-Carabot M, 'Les Immunités des Communautés Européennes' (2008) 54 AFDI 549
Benson-Rea M and Shore C, 'Representing Europe: The Emerging "Culture" of EU Diplomacy' (2012) 90 PA 480
Bentham J, *Of Laws in General* (Athlone Press 1970)
Berridge GR, *Embassies in Armed Conflict* (Continuum 2012)
Berridge GR, *Diplomacy: Theory and Practice* (5th edn, Palgrave Macmillan 2015)
Betsill MM and Corell E, *NGO Diplomacy: The Influence of Nongovernmental Organizations in International Environmental Negotiations* (MIT Press 2008)
Bicchi F, 'Information Exchanges, Diplomatic Networks and the Construction of European Knowledge in European Union Foreign Policy' (2014) 49 Coop Confl 239
Bicchi F and Carta C, 'The COREU/CORTESY Network and the Circulation of Information within EU Foreign Policy' (2010) 34 J Eur Integr 1
Bicchi F and Maurer H, 'European Cooperation Abroad' (2017) 12 HJD 1
Bindi F, 'One Year On: Assessing the European Foreign Policy and the European External Action Service' (2010) 17 BJWA 125
Biscop S and Drieskens E, 'Effective Multilateralism and Collective Security: Empowering the UN' in KV Laatikainen and KE Smith (eds), *The European Union at the United Nations: Intersecting Multilateralisms* (Palgrave Macmillan 2006)
Bjola C and Kornprobst M, *Understanding International Diplomacy: Theory, Practice and Ethics* (Routledge 2013)
Bjola C and Murray S (eds), *Secret Diplomacy: Concepts, Contexts and Cases* (Routledge 2016)
Blanke H-J and Mangiameli S, 'Article 4 [The Relations between the EU and the Member States]' in H-J Blanke and S Mangiameli (eds), *The Treaty on European Union* (Springer 2013)
Blockmans S and Hillion C (eds), *EEAS 2.0: A Legal Commentary on Council Decision 2010/427/EU Establishing the Organisation and Functioning of the European External Action Service* (Swedish Institute for European Policy Studies 2013)
Blokker N, 'International Legal Personality of the European Communities and the European Union: Inspirations from Pulic International Law' (2016) 35 Yearb Eur Law 471
Blumann C 'Citoyenneté Européenne et Droits Fondamentaux' (2006) 1 Rev Aff Eur 73
Bluntschli JC, *Das Moderne Völkerrect der Civilisirten Staten* (Beck 1868)
Boisard MA, Chossudovsky EM, and Lemoine J (eds), 'Guide de la Pratique Diplomatique à Genève' in Chef de protocole, UNOG *La Diplomatie Multilatérale* (Martinus Nijhoff 1998)

Bolewski W, 'Diplomatischer Kurier: Völkerrechtliches Instrument und Gefahren Seines Missbrauchs' (2005) 43 AVR 537
Bolewski W, *Diplomacy and International Law in Globalized Relations* (Springer 2007)
Bot BR, 'Co-operation between the Diplomatic Missions of the Ten in Third Countries and International Organisations' (1984) 10 LIEI 149
Boyle A and Chinkin C, *The Making of International Law* (OUP 2007)
Brand RA, 'Kosovo after the ICJ Opinion' (2013) 74 U Pitt L Rev 591
Breycha-Vauthier AC and Potulicki M, 'The Order of St. John in International Law: A Forerunner of the Red Cross' (1954) 48 AJIL 554
Brierly JL, *The Law of Nations: An Introduction to the International Law of Peace* (7th edn, OUP 2016)
Brinkhorst LJ, 'Permanent Missions of the EC in Third Countries: European Diplomacy in the Making' (1984) 10 LIEI 23
Brölmann C, 'The 1986 Vienna Convention on the Law of Treaties: The History of Draft Article 36bis' in J Klabbers and R Lefeber (eds), *Essays on the Law of Treaties: A Collection of Essays in Honour of Bert Vierdag* (Martinus Nijhoff 1998)
Brölmann C and Nijmann J (eds), 'Legal Personality as a Fundamental Concept of International Law' in J d'Aspremont and S Singh (eds), *Fundamental Concepts of International Law* (Edward Elgar 2017)
Brown PM, 'The Rights of States under International Law' (1916) 26 Yale LJ 85
Bruns K, *A Cornerstone of Modern Diplomacy: Britain and the Negotiation of the 1961 Vienna Convention on Diplomatic Relations* (Bloomsbury Academic 2014)
Bruter M, 'Diplomacy without a State: The External Delegations of the European Commission' (1999) 6 J Eur Public Policy 183
Burnay M, Hivonnet J, and Raube K, 'Soft Diplomacy and People-to-People Dialogue between the EU and the PRC' (2014) 19 EFAR 35
Calvo C, *Le Droit International Théorique et Pratique*, vol 2 (Durand 1870)
Campbell AIL, 'The Limits of the Powers of International Organisations' (1983) 32 ICLQ 523
Cannizzaro E (ed), *The European Union as an Actor in International Relations* (Kluwer Law International 2002)
Cannizzaro E, 'Fragmented Sovereignty? The European Union and Its Member States in the International Arena' (2003) 13 It YBIL 35
Cannizzaro E, Palchetti P, and Wessel RA (eds), *International Law as Law of the European Union* (Martinus Nijhoff 2011)
Cardinale HE, *The Holy See and the International Order* (Smythe 1976)
Cardozo MH, *Diplomats in International Cooperation: Stepchildren of the Foreign Service* (Cornell UP 1963)
Care Project, 'Consular and Diplomatic Protection Legal Framework in the EU Member States' (2010), 198–99, <www.careproject.eu/images/stories/ConsularAndDiplomaticProtection.pdf> accessed 5 May 2022
Carta C, *The European Union Diplomatic Service: Ideas, Preferences and Identities* (Routledge 2012)
Carta C, 'The EU in Geneva: The Diplomatic Representation of a System of Governance' (2013) 9 J Contemp Eur Res 406
Carter JG, *Diplomatic Immunity: Privileges and Abuses* (Nova Science 2011)
Cassesse A, 'The Status of Rebels under the 1977 Geneva Protocol on Non-International Armed Conflicts' (1981) 30 ICLQ 416
Charney J, 'International Agreements and the Development of Customary International Law' (1986) 61 Wash L Rev 971
Charnovitz S, 'Correcting America's Continuing Failure to Comply with the Avena Judgment' (2012) 106 AJIL 572
Chatterjee C, *International Law and Diplomacy* (Routledge 2007)
Chen L, *The US–Taiwan–China Relationship in International Law and Policy* (OUP 2016)
Choi SH, 'The Status, Rights, and Duties of Observers for Non-Member States of the United Nations' (1991) 19 Korean J Comp L 135
Choi W-M, 'Diplomatic and Consular Law in the Internet Age' (2006) 10 SYBIL 117

Ciobanu D, 'Credentials of Delegations and Representation of Member States at the United Nations' (1976) 25 ICLQ 351

Cloots E, *National Identity in EU Law* (OUP 2015)

Colson A, 'The Ambassador between Light and Shade: The Emergence of Secrecy as the Norm for International Negotiation' (2008) 13 Int Negot 179

Cooper AF, 'The Changing Nature of Diplomacy' in AF Cooper, J Heine, and R Thakur (eds), *The Oxford Handbook of Modern Diplomacy* (OUP 2013)

Cooper AF, Heine J, and Thakur R, 'The Challenges of 21st-Century Diplomacy' in C Cooper, J Heine, and R Thakur (eds), *The Oxford Handbook of Modern Diplomacy* (OUP 2013)

Cooper AF, Heine J, and Thakur R (eds), *The Oxford Handbook of Modern Diplomacy* (OUP 2013)

Coppieters E, *Protocole: National et International/Protocol Nationaal en Internationaal* (Institut Royal des Relations Internationales 1989)

Cornago N, 'On the Normalization of Sub-State Diplomacy' (2010) 5 HJD 11

Corten O, *The Law against War: The Prohibition on the Use of Force in Contemporary International Law* (Hart 2010)

Corten O and Klein P, *The Vienna Conventions on the Law of Treaties: A Commentary* (OUP 2011)

Cox N, 'The Acquisition of Sovereignty by Quasi-States: The Case of the Order of Malta' (2002) 6 MJLS 38

Craig P and de Búrca G, *EU Law: Text, Cases, and Materials* (6th edn, OUP 2015)

Craven M, 'Statehood, Self-Determination, and Recognition' in MD Evans (ed), *International Law* (4th edn, OUP 2014)

Crawford J, 'Israel (1948–9) and Palestine (1998–9): Two Studies in the Creation of States' in I Brownlie, GS Goodwin-Gill, and S Talmon (eds), *The Reality of International Law: Essays in Honour of Ian Brownlie* (OUP 1999)

Crawford J, *The International Law Commission's Articles on State Responsibility: Introduction, Text and Commentaries* (CUP 2002)

Crawford J, *The Creation of States in International Law* (2nd edn, OUP 2006)

Crawford J, *Brownlie's Principles of Public International Law* (OUP 2012)

Crawford J, *State Responsibility: The General Part* (CUP 2013)

Crawford J and Viles T, 'International Law on a Given Day' in K Ginther and K Zemanek (eds), *Völkerrect zwischen Normativen Anspruch und Politischer Realität: Festschrift für K. Zemanek* (Ducker & Humblot 1994)

Cremona M, 'The Union as a Global Actor: Roles, Models and Identity' (2004) 41 CML Rev 553

Cremona M, 'A Constitutional Basis for Effective External Action?' (2006) EUI Working Paper 1, 10

Cremona M, 'Member States as Trustees of the Union Interest: Participating in International Agreements on Behalf of the European Union' in A Arnull and others (eds), *A Constitutional Order of States? Essays in EU Law in Honour of Alan Dashwood* (Hart 2011)

Cremona M, 'EU External Relations: Unity and Conferral of Powers' in L Azouli (ed), *The Question of Competence in the European Union* (OUP 2014)

Cremona M and de Witte B (eds), *EU Foreign Relations Law: Constitutional Fundamentals* (Hart 2008)

Cremona M and Thies A (eds), *The European Court of Justice and External Relations Law: Constitutional Challenges* (Hart 2014)

Dahm G, *Völkerrecht*, vol 1 (W Kohlhammer Verlag 1958)

D'Amato A, 'The Theory of Customary International Law' (1988) 82 ASILPROC 242

Damro C, 'EU–UN Environmental Relations: Shared Competence and Effective Multilateralism' in KV Laatikainen and KE Smith (eds), *European Union at the United Nations: Intersecting Multilateralisms* (Palgrave Macmillan 2006)

Dashwood A, 'The Attribution of External Relations Competence' in A Dashwood and C Hillion (eds), *The General Law of EC External Relations* (Sweet & Maxwell 2000)

Dashwood D and Hillion Ch (eds), *The General Law of EC External Relations* (Sweet & Maxwell 2000)

D'Aspremont J, *Formalism and the Sources of International Law* (OUP 2011)

Davis LS and Patman RG, *Science Diplomacy: New Day or False Dawn* (World Scientific 2015)

Davis Cross MK, *The European Diplomatic Corps: Diplomats and International Cooperation from Westphalia to Maastricht* (Palgrave Macmillan 2008)

Davis Cross MK and Melissen J, *European Public Diplomacy: Soft Power at Work* (Palgrave Macmillan 2013)

De Baere G, *Constitutional Principles of EU External Relations* (OUP 2008)

De Baere G and Roes T, 'EU Loyalty as Good Faith' (2015) 64 ICLQ 829

De Baere G and Roes T, 'EU Loyalty as Good Faith' (2015) 64 ICLQ 829

De Baere G and Ryngaert C, 'The ECJ's Judgment in Air Transport Association of America and the International Legal Context of the EU's Climate Change Policy' (2013) 18 EFAR 389

De Baere G and Paasivirta E, 'Identity and Difference: The EU and the UN as Part of Each Other' in H de Waele and J-J Kuipers (eds), *The European Union's Emerging International Identity: Views from the Global Arena* (Martinus Nijhoff 2013)

De Baere G and Wessel RA, 'EU Law and the EEAS: Of Complex Competences and Constitutional Consequences' in D Spence and J Bátora (eds), *The European External Action Service: European Diplomacy Post-Westphalia* (Palgrave Macmillan 2015)

Delarue R, 'The EU–ILO Partnership and the Global Identity of the Union's Social Model' in H de Waele and J-J Kuipers (eds), *The European Union's Emerging International Identity: Views from the Global Arena Studies in EU External Relations* (Martinus Nijhoff 2013)

De Martens C, *Manuel Diplomatique ou Précis des Droits et des Fonctions des Agents Diplomatiques* (Treuttel et Würtz 1822)

De Schoutheete P, *La Coopération Politique Européene* (2nd edn, Nathan 1980)

De Schoutheete P and Andoura S, 'The Legal Personality of the European Union' (2007) LX Studia Diplomatica 5

De Sousa PC, *The European Fundamental Freedoms: A Contextual Approach* (OUP 2015)

de Vattel E, *Le Droit Des Gens, ou Principes de la Loi Naturelle, Appliqués à la Conduite et aux Affaires des Nations et des Souverains* (1758)

de Waele H, *Layered Global Player: Legal Dynamics of EU External Relations* (Springer 2011)

de Waele H and Kuipers J-J, 'The Emerging International Identity of the European Union—Some Preliminary Observations' in H de Waele and J-J Kuipers (eds), *The European Union's Emerging International Identity: Views from the Global Arena Studies in EU External Relations* (Martinus Nijhoff 2013)

de Waele H and Kuipers J-J (eds), *The European Union's Emerging International Identity: Views from the Global Arena Studies in EU External Relations* (Martinus Nijhoff 2013)

De Wicquefort A, *L'Ambassadeur et ses Fonctions* (1681)

De Wicquefort A, *Mémoires Touchant les Ambassadeurs et les Ministres Publics* (chez Pierre Du Marteau 1677)

de Zwaan JW, *The Permanent Representatives Committee* (Elsevier 1995)

Dembiński L, *The Modern Law of Diplomacy: External Missions of States and International Organizations* (Martinus Nijhoff 1988)

den Heijer M, *Europe and Extraterritorial Asylum* (Hart 2012)

Denys S, 'Les Relations Extérieures de la Communauté Economique Européenne à la Lumière de l'Arrêt de la Cour de Justice des Communautés "Commission Contre Conseill" (AETR)' in EG Pasquerelli, N Kleman, and S Denys (eds), *La Communauté Economique Européenne dans les Relations Internationales* (Centre Européen Universitaire 1972)

Denza E, 'The Development of the Law of Diplomatic Relations' (1964) 40 BYIL 141

Denza E, 'Le passeport européen' (1982) 25 Rev du Marché Commun 489

Denza E, *The Intergovernmental Pillars of the European Union* (OUP 2002)

Denza E, 'Diplomatic Asylum' in Andreas Zimmermann (ed), *The 1951 Convention Relating to the Status of Refugees and Its 1967 Protocol: A Commentary* (OUP 2010)

Denza E, 'European Practice on the Recognition of States' (2011) 36 ELR 324

Denza E, 'Art 46—Diplomatic and Consular Protection' in S Peers and others (eds), *The EU Charter of Fundamental Rights: A Commentary* (2014)

Denza E, *Diplomatic Law: Commentary on the Vienna Convention on Diplomatic Relations* (4th edn, OUP 2016)

Devroe W and Wouters J, *De Europese Unie: Het Verdrag van Maastricht en zijn Uitvoering: Analyse en Perspectieven* (Peeters 1996)

Dimier V, *The Invention of a European Development Aid Bureaucracy: Recycling Empire* (Palgrave Macmillan 2014)

Dimier V and McGeever M, 'Diplomats without a Flag: The Institutionalization of the Delegations of the Commission in African, Caribbean and Pacific Countries' (2006) 44 JCMS 483

Djupedal AK, 'Recent Developments in the EU Migration Management Policy EU–Cape Verde Mobility Partnership, Frontex and the Management of the European Borders' (2011) 7(11) ARENA 119

Do Nascimento e Silva GE, *Diplomacy in International Law* (Sijthoff 1972)

Dopagne F, Duquet S, and Theeuwes B, *Diplomatiek Recht Toegepast in België* (Maklu 2014)

Drieskens E, 'What's in a Name? Challenges to the Creation of EU Delegations' (2012) 7 HJD 51

Dugard J, 'Diplomatic Protection' in Anne Peters (ed) *Max Planck Encyclopedia of Public International Law*, 2009, <http://www.mpepil.com> accessed 4 May 2022

Duke S, 'Providing for European-Level Diplomacy after Lisbon: The Case of the European External Action Service' (2009) 4 HJD 211

Duke S, 'The Practices of Post-Lisbon Diplomacy' in M Smith, S Keukeleire, and S Vanhoonacker (eds), *The Diplomatic System of the European Union: Evolution, Change and Challenges* (Routledge 2016)

Duquet S, 'Hungary v Slovak Republic, Judgment, Case C-364/10 [2012] ECLI:EU:C:2012:630' 024 ILEC, Oxford Reports on International Law (CJEU 2012)

Duquet S, 'Raad van Bestuur van de Sociale Verzekeringsbank v LF Evans, Judgment, Case C-179/13' 078 ILEC, Oxford Reports on International Law (CJEU 2015)

Duquet S, 'Bound or Unbridled? A Legal Perspective on the Diplomatic Functions of European Union Delegations' (2018) 13 HJD 21

Duquet S, 'Immunities of Diplomatic and Consular Personnel' in T Ruys, N Angelet, and L Ferro (eds), *The Cambridge Handbook of Immunities and International Law* (CUP 2019)

Duquet S and Wouters J, 'Seeking Refuge in EU Delegations Abroad: A Legal Imbroglio Explored' (2015) 40 ELR 723

Duquet S and Wouters J, 'Diplomacy, Secrecy, and the Law' in C Bjola and S Murray (eds), *Secret Diplomacy: Concepts, Contexts and Cases* (Routledge 2016)

Duquet S and Wouters J, 'Legal Duties of Diplomats Today' in P Behrens (ed), *Diplomatic Law in a New Millennium* (OUP 2017)

Duquet S and Wouters J, 'Diplomatic and Consular Relations' in S Malone, DM Chesterman, and S Villalpando (eds), *The Oxford Handbook of United Nations Treaties* (OUP 2019)

Duquet S and Wouters J, 'What the Eye Cannot See: Justifying Limits to Freedom of Information in the Diplomatic Context' in D Mokrosinska (ed), *Transparency and Secrecy in European Democracies: Contested Trade-Offs* (Routledge 2020)

Dutheil de la Rochere J, 'The Lisbon Compromise: A Synthesis between Community Method and Union Acquis' (2007) 31 Fordham Intl L J 1143

EEAS, 'Vade-Mecum for the Use of the Diplomatic Corps Accredited to the European Union and to the European Atomic Energy Community', 2017, para III, <https://www.eeas.europa.eu/eeas/diplomatic-corps_en>, accessed 2 June 2022

EEAS, 'Missions Accredited to the European Union', 15 March 2022, <https://www.eeas.europa.eu/eeas/diplomatic-list-missions-accredited-european-union_en> accessed 2 June 2022

Eeckhout P, *EU External Relations Law* (OUP 2011)

Ehrhardt CA, 'Das Diplomatische Korps Bei Der EWG in Brüssel' (1962) 13 Aussenpolitik 659

Eilers C, *Diplomats and Diplomacy in the Roman World* (Brill 2009)

Emerson M and others, *Upgrading the EU's Role as Global Actor* (Centre for European Policy Studies 2011)

Erian AEL, 'La Conférence et la Convention sur la Epresentation des Etats dans Leurs Relations avec les Organisations Internationals: Analyse Générale' (1975) 21 AFDI 445

EU–ASEAN Strategic Partnership 2022, *Blue Book 2020: EU–ASEAN Natural Partners*, <https://euinasean.eu/wp-content/uploads/2020/04/EU-ASEAN-Blue-Book-2020-eDocument.pdf> accessed 2 May 2022

European Commission DG External Relations, 'Taking Europe to the World. 50 Years of the European Commission's External Service' (European Commission 2004)

Evans MD, 'The Restoration of Diplomatic Relations between Argentina and the United Kingdom' (1991) 40 ICLQ 473

European External Action Service (EEAS), 'Human Resources Annual Report 2016', Doc EEAS. DGBA.HR, <https://eeas.europa.eu/sites/eeas/files/eeas_human_resources_reports_2016.pdf> accessed 5 May 2022

Faizullaev A, 'Diplomacy and Symbolism' (2013) 8 HJD 91

Fauchille P, *Traité de Droit International Public*, vol 1, Pt 3 (Rousseau & C(ie) 1926)

Feld W, 'The Competences of the European Communities for the Conduct of External Relations' (1965) 43 Tex Law Rev 891

Feltham RG, *Diplomatic Handbook* (8th edn, Martinus Nijhoff 2004)

Fennelly N, 'Legal Interpretation at the European Court of Justice' (1996) 20 Fordham Int Law J 656

Fernández AM, 'Consular Affairs in an Integrated Europe' in J Melissen and AM Fernández (eds), *Consular Affairs and Diplomacy* (Brill Nijhoff 2011)

Fernández AM, 'Consular Affairs in the EU: Visa Policy as a Catalyst for Integration?' (2008) 3 HJD 21

Fidler DP, 'Challenging the Classical Concept of Custom: Perspectives on the Future of Customary International Law' (1996) 39 Ger Yearb Int Law 198

Filippini M, 'A Change for Future Intra-European Diplomatic Relations? Case C-364/10 Hungary v. Slovakia' (2013) 20 MJECL 120

Fitzpatrick J, 'The Unreality of International Law in the United States and the LaGrand Case' (2002) 27 Yale J Intl L 427

Foltea M, *International Organizations in WTO Dispute Settlement: How Much Institutional Sensitivity?* (CUP 2012)

Forni F, 'The Consular Protection of EU Citizens during Emergencies in Third Countries' in A de Guttry, M Gestri, and G Venturini (eds), *International Disaster Response Law* (TMC Asser Press 2012)

Fowler MR and Bunck JM, *Law, Power, and the Sovereign State: The Evolution and Application of the Concept of Sovereignty* (Penn State Press 2010)

Fox H and Webb Ph, *The Law of State Immunity* (3rd edn, OUP 2013)

Frederiksen J and Baser H, 'Better Aid Delivery or Deconcentration of Bureaucracy? A Snapshot of the EC's Devolution Process' (European Centre for Development Policy Management 2004)

Frid R, *The Relations between the EC and International Organizations* (Martinus Nijhoff 1995)

Frimmer S, *Delegationen Der Europaischen Union* (Grin Verlag 2013)

Garner JW, 'Some Questions of International Law in the European War' (1916) 10 AJIL 12

Garnett R, 'State and Diplomatic Immunity and Employment Rights: European Law to the Rescue?' (2015) 64 ICLQ 783

Gatti M, 'Diplomats or Fonctionnaires? The Contested Status of the EU's "Embassy" in the UK', 1 March 2021, blog post at EJIL, <www.ejiltalk.org/diplomats-or-fonctionnaires-the-contested-status-of-the-eus-embassy-in-the-uk> accessed 4 May 2022

Gautier P, 'Reparation for Injuries Case Revisited: The Personality of the European Union' (2000) 4 Max Planck UNYB 331

Gautier P, 'Article 2—Convention de 1986' in O Corten and P Klein (eds), *Les Conventions de Vienne sur le Droit des Traités* (Bruylant 2006)

Gentili, *De Legationibus, Libri Tres* (1585)

Gérard Y, 'La Coopération Politique Européenne. Méthodes et Résultats' (1987) Rev du Marché Commun 466

Ghebali V-Y, 'Le Role des Missions Permenantes auprès des Organisations Internationales Universelles' in Société Française pour le Droit International (ed), *Aspects Récents du Droit des Relations Diplomatiques* (Pedone 1989)

Gianelli A, 'Customary International Law in the European Union' in E Cannizzaro, P Palchetti, and RA Wessel (eds), *International Law as Law of the European Union* (Martinus Nijhoff 2011)

Giddens A, *The Constitution of Society: Outline of the Theory of Structuration* (University of California Press 1984)

Ginther K and Zemanek K, *Völkerrect zwischen Normativen Anspruch und Politischer Realität: Festschrift für K. Zemanek* (Duncker & Humblot 1994)

Goebel J, *The Equality of States: A Study in the History of Law* (WS Hein 2003)
Gowlland Debbas V, 'The Role of the International Court of Justice in the Development of the Contemporary Law of Treaties' in CJ Tams and J Sloan (eds), *The Development of International Law by the International Court of Justice* (OUP 2013)
Gross L, 'Immunities and Privileges of Delegations to the United Nations' (1962) 16 Int Organ 483
Grotius, *De Iure Belli Ac Pacis, Libri Tres*, vol 2 (Paris 1625)
Guastaferro B, 'Beyond the Exceptionalism of Constitutional Conflicts: The Ordinary Functions of the Identity Clause' (2012) 31 Yearb Eur Law 263
Guggenheim P, *Lehrbuch des Völkerrects*, vol 1 (Verlag für Recht und Gesellschaft 1948)
Guzman AT and Hsiang J, 'Some Ways That Theories on Customary International Law Fail: A Reply to Laszlo Blutman' (2014) 25 EJIL 553
Hamilton K and Langhorne R, *The Practice of Diplomacy* (Routledge 1995)
Hannikainen L, 'The Collective Factor as a Promoter of Customary International Law' (2006) 6 Bal YIL 124
Hanses B and Spence D, 'Structural Diplomacy and Foreign Policy: The Case of the EU Delegation in the Democratic Republic of the Congo' in D Spence and J Bátora (eds), *The European External Action Service: European Diplomacy Post-Westphalia* (Palgrave Macmillan 2015)
Harding C and Lim CL, 'The Significance of Westphalia: An Archaeology of the International Legal Order' in C Harding and CL Lim (eds), *Renegotiating Westphalia: Essays and Commentary on the European and Conceptual Foundations of Modern International Law* (Martinus Nijhoff 1999)
Hardy M, *Modern Diplomatic Law* (Manchester UP 1968)
Hardy M, 'The Diplomatic Activities of International Organisations: The United Nations and the European Communities Contrasted' (1969) 5 RBDI 44
Harris LJ, 'Diplomatic Privileges and Immunities: A New Regime Is Soon to be Adopted by the United States' (1968) 62 AJIL 98
Hart HLA, *The Concept of Law* (3rd edn, eds L Green and J Raz, OUP 2012)
Hartley TC, 'International Law and the Law of the European Union—a Reassessment' (2002) 72 BYIL 1
Hayes E, 'EU Delegations: Europe's Link to the World' in KE Jørgensen and KV Laatikainen (eds), *Routledge Handbook on the European Union and International Institutions: Performance, Policy, Power* (Routledge 2013)
Heine J, 'On the Manner of Practicing the New Diplomacy' [2006] CIGI 3
Helly D, Knoll A, and Galeazzi G, 'A Closer Look into EU's External Action Frontline: Framing the Challenges Ahead for EU Delegations' (2014) 62 ECDPM Briefing Note 16
Henrikson AK, 'Diplomacy's Possible Futures' (2006) 1 HJD 3
Hernández G, 'Federated Entities in International Law: Disaggregating the Federal State?' in D French (ed), *Statehood and Self-Determination: Reconciling Tradition and Modernity in International Law* (CUP 2013)
Hernandez-Campos A, 'The Criteria of Statehood in International Law and the Hallstein Doctrine: The Case of the Republic of China on Taiwan' (2006) 24 Chinese (Taiwan) YB Intl L&A ff 75
Hervé A, 'The Participation of the European Union in Global Economic Governance Fora' (2012) 18 ELJ 143
Hestermeyer HP, 'Vienna Convention on Diplomatic Relations (1961)' in Anne Peters (ed) *Max Planck Encyclopedia of Public International Law*, para 41 (2012). <http://www.mpepil.com> accessed 3 May 2022
Higgins R, *The Development of International Law through the Political Organs of the United Nations* (OUP 1963)
Higgins R, 'The Abuse of Diplomatic Privileges and Immunities: Recent United Kingdom Experience' (1985) 79 AJIL 641
Hill DJ, *A History of Diplomacy in the International Development of Europe*, vol II (Longmans, Green & Co 1924)
Hill C and Wallace W, 'Diplomatic Trends in the European Community' (1979) 55 Int Aff 47
Hillgruber C, 'The Admission of New States to the International Community' (1998) 9 EJIL 491

Hillion C, 'Mixity and Coherence in EU External Relations: The Significance of the Duty of Cooperation' (2009) Cleer Working Paper No 2. <https://www.asser.nl/upload/documents/9212009_14629clee09-2full.pdf> accessed 2 June 2022
Hillion C and Wessel RA, 'Restraining External Competences of EU Member States under CFSP' in M Cremona and B de Witte (eds), *EU Foreign Relations Law: Constitutional Fundamentals* (Hart 2008)
Hillion C and Wessel RA, 'Competence Distribution in EU External Relations after Ecowas: Clarification or Continued Fuzziness?' (2009) 46 CML Rev 551
Hinsley FH, *Sovereignty* (2nd edn, CUP 1986)
Hocking B, 'Catalytic Diplomacy: Beyond "Newness" and "Decline"' in J Melissen (ed), *Innovation in Diplomatic Practice* (Palgrave Macmillan 1999)
Hocking B and Smith M, 'An Emerging Diplomatic System for the EU? Frameworks and Issues' (2011) 44 Cuad Eur de Deusto 19
Hocking B and Spence D, *Foreign Ministries in the European Union: Integrating Diplomats* (Palgrave Macmillan 2016)
Hoffmeister F, 'Outsider or Frontrunner? Recent Developments under International and European Law on the Status of the European Union in International Organizations and Treaty Bodies' (2007) 44 CML Rev 41
Hoffmeister F, 'The Contribution of EU Practice to International Law' in M Cremona (ed), *Developments in EU External Relations Law* (OUP 2008)
Hoffmeister F and Kuijper PJ, 'The Status of the European Union at the United Nations' in J Wouters, F Hoffmeister, and T Ruyse (eds), *The United Nations and the European Union: An Ever Stronger Partnership* (TMC Asser Press 2006)
Hollis DB, 'Why State Consent Still Matters: Non-State Actors, Treaties, and the Changing Sources of International Law' (2005) 23 BJIL 137
Hopkins J, *Devolution in Context: Regional, Federal and Devolved Government in the Member States of the European Union* (Cavendish Publishing 2002)
Ianniello Salicetti A, 'The Protection of EU Citizens Abroad: Accountability, Rule of Law, Role of Consular and Diplomatic Services' (2011) 17 EPL 91
Institute of International Law (IIL), 'Regulation on Diplomatic Immunities' in *ILL Yearbook* (1895, rev 1929)
International Labour Organization (ILO), 'Submission of Credentials', <www.ilo.org/ilc/Credentials/lang--en/index.htm> accessed 4 May 2022
International Law Commission (ILC), 'Draft Articles on Diplomatic Intercourse and Immunities with Commentaries' (1958) II YBILC 104
International Law Commission (ILC), 'Summary Records of the Tenth Session' (1958) I YBILC, A/CN.4/SER.A/1958, 91
International Law Commission (ILC), 'Text of the Draft Articles and Commentary' (1958) II YBILC, A/CN.4/117, 131, 133
International Law Commission (ILC), 'Draft Articles on the Responsibility of States for Internationally Wrongful Acts with Commentaries' (2001) II(II) YBILC 131, 133
International Law Commission (ILC), 'Report Covering the Work of the ILC's Twelfth Session: 25 April to 1 July 1960 A/4435' (1960) II YBILC 178
International Law Commission (ILC), 'Draft Articles on the Law of Treaties with Commentaries' (1966) II YBILC 188
International Law Commission (ILC), 'Draft Articles on Representatives of States to International Organizations, with Commentaries' (1970) II YBILC 6
International Law Commission (ILC), 'Draft Articles on Most-Favored Nation Clauses with Commentaries' (1978) II YBILC 21, 37
International Law Commission (ILC), 'Draft Articles on the Responsibility of States for Internationally Wrongful Acts with Commentaries' (2001) II YBILC 104
International Law Commission (ILC), 'Draft Articles on Diplomatic Protection with Commentaries' (2006) II YBILC, 23–55
Ismail M-B, *Islamic Law and Transnational Diplomatic Law: A Quest for Complementarity in Divergent Legal Theories* (Palgrave Macmillan 2016)

Jennings RY and Watts A (eds), *Oppenheim's International Law*, vol 1 (9th edn, Longman 1992)
Jönsson C and Hall M (eds), 'Communication: An Essential Aspect of Diplomacy' in C Jönsson and R Langhorne (eds), *Diplomacy* (2nd edn, Sage 2004)
Jørgensen KE and Laatikainen KV (eds), *Routledge Handbook on the European Union and International Institutions* (Routledge 2013)
Jørgensen KE and Wessel RA, 'The Position of the European Union in (Other) International Organizations: Confronting Legal and Political Approaches' in P Koutrakos (ed), *European Foreign Policy* (Edward Elgar 2011)
Joyner DH and Roscini M, 'Is There Any Room for the Doctrine of Fundamental Rights of States in Today's International Law?' (2015) 4 CJICL 467
Kadish MJ, 'Article 36 of the Vienna Convention on Consular Relations: The International Court of Justice in Mexico v United States (Avena) Speaks Emphatically to the Supreme Court of the United States about Fundamental Nature of the Right to Consul' (2004) 36 Georget J Int Law 1
Kammerhofer J, 'Uncertainty in the Formal Sources of International Law: Customary International Law and Some of Its Problems' (2004) 15 EJIL 523
Kassim H and others (eds), *The National Co-ordination of EU Policy* (OUP 2001)
Kearney RD and Dalton RE, 'The Treaty on Treaties' (1970) 64 AJIL 495
Kelsen H, *General Theory of Law and State* (Harvard UP 1945)
Kelsen H, 'The Draft Declaration on Rights and Duties of States' (1950) 44 AJIL 259
Kerres P and Wessel RA, 'Apples and Oranges? Comparing the European Union Delegations to National Embassies' (2015) Cleer Working Paper No 2. https://www.asser.nl/media/2847/cleer15-2_web.pdf accessed 2 June 2022
Ketvel M-G, 'The Jurisdiction of the European Court of Justice in Respect of the Common Foreign and Security Policy' (2006) 55 ICLQ 77
Klabbers J, 'Qatar v Bahrain: The Concept of "Treaty" in International Law' (1995) 33 AVR 361
Klabbers J, *The Concept of Treaty in International Law* (Kluwer Law International 1996)
Klabbers J, *Treaty Conflict and the European Union* (CUP 2009)
Klabbers J, 'The Emergence of Functionalism in International Institutional Law: Colonial Inspirations' (2014) 25 EJIL 645
Klein N, 'Avena and Other Mexican Nationals (Mexico v. United States of America)' (2004) 11 Aust Int Law J 143
Kochenov D, 'The Right to Have What Rights? EU Citizenship in Need of Clarification' (2013) 19 ELJ 502
Kohler M, *European Identity* (Neuer Wissenschaftlicher Verlag 2012)
Konstadinidies T, 'EU Foreign Policy under the Doctrine of Implied Powers: Codification Drawbacks and Constitutional Limitations' (2014) 39 ELR 511
Koops JA and Macaj G, *The European Union as a Diplomatic Actor* (Palgrave Macmillan 2015)
Koutrakos P (ed), *European Foreign Policy* (Edward Elgar 2011)
Koutrakos P, 'International Agreements in the Area of the EU's Common Security and Defence Policy' in E Cannizzaro, P Palchetti, and RA Wessel (eds), *International Law as Law of the European Union* (Martinus Nijhoff 2012)
Koutrakos P, *EU International Relations Law* (2nd edn, Hart 2015)
Koskenniemi M (ed), *International Law Aspects of the European Union* (Kluwer 1998)
Koskenniemi M and Leino P, 'Fragmentation of International Law. Postmodern Anxieties?' (2002) 15 LJIL 553
Kuijper PJ, 'The Evolution of the Third Pillar from Maastricht to the European Constitution: Institutional Aspects' (2004) 41 CML Rev 609
Kuijper PJ, 'The European Courts and the Law of Treaties: The Continuing Story' in E Cannizzaro (ed), *The Law of Treaties beyond the Vienna Convention* (OUP 2011)
Kunz JL, 'Privileges and Immunities of International Organizations' (1947) 41 AJIL 828
Laatikainen KV, 'The EU Delegation in New York: A Debut in High Political Drama' in D Spence and J Bátora (eds), *The European External Action Service: European Diplomacy Post-Westphalia* (Palgrave Macmillan 2015)

Laatikainen KV and Smith KE (eds), *The European Union at the United Nations: Intersecting Multilateralisms* (Palgrave Macmillan 2006)

Langhorne R, 'History and Evolution of Diplomacy' in J Kurbalija (ed), *Modern Diplomacy* (Diplofoundation 1988)

Larik J, *Foreign Policy Objectives in European Constitutional Law* (OUP 2016)

Lauterpacht H, 'The Subjects of the Law of Nations' (1947) 63 Law Q Rev 438

Lechner S, 'What Difference Does Ius Inter Gentes Make? Changing Diplomatic Rights and Duties and the Modern European States-System' (2006) 1 HJD 235

Lee LT and Quigley JB, *Consular Law and Practice* (3rd edn, OUP 2008)

Lehmann P-É, 'Le Respect de l'Identité Nationale des États Members' in J-C Barbato and Y Petit (eds), *L'Union Européenne, Fédération Plurinationale en Devenir?* (Bruylant 2015)

Leikam F, 'A Matter of Preference: Commonwealth Africa, Britain and the EEC Association System, 1957–75' in P Winand, A Benvenuti, and M Guderzo (eds), *The External Relations of the European Union: Historical and Contemporary Perspectives* (PIE Peter Lang 2015)

Lenaerts K and Corthaut T, 'Of Birds and Hedges: The Role of Primacy in Invoking Norms of EU Law' (2006) 31 ELR 287

Lenaerts K and De Smijter E, 'The European Union as an Actor under International Law' (1999) 19 Yearb Eur Law 95

Lenaerts K and Gutiérrez-Fons JA, 'To Say What the Law of the EU Is: Methods of Interpretation and the European Court of Justice' (2014) 20 Colum J Eur L 3

Lenaerts K and Van Nuffel P, *European Union Law* (R Bray and N Cambien eds, Sweet & Maxwell 2011)

Lenaerts K, Maseliss I, and Gutman K, *EU Procedural Law* (OUP 2014)

Levade A, 'Identité Nationale ou Constitutionelle?' in M Fatin-Rouge Stéfani and others (eds), *L'Identité la Croisée des Etats et de l'Europe: Quel sens? Quelles Fonctions?* (Bruylant 2015)

Ličková M, 'European Exceptionalism in International Law' (2008) 19 EJIL 463

Lieb J, *Diplomatie Jenseits des Staates: Die EU-Außenvertretung Gegenüber Drittstaaten und der Europäische Auswärtige Dienst* (Nomos 2013)

Lieberfeld D, 'Secrecy and "Two-Level Games" in the Oslo Accord: What the Primary Sources Tell Us' (2008) 13 Int Negot 133

Lindroos A and Mehling M, 'Dispelling the Chimera of "Self-Contained Regimes" in International Law and the WTO' (2005) 16 EJIL 857

Ling Y-L, 'A Comparative Study of the Privileges and Immunities of United Nations Member Representatives and Officials with the Traditional Privileges and Immunities of Diplomatic Agents' (1976) 33 Wash & Lee L Rev 127

Lloyd L, *Diplomacy with a Difference: The Commonwealth Office of High Commissioner, 1880–2006* (Martinus Nijhoff 2007)

Lowe V, 'Can the European Community Bind the Member States on Questions of Customary International Law?' in M Koskenniemi (ed), *International Law Aspects of the European Union* (Kluwer 1998)

Lundin L-E, 'Effective Multilateralism after Lisbon: The Added Value of the EEAS and the EU Delegation in Vienna' in D Spence and J Bátora (eds), *The European External Action Service: European Diplomacy Post-Westphalia* (Palgrave Macmillan 2015)

MacLeod I, Hendry ID, and Hyett S, *The External Relations of the European Communities: A Manual of Law and Practice* (OUP 1996)

Magone JM, 'The Portuguese Permanent Representation in Brussels: The Institutionalization of a Simple System' in H Kassim and others (eds), *The National Co-ordination of EU Policy* (OUP 2001)

Mahbubani K, 'Multilateral Diplomacy' in AF Cooper, J Heine, and R Thakur (eds), *The Oxford Handbook of Modern Diplomacy* (OUP 2013)

Mainetti V, 'The League of Nations and the Emergence of Privileges and Immunities of International Organizations' in Roberto Virzo and Ivan Ingravallo (eds), *Evolutions in the Law of International Organizations* (Brill Nijhoff 2015)

Malanczuk P, *Akehurst's Modern Introduction to International Law* (8th edn, Routledge 2002)

Manin P, 'The European Communities and the Vienna Convention on the Law of Treaties between States and International Organizations or between International Organizations' (1987) 24 CML Rev 457

Manners I, 'Normative Power Europe: A Contradiction in Terms?' (2002) 40 J Com Mar St 235
Marschik A, 'Too Much Order? The Impact of Special Secondary Norms on the Unity and Efficacy of the International Legal System' (1998) 9 EJIL 212
Mathijsen P and Dyrberg P, *Guide to European Union Law* (11th edn, Sweet & Maxwell 2013)
Mattingly G, *Renaissance Diplomacy* (Dover Publications 1988)
McCaffree MJ, Innis P, and Sand RM, *Protocol: The Complete Handbook of Diplomatic, Official & Social Usage* (Durban House 2002)
McDonagh M, 'The Right to Information in International Human Rights Law' (2013) 13 Hum Rights Law Rev 25
Megiddo T and Zohar N, 'Palestinian Independence in a Post-Kosovo World' in D French (ed), *Statehood and Self-Determination: Reconciling Tradition and Modernity in International Law* (CUP 2013)
Melchior M (ed), *Les relations extérieurs de la Communauté européenne unifiée* (Université de Liège 1969)
Melissen J, *The New Public Diplomacy: Soft Power in International Relations* (Palgrave Macmillan 1924)
Melissen J and Fernández AM (eds), *Consular Affairs and Diplomacy* (Brill Nijhoff 2011)
Meloni A, *Visa Policy within the European Union Structure* (Springer 2005)
Merket H, 'From Commission to Union Delegations: A Legal-Institutionalist Analysis' European Union in International Affairs IV, Proceedings [2014] 2
Metcalfe L, 'International Policy Co-ordination and Public Management Reform' (1994) 60 IRAS 271
Michaels R and Pauwelyn J, 'Conflict of Norms or Conflict of Laws?: Different Techniques in the Fragmentation of Public International Law' (2012) 22 Duke J Comp & Intl L 349
Milanovic M and Wood M, *The Law and Politics of the Kosovo Advisory Opinion* (OUP 2015)
Miller AJ, 'Privileges and Immunities of United Nations Officials' (2007) 4 IOLR 169
Monaco R, 'Les Relations Extérieures de la CECA' in *Annuaire Européen/European Yearbook* (Springer 1958)
Monar J, 'EU International Security Governance: The Case of Counter-Terrorism' (2013) 23 European Security 195
Moran J-Y, 'La Représentation des États Fédérés: L'Exemple du Québec' in C Blumann (ed), *Aspects Récents du Droit des Relations Diplomatiques* (Pedone 1989)
Moreno-Lax V and Costello C, 'The Extraterritorial Application of the EU Charter of Fundamental Rights: From Territoriality to Facticity, the Effectiveness Model' in S Peers and others (eds), *The EU Charter of Fundamental Rights: A Commentary* (2014)
Morris WG, 'Constitutional Solutions to the Problem of Diplomatic Crime and Immunity' (2007) 36 Hofstra Law Rev 601
Mouton JD, 'L'Identité, un Concept Pertinent au Regard du Droit International?' (2014) 118 RGDIP 501
Muller S, *International Organizations and Their Host States: Aspects of Their Legal Relationship* (Martinus Nijhoff 1995)
Murray D, *Human Rights Obligations of Non-State Armed Groups* (Hart 2016)
Naert F, *International Law Aspects of the EU's Security and Defence Policy* (Intersentia 2010)
Nahlik SE, *Development of Diplomatic Law: Selected Problems* (Martinus Nijhoff 1990)
Nelson CM, '"Opening" Pandora's Box: The Status of the Diplomatic Bag in International Relations' (1988) 12 Fordham Intl LJ 494
Nicolson HG, *The Evolution of Diplomatic Method: The Chichele Lectures Delivered at Oxford, November, 1953* (Greenwood Press 1954)
Nicolson HG, *Diplomacy* (OUP 1988)
Nolte G, *Treaties and Subsequent Practice* (OUP 2013)
Norberg S and Johansson M, 'The History of the EEA Agreement and the First Twenty Years of Its Existence' in C Baudenbacher (ed), *The Handbook of EEA Law* (Springer 2016)
Novotna T, 'Women in the EEAS and EU Delegations: Another Post-Westphalia Change?' in D Spence and J Bátora (eds), *The European External Action Service: European Diplomacy Post-Westphalia* (Palgrave Macmillan 2015)
Nussbaum A, *A Concise History of the Law of Nations* (Macmillan 1954)

Nuttall SJ, 'The Commission: Struggle for Legitimacy' in C Hill (ed), *The Actors in Europe's Foreign Policy* (Routledge 1996)
Nuttall SJ, *European Political Co-operation* (Clarendon Press 1992)
Nye JS, 'Redefining the National Interest' [1999] Foreign Aff 22
Nys E, *Les Origines de la Diplomatie et le Droit d'Ambassade Jusqu'a Grotius* (Librairie Européenne C Muquardt 1884)
O'Connell D, *International Law*, vol 2 (2nd edn, Stevens 1970)
Odell AL, 'Enforcing Reciprocity in US Diplomatic Relations: The Foreign Missions Act of 1982' (1984) 17 NYUJILP 817
Odermatt J, 'The EU's Accession to the European Convention on Human Rights: An International Law Perspective' (2014) 47 NYUJILP 59
Odermatt J, 'The Development of Customary International Law by International Organizations' (2017) 66 ICLQ 491
Odermatt J, *International Law and the European Union* (CUP 2021)
Ohlin JD, *The Assault on International Law* (OUP 2015)
Onestini C, 'A Hybrid Service: Organising Efficient EU Foreign Policy' in D Spence and J Bátora (eds), *The European External Action Service: European Diplomacy Post-Westphalia* (Palgrave Macmillan 2015)
Oppenheim L, *International Law. A Treatise*, vol 1 (1st edn, Longmans, Green & Co 1905)
Ott A, 'The Legal Bases for International Agreements Post-Lisbon: Of Pirates and the Philippines' (2014) 21 MJECL 739
Pancracio J-P, *Droit et Institutions Diplomatiques* (Pedone 2007)
Panke H, 'The European Union in the United Nations: An Effective External Actor?' (2014) 21 Eur J Public Policy 1050
Pellet A, 'The Opinions of the Badinter Arbitration Committee: A Second Breath for the Self-Determination of Peoples' (1992) 3 EJIL 178
Perez A, 'The System of Privileges and Immunities Applicable to the International Organisations in Switzerland and to the Permanent Foreign Delegations in Geneva' (Eidgenössisches Departement für auswärtige Angelegenheiten 1997)
Pernice I, 'The Treaty of Lisbon: Multilevel Constitutionalism in Action' (2008) 15 Colum J Eur L 349
Pescatore P, 'Les Relations Extérieurs de La Communauté Européenne' (1961) 103 Hague Recueil 1
Pescatore P, 'La Personnalité Internationale de la Communauté' in M Melchior (ed), *Les relations extérieurs de la Communauté européenne unifiée* (Institut d'études juridiques européennes de la faculté de droit de l'Université de Liège 1969)
Pescatore P, *The Law of Integration: Emergence of a New Phenomenon in International Relations, Based on the Experience of the European Communities* (Sijthoff 1974)
Petersen LO, *Europäisierung der Diplomatie: völker- und europarechtliche Rahmenbedingungen* (Duncker & Humblot 2011)
Peterson J, Sjursen H, and Allen D (eds), 'Who Speaks for Europe?' in *A Common Foreign Policy for Europe* (Routledge 1998)
Pierre X and Paulauskas R, 'Enhancing Teamwork within the European Union Diplomacy and Including Key external Partners in the EU Coordination Process in Geneva' (2014) 12 Lith Foreign Policy Rev 106
Pintos EV, 'Representación Exterior y Cooperación Diplomática y Consular en el Tratado de la Unión Europea' (1995) 22 Rev Inst Eur 417
Plantey A, *Principes de Diplomatie* (2nd edn, Pedone 2000)
Portmann R, *Legal Personality in International Law* (CUP 2010)
Posner EA and Goldsmith JL, 'A Theory of Customary International Law' (1999) 66 UCLR 1113
Potter PB, 'Permanent Delegations to the League of Nations' (1931) 25 Am Polit Sci Rev 21
Pouliot V, 'Diplomats as Permanent Representatives: The Practical Logics of the Multilateral Pecking Order' (2011) 66 Int J 543
Pozen DE, 'Deep Secrecy' (2010) 62 Stan L Rev 257
Preshova D, 'Battleground or Meeting Point?: The Respect for National Identities in the European Union—Article 4(2) The Treaty on European Union' (2012) 8 CYELP 267

Prokhovnik R, 'Internal/External: The State of Sovereignty' (1996) 2 Contemp Politics 7
Quadri R, 'La Personnalité International de la Communauté Européenne' in M Melchior (ed), *Les Relations Extérieurs de la Commnauté Européenne Unifiée* (Institut d'Études Juridiques Européennes de la Faculté de Droit de l'Université de Liège 1969)
Quigley JB, 'LaGrand: A Challenge to the US Judiciary' (2002) 27 Yale J Intl L 435
Quigley JB, 'The United States' Withdrawal Form International Court of Justice Jurisdiction in Consular Cases: Reasons and Consequences' (2008) 19 Duke J Comp & Intl L 263
Quigley JB, *The Statehood of Palestine: International Law in the Middle East Conflict* (CUP 2010)
Rasmussen SB, 'The Messages and Practices of the European Union's Public Diplomacy' (2010) 5 HJD 263
Raux J, *Les Relations Extérieures de la Communauté Économique Européenne* (Editions Cujas 1968)
Reichling C, *Le Droit de Légation des Communautés Européennes* (UGA Éditions 1964)
Rey J, 'La Politique Commerciale de la Communauté Européenne' in M Melchior (ed), *Les Relations Extérieurs de la Commnauté Européenne Unifiée* (Institut d'Études Juridiques Européennes de la Faculté de Droit de l'Université de Liège 1969)
Richtsteig M, *Wiener Übereinkommen über diplomatische und konsularische Beziehungen: Entstehungsgeschichte, Kommentierung, Praxis* (2nd edn, Nomos 2010)
Riveles S, 'Diplomatic Asylum as a Human Right: The Case of the Durban Six' (1989) 11 HRQ 139
Roberststs A, 'A Partial Revolution: The Diplomatic Ethos and Transparency in Intergovernmental Organizations' (2004) 64 Public Adm Rev 410
Roberts I (ed), *Satow's Diplomatic Practice* (6th edn, OUP 2011)
Robinet B, *La Représentation Permanente Belge auprès de l''Union Européenne: Une Cheffe d'Orchestre à Bruxelles* (Presses Universitaires de Louvain 2021)
Roes T, 'Case Note: Hof van Justitie—16 Oktober 2012' (2014) 77 RW 518
Rosamond B, 'Conceptualizing the EU Model of Governance in World Politics' (2005) 10 EFAR 463
Rosas A and Armati L, *EU Constitutional Law: An Introduction* (Bloomsbury Publishing 2012)
Rosenne S, 'Recognition of States by the United Nations' (1949) 26 BYIL 4377
Rossi LS, 'EU Citizenship and the Free Movement of Heads of State: Hungary v Slovak Republic' 50 CML Rev 1451
Ruffert M, 'Diplomatischer und Konsularischer Schutz zwischen Völker- und Europarecht' (1997) 35 ADV 459
Rummel R, 'The Intergovernmental Conference, 1966—How to Reform CFSP?' in E Regelsberger, P De Schoutheete, and W Wessels (eds), *Foreign Policy of the European Union: From EPC to CFSP and Beyond* (L Reiner 1997)
Ryngaert C, 'The Legal Status of the Holy See' (2011) 3 GoJIL 829
Ryngaert C, 'Imposing International Duties on Non-State Actors and the Legitimacy of International Law' in M Noortmann and C Ryngaert (eds), *Non-State Actor Dynamics in International Law: From Law-Takers to Law-Makers* (Ashgate 2013)
Salicetti AI, 'The Protection of EU Citizens Abroad: Accountability, Rule of Law, Role of Consular and Diplomatic Services' (2011) 17 EPL 91
Salmon J, 'Les Représentations et Missions Permanentes auprès de le CEE et de l'Euratom' in M Virally, P Gerbet, and J Salmon (eds) *Les Missions Permanentes auprès des Organisations Internationales*, vol 1 (Dotation Carnegie 1971)
Salmon J, *Manuel de Droit Diplomatique* (Bruylant 1994)
Salmon J, 'Les Immunités Diplomatiques dans la Tourmente' in *Liber Amicorum Jean-Pierre Cot: Le Procès International* (Bruylant 2009)
Sands PJ and Klein P, *Bowett's Law of International Institutions* (6th edn, Sweet & Maxwell 2009)
Sandström J, 'Report on Diplomatic Intercourse and Immunities' (1955) II YBILC, A/CN.4/91, 10
Sari A, 'Status of Forces and Status of Mission Agreements under the ESDP: The EU's Evolving Practice' (2008) 19 EJIL 67
Sassòli M, 'The Implementation of International Humanitarian Law: Current and Inherent Challenges' (2007) 10 Y Intl HL 45
Satow E, *A Guide to Diplomatic Practice*, vol 1 (1st edn, Longmans, Green & Co 1917)

Schachter O, 'Entangled Treaty and Custom' in Y Dingtein and M Tabory (eds), *International Law in a Time of Perplexity: Essays in Honour of Shabtai Rosenne* (Martinus Nijhoff 1989)

Schermers HG and Blokker NM, *International Institutional Law: Unity within Diversity* (5th edn, Martinus Nijhoff 2011)

Schmalenbach K, 'Article 6: The Capacity of States to Conclude Treaties' in O Dörr and K Schmalenbach (eds), *Vienna Convention on the Law of Treaties: A Commentary* (Springer 2012)

Schumaker M, *Sharing without Reckoning: Imperfect Right and the Norms of Reciprocity* (Wilfrid Laurier UP 2006)

Schütze R, 'Lisbon and the Federal Order of Competences: A Prospective Analysis' (2008) 33 ELR 709

Schütze R, *From Dual to Corporate Federalism: The Changing Structure of European Law* (OUP 2009)

Schütze R, 'On "Federal" Ground: The European Union as an (Inter)national Phenomenon' (2009) 46 CML Rev 1069

Schütze R, *European Constitutional Law* (2nd edn, CUP 2015)

Seidl-Hohenveldern I, *Völkerrecht* (9th edn, Carl Heymanns Verlag 1997)

Sen B, *A Diplomat's Handbook of International Law and Practice* (3rd edn, Martinus Nijhoff 1988)

Serres J, *Manuel Pratique de Protocole* (de la Bievre 2016)

Seyersted F, 'Treaty-Making Capacity of International Organizations: Article 6 of the International Law Commission's Draft Articles on the Law of Treaties between States and International Organizations or between International Organizations' (1983) 34 ZöR 261

Seyersted F, *Common Law of International Organizations* (Martinus Nijhoff 2008)

Sharp P, 'Who Needs Diplomats? The Problem of Diplomatic Representation' in C Jönsson and R Langhorne (eds), *Diplomacy*, vol 3 (2nd edn, Sage 2004)

Sharp P, *Diplomatic Theory of International Relations* (CUP 2009)

Shaw M, *International Law* (CUP 2014)

Shen S, 'Hong Kong's Sub-Sovereign Status and Its External Relations' in P Sevastikr (ed), *Aspects of Sovereignty: Sino-Swedish Reflections* (Martinus Nijhoff 2013)

Sibert M, *Traité de Droit International Public*, vol 2 (Dalloz 1951)

Sieberson SC, *Dividing Lines between the European Union and Its Member States: The Impact of the Treaty of Lisbon* (TMC Asser Press 2008)

Silverburg SR, 'Diplomatic Recognition of States in Statu Nascendi: The Case of Palestine' in SR Silverburg (ed), *Palestine and International Law: Essays on Politics and Economics* (McFarland & Co 2002)

Simma B, 'Self-Contained Regimes' (1985) 16 Neth Yearb Int Law 111

Simma B and Pulkowski D, 'Of Planets and the Universe: Self-Contained Regimes in International Law' (2006) 17 EJIL 483

Sivakumaran S, 'Binding Armed Opposition Groups' (2006) 55 ICLQ 369

Skubiszewski K, 'Forms of Participation of International Organizations in the Lawmaking Process' (1964) 18 IO 790

Sloane RD, 'On the Use and Abuse of Necessity in the Law of State Responsibility' (2012) 106 AJIL 447

Smith KE, 'Speaking with One Voice? European Union Coordination on Human Rights Issues at the United Nations' (2006) 44 JCS 113

Smith M, 'The European Union and International Order: European and Global Dimensions' (2007) 120 EFAR 437

Smith M, 'Still Rooted in Maastricht: EU External Relations as a "Third-Generation Hybrid"' (2012) 34 J Eur Integr 699

Smith MH, 'The EU as a Diplomatic Actor in the Post-Lisbon Era: Robust or Rootless Hybrid?' in JA Koops and G Macaj (eds), *The European Union as a Diplomatic Actor* (Palgrave Macmillan 2014)

Smith MH, 'Does the Flag Still Follow Trade? Implications for European Union Diplomatic Practices in Third Countries' (2018) 13 HJD 41

Smith M, Keukeleire S, and Vanhoonacker S, *The Diplomatic System of the European Union: Evolution, Change and Challenges* (Routledge 2015)

Sobrino Heredia JM, 'La actividad diplomática de las delegaciones de la Comisión en el exterior de la Comunidad Europea' (1993) 20 Rev Inst Eur 485

Sola NF, 'The Stakes of the European External Action Service. What is Needed in Order to Become a European Diplomatic Corps?' in JM Beneyto (ed), *La Unión Europea como Actor Global: Law Nuevas Dimensiones de la Política Exterior Europea* (Instituto Universitario de Estudios Europeos de la Universidad CEU 2011)

Sofer NF, 'Old and New Diplomacy: A Debate Revisited' in C Jönsson and R Langhorne (eds), *Diplomacy* (2nd edn, Sage 2004)

Spence D, 'Taking Stock: 50 Years of European Diplomacy' (2009) 4 HJD 235

Spence D, 'From the Convention to Lisbon: External Competence and the Uneasy Transition for Geneva Delegations' in D Spence and J Bátora (eds), *The European External Action Service: European Diplomacy Post-Westphalia* (Palgrave Macmillan 2015)

Spence D, 'The EEAS and Its Epistemic Communities: The Challenges of Diplomatic Hybridism' in D Spence and J Bátora (eds), *The European External Action Service: European Diplomacy Post-Westphalia* (Palgrave Macmillan 2015)

Spence D and Bátora J (eds), *The European External Action Service: European Diplomacy Post-Westphalia* (Palgrave Macmillan 2015)

Sobrino Heredia JM, 'La Actividad Diplomática de las Delegaciones de la Comisión en el Exterior de la Comunidad Europea' (1993) 20 Rev Inst Eur 485

State Department (US), 'Diplomatic and Consular Immunity: Guidance for Law Enforcement and Judicial Authorities', 17, <https://2009-2017.state.gov/documents/organization/149734.pdf> accessed 4 May 2022

Stavridis S and Thouez C, 'The International Protection of the EU Citizen: Problems and Prospects' In R Bellamy and A Warleigh (eds) *Citizenship and Governance in the European Union* (Continuum 2005)

Steiner RC, 'A Jewish Aramaic (or Hebrew) Laissez-Passer from the Egyptian Port of Berenike' (2004) 63 J Near East Studs 277

Stockston CH, *Outlines of International Law* (Charles Scribner's Sons 1914)

Stoll JA, 'Le Statut Juridique du Représentant-Résident du Bureau de l'Assistance Technique des Nations Unies dans l'État où il est Accredité' (1964) 10 AFDI 14

Steinbach A, 'The Lisbon Judgment of the German Federal Constitutional Court—New Guidance on the Limits of European Integration?' (2010) 11 Ger Law J 367

Streinz T, 'Fraternal Twins: The European Union and the Council of Europe' in H de Waele and J-J Kuipers (eds), *The European Union's Emerging International Identity: Views from the Global Arena Studies in EU External Relations* (Martinus Nijhoff 2013)

Stuart GH, *American Diplomatic and Consular Practice* (Appleton-Century Co 1936)

Stuart G, 'Le Droit et la Pratique Diplomatiques et Consulaires' in The Hague Academy of International Law (ed), *Collected Courses of The Hague Academy of International Law* (first published Librairie du Recueil 1935)

Suy E, 'The Status of Observers in International Organizations' (1978) 160 Recueil Des Cours de l'Academie de Droit International 75

Swiss Confederation, 'Practical Manual of the Regime of Privileges and Immunities and Other Facilities', <www.eda.admin.ch/missions/mission-onu-geneve/en/home/manual-regime-privileges-and-immunities/introduction/manual-opening-mission/mission-wto.html> accessed 4 May 2022

Tannous I, 'The EEAS, EU External Assistance and Development Aid: Institutional Dissonance or Inter-Service Harmony?' in D Spence and J Bátora (eds), *The European External Action Service: European Diplomacy Post-Westphalia* (Palgrave Macmillan 2015)

Taylor H, *A Treatise on International Public Law* (Callaghan & Co 1901)

Taylor T, 'The EU in Geneva: Coordinating Policy int eh Economic and Social arrangements of the United Nations System' in KV Laatikainen and KE Smith (eds), *The European Union at the United Nations* (Palgrave Macmillan 2006)

Thomas MA, 'When the Guests Move In: Permanent Observers to the United Nations Gain the Right to Establish Permanent Missions in the United States' (1990) 78 Cal L Rev 197

Thompson H, 'The Case for External Sovereignty' (2006) 12 Eur J Int Relat 251

Tichy-Fisslberger E, 'Der Schutz der EU–Bürger durch die Diplomatischen und Konsularischen Vertretungsbehörden' (2012) 13 Europarecht 217

Tiilikainen R, 'To Be or Not to BE?: An Analysis of the Legal and Political Elements of Statehood in the EU's External Identity' (2001) 6 EFAR 223

Tizzano A, 'The Foreign Relations Law of the EU between Supranationality and Intergovernmental Model' in E Cannizzaro (ed), *The European Union as an Actor in International Relations* (Kluwer 2002)

Tobin H, 'The Problem of Permanent Representation at the League of Nations' (1964) 48 Polit Sci Q 481

Tolksdorf D, 'EU Special Representatives: An Intergovernmental Tool in the Post Lisbon Foreign Policy System?' (2013) 18 EFAR 471

Topić M and Rodin S (eds), *Cultural Diplomacy and Cultural Imperialism: European Perspective(s)* (Peter Lang 2012)

Tournier A, 'Le Droit de Légation Passive de l'Union Européenne' in M Benlolo-Carabot, U Candas, and J Cujo (eds), *Union Européenne et Droit International* (Pedone 2012)

Touzé S, 'Aspects Récents (et Choisis) de la Protection Consulaire des Citoyens de l'Union européenne' (2011) 1 Rev Aff Eur 79

Turk D, 'Recognition of States: A Comment' (1993) 4 EJIL 66

UN Protocol and Liaison Office, 'Manual of Protocol', <www.un.int/protocol/pm/manual-protocol> accesse. d 4 May 2022

US Department of State Office of Foreign Missions, *Diplomatic and Consular Immunity: Guidance for Law Enforcement and Judicial Authorities*, rev May 2015, <www.state.gov/documents/organization/150546.pdf> accessed 2 May 2022

Van Bogaert ERC, *Volkenrecht* (Elsevier Sequoia 1973)

Van der Pluijm R and Melissen J, *City Diplomacy: The Expanding Role of Cities in International Politics* (Clingendael 2007)

Van Elsuwege P and Merket H, 'The Role of the Court of Justice in Ensuring the Unity of the EU's External Representation' (2012) Cleer Working Paper No 5. https://www.asser.nl/media/1634/cleer2012-5book_web.pdf

Van Grasstek C, *The History and Future of the World Trade Organization* (World Trade Organization 2013)

Van Vooren B and Wessel RA, *EU External Relations Law: Text, Cases and Materials* (CUP 2014)

Vanhamme J, 'Formation and Enforcement of Customary International Law: The European Union's Contribution' (2008) 39 Neth Yearb Int Law 127

Vanhoonacker S and Reslow N, 'The European External Action Service: Living Forwards by Understanding Backwards' (2010) 15 EFAR 1

Vaurs-Chaumette A-L, 'La Question de la Reconnaissance' in M Benlolo-Carabot, U Candas, and E Cujo (eds), *Union Européenne et Droit International* (Pedone 2012)

Verellen T, 'The ERTA Doctrine in the Post-Lisbon Era; Note under Judgment in Commission v Council (C-114/12) and Opinion 1/13' (2013) 21 Colum J Eur L 383

Verhagen M and Bleker H, 'Economic Diplomacy in a Changing World' (2006) 1 HJD 1

Verhoeven J, *Droit International Public* (Larcier 2000)

Vermeer-Künzli A, 'Where the Law Becomes Irrelevant: Consular Assistance and the European Union' (2011) 60 ICLQ 965

Verschaeve J and Takács T, 'The EU's International Identity: The Curious Case of the OECD' in H de Waele and J-J Kuipers (eds), *The European Union's Emerging International Identity: Views from the Global Arena Studies in EU External Relations* (Martinus Nijhoff 2013)

Verwey DR, *The European Community, the European Union, and the International Law of Treaties* (TMC Asser Press 2004)

Vicuna FO, 'Diplomatic and Consular Immunities and Human Rights' (1991) 40 International and Comparative Law Q 34

Vilariño Pintos E, 'Representación Exterior y Cooperación Diplomática y Consular en el Tratado de la Unión Europea' (1995) 22 Rev Inst Eur 417

Villiger ME, *Commentary on the 1969 Vienna Convention on the Law of Treaties* (Martinus Nijhoff 2009)

Viltard Y, 'Conceptualiser la "Diplomatie des Villes": Ou l'Obligation Faite aux Relations Internationales de Pense l'Action Extérieure des Gouvernements Locaux' (2008) 58 RFSP 511

Von Bogdandy A, 'The European Constitution and European Identity: Text and Subtext of the Treaty Establishing a Constitution for Europe' (2005) 3 ICON 295

Von Bogdandy A and Schill S, 'Overcoming Absolute Primacy: Respect for National Identity under the Lisbon Treaty' (2011) 48 CML Rev 1417

Von Martens GF, *Précis du Droit des Gens Moderne de l'Europe Fondé sur les Traités et l'Usage* (2nd edn, Librairie de Dieterich 1801)

Von Redlich MDAR, *The Law of Nations* (World League for Permanent Peace 1937)

Wagner N, Raasch H, and Pröpstl P, *Wiener Übereinkommen über Diplomatische Beziehungen Vom 18. April 1961* (BWV 2007)

Walker N, 'Late Sovereignty in the European Union' in N Walker (ed), *Sovereignty in Transition* (Hart 2003)

Webb P, 'Treaties and International Organizations: Uneasy Analogues' in CJ Tams, A Tzzanakopoulos, and A Zimmermann (eds), *Research Handbook on the Law of Treaties* (Edward Elgar 2014)

Weiler JHH, 'A Constitution for Europe? Some Hard Choices' (2002) 40 JCMS 563

Weiss R, 'Remarks on the Draft Council Decision Establishing the Organisation and Functioning of the European External Action Service' in S Faro, MP Chiti, and E Schweighofer (eds), *European Citizenship and Consular Protection: New Trends in European Law and National Law* (Editoriale Scientifica Napoli 2012)

Wellens K, 'Diversity in Secondary Rules and the Unity of International law: Some Reflections on Current Trends' (1994) 25 Neth Yearb Int Law 3

Wessel RA, *The European Union's Foreign and Security Policy: A Legal Institutional Perspective* (Kluwer 1999)

Wessel RA, 'Revisiting the International Legal Status of the EU' (2000) 5 EFAR 507

Wessel RA, 'Reconsidering the Relationship between International and EU Law: Towards a Content-Based Approach?' in E Cannizzaro, P Palchetti, and RA Wessel (eds), *International Law as Law of the European Union* (Martinus Nijhoff 2011)

Wessel RA, 'The Legal Framework for the Participation of the European Union in International Institutions' (2011) 33 LIEI 621

Wessel RA, 'Can the European Union Replace Its Member States in International Affairs? An International Law Perspective' in I Govaere and others (eds), *The European Union in the World: Essays in Honour of Marc Maresceau* (Martinus Nijhoff 2013)

Wessel RA, 'Immunities of the European Union' (2013) 10 IOLR 395

Wessel RA and Larik J (eds), *EU External Relations Law: Text, Cases and Materials* (Bloomsbury 2020)

Wessel RA and Van Vooren B, 'The EEAS's Diplomatic Dreams and the Reality of European and International Law' (2013) 20 J Eur Public Policy 1350

Wesseling M and Boniface J, 'New Trends in European Consular Services: Visa Policy in the EU Neighbourhood' in J Melissen and AM Fernández (eds), *Consular Affairs and Diplomacy* (Brill Nijhoff 2011)

Weyland J, 'La Protection Diplomatique et Consulaire des Citoyens de l'Union Européenne', in Epaminondas A. Marias (ed) *European Citizenship* (EIPA 1994)

Wheaton H, *Elements of International Law: With a Sketch of the History of the Science*, vol 1 (B Fellowes 1836)

Whitcomb EA, *Napoleon's Diplomatic Service* (Duke UP 1979)

Whitman R (ed), *Normative Power Europe: Empirical and Theoretical Perspectives* (Palgrave Macmillan 2011)

Wickremasinghe C, 'Immunities Enjoyed by Officials of States and International Organizations' in MD Evans (ed), *International Law* (4th edn, OUP 2014)

Wildhaber L, 'Sovereignty and International Law' in R MacDonald and DM Johnston (eds), *The Structure and Process of International Law: Essays in Legal Philosophy, Doctrine and Theory* (Martinus Nijhoff 1986)

Wiseman GR, 'Polylateralism and New Modes of Global Dialogue' in C Jönsson and R Langhorne (eds), *Diplomacy*, vol 3 (2nd edn, Sage 2004)
Woolcock S, *European Union Economic Diplomacy: The Role of the EU in External Economic Relations* (Ashgate 2012)
Wouters J, 'The EU Charter of Fundamental Rights—Some Reflections on Its External Dimension' (2001) 8 MJECL 3
Wouters J and Duquet S, 'The EU and International Diplomatic Law: New Horizons?' (2012) 7 HJD 31
Wouters J and Duquet S, 'The Arab Uprisings and the European Union: In Search of a Comprehensive Strategy' (2013) 32 Yearb Eur Law 230
Wouters J and Duquet S, 'Unus Inter Plures? The EEAS, the Vienna Convention and International Diplomatic Practice' in D Spence and J Bátora (eds), *The European External Action Service: European Diplomacy Post-Westphalia* (Palgrave Macmillan 2015)
Wouters J and Hermez M, 'The EU's Contribution to the Strict Observance and the Development of International Law at the UNGA Sixth Committee' (2016) GGS Working Paper No 177. <https://www.law.kuleuven.be/iir/nl/onderzoek/working-papers/wp177-wouters-hermez.pdf> accessed 2 June 2022
Wouters J and Meuwissen K, 'The European Union at the UN Human Rights Council. Multilateral Human Rights Protection Coming of Age?' (2014) 2 Eur Hum Rights Law Rev 135
Wouters J and Raube K, 'Towards an Inter-Parliamentary Scrutiny of CSDP' (2012) 47 The International Spectator 149
Wouters J and Van Eeckhoutte D, 'Giving Effect to Customary International Law through European Community Law' in JM Prinssen and A Schrauwen (eds), *Direct Effect: Rethinking a Classic of EC Legal Doctrine* (Europa Law Publishing 2004)
Wouters J, Coppens D, and De Meester B, 'The European Union's External Relations after the Lisbon Treaty' in S Griller and J Ziller (eds), *The Lisbon Treaty: EU Constitutionalism without a Constitutional Treaty?* (Springer 2008)
Wouters J, Nollkaemper A, and De Wet E (eds), *The Europeanisation of International Law: The Status of International Law in the EU and Its Member States* (TMC Asser Press 2008)
Wouters J and others, *The Organisation and Functioning of the European External Action Service: Achievements, Challenges and Opportunities* (European Parliament 2013)
Wouters J, Duquet S, and Muewissen K, 'The Vienna Conventions on Diplomatic and Consular Relations' in C Cooper, J Heine, and R Thakur (eds), *The Oxford Handbook of Modern Diplomacy* (OUP 2013)
Wouters J, Duquet S, and Meuwissen K, 'Caring for Citizens Abroad: The European Union and Consular Tasks' (2014) 19 EFAR 563
Wouters J, Duquet S, and Hachez N, 'International Investment Law: The Perpetual Search for Consensus' in O De Schutter, J Swinnen, and J Wouters (eds), *Foreign Direct Investment and Human Development: The Law and Economics of International Investment Agreements* (Routledge 2012)
Wouters J, Odermatt J, and Ramopoulos T, 'Worlds Apart? Comparing the Approaches of the European Court of Justice and the EU Legislature to International Law' in M Cremona and A Thies (eds), *The European Court of Justice and External Relations Law: Constitutional Challenges* (Hart 2011)
Wouters J and others, *The Organisation and Functioning of the European External Action Service: Achievements, Challenges and Opportunities* (European Parliament 2013)
Wouters J and others, 'Improving the EU's Status in the UN and the UN System: An Objective without a Strategy?' in C Kaddous (ed), *The European Union in International Organisations and Global Governance* (Hart 2015)
Wouters J, Odermatt J, and Ramopoulos T, 'The EU in the World of International Organizations: Diplomatic Aspirations, Legal Hurdles and Political Realities' in M Smith, S Keukeleire, and S Vanhoonacker (eds), *The Diplomatic System of the European Union: Evolution, Change and Challenges* (Routledge 2016)
Wouters J and others, *The Law of EU External Relations* (3rd edn, OUP 2021)
Wu L, 'Limitations and Prospects of Taiwan's Informal Diplomacy' in J-M Henckaerts (ed), *The International Status of Taiwan in the New World Order* (Kluwer 1996)

Young E (later Denza), 'The Development of the Law of Diplomatic Relations' (1964) BYIL 141.
Zieck M, 'Diplomatiek en Consulair Recht' in N Horbach, R Lefeber, and O Ribbelink (eds), *Handboek Internationaal Recht* (TMC Asser Press 2007)
Zeidman A, 'The Abuse of the Diplomatic Bag: A Proposed Solution' (1989) 11 Cardozo L Rev 427
Zidar A, *Diplomatie Contemporaine: Entre Secret et Publicité Secrets et Le Droit* (Universités de Berne, Fribourg, Genève, Lausanne, et Neuchâtel 2004)
Ziegler KS, 'Beyond Pluralism and Autonomy: Systemic Harmonization as a Paradigm for the Interaction of EU Law and International Law' (2016) 35 Yearb Eur Law 667

# Index

*For the benefit of digital users, indexed terms that span two pages (e.g., 52–53) may, on occasion, appear on only one of those pages.*

Tables are indicated by *t* following the page number